Using UNIX

Developed by Que Corporation

CORPORATION
LEADING COMPUTER KNOWLEDGE
CARMEL, INDIANA

Using UNIX
Copyright © 1990 by Que® Corporation

Library of Congress Catalog No.:

ISBN No.: 0-88022-519-x

93 92 91   8 7 6 5 4 3 2

Interpretation of the printing code: the rightmost double-digit number is the year of the book's printing; the rightmost single-digit number is the number of the book's printing. For example, a printing code of 90-1 shows that the first printing of the book occurred in 1990.

Using UNIX can be used with most implementations and versions of UNIX.

About the Authors

David W. Solomon, the principal author of *Using UNIX*, is a Que product development specialist and staff writer who specializes in operating systems, database management, and programming. Since 1978, he has worked with a variety of operating systems on both minicomputers and microcomputers, and he has developed and written custom software for scientific and business applications on a worldwide basis. In addition to being the principal author of this book, he is also the author of *Using DOS, MS-DOS QuickStart*, the principal author of *MS-DOS User's Guide*, Special Edition, the coauthor of *dBASE IV Applications Library*, 2nd Edition, and a contributing author of *Using dBASE IV* and *Using Turbo Prolog*, all published by Que Corporation. In addition to authoring and coauthoring a number of Que titles, Solomon has served as Product Development Director for many of Que's operating system and database titles.

Tanya Rodrigue, who wrote the Command Reference of *Using UNIX*, is currently living in England where she serves as the Manager of International Channel Operation for the Santa Cruz Operation. She has experience with database applications and programming languages, as well as with the DOS, XENIX, and UNIX operating systems. While with the Santa Cruz Operation in California, Rodrigue facilitated domestic and international seminars regarding computer technology and SCO operation. Her recent projects have included technical and sales training for XENIX and UNIX. Other than computers, Rodrigue is absorbed in sports medicine and athletic nutrition. This is Tanya Rodrigue's first book for Que.

Mark Schulman contributed the chapters on shell programming and assisted with the final review of the Command Reference for *Using UNIX*. Schulman is a computer programmer and instructor with Cincinnati Bell Information Systems (CBIS). He has worked with a wide range of computer hardware and operating systems from microcomputers to mainframes. Since 1983, he has worked with UNIX and XENIX, written software for a variety of applications, and taught classes in UNIX and the C and C++ programming languages. Schulman lives in Orlando, Florida with his wife Dierdre, children Douglass and Belinda, and assorted animals. This is Mark Schulman's first book for Que.

Rosemary Colonna contributed material on office automation and multitasking for *Using UNIX*. Colonna is a software engineer who has developed course materials and trained instructors on networking and operating systems such as DOS, UNIX, and ULTRIX. She has worked as a software quality assurance engineer for several computer companies, and is the author of user and system administrator manuals for a variety of computer products. In addition to contributing to this book, Colonna has served as contributing author to *Using Symphony*, Special Edition, and *Using 1-2-3, Release 3.1*, all published by Que Corporation.

Dennis Fairclough contributed the material on the `ed` and `vi` text editors for *Using UNIX*. Fairclough teaches in the Computer Science and Information Systems Department at Utah Valley Community College. His research includes object-oriented programming and UNIX operating systems for parallel RISC architectures. Fairclough is also Chairman of the Board of CodeMaster Corporation, a company which develops and markets personal computer-based document management software. This is Dennis Fairclough's first book for Que.

David H. Lender contributed material on file and directory management for Part Two of *Using UNIX*. Lender is a self-employed writer, educator, and computer consultant in Atlanta, Georgia. He has worked with a variety of operating systems on personal computers, minicomputers, and mainframes and has written systems and communications software for the utilities, finance, and office-systems industries. Lender has written articles on technology for a variety of magazines. This is David Lender's first book for Que.

Publishing Director

David Paul Ewing

Acquisitions Editor

Terrie Lynn Solomon

Product Development Director

David W. Solomon

Developmental Editor

Mary Bednarek

Editors

Tim Huddleston
Jeannine McDonel
Lois Sherman

Technical Editor

Steve Pryor

Acquisitions Editorial Assistant

Stacey Beheler

Book Design and Production

Dan Armstrong
Don Clemons
Tom Emrick
William Hartman
William Hurley
Chuck Hutchinson
Betty Kish
Bob LaRoche
Dennis Sheehan
Bruce Steed

Indexer

Kathy Murray

Composed in Garamond by

Hartman Publishing

Page Design and Production

William Hartman, Hartman Publishing

Contents at a Glance

Table of Contents

Part One: Introducing UNIX

5 Understanding the Shell, Commands, and Syntax 103

Part Two: Using the UNIX Commands

Part Four: Programming the Shell

Part Five: Command Reference

Part Six: Appendixes

Acknowledgments

Que Corporation thanks the following individuals for their contributions to this book. All of the people who worked many long, hard hours deserve special thanks.

Publishing Director Dave Ewing for his guidance and support through all phases of the project.

Acquisitions Editor Terrie Solomon for her communication, coordination, and troubleshooting talents, and most of all, for her patience.

Stacey Beheler for keeping disk files, modem and fax transmissions, and international shipments in order and delivered to the right people at the right time.

Bill Hartman, for his dedication to producing a quality book in a timely fashion.

Mary Bednarek, for her steadfast resolve to put a quality book in the hands of UNIX users. Mary made many contributions to developing the content and structure of the book and was dedicated to ensuring high quality in the final manuscript.

Jeannine McDonel, for her cheerful patience in sorting through many commands (and variations of commands) to expertly fine-tune the UNIX Command Reference.

Tim Huddleston, for his willingness to roll up his sleeves and pitch in to do a great editing job whenever he was needed.

Lois Sherman, for her experienced editing skills.

Steve Pryor, for his careful and thorough technical review of the manuscript.

Thanks also to all the members of the production department who worked hard to get this book out on time.

Que also thanks the following vendors who supplied software and expertise:

Bridget Fuller of The Santa Cruz Operation for supplying SCO UNIX System V/386.

Greg Haerr of Century Software for providing the TERM communications program.

Mary Ann Carlton of AT&T, for supplying AT&T System V/386 and an AT&T 6386/25 WGS computer system.

Ann Morgan of Sun Microsystems for supplying SunOS and a Sun 4/110 workstation.

Bob Webster of AIX Operation International Business Machines for supplying AIX for the IBM PS/2.

Trademark Acknowledgments

Que Corporation has made every attempt to supply trademark information about company names, products, and services mentioned in this book. Trademarks indicated below were derived from various sources. Que Corporation cannot attest to the accuracy of this information.

1-2-3 and Lotus are registered trademarks of Lotus Development Corporation.

3Com is a registered trademark of 3Com Corporation.

386 and 486 are trademarks, and Intel is a registered trademark of Intel Corporation.

AIX and IBM PC/XT are trademarks, and IBM, IBM PC, IBM AT, PS/2, Personal System/2, and OS/2 are registered trademarks of International Business Machines Corporation.

Apple, Apple A/UX, Mac, and Macintosh are registered trademarks of Apple Computer, Inc.

AT&T, AT&T 3B2/600, FACE, Open Look, System III, System V, and UNIX are registered trademarks of AT&T.

ANSI is a registered trademark of American National Standards Institute.

BSD is a trademark of the University of California at Berkeley.

COMPAQ is a registered trademark of COMPAQ Computer Corporation.

CP/M, DEC PDP-7, DEC vt100, and VAX are registered trademarks of Digital Equipment Corporation.

dBASE is a registered trademark of Ashton Tate Corporation.

Disneyland is a registered trademark of the Walt Disney Company.

EtherNet is a registered trademark of Xerox Corporation.

Fox Base is a trademark of Fox Software.

Gateway is a registered trademark of Gateway 2000.

Hayes is a registered trademark of Hayes Microcomputer Products.

Hercules Graphics Card is a trademark of Hercules Computer Technology.

HP, HP-UX, HP LaserJet, HP LaserJet II, and Motif are trademarks, and HP Apollo is a registered trademark of Hewlett Packard Co. Apollo is a registered trademark of Apollo Computer, Inc., a subsidiary of Hewlett Packard Co.

JSB MULTIVIEW is a trademark of JSB Computer Systems.

MS-DOS and XENIX are registered trademarks of Microsoft Corporation.

Motorola is a registered trademark of Motorola, Inc.

"The Ordinary Man," by Robert W. Service, is taken from *More Collected Verse*, by Robert W. Service (New York: Dodd, Mead, and Co.), 1918.

Introduction

Even though UNIX has been around since the late 1960's, the operating system has seen considerable growth in recent years. Computer systems based on UNIX offer some of the most attractive cost-per-user figures in the industry. The advent of the powerful microprocessor enabled UNIX to be affordable to millions of users. People from all walks of life are becoming UNIX users as UNIX makes inroads to the business desktop, scientific lab, educational facility, and engineering shop. If you've never learned anything about UNIX, there is no better time to begin than now.

Using UNIX represents Que Corporation's commitment to people who want to learn how to use UNIX and UNIX-based operating systems. Millions of readers throughout the world have turned to Que's *Using* books as a source of fast, efficient learning and reference. *Using UNIX* is the first Que UNIX book to bear the *Using* title.

This book offers UNIX users a source of information to help them organize their UNIX work more effectively. Hundreds of example commands and basic operations are presented in *Using UNIX*. You will want to reserve an accessible place on your bookshelf or desktop for the book, because *Using UNIX* will serve as a valuable reference for your everyday UNIX questions. Although UNIX has a reputation in some circles as a difficult-to-learn operating system, *Using UNIX* covers topics that everyday users need to know, while it bypasses the more esoteric UNIX topics and concepts. The result is a no-nonsense guide to using UNIX.

Who Should Read This Book?

Using UNIX is written for the UNIX user who needs a tutorial reference to UNIX. This book explains the key concepts of UNIX without being technical and

1

intimidating. *Using UNIX* will also serve as an excellent companion text for UNIX course work.

Using UNIX was developed to address most of the needs of the typical UNIX user. The book recognizes that your learning time is limited. Whether you are just learning to use UNIX, or you are a UNIX user who wants a better understanding of the operating system, *Using UNIX* is for you.

What Software Versions Are Covered?

Using UNIX was written with examples from System V Release 3.2. However, the book is sensitive to the needs of users working with earlier releases and different implementations. The primary shell discussed is the Bourne shell. Although some users may find minor variations in their implementation of UNIX-based software, this book will fit most of their needs.

What Hardware Is Needed?

Using UNIX assumes that you have access to a terminal or modem connection to a UNIX system. Your learning experience is reinforced by examples which you are encouraged to try. However, even if you do not have access to UNIX hardware, you can still learn about UNIX by reading the book. *Using UNIX* makes extensive use of screen dialogue that appears just as it would on your terminal. If you don't have a terminal, the screen dialogue is the next best thing.

What Is Not Covered

Although *Using UNIX* covers over 100 commands, many UNIX systems offer over 300 commands. Most of the additional commands are either specific for certain implementations of UNIX, or are commands that programmers or system administrators are more likely to use.

The book includes an introduction to the `ed` and `vi` editors, but does not provide a comprehensive guide. Likewise, although simple shell programming techniques are presented, the book does not cover the more advanced programming aspects of UNIX.

The Details of This Book

You can flip quickly through this book to get a feeling for its organization. *Using UNIX* is divided into six parts. Parts One through Four begin with fundamentals and build your UNIX capabilities to a practical level. Part Five, the Command Reference, provides you with ready access to commands as well as an information base to complete your UNIX expertise. The final part of the book includes a set of useful appendixes.

Part One—Introducing UNIX

Part One includes introductory material and background information on UNIX and its place as an operating system. The chapters in this part provide a knowledge base that covers UNIX's history, its place in the world of computer operating systems, and the process of administering UNIX systems. The final chapter in Part One lays a foundation of understanding about commands and command syntax that you will draw upon as you learn the commands and utilities in Parts Two, Three, and Four.

Chapter 1, "Introducing UNIX," introduces you to UNIX and takes a brief look at UNIX's history. As the first of five chapters that give you a foundation of practical understanding, Chapter 1 demonstrates that learning UNIX can be a fascinating and fulfilling experience. As you learn about the history and folklore of UNIX, you will find that UNIX isn't difficult to incorporate into your work.

Chapter 2, "Understanding Computer Systems," provides a tutorial on computer hardware and software. Although the chapter looks at computers in the context of the UNIX operating system, you can generalize the information presented in this chapter to nearly all computer systems. The chapter is not intended to make you a computer expert, but a little computer-system understanding can make learning UNIX an easier exercise. After reading this chapter, computers—and their role in your work—may seem a bit less mysterious. If you already know about computers to some extent, you can consider Chapter 2 a review.

Chapter 3, "Understanding UNIX," focuses on UNIX's features and the software components that make these features available to you. Developing a good understanding of UNIX's underlying design will help you learn to use the system. Although the whole of UNIX is complex, no single part of UNIX is difficult to understand. A UNIX system is not a seamless monolith of hardware and software, but rather a hardware core, with layers of functionality built upon that core. This chapter describes those layers and their purpose. This chapter also introduces one of the most important and beneficial features of UNIX—the hierarchical file system—and provides an overview of the various typical UNIX systems, based on their size. With this perspective, you'll have a more global understanding of your place in the growing UNIX community.

Chapter 4, "Administering UNIX Systems," discusses UNIX system administration from an ordinary user's point of view. The chapter takes a general look at many of the complicated operations and duties the system administrator undertakes. The chapter does not try to teach you how to administer a UNIX system, but instead gives you a brief overview of UNIX system administration. As you learn about system administration, you will gain additional insight into the kernel and utilities, the file system, and devices.

Chapter 5, "Understanding the Shell, Commands, and Syntax," is an important chapter that rounds out your fundamental knowledge by showing you how the UNIX shell interprets your commands. UNIX commands enable you to manage and report on your part of the UNIX computing environment. In fact, when most users think of UNIX, they usually think of the UNIX commands. The chapter explains commands as interpreted by the shell. You learn what the parts of a command mean to the shell and learn the general guidelines for logging in to the system and issuing commands. After you read this chapter, which prepares you for the expanded discussion of individual commands in Part Two, you will be comfortable accessing your UNIX system and ready to use UNIX commands for useful work.

Part Two—Using the UNIX Commands

Part Two of this book assumes that you have learned the basics of UNIX presented in Part One. You will see command examples emphasizing the most common UNIX commands. The chapters in Part Two are based on specific categories of commands. For a quick reference of any command, you can flip to the Command Reference section and find the command alphabetically.

Chapter 6, "Managing Files," introduces you to your work with disk files. Files are the basic units of the UNIX system, so the commands that manage files are an important part of UNIX. Most users soon develop a large collection of files that they must manage in order to keep their UNIX work orderly and efficient. This chapter discusses the types of files you are likely to work with, and further expands the information on directories presented in Chapter 3. The chapter shows you how to view your files and produce a complete listing of their contents, how to use redirection in creating new files, how to modify the creation times associated with your files, and how to save disk space by compressing your files.

Chapter 7, "Managing Directories," contains information on managing your directories rather than specific files. Chapter 7 shows you how you can use file-name arguments that cross directory lines as you explore the UNIX world beyond your home directory. In this chapter, you learn how to create and remove directories, as well as move or copy files to the directories you create. You also learn to delete files and directories you no longer need. As you learn to navigate through the directory structure, you will see methods of searching for files in different directories.

Chapter 8, "Managing Devices," presents the device-related commands that you may need to use during your UNIX system-level work. These commands inform you about your terminal-to-UNIX communications link and disk-storage resource. In addition, you'll learn a bit more about disk drives, the file system, and your terminal. You will learn how to set options on your terminal, such as the display of colors, tabs, and other features. You will also learn how to find out how much disk space you have.

Chapter 9, "Participating in a Multiuser Environment," introduces you to UNIX's multitasking capabilities. Because the UNIX operating system can support many users on one system and work on several tasks concurrently, the system is considered *multiuser* and *multitasking*. In this chapter, you learn how UNIX arranges for tasks to be performed, and how you as a user fit into the overall multitasking lineup. You learn how to run programs in the background so that you can continue *your* work while UNIX does *its* work. This chapter presents the commands you will find useful for handling the multiprocessing capabilities of UNIX. You learn how to change your password, find out who is on the system and who is doing what, control your file and directory permission settings, switch between groups, print your work to a printer, and schedule tasks and priorities. Being able to use these commands puts you in control of task management with UNIX.

Chapter 10, "Processing Files," presents several commands that you can use with text files to perform useful tasks at the operating-system prompt. These tasks include identifying the type of file you are working with, sorting the contents of your files into alphabetical or numeric order, comparing the contents of your files and listing the differences between them, chopping up a file into pieces—either horizontally or vertically—putting those pieces of files together, and adding line numbers to files.

Chapter 11, "Automating the Office Environment," is the final chapter in Part Two. The chapter rounds out your understanding by taking you back to the basics of being a member of the UNIX community. You learn to use the UNIX office-automation commands to "talk" with other people on your system (and on remote systems), set up an automatic reminder service to help you keep track of your appointments, display a calendar at your terminal, use your computer as a desktop calculator, and print banners for reports, messages, and displays.

Part Three—Using Text Editors

Part Three introduces you to two of the basic text editors provided with your system—ed, the UNIX line editor, and vi, the UNIX full-screen, visual editor. In your work with UNIX, you will often find the need to create and modify ASCII text files. Such files can be anything from a short memo or shell procedure to a long report or a complete shell script that can automate your daily work. As you gain experience with UNIX, you will find many occasions to create new text files or change existing text files to suit your purposes. A text editor is your primary tool for creating and modifying text files, and Part Three introduces two of the more common UNIX text editors—ed and vi. In Part Four, you learn about the basics of shell programming. You can create many of the simple shell scripts and procedures described in Part Four by using either ed or vi.

Chapter 12, "Using ed, the UNIX Line Editor," introduces you to the most universally available of the UNIX editors, ed. Line editors such as ed enable you to enter, modify, search through, substitute, copy, and delete text. The editor's commands are brief, effective, and powerful. This chapter provides a basic introduction to the ed editor; the chapter does not provide comprehensive descriptions of all the editor's facilities and capabilities.

Chapter 13, "Using vi, The UNIX Visual Editor," introduces you to another class of editor, the full-screen or visual editor, vi. If you have used word processing programs, you'll feel more at home with vi than ed. Like most word processing programs, vi is active on the complete screen. vi incorporates powerful editing features, such as search and replace, text-block moves, insert and append modes, extensive cursor-positioning commands, and customized terminal setup. The chapter does not cover the more advanced features of vi, but it does introduce you to the program in an easy-to-learn, easy-to-use manner. If you want more information on advanced features and advanced text-editing operations, consult Appendix F and the Reference Manual supplied with your system.

Part Four—Programming the Shell

Part Four introduces you to shell programming procedures that you will find useful in your daily work with UNIX. In Chapters 14 and 15, you will explore some of the capabilities of shell programs. Programmers find many familiar concepts in shell programming, but most users can make good use of shell programming features without any knowledge of programming.

Chapter 14, "Understanding the Basics of Shell Programming," teaches you how to create and execute simple shell programs (also known as *shell scripts* or *shell procedures*) and use some of the basic shell programming features. You also see a bit of the history and diversity of the UNIX user interface.

Chapter 15, "Increasing Your Productivity with Advanced Programming," presents techniques that greatly expand the power of shell programs for your UNIX work. In this chapter, you learn additional commands, such as decision-making and looping commands, that are more programming-oriented and powerful than those in Chapter 14.

Part Five—Command Reference

Part Five is the UNIX Command Reference, a guide that indexes and describes over 100 UNIX commands. The commands, which are arranged in alphabetical order, are shown with syntax, applicable rules, examples, and notes. You can use the Command Reference both as a reference when you have problems and as a source of practical advice and tips during a "browsing session." In all, the Command Reference is a complete, easy to use, quickly accessed resource on the proper use of UNIX commands.

Part Six—Appendixes

Using UNIX includes six appendixes containing useful summary information that will serve as a ready reference.

Appendix A, "DOS-to-UNIX Command Conversions," is a command conversion table that MS-DOS users may find convenient for issuing UNIX commands. Appendix B, "Chart of ASCII Values," lists the ASCII codes used by UNIX. Appendix C, "Command Finder," categorizes the UNIX commands both alphabetically and by their function in the program. Appendix D, "Special Keys and Characters," includes several useful tables that list the typical names and functions of keys, key combinations, and characters that have a special meaning to UNIX. Appendix E, "Summary of `ed` Commands," and Appendix F, "Summary of `vi` Commands," provide a list of start-up options, commands, and options for the UNIX text editors `ed` and `vi`. Neither appendix is intended as a complete reference.

Conventions Used in This Book

Certain conventions are used in this edition to help you more easily understand the discussions. The conventions are explained again at appropriate places in the book.

Special Typefaces and Command Representations

This section describes the special typefaces and command representations used in *Using UNIX*. Note that UNIX is case-sensitive. In many cases, commands and options are interpreted by UNIX in a certain manner depending on case.

Typeface	Meaning
`special font`	This font is used for UNIX commands, the names of files and directories, and system output, such as prompt signs and screen messages.
`bold special font`	This font is used for user input, such as commands, options to commands, and names of directories and files used as arguments.
`italic special font`	This font is used for the names of variable elements to which values are given by the user, such as *`filename`* or *`increment`*.
<input>	User input that does not appear on-screen when it is typed is enclosed within angle brackets. Such input can be <passwords>, special keys such as <Return> or <Del>, or control characters such as <^C> or <^G>.

Prompts

The UNIX system prompts appear in the special typeface. In most sample commands, the Bourne-shell dollar sign ($) is used as the default system prompt. Your prompt may be different. In addition, the > and # are also used as prompts under various circumstances. You do *not* type the prompt.

Keyboard Keys

Most keys are represented as they typically appear on keyboards and are shown enclosed within angle brackets. Such keys include <Backspace>, <Return>, <Esc>, and so on. Your terminal may have different names for these keys. You do *not* type the angle brackets.

Control Keys

Control keys are represented both on-screen and in text by a caret or circumflex character (^) and enclosed in angle brackets <^K>. You do *not* type the angle brackets. To enter a control key, you hold down the Ctrl key and press the specified key. For example, to enter <^C>, you hold down the key marked Ctrl on your keyboard and press the C key.

Command Syntax and Examples

The syntax for a command appears as follows:

```
news [-ans] [item]
```

In this syntax line, the news command is shown in the special typeface. Also shown in the special typeface and enclosed within square brackets are the options [-ans] available with the command. (Note that you do *not* type the square brackets.) You do not need to use the options to execute the command. The options, however, are represented in a literal manner. In order to use the -a option, for example, you type **-a** on the command line.

Another syntax element involves the use of variable arguments. This information cannot be represented in a literal manner because the user actually substitutes her or his information for the variable argument. For this syntax line, the element [item] represents an argument the user supplies with the command. In this case, item specifies the name of the news file you want to view. You supply the name of the news item.

Note: In this example, the item argument is variable *and* optional. With certain other commands, the variable argument may be *required*. In such cases, the variable argument is *not* enclosed within square brackets. When ellipsis dots . . . follow an argument on a syntax line, the ellipses indicate that more than one argument can be used on a single command line.

The following examples show how each of these syntax elements are used in a command.

To display all news items, type the following at the prompt:

    $ **news** <Return>

In this example, you type the command—**news**—at the Bourne-shell prompt ($). (Remember that your prompt may be different.) The <Return> indicates that you press the Return key (or <Enter> or <CR>, depending on your system) to execute the command.

To display a specific news article called bonus, at the prompt type the following:

    $ **news bonus** <Return>

In this example, the *item* argument is included. The user specified the file name bonus for *item*.

To display the number of new items that you have not read, at the prompt type the following:

    $ **news −s** <Return>

In this example, the −s option is used to display how many current news items you have without displaying their names or contents and without changing the modification time. Note that the **−s** was typed literally on the command line.

Icons and Asides

Throughout the book, you will find the following special icons used to identify certain text. These items are brief digressions.

A note provides brief, additional information relating to the topic in the surrounding text. A note can also serve as a reminder or to clarify a point.

A warning serves as a caution to the reader. The warning points to the careful use of a procedure or perhaps to some event that could cause a loss of files or work for the user.

A tip is an insight that can help you more fully realize and benefit from the features of UNIX.

In addition, certain discussions are expanded by the use of "asides." The aside is an extended discussion of some item. The information in an aside may be of a somewhat technical nature, or perhaps serves as an elaboration of some element being discussed. This elaboration might be somewhat "out of context" if included in-line with the rest of the text, but if used as an aside, can provide additional information for the reader who wants to know more about the topic. The text for the aside, which bears a headline pointing to its subject matter, such as ***About Booting . . .***, is enclosed in a shaded box.

— Part —
One

Introducing UNIX

Introducing UNIX

Understanding Computer Systems

Understanding UNIX

Administering UNIX Systems

Understanding the Shell,
Commands, and Syntax

Introducing UNIX

A small crowd of people gathers in the office cafeteria for a hastily called 10 o'clock meeting. The company's vice president of operations walks to the head table and begins to speak. "Some of you have noticed visitors looking over our operation and asking questions about how we do things," says the vice president. A few managers nod in acknowledgment.

"These visitors are from Gromley and Associates; we have just purchased a UNIX-based computer system from them. You'll use the new UNIX system to do many of the jobs that you are now doing manually. This new departmental computer will make your lives much easier," continues the vice president.

A few individuals in the group repeat the word "UNIX." Some say the word with suspicion—some with relief. A few say the word in complete ignorance. The vice president then introduces a representative from Gromley, who speaks about "multiusers" and "multiprocessing." The staff hears about office automation, electronic mail, and security. After a brief explanation of plans, the vice president dismisses the group, and the people resume their jobs.

By 1 o'clock, rumors already are spreading about the new computerization plan. Most rumors involve UNIX. "UNIX is hard to learn." "UNIX is easy to learn." "UNIX is for scientific types." "UNIX will eventually replace all other kinds of computers." "Unless you're a UNIX expert, you'll make a mistake and ruin the computer." Like most rumors, these are based on the thinnest thread of truth.

This scenario is repeated in working environments everywhere. The fine points of the scenario change, of course, but the reputation of UNIX continues. This chapter, which introduces you to UNIX and takes a brief look at UNIX's history, is the first of five chapters that prepare you to become a UNIX-system user.

After reading this introduction, you should have a practical understanding of what it means to be a UNIX user. Using UNIX can be a fascinating and fulfilling experience. In fact, UNIX is known for instilling a certain "spirit" in its users. Now it is time for you to catch the UNIX spirit.

Key Terms Used in This Chapter

UNIX   An operating system. UNIX is software.

Standard   A point of reference that is used to determine the similarity of software originating from different sources.

Software standard   A standard for computer software that enables the uniform operation of different software.

AIX   Advanced Interactive Executive. This operating system is the IBM variant of UNIX.

XENIX   A variant of UNIX suited to personal computers. XENIX was developed by Microsoft, and is now developed by the Santa Cruz Operation.

BSD   The Berkeley Software Distribution variant of UNIX, developed by the University of California at Berkeley.

System V   UNIX System V (five) is the official AT&T UNIX operating system.

SVR4   An acronym for System V Release 4. SVR4 is the latest version of AT&T UNIX.

Sun OS   An adaptation of BSD by Sun Microsystems for use on Sun workstations.

What is UNIX?

UNIX is an operating system. Operating systems are a kind of computer software program. UNIX is the software foundation upon which computer programs are built. You'll read more about computers and software in the next chapter.

UNIX is a registered trademark of American Telephone and Telegraph Corporation, better known as AT&T. Officially, AT&T owns the name UNIX, and AT&T decides which companies can use the name UNIX. To most computer users, UNIX refers to computer software that is based on AT&T's UNIX System. The actual name of the software that the users refer to as UNIX may vary. The name may be AIX, XENIX, BSD, or one of dozens of other names.

It is important for you to note that many products that users call "UNIX" are products based on UNIX, or products that perform like UNIX. The UNIX System is a set of computer programs licensed by AT&T. Vendors of computer software who license the UNIX System incorporate their own modifications to produce their own UNIX-based system. When this book refers to UNIX, you can assume that the book is referring to either the "official" UNIX or one of the operating systems based on UNIX.

A Brief History of UNIX

You will not find a single, unified form of UNIX. UNIX has evolved over the years in more than one direction. What you will discover, however, is that today's variations are direct descendants of the original version of UNIX. As you will see, UNIX has an interesting history, which has much to do with its reputation and general folklore.

UNIX was developed by programmers at Bell Laboratories in Murray Hill, New Jersey in 1969. By today's standards, you can consider UNIX a fairly *old* operating system. Of course, UNIX has evolved since 1969. In fact, there is much effort in the UNIX community to incorporate the latest desirable features into UNIX. Still, the core of UNIX has remained stable all these years.

You might imagine that such an enduring operating system originated as being the center of attention of a large group of computer specialists. You could picture the debut of UNIX as a full-scale media event complete with a four-color magazine campaign. But like many "legends," UNIX was born in quiet obscurity. UNIX was not developed by a huge team of programmers working with the ultimate specifications of the day. Rather, UNIX was developed by a handful of people, working under the guidance of a programmer named Ken Thompson.

The original UNIX ran on a single type of minicomputer, Digital Equipment Corporation's (DEC) PDP-7. Today, UNIX runs on many different kinds of computers.

Many users think that the name "UNIX" must be a clever acronym for some descriptive phrase, which underscores the operating system's features. In fact, the name "UNIX" is merely an offshoot of the operating-system name "MULTICS." Ken Thompson worked with the multiuser MULTICS operating system before creating UNIX. UNIX folklore has it that Thompson jokingly referred to his original version of UNIX with the "UNI" part of the name meaning *one* or *single* user, as opposed to the "MULTI" part of MULTICS, which referred to many users. It is ironic that MULTICS is remembered chiefly as the source for the pun that created the term UNIX, while UNIX continues to gain acceptance.

As you can see, UNIX had rather humble beginnings. These humble beginnings, along with an unusual evolution, gave UNIX a much different framework for evolution than that experienced by most other operating systems.

The UNIX operating system caught on quickly within Bell Labs, and seemed to have all the ingredients needed to become a rapid commercial success. UNIX was a flexible and complete operating system that was well suited to programmer's activities. Further, UNIX could be moved to different types of computers. By 1973, most people who used UNIX considered it to be a viable product. By all rights,

UNIX was ready to become a commercial success. Yet, UNIX was not to make commercial inroads for several years.

During its first years, UNIX was not a commercial product. Because the business of AT&T was telecommunications rather than computer-related products, Bell Labs and AT&T were restricted as to what commercial products they could offer. Despite these external limitations, UNIX continued to flourish within Bell Labs.

In 1974, UNIX was licensed to universities for use in education. AT&T also made UNIX available to research labs. Although UNIX had finally left the confines of Bell Labs, its use was still not commercial. But the university environment helped further prove UNIX's viability as a serious operating system. Even today, UNIX plays an important role in the computer programs of most universities.

UNIX also enjoys much popularity in the scientific and research laboratory environments. Many of the commands and utilities that evolved with UNIX were developed by the scientific and academic communities. By the nature of its design, UNIX is *extensible*, meaning that UNIX programmers can add new utilities. In the scientific and academic environment, a constant trickle of new utilities aided in UNIX's evolution. Some of these utilities have names composed of their developer's initials. Others have names that are acronyms for describing what the utilities do. To many users today, these UNIX command names seem unnecessarily cryptic. Yet when you consider the freedom of early users to extend UNIX, unusual command names were to be expected. The "individual touches" of contributed commands help underscore the openly extensible nature of UNIX.

AT&T released an improved version of UNIX, *Version 7*, in 1978. Although the licensing arrangements for Version 7 were more constrained than licensing arrangements for UNIX today, UNIX was now available to the world. Restrictions on AT&T's computer business were lifted as a result of the breakup of the Bell companies. Within a few years, Version 7 was upgraded to *UNIX System III* (pronounced 3). UNIX was now a full-fledged product that created a great deal of commercial interest.

By the time System III was introduced, AT&T had reduced the licensing costs of UNIX to a degree that made UNIX a viable commercial product for third-party vendors to sell. By virtue of its underlying program language, UNIX could be moved to a variety of computers. Soon, UNIX was available for a growing number of computers. As part of the licensing arrangement with AT&T, vendors of UNIX-based products gave the resulting product distinct names. For example, Hewlett Packard's HP-UX is a UNIX system-based product; so is Microsoft's XENIX.

Some companies eliminated licensing costs altogether by developing UNIX "look alikes." These UNIX-like operating systems had the feel of UNIX, but did not rely on the AT&T software code.

In 1983, *UNIX System V* (pronounced 5), the latest version of AT&T UNIX, made its debut. AT&T no longer was constrained from the computer business. System V became AT&T's commercial UNIX force, leaving previous versions to fade out of the picture. Since its introduction, System V has been the focus of AT&T's concentrated UNIX efforts.

From a historical perspective, you get a sense that UNIX is really a seasoned operating system. Of course, you don't have to commit the history of UNIX to memory. Just carry away from this section an appreciation of the folklore and the following that UNIX has acquired since 1969. Many computer users who are now discovering the flexibility of the UNIX system were not yet born when Ken Thompson ran his first UNIX-supported program.

The Leading Standard Versions of UNIX

Not all of UNIX's evolution has been controlled by AT&T. Many UNIX licensees have added features to the operating system for their own enhancement purposes. Perhaps you've heard of a situation in which a story was told to three people, and each of those people then told the story to three more people. The result is still the story, but with twelve different variations. In some respects, UNIX has evolved in the same way. The core of UNIX remains the same, but internal and external features vary from vendor to vendor. This section introduces you to the primary standard versions of UNIX. Most other "flavors" of UNIX are based on one of these main standard versions.

A *software standard* is a point of reference that is used to determine the similarity of software originating from different sources. As a UNIX user, you may not see much difference in the UNIX offered by one source as opposed to another. Many of the differences that developed during the fairly recent past are disappearing. In any case, you will concentrate on your current version. You will, however, have a greater appreciation of UNIX if you are aware of the different UNIX standards.

AT&T System V

You already have read about UNIX's emergence from Bell Labs within AT&T in 1969. More recently, AT&T released UNIX System III in 1981. System III is an upgrade of UNIX Version 7, or 7th Edition. In 1983, AT&T released UNIX System V. System V is now the primary version of UNIX. Many vendors license System V and base their UNIX products on it. System V contains work done by AT&T and incorporates improvements and suggestions of others.

Since 1983, System V has been improved several times. To differentiate smaller steps of improvement within System V, AT&T refers to a particular release level of UNIX System V. The current release level is Release 4. System V Release 3, however, is still in wide use. Small differences can occur even within individual release levels. To indicate these small steps, a period followed by a minor release number is given. For example, System V Release 3.2 (pronounced 3 dot 2) is a common form of UNIX. Another form of reference to System V releases uses an acronym. *SVR4* is the acronym for System V Release 4.

Berkeley Software Distribution

As you recall, AT&T licensed UNIX to universities during the period when AT&T complied with restrictions that kept UNIX from being a commercial product. The University of California at Berkeley was to be a major force in the evolution of UNIX. In 1979, Berkeley moved Version 7 to a new supermini computer at the university. The resulting enhanced UNIX was called *3 BSD*. BSD is an acronym for *Berkeley Software Distribution*. BSD, sometimes called *Berkeley UNIX*, has evolved along its own path since 1979. In 1981, 4.1 BSD was produced at Berkeley, followed by 4.2 BSD in 1984. Today, 4.3 BSD is the current version, but a newer release is expected soon.

The Berkeley developers added certain enhancements that made UNIX more user friendly, programmer friendly, and real-world capable. By virtue of these enhancements, AT&T UNIX and BSD have not been entirely compatible with each other during their evolutions. You could spend a lot of time reviewing the technical differences between BSD and UNIX, but you probably would not benefit much from the knowledge. As a UNIX user, you will be more interested in the practical differences in commands and operations. Fortunately, many of the practical differences between versions of UNIX have been dissolved in newer releases. You will soon understand why such differences are less of an issue today.

BSD is the de facto standard UNIX in the academic community. The so-called *Berkeley enhancements* to UNIX are not just for the academic environment, however. Vendors such as Sun Microsystems have based their forms of UNIX on BSD. Sun's Sun OS is the name of a BSD-derived operating system. BSD is a fine example of how the academic community can contribute to the computer industry in a tangible way.

XENIX

The final major variant of UNIX was developed initially from System III by Microsoft Corporation. Microsoft calls this variation of UNIX the *XENIX* operating system. Later, Microsoft adopted System V for the basis of XENIX. Microsoft is perhaps better known for its MS-DOS and OS/2 operating systems than for XENIX. MS-DOS, OS/2, and XENIX were made to operate on small personal computers. In fact, XENIX's emergence as a commercial success and UNIX standard is due largely to the microcomputer revolution of the 80s. You recognize personal computers from IBM, COMPAQ, and others like them from seeing these computers in all types of business settings.

Early XENIX versions could operate successfully on an IBM PC-XT or equivalent computer. The large-scale availability of small computers and a mainframe-capable operating system was revolutionary. In the last 10 years, the power available from a desktop computer has risen 50-fold. XENIX has grown as well, to take advantage of the greater power available from these new computers. Today, a personal computer running XENIX has more computing power than many mainframes and minicomputers of just a few years ago. To the end user of XENIX, more power means faster response from programs.

The Santa Cruz Operation (SCO) has joined with Microsoft as the co-developer of XENIX. SCO has added a great deal of commerical viability to XENIX. Today, XENIX is one of the most successful variations of UNIX.

Hybrid Versions (Toward Standards Unification)

Today, many versions of UNIX contain enhancements from other versions. In a sense, these blended versions are hybrids of many UNIX contributions. UNIX made inroads into computer activities around the world in the form of AT&T UNIX, BSD, XENIX, and their licensed derivatives. Although the varieties were different, each of these major varieties of UNIX had the essential UNIX core. This core gives UNIX its "feel" as an operating system. The UNIX "feel," in turn, gave a unity to the UNIX community. As each variety evolved, each incorporated parts of the others. This incorporation enabled many useful features to become available to a wide audience of UNIX users. Exchanged features also gave UNIX an open-system appeal. In an open system, a variety of interests have input to the standard. Today's versions of UNIX reflect this cross-pollination of features. You benefit from the interchange of features between the major variants of UNIX by having access to many parts of each.

Vendor Consortia

Because UNIX-based operating systems are a proven commercial commodity, vendors have divided into groups to promote their interests in the evolution of UNIX. As computer users and implementors strive to get more computing power for fewer dollars, UNIX's features make the operating system a good choice. Most major companies that sell computers or operating systems offer some form of UNIX for their customers. Customers, in turn, are pushing the computer vendors for more open versions of the vendor's UNIX. In an open version of UNIX, customers can "mix and match" hardware and software from many vendors. In response to this demand, two main groups of vendors have formed organizations to provide a standardized UNIX. The first group, which has focused its efforts on System V, is called *UNIX International*. The second group, called the *Open Software Foundation*, focuses on the OSF/1 operating system.

UNIX Verification Suite Standards

To aid in the standardization of UNIX, AT&T published the *System V Interface Definition*, or *SVID*. Companies that want their versions of UNIX to be compatible with System V are able to follow the SVID guidelines. In addition, AT&T produced a *System V Verification Suite*, or *SVVS*. Those companies that want to verify compliance with SVID can obtain the SVVS as a benchmark testing-program set. The SVVS programs verify that the tested programs are compliant with the System V standards as outlined in SVID. Both the SVID and the SVVS have been expanded to include new features of System V.

Berkeley UNIX and System V have become very close because of the cooperative work of AT&T and Sun Microsystems. System V Release 4 (SVR4) includes compatibility with BSD. Sun Microsystems produces UNIX-based work stations, which use Sun's Berkeley-based Sun OS operating system.

AT&T also worked with Microsoft to bring XENIX into the System V standard. The new XENIX operating system officially uses the UNIX name and operates on computers based on the powerful Intel 80386 family of microprocessors. Through the AT&T and Microsoft alliance, XENIX and UNIX are quite close today.

Many vendors of UNIX-based operating systems have joined with AT&T to form *UNIX International*, or *UI*. As an advisory group, UI has established a standard for UNIX System V. UI has published *Road Map*—a list of firm goals, which calls for staged release of new System V features. Vendors can use *Road Map* to incorporate new features that are in the same vein as the UI plans.

The Open Software Foundation

The *Open Software Foundation*—or *OSF*—is a consortium of vendors who are developing their own version of a UNIX standard. The OSF's operating system is called *OSF/1*, and is based on software developed at Carnegie-Mellon University. Elements of OSF/1 are based on IBM's AIX operating system. The OSF has announced a plan for future features similar to UI's *Road Map*.

The Combined Effects of Standardization

At first, UNIX-based operating systems evolved on divergent courses; today, these systems are evolving toward a uniform standard. To you, this standardization promises greater availability of "off-the-shelf" software. To the equipment and materials purchaser, this standardization promises open choices and reduced costs. To the UNIX trainer, standardization promises more concise presentations with fewer exceptions to the rule. To the UNIX community as a whole, standardization promises the same market leverage enjoyed by DOS-based computer commerce.

Even though the vendors of UNIX-based systems have made great strides toward a single UNIX standard, some question remains as to the final standard. The rival UI and OSF organizations have outlined a very similar future for their versions of UNIX. The UNIX community eagerly awaits a single standard. Both UI and OSF look to formal standards organizations for a clearer definition of an open UNIX's underlying features.

The Formal Standards Organizations

Formal standards organizations define standards that the organizations want vendors to consider when designing systems. Formal standards organizations aren't controlled by any particular vendor or group of vendors; vendors, however, can be represented in the organization. The strength of these organizations' proposed standards is tied directly to the credibility of the organization. UNIX vendors generally cite compliance with the standards of one or more organization's guidelines. It isn't uncommon to hear in UNIX conversations the names or acronyms of UNIX standards organizations and their guidelines. The next few sections will give you a fundamental understanding of these organizations and their work. Chances are that you will not have direct interest in the standards organizations, but as a UNIX user, you may eventually be affected by their activities.

IEEE 1003.1

While AT&T was developing SVID, the IEEE (Institute of Electrical and Electronics Engineers) formed a standards committee to develop a standard for a portable operating system. The IEEE committee published its standard, numbered *1003.1*, in 1986. The standard was named *Portable Operating System Standard for Computer Environments*, and often is referred to by the acronym *POSIX*. The IEEE also published other standards for peripheral aspects of UNIX soon after the initial standard. POSIX is an important standard because it is recognized by the U.S. Federal Government as an indication of one particular UNIX's compatibility with others. Although it is American in origin, POSIX has international influence.

X/Open

Whereas IEEE is an American organization, X/Open is strongly European. X/Open is a collaboration between European computer companies and American computer companies with strong ties to the European computer market. X/Open standards include computer aspects other than UNIX, but X/Open standards are important to European UNIX development. The X/Open *Portability Guide* guidelines are very close to POSIX guidelines for UNIX.

ISO

ISO is the International Standards Organization. ISO creates standards for many items, ranging from photographic film to operating systems. ISO has adopted standards for UNIX similar to IEEE's standards.

Summary

UNIX, UNIX-based operating systems, and UNIX "work-alikes" all trace their lineage back to the early UNIX from AT&T Bell Labs. UNIX has evolved for more than 20 years, and this evolution has taken many paths. With 20 years of history, UNIX has developed its own folklore. While some users greet UNIX with enthusiasm, others avoid it out of uncertainty. It is important for you to realize that UNIX's history and recent stormy standardization activities have much to do with users' perceptions. As you learn to use UNIX, you will find that UNIX isn't difficult to incorporate into your work.

In this chapter, you learned the following key points:

- ❑ UNIX is an operating system that has evolved over several years.
- ❑ Several UNIX-based operating systems have evolved from the original UNIX operating system.
- ❑ BSD (Berkeley UNIX) is a major UNIX variant developed at the University of California at Berkeley.
- ❑ XENIX is a major variant of UNIX developed by Microsoft. XENIX runs on small, personal computers.
- ❑ System V is the official UNIX from AT&T.
- ❑ The two primary groups offering their own standard UNIX-based operating systems are UNIX International and the Open Software Foundation.
- ❑ Formal standards organizations such as IEEE, X/Open, and ISO have adopted standards recommendations for vendors to use.

The next chapter provides a tutorial on computer hardware and software. Computers can be somewhat mysterious. Although the next chapter won't make you a computer expert, it will make computers seem a bit less mysterious. With a historical perspective and a basic understanding of hardware and software, you'll be well on your way to catching the UNIX spirit.

Understanding
Computer Systems

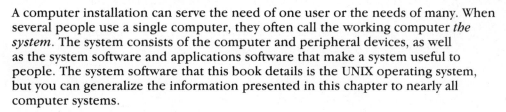

A computer installation can serve the need of one user or the needs of many. When several people use a single computer, they often call the working computer *the system*. The system consists of the computer and peripheral devices, as well as the system software and applications software that make a system useful to people. The system software that this book details is the UNIX operating system, but you can generalize the information presented in this chapter to nearly all computer systems.

To gain a better understanding of UNIX, you will learn about some computer fundamentals in this chapter. Don't worry—you won't need to become a computer expert to use UNIX. Everyday users of UNIX aren't often computer specialists. Yet, some understanding of computer systems will help you do everyday computer work.

If you already know about computers to some extent, consider this chapter a review. In any case, you will give yourself an edge in learning UNIX if you acquire a good foundation for your learning. To help clarify this discussion, review the key terms listed in the next section. Before long, you will be using UNIX confidently.

Key Terms Used in This Chapter

Hardware	The mechanical, electrical, and electromechanical components of a computer system.
System hardware	The components of a computer directly involved in the action of computing.
Peripheral hardware	The components of a computer involved with input and output.

Binary	A two-state (0 and 1) number system that computers use to represent values.
Instruction	A binary pattern that the central processing unit decodes and executes to accomplish computing an operation or task.
Bit	An acronym for *Binary Digit*. A bit is 0 or 1.
Byte	A pattern of eight bits, which are stored and manipulated as a unit.
Random-access memory	Also called *RAM*, the electronic storage units that the CPU addresses in order to store and retrieve data and instructions. The contents of RAM are lost when the power source is turned off.
Read-only memory	Also called *ROM*, the electronic storage units the CPU can address as it does RAM, but can only retrieve values from. The contents of ROM are not lost when the power source is turned off.

Understanding Hardware

Hardware is one of those computer terms that people who work with and around computers use with ease. Yet many people don't really know what computer hardware is. In the most general sense, hardware refers to the computer equipment that sits in the computer room. If you have a personal computer, such as an IBM PC or an Apple Macintosh, the hardware sits on your desk.

Hardware is made up of the nuts, bolts, circuit boards, keyboards, and screens of a computer system. Of course, all these mechanical, electomechanical, and electronics components are highly integrated into a computer design. The computer that supports a large UNIX system can be quite sophisticated. Fortunately, you don't have to be a hardware specialist to understand why hardware is important in a system.

Hardware can be divided into two general categories: *system hardware* and *peripheral hardware*. When you have the right members of these two hardware groups, you have the basis for a working computer. The next two sections provide more detail.

Understanding System Hardware

System hardware consists partly of the circuits and support components that perform the actual computing operations. The most notable component of system hardware is the *central processing unit*, or CPU. Other components of system hardware include system memory, peripheral-controller circuit boards, and power supplies. Computer systems vary in the exact makeup of system hardware, but the fundamental components are almost always in place.

The CPU

The central processing unit of a computer system is the "brain" of the computer. Although the CPU is incapable of thought as you know it, it is capable of logical and arithmetic operations that seem intelligent.

The electrical signals can be routed in many directions within a computer. The CPU acts as a master switcher, much like the master switcher at a busy rail yard. The CPU throws the proper switch to route a value for manipulation. When the computation is complete, the CPU throws a switch to route the value to its next destination.

The exact steps for doing its job are external to the CPU. The CPU has no "built-in" plan to do word processing, accounting spreadsheets, order entry, or other kinds of user-based tasks. The CPU relies entirely upon programs to instruct it to do useful work for users. You will read about programs later in this chapter, but for now, just understand how programs and the CPU work together.

Today's computer systems employ CPUs that consist of a single integrated circuit called a *microprocessor*. Microprocessors have significantly reduced the size of the system hardware. A small desktop computer can outperform many of yesterday's large rack-mounted computers and even the room-sized computers of the 60's and 70's. If you hear the term microprocessor or just processor, you can take the term to mean the CPU. All forms of CPUs execute programs in a computer system.

The programs executed by CPUs are collections of *instructions* which, taken as a whole, instruct the CPU to apply its arithmetic, logical, and control capabilities to doing useful work. Each instruction is a *binary* code that the CPU understands.

Binary is a method of representing values with two possible states. A binary element is either on or off. If you were to count in binary, you would use only 0 and 1 as the numbers. Each digit in a binary number is called a *bit* for *binary digit*. An instruction is seen by the CPU as a pattern of on-and-off electrical values. The CPU is designed to decode the meaning of these bits and carry out the instruction. The *data*, or information that the CPU uses and produces, also is in a binary form.

At first, the concept of binary representation may be hard to grasp. Binary number systems, computer instructions, and binary digits seem a bit abstract. If you stop and think about it, however, you may be more familiar with the concept of binary representation than you think.

Envision a theater marquee with the name of the movie moving across the front. The lit name is a real eye-catcher. If you stand close to the marquee and look at one of its lights, however, you will just see a light blinking on and off. On-and-off is the same as binary. Just one light blinking doesn't mean anything to you. It is only when you stand back and view the combination of many lights—some on (1) and some off (0)—that you see moving words. Your eyes are able to decode the patterns of lights as letters and words.

Computers do not work with data (information) like people do. You count to 9 and carry the next digit to the next column to get to 10. You use alphabetical characters to write words. Internally, computers count to 1 and carry the next digit to get to binary 10, which is the computer's way of expressing the value of 2. Computers work with alphabetical characters as distinct patterns of 0's and 1's. But don't worry—you don't have to learn to count in or read binary numbers or letters. Computers translate their binary representations to readable output for you to work with.

People have 10 fingers, which are useful for counting. Thus, the decimal number system, based on 10, is comfortable (and natural) for people, but the number system based on two states (0 and 1) is natural for computers. You can think your way, and the CPU can "think" its way because you see the results of computation as familiar letters and numbers. The CPU, through a part of a program, translates binary data into people data. Perhaps if people had evolved with 8 fingers, you would find it natural to use the *octal*, or *base 8*, number system.

You will read more about how the computer and people points of view are merged in a moment, but for now, remember that the CPU, as well as most of the rest of the system hardware, works with binary representations based on on-and-off electrical states.

About Binary Shorthand . . .

Some computer users, such as programmers and system designers, must work with binary values directly. Writing or speaking a binary value such as 00101011 is cumbersome. Just try repeating quickly that binary number three or four times, and you'll see! To make working with binary values easier, computer people have worked out a shorthand notation for binary numbers. This shorthand notation divides a binary number into two 4-bit pieces. In this example, the division is 0010 1011.

Each 4-bit piece can contain 16 possible combinations of 0's and 1's. Computer people take advantage of the 16 possible combinations by representing the 4 bits as *hexadecimal* or *base 16* numbers. To count in hexadecimal (or *hex*), you count from 0 to 9 as you normally do. Instead of carrying the next number to the 10's column and beginning at 1 again, however, you keep counting. Hex uses the letters a through f for the decimal values 10 through 15. You would count to "10" in hex as follows:

```
1 2 3 4 5 6 7 8 9 a b c d e f 10
```

In hex, it takes 16 counting steps to reach "10."

About Binary Shorthand . . .(continued)

To see how a hex value is assigned to 4 bits, look at the value of each digit of a 4-bit value consisting of all 1s.

	Binary value	1	1	1	1
		×	×	×	×
Decimal value of each digit		8	4	2	1
	Total		8+4+2+1	=	15 decimal or f hex

Notice that each decimal digit is two times the value of the digit to its right. In binary numbers, each digit is a power of 2, or *twice* the value of the digit to its right. When there is a 1 in a position in a binary number, that number is "worth" the decimal value of that position. The decimal values are 1, 2, 4, 8, 16, and so on. When there is a 0 in a position in a binary number, the decimal value of that position is 0. Adding the decimal values of each digit of binary 1111 gives you 15 or hex f. With the additional value of 0, this computation provides the 16 possible combinations in a hex digit. Now apply the hex conversion to the original binary number in this section:

	Binary value	0	0	1	0		1	0	1	1
		×	×	×	×		×	×	×	×
Decimal value of each digit		8	4	2	1		8	4	2	1
	Total	0+0+2+0	=	2			8+0+2+1	=	b	

The shorthand hex value for 00101011 is 2b.

In computers, electrical signals are processed meaningfully through the on-and-off states of the signals. Any one of these signals is not very informative to you or the computer. But when the CPU is presented a pattern of several binary signals, it can decode the meaning of the signals and carry out work or interpret a value.

The manufacturers of different computers have different ideas concerning how their CPUs should decode binary instructions. A binary pattern that is meaningful to one computer may be completely incomprehensible to a different computer. Each CPU in a manufacturer's computer line understands its own specific binary instructions and no others. This set of understood instructions is referred to as the computer's *instruction set*.

The individual instructions that make up the core of UNIX can be translated to various computers. As you will see, UNIX can operate on a variety of computer CPUs using a variety of instruction sets. Nonportable operating systems work with one instruction set only. For instance, the MS-DOS operating system works only on computers with CPUs from the Intel family of 8086 microprocessors.

System Memory

Instructions are presented to a CPU as a program runs. A running program is actually the CPU executing a series of instructions. The CPU fetches the instructions in a predetermined order. These instructions must come from some place that the CPU can access; that *some place* is the computer's *memory*. In fact, when the CPU develops the results of computations, it must store those data results in memory as well. The component of system hardware that stores instructions and data in a location accessible to the CPU is called *random-access memory*, or RAM.

RAM is a collection of electrical binary storage units held within integrated circuits or chips. As long as power is supplied to these chips, they can retain their stored contents. In simple terms, RAM remembers.

RAM stores binary data in locations that the CPU can electrically *call out*, or *address*. To make more efficient the CPU's accessing of binary data, each address in RAM is able to store eight or more binary digits or bits. The number of bits stored at each RAM address is almost always some multiple of eight.

The grouping of eight binary digits is so common in computing that eight associated bits have their own term. A *byte* is eight binary digits. RAM stores data in one or more bytes per address. The CPU accesses the contents of a RAM address in an operation called *reading*, and the CPU provides the contents of a RAM address in an operation called *writing*. Because RAM accommodates both reading and writing, it is known as *read/write memory*. RAM gets its name because the CPU can *randomly* read from or write to any of the RAM's addresses.

About Memory Capacity . . .

Today's UNIX-system computers contain millions of bytes of RAM. A program contains thousands of bytes of instructions. To make byte capacity or quantity more meaningful, computers use prefixes to indicate relative numbers. A kilobyte, abbreviated as K or KB, is 1024 bytes. A megabyte, abbreviated M or sometimes MB, is 1024 kilobytes. The multiples are not in even 1000's because 1024 is a power of 2 (binary). When you see a number such as 640K, you can multiply the number by the 1024 multiplier to get the total capacity or size in bytes.

The links between the CPU and RAM (as well as between most electrical components of the system hardware) are called the *buses*. A bus is like a multilane electrical highway on which signals can move from one component to another quickly and efficiently. The number of electrical lines (lanes) in a bus is related to the number of bytes the system is capable of moving. The CPU uses an *address bus* to encode the address of a desired memory location. RAM picks up this address and ensures that only the content of the memory location corresponding to that address is active.

If the CPU is reading the memory address, the RAM hardware places the current contents of the addressed location on the data bus. The *data bus* is separate from the address bus. The data bus delivers the contents of the addressed memory location to the CPU. The delivered data may be an instruction that the CPU carries out, or the data may be a value that the CPU needs to perform a computation. In any case, the CPU, the buses, and the random-access memory are designed to interact in a highly organized manner.

Although RAM is well suited for storage that the CPU can immediately access and alter, RAM cannot provide the complete storage solution in a computer system. RAM's major shortcoming is its dependence on electrical power to retain stored values. When RAM loses power, such as when the computer's main power switch is turned off, all of the data and instruction contents of RAM vanish.

A computer can make good use of memory that doesn't "forget" when the power is turned off. Normally, RAM's loss of content is of no consequence, because the loss is a natural part of turning the system off. Still, a computer with absolutely no "recollection" of what happened before the electrical power went off is handicapped. All UNIX systems need some initial information available as soon as the power is restored.

A special family of memory called *Read Only Memory*, or *ROM*, does retain its stored values when power is turned off. Like RAM, ROM is randomly accessible by the CPU via the buses. Unlike RAM, however, ROM can only be read from—not written to. In some computer operations, such as the execution of start-up instructions, ROM is ideal. Because ROM retains its values, and therefore any instructions, the CPU is able to use ROM in place of RAM to establish the computer in an operationally ready state.

Both ROM and RAM are relatively costly methods of storing massive amounts of computer information. In most UNIX systems, as well as in other types of systems, mass storage of data is delegated to magnetic devices, such as disk drives.

About Booting . . .

In computer terms, *booting the system* refers to starting the computer. UNIX resides on the disk (see the next section) until power is applied to the computer. Remember that when power is off, RAM loses its contents and therefore any instructions. When power is restored, the CPU executes the instructions in a special ROM, called the *bootstrap ROM*. Like other ROM, the bootstrap ROM does not lose its contents when power is switched off. The bootstrap ROM enables the CPU to access the main loading program on the disk. When the main loading program is loaded into memory and executed by the CPU, the rest of UNIX is loaded into memory by the main loader program. The UNIX system is then booted. If you use your imagination, you can see how the computer has "pulled itself up by the bootstraps."

Another expression for booting is *Initial Program Load* or *IPL*. Before any user can access the services of a UNIX system, the system must be IPLed or booted.

Disk Drives

A *disk drive* is a unit of computer hardware that enables the storage of massive amounts of instructions and data. Disk drives often are housed within the same enclosure as the CPU, memory, and other electrical-system components (see fig. 2.1). In many cases, disk drives have their own enclosures and are physically located close to the system-unit enclosure. Although disk drives are peripheral to the main system hardware, it is convenient to think of disk drives as part of the system hardware.

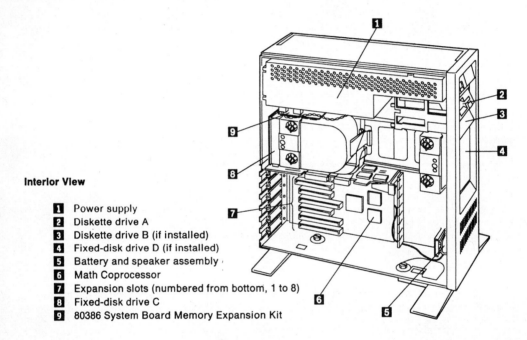

Interior View

1. Power supply
2. Diskette drive A
3. Diskette drive B (if installed)
4. Fixed-disk drive D (if installed)
5. Battery and speaker assembly
6. Math Coprocessor
7. Expansion slots (numbered from bottom, 1 to 8)
8. Fixed-disk drive C
9. 80386 System Board Memory Expansion Kit

Fig. 2.1. An interior view of a system unit, showing positions of floppy and hard disk drives.

Disk drives use magnetics to store binary information. A special circuit converts electrical bits taken from the data bus to magnetic patterns in the surface of a disk. The surface of the disk is a special oxide coating that lends itself to being magnetized quickly. Within the oxide coating are billions of particles. Each of these particles is capable of acting like a miniature magnet.

If you dust off your physics knowledge for a moment, you'll recall that every magnet has two stable poles— a north pole and a south pole. With two poles, magnets are natural binary storage units. With billions of particles to magnetize, disks are capable of storing huge masses of binary information.

The work of converting the electrical signals of the computer to the magnetic poles on a disk's surface is done by the drive's *head*. The head is capable of exerting a magnetic force on the particles on the disk's surface. The disk itself is spun on a center hub, as is a record on a phonograph. The head is positioned over the disk like the phonograph's pick-up arm. As the disk spins below the head, the head can magnetize clumps of oxide in north- or south-pole orientation. In other words, the head magnetizes binary patterns. When a disk head is recording data on the disk, the head is writing the disk. Figure 2.2 shows the multiple read/write heads of a hard disk drive.

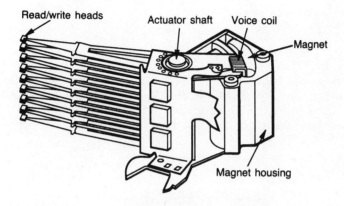

Fig. 2.2. *Each head reads data from and writes data to the disk.*

Once written, the magnetic data is very stable. Because the written data relies on magnetism to retain its values, the disk retains data even with the power off. Once power is reapplied to the computer system, the drive can position the head above the magnetic data and extract an electrical signal induced by the magnetic clumps. The drive electronics then convert the electrical signal to binary data suitable for use by RAM or by the CPU. Although data stored on a magnetic disk takes a round-about route to get to the business end of computing, data storage on disk is useful, and the data is accessed reasonably quickly by the system. Disks can store data for a few cents per kilobyte.

To make the job of storing and retrieving disk data more uniform, disks are divided into concentric tracks. Each position accessible by the drive's head contains a *track* (see fig. 2.3). Tracks are further divided into *sectors*. In other words, each track contains many sectors. The electronic controller can use the track/sector "address" of each disk to store and retrieve data (or instructions).

A special UNIX program prepares the track and sector information for the disk before the disk can be used. You will not have to see to the preparation of disks because disk formatting is done by a system administrator.

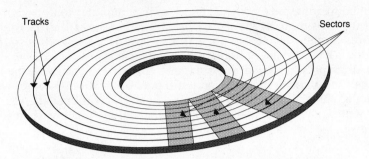

Tracks   Sectors

Fig. 2.3. Concentric tracks on a disk's surface.

Small removable disks, called *floppy disks* (see fig. 2.4), are employed in many UNIX systems. Floppy disks get their name because of their semi-rigid nature. The actual recording surface (the *media*) is a flexible Mylar disk housed in a square jacket. Floppy disks and disk drives are available in 8-inch, 5 1/4-inch, and 3 1/2-inch sizes. Floppy disk storage capacity is relatively low, ranging from around 128K to just over 2.4M.

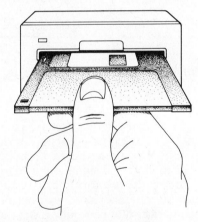

Fig. 2.4. Inserting a 3 1/2-inch floppy disk into a disk drive.

Most high-capacity disk drives have several fixed disks or rigid platters permanently fixed on a single shaft within the sealed drive. These types of drives are called *fixed* disk drives, *hard* disk drives, or *Winchester* disk drives (see fig. 2.5). Each of the rigid platters is divided into tracks and sectors. Each platter is read to or written by an individual head. Hard disk drives can store hundreds of megabytes of data.

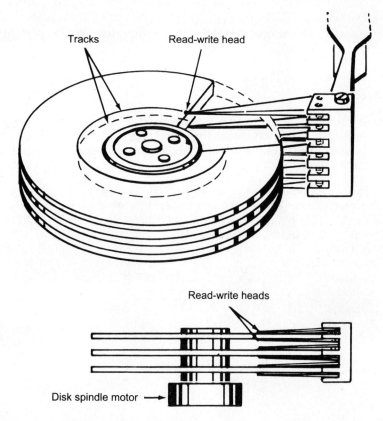

Fig. 2.5. *A typical hard disk drive.*

Understanding Peripheral Hardware

Thus far in this discussion of hardware, it sounds like the computer does most of its work supporting its own subsystems. When you think of a computer, you think of how the computer can help you do your work. The data and instructions that are used by the CPU are intended to provide you with meaningful results.

Actually, nothing meaningful can be done by the computer unless information is passed to and from the outside world. Normally, the outside world means *you*. You type in memos at the keyboard as you monitor your work on-screen. You look at the results of a financial model when you read the computer-generated, printed report.

The keyboard, screen, and printer that accept and display computer information are called *peripheral hardware*, or *peripherals*. Peripherals are involved in *input/output*, or *I/O*. You communicate with your UNIX system through peripherals. In fact, of all the components in your computer system, peripherals are the components you directly operate.

Terminals

By far, the most frequently employed hardware used to communicate with a UNIX system is the *terminal*. The terminal, as the name suggests, is the component at the end point of a computer system. Beyond the terminal, the computer expects to find human eyes and fingers!

Terminals consist of a display unit and a keyboard. The display unit may be a paper-printing mechanism, like a teletype printer, but most likely it is a *video display unit* or VDU (see fig. 2.6). Some people refer to the VDU as a *CRT* for *cathode ray tube* (also used by a television set).

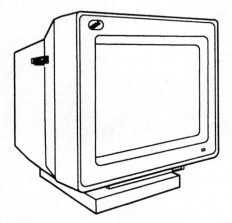

Fig. 2.6. *A video display unit.*

Most VDUs employ a cathode ray tube. In new designs, the display may be a flat-panel display, using liquid-crystal or gas-plasma technology. Regardless of the underlying design, the VDU screen displays text (and sometimes graphics) which has been output by the system hardware. Thus, the VDU screen is an output-only peripheral. Many people use the terms VDU and terminal interchangeably. Using these terms interchangeably is acceptable as long as everyone understands the intended meaning.

The other half of the terminal's functional parts is the *keyboard* (see fig. 2.7). The keyboard is an input device. Keyboards usually come packaged with the VDU. In many cases, the keyboard is located in the same physical enclosure as the VDU screen. In other cases, the keyboard is a separate unit that attaches to the VDU by means of a coiled cord. As far as UNIX is concerned, the keyboard's method of attachment is not important.

Certain keys on the keyboard have special meanings for UNIX. Chapter 5 covers the meanings of these keys and key combinations.

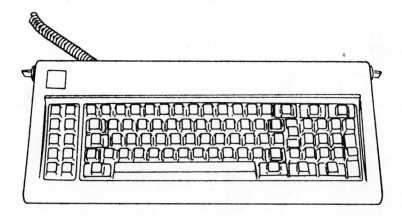

Fig. 2.7. *A standard keyboard.*

A UNIX system may have several terminals attached to it. From the user's point of view, the terminal is the standard peripheral used to provide keystroke input and to receive visual output. As you will discover as you use UNIX commands, the concept of standard input and standard output is important. For now, make sure that you understand that typing at the keyboard is considered standard *input* and that seeing characters displayed on-screen is considered standard *output*.

One terminal, the *system console terminal*, has an important role in UNIX installations. The system console terminal is the primary terminal for starting a UNIX system's operation. Normally, a person administrating the UNIX system will use the system console. On some single-user UNIX systems, the user terminal and the system console will be the same terminal. In effect, the console on a single-user computer system does double duty.

Printers

Printers provide a means of obtaining a permanent copy of output. Printed output can be anything from an instruction manual to the contents of one of UNIX's configuration tables. Printers are output-only peripherals. A UNIX system may have more than one printer.

Today, printers have become specialized. The specialization is based on output quality and speed. It is not uncommon for a UNIX system to have one printer for high-quality text, such as correspondence, and another printer for large-volume reports, such as accounting audit trails. The high-quality printer is often a laser printer, whose quality begins to rival that of typeset text (see fig. 2.8). The high-volume printer is often a dot-matrix line printer (see fig. 2.9), whose speed can produce copy at as much as 600 lines per minute (lpm). When you are ready to use a printer, ask the person in charge of administrating your system about the availability of specialized printers.

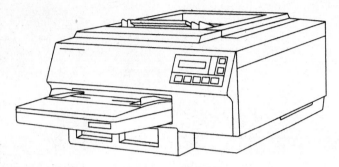

Fig. 2.8. *A laser printer.*

Fig. 2.9. *A dot-matrix printer.*

Modems

Wouldn't it be handy to sit down at a terminal and access a UNIX system across town, or even in another state? Through the use of modems, you can. The term *modem* is made up of the terms *mod*ulate and *dem*odulate. Modulation is a method of imposing an information signal on top of a carrier signal. Radio and television systems work through the transmission of modulated signals and subsequent demodulation by a radio or TV.

Radio and television systems modulate airwaves (electromagnetic waves), whereas modems modulate sound waves. In fact, modems are designed to work with sound waves carried over telephone lines. When you press a key on your local keyboard, the modem sends a series of sounds to the distant modem you called. The distant modem demodulates the sounds and translates the sounds into the binary representation of the key you pressed. When the distant UNIX system receives the character from the distant modem, the system accepts the character as though the character had been entered from a terminal a few feet away. Likewise, the distant UNIX system sends character output to your remote terminal. Again, the method of transfer is sound, and the transfer is fully supervised by the modems. Because modems enable input and output operations, the output capability can be used to connect distant printers through modems (see fig. 2.10).

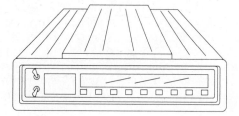

Fig. 2.10. A modem.

The Mouse

Some computer-input operations involve choosing an item from an on-screen display. Other input operations involve the creation of lines for drawing or drafting input. A popular device to provide these input operations is the *mouse*. A mouse gets its name from its general shape (see fig. 2.11). You have to have a good imagination, but you can visualize the curved, tapered body of a mouse when you look at this input device. Of course, the trailing connection wire is supposed to resemble the mouse's tail.

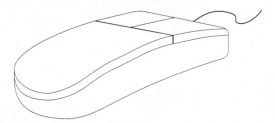

Fig. 2.11. An optical mouse.

The mouse's job is to translate its movement across a surface into input signals that the computer can use to operate a program. Two or more switch buttons on the mouse enable secondary functions, such as selection or cancellation of screen items. You coordinate the movement of the mouse with your hand by watching the corresponding movement of an arrow or other on-screen icon. The mouse-screen pointer works with the software to direct and select items on-screen. Selecting items, such as menu options, with the mouse pointer, is often called *point-and-shoot operation*. Not all programs work with a mouse, however. If you execute a program that doesn't support a mouse, the mouse does nothing.

Understanding Software

Hardware provides electrical and electro-mechanical computing capabilities, but *software* provides the blueprint for the exact way the computing is done by the hardware. Actually, software provides instructions for the CPU to follow. These binary software instructions are held in files on a disk. When you load the software, it is read from the disk file into RAM. Because the CPU can randomly access memory, the CPU can access a sequence of instructions and execute the sequence to "run" the program.

The following explanation is quite a simplified view of how software and hardware operate together in a working computer system, but this explanation is sufficient for your basic understanding. You will see a more detailed view later in this chapter and in other chapters.

The software used with a UNIX-based system can be divided into three broad areas:

- System and utility software
- Development software
- Applications software

The core of UNIX is system software and utility software. Another area associated with UNIX-based systems is development software. Development software enables programmers to devise new programs for the system. The third broad area is applications software. Applications software consists of programs that apply the computer's capability to automate your work. The next sections look at the three broad areas of UNIX software in a bit more detail.

Understanding System Software

In the daily work of computer systems, many of the fundamental computing tasks are repetitive. The computer's placement of characters on the display and your copying a file are examples. Specialized system software is the part of the division of software labor that handles the fundamental computing tasks. System software can be further categorized as operating-system software and utilities.

Operating-System Software

System software handles routine repetitive tasks and resource allocation. For example, the computer places thousands, if not millions, of characters on a display during the computer's lifetime. Displaying characters is just one repetitive task that is fundamental to a working computer system.

Remember that the display, or VDU, is an item of hardware. Also remember that software, through instructions, controls the CPU. In fact, each time a character is displayed on-screen, the CPU and the software work together to accomplish the display job. Similarly, reading or writing data onto the disk is a constant computing task. Placing a character on a screen and reading bytes of data from a disk seem like a trivial job when you compare those jobs with calculating the launch window of a space probe or with some other exotic application of computer power. Yet working computers do scores of such repetitive tasks while providing you (or your program) with sophisticated results.

Operating-system software, such as UNIX, takes responsibility for doing many of the repetitive and fundamental jobs of program execution and reporting any problems along the way. A programmer writing a program to capture information from a lab instrument does not have to contend with the low-level programming details or the numerous instructions necessary to display a character or read an exact section of a disk. Operating-system software sees to these and other low-level details. The programmer needs to know only how to call upon system software for low-level services.

If you think of the computer hardware as a theater's empty stage and a working program as an ongoing play, you can see a void between them. There is a lot of support behind the "scenes." Operating-system software does the computer-equivalent job of the set-preparation crews, the lighting crews, the stage hands, the makeup artist, and even the janitor. All the services that must bridge the hardware and the user's program are performed by the operating-system software. The program is not burdened with routine details. Can you imagine the lead actress having to push her own backdrop onto the stage just before the curtain goes up?

Much of the software that makes up an operating system such as UNIX provides low-level service to other programs. Other programs don't need to include instructions for low-level, repetitive operations because the programs can rely on the foundation of the services the operating system provides. In Chapter 3, you will read in more detail about UNIX as an operating system. For now, you should begin to understand that UNIX has an important role as a detail-oriented foundation for other software.

Utilities

Just as a carpenter has a set of utility tools for building, maintaining, and repairing items, UNIX and other operating systems have a set of *utility programs*, or *utilities*, that enable you to manage the aspects of your computing work. Utilities are not considered operating-system software, but they are considered system software because utilities are provided with operating-system software.

UNIX utilities enable you to manage files, directories, user environments, security, and many other computer considerations. Part Two of this book is dedicated to the UNIX utilities and commands. You will see utilities in detail in Part Two. For now, just think of utilities as the useful tools provided with an operating system. Chapter 3 will show you how utilities fit into the UNIX operating-system picture.

Understanding Development Software

Programmers use development software to create new programs and to manage the creation process. Normally, a typical UNIX user does not use the development software. You will, however, want to be aware of development software and understand its basic use. Using computers is less mysterious when you have insight into the software. The next few sections give you a brief glimpse of program development and the software that makes the development possible.

Compilers

Nearly all programming done for large systems, such as UNIX systems, is done by programmers using high-level languages. A *high-level language* (*HLL*) is a symbolic description of processing steps. This symbolic description is also known as *program code*. Such programming languages as Fortran, COBOL, BASIC, Pascal, and C are examples of HLLs.

A programmer writes source program code in an HLL using a text editor. The coded "words" contained in the source program are specialized notations for the steps the programmer wants the computer to carry out. To people other than programmers, the source program may look like Greek, but programmers are trained to be conversant in HLLs.

A programmer cannot immediately execute on the computer a program he has written in an HLL. As you read in a previous section, computers understand binary values, rather than words and symbols. In order to obtain a binary version of the source program that the computer understands, the programmer submits the source program code to a special program called a *compiler*.

The compiler translates the written source code into a set of binary instructions and data that the CPU can use. In their binary form, programs are in the CPU's native tongue. A compiler can translate (compile) operating-system software source programs, utilities source programs, applications source programs, or any program. Compiled programs are often referred to as *binaries*. In fact, you later will read about a file directory in most UNIX systems named /bin for *bin*ary. Many of the system's executable programs are stored in /bin.

There are many computer languages (compilers). BASIC, ADA, Fortran, COBOL, and Lisp are just a few. The most common compiler available in UNIX systems is the C compiler. C is a programming language that has been adapted to many different hardware platforms. UNIX is written in the C language. You may not care about C or other programming languages, and that's perfectly all right. Just understand that UNIX can be functionally implemented or ported to any computer that supports a C compiler. As you will see in Chapter 3, UNIX is quite portable. UNIX owes much of its portability to C.

Source Code Control Systems

In large systems, several programmers may work on various parts of a single programming project. A Source Code Control System, or SCCS, is a software utility that keeps track of the source code for projects. A single project can have hundreds of source-code files, each representing a small portion of the final program. Each programmer tests and modifies his portion of the source files several times before the program is completed. The SCCS identifies the most current version of each source-code file, to enable the newest version to be incorporated into the program. Program documentation and definition are usually incorporated into an SCCS. The SCCS also can track the dependencies of the source programs, where one source file refers to another in order to complete its function. You can think of the SCCS as a kind of combination source-code librarian/project-management system for programs.

Understanding Applications Software

Applications software is the software you utilize to do your daily computer work. Applications software does a focused job of dealing with real-world problems. Word processors, spreadsheets, inventory systems, and CAD/CAM programs are all examples of applications software. From your point of view, applications software does the useful work, whereas the system software supports that work.

The range of applications software is growing. You may use programs used by hundreds or thousands of other UNIX users. Other programs that you use may be unique to your location or even unique to you. The next sections look at some of the popular categories of UNIX applications software.

Accounting

Accounting software is used to track the financial side of company operations. Most accounting packages consist of several distinct parts. Although the exact makeup varies, accounting applications usually include accounts payable (AP), accounts receivable (AR), general ledger (GL), fixed assets (FA), and payroll modules. By the time a company has a dozen employees and a dozen accounts, the company can benefit from a computerized accounting system.

Order Entry

Order-entry software handles the tracking and management of customer orders. Any company that sells a product, whether the sales are wholesale or retail, can implement an order-entry system. Most order-entry systems have the capability to track an order through its progress until the order is filled and shipped. It is not uncommon for order-entry software to tie into accounting and inventory software. Applications that plan materials requirements are often linked to order-entry applications—to track the goods ordered. This linking of program modules enables distinct departments to benefit from the information activities of other departments.

Inventory Control

Inventory-control applications provide a crucial role in accounting for materials. Inventory control provides information about items, quantities, bills of materials, stocking levels, inventory turns, inventory values, and more. It is hard to picture a modern business of any size remaining competitive without inventory-control software.

Machine Control

In today's modern manufacturing and testing environments, machine-control applications provide a means to coordinate a complex operation with a minimum of human intervention. Machine-control applications automate factory floors, give directions to robots, monitor alarm-system switches, and perform many other specialized control tasks. Machine-control applications make extensive use of I/O that is not *user* input and output. Much of a machine-control application's I/O is associated with sensors, machine interfaces, and other computers.

Database Management

Database-management applications provide a means for users to design data forms and enter information into the forms. The forms provide a uniform method for entering and viewing a particular category of information. The actual storage file or files for each form is called the *database*. One of database management's strong suits is its capability of assuming responsibility for the complex nature of storing information, while presenting an easy-to-use user interface. Figure 2.12 shows a typical database screen.

When information (data) is in the database, the user of a database-management application can query, modify, relate, and report the stored information. The user may work directly with the database-management software in an *ad hoc* mode, or the user may work with programmer-developed, stand-alone applications that use the active core or engine of the database-management software.

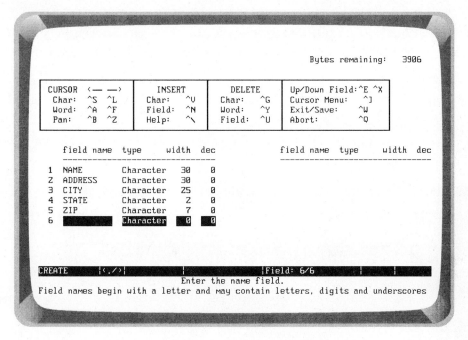

```
                                      Bytes remaining:    3906

 ┌─────────────────┬──────────────┬──────────────┬──────────────────────┐
 │ CURSOR  <— —>   │  INSERT      │  DELETE      │ Up/Down Field:^E ^X   │
 │  Char:  ^S ^L   │  Char:   ^V  │  Char:   ^G  │ Cursor Menu:     ^]   │
 │  Word:  ^A ^F   │  Field:  ^N  │  Word:   ^Y  │ Exit/Save:       ^W   │
 │  Pan:   ^B ^Z   │  Help:   ^\  │  Field:  ^U  │ Abort:           ^Q   │
 └─────────────────┴──────────────┴──────────────┴──────────────────────┘

        field name    type      width  dec          field name  type      width  dec
        ────────────────────────────────            ────────────────────────────────
    1   NAME          Character   30    0
    2   ADDRESS       Character   30    0
    3   CITY          Character   25    0
    4   STATE         Character    2    0
    5   ZIP           Character    7    0
    6   ▮▮▮▮▮▮▮▮       Character    0    0

 ───────────────────────────────────────────────────────────────────────────
 CREATE       |<./>|         |              |Field: 6/6     |        |
                        Enter the name field.
   Field names begin with a letter and may contain letters, digits and underscores
```

Fig. 2.12. A typical user-generated database-management form.

Many database managers support *Structured Query Language* or *SQL*. SQL is a standard method for managing databases without regard to the exact database engine that supports any particular database. Through SQL, two different database-management programs can exchange data. If SQL interests you, you might want to pick up a copy of Que's *Using SQL* for useful reading.

Spreadsheets

The spreadsheet is one of the biggest success stories in software. Millions of users find their spreadsheet software a valuable tool for business. Spreadsheets get their name from the concept of the accountant's columnar pad or tablet. The tablet is ruled with rows and columns to provide boxes for entries. The use of boxes or *cells* keeps entries neat, aligned, and segregated.

Spreadsheet software takes the idea of the accountant's columnar pad and adds provisions that take advantage of the computer. Not only can each cell contain a literal value, like the accountant's entry, but the cell can also contain a formula based on the contents of other cells. When a value is changed in a formula-referenced cell, the value of the cell containing the formula changes accordingly.

With a little imagination, spreadsheet users have devised thousands of ways to combine data values and formulas into spreadsheets. The result has been an unprecedented information and decision-support resource for business. Spreadsheets are used for everything from modeling sales forecasts to tracking students' grades.

Some popular DOS-based spreadsheets, such as Lotus 1-2-3, are now available for some UNIX systems (see fig. 2.13). If you use 1-2-3 or a 1-2-3 work-alike on your system, you can find useful guidance to spreadsheet operations from *Using 1-2-3 Release 2.2*, Special Edition, *Using 1-2-3 Release 3*, and a variety of other books about 1-2-3 published by Que.

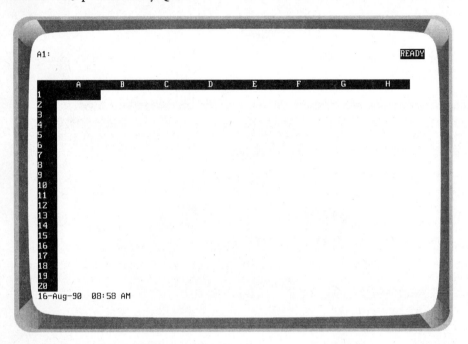

Fig. 2.13. *A blank 1-2-3 worksheet.*

Automatic Securities Trading

Thanks to their rapid processing speeds, UNIX-based computers can utilize special applications that enable the computer to buy and sell securities automatically via electronic data exchange. These securities-trading applications accept parameters that act as the rules for making decisions. The computer analyzes input information and uses the rules set by the parameters to take any action. A typical trading application can buy or sell securities hundreds of times per day. Don't spend too much time looking for such an application for personal use, however. These programs are used by specialized companies, which have people with the expertise to devise sound rules.

CAD/CAM

UNIX has been popular in the scientific and engineering communities for a number of years. One popular family of applications programs that has roots in these communities is CAD/CAM. *CAD* or *Computer Assisted* (or *Aided*) *Design*, and *CAM*, or *Computer Assisted Modeling*, harness the computer for work that previously required tedious human endeavor. CAD/CAM is used for mechanical and architectural drawing, circuit design, stress modeling, printed circuit-board layout, prototyping, and other engineering activities.

Summary

This chapter has presented some basic information about computer systems. Although no one expects you to be a computer expert, a little computer-system understanding can make learning UNIX an easier exercise. Following are the key points covered in this chapter:

❑ Working computer systems consist of hardware and software.

❑ Hardware falls into the categories of system hardware and peripheral hardware.

❑ System hardware is centered around the CPU, RAM, ROM, and buses.

❑ Peripheral hardware connects the system hardware to the outside world for input and output. Terminals and printers are examples of peripheral hardware.

❑ Software contains instructions that tell the CPU how to compute.

❑ System software, such as UNIX, oversees the repetitive details of computing by providing common services to applications software.

❑ Applications software addresses specific computing needs. Applications focus their instructions on one area, such as accounting or database management.

In the next chapter, you'll use the insight you gained in this chapter as you take a conceptual look at UNIX.

Understanding UNIX

3

In Chapter 1, you learned about UNIX's evolution and current efforts to standardize the operating system. Chapter 2 taught you about computer systems and the types of software that make them useful. This chapter focuses on UNIX's features and the software components that make these features available to the user.

Some UNIX users say that UNIX is difficult to learn. When a user is thrown into a "sink-or-swim" learning experience, learning may very well be difficult. If the user does not start by developing a good understanding of UNIX's underlying design, he or she will not be able to build on these concepts later. UNIX lends itself to a building-block method of learning and understanding. Although the whole of UNIX is complex, no single part of UNIX is difficult to understand. A UNIX system is not a seamless monolith of hardware and software. It is a hardware core, with layers of functionality built on that core. This chapter describes those layers and their purpose.

Unlike most other operating systems, UNIX is employed on a variety of computer systems. As you read this, thousands of UNIX systems are providing computer services to more than a million users. Although you might think that all those UNIX systems are large networks or supercomputers, such is not always the case; there is no "standard size" UNIX system. UNIX can be implemented on many sizes of computers, ranging from PCs to powerful supercomputers. This chapter gives you an overview of the various typical UNIX systems, based on their size. With this perspective, you'll have a more global understanding of your place in the growing UNIX community.

Key Terms Used in This Chapter

Core dump	A system action—in response to a detected problem—during which memory contents and other information are written to a disk. The core-dump file is then available for use by the technical staff in diagnosing the system problem.
Swapping	The transferring of an active program from memory to a disk file to enable another program to utilize memory resources.
Virtual memory	A memory-management technique that enables programs to appear to utilize more memory than is physically available.
Track	One circular data-storage section of a disk's platter surface.
Cylinder	The imaginary alignment of two or more tracks when two or more disk surfaces are employed in a disk drive.
Sector	The electrical division within each track that comprises the disk drive's most fundamental data-storage unit.
Block	The multiple of sectors that UNIX uses as its minimum disk data-handling unit. Block size can vary from implementation to implementation.
Data-transfer area	An area of system memory used to temporarily hold data that is being transferred to or from a device such as a disk drive.
Buffer	An area of memory storage dedicated to holding device data that is being read or written. Buffers accept data at one rate and deliver it at another.
Device management	The configuration, maintenance, and operation of system devices. On UNIX systems, device management includes making devices available to users on a shared basis.
Device driver	A software component of the UNIX kernel that contains the instructions necessary to integrate the device into UNIX.
Kernel	The essential core software component of UNIX. The kernel contains instructions and data tables necessary to provide higher-level programs with low-level access to computer services.
Shell	The command-interpreter software component of UNIX. The shell accepts your commands and arranges for their execution.
Utility	A command or program that performs a common and useful service. UNIX commands are often called UNIX utilities.

Command	A utility software component of UNIX. A few commands are built into the shell. Most commands are executable program files that load and execute when you type their names to the shell. Commands do utility work with files and devices.
Process	A UNIX program and its associated data in the act of executing.
Applications program	A program or related set of programs that focuses on one particular computing activity. Examples of applications include word processors, accounting packages, spread-sheets, and database managers.
C language	The high-level language used to create UNIX.
Multitasking	The capability to perform more than one task at a time. Multitasking operating systems enable the independent execution of simultaneous processes.
Multiprocessing	Another term for multitasking. Because executing UNIX programs are processes, multiprocessing more accurately describes UNIX.
Security	The ensuring of the integrity of programs, data, operating-system components, device access, and user identity. Secure computer systems reduce the exposure of system integrity to accidental or intentional damage.
File system	A collection of files organized into directories. File systems are stored physically on disks and viewed logically as a tree-structured hierarchy of directory and file names.
Directory	A special type of file containing the names and links to the locations of other directories and files.
Subdirectory	A directory that is contained within another directory in a hierarchical file system.
Hierarchy	An organization of tree-structured dependencies, similar to a family tree. In file systems, all directories can trace their identities back to a root directory in a child-to-parent fashion.
Root directory	The highest-level UNIX directory. The root directory is often called simply the "root." The root has no parent directory, and all other file system directories descend from the root.
Home directory	The directory a user accesses directly when the user logs into the system. The home directory is also known as a login directory. Each user has an individual home directory.

Looking More Closely at Operating Systems

Chapters 1 and 2 gave you a very basic idea of what an operating system is and what an operating system does. Because you're reading a book about an operating system, you'll benefit from having a good understanding of operating systems in general. Don't get the impression that you'll have to become a computer scientist in order to use UNIX. On the other hand, a little knowledge about operating systems will keep you from falling into the "technology gap."

The "technology gap" is the imaginary hole of understanding that adults sometimes find themselves in, and their sixth-grade children seem to avoid. The technology gap is similar to the "new math gap."

Memory-Management Mechanisms

As you recall from Chapter 2, the computer's central processing unit—or CPU—actually executes applications programs. While it is being executed, an applications program resides in random-access memory, or RAM. The operating system is responsible for loading the program into RAM so that the program can be executed. Because the operating system oversees the entire computer system, the operating system alone is in a position to allocate memory resources for use by programs. Typically, several programs reside in memory at any one time. If each program could allocate the system's RAM for its own use, problems would occur. Two programs might try to use the same locations in RAM, for example, but only one would succeed. The other program would be out of luck.

In its management of the computer's memory, the operating system maximizes memory usage and avoids wasted memory space. If programs selected their own memory, they might leave small gaps between themselves and their neighboring programs. By itself, one of these gaps would be too small to hold another program; if you put them all together, however, these little gaps would add up to a great deal of wasted memory space.

To visualize this "gap" situation, imagine what happens when people pick their own seating positions on a bench seat in a waiting room. If two people seat them-selves wastefully on a three-person seat, there isn't enough room left for a third person to sit. Still, there are gaps of space left on the seat, and these gaps are wasted space. If someone is responsible for assigning seating, however, it is likely that three people are given the three seating positions on the bench. When the computer's memory is involved, the operating system is in charge of "seating" the programs, much like a person in charge of assigning seating positions.

In the "olden days" of computing (that is, until the 1970s) computers used a type of memory called *core plane memory*. Core-plane memory—also called simply *core*—is made of thousands of tiny doughnut-shaped rings, each of which is magnetized as a binary 1 or 0. Although core memory is rarely used today, the term "core" often is used interchangeably with the term "RAM." When an operating system detects a serious problem in operating integrity, the operating system stops the offending program (or the program that is using the services of an offending item of hardware). If possible, the operating system sends a warning message to the system's main terminal. Then, the operating system sends the contents of memory to a printer or a disk, for examination by computer specialists who are troubleshooting the problem. When an operating system sends this type of "snapshot" of the memory's contents to a printer or disk, the operation is called a *core dump*. Not all operating systems perform core dumps. MS-DOS, for example, does not, but UNIX does perform core dumps.

Computers have varying amounts of RAM. In order to allocate memory effectively, the operating system must continually determine how much memory is available. The more memory a system contains, the more programs the operating system can place in memory for execution. Because most users run at least one program while they do their work, a direct correlation exists between the amount of memory in a system and the number of users the system can support at any one time. When memory is completely allocated, an additional user must wait until one of the current users finishes work. The operating system then can release the finished program's memory for use by the new user.

Many operating systems get around this memory limitation by using a technique called *swapping*. When swapping takes place, the operating system checks the activity of memory-resident programs and writes inactive or low-priority programs temporarily to the disk. In other words, the operating system snatches the program out of memory—complete with its intermediate data—and writes the program to a disk-based swap file. A "swapped" program is in "suspended animation" while it is in temporary storage on the disk. Another user's program then can be loaded into the newly freed memory space. The other user's program may be a new program, or it may be a previously swapped-to-disk program that is swapped back to memory to begin exactly where it left off. The effect of this swapping mechanism is that the operating system can support more simultaneous users than the system's total memory indicates is possible. UNIX takes advantage of this type of swapping mechanism so that more users can work with a fixed amount of memory. If you use a system in which swapping is taking place, you will notice a degradation of system response as the swapping overhead "tugs" at the system's computing resources.

More sophisticated operating systems take the idea of swapping a bit further by incorporating a mechanism called *virtual memory*. Virtual memory is memory that *appears* to be present, but in reality is only *simulated* in software. Virtual-memory management takes advantage of the fact that most programs are executed as a progression of memory-location accesses. That is, the CPU executes the instruction being held in the first memory location, then the second, then the third, and so forth. Only occasionally does the CPU "jump" out of sequence to an instruction that is located very far from the last instruction's memory location.

When virtual memory is used, the operating system allocates an area of RAM that is smaller than required to hold a large program. The operating system then loads as much of the program as possible into the allocated memory space and places the remainder of the program—in a virtual storage location—on the disk. Because the CPU begins execution in the memory-resident portion of the program, and only occasionally needs to access the portion stored on the disk, the program still executes rapidly.

When the disk-resident portion of the program is needed, the memory-resident portion is sent to disk, and the disk-resident portion is loaded into memory. The program itself doesn't "know" that it is being divided between RAM and the disk. The operating system supervises the virtual memory that the program uses. You won't be aware if your system employs virtual-memory management. From the program's point of view, it has as much memory as it needs to do its job.

Virtual memory is more efficient than swapping, because virtual memory does not swap the user's entire program to disk and then hold it in "suspended animation." Only the inactive portion of a virtual memory program is sent to disk, and then only when memory resources become short. Because the program's active portion continues to run, the user sees less lag in the system's response. More sophisticated UNIX-based systems incorporate virtual-memory management.

You won't see the operating system's memory-management mechanism at work. Memory management is a detail that an operating system handles behind the scenes. However, you may experience increases or decreases in system response to your programs and commands. Much of this response variance is due to the number of users and their programs' demands on memory.

Disk-Management Mechanisms

You should have the idea by now that disks (and their close relatives, tapes) are key hardware components. Disks store data and programs in magnetic form. In order to be useful, the data and programs must be accessible to the system hardware. The operating system is responsible for moving data and programs between disk drives and system RAM. Further, the operating system maintains "bookkeeping" records of each disk's contents and the location of each program and data file on the disk. Each operating system has its own way of performing such tasks.

Data and programs are stored on disks as files. You access a file by referring to the file's name in a command. Disk-drive electronics are not capable of accessing files by name. To a disk drive, the file you want is physically located in a sector of a track of a cylinder. In fact, a file can span several sectors. You'll learn about the physical attributes of disks in a moment. For now, just understand that the way you reference disk data and the way that a disk drive references the data are very different.

To understand the principle, think of a house in a housing addition. You may refer to the house as "the house on lot 66." Lot 66 is a distinct identifying name. When you look at the directory of available properties, you see the entry for lot 66. You and the realtor can speak of lot 66 with no misunderstanding.

In a similar way, UNIX files have names. You can see file names in a directory listing. When you and another user refer to a file name in a directory, there is no misunderstanding.

In the example of the house on lot 66, understand that the agencies responsible for dividing and recording the physical land that makes up housing additions must reference property in a more physical manner than you and the realtor. Property is referred to as a portion of a county; a township is a portion of a county. Likewise, a range is a section of a township, a section is a portion of a range, and a quarter is a portion of a section. In the surveyor's view, lot 66 is a physical division of land located 120 feet from the edge of the southwest quarter of section 3, range 2, of Orange township, Rush county.

Like the agency, the disk accesses data based on a physical division of the disk's surface. And just as the surveyor has no idea of the final disposition of land, the disk drive has no "idea" of the names of files stored on the disk's surface.

In real estate, official property logs keep track of physical property such as the example lot 66. The property log records not only the reference to the lot number, but also the reference to the county, section, quarter, and so on. The property log acts as a translation mechanism for two different methods of referencing lot 66. Through the translation mechanism, both the surveyor and the home buyer can reference the same place.

Nearly all operating systems incorporate some form of translation mechanism to equate the divided "real estate" of a disk's physical layout with the names of files that the disk stores. To understand how the operating system interacts with disks, you need to understand the disk's physical layout.

You may recall the discussion in Chapter 2 of disk drives as hardware items. Disk drives are important storage devices because they store millions of bytes of data and programs. Typically, a mass-storage disk drive has several circular disks or platters, which are mounted on a spindle. The platters and associated parts are sealed in a closed case. In operation, the platters spin at 3,600 revolutions per minute, while movable heads "float" on the air currents created by the spinning platters. The floating heads ride on a microscopic cushion of air just above the surface of the platters. In this position above the platters, the heads can read or write magnetic data on the platters.

The disk's read-write heads are connected to a common support and actuation mechanism, so that all heads are offset from the edges of their respective platters by the same distance. The head-actuation mechanism can incrementally move—or step—the position of the heads toward the center of the platters and back to the outside edges of the platters. At each stepping-position stopping point, a head can read or write as much data as will fit into one rotation of the platter. Beyond one rotation of the platter, of course, the data would repeat. The circular band of data at each stepping-position stopping point is called a *track*.

All the heads are aligned at the same offset of all the platters, so you can visualize that the same stepping-position stopping point on each platter aligns through the platters. This imaginary alignment of each track through all the platters is called a *cylinder*. Tracks themselves are divided into smaller slices or segments, called *sectors*. The drive's controlling electronics physically address data items stored on the disk by stepping to a predetermined cylinder, activating a predetermined head, and reading a predetermined sector's data. Using this cylinder-, head-, and sector-coordinate system, the drive can map every segment of data that the disk drive can access.

Although coordinate systems might be fine for electromechanical devices, many people find such systems quite difficult to use. Suppose that you have just moved into a new house, and your family is unpacking boxes. When you are ready to begin working in the new family room, you may ask for the box labeled "FAMILY ROOM STUFF;" you probably would not ask for the box from "truck load 2, level 1, 4th row back." Storing by truck, level, and row is good for efficient moving, but such a system is not very helpful when someone simply needs to find something.

Because disks use such a coordinate system to store your files, the operating system takes responsibility for maintaining a list of the names that you or your programs give to your files. You "converse" with the operating system about your files by referring to the files by name. In order to "converse" with the disk drive, however, the operating system must translate a file's name into the unfriendly—but practical—coordinate system required by the disk drive.

The operating system establishes a format on the disk by recording place-holding information in each sector on the disk. When actual data is written to the disk, the place-holding information is overwritten. The operating system then sets up bookkeeping tables that link the file names you use with their sector locations on the disk. Because each sector has a distinct disk address, it can be represented by a sector number. As a final step for reading or writing a file, the operating system translates the file's sector numbers into the coordinates that the disk drive understands.

Like its memory-management mechanism, the operating system's file-storage mechanism does its job invisibly. As a system user, you simply work with file names and let the operating system provide the disk services. You will become aware of the process only if the operating system has deficiencies—for example, when too few file-name entries are available, or when the disk's space is improperly allocated. If the operating system uses a poor file-management method, you eventually will find out about the problem. UNIX, however, uses a highly respected method for handling disk files. You probably never will find UNIX's file-management mechanism lacking.

Device Management

The operating system takes responsibility for many types of peripheral devices, not just disk drives. Serial communication ports, mice, parallel printer devices, keyboards, displays, card and bar-code readers, light pens, network-interface cards (NICS), and digitizer pads are just a sampling of the many devices that operating systems manage. In fact, a *device* is any piece of electronic or electromechanical hardware (or software simulation of hardware) that provides input and (or) output.

Operating systems generally employ two basic types of device management. The first type is called *block-device management*. Block devices transfer data in groups of bytes called *blocks*. Disk drives are the most common block devices. To accommodate block devices, operating systems set aside enough memory to hold one or more blocks of data and (sometimes) administrative information about the data. This memory is often called the *data-transfer area* or *file-control block*. Temporary storage areas also are called *buffers*. The operating system stores block data from a file in buffers until the requesting program can handle the data. Block devices generally read and write data at great speeds. A typical disk drive, for example, can deliver millions of bits per second.

The second type of device management is *character-device management*. Character devices deliver data one byte at a time. Your terminal is a typical character device. The terminal is attached electrically to a communications port on the system.

The communications port is also a character device. A key electronic component in the port circuitry is the Universal Asynchronous Receiver Transmitter, or UART. When it receives a character from your key press, the UART captures and stores the character's bit stream until the full character is received. The UART then signals the operating system that a character is available in the UART's receive buffer. The operating system is responsible for accessing the character and making it available to the appropriate program. When the program sends data to your terminal, an opposite operation takes place. The operating system takes the character from your program, and then takes steps to place the character in the UART's transmit buffer. The UART then transmits the character to your terminal as a serial bit stream. When you consider the ease with which you can type on a computer, you might be surprised at the work the operating system does just to manage one communications port.

Terminals attached to ports are just one type of character-data device. Most operating systems provide services for several character devices. You and your programs don't need to be concerned with the details of using these devices. Some operating systems are designed to manage a fixed set of devices, so you may find it impossible to add a new device to the established set. Other operating systems, such as UNIX, incorporate special device-handling programs called *device drivers*. A device driver can be written for a new device and then added to the operating system. With the correct device drivers installed, UNIX can manage a host of peripherals.

Examining the Software Components of UNIX

The previous sections gave you a general overview of the responsibilities of a typical operating system. Your specific interest, however, is UNIX. Like all operating systems, UNIX is software. UNIX's operations are very visible in some ways, but very secretive in others. You see the operation of your commands and programs, but you do not see the supervision of memory allocation, disk services, or device drivers. Although they are invisible to you, all these activities are important. To understand why some operations are performed behind the scenes while others are not, you need to realize that UNIX functions on your computer system in conceptual layers. You simply can't "see" through the surface layers of your programs and commands to the deeper operating-system components that work with the hardware. One way to get an understanding of this "layered machine" is to see how UNIX's software components relate.

The Hardware Core

At the center of a UNIX system lies the computer hardware. The hardware includes the CPU, memory, and interconnecting buses, as well as disk drives, auxiliary processors (such as math coprocessors), and other devices. The combinations of core hardware components can vary significantly from system to system. Even individual components of the same class can be different. For example, one disk drive may have nine platters, while another has only two. One CPU may incorporate an instruction set that another CPU cannot execute. Regardless of the hardware's exact makeup, the operating system is designed with the hardware in mind, so that you do not have to deal with the hardware-specific details of computing.

The UNIX Kernel

The UNIX *kernel* is the heart of UNIX. In the strictest sense, the kernel *is* UNIX. All other software components of UNIX are programs that call on the kernel's services. The kernel knits together the features of UNIX. When the system is booted, the kernel is read into memory and remains there as long as the system is running. From your point of view, the kernel is invisible. You don't work directly with the kernel. Rather, your programs and commands call on the kernel's services. The kernel, in turn, consults its data tables as it schedules your program, allocates resources to your program, and manages the low-level exchange of data with the computer's hardware.

Admittedly, you may not be able to picture a "hidden" program's workings very easily. You might get the picture, however, if you look at an example that's easier to relate to than an operating system. For such an example, you needn't look any farther than your favorite fast-food restaurant.

Suppose that you drive to the restaurant's drive-up order station and look at the menu, which offers a fixed number of items. When you give your order at the drive-up speaker, you don't worry about the steps involved in providing your food. You expect that the restaurant deals with the details of procurement, cooking, inventory, packaging, and efficiency. After you place an order, you need only to pick up your food.

You may be wondering how a fast-food restaurant is like an operating system. To find out, you should make a head-to-head comparison of the process of executing a system command and the process of ordering lunch. When you issue a command, your command carries out its work by making requests to the operating system for service. You make your request through a drive-up speaker. Your program or command makes its requests through kernel-system calls. You request only items that are available from a menu. Your program or command makes only system calls for services available from the kernel. You aren't burdened with the steps, for example, of turning on the stove, flipping the burgers, or putting the finished sandwich together. You don't have to package your order so that it doesn't get confused with someone else's order. You may be aware that such activities are taking place inside the restaurant, but you catch only a glimpse of the activity.

When a program requests kernel services, the kernel takes the detailed steps required to fulfill the request. When a program requests a file service, for instance, the program gives the kernel a system call. The kernel supervises the accessing of the disk drive where the file resides. The kernel extracts the correct data and ensures that the data is not "mixed up" with another program's requested data. Finally, the kernel delivers the data to a buffer, where your program picks up the data. Like you at the drive-up window, your program does not have to contend with the details of the kernel's internal workings. The final delivery is the result of many elemental operations.

If you envision the relationship of the kernel with the underlying hardware, you get a picture like that in figure 3.1. At the center of this figure, you see a representation of the system's hardware core. The kernel is built upon and adapted to this hardware core. Parts of the kernel can be configured to accommodate variations in hardware. To accommodate the combination of numerous devices, the kernel contains a changeable set of device drivers. At this lower hardware level, the kernel is equipped to work effectively with the system hardware and peripherals. You can think of this work as the kernel's knowing exactly how to operate the french-fry machine, the milkshake machine, and other specific pieces of restaurant equipment.

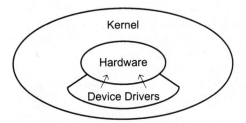

Fig. 3.1. *The UNIX kernel, built upon the system's hardware core.*

Within the kernel, individual segments of programs, or *routines*, carry out the kernel's work. These kernel routines allocate memory resources, schedule CPU time, and manage smooth and fair access to system resources for user programs.

The kernel routines also monitor the system for error conditions and hardware problems so that the kernel can report errors to your terminal or to the system's main terminal.

At a higher level, the routines provide programs with entry points to kernel services. This high-level interface is where programs use system calls to get the kernel's attention. This high-level interface is the equivalent to the drive-up order station. The kernel provides this high-level interface for all programs to use, just as the fast-food restaurant provides the drive-up station for all customers to use. All UNIX programs use the kernel's system calls. You don't use the kernel's system calls, because your program does the calling for you. To the kernel, all programs are the same, because they all call on services of the kernel. To you, programs are very different. Some are shells, some are commands, and some are applications. For UNIX work, the most common program that you will use is the UNIX shell.

The UNIX Shell

Because most users do not want to contend with the details of the kernel, UNIX features a special program that gives you access to the kernel's functions. This program, called the *shell*, begins to operate as soon as you log onto the system. When you think of a UNIX shell, you can picture a thin, shell-like separator that covers the kernel and hides it from your view. The shell carries out its primary tasks by acting as a command interpreter. You do your routine UNIX work by issuing commands; the shell interprets the commands before loading them into memory. Although the kernel allocates the necessary computer resources to a command, the shell accepts your keystrokes and essentially arranges for the kernel to run a command as you intend. You'll learn about the shell in detail in Chapter 5. Chapters 14 and 15 show you how to create shell programs that the shell runs.

A UNIX system commonly employs the Bourne shell, the Korn shell, or the C shell. Some systems offer you a choice of shells. For your understanding of the shell as a UNIX software component, you need only know that one of these shells acts as your *command interpreter*.

The kernel loads and executes the shell just as it would any other program. From a purely technical point of view, the shell isn't special. From a user's point of view, however, the shell plays a very important role. The shell is the "launching pad" for the rest of your programs. For the most part, you use the keyboard to set other programs in motion from within the shell. You can even use the shell to start additional copies of the shell and run multiple copies of the shell at the same time.

From a user's perspective, the shell forms a layer above the kernel. This layer interacts with the kernel by passing command names and other information (called *arguments* or *parameters*) to the kernel. The kernel, in turn, loads programs and commands and ensures that the commands have access to the parameters and other information. As you will learn later, the new program "inherits" much of the previous program's information. For example, a command inherits the type of terminal you use. The command can use the terminal type if the command can use special terminal features, such as the capability of making characters blink. When the shell is active, the shell's relationship with the kernel can be viewed as shown in figure 3.2.

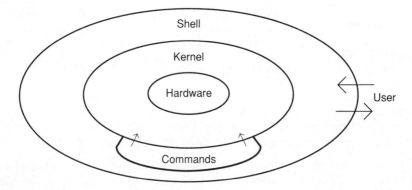

Fig. 3.2. *The relationship of the active shell with the kernel.*

As the shell accepts your keyboard instructions, it "hides" the kernel from you. That is, the shell provides you with a user interface to the kernel and its capabilities. The kernel is not programmed to accept "human" requests, such as assigning a new name to a file or erasing all files that contain the letters `temp`. The shell accepts your "human" requests as command lines and arranges for the kernel to load the proper commands to carry out your requests. Although the shell does have a few commands "built-in," the real power for your system-level work comes from external commands or utilities.

UNIX Commands and Utilities

Commands—which sometimes are called *utilities*—are programs that perform specific operating-system chores. As mentioned previously, the shell does feature a few built-in commands, but most commands reside in disk files until you type their names to the shell. When you issue such a command, the kernel loads the appropriate disk file's contents into memory and executes the command.

Some computer users use the term "utility" to describe a command that provides several features, like larger applications programs do. The `vi` command, for example, invokes UNIX's visual editor utility. The visual editor features its own command structure, which you can use to create and modify text files such as books, memos, reports, shell procedures, and other character-based files. The capabilities of `vi` give it more *utility* than "ordinary" UNIX commands such as `copy` (which is used to copy files), or `ls` (which is used to list files). For the purposes of this text, however, you can use the terms "command" and "utility" interchangeably.

When a command (or even a shell or applications program) executes, it is called a *process*. The kernel schedules processes, provides them with the required system resources, and services the system calls made by those processes. When a command is operating on your terminal, the command receives its standard input characters (if any) from your keyboard, and sends its output information and error messages to your screen. In fact, a command does its work as a kind of "offshoot" of the shell. The shell sets up the command's execution, but when the kernel executes the command, the shell "sleeps" in the background while the command works. The shell does not "awaken" until the command finishes its operation.

> The kernel also can execute commands as background processes. Background processes do their work behind the scenes; the shell continues to accept commands (and does not "go to sleep") while background processes work. You will learn about background processes in greater detail later in the chapter.

Figure 3.3 shows the relationship between commands and other programs and the kernel. Notice that a shell process is still indicated, but is shaded to show that the shell is not active. The command and other programs, however, are active. Commands, as processes, have the full services of the kernel through system calls to the kernel's entry points.

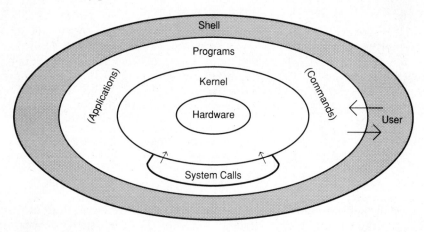

Fig. 3.3. *The relationship between commands and the kernel.*

Keep in mind that a command's relationship with the kernel is a temporary one. When the command process finishes and the shell is again waiting for your input, you can run the command again just by typing its name.

UNIX Applications

Recall from Chapter 2 that an *applications program* is a program that performs a specific type of task. Word processors, spreadsheets, database managers, and

CAD/CAM programs are all examples of applications. But as far as the kernel is concerned, applications are just programs, as are shells and commands. That's why you see applications and commands together in figure 3.3. To start an application, you enter its name into the shell just as you would enter a command's name. When compared with commands and shells, however, applications are distinct because of the scope of work they do and the ancillary data they require.

Generally, an applications program maintains its own set of data. The data might be in the form of a memo, a budget spreadsheet, an employee database, or another collection of information. If an application maintains its own data, it keeps the data in disk files. The kernel does not apply any conditions on an application's method of composing the data in the files. The kernel simply services the application's system calls and stores or retrieves the files that the application requests. If you use applications programs, you probably will use UNIX commands to maintain the files that the programs create.

Each applications program has its own interpretation of words, keystrokes, mouse movements, input prompts, and other forms of communication with you. In other words, something that works with the shell won't necessarily work while you're using an application. An applications program's internal program logic guides the application through its work. Still, when a program needs to "talk" to a device—such as a modem, a printer, or even the screen—the program must call upon the kernel services to access the device. For all practical purposes, commands and applications request services in the same way.

To use an applications program successfully, of course, you must learn how the program works. It is beyond the scope of this book to teach you how to use any specific applications programs. If you want to use an applications program, consult the program's manual for details and instructions. What you should remember from this discussion, however, is that UNIX applications programs are built upon the kernel and the kernel's system calls. When you run a program on your system, you will know that UNIX is working behind the scenes.

Examining the Features of UNIX

With all the discussion so far about hardware and software, shells and commands, and applications and utilities, you may wonder what practical attributes UNIX can possess to merit its popularity. UNIX has many desirable features that make it a good solution to an operating-system need. As you read about the features of UNIX in the next few sections, you can apply some of your knowledge from Chapters 1 and 2 and this chapter to help you see the benefits of UNIX's features.

The Portability of UNIX

The UNIX kernel and many UNIX commands are written in a high-level programming language called *C*. C may seem to be a peculiar name for a language when you consider the names of other popular programming languages such as COBOL, BASIC, and FORTRAN. But when C was developed at Bell Labs, its creators did not count on C's commercial success when they gave the language its odd name. Yet C is a popular computer language, for many reasons. C is one step better than its predecessor, the B language. C also can be implemented on a wide variety of computer systems. Because UNIX is written in C, UNIX, too, can be implemented on a wide variety of computer systems. The act of moving UNIX (or another program) from one computer system to another is called *porting*.

Today, UNIX has been ported to virtually every popular computer-hardware platform. UNIX runs on many types of computers, including Apple, DEC, Wang, IBM, Cray—and the list goes on. All these computers are different from one another, yet to their UNIX users, they all look very similar.

The Device Independence of UNIX

Not long ago, computers utilized a few "standard" peripherals, such as terminals, disk drives, modems, and printers. Today, the numbers and types of peripherals are growing as quickly as technology can expand. An operating system is at a disadvantage if it is "stuck" with using the old devices. Because of its kernel, however, UNIX is independent of a set group of devices.

The UNIX device drivers are designed as separate components of the kernel. When changes are required to accommodate new or improved devices, the engineer or system administrator links new device drivers with the kernel. This linking, in essence, forms a new kernel, which is capable of supporting the new device. The UNIX kernel is so malleable in its device support that your system may have several kernel files with one kernel file as the boot kernel.

Programmers who design and code device drivers follow a very specific set of guidelines. These guidelines ensure that the device driver and the kernel will merge in a standardized fashion. With such standardized device handling, the kernel can simplify the manner in which commands request device-related services. The system calls that arrange kernel services rely on this standardization. Device drivers enable the kernel to provide for devices certain services that are very similar to kernel file services. As a result, you can use a device argument in most commands that accept a file argument. In fact, the kernel's device-management mechanisms treat devices as special files, which have directory entries in the file system.

The Multitasking Features of UNIX

Multitasking is the performance of more than one task at a time. Multitasking operating systems can run more than one copy of the same program at one time. UNIX is a multitasking operating system. Because UNIX deals with processes, however, it is more accurately called a *multiprocessing* operating system. UNIX enables you to print a report, for example, while you are entering commands to the shell. Depending on your system's computing "horsepower," UNIX can schedule and run hundreds of processes at the same time. To understand exactly what is meant here by the phrase "at the same time," you need to consider appearances. Appearances can be deceiving.

When you watch a movie at the theater, you see pictures of people and objects moving across the screen. What happens when the film breaks and a frame gets stuck in the projector's film gate? The picture on the screen looks like a photograph. (At least it does until a hole burns through it.) You then realize that, while the film was running, the movie created the illusion of movement because each frame of the film was seen for only a short time. In each new frame, the elements occupy slightly different positions than they did in the preceding frames.

A UNIX system appears to be performing several processes at the same time because UNIX uses the computer's inherent speed to switch its attention among individual processes. The CPU's resources are devoted to only one process at any instant. By switching rapidly among processes, UNIX gives all processes timely computing resources. The switching occurs so fast that all processes appear to be progressing at any point in time. In reality, each process shares CPU time with the rest.

To the individual user, multitasking is a great benefit when a multiple-window screen environment is in use. In such an environment, the screen is divided into framed areas, or windows, and each window runs a separate process. If each window is running a program that draws an individual geometric form, then all the forms appear to progress at an even rate. If one window is running a spreadsheet and another window is running a word processor, the user can select spreadsheet data (using a mouse) and "paste" that data into a report in the word processor's window. In a multiprocessing windowing environment, a user is able to direct several programs "at the same time." You'll see other benefits of multiprocessing when you read about background commands in Chapter 5.

The Multiuser Features of UNIX

When an operating system handles the time and resource scheduling required for multitasking, the logical extension of that operating system is its *multiuser capability*. When a system has multiuser capability, more than one individual can directly access the system's computing capabilities at the same time.

To gain access to a multiuser system, each user must first identify himself to the system, so that UNIX can track each user's activities separately. In UNIX, this introduction and identification procedure is called *login*.

Thereafter, UNIX ensures that any process started by a user is linked to that user. As each user creates files, UNIX includes the owner information in its record of each file, so that many users can create and manipulate files without causing confusion. UNIX tracks the terminal used by each user and makes sure that the user's terminal input/output is routed to the correct terminal. The UNIX kernel is responsible for keeping one user's computing activity separate from the other users' work.

Multiuser operating systems have been in existence for several years. Recently, microprocessors have brought computing power to the world's desktops. Many of the personal computers that incorporate microprocessors operate with a single-user, single-tasking operating system. As the power of personal computers has increased, they have developed the capability of supporting multiple users. UNIX is a logical choice as the operating system to operate a multitasking environment on these desktop microcomputers. Running UNIX, a PC designed for a single user can support from 4 to 16 terminals. Some can even support more users.

The Programmable Shells

You've learned that the shell is a command interpreter. Nearly all operating systems have command interpreters, of course, but the UNIX shell is a very special command interpreter. Not only can the UNIX shell interpret commands from your keystrokes, but it also can interpret commands from a text file. This capability means that you can create a command file—or *procedure file*—and then mark the file as executable. Your new procedure file becomes a new command. After the executable procedure file is established, you can enter the new file's name as a command—just as you would enter any UNIX command. The shell then creates a copy of itself (a subshell), and the copy executes the commands in the procedure file. Because the shell is programmable, you can extend the utility of available UNIX commands by creating your own "customized" commands.

Although many operating systems feature shell-command programming, the UNIX shells offer programming capabilities well beyond most. Chapters 14 and 15 discuss shell programming in detail, but for now, just remember that you can write very complete programs for the shell. Even if you never considered yourself a programmer, you'll be able to create your own simple "custom" commands with very little effort.

 If you are an MS-DOS user, you'll find numerous similarities between DOS batch files and UNIX shell procedures.

The UNIX shell itself is actually a file-based command like other UNIX commands. A shell is started for you when you log onto the system. The shell has a wide range of capabilities, and you should become familiar with these capabilities as you use the shell. Chapter 5 provides a detailed discussion of the way the shell interprets your commands.

The Wealth of UNIX Utilities

Although UNIX features many "hidden" capabilities such as multitasking, multiprocessing, and device independence, your primary focus as a UNIX user is issuing commands to do useful work. UNIX comes complete with a base set of commands and, optionally, with an extension set of commands. In all, UNIX responds to more than 200 commands.

In your daily UNIX work, you probably will concentrate on a couple of dozen commands. Experienced users, on the other hand, may appreciate the large (and growing) selection of UNIX commands as they involve themselves in more detailed operating-system work. As you will discover, many UNIX commands or utilities are not specific to operating-system work at all. UNIX utilities—such as desktop calculators, calendar reminder services, text processors, and electronic mail—are programs that can make your working life easier.

UNIX utilities are individual programs that the shell and other programs can invoke. Because most commands and utilities are external to the shell and the kernel, you do not need to modify the entire operating system in order to add a new command. The internal procedure that loads and executes a command works equally well for new and existing commands. For this reason, adding a new UNIX command (besides a shell procedure) is as straightforward as adding an applications program to the system.

This flexibility has been a benefit to developers who create specialized commands for different implementations of UNIX. Each implementation may include commands that are unique to that individual implementation. Implementation-specific commands generally operate on an unusual feature of the hardware or software of a certain computer. Even though these special commands are not already built into UNIX, UNIX's open architecture allows the developer (or even a relatively sophisticated user) to modify the operating system's personality easily and naturally.

The Built-In Security Features

In computer terminology, *security* means enabling access to resources on an individual basis. The resources might be files, commands, programs, administrative information, or even access to the system itself. If you take the idea of security a step further, you can even include the logging of "comings and goings" of the system's users. UNIX's security features enable users to operate in a secure, trustworthy computing environment.

Security is important for many reasons. Entry-level security minimizes unauthorized access to the system. An unauthorized user may want sensitive information from the system's files. An unauthorized user may want to "vandalize" the system by erasing files or by substituting "dummy" commands for the real ones. An unauthorized user may want "free" access to computer time to do his work. Obviously, if a would-be unauthorized user cannot access the system, then he cannot perform any of these activities.

When a UNIX user creates a file, the file is "owned" by that user. Perhaps a better view would be that the user owns the permission to share the file with other users;

that is, the file's owner can grant other users access to the file. Because every data file, program, and device in a UNIX system is subject to permissions, the system is capable of maintaining secure file, command, and resource access.

The kernel is responsible for maintaining security by checking the permissions associated with files. UNIX provides administrative security through tables, which are supervised by administrative personnel. Newer implementations of UNIX provide remedial security, which logs significant events that concern the security of the system. Although logging events does not prevent a security breach, it does act like a security camera in a bank by identifying "violators."

Login security is introduced in Chapter 5. Chapter 9 introduces the commands that control the permissions associated with files and file security. Most other UNIX security provisions are administered by your system administrator or a member of the administrative staff.

Understanding the UNIX File System

When you use UNIX, you and your programs use the *file system* to work with disk-based data. One of UNIX's most important jobs is to provide you with file-based services. In order to manage your files through UNIX commands, you need to know how the file system stores files.

The UNIX file system is a *hierarchical* file system. Although you probably see the file system as a hierarchy of directories containing files and other directories, UNIX sees the file system as a bookkeeping system that links file names with their data locations on disk. You need to understand the file system in order to use many UNIX commands. The file system's arrangement may seem confusing at first, but you soon will find it to be both convenient and useful. In no time, you'll be using commands both to manage your files and to manipulate file-based data.

Understanding Files

Ordinarily, a *file* is a disk-based collection of data that is managed under a single name. The collection of data can be a program, a memo, a configuration table, a database, or any other collection of bytes. UNIX, as a product, is delivered as a group of disk files for installation on a system. You create files as by-products when you use commands and applications programs.

Each file must have a file name, which can include from 1 to 14 characters. When you create a new file, give it a descriptive name. File names such as `memo1` and `memo2` are good to describe memos. `boss` and `file22`, on the other hand, give little indication that they name memo files.

Remember also that UNIX treats upper- and lowercase letters differently. The file names `Memo1` and `memo1`, therefore, represent two different files. As a rule of thumb, name your files using the characters a-z and 0-9. You also can use the period character (.) and the underscore character (_) anywhere in a file name. The period and underscore make good separator characters in file names such as `schedule.old` and `memo_to_boss`. UNIX doesn't limit you to these characters, but other characters may interfere with the shell's interpretation of file names from the command line.

When you need to name a file, keep the following guidelines in mind:

- File and directory names can be from 1 to 14 characters long.
- You can use all characters except the slash (/).
- As a practical point, avoid using <spacebar>, <Tab>, and <Backspace> in file names, as well as the following characters:

  ? @ # $ ^ & * ( ) [ ] \ | ' ` " ; < >

- Avoid using a plus sign (+) or a period (.) as the first character of a file name.
- Upper- and lowercase characters are treated differently in file names.

About Special Device Files . . .

As discussed in a previous section of this chapter, UNIX includes devices as special files in the file system. Unlike ordinary files, however, device files do *not* contain data. A device file contains information that enables UNIX to send output *to* or receive input *from* the device. As far as their use in UNIX commands, device files are interchangeable with ordinary files. The use of a device file name in a command extends the command's capabilities without introducing additional command complexity. Device file names follow the same rules as ordinary files, but you don't have to worry about creating device files. All the devices that your system uses (and includes in the file system) are already present in the file system.

A *directory* is another special UNIX file. A directory, however, does not contain user data. Rather, a directory contains entries that describe other user files, devices, and directories that are contained in that directory. Directory names follow the same rules as ordinary file names. Directories also are called *subdirectories* because they are listed as entries in another directory. The inclusion of special directory files is the foundation of the UNIX hierarchical file system. From your point of view, UNIX's file-storage system is not a flat list of file names. UNIX stores a file as an entry in one of many directories. The next section will help you understand the hierarchical directory structure.

Understanding the Hierarchical Directory Structure

A *hierarchy* is an organization or arrangement of entities (things). Entities can refer to people, objects, processes, files, or many other things. Coins, for example, can be arranged by denomination, and soldiers can be organized by rank. There **are**, of course, many ways to organize entities besides hierarchically. Stones in a driveway are arranged randomly; bricks in a wall are arranged in parallel rows; and telephone book listings are arranged in alphabetical order. The arrangement **of the** stones, bricks, and listings is not hierarchical. Hierarchical organization is useful, however, because you can identify each entity by its relationship to other **entities**. If this organization confuses you, don't despair. It will soon become clear.

To a genealogist, entities may be people in a family tree. To UNIX, entities are directories in a directory system. In either case, the hierarchy begins with the essential core, or root entity. In a family tree, the core entity might be great-**great**-grandfather Isaac Watson. In UNIX, this core entity is the *root directory*, or **simply** "root." In genealogy, people can trace their roots through their parents and **their** parents' ancestors. People can identify their forefathers, based on the **relationships** in the family tree. In UNIX, subdirectories can trace their paths back to the root directory. UNIX subdirectories and their files can be identified by their relation-ships to other subdirectories.

It is easy to see why the UNIX hierarchical file system is called a *tree-structured* **file** system. At the base of this tree structure is the root directory. Directories that contain other directories are the parents of the those directories. Directories **that** have parent directories are the child directories of their parents. Just as some children can be parents, most UNIX directories are both children of higher **direc**-tories as well as parents of lower directories. In UNIX, the parent/child **relationship** of directories forms the directory hierarchy. Figure 3.4 shows an imaginary **direc**-tory structure that is made of directories bearing people's names. You can **view** these names as members of a family tree.

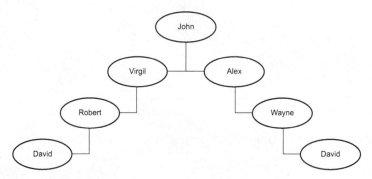

Fig. 3.4. *A directory family tree.*

In a family tree, David might be child of Wayne, who is child of Alex, who is child of John. John is the head or root of the family tree for David. Another way to repre-sent David's identity in this family tree is to separate each level in the family hierarchy with a slash character (/), as follows:

John/Alex/Wayne/David

In this example, each level of the family tree is separated by a slash character because UNIX uses the slash character to separate directories. This David is different from the following David:

John/Virgil/Robert/David

Both share the name David, but their relationships to their parents are unique. By giving the full family-tree list of names, you can positively identify David. UNIX directories share the same kind of identity relationships as families. In fact, every UNIX system is capable of having a "family" of subdirectories stemming from the root directory. Every file in every directory has a unique identity because UNIX does not allow duplicate file names in a directory, nor does UNIX allow full directory names to be duplicated.

UNIX establishes some directories and files when the system is installed. Figure 3.5 shows this initial level of the directory tree.

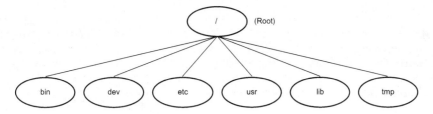

Fig. 3.5. *UNIX's first-level directories.*

Notice that this directory tree is inverted (the root of the tree is at the top). UNIX directory trees usually are presented as inverted trees. The root directory is a higher directory and the root's child directories are lower directories. In an actual system, the second-level directories shown in figure 3.5 would also contain lower-level subdirectories. Table 3.1 matches the typical first-level directory names with the nature of the files that each contains.

Table 3.1.
The UNIX First-Level Subdirectories and Their Contents

Directory Name	Contents
/bin	Executable command files
/dev	Device files
/etc	Miscellaneous commands and system files
/lib	Programming-library files
/tmp	Temporary files (removed regularly)
/usr	User-oriented files and user subdirectories

Your system's directories may differ from those directories shown in table 3.1, but most of the listed directories should be in your system. The /bin directory contains the files that hold the commands that you will use. As you recall, commands and programs are executable binary files. The *bin*ary nature of these files is the source of /bin's name.

/dev is the home of the device files. Because UNIX uses device files in the file system, you can use devices in commands. The /etc (pronounced *et-see*) directory holds miscellaneous system files and commands. When UNIX first boots, the operating system searches the /etc directory for tables of information. The /lib directory contains files associated with program development, and /tmp temporarily holds files that are created by system activity as intermediate steps in doing system work. Because the files in /tmp have no long-term value, they are removed from time to time. You will find that /usr is the parent directory of much of your file activity. The /usr directory—or /u or /usr1 or some similar name—is the subdirectory branch of the file system that contains user-related files.

When you become a user on a UNIX system, you automatically are assigned your own base directory as an entry in /usr. This assigned directory becomes your *home directory*. Your home directory is named the same name that you use to identify yourself to the system when you log on. You will read about the login process in Chapter 5, but a brief explanation will be useful here. If your login name is david, for example, then your home directory is /usr/david. The first slash (/) stands for the root, but any other slashes in the full directory name act as the directory separators for UNIX to use when looking for files. UNIX positions you in your home directory when you log onto the system. Your home directory is your working directory at the time of login. While you are working within the home directory, you can access its files by using their simple file names. You don't have to give the full file name, including the root and all parent directory names, in order to use a file in your working directory.

The provision for a working directory enables you to work with the files in that directory as if they were the only files in the file system. At any point in your operating system-level work, you can change to a different directory in the directory tree, and that directory will become your working directory. Chapter 7 shows you the commands that you use to create, manage, and remove your own directories.

You can create many directories from your home directory, and your home directory will be the parent of each of the newly created directories. You also can create subdirectories that stem from other subdirectories—in effect, adding branches to your branch of the subdirectory tree. The files in each subdirectory can be viewed as the "leaves" on a branch. This tree analogy is why the UNIX directory system is often called a tree-structured directory system.

Two additional levels of subdirectories are represented in figure 3.6. The new levels are added to /usr. A user named david has a subdirectory of /usr. From his home directory, David has created a subdirectory called letters. The full name for the letters directory, therefore, is /usr/david/letters. The letters directory holds letters, memos, and various documents.

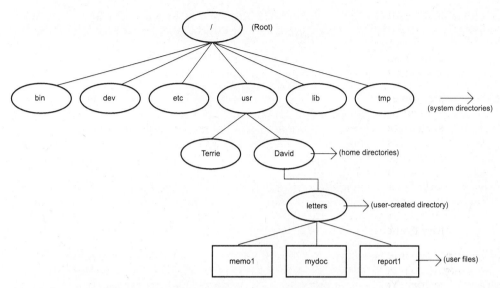

Fig. 3.6. *System directories with user directories added.*

UNIX does not require that a directory's files follow the theme of the directory's name. In fact, there is no way for UNIX to tell what a user puts into a directory. However, most users group similar files into an appropriately named directory for convenience. Because you determine the number and types of subdirectories that will be created from your home directory, your directory tree branch may have more or fewer levels. Regardless of the number of levels, the relationship of the subdirectories is important. Each subdirectory, as well as the root directory, can contain user files. Two files can have the same file name, as long as the files reside in different directories.

Suppose that you have given two files the same name. (Of course, the two files reside in different directories.) Next, suppose that you want to include one of the files in a command. Because UNIX needs to know which of two files your command specifies, you also must supply the names of the directories, starting from the root, that lead to the desired file. This sequence of directory names leading to a file is called a *path*. The concept of the path is discussed in the next section

Understanding Path Names

A path name is a chain of directory names that tell UNIX how to find a file that you want. Each directory is separated from the others by a slash (/) character. The / is UNIX's directory delimiter. A file's full path name is the absolute indicator of where the file is located. Using symbolic notation, the path name for a file looks like this:

```
/dir1/dir2/dir3. . ./filename
```

In this generic syntax, the first / is the UNIX name for the root. The list `dir1/dir2/dir3. . .` indicates a chain of directories in which the directory to the left of another directory is the parent. The ellipses (. . .) indicate that more (or fewer) directory names may be needed to address a particular file. All characters between the first / and the final / comprise the directory path. `filename` is the name of the file that is in the final directory of the directory path.

Remember that your home directory is your working or current directory when you log onto the system. If you want to see or use the files in a different subdirectory—`/bin`, for example—you must include the path specifier in the file name. In other words, you must give UNIX an *absolute* path name to find a file. When you include a path specifier in the command, UNIX looks only at the specified directory for the files. To see the name (listing) of the `find` file in `/bin` while your home directory is the current directory, you would issue the following command:

$ **ls /bin/find** <Return>

You do not need to worry about the formation of the commands in these examples for now. You will learn about command formation in Chapter 5. (For your information, however, the $ represents the UNIX prompt, and the <Return> simply indicates that you press the Return key after issuing the command.) For now, just notice that this sample `ls` command includes the full path to the desired file. Suppose, on the other hand, that you issue the command in the following form:

$ **ls find** <Return>

This command tells UNIX to look for the file in your working directory; because `find` is in the `/bin` directory, however, UNIX would not be able to find the file.

If you use the `cd /bin` command to change to the `/bin` directory, `/bin` becomes the current directory. UNIX knows that if you omit the path specifier, `/bin` is the default directory to use. Now, when you want to see the `find` command's file in the `/bin` directory, you can issue the following command:

$ **ls find** <Return>

This command produces the same output as the command `ls /bin/find` issued from your home directory. Because `/bin` is now the current directory, UNIX supplies the `/bin` path specifier by default. Most UNIX commands work with optional path specifiers. If you do not supply a path, UNIX automatically uses the current directory.

Helping UNIX Find Commands and Programs

As noted in previous sections, most UNIX commands reside in files, which must be loaded and executed when you want to use the commands. When you issue an external command, UNIX must know where to find the file that contains the command's program code before the file can be loaded and executed. A command may be in one of several directories. You can tell UNIX where the command is located in one of the following ways:

- Change to the directory that contains the command.
- Supply the command's path in the command line.
- Establish a UNIX search path to the command's directory.

If you want to use an external command that is located in a directory that is not the current directory, you can supply path information directly in front of the command's name in the command line. Suppose, for example, that you want to list the files in the /etc directory while you are logged into your home directory. Issue the following command:

$ **/bin/ls /etc** <Return>

UNIX looks for the ls command's program in the /bin directory, and then executes the command to list the files contained in /etc. Because you have given UNIX the absolute path to find ls, UNIX has no trouble locating the command.

The most convenient way to help UNIX find external commands is to rely on the established search-path specification that UNIX uses. Through the PATH environment variable, the command search path list is established for you when you log onto the system. UNIX designers anticipated that you would not want to log to a directory containing an external command, or give the command's path in order to use the command. The PATH variable enables you to inform UNIX which directories are most likely to contain external commands, procedure files, and program files. The contents of the PATH variable consist of alternative path names.

When you enter a command's name without the command's path, UNIX consults the PATH variable and begins to look in each directory listed. If the consulted directory doesn't contain the command, UNIX searches the next alternative directory. If you enter a command with a typographical error or a name that doesn't exist, UNIX will look in every directory in every path alternative indicated by the PATH variable. Of course, when UNIX finds a command using one of the alternative paths, it looks no further.

NOTE The PATH variable enables UNIX to locate executable (program) files for execution. Shell procedure files (scripts) also can be located and executed through the search path. If you *don't* supply a path to a command on the command line, UNIX will use the PATH variable to attempt to locate the command. If you *do* supply a path to a program on the command line, UNIX will not search the path alternatives, even if the program is not in the directory you specified.

If you are unsure of the current PATH setting, you can issue the set command at the UNIX prompt. UNIX displays the PATH setting as well as any other settings (such as HOME) in a screen report. The set command reports variable values from an area of special memory called the *environment*. All programs, as well as UNIX commands, may consult the environment to find the current values of environment variables. Chapter 4 discusses the environment and its common variables. UNIX provides a default PATH that enables you to issue all common commands without the need to include the path in the command line. Remember, however, that the PATH specification does not help UNIX find data files. When you want to access data files that reside outside the current (working) directory, you must include their paths as part of their full name.

The PATH assignment takes the following form:

```
PATH=path1/:path2/:...
```

The equal sign (=) (assignment character) assigns the value on the right to the name on the left. In this generic syntax, *path1/* is the first alternative search directory. The colon (:) character following *path/* tells UNIX that the end of the first path has been reached in the assignment. *:path2/* is a second alternative drive and path combination for UNIX to search if the desired program is not in the first path. The : . . indicates that you can add other alternative paths to the assignment. UNIX searches the path specification from left to right when searching for an executable file.

A typical PATH assignment command looks like the following:

```
PATH=/usr/bin:/bin:/etc:
```

This PATH assignment is typical because most commands and programs that ordinary users execute are located in either /usr/bin, /bin, or /etc. If you are in doubt about your command search path, ask your system administrator to clarify your settings.

Comparing the Sizes of UNIX Systems

To gain a better understanding of your system's place in the scale of UNIX systems, you should review the next few sections. To appreciate UNIX, you must appreciate the wide range of hardware platforms that accommodate UNIX. Considering the range of computers that run UNIX, it is remarkable that you can move from one system to another and experience the same core response from UNIX. Naturally, variations exist in UNIX; the operating system is not yet sufficiently standardized for you to see no differences in systems of different sizes or from different manufacturers. If you're like many UNIX users, you will find yourself using a new UNIX system before long. Then you will no doubt appreciate the similarities with your previous system.

Personal Computers

The personal computer is considered the entry-level UNIX system. Most UNIX-based personal computer systems are members of the IBM-PC family of computers. This family of personal computers includes the PC-XT, Personal Computer AT, and PS/2. Many companies offer computers based on the de-facto industry standards established by the popularity of these computers. All of these computers incorporate microprocessors made by (or licensed from) Intel. The latest 32-bit microprocessors from Intel, the 80386 and 80486, provide UNIX-based personal computers with the computing power attained by minicomputers only few years ago. Although UNIX-based personal computers retain the shape and size of personal computers, they are capable of full multiuser, multiprocessing operation. Systems supporting 8 to 16 users are common.

XENIX and UNIX System V/386 are the predominant variations of UNIX for personal computers. Development of XENIX is in the hands of the Santa Cruz Operation, or SCO. Much of the testing and developmental work for this book was done using SCO UNIX System V/386 running on an Gateway 80386-based microcomputer. Many other companies offer UNIX or UNIX work-alikes for personal computers.

IBM's AIX implementation of UNIX operates on a wide range of IBM hardware. The microcomputer version of AIX runs on the 80386 based PS/2 computers. Having been long recognized for its excellent proprietary operating systems, IBM has stated a strong commitment to UNIX-based computing. IBM AIX running on a PS/2 Model 80 computer was also used in the testing and developmental work for this book. AIX is implemented in multiuser configurations as well as single-user workstation configurations.

Until the divestiture of Bell Telephone, AT&T was enjoined from selling computer products. It is ironic that the originator of UNIX could not sell the product commercially. Today, AT&T offers a complete line of UNIX products and services. AT&T WGS (Work Group Systems) provide an 80386-based personal computer system running UNIX System V/386. Like other 80386-based systems, the WGS systems support up to 16 UNIX users in a typical installation. Some of the testing and developmental work for this book was done on an AT&T WGS UNIX system.

Many supporters of Apple Computer's popular Macintosh family of microcomputers use Apple's A/UX implementation of UNIX on their machines. Unlike the IBM PC, the Macintosh is based on the Motorola 68000 microprocessor family. The Macintosh is noted for its graphical user interface (GUI), and A/UX provides a graphical environment for the computer's user.

UNIX-based personal computers, however, make up one of the fastest-growing segments of the UNIX market. Because of the increasing number of PC-based UNIX users, this book highlights the 80386-based UNIX implementations from SCO, IBM, and AT&T.

Workstations

A workstation is a powerful version of a personal computer. Workstations, however, are not PCs. Workstations employ very high-resolution displays and powerful processors. Workstations utilize special math-calculating electronics called *floating point units*, or FPUs. Most often, workstations are equipped with network interface cards, and most workstations have a mouse. With crisp displays, powerful processing capabilities, work-group interconnectability, and graphical user interfaces, workstations are ideal for scientific and engineering work. For workstations, UNIX's multiprocessing and multiuser capabilities create an excellent marriage between operating system and specialized machine.

Workstations from Sun Microsystems and HP Apollo are well known in scientific and engineering circles. Other manufacturers, such as IBM, DEC, Data General, Unisys, Sony, Wang, and many others sell workstations. Some of the testing for this book was performed on a Sun Microsystems workstation.

While most of the applications software for workstations has historically been of a scientific or engineering orientation, business software is becoming increasingly available for workstations. Because of a workstation's inherent power and connectability with other workstations on a network, many businesses consider workstations to be ideal. The number of workstations running UNIX is increasing every month; further, their price continues to decrease in relation to their performance.

Minicomputers

When most people think of multitasking computers, they think of minicomputers. Minicomputers are the class of computers that provide more departmentalized computing than their larger mainframe cousins. A typical minicomputer provides computing services for 16 to 256 users. Minicomputers contain circuitry designed to accommodate multiuser, multitasking operating systems. Minicomputers are often equipped with disk drives capable of storing hundreds of megabytes of data. Unlike workstations and personal computers, minicomputers do not contain built-in displays, keyboards, disk drives, or mice. The main circuitry in a minicomputer is contained in a chassis enclosure, and much of the peripheral support hardware is contained in enclosures of their own. You will not find a minicomputer on a desktop very often. Minicomputers normally are located in a special environment, such as a computer room.

Many manufacturers make minicomputers. Berkeley UNIX was implemented on DEC's popular VAX computers. IBM supports their AIX operating system across a line of minicomputers. AT&T offers a 3B series of minicomputers. Unisys, Data General, Wang, and many other companies have loyal minicomputer customers. Until personal computers and workstations came along, UNIX was most commonly implemented on minicomputers.

Mainframes

As far as computing power goes, the mainframe computers are at the top of the spectrum. One mainframe computer can provide service to hundreds of users. The most powerful of these mainframes are called *supercomputers*. One supercomputer has more computing power than a room full of workstations! Like most mini-computers, mainframes and supercomputers are located in computer rooms or computer facilities. Mainframe computers require greater temperature and humidity control than is required by smaller computers. Some supercomputers require very cold operating environments. To attain their tremendous computing power, these large computers push electron flow through their components to the limits of physics.

Summary

This chapter has presented you with a view of the underlying design of the UNIX operating system. You have seen that UNIX is not a single software item, but rather, a composite of many software components. The UNIX operating system has many useful features that provide you with computing benefits. There is no single example of a "typical" UNIX system size, yet UNIX systems of all sizes share common UNIX characteristics.

This chapter presented the following key points:

- ❏ UNIX manages system memory resources.
- ❏ UNIX manages disk storage and file bookkeeping.
- ❏ UNIX manages hardware devices through device drivers.
- ❏ Hardware is the core upon which UNIX is built.
- ❏ The kernel is the memory-based software component that is the essential nucleus of UNIX.
- ❏ The UNIX shell is the command-interpreter software component of UNIX. You interact with UNIX through the shell.
- ❏ You use the UNIX commands and utilities to do your operating system work. Commands and utilities, in turn, use the services of the kernel to do their detailed work.
- ❏ You use applications programs to do your daily computer work. Applications perform useful computer tasks that apply to real-world problems such as accounting, word processing, CAD/CAM, and database information management.
- ❏ UNIX features include portability, device independence, multi-processing, multiuser capabilities, programmable shells, a wealth of utilities, and built-in security.

❑ One of the most important and beneficial features of UNIX is the hierarchical file system. The UNIX file system includes many directories arranged in a tree structure. Each file in the file system has a distinct path name that includes the directory names that lead to the file name.

The next chapter discusses UNIX system administration from an ordinary user's point of view. The chapter takes a general look at the many of the complicated operations and duties that a system administrator undertakes. As an ordinary user, you will appreciate the nature of the work that the system administrator performs on your behalf.

Administering UNIX Systems

Life with a typical UNIX system involves more than simply running applications and issuing commands. A UNIX system requires initial configuration and continuous attention to ensure that the system remains effective, trustworthy, and efficient for all users. The system administrator is the person responsible for attending to the UNIX system's needs.

You now have a working understanding of computer basics and the general makeup of UNIX. As an ordinary user, you need only to learn some basic UNIX commands to become productive on a UNIX system. The system administrator, on the other hand, must be able to do in-depth work on the file system, tune the kernel's changeable parts, add new applications software, manage the terminal devices, and perform many other duties.

This chapter discusses the role of the system administrator and, in some cases, the system administrator's staff. The chapter does not try to teach you how to administer a UNIX system; that subject would require hundreds of pages. At any rate, all UNIX systems are different in one way or another, and each one is unique in the way it must be administered. The manuals supplied with UNIX are the system administrator's guide to his system. You will benefit, however, from the following brief overview of UNIX system administration.

System administration is often a dark secret to the ordinary user. Some users feel tentative about using UNIX when they worry about aspects of security, the file system's integrity, or even the ramifications of a sudden power outage. As you learn about system administration, you will gain additional insight into the kernel and utilities, the file system, and devices.

Key Terms Used in This Chapter

Superuser	The highest privileged user of the system. Also called the *root user*.
Kernel parameters	The configurable parts of the UNIX kernel, which are "tuned" by the system administrator for optimum system operation.
Pseudo-terminal	A software-produced function that UNIX sees as a terminal device. Often used in multiscreen-system extensions.
Hardware support	Contracted technical help for maintaining computer hardware components.
Software support	Contracted technical help for maintaining and operating computer software.
Up time	Any time when the system's services are available to users.
Down time	Any time when the system's services are not available to users.
Information node	An entry in the information node table that holds information about a file, based on the file's information number. Also called an *i-node* or *inode*.
Mountable file system	A file system that is added to the root file system. The extra file system is attached as a branch of the root file system through a mount command.
Print queuing	A method of holding output for printing until a shared printer can print the output. In a multiuser environment, print queuing enables simultaneous printing requests.
Disk formatting	The electronic preparation of a disk's surface for storing data.
Sector	A formatted division of a disk's surface.
Network	A collection of two or more computers connected for the purpose of information interchange.
Point-to-point network	A network in which one computer connects to another only for the duration of the interchange. Point-to-point connections typically are made via a modem.
Forward and hold	A method of sending mail and other information over a point-to-point network, in which the receiving system holds the information until it can be forwarded to the destination system.

Broadcast network	A network in which all computers are attached to a common medium. All computers "hear" the transmissions of other systems. This type of connection is commonly used in a Local Area Network (LAN).
Token-passing network	A network in which each computer passes all messages to its neighbor. Each message is attached to an electronic token. Only the intended receiving computer acts on the message.
Internetwork	A network consisting of independent networks connected by gateways. UNIX internetworks communicate using TCP/IP protocols.

Understanding the Superuser

Each UNIX system has a single user who can perform virtually any operation he or she wants on the computer. This user is called the *superuser*. The superuser has a special login name, called *root*. The user named root is logged to the root directory of the file system when he or she logs on to the system.

Many programs, commands, and utilities that are inaccessible to an ordinary user are open to the superuser. The system administrator performs system-administration actions as the root user. Even on large UNIX systems, only a few users know how to log on as root. When any person is logged on the system as root, that person is the superuser and has absolute privilege on the system. With this privilege, the superuser can change the attributes of any file, stop the system, start the system, make backups of the system's data, and perform many other tasks. The system administrator's tasks fall into the following general categories:

- Keep the system secure by administering security
- Back up user files and store the backups for possible restoration if the system's files are lost or damaged
- Configure the system to permit the maximum number of users to use the system's hardware and software resources
- Manage any network connections
- Add new applications programs, operating-system updates, and maintenance corrections to the system
- Record or log any significant activity concerning the system
- Work with vendors of software, hardware, and training contracts
- Act as the "local expert" as an aid to the system's ordinary users

The system administrator logs in as the superuser to perform privileged work. For normal system work, the system administrator logs in as an ordinary user. The superuser login—root—is used for limited special purposes only.

Understanding the Administrative Role

So far, you have read about just a few of the system administrator's many possible tasks. To get a better understanding of the administrator's role, you can compare a working UNIX system to a large amusement or theme park. As an ordinary user, you access the facilities of UNIX as you would access the rides or exhibits at a theme park. Your interest is in using the available facilities.

When you want to visit a theme park exhibit, you simply follow the procedure for getting into the exhibit. Similarly, when you want to use a UNIX facility, you follow the procedures for issuing commands and operating programs. When you board a ride at an amusement park, you follow rules, such as holding the safety rail and getting off when the ride is over. When you work with UNIX, you follow the rules of logging on to the system, forming commands, and logging off.

When you stop and consider the complexity of rides and exhibits at a theme park, you realize that a great deal of work goes into keeping everything working smoothly, so that the visitors can enjoy themselves. Much of the behind-the-scenes work is done by the UNIX system manager as well, so that the system's users can enjoy the benefits of working with the system.

You don't worry about the details of managing the ride or the exhibit. Rather, you assume that the park's manager makes sure that all the necessary resources are allocated, and that maintenance is performed to keep the ride and the exhibit ready for public use.

Keeping a UNIX system in good operating condition requires the allocation and management of resources, too. Ordinary users don't involve themselves in management details, such as mounting file systems or establishing the printer device for accepting user output. The system administrator handles such details, just as the theme park's manager ensures that the rides are maintained and ready for use.

A vast behind-the-scenes system of administration exists at the popular theme park, Disney World. Even in the park's public areas, certain doors are not accessible to the ordinary visitor. Disney World personnel use these doors to gain access to the park's inner workings, where park administration takes place. In a very similar fashion, certain UNIX commands provide access to the "underground" world of system administration. Only privileged users (that is, those users who have received the required authorization from the superuser) can access these privileged commands and utilities.

In the following sections, you will get an idea of the many responsibilities a UNIX system administrator assumes. The discussion assumes that your system is administered by a single person. Your system may be administered in a somewhat different way, but for purposes of understanding, you can generalize the single-administrator paradigm to your system.

The delegation of administrative responsibilities varies from system to system. On larger systems, system administration tasks can be divided among several people. Some smaller systems do not even require a full-time administrator; such systems simply designate a certain user to act as system administrator. If you work in a networked environment, your system may be administered over the network by a network administrator. You should find out how system administration is delegated on your system.

Administering System-Level Considerations

An end user might easily underestimate the system administrator's role, because the administrator does much work behind the scenes. Nevertheless, the administrator must juggle a formidable list of system-level responsibilities. Remember that a UNIX system is a configured blending of hardware, system software, and applications software. The system administrator must make sure that all the major elements of this blend are properly managed.

A typical UNIX installation does not maintain the same configuration for long. As hardware, software, and user loads change, the system administrator checks and tunes the system kernel. The administrator manages the installation of additional hardware and ensures that the kernel is capable of supporting the new devices. Tracking software updates and making sure that the system is running the appropriate versions of software are also part of the job. In addition, the administrator acts as the contact for hardware and software support contracts from outside vendors. The next few sections take a closer look at these important parts of system administration.

Reporting System Information

The system administrator knows the names and directory locations of many key data files, which constitute tables of the system's configuration and activity. For example, most UNIX systems log system messages to a text file. Most system messages are simply routine status reports, but some are indicators of problems in the system. All systems experience minor problems on occasion, but a consistent problem report or a pattern of seemingly unrelated system messages may indicate that corrective action is required. Often, system messages are good indicators of a subtle problem in the system's configuration. The system may halt during the night and then restart automatically. Without the logging of the messages that the system issued before it halted, a system administrator would be left to speculate about the nature of the problem.

About Administrative Shells . . .

SCO System V/386 includes a program for accomplishing main system administration duties. This program is known as the *System Administration Shell* and has the command name `sysadmsh`. Many other UNIX-based systems have similar programs to assist with system administration. Some AT&T systems include the FACE utility, which features system administration functions.

Administrative personnel use the System Administration Shell to initiate tasks rather than issuing UNIX commands that initiate the same tasks. The `sysadmsh` and FACE programs present menus of items to select on the administrator's screen. To many administrators, this type of presentation is easier to use than standard UNIX commands. A typical system administrator must have a broad knowledge of UNIX to administer a system effectively. Wide-ranging administrative commands can be difficult to remember, and administrative programs relieve the administrator from the burden of remembering esoteric command names.

Configuring the Kernel

You learned that the UNIX kernel is a single component of system software that loads into system RAM at boot time to provide the core operating-system services. The kernel includes variable (or tunable) *parameters* that affect the efficiency and functionality of the kernel. These parameters control resources that the kernel uses, releases, and then recycles during system operation.

An example of these system resources is the cache of memory-based storage locations called *disk buffers*, which temporarily house recently used disk data. When a program calls for disk data, the kernel first consults the disk buffers in case the requested data is held in the buffer as the result of a previous disk access. Data can be retrieved from the buffer much more quickly than it can be read from a disk drive. If the system does not have a sufficient number of buffers, the system must depend on slower disk accesses to retrieve data. As a result, system throughput slows. When too many disk buffers are allocated, less system memory is available for user programs, and more user programs must be swapped, or *paged*, to the disk. Excessive program swapping slows system throughput even more than repeated disk accesses for nonbuffered data.

When system memory is short, or when user load is high, the choice between using memory for buffers or user programs becomes critical. The system administrator must monitor buffer access and swapping activity in order to tune buffer resources to an optimum size. Buffer allocation is just one kernel resource that the administrator monitors. When the system administrator sees persistent error messages indicating that system resources (such as space for the i-node table) are exhausted, he must consider reconfiguring the kernel. To establish a new set of kernel parameters, he uses diagnostic programs and monitors error messages.

To reconfigure the kernel, the system administrator generates an additional kernel program to replace the existing kernel. This procedure, however, does not destroy the old kernel program. The administrator then renames the old kernel, and the new kernel takes its place as the new UNIX. The system administrator can test the new kernel and, if necessary, revert to the old kernel. If the new kernel operates satisfactorily, it becomes the new heart of the system. You can see that a modular kernel offers flexibility in the form of a replaceable software component.

Installing Additional Hardware

Installing additional hardware on a UNIX system is not a simple undertaking. Pushing a new circuit board into the computer's chassis is only part of the procedure. There are software considerations to installing hardware, as well. You'll recall from the earlier discussion of system software that the device-driver programs provide a consistent interface between the hardware and the parts of the kernel that request hardware services. Before a new item of hardware can provide service to the system, its device driver must be linked to the kernel.

Not all devices represent physical hardware. Multiscreen capability, for example, is achieved through software manipulation. In a system which supports multiscreen sessions, a user can log onto a terminal several times, without logging off between logins. Each login appears to be a different login to the system. The user presses a special action-key sequence at the terminal, and then the terminal prompts for another login as though the user had moved to another terminal. The user's first session, however, remains active behind the scenes on the same terminal. The user sees the current session as though it were the only session. By pressing the action-key sequence again, the user can toggle the first session back to the screen.

A system with multiscreen capability treats a single physical terminal as multiple logical terminals. To the system, each logical session has its own *pseudo-terminal*, even though only one physical terminal is present. A pseudo-terminal is a software "simulation" that UNIX recognizes as a real terminal. The user may be running a word processor on one logical terminal, a database program on another, and compiling a C program on a third. The user can switch to any of these activities with a simple key sequence rather than moving to another terminal. Like any other device, however, multiscreen pseudo-devices must be linked to the kernel. The system administrator must configure the resources allocated to multiscreens just as he would configure other resources.

The system administrator must configure the system to utilize other devices such as a mouse and a network interface card. When the system administrator installs other devices, he or she accepts the fact that the system will be a bit more complicated than before.

Arranging Support Contracts

Managing a UNIX system is a complex undertaking for the system administrator. Many managers arrange for support from the system's manufacturer or a third-party support organization. Support contracts are agreements between the operators of the UNIX system and a professional provider of support services. System support is divided between *hardware support* and *software support*. Support may be rendered on-site by traveling personnel or over the phone by phone support personnel.

System managers rely on hardware support to isolate and repair defects in system hardware components such as circuit boards, disk drives, terminals, and power supplies. Although many system managers know a great deal about hardware, they do not have access to the specialized diagnostic tools used by professional hardware support personnel. Hardware support organizations also have quick access to spare parts. If a system manager must purchase a new disk drive to replace a defective one, the system might be "down" for several days. A hardware support organization, on the other hand, probably can replace the same disk drive in a matter of hours. If a hardware item is in the process of failing, the support organization may be able to detect the failure by monitoring the system over a modem connection. Modem support offers the advantage of eliminating the time a technician must spend traveling to and working at a UNIX site.

Software support is most often done over the phone or through a modem connection. A typical UNIX system offers dozens of applications programs and stores thousands of files. The system manager may have to configure each application to the system's unique situation. When a program appears to be working incorrectly, and the system administrator cannot determine the problem, the expertise of phone-based software support personnel can be of immeasurable value. Software support people must examine all types of software problems and determine their solutions. Because these experts repeatedly encounter many problem situations in the use of a software package, they generally can determine the nature of the problem in a short time.

A busy system administrator cannot be an expert on every "nut and bolt" in the system. By working with contracted support personnel, the administrator doesn't have to be a master of every aspect of the system. To the end user, the value of outside support is measured in the increased amount of *up time*, or time when the system is available. When the hardware or software is "broken," the extra support minimizes the amount of *down time* users must spend waiting for the system to become available for use again.

Ensuring Timely Backups

When you run programs and commands on a UNIX system, you generally produce files as a natural by-product of your computing activity. Of course, you assume that your files will be accessible when you need them. Occasionally, however, a file or group of files can be lost. File loss occurs for many reasons. You might accidentally erase a file or group of files. An item of hardware might fail and corrupt UNIX's internal file-storage bookkeeping tables. In rare instances, an unauthorized user might delete files as a deliberate act of sabotage. In any case, the only reliable way to recover the lost files is to restore them to the file system from a *backup* set of files. The `sysadmsh` program and similar utilities help the system administrator perform important backup chores regularly.

Creating Backups

As you recall, the primary storage devices for UNIX systems are fixed or hard disk drives. Hard disk drives store data on a magnetic medium. In order to create a usable copy, or backup, of a hard disk's files, the system administrator selects an alternative removable medium on which to store the backed-up files. The two most commonly used media are magnetic tape and floppy disks. Both tape and floppies are available in various formats, but all can be removed from the system and stored in a safe place.

Magnetic tape cartridges can store from tens to hundreds of megabytes (M); a single floppy disk can store about 1M to 1.5M. Larger systems in the minicomputer and mainframe classes employ magnetic tape units, whereas smaller systems employ floppy disk drives or 1/4-inch tape cartridges. Each 20M of data requires about 15 5 1/4-inch 1.2M floppies. A single 450-foot tape cartridge can hold 40M.

Although UNIX offers provisions for making backups of files, you should not become complacent about referring to your files in commands that manipulate them. You have no guarantee that a deleted or overwritten file can be restored from the backup. Even if the file exists on a backup, the backup file probably will be an older version and may not contain recent changes.

Whenever you save a newly created or recently modified file, UNIX "stamps" the file with the current time and date. Most system administrators use this time and date information to determine which files should be included in a particular backup. User files can change daily, and therefore should be backed up daily. System files—such as commands, programs, initialization and configuration tables, and shell procedures—do not change often, and therefore do not need to be backed up as often as data files.

To accommodate smaller backups, the administrator may make a daily backup of only those files that have been created or changed since the day before. This daily approach results in several "sets" of backup files on individual tapes or sets of floppies. In any given week, files changed or created during that week will be included on at least one daily backup. If a file changes more than once a week, a copy of its most recent version will reside on a later backup. Even if daily dated backups are maintained, most system administrators still perform a complete backup of all files as a safeguard against a total failure of the disk(s).

Although system administrators may elect to suspend use of the system temporarily to perform a backup, they usually establish an automatic process that uses a schedule to perform backups when the system is not in use. Backup time normally is scheduled at night, when user load is minimal or nonexistent. You can easily understand why backups are best performed when no users are on the system. With users changing, adding, and deleting files, the backup operation would be like "shooting at a moving target."

Make a mental note whenever you change or add a file. If you accidentally erase or overwrite a file, you can help the system administrator make sure that the most recent backup copy is used to restore the file. If you're changing or deleting a file critical to your work, you might want to jot the file's name down in a notebook.

Restoring Files from Backups

The restoration process is the reverse of the backup process. Through file restoration, the system administrator can move a file from the backup medium to the system's fixed disk. You recall from the discussion of backing up files that not every file in the file system needs to be backed up. The same is true of the restoration process. When a single file or a group of similarly named files must be restored, only those particular files are restored. If an entire file system is damaged during system operation, the entire file system is restored. The system administrator cannot tell if you have erased important files from one of your directories. It's *your* responsibility to inform the administrator. If the entire file system is damaged, UNIX will most likely detect the problem and inform the system administrator with a message or series of messages.

About the Workings of the File System . . .

UNIX employs an internal bookkeeping system to store and retrieve files. You don't see much of this system at work because much of the file-storage mechanism is handled by the kernel. When you create a file in one of your directories, UNIX creates a directory entry containing the file's name. In addition to the file's name, UNIX links the file name to a storage table called the *Information-Node* (or simply *i-node*) table. The Information-Node table contains an entry for each file in the file system. The file's i-number is the link between the directory entry for a file and the i-node table. The i-number simply identifies the i-node that contains the remaining information about the file. While you will often work with directory and file names, you will seldom work with i-numbers.

Each file system has a predetermined number of i-node entries. Each entry contains file ownership information, the time and date of the last modification and access, and a link count that indicates the number of names in different directories that contain a file name that represents this i-node as their i-number. Through the use of i-numbers, it is possible to link two file names in two different directories to the same file. All files and directories have i-numbers that link them with i-nodes in an i-node table. You don't have to contend with the i-node or the i-node table. Your work with files and directories takes place at the directory level.

UNIX enables the use of more than one file system by mounting additional file systems to a branch of the root file system. A common use of a separate, *mountable file system* is to separate user files from system files by giving the user files their own file system. The separate user file system is often named /u or

About the Workings of the File System . . . continued

/usr2. System administrators then can use a backup command to copy entire file systems. With a separate file system for user files, the file-system backup command is ideal for backing up only the user files.

Each file system contains a data structure called the *superblock*. The superblock describes the makeup of the file system. The superblock stores information such as the size of the file system in blocks and the number of i-nodes allocated to the file system. The superblock also keeps track of the next available i-node and the next available block. Each file system maintains its own i-node table. Files cannot be linked by i-number from one file system to another because the i-numbers are not exclusive. Files can be symbolically linked between file systems, however. In a symbolic link, the linked file's name serves as the internal identifier of the file in place of the i-number.

Administering backups is one of the system administrator's most important jobs. This task goes largely unnoticed by ordinary users. Typically, an end user becomes aware of the importance of backups only after the first time he or she inadvertently erases a file containing a 60-page report. The user breathes a sigh of relief when the system administrator restores the file from yesterday's backup set.

Administering Accounts

At the core of UNIX system security is an identification process that matches people to the system's resources. Because a user must properly identify himself to the system, UNIX can prevent unauthorized persons from using the system. Security improves when the user must receive authorization to access or execute data files, directories, and programs. The system administrator establishes information about each authorized user and stores this information in individual user accounts. Because you have or will have an account on your UNIX system, you should become familiar with the basics of account administration. Each system has its own criteria for security; talk to your system administrator about the specifics of your account.

Identifying and Managing User Accounts

With few exceptions, a person must identify himself to the system before he can attain access to the system's resources. Central to this identification procedure is the user's login name and password. Chapter 5 discusses login names and passwords in detail; for now, you need to know only that secure systems require users to supply correct login names and passwords. UNIX relies on the user's unique ID number to track the user internally. UNIX associates your user ID number with your login name, password, the programs you run, and the files you create. Your user ID is the only absolute "identity card" that will get you through UNIX's various security mechanisms.

Your system administrator establishes your login name—and usually, your password—when your account is set up. You don't have to do anything. You will be notified when your account is added to the system. You'll learn more about your personal account in the next chapter.

Setting Up Account Defaults

The system administrator establishes *system defaults* for user accounts. System defaults are values that the system automatically uses unless the system administrator overrides them. The administrator may choose to override certain default settings when your account is established.

A wide variety of default settings deal with account security. One default setting, for example, determines the number of unsuccessful login attempts you are allowed before the account locks up. Another concerns the length or nature of your password. The program that is your shell is an established default, as is the content of your login initialization files. Don't worry about the exact nature of your defaults; you'll learn more about your account in the next chapter. As you read about logins and security later in this text, just remember that the system administrator tailors your access according to the system's predetermined security policy.

Administering Terminal Ports

Chapter 2 explained that terminals are connected to the system through serial communications ports. Other peripherals also attach to UNIX systems through serial ports. The system administrator must configure each port so that UNIX operates the port in a way that is proper for the device. For instance, a modem must be initialized to answer incoming calls automatically. A port dedicated to a digitizer pad for CAD/CAM applications cannot be treated like a terminal port, because the pad's output takes the form of digitized position information rather than user-entered keystrokes.

The system administrator selects certain ports and enables logins for those ports. A file named /etc/inittab lists the system's serial communications ports and provides initialization parameters for each port. If a port is dedicated to a device other than a terminal, the system administrator must disable user logins on that port. Otherwise, the system might mistake the device's data output for terminal activity and treat the output as though a user had typed characters on a keyboard. If this happens, the attached device cannot work with the system as the application intended.

Administering Printers

Printers are a computer system's hardest-working output devices. Printed output—or "hard copy"—usually is a variety of information that appears in a variety of formats. UNIX-system printers print everything from inventory lists to address labels and bar-code labels. For high-volume output, most systems employ dot-matrix printers or high-speed line and page printers. For high-quality output, many systems rely on laser and ink-jet printers. Nearly all UNIX systems utilize at least one printer, and most larger systems have multiple printers.

In the multitasking/multiuser environment of UNIX, it is quite possible that more than one program will attempt to send output to the same printer at the same time. Of course, a printer can accept output from only one program at a time. Otherwise, printed lines from contending programs would be mingled together on one page. So that users do not have to wait until the printer is no longer busy with the current printing job, UNIX employs a *print-queuing* mechanism.

When a program utilizes the print-queuing mechanism, UNIX intercepts program output that is destined for the printer, and places that output in a file. The program behaves as though the output has successfully gone to the printer. When the printer is no longer busy with the current print job, another queued job is taken from its file and sent to the printer. To UNIX, print queuing and printing are just another running process. To the user, print queuing is a transparent extension of a command or applications program. To the system administrator, print queuing is another UNIX subsystem that must be configured, checked, and maintained.

Configuring Printers

In a UNIX system, one printer is identified by its device name as the primary or default printer. When a program sends printer output to the printer service, this printer is used by default. If the system has one printer, that printer is the default printer. When configuring printers, the system administrator must consider the means by which printers are attached to the system. Printers are connected to a UNIX system by means of a parallel interface or a serial interface. The system administrator identifies each printer by name, and then associates the printer with a serial or parallel device name. Users can give the printer's name as part of a print command or as a configuration option to programs that print. The printer service then routes output to the named printer.

You should ask your system administrator for the possible print destination names on your system, and for the name of the default system printer. Also, if you need to produce high-quality output, you will want to know the name of your system's laser printer.

Managing Printer Operation

Like any other mechanical device, printers require maintenance. Printers can jam, run out of paper or toner, or simply fail. If a printer must be taken out of service temporarily, the system manager may route printing requests to another printer. This flexibility enables the administrator to maintain printers while printing activity goes on relatively undisturbed. You also should be aware that, when necessary, the administrator can cancel a print job before it starts. If your print job is canceled, you should receive a message explaining the action.

Sometimes, when many print jobs are waiting in the print queue, an important report may need to be moved forward in the queue. When this need arises, the system administrator can adjust the priority of pending print jobs, so that more important jobs are printed before less important jobs. Prioritizing the print requests, however, is often a subjective call. You may think that your report is more important than the accounting department's quarterly financial statement; nevertheless, your report's priority might be changed.

Managing Magnetic Media

Because a UNIX system uses magnetic media for data storage, the system administrator spends a great deal of time working with disks and tapes. All UNIX systems (except stand-alone systems such as workstations) share peripheral devices such as disk drives among all users. Sometimes, however, a user may need to move a copy of his files to another UNIX system. Or, a user might need to keep some files on a floppy disk for historical purposes. Normally, an ordinary user does not have direct access to the disk drives or to the commands that manage them. The system administrator is responsible for managing the system's magnetic media.

Maintaining Complete File Listings

Many system administrators print a complete listing of all the files in the system. In a way, the listing is a form of system logging. Although the system administrator can view lists of files on his terminal, a hard-copy listing is often easier to use. You can imagine the difficulty of referencing thousands of files on a screen that can display only a few dozen files at a time.

The system administrator may choose to keep more than one listing. A primary listing shows the name of each file, complete with path names in the directory tree system. The primary listing shows the files in the hierarchical order of the directory structure. Further, the primary listing may show the time and date of each file's creation, as well as each file's size, i-number, and other administrative file attributes.

Secondary file listings may list files in order, either alphabetically, by size, or even by user. Such secondary listings (that is, listings that show files in an order other than the system's hierarchical order) can help the administrator generalize the composition of the system's files. Using information from secondary listings, the administrator can see which files occupy the most space, who owns the most files, and which files are accessed or changed most or least often. This type of information can help the administrator determine which files should be removed from the system and placed on tape or floppy disk. The administrator may take care of file removal himself, or he may ask you to remove files that you have created but do not seem to use. At the very least, a file listing is a convenient reference of each file's place in the file system.

Archiving Files

When the system administrator elects to store files on tape or floppy disk, he may use UNIX's archive facilities. The archive facilities are based on the `tar` (*tape archive*) command. Archived files are stored in a special format on floppy disks or tape. The archive format is not the same as the format used for the daily storage of files on the hard disk. The UNIX file system cannot directly access archived files. Files are archived to reduce the main disk requirements, to provide a means of physically transferring files to another system, and to provide a means for the distribution of programs, updates, and problem fixes. Backups provide a safety net for the possible loss of files that remain on the hard disk after backing up. In contrast, archived files represent information that is not immediately needed, but too important simply to erase.

If the system administrator elects to return archived files to the file system, he can use a utility (based on `tar`) to extract the desired files from the tape or floppy disk. A file-extraction utility can place extracted files back into the file system in a relative position.

What does this mean? In a hierarchical file system, relative file names are taken as being additional to the current path. If the current directory is `/usr`, for example, then a relatively extracted file named `bin/dojob` becomes `/usr/bin/dojob` in the file system. By using relative file names, the administrator can "graft" a new branch to the current directory tree. Relative extraction is an ideal technique for distributing programs and associated data files from a source system to any number of destination systems. The system administrator can determine the best location in the system for extracted files, without worrying about the exact location of the source files in the source UNIX system's directory tree.

Formatting Disks

Before a disk can be used with a UNIX system, it must be prepared electronically—or *formatted*—so that it can store files. Formatting divides a disk's tracks into sections called *sectors*. The UNIX kernel can translate a file's directory location (that you use in commands) to a sector or series of sectors (that the disk hardware uses to access data). When a disk is "factory new," the disk has no sector divisions. The disk must be formatted to be useful.

In very basic terms, formatting a disk is like drawing horizontal rule lines on a blank sheet of paper, so that someone can write on the paper in an ordered manner. Although formatting a disk is much more complicated than drawing lines across a piece of paper, the two operations produce similar results. The formatting procedure organizes a disk's blank surfaces into clearly divided areas, into which information can be written.

Duplicating Disks

System administrators spend a great deal of time duplicating floppy disks. Duplicate disks are necessary when the administrator wants to distribute multiple copies of archived files, when extra copies of files are needed for security reasons, or whenever someone needs a mirror image of a floppy disk. A duplicated disk is a mirror image of the original disk because the original disk's sectors are copied—in order—to the duplicate. The duplicate disk can be an archive disk, a backup disk, or a mountable file system. Of course, the system manager must carefully label any floppy disk to eliminate confusion about the disk's contents.

Using the Tapedump Facility

A *tapedump* is the outputting—or "dumping"—of a magnetic tape's contents to a file, the screen, or a printer. A tapedump facility is an important tool in the management of a UNIX system, because the facility enables the system to use magnetically stored data that was originally generated by a "foreign" operating system. Generally, the original data is written to the tape on a non-UNIX computer system. The original data might be a mailing list of names and addresses, for example, or data from some sort of instrumentation. In any case, the tapedump facility makes the data available to programs on the UNIX system.

As you recall, UNIX uses the ASCII coding system to store character data. Some computer systems (including many IBM systems) use an extended form of character encoding known as EBCDIC (pronounced *ebb si dick*). The tapedump facility enables the conversion of tape data to and from EBCDIC. With the help of this conversion facility, a UNIX system can use tapes written by an IBM mainframe.

Managing Jobs

A *job* is a program that is scheduled to be executed at a specified time or during a predetermined low point in system activity. The system administrator (and ordinary users on some systems) can initiate jobs to run unattended at a convenient time. A job is different from a program in that a program runs when a user enters the program's name on the command line. A job's execution is delayed until a later time. The job's function, however, usually is the same as a UNIX command or some other program.

The system administrator might order UNIX to start a program at midnight, for example, to print the daily invoice file on the system printer. By using the job facility, the administrator can initiate the printing, but does not have to be at a terminal at midnight to start the printing program. A job may be a simple command, or a job may consist of several tasks linked together in a shell procedure file.

The system administrator can establish a table of commands that UNIX executes at regular intervals. A command that typically runs at regular intervals is the `sync` command. Every few seconds, the `sync` command tells UNIX to write the contents of buffer-based files to the disk. The file system's bookkeeping tables are updated when the disk buffers are emptied (flushed). By regularly flushing the disk buffers, the `sync` command ensures that only the last few seconds of disk file activity are lost in case of a system power failure.

Another example of a scheduled event is the forwarding of electronic mail to another UNIX system. A sending system initiates a program that controls a modem link to a receiving system. Any mail that is addressed through the second system is then transferred. The second system may then forward mail to other systems. The forwarding and holding events take place without intervention from any of the system administrators.

Managing the File System

The file system is an essential part of UNIX. If users are to trust their data to the files that make up the file system, the file system must be in proper operating order.

The file system consists not only of files—the system is also made up of the UNIX bookkeeping mechanisms that record essential information about the files. The bookkeeping mechanism includes data structures, such as directories, i-node tables, and the superblock. All of these data structures must faithfully reflect the actual condition of the file system. If the superblock loses track of the next available block, the next file that a user creates may destroy someone else's file. If an i-node records the wrong data block number of its file, the contents of the file are inaccessible.

The system administrator is responsible for testing the integrity of the file system and correcting problems. The most common problem with file-system integrity stems from the loss of power while files are in use. Because part of an active file is held—in disk buffers in system memory—a power loss can catch a file with part of its contents not committed to disk. UNIX periodically "flushes" the buffer contents to the disk in order to keep the disk up to date. At that time, UNIX also updates the superblock on the disk from a copy held in memory. A power loss, therefore, can lead to a discrepancy between UNIX's records of the file's contents and the file's actual contents. The system's disk-based records may not match the disk-based file contents because the memory-based buffers, i-nodes, and superblock contents were lost before the power failure. Automatic periodic flushing of the memory-based disk buffers and superblock updating minimize such discrepancies, but problems can still arise.

The system administrator can utilize the `fsck` (*file system check*) command to detect and fix file system problems. If the file system's problems are so serious that `fsck` cannot repair them, the system administrator may resort to other file system repair commands. At the very least, the administrator must be prepared to restore the entire file system from backups. Needless to say, the duties associated with maintaining the file system are important. You count on the system administrator to ensure that your files' integrity is maintained.

The system administrator is normally responsible for creating mountable file systems. Remember that every UNIX system has a default root file system, but additional file systems can be linked to the root file system. The system manager must determine the number of disk blocks (1,024-byte sector groups) that the new file system can occupy. He must reserve a sufficient number of i-nodes in the i-node table, but not so many as to be wasteful. He must establish a mounting point in the directory-system tree for the new file system. If the new file system is to be mounted automatically when the system boots, he must make proper administrative table entries to ensure that the system mounts the new file system. If the new file system is to be unmounted from the root file system, he must ensure that all user activity with the new file system is complete.

From your vantage point, the additional mounted file systems are largely transparent. You aren't aware that you are accessing files from an additional file system. From the system administrator's point of view, however, additional file systems are another element of UNIX that must be managed.

Installing Software

Normally, a UNIX system initially contains only a core set of utilities and data files. The system administrator installs additional commands, applications, and associated data files after the system is built. Most UNIX system vendors provide a command, such as AT&T's `installpkg`, which enables the system administrator to install new programs easily. The administrator should maintain a log of the name and revision level of each program as it is installed.

Most applications programs (except for very simple ones) must be configured to the system before they can be used. The system administrator, for example, may have to identify users and users' configurations to an application's initialization tables. In some cases, the administrator must create new directories to house the application's files. Some applications require the configuring or reconfiguring of system devices, such as mice or terminal settings. Whereas end users are primarily concerned with learning to operate the new program, the system manager must make sure that the system's resources are properly set up and maintained for the program.

Administering Networks

Many UNIX systems have hardware and software facilities that enable them to communicate with other UNIX systems. Two or more interconnected systems form a *network*. Networks communicate at various speeds and through various methods of electronic communication interchange. The slowest networking facilities communicate via modem link at speeds of 300 to 2400 baud. Faster 9600-baud modems are commonly used today for modem links. Fast networking facilities can communicate at speeds greater than 10 million bits per second over dedicated cables. A network's speed is primarily a function of the networking hardware.

To you, greater accessibility is the benefit of operating in a networked environment. Depending on the type of network you use, you can access anything from a remote system's files and mail services to the processing time of a remote system's CPU. A modern, full-function network can even create the illusion that the entire network resource is your computer. To the system administrator, however, the work involved in configuring and maintaining a networked environment means challenges that reach far beyond the normal UNIX responsibilities. This book is not a tutorial on the use of networking facilities. If you are working in a networked environment, ask the system manager for the documentation that describes your networking facilities.

About Network Security . . .

UNIX's extensive security features enable the system administrator to maintain a secure, trustworthy system. On non-networked systems, the greatest risk of security breach comes from a breakdown in password secrecy. An administrator generally knows all users on a non-networked system and can consult logs and audit trails to explain any unusual user activity.

When a system is part of a network, however, the number of possible users grows in relation to the size of the network. If someone wants to break into the system, that person will exploit any security lapses to gain the privileges of the superuser or another highly privileged user. A person with superuser privileges can do as he pleases on a system. He may view sensitive files or perform acts of vandalism. He may leave programs on the system that mail themselves to other systems, thereby spreading the problem. Destructive programs or viruses often masquerade as common UNIX commands, and an unsuspecting user entering one of these commands can unwittingly destroy files or even the entire file system.

The security measures that system administrators employ to keep their systems secure can sometimes seem cumbersome to users. System users must understand, however, that as more people gain access to privileged commands and data, the risk of security breaches increases. If you notice that a command acts oddly, or if you see any unusual files in your work area, notify your system administrator. If you operate in a networked environment and have access to superuser privileges, be especially careful with your passwords.

Understanding UUCP

The most basic UNIX networking utility is a collection of commands and tables called *UUCP* (for *UNIX-to-UNIX Copy*). UUCP is actually a UNIX command when entered in lowercase letters at the command prompt. The name UUCP is a generalized name given to uucp and other basic networking commands. UUCP has been available on UNIX systems for several years and enjoys a well-established following. Systems connected via UUCP communicate over serial communication lines, either directly or through modems. Networks that consist of individual computers that connect to other individual computers when communication is desired are called *point-to-point* networks.

The system administrator configures one or more of the system's ports as the network port, and then enters the machine names of the systems to which connections can be made. These systems are called the *remote systems*. To accommodate requests for command execution from remote systems, the administrator establishes authorizations and permissions that provide security from remote commands. Of course, the system administrator creates any necessary directories for UUCP and installs the appropriate basic networking facility commands and data files. UUCP networks are informal and rely on the cooperation of system administrators to permit access to their systems.

One of the most common reasons for establishing a connection to a UUCP network is electronic mail. If your system is connected to other systems (sites) through UUCP, you can send electronic mail to users at those sites. To facilitate the exchange of electronic mail, each site's administrator gives his system a name. As a result, both you and your system (as well as other users and other systems) have an identity on the network.

Suppose, for example, that a user named David works at Que Corporation. He may have a unique UUCP address of queps2!david. The site name or machine name for Que is queps2, which happens to be an IBM PS2 Model 80 computer running AIX. The ! character follows the machine name and is immediately followed by the user's name, david. Now, suppose that another machine named andiron has a user named terrie. The two machines are capable of connecting by modem in a UUCP network; David's machine has UUCP tables that contain information about accessing Terrie's machine (and the machines of other users in the network), and vice versa.

If Terrie wants to send David a memo through electronic mail, she uses the address queps2!david as the memo's mail destination. When Terrie completes the mailing, her system stores (holds) the memo temporarily. Terrie's machine, andiron, is programmed to dial David's machine, queps2, every four hours to exchange any mail that is being held. When the two machines connect, the UUCP programs forward all the mail, and the appropriate machines deliver the mail to the appropriate users. David then receives Terrie's memo. This *hold-and-forward* mailing method is efficient because the time that the two machines are "tied together" is limited to the mail exchange time, which occurs once every four hours.

The four-hour interval, however, is not fixed. The system manager could opt, for example, for an exchange every hour or once a week.

By taking the hold-and-forward technique one step further, the `queps2` machine can establish a connection with a much larger system, `bigvax`, at the local university campus. The UNIX system at the campus has established mail-forwarding connections with dozens of smaller sites. One of the smaller sites is named `amc3b2`, where Steve is a user. Although no modem connection exists between `andiron` or `queps2` and `amc3b2`, both `queps2` and `amc3b2` can connect with `bigvax`. Remember also that `andiron` connects to `queps2`.

Figure 4.1 illustrates the physical layout (topology) of this networking scenario. Notice in the figure that there is no direct line between the `queps2` box and the `amc3b2` box. No direct line exists between `andiron` and `amc3b2`, either. Through hold-and-forward techniques, however, any of these systems' users can send mail to any other user on the network.

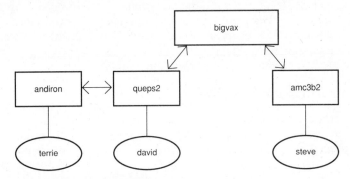

Fig. 4.1. *A sample UUCP network.*

In this sample scenario, Terrie (`andiron`) composes and sends a mail message to Steve. The message is addressed to `queps2!bigvax!amc3b2!steve`. Terrie finishes the message at 8:55 a.m. At noon, `andiron` calls `queps2` for mail exchange. Terrie's message to Steve is now held by `queps2`. The `queps2` machine forwards mail to `bigvax` every other hour; therefore, at a few minutes after 2 p.m., Terrie's message to Steve is held by `bigvax`. At 4 p.m., `amc3b2` calls `bigvax` to exchange mail. In the exchange, the message is delivered to `amc3b2`. A few minutes later, the message is delivered to Steve's mail box. The time is 4:03 p.m. More than seven hours after it was written, Terrie's message to Steve has completed its journey through four UNIX systems.

In actual UUCP mail operations, a user can connect to thousands of potential sites. The system administrator of an active UUCP system is often caught between limiting access to his system for security reasons and keeping his system open for information interchange. All UUCP sites, however, do not offer the same access to outsiders. Many larger installations require the services of a full-time network administrator in order to maintain openness while ensuring security and efficient network operations.

Understanding Local Area Networks

A local area network (LAN) is a group of computers that are connected electronically through high-speed network interfaces. The networked computers are physically close to each other. A typical LAN covers a building or a set of buildings. In a UNIX environment, workstations are typical LAN computers, although PC-based systems are often networked in a LAN.

While UUCP networks are, by design, point-to-point networks, LANs are either *broadcast* or *token-passing* networks. Point-to-point networks rely on an individual computer to contact another computer to exchange data. Broadcast and token-passing networks rely on all connected computers to read communicated data while only the intended recipient of the data responds. LAN communication is like communication that takes place when several people are in a room talking. Everyone in the room can hear everyone else talking. Yet an individual responds only to conversations that are directed at him or her. Point-to-point networks act more like students who are passing a note during study hall. The note gets forwarded from one point to another, while individuals who are not forwarding the note are unaware of the communication.

LANs offer the advantage of speed. Mail delivery over a LAN seems instantaneous. A LAN's major disadvantage is its effective size. Because one system on a LAN must be within a few hundred meters from the other systems on the LAN, the network's total coverage is limited to a few thousand meters. While a few thousand meters may cover several buildings, it is not nearly enough to accommodate the networking of regional offices or remote university campuses.

Many networked systems employ an extension to the normal UNIX file system to enable mounting of remote file systems to the user's system. Sun Microsystems Network File System (NFS) software and AT&T's Remote File System (RFS) software are examples of file-system extensions. If your system utilizes NFS or RFS, you have access to special commands that enable convenient use of another system's files. Check with your system administrator to learn about these commands.

Understanding Internetworking

An *internetwork* is created when independent networks, such as individual LANS, join to form a single large network. Individual networks are connected together through `gateways`. Gateways are systems that can determine the best routing for information, and can forward the information to other gateways or destination systems. As with other networking models, every internetworked system has a machine name and corresponding address. Internetworking uses both point-to-point and broadcast methods of networking.

Figure 4.2 shows a general view of an internetworked group of systems. The figure shows two independent networks and provisions for additional independent networks. Each network has a gateway that links it with the gateway of another network. In practice, such an internetwork can be expanded to include hundreds of networks.

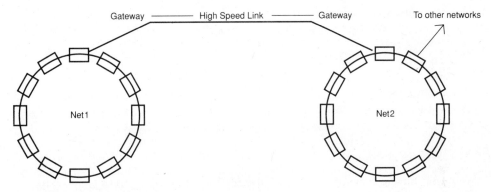

Fig. 4.2. *A sample internetwork.*

The largest and most well-known internetwork is the DARPA (Defense Advanced Research Projects Agency) Internet. Internet is made up of several thousand systems, which are connected to hundreds of networks across the United States and other countries. Internet uses a set of communications rules, or protocols, called the *TCP/IP suite*. TCP/IP is an acronym for Transmission Control Protocol and Internet Protocol. The major users of Internet are government, academic, and industrial laboratories. If you use a system that is linked to Internet, you may have to follow special procedures to access the network's resources. Your system or network administrator can best instruct you how to access network resources.

Summary

This chapter gave you some insights into system administration. System administrators rely on you to use system resources in a cooperative and professional manner. You rely on the system administrator to keep your system operational and well-managed.

This chapter discussed the following key points:

❏ The superuser is the UNIX system's most privileged user.

❏ The system administrator's role is managing and maintaining the system's computing resources for other users.

❏ The system administrator tests and tunes the kernel, installs additional hardware, and arranges outside support for the system.

❑ The system administrator ensures that all data and programs are regularly backed up and restored when necessary.

❑ The system administrator provides system security features by administering user accounts and terminal ports.

❑ The system administrator makes shared multiuser services, such as printing devices, available on a timely basis.

❑ The system administrator manages the system's magnetic media as the foundation for the integrity of the file system and backups.

❑ The system administrator schedules UNIX jobs.

❑ The system administrator installs and configures new software, maintenance patches for existing software, and interim releases of applications software.

❑ The system administrator configures and controls the system's network connections to provide a secure yet useful networking environment.

By now, you have a good fundamental understanding of what UNIX is and what UNIX does. You know UNIX's history. You know how computer hardware and software work together. You understand what an operating system is and how a UNIX system is administered. In the next chapter, you will complete your fundamental knowledge by learning how the UNIX shell interprets your commands. By the end of the next chapter, you will be ready to use UNIX commands and move to Part Two.

Understanding the Shell, Commands, and Syntax

As a UNIX user, you will issue commands to do useful operating system work. Although commands are just one part of UNIX, they are a very important part. As you recall, UNIX commands, also called *utilities*, enable you to manage and report on your part of the UNIX computing environment. In fact, when most users think of UNIX, they usually think of the UNIX commands.

This chapter explains commands as interpreted by the shell. You learn what the parts of a command mean to the shell and learn the general guidelines you need to issue commands for UNIX to carry out for you. When you have absorbed the information in this chapter, you will be comfortable accessing your UNIX system and doing useful work. (Chapters 14 and 15 discuss the shell in greater detail and introduce shell programming.)

Before any UNIX user can begin to enter commands at the keyboard, the user must establish a connection with the UNIX system. Connecting may be as simple as turning on your terminal, or as involved as establishing a modem connection through your terminal. If you are a first-time UNIX user, you'll want to pay close attention to the preliminary steps in establishing your UNIX connection.

Communicating your wishes to a computer can be one of life's frustrating experiences. If you're like most people, you don't need additional frustration. When you use UNIX, you communicate your wishes to the system in the form of commands. Using a computer is intended to increase your productivity. You will find that the more confident you are about using UNIX commands, the less frustrated you will be.

This important chapter prepares you for the discussion of commands in Part Two. When you are satisfied with your learning here, you'll be ready for Part Two.

103

Key Terms Used in This Chapter

Login name	The name assigned to you as your identity to the system.
Account	The record of your access to the system.
Password	A secret "word" that verifies your login name during the process of logging on to the system.
Parity	A method of detecting errors in serial communications.
Baud rate	A measure of the speed at which characters are transmitted and received.
Duplex	Simultaneous sending and receiving of characters in which the system echoes to the screen the characters you type.
Command prompt	The $, %, #, or other character string that indicates that UNIX is waiting for a command.
Parsing	The "breaking apart" of a command line in order to extract its meaning.
Syntax	The rules of proper formation for a command.
Delimiter	A character that separates parts of a command. A space is a delimiter to UNIX.
White space	A space, multiple spaces, or tab characters that delimit parts of a command.
Argument	An item or items given as parts of a command. An argument tells a command what to operate on or where to send the results of an operation.
Option	A type of argument that modifies the basic way a command operates. Options follow a minus (–) character.
Expansion	Interpreting special characters in file names to generate a list of file-name arguments.
Substitution	Interpreting special characters in commands by substituting another meaning for the literal letters.
User-defined	A method that stores a string value in a named variable so that the name's value can be substituted as part of a command.
Command category	A subjective grouping of commands that perform related tasks. Command categories are useful when you are learning commands.

Accessing a UNIX System

UNIX is a secure, multiuser operating system. Your UNIX system provides built-in methods to keep the activities of various users separate and distinct. The key to UNIX's differentiation of its users is each user's *login name*. You identify yourself with your login name when you access your UNIX system. Of course, you communicate with the system through your terminal's keyboard and screen. If your terminal is directly connected or "hard-wired" to the system, you need not concern yourself with the details of the terminal-to-system link. If your terminal is connected to the system through a modem, you need to establish a phone link with the system before you can actively access UNIX. Once connected to the UNIX system, you can attempt a login and begin your UNIX session.

Single-user systems, such as workstations, use the computers' screens and attached keyboards as their terminals. If you use one of these dedicated UNIX systems, you don't have to worry about serial terminals.

Accessing your system will be routine to you in a short time. Yet, accessing a system may seem confusing to a beginner. The next few sections cover the preliminary steps for connecting to your UNIX system. You should familiarize yourself with this information before you sit down in front of your terminal for the first time. If you are already using UNIX, it would be a good idea to review this preliminary information before you continue.

Obtaining a Login Name and Password

When you use UNIX, you are likely to be one of many users sharing the resources of the system. One of UNIX's main jobs is to allocate system resources fairly among its users. When it comes to the computer's resources, UNIX is a sharing operating system. At the same time, UNIX assumes that you do not want to share your work, such as memos or data, with other users. UNIX must identify you and other users in order to give each user the system resources to do useful computing while maintaining the individual integrity of each user's work. Your login name identifies you to your system and acts as the identifier for resource allocation and system security.

You also may hear the term *login name* referred to as a *log name* or just *login*. In the context of your identity to UNIX, these "log" terms mean the same thing.

If you are new to a UNIX system, ask the system administrator to set up an *account* on the system for you. An account is a record of who you are and what you can access. The system administrator establishes an account for a new user and assigns the new user a login name. In most systems, each user is assigned a *password* in conjunction with the login name. The user's password serves as a verification of the user's login name.

Login Names

Your login name is a set of numbers and letters. You cannot use blank spaces in a login name. Your system may have an established precedent for login names, such as the user's first name and last initial or first name and a number. Examples are terries and terrie3. Other systems have login names that are a bit more abstract, such as 4yp9gt. On some systems, login names have a symbolic flavor, such as bladerunner or big_deal. Your system administrator can tell you what kinds of login names are appropriate for your system.

As you choose your login name, keep a few things in mind. First, UNIX establishes a home directory for you and gives this home directory the same name as your login name. Therefore, don't pick a name that will be cumbersome to type when you are navigating through the file system to your home directory.

Consider also that other users may send you messages or mail by using your login name as the destination for messages or mail. You wouldn't want to receive mail from your boss knowing that the boss addressed the mail to goofball! Also, pick a login name that you will be satisfied with for the long term. To change your login name, the system administrator must delete your existing account and establish a new one for a new login name. Any files or directories that you own may require ownership modification before you can access them under your new login name.

UNIX records your login name in your user-account file along with other information. As part of the process of establishing an account, UNIX assigns each user a unique user number. The user number helps ensure secure multiuser operation. UNIX also establishes a group identifier for each user. To UNIX computing, a group is simply a group of users related by some arbitrary guidelines. All users in the purchasing department might be members of the purchase group, for instance. Like the user number, the group number corresponds to the character-based group name.

Don't worry about your group for now; the system administrator will attend to your group identification. Ask the administrator whether you have a special group affiliation. You may have such an identification, which is likely to be based on your department or the nature of your computing activity.

Passwords

One aspect of your user account that you normally can control is your password. A password is the second part of UNIX's two-level login security. After you enter your login name, you are prompted for your password. Although your login name is public information, your password is secret. You won't even see its characters on-screen when you type it during the login process. Of course, someone standing over your shoulder won't see the password, either. Passwords are UNIX's most important login security measure. Users who are not authorized to use your system may do so anyway if they can get your login and password. You should always treat your password as a secret.

 Some UNIX systems do not require a password. In these systems, the system administrator has decided to relax the security provisions of UNIX. If the system administrator chooses, some terminals are automatically logged on when the system is up.

In all likelihood, the system administrator will assign you a password to get you established as a system user. Your initial password may be temporary. When you try your first login, UNIX may ask you to pick your own password to replace a temporary one. If UNIX doesn't prompt you for a new password, you can use the `passwd` command to select a new password. (Chapter 9 discusses the `passwd` command.) When you pick your password, avoid an obvious set of characters like a common name or object. For someone intent on a security breach, common names are easier to guess. So are birth dates, and husband's, wife's, and children's names. Your favorite color may be easy to remember as a password, but passwords that are the same names as colors aren't too difficult for an outsider to breach.

Different systems have different requirements for the content of passwords and the length of time for which a password is valid. Your password may be good forever, or you may be prompted by the system to change it from time to time. Some systems allow simple passwords of two or three characters; other systems require that passwords contain at least six characters. In more secure systems, each password must contain at least one number or special character and at least two alphabetical characters. Some systems do not allow passwords that are comprised of all numbers, all letters, or the reverse or circular shift of the login name. These restrictions make guessing a password more difficult. If you are in doubt about what password to use for yourself, consult your system administrator. He or she can supply you with the details of your system's requirements.

Be sure to memorize your password. If you write down your password, keep the written copy in a secure place like your purse or billfold. Don't leave your written password on your terminal, in your desk drawer, in your address book, or anywhere else probing eyes might find it. Remember that the integrity of your system—and especially the integrity of your files—depends on your keeping your password secure. Letting someone "borrow" your login name and password for a UNIX session is asking for trouble.

Understanding Your Terminal

Assuming that you have a valid account established through your system administrator, you are ready to sit down at your terminal and try a login. But before you jump into entering your login name and password at the prompts, take a few moments to familiarize yourself with your terminal.

NOTE   Most terminals have *setup switches* or a *setup mode*. Chances are good
that your terminal's setup is correct, but an incorrect setup can cause
improper operation. Consult your terminal's manual or ask your system
administrator for help.

You recall from Chapter 2 that a terminal is an input/output peripheral hardware
device. Terminal design exhibits quite a bit of variability; no standard design is
available. Some terminals display system responses by printing output on paper.
Most terminals use a video display to show system responses. This book assumes
that you have access to a video display unit, or VDU. In either case, there is little
difference between user input and system response whether you are using a VDU
or a printing terminal.

Terminals communicate with their UNIX system using the process of serial
communication. During serial communication, a stream of electrical 0's and 1's
travels through the connecting wires. Recall the discussion of binary data in
Chapter 2. Binary representation is a computer's native tongue. Through a serial
stream of binary data traveling to and from the terminal and the system, you
communicate with UNIX.

For the most part, terminals are character-based devices. In other words, they send
and receive letters, numbers, and special characters while communicating with the
system. UNIX systems use ASCII character representations. ASCII (pronounced
As-kee) is an acronym for *American Standard Code for Information Interchange*.
ASCII consists of 128 binary-coded combinations capable of representing lowercase
letters, uppercase letters, numbers, punctuation symbols, and special control
characters. In other words, nearly all the keys on a typical terminal have a corresponding ASCII value. In binary representation, 128 requires 7 digits of binary value.
You recall that computers often package bits in patterns of 8 bits called *bytes*.
ASCII's 7-bit characters can be efficiently stored and manipulated as bytes by the
electronics of a computer. Appendix B lists the ASCII values and their character
equivalents.

Parity

When a terminal and a UNIX system communicate, they effectively exchange data
one character at a time. Characters being communicated travel serially as bits of a
byte. Of the eight bits in each character's byte, seven bits represent the character;
the eighth bit represents the *parity*.

Parity is a simple indicator of data-transmission integrity. If an electrical disturbance
causes one of a character's bits to be altered during transmission, such as from a 0
to a 1, the receiving end can check the parity bit to determine whether an error
occurred. With seven bits of character data and one bit of parity, each byte of serial
communication is filled. Your system administrator or hardware specialist can assist
you if you need to alter your terminal's parity. Most UNIX systems are set to a parity
setting of "none."

You do not have to know the technical details of parity to ensure the proper parity setting on your terminal. The key is to match your terminal's setting with the setting of the UNIX system.

About Parity . . .

Parity is one of the technical aspects of serial communications that users often encounter. While most ordinary users don't need to be concerned with parity, some insight into the role of parity is helpful when a user is required to set a terminal's operating parameters. Determining a character's parity is really quite simple if you know the value of the seven bits that make up the character.

To determine parity, first add the seven bits. If the resulting number is odd, the character's parity is odd. If the resulting number is even, the character's parity is even. The value of the parity bit can now be determined for the character in two basic ways.

If the communications parameters for the serial device are set to *even* parity, you (or the communications equipment) always assign a value of 0 to the parity bit of a character whose 7-bit parity is already even. Adding all 8 bits, while the 8th or parity bit is 0, still results in an even number. A character whose 7 bits are odd has a value of 1 for the parity bit. Now all 8 bits add up to an even number. For even parity, the parity bit is forced to the value that makes all 8 bits of the byte even.

If the communications parameters for the serial device are set to *odd* parity, the parity bit must be forced to a value that makes all 8 bits of the character's byte add to an odd number. A character with the parity bit set to 1 in even parity has its parity bit set to 0 in odd parity.

There are three other settings for parity. *Mark* parity has the parity bit always on. *Space* parity has the parity bit always off. *None* parity completely ignores the parity bit.

Baud Rate

During the process of serial communication, your terminal and the system communicate at an established speed, which is measured by the number of bits transmitted per second. A terminal's bits-per-second or *bps* rate can vary from 300 bps to 19200 bps. The serial communication's *baud* rate is essentially equivalent to the bps rate.

In addition to the 8 bits of character and parity data, serial communications devices transmit a start bit and a stop bit to enable the receiving end to correctly frame the transmitted character. Each character therefore has 10 bits in a transmission stream. By dividing the baud rate or bps rate by 10, you can determine the character-per-second (*cps*) transmission rate of the terminal's setting. Most directly connected

UNIX terminals are set to 9600 baud and therefore are capable of communicating at a 960 character-per-second rate. At 960 cps, your screen shows messages and responses almost instantaneously. At lower baud rates, you will notice a delay as UNIX writes to your screen. Of course, the baud-rate setting of the terminal must match that of the system's communications electronic entry point or *port*. When the terminal and system have mismatched baud rates, characters are scrambled and incorrect.

Duplex and Echo

Most terminals have a setting for half or full *duplex*. Duplex refers to simultaneous two-way communications. Full-duplex terminal operation enables a terminal to send and receive characters at the same time. In full-duplex operation, the characters you type on the keyboard are sent serially to the system. The system then echoes or re-sends the same characters back to the terminal where they are displayed on-screen. The echo operation is so fast that at nearly all baud rates, you will think that the character appears on-screen as soon as you type it. UNIX system terminal communication defaults to full duplex. You should have your terminal set to *full duplex* or *no local echo*.

If your terminal is set to half duplex while the UNIX system is expecting full duplex, you may see two of each character that you type. In half duplex, or *local echo mode*, the terminal provides its own screen echo of the keys you press. To correct double characters, switch your terminal to full duplex. Your terminal's manual will tell you how to make the switch.

Keyboards

Before you try to use the system, you should familiarize yourself with the layout of your terminal's keyboard. Unfortunately, there is no standard key layout for terminals. You will discover with experience that nearly all terminals contain keys, or key combinations, for the 128 ASCII characters. Most of these ASCII characters appear on an ordinary typewriter. In addition to the normal punctuation symbols, numbers and letters, terminals have special keys.

Table 5.1 lists the typical names and functions of the special keys. Remember that your keyboard may have other special keys or fewer special keys. Remember also that you do not type the angle brackets (< >) that enclose some of the key names shown here. The angle brackets appear in the text to cause the key names to stand out.

Different programs use special keys in different ways. Many keys on elaborate keyboards, such as those found on graphics terminals, are not recognized or used by UNIX. In fact, some terminals can switch into modes of operation that make the terminal seem inoperable. If your terminal displays unusual characters or seems unresponsive after it has been working well, you may have to perform a reset operation. Each terminal has its own method of reset, so ask your system administrator about your particular terminal's "personality" traits. You may also find that other users can provide useful insight into a terminal's "quirks."

Table 5.1

Special Terminal Keys and Functions

Key Name	Function
Esc (Escape)	Causes a return to a previous function in an applications program and some UNIX utilities.
Ctrl (Control)	Pressed simultaneously with a letter key to indicate that a terminal-control function is desired. In this book, the Ctrl key is indicated in text by the circumflex (^). For example, Ctrl-D is shown as <^D>. Note that the letter typed at the same time as Ctrl may be typed in either upper- or lowercase letters.
Enter	Terminates an input you are typing and sends the line to the system for processing. You must press <Enter> or <Return> before UNIX will execute your command.
Return	Return is an alternate name for <Enter>. The name Return is derived from a typewriter's carriage return (CR) action. In this book, <Enter>, <Return>, and <CR> all indicate the end of input.
Del (Delete)	Deletes the current command line or, on some systems, erases the character under the cursor.
Break	The Break key stops the execution of most UNIX programs and commands. During the login process, <Break> signals the system to try an alternative baud rate.
Alt (Alternate)	Pressing <Alt> simultaneously with another key gives the system an alternative value for the other key. <Alt> is often found on IBM PC-type keyboard layouts.
Backspace	Pressing <Backspace> backs the cursor one character to the left while erasing the character. On most terminals, use <Backspace> to correct mistakes.
Arrow Keys → ← ↑ ↓	Some applications programs use the arrow keys to move the cursor on-screen.
Cursor-Control Keys	Like the arrow keys, the cursor-movement keys (PgUp, PgDn, Home, and End) are used by some applications programs to move the cursor on-screen.
Function keys (F1-F12)	The function keys signal the system to perform a predetermined function. The exact function assigned to each function key is determined by the application that uses function keys.

TIP

Don't forget that producing some ASCII characters requires you to press and hold down the Ctrl key while you press another key. All Ctrl-combination letters can be typed in lowercase or uppercase letters.

When you are issuing UNIX commands, you will find that several keys provide useful command-line control. Table 5.2 lists the keys and key combinations that are useful while you are working with UNIX commands. Be aware that keys shown in this text enclosed in angle brackets (< >) are nonprinting. In other words, you won't see a character on-screen when you type a nonprinting character.

Table 5.2
Special Command Keys and Functions

Key	Meaning to UNIX
# (sharp or pound)	Erases a character to the left. # is used on systems without active Backspace keys.
@ (at sign)	Deletes (kills) the current line. The system ignores the contents of the line.
^C (Ctrl-C)	Interrupts the current process by stopping it. <^C> is called the UNIX *interrupt* character.
Del	The Delete key. Acts as the interrupt character in place of <^C> on many systems.
^D (Ctrl-D)	Stops input from the input sources of some commands, or logs you off the system. <^D> is UNIX's end-of-file (EOF) indicator.
^H (Ctrl-H)	Acts the same as the Backspace key. Use <^H> if your terminal does not have a Backspace key.
^I (Ctrl-I)	Performs a horizontal tab operation on terminals that do not have a Tab key.
^S (Ctrl-S)	Stops display output until <^Q> is pressed. In communications terminology, <^S> is called *XOFF*. Use <^S> to temporarily stop screen output from scrolling off the screen.
^Q (Ctrl-Q)	Restarts a display that you have temporarily stopped by pressing <^S>. If your terminal appears to be locked, pressing <^Q> will sometimes restore normal operation. In communications terminology, <^Q> is called *XON*.

Terminal Emulations

An emulation is a type of behavior. *Terminal emulation* refers to the copying of one terminal's functions by another terminal or computer. Some "terminals" may actually be personal computers (PCs) running terminal-emulation software. If you are using a PC, you need to start the terminal emulation software and check the emulation's configuration before you can access UNIX. Terminal emulation is an effective way to use a personal computer to connect to a UNIX system. In fact, many of the screens reproduced in this book were produced from a PC running a terminal emulation program called TERM.

As you familiarize yourself with your keyboard layout, don't become intimidated by the variety of keys. Command examples shown in this book step you through keyboard input; you will soon be comfortable with issuing commands.

Understanding Your Modem

Many terminals do not directly connect to a UNIX system. Rather, these terminals connect by telephone lines via modem. From a practical point of view, a modem is the device that supervises the telephone connection. The modem establishes a connection with another modem attached to the UNIX system. Serial-data communications take the form of sound waves. The sounds made by the modem connection often sound like whistles and screeches. What is noise to your ears, however, is intelligible communication to the modem.

 If your UNIX connection does not use a modem, you can skim this discussion of modems.

There are two basic types of modems. The first and oldest design is the *acoustic coupler*. An acoustic coupler is a cradle containing two cups. You use a standard phone to dial the UNIX modem and transfer the handset to the cradle when the whistle of the carrier is present.

The most common type of modem is the self-contained, *autodialing* modem. The autodialing modem is the primary focus of this discussion. Your terminal's serial cable connects to the modem, and the character stream moves to and from the UNIX system as sound waves over a telephone line.

Make sure that your terminal and modem are powered on and that the serial and phone cables are properly connected. It is easy to confuse connectors. The modem jack labeled "line" is connected to the phone-service jack on the wall. If your modem phone line is sharing service with a standard phone, be sure that no one is using the phone. If you have call waiting, disable this feature. Call-waiting activity can disturb the modem connection's integrity and you can be inadvertently logged off when an outside call comes in on your line.

When the equipment is ready, you can dial your UNIX system's number. If your modem is a Hayes-type modem, you type **ATDT** followed by the phone number. Through the built-in speaker, you should hear the modem pick up the dial tone and then dial the number. If you hear a busy signal, the UNIX modem is in use. Try again in a few minutes. If you hear ringing, but no answer, the UNIX modem is either turned off, or the UNIX system is not accepting logins at this time. Try again in a few minutes. If the UNIX modem doesn't answer again, you may want to call a voice number at the UNIX site to determine when the system is available for modem logins.

When the UNIX modem answers, you will hear the modems' carriers whistle and screech. Your screen may say `Connect` or `Connect 1200` or `Connect 2400`. The numbers following the `Connect` message indicate the baud rate of the connection. Most modems operate between 300 and 2400 BPS. Some later-model modems are capable of 9600 BPS. All the messages you see on-screen to this point originate from your modem. You will know you are communicating with UNIX when you see the login banner; that is, when the word `login:` appears on-screen.

Logging On to the System

Logging on to the system is the method that you use to gain access to the system's computing resources. By logging on, you identify yourself as a legitimate system user; your secret password confirms that identity.

The Program Sequence of Login . . .

When your UNIX system is booted, the system is in single-user mode for the first few seconds. Through system administration settings, the system initiates the multiuser mode. A program named `init` consults an initialization-table file to establish defined system-operating considerations. If `init` finds that terminals are enabled for logins, `init` starts a program named `getty` (for *get* tty) to monitor each enabled terminal port for keyboard activity.

UNIX consults several files during this initializing activity. When you press a key on a terminal, `getty` starts a program named `login`. The `login` program conducts the actual interaction with you during your login. When you have successfully logged onto the system, `login` gives up its place to the shell program, usually `sh` or `csh`. The shell program initializes its environment and presents you with the command prompt. You are then able to enter commands.

As an ordinary user, you don't have to be concerned with the sequence that enables your login. Yet you may find that knowing that a defined sequence is taking place during the login process enhances your appreciation of UNIX's services to you.

If your terminal (or modem) is connected to an enabled communications port, UNIX displays a login-prompt message on-screen. If you have just turned on your terminal, and you don't see a login prompt, press <Return> once or twice. The login prompt may have been on-screen before the terminal's power was switched off, but screen information is lost when power is removed from the terminal. Pressing <Return> alerts the system that you are trying to log on to the system.

The actual login screen varies from system to system. The system administrator can modify the login message's default text to include useful information or welcoming text. Figures 5.1 and 5.2 show two login screens. As you can see from the figures, the text varies. In nearly all cases, the login screen contains the word `login:` as the final text. The cursor appears next to the word `login:`.

Locate the word `login:` (or similar prompt) and the position of the cursor on-screen. You are now ready to enter your login name.

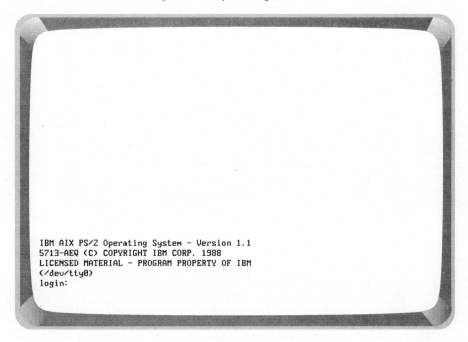

```
IBM AIX PS/2 Operating System - Version 1.1
5713-AEQ (C) COPYRIGHT IBM CORP. 1988
LICENSED MATERIAL - PROGRAM PROPERTY OF IBM
(/dev/tty0)
login:
```

Fig. 5.1. *The default AIX login screen.*

WARNING

At login, remember to make a quick check to be sure that the Caps Lock key is not activated. Remember that UNIX is case-sensitive; the program sees upper- and lowercase letters as being different in meaning. If you enter an uppercase login name, UNIX may incorrectly assume that your terminal has no lowercase capability.

You can see that both screens have the word `login:` as their final text. Notice that figure 5.2 presents the login prompt as `andiron!login:`. The `andiron` portion of this prompt is the UNIX name of the computer (machine) on which this version of UNIX is operating. The `!` character separates the machine name from the login prompt. Many UNIX systems show the machine name as part of the login message, and as part of the command prompt. If you are accessing different UNIX systems, the machine name reminds you which computer you are using.

```
$
andiron

Welcome to SCO System V/386

andiron! login:
```

Fig. 5.2. The default SCO login screen.

The (/dev/tty0) text in figure 5.1 displays the name of the terminal device that the user is logging on to. If this were a modem connection, the user might make a mental note of the terminal device for this login. The next time the user connects to this system, the device might be different because another terminal or modem is used.

Entering Your Log Name

When you locate the cursor, carefully type your assigned log name. The characters echo to the screen as you type. If you make a mistake, use the <Backspace> key (or its equivalent on your keyboard) to correct the mistake. When your log name is correct, press <Return> once, and then wait for the system to prompt for your password. If you have been assigned a temporary password, be prepared to select one of your own choosing in case your system requires you to change from the temporary password to a new one.

Some UNIX systems do not require a password. Some systems provide automatic logins for certain terminals. If either situation applies to you, read the information on password procedures anyway. You may need to know how to login with a password in the future.

Entering Your Password

When the system displays the `password:` prompt, UNIX is ready to accept your password. Carefully type your password. Notice that the password's characters are *not* echoed to the screen. This invisible treatment of your password ensures that no one else can see it when you type it; unfortunately, you can't see the password, either. Because the password is invisible, you cannot see your current position on-screen as you type the password. If you make a mistake while typing your password, you can make corrections by backspacing to the error and retyping. Because you can't see the exact position of errors, however, you may find it easier to press <Return> and try another login. When you have typed your password correctly, press <Return> once. You should now be logged on the system.

 Some systems mail an electronic message to new users to welcome them to the system and provide general operating information. When you log on the system, you may see a message similar to the following:

    You have mail.

You will see how to access this message in Chapter 11.

What To Do In Case of Problems

If you can't get logged on, one of several things may be keeping you from being successful. Table 5.3 lists the most common reasons for unsuccessful logins, as well as some remedies. Use this table as a reference if you have problems.

Table 5.3
Login Problems and Corrective Actions

Problem	Corrective Action
Terminal is off.	Turn on power and try again.
Won't accept password.	Your account hasn't been established yet. Ask the system administrator to inform you when your account will become valid.
System is down. No response.	Try again later or call computer personnel to determine the next availability of the system.
Characters are garbled (Greek).	Terminal settings are wrong. Ask computer personnel for assistance in setting your terminal.
Login Incorrect message appears.	You made a mistake entering a log name or password. Try again. If you entered the information correctly, check with the system administrator.
Extra characters appear without your typing them.	If you are making a modem connection, you have a poor phone connection. Hang up and try again.

Your account also may have been locked for some reason. If you suspect that your account has been locked, contact the system administrator. If your keystrokes don't seem to be getting to the system, and you know that the system is operational, you may have a loose communications cable at your terminal. If a terminal has been placed "off-line" or "local," the system cannot receive the terminal's keystrokes. In some cases, an unresponsive keyboard is due to communications being halted by a <^S> (the XOFF character). Try typing <^Q> (the XON character) to see if characters again flow.

Most important, remain calm when you have a failed login experience. Try again. If you can't seem to correct the problem, ask for assistance.

Viewing the Opening Screen

When you've made it through the login exercise successfully, the UNIX system generally greets you with an opening screen. The opening screen (which simply may be additional text on the current screen) often contains a message of the day. Figure 5.3 shows the opening screen of an AIX login.

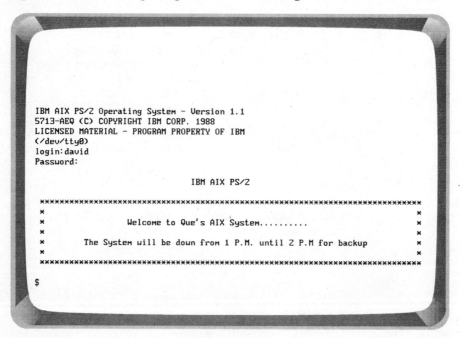

```
IBM AIX PS/2 Operating System - Version 1.1
5713-AEQ (C) COPYRIGHT IBM CORP. 1988
LICENSED MATERIAL - PROGRAM PROPERTY OF IBM
(/dev/tty0)
login: david
Password:

                        IBM AIX PS/2

*********************************************************************************
*                                                                             *
*                Welcome to Que's AIX System.........                         *
*                                                                             *
*         The System will be down from 1 P.M. until 2 P.M for backup          *
*                                                                             *
*********************************************************************************
$
```

Fig. 5.3. *The opening screen for an AIX session.*

The opening screen shown in figure 5.3 shows a message enclosed in a box. This message is called the *message of the day*. Figure 5.3's message of the day welcomes users and then informs them that the computer will be unavailable for an hour to accommodate system-level maintenance. Notice that the space following the `Password:` prompt is empty. UNIX did not echo the actual password characters back to the screen.

On the final printed line of your screen, you see the UNIX prompt. The UNIX prompt is generally the $ or %, but can also be # or another string of characters. In this book, the $ symbol is used to represent the UNIX prompt in most cases. If your system presents a different prompt, use your prompt in place of the $.

The $ prompt is actually presented by the UNIX shell. As you recall, the shell is the interactive command interpreter that accepts your commands, carries them out, and provides prompts and messages. The $ (or your equivalent) is therefore the *command prompt*. When you see the command prompt at the left margin of your screen, the UNIX shell is ready to receive your command. You soon will be reading more about the shell and commands. Before you try some commands, however, you should learn how to log off (log out of) the system.

Logging Off the System

Logging off is your way of completing your UNIX session. Logging off returns the system resources that you were using to the remaining active users. Logging off ensures that commands and files that you were using have been stopped and closed properly.

One of the most important aspects of logging off is that your account is no longer "live" on your terminal. Until you log off, anyone can sit at your terminal and use your user privileges as though that person were you. The system will not know the difference. An uninvited user can erase or rename your files, look at your mail, or even change your password! When you leave your terminal, even for a short time, it's a good practice to log out.

You might be tempted to simply turn off your terminal to end your session. In most systems, turning off a terminal (or hanging up the modem) will log out the current user. However, if the terminal settings or communications wiring enable it, an active session will continue with the terminal off or the modem hung up. In this non-logged out condition, the port still behaves as if you were using it. The next person to turn on the terminal or dial the modem line will have your login. The simplest way to ensure against someone using an abandoned terminal or login is to log out.

Logging out is simple; just press <^D> at the command prompt. Your session will end gracefully with files closed and commands (if any) stopped. You know that you are logged off because UNIX displays the login message again.

If by some chance you have started additional shells, the <^D> command terminates the current shell and returns you to a lower (previously started) shell rather than logging you off. You know if you are terminating an additional shell because another command prompt appears when you press <ˆD>. Don't worry. You will learn about additional shells later. For now, just be aware that UNIX allows multiple versions of the shell to be running at the same time. Keep pressing <ˆD> until you see the login message. In most cases, you need to press <ˆD> just once to log off. Remember that you can use a lowercase D in the <ˆD> sequence.

TIP

When you type the exit command, some systems respond as though you have pressed <ˆD> for logging out.

Try logging out and then logging back in again a few times. Practice helps you learn your password so that you won't have to refer to a paper to remember it. When you are comfortable with logging in and logging out, you are ready to learn about and use the shell.

Understanding the Shell

When you are doing operating-system level work in UNIX, you do that work through the shell. From your vantage point, the shell accepts your commands, arranges for loading and executing the programs that carry out those commands, and directs the commands' input and output. Because your UNIX experience is so closely related to the shell, you need to know many aspects of the shell to be a competent UNIX user.

When you successfully log on to the system, a shell is automatically started for you. The shell is *not* part of the operating system kernel. In all technical respects, the shell is just another UNIX command (program). In a functional respect, however, the shell is a very special program. The shell acts as your "go-between" for accessing the services of the kernel. With this command-interpreting role, the shell is indeed an important component of UNIX. All UNIX systems have at least one type of shell program available. Many systems have more than one type of shell program. An entry in the password file determines which shell you initially use.

System V-based systems generally incorporate a shell called the *Bourne shell*. BSD-based systems generally use a shell called the *C shell*. This book's primary focus is the more common Bourne shell. Take note if your system uses the C shell because the C shell differs somewhat from the Bourne shell. In some instances, this book includes specific references to the C shell. A third type of shell, called the *Korn shell*, is much like the Bourne shell. Korn-shell users can follow Bourne-shell examples. Regardless of the shell, you enter commands at the shell's command prompt in the same fashion.

As you will see, command lines can be made of several parts. The shell scans command lines for the proper formation of the command's parts in a process called *parsing*. The ordering and form of the command line is called its *syntax*. The shell observes several character conventions in which special characters convey additional meaning to the shell. The shell expands or translates these characters into their meanings during command-line parsing. You may have occasion to use these special characters to make your UNIX work more versatile and efficient in some operations. You will want to understand the shell, the syntax, and the general rules for commands before you go very far in your UNIX work. The rest of this chapter will aid your understanding.

UNIX automatically starts a private copy of sh (Bourne shell) or csh (C shell) as your login shell. The shell process continues to run throughout your session. (As you recall, a process is a program in the act of execution.) The most commonly available UNIX shell is the Bourne shell. Like the other popular shell, the C shell, the Bourne shell provides important computer services for you as it shields you from the technical details of the UNIX kernel. Either shell can be referred to as *the shell*.

The shell provides the following important services:

- Parsing your command-line text and interpreting your command through the command's syntax
- Loading and executing a command or program in the foreground or background
- Redirecting the input and output of a command when you specify redirection
- Managing the flow of the inputs and outputs of a program through a pipe or filter when you specify a pipe or filter
- Tailoring your computing environment through variables that the shell interprets with special meanings
- Interpreting and executing programs you write in shell procedure (script) format

Shell-procedure programming is covered in more detail in Chapters 14 and 15.

How the Shell Sees Commands and Special Characters

The shell's view of a command line is conceptually like your view of a written sentence. A *simple* command begins with a command followed by "words." All the "words" in a simple command are separated by spaces (or tab characters). The "words" of a simple command are the command's parts. In a written sentence, you might instruct a worker through the order "Show me the length of these three reports." On a UNIX command line, you would type the following command:

```
$ ls -l report1 report2 report3 <Return>
```

This command instructs the shell to display on-screen a report containing file information. When you communicate a "sentence" to the shell, the shell immediately scans the "words" to extract their total meaning. With the simple command's meaning extracted, the shell can arrange to execute the command. If you "communicate" your request to the shell accurately, UNIX fulfills the request.

The space character or the tab character separates—or *delimits*—the words of a simple command. The shell relies on *delimiters* being in appropriate positions in order to parse a command line correctly.

The space between parts of a command line is often called *white space*. When words are written on white paper, the blanks between words are obviously white. This white space is white whether it is one blank space or ten. In most instances, the shell does not care how many space characters separate the parts of a command. For readability, you normally type one space between command parts, but you can use two or more if you want. The shell is "trained" to scan over intervening space delimiters.

When the shell has separated a simple command into its component parts, the shell constructs a list of the parts to pass to the command you issued. The list, consisting of the correctly positioned parameters, is the information that the command uses to do what you want. The shell "remembers" the positional parameters by assigning each parameter to a special variable. Programs and shell procedures can use the variable information to further instruct the programs or shell procedures. You learn more about positional parameters and their use in Chapter 15.

The shell doesn't always take each part of a command at its face value. Certain characters convey special meanings to the shell. When the shell encounters special characters on the command line, the shell translates the literal characters into their special meanings. This translation process is called *expansion* and *substitution*.

Expansion and substitution are not as cryptic as they sound. In spoken communication, you regularly expand or substitute the meaning of certain words. When someone says, "Bring those here," you expand the meaning of "those" to "paper and pen," "hammer, nails, and wood," or to whatever group of things that the word "those" might refer.

Likewise, when you say, "Send a birthday card to Mary's husband," you count on the sender to substitute "Bob Smith" or "Jon Arthur" as the true meaning of "Mary's husband." When the doctor hands a specimen to a technician and says, "Send me the results," the technician substitutes the meaning of "results" with "first run the tests and then send the test results." The technician performs two tasks to fulfill the doctor's single request.

Unlike a human, the shell cannot extract by conversational context the meaning of command words. The shell must rely on the meaning of special characters to signal expansion and substitution. By recognizing special characters, the shell can translate special command-line words into their literal meanings. The shell passes only the literal meanings to a command for the command to use.

Understanding the Shell's Special Characters

Often, you want the shell to take an action with your command line that a literal interpretation would not provide. Special characters enable the shell to parse a command line and to interpret the command's elements in ways that are different from the literal interpretation. Table 5.4 lists the shell's special characters and the interpretation that the shell makes when those characters are used. As you review the table, remember that the special interpretation occurs when the character(s) are encountered as part of command-line input. At other times, such as when you are running a program, these characters have no special meaning.

Table 5.4
Bourne Shell Special Characters and Interpretations

Character	Interpretation
$	Use the rest of the word as the contents of a previously defined variable
;	Break the command line into separate commands using the ; as the separator
\	Remove the special meaning of the character that immediately follows
"	Remove the special delimiting meaning of spaces and certain other special characters contained between a pair of " characters
'	Remove the special meaning of any special characters contained between a pair of ' characters
`	Execute the command contained between a pair of ` characters and use the results as the argument for this position of the command line
&	Execute this command as a background process

Don't get the impression that UNIX command lines will be littered with special characters and that you will be lost. In actual UNIX work, most beginning users do not use these special characters with any great frequency. You should learn about each special character, though, because each one can give more power to many of your command lines. Each special character is discussed in its own section.

Substituting the Value of a Variable with $

When the shell encounters on the command line a string of characters that begins with $, the shell interprets the string to mean the *value* of the variable, not the literal characters of the string. This type of interpreted string is called a *metastring*.

To the shell, a metastring says "Don't use me. Use what I contain." In the Bourne shell, you assign a value to a variable by using the following form:

```
variable=value
```

You assign a value to a variable in the C shell by using the following form:

```
set variable=value
```

variable is simply the name you choose to contain the value. By convention, variable names are in uppercase. The name should be short and should not conflict with other variable names or command names. *value* is a string of characters that you want to store in *variable*. If the string of characters contains any embedded spaces, enclose the string in quotation marks ("). Quotation marks, as well as certain other characters, are interpreted by the shell as having special significance. You will get a full explanation in a moment. For now, just remember that variable string values need to be enclosed in quotes if the values contain spaces. Here's an example of a Bourne shell variable assignment:

```
$ REMINDER="Call home during lunch." <Return>
$
```

An easy way to see the contents of REMINDER is to use the echo command with an argument containing the special character $. The echo command sends any accompanying argument string to the screen. When you precede a variable name with the $ character, the shell substitutes the variable's value for the literal text (variable name) that you typed. In conjunction with the echo command, the argument $REMINDER prints the contents of REMINDER on-screen. The command and response look like this:

```
$ echo $REMINDER <Return>
Call home during lunch
$
```

Remember that you must use the $ character *before* the variable name to echo its contents. If you forget to include the $, you see something like the following:

```
$ echo REMINDER <Return>
REMINDER
$
```

In this case, echo does its job and echoes literally what you have entered as its argument.

Prefixing a variable with the $ to make it a metastring is the way that UNIX users include the current values of variables in commands. The echo $REMINDER command is just one example of the use of a metastring. Many commands can benefit from variable substitution. You will see other examples of the use of metastrings in Part Two.

Don't confuse the shell's $ prompt with the $ that you input on a command line. The prompt, which is printed on-screen, is *not* part of the command line's input.

Running Commands in Sequence with ;

A simple command performs just one task. Many UNIX users find it handy to issue several commands at one time in order to perform several tasks. To accommodate multiple commands on the command line, the shell recognizes the ; (semicolon) character as a command separator or delimiter. To utilize this shell feature, the user types the first command, types a semicolon, and then types another command. If additional commands are needed, the user can add them to the command line and separate them with semicolons. When the user presses <Return> after the final command, the shell begins executing each command from the command line in single-file order from left to right. When the currently executing command finishes, the next command to the right runs.

The two commands in the previous $ example can be combined on one command line, as follows:

```
$ REMINDER="Call home during lunch.";echo $REMINDER <Return>
Call home during lunch
$
```

Another example uses the ls file-listing command in sequence with echo, as shown here:

```
$ ls;echo "File list complete..." <Return>
memo_to_boss
resume.doc
salary.study
resignation
File list complete...
$
```

The ls command displays the directory's contents, and then the echo command displays the File list complete message.

Hiding Special Meanings with \

To prevent the shell from interpreting a special character, place the \ (backslash) character immediately before the special character on the command line. The backslash is called the shell's *escape* character because the character that \ precedes "escapes" the special interpretation. Not all the special characters, however, can be successfully "escaped" with \. You can use \ with the following characters:

```
*   ?   [   ]   ;   &   <   >   |
```

If you want to use echo to print a string containing a ; character, you can hide the normal "command separator" meaning of ; by escaping the character. The command line and reply look like the following:

```
$ echo WELCOME\; <Return>
WELCOME;
$
```

Notice that, in the example, the shell accepts the ; as an ordinary character. When the string is echoed, the \ is not echoed.

NOTE

Don't confuse using a \ to "escape" a character with the process of pressing <Esc> (the Escape key). The two actions are entirely different. Escaping a character enables the character to "escape" the shell's interpretation; pressing the <Esc> key normally changes the operation modes of an applications program.

Embedding Spaces with "

When you enclose command-line characters within a set of double quotation marks ("), the shell does not interpret the space characters as delimiters. Normally, a space character tells the shell that the last part of the command line has ended and that a new part of the command line is beginning. The shell considers all the characters enclosed in quotation marks to be a single part of a command. The shell's provision for ignoring quotation-embedded special characters is called the *quoting mechanism*.

You also can use quotation marks to turn off the special characters' meaning to the shell. The use of pairs of single quotation marks is also a quoting mechanism. When a special character (except $ and `) is enclosed in double quotation marks, the shell reads the character literally. The shell can still "look inside" the double quotes to find $-formed metastrings as well as the ` (back apostrophe or accent grave) for command substitution. Command substitution is discussed in an upcoming section.

Making All Special Characters Normal with '

A pair of ' (single quotation mark) characters enclosing a string of characters has a meaning to the shell that is similar to the use of double quotation marks. You use single quotation marks when you want to hide the special meanings of all special characters. Embedded spaces are not treated as delimiters when they are enclosed within single quotation marks. All the meanings of the special characters are turned off when they are enclosed within single quotation marks. An advantage of using single (and sometimes double) quotation marks rather than the \ escape character is that you save many keystrokes by not having to type \ when you are typing many special characters that you want the shell to treat as normal characters.

Unless you want the shell to interpret $ and ` characters, you should get into the habit of using single quotation marks to hide special character meanings.

Using Command Output as Arguments with `

The ` character, called the back apostrophe, the backquote, or the accent grave, encloses characters much like the single and double quotation marks. The ` characters are used in pairs. The shell interprets the characters enclosed within the accent grave marks as the output of the command the characters name. When the shell encounters a command enclosed in a pair of ` characters, the shell executes the command and substitutes the command's output for the positional argument. This action is called *command substitution*. You position the string enclosed in backquotes on the command line where a command argument would appear. Consider the following command:

```
$ echo `ls` <Return>
```

This command is interpreted by the shell as meaning "execute the `ls` command."

Running Commands in the Background with &

UNIX is a multiprocessing operating system. In a practical way, multiprocessing means that UNIX can do more than one thing for you at a time. As you learn more UNIX commands, you will find that some commands take a noticeable time to complete. If you simply enter a long-running command, you're stuck waiting for the system prompt.

The shell, however, can execute a command behind the scenes, or in the background. You enable background processing of a command by placing the & (ampersand) character at the end of the command. UNIX then assigns a process number to the command and displays the number for you to see. The shell then presents you with the command prompt again even though the last command is running in the background. You are free to enter another command without waiting. If for some reason you want to stop the processing of your background command, UNIX provides a command that uses the process ID number to stop the background command. An essential difference between issuing a command to run in the background and issuing a command as part of a sequence of commands is that background commands execute immediately. Commands in a sequence normally wait to execute when the preceding command is finished. Background processing is very common, and you'll see several examples of it in this book.

The & character is a command delimiter, much like ; . In fact, the shell looks for the presence of & before it looks for ; . The shell gives higher precedence to & than to ; .

Consider the following command:

```
$ ls;pwd &;echo done <Return>
```

In this command, the ; between & and echo isn't necessary because & delimits the pwd command from the others. The pwd command runs in the background in this instance; the other commands run in the foreground. Normally, you wouldn't place pwd in the background. It is done here to illustrate &'s delimiting capability. The command **ls;pwd & echo done** <Return> does the same work as the previous command.

Understanding Special Characters for File-Name Arguments

Many UNIX commands operate on files and therefore accept file names as arguments. As a result, you can work with groups of files to increase your file-management and file-processing efficiency. When you need to copy several files from one directory to another, for instance, you don't want to have to issue one command per file to get the job done.

The key to using commands to manipulate groups of files is the similarity of the names of the files. The files in any one of your directories may have similar, though not duplicate, file names. Similar file names have groups of characters or patterns that are the same, while the remaining characters are different.

The shell accepts special characters that accommodate patterns in file-name arguments. As with other special characters, the shell does not interpret these special characters literally. These file-name related characters are called *metacharacters*, or *expansion characters*. When the shell encounters an expansion character in a file-name argument, it uses the expansion character's meaning to find the actual file names for use as the file-name argument. This expansion process is also known as *file-name generation*, because a list of file names is generated by pattern matching.

TIP

The expansion characters are often called "wild-card" characters because of their matching capability.

Table 5.5 lists the file-name argument expansion characters and their meanings to the shell. In a command, these characters enable the matching of file names and parts of file names based on the position of the expansion character relative to the same character position in the file names in a directory. Non-expansion characters in file-name arguments must exactly match their counterparts in the file-name pattern. This pattern-matching process is one of the shell's handiest features.

The *Character* column of table 5.5 contains the expansion characters you include in file-name arguments. The *Meaning to the Shell* column contains the pattern-matching effect on files in the directory that the command is accessing.

Table 5.5
The Expansion Characters and Their Meanings

Character	Meaning to the Shell
?	Match any character in this position.
*	Match any characters.
[characters]	Match one character of the sequence of characters contained within the brackets, or one character of the range of characters contained within the brackets. If the characters are preceded by the ! character, match characters are *not* included.

NOTE   When a file name begins with the . (period character), as in the file name .profile, the expansion characters will not match the period character. You must specify the period character in the file-name argument to match it as the first character of a file name.

Matching a Single Character with ?

You recall that UNIX file names can contain up to 14 characters. When you use UNIX commands to manage or process files, you must identify the files you want to work with by using the names of those files. The file names are given on the command line as command arguments.

Normally, UNIX locates the file you name in the command's argument by taking the literal name you provide. If you type the ? at any character position in the file-name argument, the shell matches any character in the same position as the ? in the directory that the shell searches. Any file whose characters match the literal characters that you gave in the file-name argument are processed by the command. You can include more than one ? character in the file-name argument. You will get a better idea by looking at table 5.6. Table 5.6 is a sampling of file names that might be included for processing by a command when ? is used.

Table 5.6
Matching File Names Using the ? Expansion Character

Argument	Match	No Match
letters?	letters1, letters2	letter1, letters12
???bills	janbills, febbills	duckbills, marbill
?????	david, paper	memo, budget, io.o

In the first example of table 5.6, the argument `letters?` matches file names like `letters1` and `letters2` because the literal part of the argument, `letters`, matches all but the last character of either `letters1` or `letters2`. The `?` character matches any character in its relative position, so it matches both the 1 and the 2. You can see how the shell selects matches when you line up the argument with the various file names:

```
letters?  letters?  letters?  letters?
letters1  letters2  letter1   letters12
```

The file name `letter1` does not match this first argument because there is no s in `letter1` to match the one in the argument. The file name `letters12` does not match because it contains an extra character in the position following the one that corresponds to the `?` in the argument.

Now look at the match-up of the second example from table 5.6.

```
???bills  ???bills  ???bills   ???bills
janbills  febbills  duckbills  marbill
```

The last two file names do not match the pattern of the argument.

The last example from the table uses five `?` characters as the argument. Any file name consisting of five characters matches this argument. See how the patterns match in this last example from table 5.6.

```
?????  ?????  ?????  ?????   ?????
david  paper  memo   budget  io.o
```

As you can see, the last three do not match.

Matching Multiple Characters with *

Although the `?` is handy in specifying file names as command arguments, it does have its limitations. You will find plenty of occasions when you want match parts of file names without regard to the number of characters before or after the part you want to match. The `*` metacharacter does exactly this kind of matching job. In a file-name argument, the * matches all characters between the last literal character and the next literal character. In other words, only the part of the file name that you give is compared. Of course, if you use other metacharacters, such as ?, along with *, the other metacharacters are still given special treatment by the shell. To understand the role of *, see table 5.7. Again, this table shows examples of file names that match arguments.

Table 5.7
Matching Using the * Expansion Character

Argument	Match	No Match
`*.old`	`.profile.old  memo.old`	`cold  memo.new`
`jan*`	`janbills  january`	`old.jan  june`
`*old*`	`jan.old  jellomold  oldie`	`lode  dole`
`*`	`nearly every file`	`.profile .login`

To see why some names match and others do not, align the literal part of the argument with the same characters (if any) in the file names. The first example looks like this:

```
       *.old      *.old  *.old    *.old
  profile.old  memo.old   cold  mo.new
```

As you can see, as long as the literal characters following the argument's * character match, the pattern is a successful match. Even if one of the literal characters does not match, the pattern is not a successful match.

The second example positions the * at the end of the literal characters in the argument. Again, by lining up the literal parts, you can see the matches.

```
  jan*       jan*        jan*   jan*
  janbills   january  old.jan   june
```

When the * is used before and after the literal part of an argument, matches will be made with file names that contain those literal characters in the same order, regardless of any other characters in the file name. Here's how the third example from the table aligns.

```
   *old*       *old*   *old*    *old*    *old*
  jan.old  jellomold   oldie   lode    dole
```

By using ? with *, you can fine-tune pattern matching even more than with either metacharacter alone.

Matching Ranges and Sequences with [ ]

The third type of metacharacter is actually a pair of characters: the opening square bracket ([) and the closing square bracket (]). Because the pair is always used together, you can think of them as a single metacharacter function.

You use the [ ] pair in two basic ways. One way specifies an enclosed range of numbers that a character in a file name will match if it is included in the range. An example of a range is [a-Z]. Notice that the last letter in the range is a capital letter. On most systems, lowercase letters are alphabetized before uppercase letters.

The other basic way to use the [ ] pair is to enclose a sequence of characters as a list of sorts. An example is [ace], where the list contains the letters *a*, *c*, and *e*. If the corresponding character position in the file name matches any of the characters in the sequence, the character is considered a match. The case of the characters must match the same character and case in the file name. Table 5.8 shows how a range of characters might be specified in a file-name argument.

Table 5.8
Matching File Names Using Specified Ranges

Argument	Match		No Match	
budget[1-6]	budget3	budget6	budget7	budget12
[a-Z]*	alphafile	ZIPPER	.profile	123file

In the first example in table 5.8, the range specified is any character from 1 to 6, including 1 and 6. The files budget3 and budget6 match the argument budget[1-6] because both sample file names match the budget portion of the argument exactly. The file names also have a remaining character that falls within the inclusive range of the [1-6] range portion of the argument. The file name budget7, however, does not match because the 7 portion of the name is out of the range it needs to match. The file name budget12 does not match either.

Be sure that you understand that budget12 fails to match because it has the extra character—2—which has no literal or implied position in the argument. You might be tempted to think that 12 is out of the range of 1 through 6, but the failed match is not due to the range. Remember that only one character of the file name can compare to one character of the range. The 12 portion of the nonmatching file name is two characters. In reality, the 1 character matches the argument range, but the 2 character matches nothing in the same position in the argument.

The second example uses the range [a-Z] along with the "match anything" metacharacter, *. To interpret this argument as if you were the shell, you would say, "Match any file name that begins with any alphabetic character." Recall that the shell observes the case of characters. If you use an argument such as [a-z]*, the shell does not match file names that begin with a capital letter. Remember that ranges are based on the alphabetical order of the given range. The order in which your computer alphabetizes ASCII characters is called its *collating sequence* or *order*.

UNIX systems order all lowercase letters before uppercase letters. The collating sequence is changeable, however. You may find that your system uses a collating sequence that places each uppercase letter immediately after the corresponding lowercase letter. This alternating system sorts letters in a sequence such as aAbBcCdD. . . . On a few UNIX systems, upper- and lowercase letters are equivalent. Make a note to yourself to test the collating sequence with a range argument, or just ask your system administrator how your system sorts alphabetical sequences.

Notice that all the matching files in the second example of table 5.8 begin with an alphabetical character. The nonmatching file names begin with a character other than an alphabetical character. Don't forget that all the characters that appear on-screen, including numbers and punctuation, are ASCII characters. The collating sequence includes all ASCII characters, so you can use nonalphabetical characters in range arguments. Appendix B lists all ASCII characters in their normal collating sequence. You can use Appendix B to help you determine range arguments that are not based on alphabetic characters.

When you want to include all ASCII characters up to and including a certain character, such as M, you can give the range portion of your file-name argument as [-M]. Likewise, you can include all ASCII characters from a certain character with [M-].

Although using ranges of possible matching characters is handy in many file-matching command arguments, ranges cannot match a portion of the file names within the range while excluding others. Fortunately, the shell interprets a series of characters within the [ ] expansion characters as candidates for a match. These characters do not have to be in alphabetical order, nor do they have to be members of an inclusive range. If you're a bit confused, look at the examples in table 5.9. The examples in table 5.9 illustrate how the shell matches possible file names using one of the characters in the argument's sequence portion.

Table 5.9
Matching File Names Using A Specified Sequence

Argument	Match		No Match	
[hm]ouse	house	mouse	louse	spouse
[dm]emo	demo	memo	demo1	emotion
letter[135]	letter1	letter5	letter2	letter4

You can use a comma to separate characters in a sequence. The shell ignores the commas. To the shell, [adp] and [a,d,p] have the same meaning.

In the first example in table 5.9, the two characters, h and m, are bracketed in the file-name argument as the sequence or list of possible matches. The letter portion of the file name is literal, and as you know, possible file names must match the literal portion of a file-name argument exactly. The file name house matches because it begins with h and matches the ouse portion of the argument exactly. The file name mouse begins with m, which matches the second character in the argument's bracketed sequence. Again, the ouse is a literal match. The file name louse fails to match because the l at the first character position is not a member of the sequence in the argument. The file name spouse doesn't match, even though the literal portion ouse matches. The sp portion of spouse is two characters while the sequence argument provides for matching only one character.

You will notice in the third example that the argument letter[135] matches letter1 and letter5, but doesn't match letter2 and letter4. This example shows how a sequence can include some files in a range while excluding others. If you want all the file names used in this third example to match, give the argument letter[12345]. If you stop and think about the sequence, you will notice that the sequence is actually a range. The argument letter[1-5] matches the same files as the argument letter[12345].

Combining Wild-Card Characters in File-Name Arguments

UNIX doesn't limit you to using just one type of special character in a file-name argument. The tables and examples emphasize the use of one type of expansion character, but remember that you can mix wild cards in your file-name arguments. Much of the versatility of commands that manage or operate on files comes from your ability to construct file-name arguments with multiple pattern-matching characters. When you name files, you should consider how easily you can match those file names at some later time.

It's much easier, for example, to copy all your word processing files if the file names all contain the characters doc. You can form an argument that will always match as *doc*. This argument matches file names such as budgetdoc, speech.doc, document2, and 5_22_doc.let. The double use of * in this example is interpreted by the shell to mean "match any characters before doc, and match any characters after doc." In other words, this file specification matches any file name that contains doc.

The argument [a-df-z]* matches all lowercase file names with the exception of those that begin with e. You can form the same effective argument by using [!e]*. Within the square brackets, the ! character means "excluding" or "not."

To experiment with the expansion characters, you first can issue the ls command with no arguments. The ls command with no arguments lists all files in a directory except those beginning with the period character (.). When the files are printed to your screen, pick some combinations of file names. Then, issue the ls command with a file-name argument consisting of the wild-card pattern that lists the files you picked. You will gain skill in formulating wild-card arguments while using a command that won't harm files.

WARNING

Some UNIX commands can be destructive. The `rm` (remove file) command, for example, has the potential to destroy all your files when issued with wild-card arguments. You must exercise caution when using commands that overwrite or erase files. When you include wild-card arguments in destructive commands, exercise extreme caution so that you do not inadvertently remove or overwrite files that you didn't expect the file-name argument to match. It is a good practice to use a nondestructive command (such as `ls`) prior to using a destructive command (such as `rm`) to test the validity of a wild-card combination.

Using >, >>, and < for Redirection

Recall from Chapter 2 that your terminal is the standard input and output device for your UNIX activities. Commands get their arguments and parameters from your keystrokes. Your terminal's keyboard is the standard input device; the screen is the standard output device. Any messages or error information is displayed on-screen.

Most commands are not "aware" of the source of their input, nor are they aware of their output's destination. The shell acts as the director of the input and output of commands. The shell enables you to re-route input and output from their standard locations in an operation called *redirection*. As the name implies, input or output of a command comes from or goes to somewhere other than the standard device. In other words, through redirection, you can enable a command to get its input from a file, and you can enable a command to send its output to a file. The shell interprets the characters <, >, and >> as meaning "redirect."

You may wonder why anyone would want to use redirection. Why not just type the input and read the output? The answer is that normally, you type input on your keyboard and read output from your screen. On occasion, however, you run a command in the background and want the command to get its input from a file of arguments that you prepared at an earlier time. You redirect the command's output to another file, which you can inspect later. Because UNIX treats devices as special files, you can redirect a command's output to a printer device.

To get an idea of the usefulness of background processing and redirection, just think about a telephone answering machine. You pre-record a message (the input) for the machine to play for a caller. You then turn on the machine's answering capability and let it monitor incoming calls. You are then free to do other activities. When the machine answers the incoming calls, it plays the message and accepts any return message (output) as a recording. At some later point, you play back the machine's output from the recording. Like a redirected input command, the answering machine gets its input from information stored earlier. Like a background command, the machine does not need your immediate attention to operate. Like a redirected output command, the machine redirects the callers' messages to storage for you to inspect later.

Redirecting a command's output to a device can be illustrated in another everyday situation. When you take a bath, you turn on the water to your tub's fill spout. Like your terminal, the spout is the standard output device. If you take a shower, you turn the water on in the same way as you do when taking a bath. The difference is that you redirect the water to the shower head device by using the shower lever. The water then flows out of the shower head. In redirected UNIX commands, the output flows to a file such as a printer device or ordinary text file, rather than to your screen.

NOTE

Not all commands support redirection. Some commands support only input or output redirection.

To use redirection, you issue a command in the following form:

```
command <infile >outfile
```

In this generic syntax, `command` is a UNIX command. The < character is interpreted by the shell to mean "Get the input from the file or device that follows." The `infile` is the file or device that provides the input to `command`. The character > is interpreted by the shell to mean "Send the output of this command to the file that follows." The `outfile` is the name of the file that will contain `command`'s output when the command is completed. Notice that no space is required between the redirection symbols and their associated arguments.

If `outfile` doesn't exist before the command is executed, UNIX creates it. If `outfile` does exist before the command is executed, UNIX erases its old contents and places the new output in the file. If you want to add contents to `outfile` rather than replace the the file's existing contents, you can use the >> output redirection symbol. Note that this additive redirection symbol is just a double > redirection symbol. Don't worry if you use >> to additively redirect output to a file that doesn't exist. If the output file doesn't exist, UNIX creates it.

Forming Command Pipelines with |

You can redirect a command's output to a file, and then use that file as the redirected input for another command. This means, in effect, that you can use one command's output as another command's input. To use two commands in this way, you must issue the two commands in two separate steps. UNIX provides a single-step means to accomplish the same combination of two redirected commands. The shell interprets the | character to mean, "Pipe the output command in front to the input of the command that follows." The command line takes the following form:

```
command1 | command2 . . .
```

In this generic syntax, *command1* is the first command in the pipeline, whose output is piped through the | character as input to *command2*. The ellipses (. . .) indicate that other commands can be piped together in the command line. Through the use of the | pipe character, one command's output is sent directly to another command's input without your having to specify a redirection file. When you specify a pipe between commands, UNIX handles the details of redirecting the first command's output to the second command's input, and so forth.

As an example of pipelining, you can combine the file-displaying command cat with the alphabetizing command sort to see a text file sorted in alphabetical order. If the file thoughts were given as a file-name argument with the cat command, the screen might appear as follows:

```
$ cat thoughts <Return>
Zelda will call me tonight.
A call would be nice.
Otherwise, I'll watch cable TV.
$
```

As you can see, the file's content is three sentences of no particular importance. When the same command is piped through sort, the lines are alphabetized based on the first letter of each sentence. The new text on-screen looks like the following:

```
$ cat thoughts | sort <Return>
A call would be nice.
Otherwise, I'll watch cable TV.
Zelda will call me tonight.
$
```

In this example of pipelining, the shell processes the command line normally, from left to right. The cat command's output does not go to the screen, but is presented to sort because of the special | character. The sort command acts on the input by sorting the lines in alphabetical order. The sort command then sends its output to the standard output device, the screen.

 Commands that manipulate their input to produce output are called *filters*. The sort command is an example of a filter. UNIX filters are often used in pipelines. You will be introduced to other UNIX filters in Part Two.

Diverting a Pipeline with tee

Normally, each command in a pipeline sends its output to the following command, continuing in a chain until the last command is reached. Occasionally, however, a user wants to see or save the intermediate output from a pipeline. The tee command enables users to divert the flow of output to input as an additional output stream. A tee in a pipeline does not interrupt the flow from one command to another. Rather, a tee simply creates a copy of the output at the point of the tee. The tee output goes to the screen unless the user gives a file name as an argument.

In a pipeline, the `tee` command takes the following form:

```
command1 | tee teefile command2 . . .
```

In this generic syntax, `command1` is the first command of a pipeline, and `|` is the pipe character. `tee` diverts a copy of the piped output of `command1` to the file represented by `teefile`. The output of `command1` also is piped to the input of `command2`, just as if `tee` were not present. The ellipses (`. . .`) indicate that more piped commands and tees may be entered. When the command-execution line is complete, the file named in `teefile` will contain the output from the teed point in the pipeline.

As an example of the `tee` command in a pipeline, consider the `grep` command. The command name, `grep`, is an acronym for *general regular expression print*. You can think of `grep` as the "match this" command. In operation, `grep` looks at the input stream for a match for characters that you provide as an argument. Building on the sample pipeline command line you saw in the last section, the command line including `tee` and `grep` looks like this:

```
$ cat thoughts | sort | tee sortfile grep "call" <Return>
A call would be nice.
Zelda will call me tonight.
$
```

Again, the contents of the text file `thoughts` is piped to `sort`, where the input lines are sorted in alphabetical order. The sorted output is then piped into `tee`, where a copy of the output is sent to `sortfile`; the output is also sent to `grep`. The `grep` command compares each of the sorted input lines for a match for the quoted argument `call`. The `grep` command passes to the screen only the lines that contain `call`. When the command line finishes executing, the user can see the contents of `sortfile` by issuing the `cat` command as follows:

```
$ cat sortfile <Return>
A call would be nice.
Otherwise, I'll watch cable TV.
Zelda will call me tonight.
$
```

As you see, the file contains a copy of the output of the pipeline just before `grep` selected the lines containing the word `call`.

You cannot tee into a pipeline. Tee output must go to a file or the standard output. The item following the `tee` must be a file name or the next command.

Understanding Your Profile and the Shell

The term *profile* is often used to mean a descriptive outline. A profile provides insight into the nature of something's make-up. The shell initializes your session by using the concept of a profile. In UNIX's case, the profile is the contents of a file. When you log in to a UNIX system, the system automatically makes your home directory your working (current) directory. The Bourne shell then looks for a file in your home directory named `.profile`.

Note that the `.profile` file begins with the period character (.). As its name suggests, the file establishes a starting profile for your session. If this file is found, the shell executes commands that the file contains. Users of the C shell have a similar file named `.login`, as well as `.cshrc`. These files serve the same purpose as `.profile`. Because the `.profile` file can be located in each user's home directory, every user can have his own initialization.

MS-DOS users may note that the purpose of the `.profile` file is conceptually the same as that of MS-DOS's AUTOEXEC.BAT file. The AUTOEXEC.BAT file also establishes session settings each time a user boots a personal computer based on MS-DOS.

The commands contained in `.profile` establish the values of variables that you (or your UNIX session) use during your work at the operating-system level. Other `.profile` commands may check to see whether you have mail, or establish operating parameters for your terminal. Some `.profile` files contain commands that start applications programs.

Systems based on the C shell normally do not have a `.profile` file in a user's home directory unless the Bourne shell is also available. C-shell users can substitute `.login` for `.profile` for the examples in this section.

There is no one format for the contents of a `.profile` file. Each system, however, may contain established contents by convention. Experienced users often modify the contents of their `.profile` file to suit their individual needs. Users add commands to `.profile` and assign environment variables to the file. Some new users find that they automatically have a `.profile` in their home directory. Others do not. If you do not have a `.profile` file, you may want to create one later.

You create a `.profile` file by using a text editor, such as `ed` or `vi`. (Chapter 12 shows you how to use `ed`; Chapter 13 covers `vi`.) As soon as the shell processes the contents of `.profile`, the shell accepts input from your keyboard (the standard input) and outputs system responses to your screen (standard output). Error messages are output to your screen (the standard error or diagnostic).

When you log onto the system, your initial shell automatically consults the file `/etc/profile` or `/etc/login` to obtain system-level initialization instructions before acting on the contents of `.profile` or `.login`.

Checking for a `.profile` is easy. You can do the check now and, in the process, see how easy it is to enter a UNIX command. As a preliminary step, of course, you should log on to your system.

When you are logged on to the system, you should see the Bourne shell's $ prompt or the C shell's % prompt, with the cursor next to it. (As mentioned previously, most of the examples in this book display the Bourne shell's prompt: $.)

Make sure that your Caps Lock key is off and type this simple UNIX command line:

    $ **pwd** <Return>

Don't forget that the <Return> stands for the Return, CR, or Enter key. You do not type the literal word Return or the angle brackets. pwd is the *print working directory* command. The pwd command instructs UNIX (through the shell) to display the full name of your working (current) directory. Your working directory will be your home directory after you log in and until you change to another directory. If your login name is david, for example, pwd responds as follows:

    /usr/david
    $

Try the pwd command to see whether the last part of your current working directory's name is your login name. Notice that the next command prompt is printed by the shell as soon as the pwd command finishes printing the directory name. Remember that /usr or /u is the normal parent directory for users' home directories.

The next command line determines whether the .profile file exists in your home directory. At the command prompt, type the following:

    $ **ls .profile** <Return>

The ls command is the *list* files command. After the space following the ls command, you include the file name .profile as an optional argument to the ls command. In this case, you are telling ls to list (operate on) only the file named .profile. Remember that you do not literally type the word Return or the angle brackets.

 Within the UNIX command line, the command name is called the *command argument*. You can think of the command argument simply as the command.

NOTE

If you have a .profile file, the system responds with something like the following:

    .profile
    $

If you do not have a .profile, the system responds with a message similar to this:

    .profile not found
    $

Although this exercise is very simple, it does illustrate how you can issue a command to test for your .profile or .login. Part Two of this book discusses the ls command in greater detail.

Understanding the Shell's Variables and Environment

One useful feature of the shell is its capability to retain values that have been assigned to named variables. Such named variables are also known as *user-defined* variables. The REMINDER variable example you saw in a previous section was a user-defined variable. Variables are an important feature of the shell. The shell and other UNIX programs assign and use many variables without your being involved. Some variables are assigned values during the processing of /etc/profile and .profile. UNIX uses assigned values in variables as it carries out your work.

The following command line is an example of a variable assignment in the Bourne shell:

$ **TERM=ansi** <Return>

Each variable has a variable name. In this example, the variable's name is TERM. The name of a variable remains constant during your session, but you can change the contents of most variables any time you are at the command prompt. The variable TERM is given the character-string value of ansi.

All user-defined variables store their information in a character-string form. UNIX stores in memory both the names and values of variables. When you log off or when power is removed from the system, the names and values of all of your variables are gone. Don't worry about losing "UNIX information," however, when you log out. Important variables are initialized for you each time you log in.

Although all users have variables with the same names as most of your variables, UNIX keeps the values of your variables separate from the values of those of other users. You do not have to worry about assigning a value to a variable that will affect your computing neighbor.

The collection of variables "known" by the shell is called the *environment*. You or your program can start additional shells, called *subshells*, during your session. Each shell has its own environment. When any shell arranges for the execution of a program or command, the shell passes part of its own environment to the new program or command.

The program may consult the values passed to it in order to get additional local information about how to do its job. For instance, the environment might contain a variable called LEX, which contains the name of the directory that contains the user's word processor dictionary. The program can use the named directory when consulting the dictionary file as the user spell-checks a memo.

Each shell that is running keeps or stores its assigned variables locally. The name of the variable and its value can be made globally available to additional shells or programs through the export command. If you (or your program) start an additional shell at the command line, the new shell inherits the exportable variables from the current shell's environment.

The environment and its variables are aspects of UNIX that confuse many users. The concept, however, is simpler than you might suspect. Consider the following example. You are an individual with an occupation, name, address, phone number, and so on. You know this information, but a stranger doesn't know it. If a person filling out a college registration form asks you where you call home, you usually name your address. The name "home" on the form is a variable name. When the person writes your name in the blank by the name "home," the value of your name is being assigned to "home." The meaning of "home" is variable, however. The next person filling out the form will have a different value for "home." Yet, the word "home" can be used universally as having a meaningful value. The same is true of the terms "Social Security number," "name," and other "stand-ins" for individual values. When the form is complete, several values have been assigned to variables.

When you take your form to the class assignment station, you can give it to a new person; that person consults the form to find your name and other information. In effect, you have *exported* your variables to a new process. The person conducting the new process can use your values to make decisions about which classes to assign you.

To UNIX, the location of your home directory can be represented by the variable HOME. When the value of your home directory is exported, a new program needs only to consult the HOME variable to find the name of your home directory. Because your environment is separate from that of other users, your HOME is distinct from others. The program might use HOME and other variables to decide where to store your data files.

By convention, all letters in UNIX variables' names are uppercase characters. However, you can use variables typed in lowercase characters. Note, however, that term and TERM are different variables.

In some cases, an assigned variable is of no use to programs outside the current shell; therefore, the variable is not exported. The name and value of this variable are local. All user-defined variables are local until they are exported. Local variables are useful for holding temporary or short-term values. You can assign the current time to a variable so that you can later calculate how much time has elapsed. You can store a long file name in a variable and then use the variable's name (preceded by a $) as a file-name argument for a series of commands. Your use of variables is limited only by your ingenuity. The current time or long file-name variables are likely to be of no use to commands or programs, so you would not export them to the environment.

You are used to working with variables like names and addresses, but you don't know the kind of variables that UNIX is looking for. Don't worry that you will have to identify all your variables. UNIX defines all important variables and assigns their values for you; these variables are exported if necessary.

Not all UNIX systems assign the same variables for logged-on users. Some variables are common, however. Table 5.10 lists common environment-variable names and the meaning of their assigned values. Be aware that your environment may have many variables assigned that are of little or no interest to you in your daily work. UNIX uses these variables internally. Until you gain experience, just remember the meanings of your common variables.

Table 5.10
Common Environment Variables and Their Meanings

Variable	Meaning of Assigned Value
HOME	The full name of the user's home directory.
PATH	The search path to be used by UNIX when searching for the program file of an executable command.
TERM	The name of the user's terminal to be matched against a table of terminals to determine the capabilities of the terminal.
MAIL	The full name of the directory in which the user's electronic-mail files reside.
LOGNAME	The name the user used when logging on for the current session.
PS1	The primary command-prompt string that the user sees. Normally, $ is assigned to PS1.
PS2	The prompt string the user sees if the command line is continued to the next line. Normally, > is assigned to PS2.

You can see which variables are associated with your current shell by entering the Bourne shell's built-in `set` command. When issued with no arguments, the `set` command displays the current variable names and their values. The command is simple. At the prompt, enter the following:

```
$ set <Return>
```

UNIX responds with the current setting, similar to the following:

```
HOME=/usr/david
HZ=100
IFS=

LOGNAME=david
MAIL=/usr/spool/mail/david
MAILCHECK=600
PATH=/bin://usr/bin:/usr/david/bin:.
PS1=$
PS2=$
TERM=ansi
TZ=EST5
```

Remember that the preceding output is for the user named `david`. Your screen will be different. Don't worry about the meaning of these variables for now. The exact variables vary from system to system and from user to user. Some of the variables shown with the set command may not be exportable from your current shell's environment.

NOTE

You learn more about variables and their uses in shell procedures (scripts) in Chapter 15.

Understanding Syntax

Earlier in this chapter, you learned that the shell reads an input line from your keystrokes (or from a redirected input file) and then breaks the command line into distinct parts. The act of breaking apart the command line is called *parsing*. The shell follows a predefined set of rules concerning the ordering and the contents of the command line. This set of rules is similar in purpose to the rules concerning spoken or written words.

To the shell, a command line is like a sentence that contains words. The form and order of parts of a command line is called its *syntax*. When you speak or write, you use proper syntax so that the person with whom you are communicating can understand exactly what you are saying. If you make a minor mistake in spoken syntax, however, your listener will probably still understand you. The shell, on the other hand, is more reliant on proper command-line syntax than people are on language syntax. People can use context and previous experience to help them understand words that are presented in incorrect syntax; UNIX cannot. Computers rely on exact adherence to syntactic rules to carry out your intentions.

UNIX command lines always begin with the name of a UNIX command. Most commands are held in named files; a few commands are actually "built-into" the shell. Commands that are held in files are called *external* commands; built-in commands are called *internal* commands. External commands are either *executables* or *shell procedures*. Executables are compiled binary programs that require no additional translation to run. Shell procedures are text files that contain commands. The shell executes the procedure file's commands in a *subshell*. A subshell is a child shell belonging to the parent shell. Built-in commands are executed in the same shell that processes the command line for the command.

All users have access to internal commands. A user can execute external commands only if the user has been granted execute permission for the command's file. Remember that not all UNIX systems have all possible commands. Also, each system enables its own selection of commands for ordinary users. UNIX looks in your current directory for an external command. When you first log in to the system, your current directory is normally your personal directory and has the same name as your log name. Most executable commands and shell scripts are located in /bin, /usr/bin, and /etc.

Your PATH variable indicates to the shell where to look for external commands, programs, and shell scripts. PATH is usually assigned for you during login, when your .profile is processed. Of course, you can eliminate the path search by giving the full path name for the command on the command line. Command examples in this book assume that your PATH variable enables UNIX to search the directory in which commands reside. When you see sample syntax or actual commands, you should consider the search path.

Many UNIX commands are accompanied on the command line by additional groups of characters or words called *options*, or *flags*. Options modify or clarify the standard way that a command operates. Options begin with a dash (-), also called a minus sign. The dash is then followed immediately by one or more characters that define the option. Use a delimiting space to separate an option (flag) from a command. The use of options is optional, as their name implies. Not all commands take options, however. Some commands have many options. When commands are presented in Part Two and the Command Reference, you will see each command's common options.

An example of an option given with a command is the ls -l command line. The ls command, as you recall, lists files in a directory. The -l option modifies the standard way that ls operates. The -l option causes the ls command to format its output in a wide listing. The wide listing contains additional information about the files included in the list. Chapter 6 discusses the ls command with the -l option.

If you were to issue the command ls-l, you would have entered a syntax error. The shell would not find a space between the command and the option and therefore would not parse the command as you intended. UNIX would try to locate a command named ls-l, which does not exist. Although the errant command line is close to being correct, the shell still cannot find the command and the option. Forgetting the space between a command and an option is a common mistake.

TIP

UNIX options or flags are equivalent to MS-DOS command-line switches.

You can issue ls and other commands with more than one option. When used with ls, the -a option includes in the output *a*ll files, including those beginning with a period character (.). For a long, all-inclusive list of files in the current directory, issue the following command:

    ls -a -l

To make the command line more efficient, you can issue the same command as follows:

    ls -al

Notice that the option letters are grouped immediately after the minus character. Multiple options for a command are implemented immediately in the command's operation, regardless of how you enter them on the command line. In most cases, you can group options on the command line with only one minus sign (-). Some options accept additional arguments. Options that accept arguments must either be last in the group, or separate from other options.

Many UNIX commands use the same letter as an option, but the meaning of the letter varies from command to command.

Arguments, as you learned in a previous section, give the command (and sometimes options) information about what to operate on or where to send the results of the command's operation. Arguments are delimited from other parts of a command line by a space or tab character and sometimes by a redirection or pipe character. Arguments are often file names, but arguments also can be times, dates, colors, or other character strings. Each command that accepts arguments has its own class of arguments. When you learn about commands in the other chapters of this book, be sure to look at the arguments in the examples to get a feel for the various classes of arguments that UNIX commands accept.

Understanding Command Categories

Over the years, more than two hundred commands have evolved within UNIX. As in any evolutionary situation, some commands have fallen by the wayside while newer, better commands have taken their places. An ordinary user of UNIX has occasion to use a few dozen commands regularly. The commands presented to you in this book represent a high percentage of your UNIX command-prompt work. To help you understand the scope of the capabilities and uses of UNIX commands, this section groups commands by general utility. The next few sections introduce the categories. Bear in mind that some commands fit well in more than one category.

The File-Management Commands

The category of file-management commands includes commands that you use to copy, delete, archive, and manage other aspects of your files. Chapter 6 is dedicated to these commands. Table 5.11 lists the file-management commands.

Table 5.11
File-Management Commands

Command	Action
cp	Copies files
join	Joins the output of files on a relation
ls	Lists files in directories
pack	Compresses file size
touch	Updates the access and modification times of files
unpack	Expands packed files

The Directory-Management Commands

One of UNIX's most desirable features is its hierarchical file system. You can use the operating system's directory-management commands to manage the directories that you add to the file system. Other directory-management commands enable you to navigate efficiently through the directories in the file system. Table 5.12 lists the directory-management commands and their actions.

Table 5.12
Directory-Management Commands

Command	Action
cd	Changes the working directory
copy	Copies files and directories of files
dircmp	Compares directories
ln	Makes a link to a file
mkdir	Creates a new directory
mv	Moves (renames) files
pwd	Displays the name of the working directory
rm	Removes (erases) files
rmdir	Removes an empty directory

The File-Processing Commands

File-processing commands perform operations on files. File-processing commands are closely related to file-management commands. You use file-processing commands to work with a file's contents rather than managing the file itself as a whole. Table 5.13 lists the file-processing commands and their actions.

Table 5.13
File-Processing Commands

Command	Action
cat	Concatenates (appends) files
cmp	Compares two files for equality
comm	Processes lines common to two files
crypt	Encrypts the contents of a file
cut	Cuts selected text from lines in a file
diff	Displays differences in two text files
egrep	An extended grep command

Table 5.13—(continued)

Command	Action
fgrep	A grep command for fixed strings
file	Displays the type of files
find	Finds files in the directory tree
grep	Searches a file for a matching pattern
head	Displays the beginning of a text file
more	Displays text a screen at a time
nl	Provides line numbers for lines of a file
pcat	Views files previously compacted with the pack command
pg	Displays text a screen at a time
sort	Collates (alphabetizes) lines of a file
split	Divides a file into smaller parts
tail	Displays the end of a text file
uniq	Reports repeated lines in a file

The Device-Related Commands

Normally, the system manager works with device commands to establish the proper computing environment. There are a few device-related commands that ordinary users find useful, however. Most of these commands concern themselves with the operation of the terminal. Two commands inform users about the storage status of the disk drive. The device-related commands and their actions are shown in table 5.14.

Table 5.14
Device-Related Commands

Command	Action
clear	Erases the terminal display
df	Shows amount of disk space still free
display	Selects the display colors (AIX)
du	Shows disk usage
setcolor	Selects the display colors (SCO)
stty	Makes or displays terminal port settings
tabs	Sets the default tabs
tty	Shows the device name of the terminal

The Multiprocessing/Multiuser Commands

By design, UNIX is a multiprocessing/multiuser operating system. All commands are designed to work within this environment. The multiprocessing/multiuser command category includes commands that are more directly involved with or related to the multiprocessing/multiuser aspects of UNIX. These commands are listed in table 5.15.

Table 5.15
Multiprocessing/Multiuser Commands

Command	Action
at	Executes commands at a given time
batch	Executes commands when system load allows
cancel	Unschedules printer jobs
chgrp	Modifies the group IDs of files
chmod	Modifies permissions (attributes) of files
chown	Modifies the owner IDs of files
cron	Executes scheduled commands
kill	Stops processes
lp	Sends output to a system printer
lpstat	Reports the status of the printer queue
news	Displays text items of interest to users
newgrp	Changes (logs) user to a different group
nice	Adjusts the priority of a process
passwd	Maintains user passwords
pr	Prints files to the screen or printer device
ps	Displays process information
su	Enables superuser privilege
sync	Flushes (writes) disk buffers to disk
umask	Establishes the file-creation mode for a user
uname	Prints the name of the UNIX system
who	Displays the system's logged users
who am i	Reports a user's log name
whodo	Determines which user is doing what process

The Office-Automation Utility Commands

Office automation is a term given to computer activity that assists or automates typical office overhead work. Many UNIX commands fit this description. The office-automation commands enable users to handle the overhead of daily office communications, calculations, scheduling, and time management. Table 5.16 lists the office-automation commands and their actions.

Table 5.16
Office-Automation Commands

Command	Action
at	Executes commands at a given time
banner	Prints large letters on screen or printer
bc	Invokes a basic calculator utility
cal	Displays calendars
calendar	Manages a calendar-based reminder service
cu	Calls another UNIX system or terminal
date	Displays (sets) the system date
dc	Invokes a desktop calculator utility
mail	Initiates the electronic mail system
mesg	Controls message printing on a terminal
wall	Writes a message to all users
write	Outputs a message on another user's terminal

The Shell-Programming Commands

Shell programs—or *scripts*—are executable text files that contain UNIX commands. Through the creation of appropriate shell scripts, you can automate sequences of commands. Shell scripts are very similar to MS-DOS's batch files. Although no command is dedicated to exclusive use in shell scripts, some commands lend themselves to inclusion in scripts. The shell-programming commands and their actions are listed in table 5.17.

Table 5.17
Shell-Programming Commands

Command	Action
csh	Invokes the C shell
echo	Displays text on the terminal
env	Sets and reports the environment
false	Returns with a non-0 exit value
line	Reads one input line
paste	Merges lines of text
read	Reads one item into a variable

Table 5.17—(continued)

Command	Action
sh	Invokes another command shell
sleep	Suspends execution for a specified time
tee	Copies output from a pipeline to a file
test	Tests conditions
time	Reports the elapsed time of a command
true	Returns with a 0 exit value

The Text-Editing Commands

One of the computer's most widely appreciated capabilities is the capability to edit text. UNIX includes two text editors, each with its own strengths, which you can use to create reports, memos, documents, or anything done in writing. When text editing is coupled with text formatting, spell checking, and printing, the full capabilities of word processing are available to you. Table 5.18 lists the text-editing commands and their actions.

Table 5.18
Text-Editing Commands

Command	Action
ed	Simple line editor
spell	Checks spelling of words in a file
wc	Counts lines and words in a file
vi	Full-screen visual editor

Learning By Doing

Now that you have seen how the shell interprets special characters, matches file names, and provides for pipes, tees, and redirection, you may feel that using UNIX is going to be difficult. Granted, the shell is somewhat complex. But if you're worried that you will need to master the more complex aspects of the shell in order to use UNIX, just relax. UNIX works equally well for beginners and experts alike. You will use only the shell features that you need and understand. As you do UNIX work at the operating-system level, you will find situations in which you can take advantage of special characters, pipes, tees, and redirection. When that happens, you can refer back to this section to refresh your memory. When you are working with UNIX, experience is the best teacher. Give yourself the time to work at the shell level. Before long, you will be comfortable with UNIX.

Summary

In this chapter, you learned the last of the fundamental information necessary to have a good foundation to use UNIX commands. This chapter discussed the following key points:

- ❏ You gain access to a UNIX system by logging on.
- ❏ Your login identifier is your login name.
- ❏ You verify your login name with a secret password during the login process.
- ❏ You must log off the system to terminate your session gracefully.
- ❏ The shell is the "go-between" for you and the kernel. The shell presents the command prompt and interprets command lines that you type.
- ❏ The shell parses command lines and applies syntax rules to the command's formation.
- ❏ Through special characters, the shell expands and substitutes parts of the command line.
- ❏ The shell provides for the re-routing of command input and output through redirection.
- ❏ The shell enables one command's output to be another command's input in pipelines.
- ❏ Each shell's environment contains values held in variables.
- ❏ Many of your variables are initialized in the `.profile` or `.login` file.
- ❏ Commands consist of command names, options, and arguments.
- ❏ Commands can be grouped by action or activity.

The next chapter begins Part Two of this book. Part Two assumes that you have learned the basics of UNIX presented in Part One. You will see command examples emphasizing the most common UNIX commands. The chapters are based on command groupings, such as those listed in tables 5.11 through 5.18. For a quick reference of any command, you can flip to the Command Reference section and find the command alphabetically. Because commands that manage files are such an important part of UNIX, the next chapter will introduce them to you.

— Part —
Two

Using the UNIX Commands

Managing Files

Managing Directories

Managing Devices

Participating in a Multiuser Environment

Processing Files

Automating the Office Environment

Managing Files

The UNIX file system works with many kinds of files. The term "file" can refer to device files, standard input and output files, and ordinary disk files. This chapter introduces you to your work with ordinary disk files. When this chapter talks about a file, you can take the meaning of the word "file" to mean "ordinary disk file."

As you work with UNIX, you will create files. Files are the basic units of the UNIX system. As a user, you create files in many ways. For example, you create files when you redirect output to a file. Your applications create files to store the data or text that you develop while working with the applications. And the UNIX file-related commands create files when you copy source files to new destination files.

It won't take you very long to create dozens of files. Most users, in fact, soon develop a large collection of files. Like any other large collection, however, you must manage your files in order to keep your UNIX work orderly and efficient.

Recall from Chapter 3 that you identify a file by its name. A file name can include up to 14 characters. Because the UNIX file system is a tree-structured, hierarchical directory system, a directory path name exists for every file. You give a file a full path name by using a path name and a file name. Whenever possible, you should use a file name that describes the contents of the file.

The UNIX file system is like a filing cabinet. In the process of creating files, the UNIX filing mechanism in the kernel enters the name of the file in a *directory*. A directory is like a "cabinet drawer" for files. When you log on to the system, you are positioned in the directory tree in your home directory. This chapter shows you how to manage the files that your home directory contains. You also can use the file-management commands presented here to work with files in other directories.

You'll learn more about directory management in Chapter 7. For now, understand that you can issue file names as command arguments without including the full path name. When you do not include the path in the file-name argument (the full path name for the file) UNIX will work in your current or working directory.

UNIX enables you to have several types of ordinary files. One of the most common file types is the text file. You can view or print the contents of a text file. Other files, such as binary files, cannot be viewed or printed. Even though you cannot see or print a binary file, it is still a good idea to learn about managing such files; you may, for example, want to copy a binary file or be able to move around a directory that contains such files.

In Chapter 5, you learned how to use the process of redirection. This chapter covers the use of redirection in creating new files. You also learn how to modify the creation times associated with your files and how to save disk space by compressing your files.

Key Terms Used in This Chapter

Attribute	A characteristic of a file, such as its type, length, name, and so on.
Backspace	The combination of the Ctrl and U keys (< ^ U>), or the key labeled Backspace on your keyboard.
Binary file	A file of numbers that can be read only by a machine or program; a binary file cannot be displayed on-screen.
Block	A unit of file information containing a multiple of 512 bytes.
Byte	Within a text file, a byte represents a single character. Within a binary file, a byte represents a number from 0 to 255.
Compression	The process of reducing the amount of disk space a file takes.
Directory	A "file drawer" for files.
End-of-file (EOF)	An indication that there is no more data in the file; EOF is indicated by the < ^ D>.
File name	A name used to specify a file.
Path name	The address of a file, specifying its directory location.
Standard output	Where most UNIX commands place their results (that is, your display screen).
Text file	A file of characters.
Underbar	The character you enter by pressing the underline key (_) on your keyboard.

Displaying File Information

In Chapter 3, you learned the UNIX conventions for file names, path names, and file attributes. When you use UNIX, you often need information on specific file names, path names, and attributes in order to perform certain tasks. In this section, you learn how to access this information by using UNIX commands.

Recall that a file name is a sequence of 1 to 14 characters consisting of letters, digits, and special characters such as the underbar (_). When naming files, be careful not to use a Backspace, < ^ S >, or other special characters that are not displayed on your terminal. As you will learn in a later section, using such characters can prevent you from easily accessing your files.

When accessing a file that is not in your working directory, you specify a full path name so that UNIX knows where to go in the file system to access your file. At login, you are assigned a home directory as your working directory. However, you may have the same file name in your home directory that someone else has in theirs. The two files with the same name, however, are distinct because they reside in two different directories. By specifying a full path name, you tell UNIX exactly which file you want.

UNIX also assigns your files certain attributes. These attributes serve as characteristics of your files, such as who owns the file, who is allowed to look at the file, and who is permitted to modify the file.

This section shows you how to find out information about your files by using commands that list file names and attributes, and commands that display part or all of the contents of a file or files.

Listing File Information with `ls`

At times, you want to see which files you have available to you in your working directory. Suppose that you want to work with a certain file but cannot remember the file name. Or, you may have a group of similarly named files and need to see a complete list so that you can decide which file you want.

UNIX provides the `ls` (*list* files) command, which, when issued with no options or arguments, provides a simple list of the files in your working directory.

NOTE

When issuing commands presented in this book, you type the characters shown in boldface characters. Where you see <Return>, you press the Return (or CR or Enter) key. The command output will follow the command line and be displayed on-screen.

To access the ls command, type the following command at the prompt. In this example, the sequence and resulting file list look like this:

```
$ ls <Return>
commands
customers
inventory
letter
lsfil
mailing
mbox
payroll
$
```

This command produces a list of the files in your current directory. This is the form of the ls command you are likely to use most often.

 If this is the first time you have used your account, there may not be any files present when you issue the ls command. In a later section, you learn how to create new files. In most cases, however, your system administrator has probably set up some files for you.

Using Options with the ls Command

As with most UNIX commands, you can alter the basic operation of the ls command by including options or flags. An option enables a more specialized operation with a command. Options are keyed in after the command's name on the command line and are normally preceded by the dash or minus sign (–) character.

Suppose that you want to know the size of a file (in bytes), when a certain file was last modified, or which permissions are assigned to the file. You can use several options with ls in order to view these attributes. The most common ls options are listed in table 6.1.

Table 6.1
Commonly Used Options for the ls Command

Option	Action
–l	Produces a *long* listing of files
–q	Replaces the nonprinting characters in file names with a *question-mark* character (?)
–a	Lists *all* file names, including directories and names beginning with the dot (period) character

The ls command issued with the –l option is called the "long" form of the ls command. As you will see, however, the command is still a "short" command that simply displays the file list in a longer format. Try entering the ls command with the –l option:

```
$ ls -l <Return>
total 48
-rw-------    1 dave    group        959 May 27 19:46 commands
-rw-------    1 dave    group       7492 May 27 20:55 customers
-rw-------    1 dave    group        263 May 27 19:49 inventory
-rw-------    1 dave    group        534 May 27 19:26 letter
-rw-------    1 dave    group       9365 May 27 20:56 mailing
-rw-------    1 dave    group        391 May 27 11:24 mbox
-rw-------    1 dave    group       1873 May 27 20:53 payroll
$
```

In this listing, the number that follows the word `total` is the number of blocks used on the disk to store the files. A block contains a multiple of 512 bytes. In most systems, a block is 1024 bytes, but a block can be 512, 2048, or 4096 bytes in size. For text files, a byte is equivalent to a single character. 48 blocks are needed to store the files shown in the preceding listing.

Each successive line of this output of the `ls-1` command contains quite a bit of information. Consider a typical line from this listing:

```
-rw-------    1 dave    group        959 May 27 19:46 commands
```

The screen display is made up of eight fields, each of which provides valuable information about the file. Figure 6.1 shows the contents of each field. Table 6.2 explains the meaning of each field.

Another form of the `ls` command is useful when you are having trouble accessing a file that you can't access with the name you see in a directory listing. Perhaps there are characters in the file name that cannot be displayed on-screen. When you issue the `ls` command with the `-q` option, `ls` replaces the nonprintable characters in file names with a *question* mark (?).

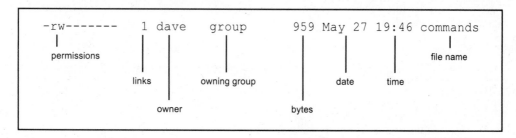

Fig. 6.1. The fields displayed by the `ls` command when issued with the −l option.

Table 6.2
Fields Displayed by the `ls-l` Command

Field	Explanation
Permissions	Characters that indicate whether you allow users to read, write, and execute the file. This particular file contains both read (r) and write (w) permission for the owner.
Links	The number of links to a file, usually 1. The file's link count comes from the i-node that records the file. A link count of 2 or more indicates that the same file is listed in a directory elsewhere.
Owner	The login name of the file's creator. This entry normally indicates your home directory, in this case, dave. In come cases, system logins such as root own files.
Owning group	The name of the group to which you (or the owner) belong. Other users may be members of your group.
Bytes	The size of the file in bytes, in this case, 959.
Date	The date and time when the file was created or last modified.
Time	In this example, the file was last modified on May 27 at 7:46 p.m.
File name	The name of the file—in this case, commands.

Recall from Chapter 5 the discussion of escaping characters using the backslash (\) character directly before each escaped character. Escaping a character hides its special meaning from the shell. The following listing shows some file names containing special characters. These special characters had been "escaped" when the files were named.

```
$ ls <Return>
bacspace
bellname
tab                    name
$
```

If you try to use any of the file names in this listing, your command will fail because each file name contains nonprinting characters.

After you check your spelling of the name(s), you can issue the ls -q command to determine whether hidden characters exist. The ls -q command looks like this:

```
$ ls -q <Return>
back?space
bell?name
tab?name
$
```

In this file listing, the ? character appears in each file name. The ? marks the position of an unseen character. In the file listed as `back?space`, for example, the hidden character is a backspace character. Notice in the first listing that the same name appeared as `bacspace`. The nonprinting backspace character contained in the file name literally backspaced over the letter `k` when the name was listed. The −q option with `ls` gives you a much better idea of the number of characters in the name.

Notice also that the file listed as `tab?name` contains a tab character in the fourth character position. When most terminals display a tab character, they display it as a series of spaces. Without the −q option, as in the first listing, the name appears to have a "space gap" in the middle.

The file listed as `bell?name` contains a < ^ G> bell character in the fifth character position. On most terminals, the < ^ G> character makes the terminal sound a beep or bell. When this file is listed by the `ls` command, the bell character is not displayed, but the terminal beeps in response to the embedded bell character. The `ls -q` command helps disclose the reason that `bellname` is not the file's name.

Spaces may appear in file names if the spaces were escaped, or if the space-containing file name was enclosed in quotes during naming. Spaces in file names will not produce ?s with the `ls -q` command. File names that contain spaces will look the same when listed by `ls` as when they are listed by `ls -q`.

Tab, Backspace, and the bell character are not the only nonprinting characters. In fact, every character produced by holding the Control key while pressing a letter key is a nonprinting character. In this book, most of these nonprinting characters are enclosed in angle brackets < >. Needless to say, you must be careful when escaping characters in a file name. You later may not remember how you named the file. Keeping the command `ls -q` in mind can be a big help.

To remove nonprinting characters from a file name, try renaming the file using the ? wild card. In the old file-name argument, use the ? wild card in the same position where the ? appears in the `ls -q` listing. In the new file-name argument, give the name that you want the file to now have. For the `bell?name` file used in the previous example, the `mv bell?name bellname` command will give the file a completely printable name. (The process of renaming files is covered in more detail in Chapter 7.)

The `ls` command normally doesn't list files or directories whose names begin with the dot or period (.) character. This feature enables you to name files using the dot as the first character, without constantly seeing these files in your directory listing. Some files don't change often, and some don't change at all. For example, once you have established your `.profile` file, you aren't likely to want to see it displayed in every `ls` command. The same rationale applies to initialization files like `.login` for C-shell users, and `exrc` for users of the `vi` screen editor.

Every UNIX directory—with the exception of the / root directory—contains an entry for itself as a single dot as well as an entry for the directory's parent as two dots (also called "dot dot" . .). These entries are useful as a form of "shorthand" notation for full file names, as you will see in Chapter 7. Like other names that begin with the dot character, you most likely won't need to see these dot directories in an ls listing.

In normal listing activity, the file names that begin with the dot character aren't very informational. You *expect* to see your .profile file, so ls doesn't clutter your screen by showing it. In effect, the dot files are hidden from ls. However, if you name files using a dot as the first character, you want a provision to include the names of these files in a directory listing. The -a (for *all*) option gives ls the capability to "see" these hidden dot files and include them in the directory listing.

Consider the following example:

```
$ ls -a <Return>
.
..
.exrc
.profile
commands
customers.z
inventory
letter
lsfil
mailing
mbox
payroll
session
$
```

Notice that some files begin with the period, or dot (.) character. You didn't see these files in previous ls listings. The -a option instructed ls to include them.

Notice the first two entries in the preceding listing. These entries, one period and two periods, both of which are not followed by a file name, indicate the current directory and the current directory's parent directory. Remember that these "dot-only" entries are a form of shorthand notation. No file is literally named . or . . You'll understand the concept of current and parent directories better after reading about them in the next chapter.

In many cases, when you issue the ls -a command, it is useful to also include the -l option to verify which names are directories. All listed directories are sub-directories of the listed directory except for the shorthand . . parent directory. When both options are issued, you can tell which files are directories simply by looking at the permissions field of the directory listing.

In the following listing, several subdirectories have now been added to the example home directory. You can see them, as well as any hidden files, by issuing the `ls` command with both the `-a` and `-l` options as follows:

```
$ ls -a -l <Return>
total 72
drwx------   7 dave     group      1504 Jun 29 01:10 .
drwxrwxr-x  19 root     auth        304 Jun 25  1989 ..
-rw-------   1 dave     group        62 May 27 19:18 .exrc
-rw-------   1 dave     group       526 Jun 25  1989 .profile
-rw-------   2 dave     group       973 Jun  9 11:44 commands
-rw-------   1 dave     group      4630 May 27 20:55 customers.z
-rw-------   1 dave     group       263 Jun 11 15:59 inventory
-rw-------   1 dave     group       534 May 27 19:26 letter
-rw-------   1 dave     group      9365 May 27 20:56 mailing
-rw-------   1 dave     group       391 May 27 11:24 mbox
-rw-------   1 dave     group      1873 May 27 20:53 payroll
-rw-------   1 dave     group         0 Jun  9 10:59 session
drwx------   2 dave     group       272 Jun 10 13:58 splitdir
drwx------   2 dave     group        48 Jun 11 16:04 subdir1
drwx------   2 dave     group        32 Jun 11 16:00 subdir2
drwx------   2 dave     group        80 Jun  9 11:18 subdir3
drwx------   2 dave     group        80 Jun  9 11:21 subdir4
$
```

TIP

You can group options that don't require their own arguments after one minus sign (–) character. For example, in the preceding list, the options are given as `-a` and `-l`—each option having its own minus sign. Alternatively, you can combine the `-a` and `-l` options with the `ls` command as `ls -al`.

Giving File-Name Arguments with the `ls` Command

Although viewing all of the files in your current directory is handy for getting a "big picture" of the directory, you often want to see only one or two specific files reported by `ls`. Recall from Chapter 5 that most UNIX commands accept file names as arguments. The `ls` command is a good example of such a command. You can specify—as arguments to the command—any and all the files you want `ls` to list.

File-name arguments follow options (if any) on the command line. You can include one file name or more than one. Most of the time, you will include one file name because you want to see information about a single file.

For examples of file-name arguments given with `ls`, you'll see files from a user whose login name is `terrie`. Terrie's home directory is therefore `/usr/terrie`. All of the reported files are located in `/usr/terrie`.

The command that shows the contents of Terrie's home directory in a columnar listing is the ls -aC command. The -C (for *columnar*) option causes the output to be displayed in columns. Columnar grouping of files takes less space than the standard listing of ls. The command and its listing looks like this:

```
$ ls -aC <Return>
.              .desk_pref    .tcap        budget.wk    mw.ini
..             .profile      boss.mem     clipdir      wastebasket
$
```

As you can see, all files and directories, including the dot names, are displayed in two rows of five columns. This listing enables you to more easily see which file names can be used as arguments for the ls command. To see a *long* listing of the budget.wk spreadsheet file, issue the ls command with the -l option and the file name budget.wk as an argument, as in the following example:

```
$ ls -l budget.wk <Return>
-rw-------   1 terrie   group      1605 Aug 20 22:20 budget.wk
$
```

Notice that only the file name given as the file-name argument—budget.wk—is listed. The listing is presented in the long format. Because this file is listed alone, however, the output of ls is much less cluttered.

To list two files with one ls command, you give the two file names as arguments. Separate the two file names with one or more spaces so that the shell can delimit the names. You enter the command as in the following example:

```
$ ls mw.ini boss.mem <Return>
boss.mem
mw.ini
$
```

This ls command, which includes no options, produces a normal output. Two file names, mw.ini and boss.mem, are given as arguments. Notice that in the command line, the file names are separated by a space. ls finds both files in the current directory and reports their names.

If you give a file name, and the name does not exist in the directory, you'll see a report that tells you ls didn't find the file. The exact report varies among implementations of UNIX, but the following is an example:

```
$ ls appointments <Return>
appointments not found
$
```

As you recall from looking at Terrie's entire directory listing, the file appointments is not included. The ls command gives you a message to that effect. If you give more than one file name as argument, and any argument files are not found, you'll see the names that ls didn't find, displayed within their own message. The following command shows an example:

```
$ ls .profile .login <Return>
.login not found
.profile
$
```

Notice the line reporting `.login not found`. The next line shows the name that `ls` did find—the `.profile` file. Both file names begin with the dot character, yet the command didn't include the `-a` option to show any hidden files. These files are processed by `ls` even though the `-a` is not given because the files are given as literal arguments. In other words, the file names are entered on the command line by their actual names. `ls` only hides dot files in full listings when you issue `ls` with no arguments. `ls`, however, is designed to include dot files when you explicitly ask for them.

File-name arguments given with `ls` give you full control over the file names reported. If a file name that you include as an argument isn't in the directory, `ls` will let you know.

Before you create, rename, or copy a file to your current directory, issue the `ls` command using the new file name first. If the name already exists, you will want to select a new file name for the copying or renaming process. Copying a file using an existing name overwrites the contents of the file that has the same name.

Using Wild Cards with `ls`

When you give file names as arguments to `ls` and other commands, the names are passed to the command by the shell as a kind of list. The list of file names is the list of work that the command must do. You'll recall from Chapter 5 that the shell reserves special characters for interpretation as pattern-matching characters in file-name arguments. These characters are *, ?, and the [ ] pair. The shell creates its own list of file names for the command to act upon by using pattern matching of wild-card arguments. The shell-created list functions the same as if you had given a list of literal file names.

You can use wild cards in file-name arguments to specify which files you want to list with the `ls` command. This capability is useful when you have a large number of files and you know part of the file name. You can use the asterisk character (*) as a "full" wild card. The asterisk wild card matches any single character or any number of characters. If you give * as the only character in the file-name argument, the * will match all file names in the directory. By specifying in the command the letter c followed by a wild card, you list all the files that begin with the letter c. The `ls` command does not care about the number of characters following the c in the matching file name. Consider the following example, which uses Dave's home directory:

```
$ ls c* <Return>
commands
customers
$
```

This command lists all the files that begin with the letter c, no matter how many characters the file name contains. The shell looks at the file names in the current directory for a match of the letter c in the first position. The names commands and customers both begin with c, but their remaining characters are completely different. Because * acts as the "match-anything" wild card, the difference in the names doesn't matter.

You can also use the question-mark character (?) as a wild card. When you use the question mark, however, you tell the ls command that the wild card matches only *one* character. Consider the following ls command issued with the ? wild card:

```
$ ls c? <Return>
$
```

Remember that the ? wild card represents a *single* character of a possible match. Because there are no file names in the directory that begin with the letter c and contain only two characters, no file names are displayed.

If, however, you specify seven question marks following the c, you will find a match:

```
$ ls c??????? <Return>
commands
$
```

Notice that only the file named commands is displayed. Unlike the asterisk wild card, which matches any number of characters, the question-mark wild card requires that you specify an exact number of characters. Because the file name customers has nine characters rather than eight, it is not included in the file listing.

Learning To Use Wild Cards . . .

Using wild cards in file-name arguments can sometimes be dangerous, especially if you are careless and accidentally overwrite some files containing important data. If you are just learning how to use wild cards in file-name arguments, the ls command is an excellent command to practice with. If you form a file argument with ls using wild cards, and you include a pattern that matches more files than you intend, you won't risk harming any of your files.

For example, try combining the * and ? characters in the file-name argument when you use ls. You will also want to try character ranges and lists by enclosing them between [and] characters. Chapter 5 will help you review the use of wild cards if you get out of practice using them.

Displaying the Contents of a File with `cat`

After you obtain a list of the files in your directory, you may want to look at the contents of some files to refresh your memory of what the file contains. The versatile `cat` command enables you to see the contents of your ASCII text files on your terminal screen. As you learned in Chapter 2, UNIX uses your terminal screen as the standard output of commands.

You also can use the `cat` command to con*cat*enate or chain files together and display them on the standard output (your terminal). This capability is a very powerful tool for displaying files.

`cat` is a simple command, and most often it is issued with no options. To look at the contents of a text file, at the prompt, type **cat**, followed by a space and the file name. Then press <Return>.

In the following example, a text file named `commands` contains the names of many UNIX commands:

```
$ cat commands <Return>
tty
umask
uname
uniq
units
uptime
uucp
uuencode
uustat
uuto
uux
vc
vi
vidi
vmstat
w
wait
wc
what
who
whodo
write
xargs
yes
$
```

Because the file contains more than a screenful of data, only the last 23 lines of the file remain displayed on-screen. The other lines of the file rapidly scroll off the top of the screen. To look at a file one screen at a time, you use the pg and more commands. These commands are discussed in the next section.

In a later section, you learn to use cat with redirection to copy and move files.

Displaying Part of a File with pg and more

When you want to look at a text file that contains more than 23 lines, you use the more and pg commands to display one screenful of information at a time. In their basic forms, the two commands are very much alike. The difference between more and pg centers around the way in which you tell each command that you want to see the next screen of information. With the pg command, you press <Return> to display the next 23 lines. With the more command, you press the space bar to display the next 22 lines. The more command also tells you the percentage of the file you have seen and enables you to look at a line at a time instead of 22 lines.

NOTE   Some implementations of UNIX offer either pg or more, but not both commands. Some implementations offer both commands. If you have only one of the two commands, you can concentrate on the description of the command you have. If you have both, use the one that you find most useful.

To understand the basic operation of the pg command, look at the following example, which lists on-screen the contents of a text file named numfile. Each line of numfile contains the characters that represent the line's number in the file. The command is issued as follows:

```
$ pg numfile <Return>
one
two
three
four
five
six
seven
eight
nine
ten
eleven
twelve
thirteen
fourteen
fifteen
sixteen
seventeen
eighteen
nineteen
twenty
```

```
twenty-one
twenty-two
twenty-three
twenty-four
:
```

You can see that 24 lines from the file are displayed. On the 25th line, you see the
: (colon) character. The colon is the prompt that pg displays after it presents a
screenful of information. To see the next page of the file, simply press the
<Return> key. pg then displays the next screen of file contents. The actual
number of lines you see on your screen depends on your terminal type. The
additional lines of numfile appear on the terminal as follows:

```
twenty-five
twenty-six
twenty-seven
twenty-eight
twenty-nine
thirty
(EOF):
```

Each time you press <Return>, pg displays the next page of the file until the final
lines of the file are displayed on-screen. When pg encounters the end of the file, it
displays the (EOF) and presents the colon prompt again. If you press <Return> at
the end of file message and prompt, pg completes its execution, and the command
prompt returns.

Now try using the more command. more is very similar to pg in that it displays a
screenful of information at a time. You respond differently to the prompt that more
presents, however. Try the more command on one of your longer files. Here's what
happens with the file named numfile:

```
$ more numfile <Return>
one
two
three
four
five
six
seven
eight
nine
ten
eleven
twelve
thirteen
fourteen
fifteen
sixteen
seventeen
```

```
eighteen
nineteen
twenty
twenty-one
twenty-two
twenty-three
--More--(67%)
```

The more command presents the prompt --More--(*nn*%) on the last output line of each screen page. The more prompt presents an approximate percentage of the file displayed thus far. To display an additional line from the file, press <Return> at the more prompt. The screen scrolls an additional line and presents the more prompt again. The additional screen dialog looks like this:

```
--More--(67%) <Return>
twenty-four
--More--(72%) <Return>
twenty-five
--More--(77%)
```

Some users prefer this line-at-a-time approach to seeing "more" of a text file. The more prompt enables screen-at-time progress through a file as well. At the more prompt, you press the space bar once to see the next screen of output. At the present location in the numfile example, the screen dialog looks like this:

```
--More--(77%) <space bar>
twenty-six
twenty-seven
twenty-eight
twenty-nine
thirty
$
```

Because numfile contains enough text lines to fit in two screens, more encounters the end of the file after presenting the remaining lines on the second output page. Unlike pg, more returns control to the shell without a final prompt. Of course, you can use more on text files containing many pages of text. If you press the <space bar> or <Return> until there are no more lines in the file, the $ prompt appears. The more command does not indicate the end-of-file as does the pg command.

Using Options with more

You can use options with both more and pg to change the number of lines to be displayed at a time. This means that you can tell UNIX what you want to be displayed as a screenful of data. The default line listings for most terminals are 23 lines for more and 24 lines for pg. Table 6.3 lists the commonly used options for the more command.

Table 6.3
Commonly Used Options for the more Command

Option	Action
-n	Causes more to display n number of lines at a time instead of the default 23 lines
+linenumber	Causes more to begin displaying lines at the line specified by linenumber

The -n option enables you to tell the more command how many lines you want to display before you are prompted to press the space bar. Use -12, for example, if you want to retain about half of the previous lines. By decreasing the number of lines of page increment, you get to see more of the previous screen; this feature can help you keep reading any new text in context.

With the +linenumber option, you can tell more where in the file you want to begin. You may not want to view the entire file, for example, and the more command allows you to specify where you want to start. This use of more is similar to the tail command, which is covered in the next section.

Using Options with pg

Table 6.4 lists the commonly used options for the pg command.

Table 6.4
Commonly Used Options for the pg Command

Option	Action
-n	Causes pg to display n number of lines at a time instead of the default 24 lines.
+linenumber	Causes pg to begin displaying lines at the line specified by linenumber.
-pstring	Causes pg to display the prompt specified by string instead of the default colon (:). An example of a prompt might be Press Return. If %d is used in the string, it is replaced by the current page number.

As you can see, the options for pg are very similar to the options for the more command. For example, to change the number of lines to be displayed, use the -n option. For example, to view ten lines at a time, you specify the more command as follows:

```
$ more -10 commands <Return>
```

To view ten lines at a time with the pg command, use the following command:

```
$ pg -10 commands <Return>
```

The pg command, however, has an additional, very useful option. The -p option enables you to specify a string of text that pg uses to request that you press the <Return> key.

An additional feature of the -p option is that you can include a page number in the prompt. Consider the following example:

```
$ pg -5 -p "Page %d, press RETURN" commands <Return>
```

This command produces the following display of the contents of the example commands file:

```
assign
at
auth
awk
banner
: Page 1, press RETURN
```

Notice that the page number is filled in by the pg command. The special %d format indicator in the prompt string instructs pg to substitute the current page number for the format indicator. The page count is based on the number of times that the colon prompt is presented. The page number is not tied to the page number that results from printing the file on a printer. If you select a page size of a few lines, the page numbers will increase more quickly than when you select a larger page number.

You might find this technique useful if you want to quickly count the number of lines in a file while you are looking at the file.

In addition, certain commands available with pg enable you to move around in the file and *peruse* the contents. You enter these *perusal* commands as keystrokes at the colon prompt. Table 6.5 lists some of the more common perusal commands that can be used with pg.

Table 6.5
Commonly Used pg Perusal Commands

Command	Action
RETURN	Displays the next page
+n	Moves forward n number of pages
-n	Moves backward n number of pages
n	Moves to the page specified by n
$	Moves to the last page
h	Accesses help
q	Quits or leaves pg

Displaying the Start and End of a File with `head` and `tail`

So far, you have used the commands `cat`, `pg` and `more` to display the contents of a file. In many cases, you want to refresh your memory about a file's contents by seeing the beginning or ending of the file. The `head` command displays the first lines of the file, and the `tail` command displays the last lines of the file. You can specify the number of lines to be displayed by using the *n* argument with either command. The default for both `head` and `tail` is to display 10 lines.

You use the `head` and `tail` commands when you don't want to page through the entire file. This feature can be useful when you want to look at the contents of a file simply to help identify it. You may not want to look at the entire file, especially if the file is extremely long.

In the following example, the `head` command is used to see the front of the file `commands`:

```
$ head commands <Return>
assign
at
auths
awk
banner
basename
bc
bdiff
bfs
cal
$
```

You can specify the number of lines you want to view. To view the first 5 lines, use the following command:

```
$ head -5 commands <Return>
assign
at
auths
awk
banner
$
```

The `tail` command displays the last lines of the file. You specify the number of lines to be displayed by including the *n* argument. As with `head`, the default number of lines displayed with `tail` is 10 lines. Following is the default listing of `tail` used with the file `commands`:

```
$ tail commands <Return>
vmstat
w
wait
wc
what
who
whodo
write
xargs
yes
$
```

You use the `tail` command when you only want to look at the last few lines of a file. This can be useful if you are keeping a daily log and want to see only the last few entries.

`head` **and** `tail` have only one common option—the *n* count argument.

Copying Files with `cat` and Redirection

You may find you want to make a copy of one or more of your files. You can accomplish this by redirecting the output of `cat`. Suppose that you have a file named `purchases`. This file contains the same information as the file named `inventory`. You can use redirection and the `cat` command to save a copy of one file and work with a different copy. In this way, you can make changes only to the new files, and keep the originals intact.

Chapter 5 discusses the use of the redirection symbol >. To copy the file `inventory` to `purchases` for example, you type the following:

```
$ cat inventory > purchases <Return>
```

The information in the file named `inventory` is now also contained in the file named `purchases`.

Another method you can use to copy a file is the `cp` command. To use `cp` to copy the file `inventory` to `purchases`, you enter the following command:

```
$ cp inventory purchases <Return>
```

Note that the `cp` command line doesn't require a redirection symbol. Both the `cat` and `cp` examples accomplish the same thing; they copy the file `inventory` into a new file called `purchases`. The `cp` command uses the file-name arguments for standard input and output. The `cat` command sends the input-file argument to your screen unless you specify redirection of the standard output to a file name. For a straight file-to-file copy, `cp` is more convenient to issue.

The `cat` command, however, gives you additional flexibility because you can direct the output of `cat` to the end of an existing file by using the append >> symbol, as in the following example:

$ **`cat inventory >> purchases`** <Return>

The results of this command will vary depending on whether the file named `purchases` exists. If `purchases` does not exist, you have made a copy of the `inventory` file. If it does exist, you have added the `inventory` file records to the end of the `purchases` file.

About Redirecting Files to Themselves . . .

Be careful *not* to copy a file to itself using the following form of the command:
`cat` *filename* `>` *filename*

For example, suppose you were to type the following:

$ **`cat inventory > inventory`** <Return>

This command erases all the data in the `inventory` file because UNIX creates an empty file to hold the output of the redirection. The empty file name is the output-redirection file name. Because the output name is the same as the input name, the contents of the `inventory` file are lost before the copy begins.

Consider also the following command:

$ **`cat inventory >> inventory`** <Return>

This statement gives you duplicate contents of your original `inventory` file in the resulting version of the `inventory` file.

Changing File Times with `touch`

At times, you may be given a set of files with which to work. These files may have been created by another user, or perhaps were set up by your system administrator. You may want to reset the dates and times associated with these files to correspond to when you actually began working with them. You use the `touch` command to accomplish this.

Or, you may want to change the times that one or more of your files were accessed and modified. The `touch` command provides you with this capability.

Before you modify the dates and times of files, it is a good idea to review the current times for your files by issuing the `ls` command with the −l flag, as in the following sequence:

```
$ ls -l <Return>
total 48
-rw-------    1 dave    group      959 May 27 19:46 commands
-rw-------    1 dave    group     7492 May 27 20:55 customers
-rw-------    1 dave    group      263 May 27 19:49 inventory
-rw-------    1 dave    group      534 May 27 19:26 letter
-rw-------    1 dave    group     9365 May 27 20:56 mailing
-rw-------    1 dave    group      391 May 27 11:24 mbox
-rw-------    1 dave    group     1873 May 27 20:53 payroll
$
```

To change the time for the file letter, use the following command:

```
$ touch letter <Return>
$
```

If you then relist the files, you will see that the time for the file has been changed:

```
$ ls -l <Return>
total 48
-rw-------    1 dave    group      959 May 27 19:46 commands
-rw-------    1 dave    group     7492 May 27 20:55 customers
-rw-------    1 dave    group      263 May 27 19:49 inventory
-rw-------    1 dave    group      534 May 29 15:21 letter
-rw-------    1 dave    group     9365 May 27 20:56 mailing
-rw-------    1 dave    group      391 May 27 11:24 mbox
-rw-------    1 dave    group     1873 May 27 20:53 payroll
$
```

You may want to use the date command to display or set the date and time. Refer to Chapter 11 for information on the date command.

Several options are available with the touch command. These options enable you to specify whether to change the access or modification times of your files. Table 6.6 lists the common options available with the touch command.

Table 6.6
Commonly Used Options for the touch Command

Option	Action
-c	Prevents the touch command from creating the file if it does not exist.
-a	Causes the touch command to update only the access time and not the modification time of the file.
-m	Causes the touch command to update only the modification time—not the access time of the file.

If you use the `touch` command on a file that does not exist, `touch` will attempt to create the file. By specifying the `-c` option with `touch`, the command will not create a new file.

Notice that the `touch` command modifies both the modification and access times for a file. If you want only one of these times to be changed, use the `-a` and `-m` options. The `-a` option causes only the access time to be changed. The `-m` option causes only the modification time to be changed.

Conserving Disk Space

When participating in a multiuser environment such as the one created by UNIX, you will want to keep the maximum amount of disk space available to you and other users of the system. You only have a fixed amount of disk space to store your files. As that space becomes full, you will need to obtain more disk space or free up some of what you are already using. The commands introduced in the following sections enable you to conserve your disk space so that the entire system can be more efficiently operated.

One way to free up disk space is to erase files you no longer need. It is good practice to erase files you don't use. This process of cleaning up after yourself ensures that too many files aren't taking up space you don't need.

If you don't clean up on a regular basis, at some point, you may need to look through each and every one of your files to determine which ones you no longer need. This process can be quite tedious, so get in the habit of keeping only those files you use and erasing the others. Chapter 7, "Managing Directories," covers the commands used for erasing files.

Before you do any "clean up," however, be sure that your files are being backed up by your system administrator on a regular basis in case you erase a file you—or someone else—may need at some future time. Chapter 4 discusses the activities involved in making and maintaining backup copies of your files.

Another way of maximizing available disk space is to compress especially large files so that they take up less room. A large file that you use infrequently, and that you must retain relatively fast access to is a good candidate for compression.

You can use the `pack` and `unpack` commands to compress your files and subsequently expand them. Not all files, however, can be packed and unpacked. The following sections discuss these commands.

Compressing a File with `pack`

Both the `pack` and `unpack` commands use a method of compression that replaces repeated characters through a method of encoding. The compression process requires some disk space for overhead, so small files can end up taking more space rather than less. When such a situation is possible, however, `pack` displays a message that indicates that no savings will be accomplished when you pack a certain file.

For this example, the `pack` command is used on a small file, named `inventory`. The file contains 263 bytes.

To attempt to pack the file named `inventory`, use the following command:

```
$ pack inventory <Return>
pack: inventory: no saving - file unchanged
$
```

The display lets you know that `pack` cannot compress the file because no space would be saved doing so. Don't worry about the need to pack small files of 1000 bytes or less. You won't be saving the system enough disk space to make any difference. If you have several large files, say 100,000 bytes in size, you should consider packing the files you don't use often.

If you try a larger file, you will see the power in using the `pack` command:

```
$ pack customers <Return>
pack: customers: 38.2% Compression
$
```

You can save 38 percent of disk space by compressing this file. Try the technique on some of your own files to get an idea of just how much space you can save using the `pack` command.

The `pack` command renames the file with a `.z` extension so that you know the file has been packed. The file named `customers` is now named `customers.z`, and the original file `customers` does not exist. Because `pack` must add the 2 characters to a file's existing file name, the existing file name must be 12 characters or less in length.

You cannot use `pack` to compress a file if a file with the same name, and if a `.z` extension already exists. You also cannot use the `pack` command on an entire directory, although you can use `pack` on each file in the directory. Refer to the Command Reference for a complete description of these and other restrictions on your use of the `pack` command.

WARNING
If you are copying a file that has been compressed (that is, one that bears a `.z` extension), be sure to include a `.z` extension in the new file name. Otherwise, it will be difficult to determine which files are packed and which are not.

In the next section, you learn how to retrieve the original file that was compressed with `pack`.

Decompressing a File with unpack and pcat

Once you have compressed a file with pack, you will eventually need to decompress it in order to work with it. There are two ways to decompress a file after you have compressed it. You can use unpack or pcat. unpack returns the file to its original form; pcat acts as a cat command for packed files.

The unpack command accepts as input the .z file you created with pack and replaces it with an unpacked file of the same name, but without the .z extension. Note that you cannot unpack a file that has not been packed, even if you have given it a .z extension.

In the following example, unpack lets you know that it has been successful in unpacking your file:

```
$ unpack customers <Return>
unpack: customers: unpacked
$
```

The customers file may be a list of customers from two years ago that was packed because a newer customer list took its place. The user can unpack the old customers file to get needed customer information and then pack the file again. The file is available for relatively immediate use, but the file doesn't take as much disk space because it is packed.

You use pcat in the same way you use cat, but pcat works on compressed files. You specify the file name with or without the .z extension, and pcat displays the file's contents on the standard output. The file itself remains packed. Like unpack, pcat works only on files that have been compressed by pack.

No options are available for the pack and unpack commands.

Summary

This chapter has shown you ways to keep your files in order so that you can be a more efficient UNIX user.

The chapter presented the following key concepts:

❑ You can use the versatile ls command to list the files in your directories. You can use ls to get a "big picture" of the contents of your directories as well as a snapshot view of a single file.

❑ The cat command enables you to look at the contents of your files. You can also use cat to concatenate files together and display them on your terminal.

❏ By using the `pg` or `more` commands, you can view the contents of a text file one page at a time, or one part at a time.

❏ The `head` and `tail` commands display the beginning and ending of a file, respectively.

❏ You can use `cat` and redirection to make a copy of a file.

❏ Use the `touch` command command to modify the dates and times of files.

❏ Use `pack` and `unpack` to compress and decompress files to save disk space.

The next chapter, Chapter 7, contains information on managing your directories rather than specific files. Chapter 7 shows you how you can use file-name arguments that cross directory lines. Chapter 10 presents more details on how to work with the contents of your files.

Managing
Directories

Chapter 6 introduced you to the process of using commands to work with file information in your home directory. Your home directory is your own "little corner" of the UNIX world. The sooner you explore the UNIX capabilities of creating and managing additional directories, the more organized your UNIX files will become. This chapter will help you explore the UNIX world beyond your home directory.

In your computing work, you may be working with tens, hundreds, or even thousands of files. How do you keep them all organized? Chapter 6 presented some methods of keeping your files in order. One method of maintaining orderly files involves listing both the contents of your directory and the contents of your files. You can always search for the files you need by using wild cards, as described in Chapter 6. This method, however, proves to be very cumbersome after the first dozen files. The more files you own, the more organized you must become.

UNIX provides you with tools for organizing your files into subdirectories. In this chapter, you learn how to create and remove directories, as well as move or copy files to the directories you create. You also learn to delete files and directories you no longer need. As you learn to navigate through the directory structure, you will see methods of searching for files in different directories.

Key Terms Used in This Chapter

Period or *dot (.)*	A shorthand notation used to indicate the current directory. The `.` character is useful for indicating the current directory in a file-name argument.
Home directory	The directory specified by the user's login—usually the directory `/usr/name`. `name` is the name used to log in.

181

Parent directory	A directory containing a subdirectory. For example, the `root` directory is the parent of the `/usr` directory. The shorthand notation for a parent directory is dot dot (. .). Dot dot is used in commands in the same fashion as dot.
Path list	Specifies one or more path names.
Path name	The directory or directories that point to a file; path names are separated by slashes (/).
Permission	The capability to perform various functions on a file or directory.
Recursion	The process of working through the same program repeatedly, using a different input each time the program is repeated. An example is to perform a search on a directory, on all directories in that directory, in all directories in those, and so on.
Root directory	The base directory for the UNIX operating system.
Subdirectory	A directory which is contained within another directory. All directories other than the root are subdirectories.
Wild card	The * and ? characters in file-name arguments; used to specify a match on characters when performing file-name comparisons.

Working with the Directory Structure

Recall the directory structure introduced in Chapter 3. You can create your own directory structure as an extension of your home directory, similar to the one the UNIX system itself uses.

Remember that UNIX has a base directory called the *root* directory. All other directories are subdirectories of this main root directory. The root directory is signified in syntax by the slash (/) character.

The directory that you log into during the login process is your *home* directory. Your home directory is your initial *working* directory. A working directory or *current* directory is where UNIX commands do their file work unless you specify another directory as part of a file-name argument. In Chapter 6, the command examples took advantage of the current directory and used as arguments only file names—not directory *and* file names.

In all likelihood, your home directory is a subdirectory of the UNIX directory called `/usr`. Some systems have a `/u` or a `/usr1` user subdirectory. In the examples in this chapter, you'll see `/usr` as the user directory name. The directory `/usr` is in turn a subdirectory of the `root` directory.

The `root` directory has other subdirectories besides the `/usr` subdirectory. Figure 7.1 shows the relative relationship between some of these directories.

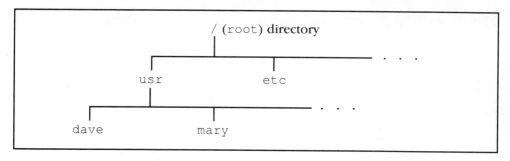

Fig. 7.1. *The directory-tree structure.*

Just as the /usr directory is a subdirectory of root, you can create subdirectories of your own home directory. This chapter shows you various ways of organizing your directories. In this section, you learn to move around the directory tree structure.

About Using Full Directory and File Names . . .

You learned that the root directory is represented by the slash (/) character. The / character has an additional meaning when used in specifying subdirectory names. The / character is also a subdirectory-name separator. For example, you refer to the file named memo in the dave subdirectory of the usr subdirectory of the root (/) as /usr/dave/memo. /usr/dave/memo is the full path name of the memo file.

Consider the path as the tracing of directory names to the file name. The first / names the root directory. The usr subdirectory immediately follows. The second / is a separator which delimits usr from dave. The subdirectory dave is separated from the file named memo by the final /.

Although UNIX ensures that the file name memo is unique in the file's directory, the name memo can appear in any other (or every other) directory in the file system. With most commands, UNIX relies on you to supply the path information in file-name arguments that indicates which file named memo you are referencing.

Files in your working directory are an exception. If a file is in your working directory, UNIX supplies the path portion of the full path file name for you when you supply the file name. To access a file in any directory other than your current directory, you must supply the path portion of the full path file name.

Displaying the Current Directory with `pwd`

When working with your directories, you often want to know which directory you are currently using. After issuing many directory-level commands and moving your working directory position several times, you easily can lose track of where in the directory tree you are. UNIX supplies the `pwd` command, which stands for *print your working directory*. `pwd` reports your current working directory, showing you its full path name. Try typing **pwd** and pressing <Return> to see which directory you are working with.

Following is an example:

```
$ pwd <Return>
/usr/dave
$
```

The example reports that `/usr/dave` is the working directory.

`pwd` is a simple command to use because it has no options or arguments. `pwd` is also one of the most frequently used UNIX commands because its function is indispensable. While you are learning to move around the directory system, you should issue `pwd` often to confirm that you are where you think you are. In the next section, you will learn to move among several different directories and will understand how useful it can be to know with which directory you are currently working.

Changing the Current Directory with `cd`

In UNIX, the directory you log into is known as your home directory. This directory generally has the path name `/usr/name`, in which `name` is the account name you use to log in. For these examples, `/usr/dave` is the home directory.

To move to a different directory, use the `cd` or *change directory* command. You can move up a level in the directory-tree structure toward the root by typing the following:

```
$ cd /usr <Return>
$
```

This `cd` command includes the `/usr` directory as an argument. You can change to other directories by naming them as arguments to `cd` commands.

The `cd` command does its work silently. It does not confirm your new directory location. You can, however, confirm your new location by issuing a `pwd` command. When you are in a different working directory, you can access all of the files in the new directory by using their simple names. You don't have to include their paths. If you want to work with files in your former working directory, however, you must provide path information in the file names.

At any point in the directory tree, you can directly return to your home directory by issuing the cd command with no directory-name argument. cd issued with no arguments changes your current directory position to your home directory—just as though you had given your home directory's name as an argument. If your working directory is /usr/bin, you can return to your home directory, as shown in this example:

```
$ pwd <Return>
/usr/bin
$ cd <Return>
$ pwd <Return>
/usr/dave
$
```

In this command sequence, the first pwd command confirms /usr/bin as the working directory. The cd command with no argument changes the working directory to the home directory. The second pwd command confirms that the working directory is /usr/dave—Dave's home directory.

The cd command does not change any contents of the file system—just your position within the file system.

 The cd command is a safe command to practice with because you can't hurt anything using it. You should explore some of the other directories and their files using cd, pwd, and ls. Practicing with these commands will give you a good sense of how extensive the UNIX hierarchical file system is.

Displaying Other Directories with ls

In Chapter 6, you learned how to list your files with the ls command. Recall that when you use the −l flag with the ls command, UNIX displays a listing of file attributes and other information. The first attribute column in the listing indicates the file's type. You can scan this column to determine whether or not any subdirectories are present in the directory you are listing.

Issued from the /usr directory, the ls command will produce something similar to this:

```
$ ls -l <Return>
total 44
drwxr-xr-x    5 adm      bin       224 Jun 11 09:15 adm
drwxrwxr-x    2 bin      bin      3088 Jun 25  1989 bin
drwx------    5 dave     group    1504 Jun 11 15:59 dave
drwxrwxr-x    3 bin      bin       128 Jun 25  1989 include
drwxrwxr-x    2 bin      bin        96 Jun 25  1989 lbin
drwxr-xr-x   31 bin      bin      1280 Jun 25  1989 lib
drwxr-xr-x   15 bin      bin       256 Jun 25  1989 man
drwxr-xr-x    7 mmdf     mmdf      160 Jun 25  1989 mmdf
drwx------    3 bin      bin        48 Jun 25  1989 net
```

```
drwxrwxr-x    2 network   network    32 Jun 25  1989 network
drwxrwxrwx    2 bin       bin        32 Jun 25  1989 news
drwxrwxr-x    2 root      sys        32 Jun 25  1989 options
drwxrwxrwx    2 bin       bin        32 Jun 25  1989 preserve
drwxr-xr-x    2 bin       bin        80 Jun 25  1989 pub
drwxrwxr-x   10 root      bin       160 Jun 25  1989 spool
drwxr-xr-x    2 sys       sys        32 Jun 25  1989 sys
drwxrwxrwt    2 sys       sys       112 Jun 11 09:29 tmp
$
```

Note that the first column of the attributes field contains the letter d, indicating that the name in the last field is a *directory*.

Remember that directories can contain file names *and* the names of other directories. The directories listed in a directory are *child* directories of the listed directory. Likewise, the listed directory is the *parent* of the child directories. The directory you are listing, unless it is the root, has a parent directory, too. In this example, the parent of /usr is / or the root. In fact, a path name, when viewed from right to left, is the listing of parent directories separated by / and ending at the root.

Every subdirectory (any directory other than the root) has an entry as . . or "dot dot." The dot-dot entry in a subdirectory is a universal name for that directory's parent directory. You can use the dot-dot name as a shorthand name for the working directory's parent directory's name.

For example, if your working directory is currently /usr/dave/data/save, you can change to the /usr/dave/data directory by issuing the following command:

    $ **cd** . . <Return>

This command means "change to the parent (dot-dot) directory." The use of the shorthand dot dot is easier than typing /usr/dave/data as an argument, but it means the same thing to UNIX.

You can form shorthand path names by using more than one dot-dot entry separated by the slash /. To get to /usr from /usr/dave/data, you can give /usr as an argument to cd, or you can use the shorthand notation, as shown in this example:

    $ **cd** ../.. <Return>

This command changes to the parent directory's parent, /usr.

If you've been trying these examples, change back to your home directory by issuing cd with no arguments. The command will list the contents of your directory, much like the following example:

    $ **cd** <Return>
    $ **ls −l** <Return>
    total 50

```
-rw-------     1 dave      group          959 Jun   9 11:31 command2
-rw-------     1 dave      group          959 Jun   9 11:31 command3
-rw-------     1 dave      group          973 Jun   9 11:44 commands
-rw-------     1 dave      group         4630 May  27 20:55 customers.z
-rw-------     1 dave      group          534 May  27 19:26 letter
-rw-------     1 dave      group            0 Jun  11 09:28 ls2
-rw-------     1 dave      group         9365 May  27 20:56 mailing
-rw-------     1 dave      group          391 May  27 11:24 mbox
-rw-------     1 dave      group         1873 May  27 20:53 payroll
-rw-------     1 dave      group            0 Jun   9 10:59 session
$
```

Notice that the example listing contains no directories. Your particular home directory, however, may have subdirectories that were already established for you. If you expand the directory structure, you'll be adding subdirectories to your home directory. You may even add subdirectories to those subdirectories. In the next section, you learn how to create subdirectories in your home directory.

Creating, Moving, and Deleting Directories

Unless you are a casual or occasional UNIX user, you will begin to accumulate files. You create files when you use applications, when you copy other files, when you redirect output to files, and when you participate in the electronic mail system. You can choose to keep these files "lumped" together in your home directory, or you can create additional directories with descriptive names to hold categories of files in smaller, easier-to-manage groups.

You aren't locked into the original organization that you create, however. You can copy and move files between directories. You can even empty a directory of its files and subdirectories and delete the directory completely. The next few sections will help you gain an understanding of how to create directories and manipulate them and their contents.

Creating New Directories with `mkdir`

To create a new directory as a subdirectory of your home directory, you issue the `mkdir` (for *make directory*) command. The command takes as an argument the name of the directory you want to create. The names used in the examples use the characters `dir` within the name to make the listings easier to follow. Of course, you will want to use more descriptive directory names, such as names that indicate the contents of the directories you create.

Directory names follow the same naming rules as file names. Review Chapters 3 and 6 for information on file-naming rules.

About Relative and Absolute Path Names . . .

You have learned that a full path name consists of the directories, starting from the root, that lead to the desired file or directory. Path names that begin from the root (those that begin with a / character) are called *absolute* path names. You can identify to UNIX any file in the system by referring to it by using the file's name and its absolute path name. UNIX traces the entries in each directory in the path name to locate the directory component of the path name. The action is a kind of "scavenger hunt," in which each found clue (the directory entry) tells where the next clue (the next directory entry) can be found. Ultimately, the last clue is the file name in the final directory name of the path.

Although it is convenient to access files using an absolute reference in completely unrelated branches of the file system, it becomes extra work when the file is in a subdirectory of the current directory. UNIX always keeps track of your working directory; when you change your working directory, UNIX changes to match. When you give a path name that does *not* begin with a /, UNIX doesn't trace the path from the root. Instead, UNIX uses the absolute path that it is tracking to fill in the beginning of the path you gave as an argument.

The concept of a relative path is similar to the concept of getting directions. When you're on the third floor of an office building, asking a person how to get to "Dr. Tolliver's office," you expect to get directions to the office based on where you are currently located. The directions might be, "Go from here to the fourth floor to room 422." Those directions are relative. The information started from "here," your current location.

If, however, the person says, "Start on the first floor, pass the second floor, pass the third floor, stop on the fourth floor, and then go to room 422," the directions are absolute. To you, the absolute directions contain certain information that you already know. In fact, you've already followed the path from the first floor to the third floor. The directions that are meaningful to you can begin with your current location.

If your current directory location is /usr, UNIX knows that your working directory is /usr. You can give UNIX directions to change to /usr/bin by supplying UNIX with the part of the absolute path that UNIX doesn't know. In other words, you can change to the /usr/bin directory by issuing the following command:

```
$ cd bin <Return>
```

Because UNIX didn't find a leading / in front of bin, UNIX knew that the path argument was relative from the working directory. UNIX supplied the /usr/ part of the absolute path name to the part you entered.

You can use a relative path argument anywhere you would use an absolute path argument. When using a relative path, however, it is important that you know your working directory's name. UNIX will use a relative path as directions from where you are, not from where you *think* you are.

It's a good idea to verify which directory you are working in by using the `pwd` command before you create a new directory, as illustrated in the following sequence:

```
$ pwd <Return>
/usr/dave
$
```

The working directory is `/usr/dave`. To create a subdirectory of `/usr/dave`, named `subdir`, you can use the `mkdir` command with a relative path argument as in the following:

```
$ mkdir subdir <Return>
$
```

Notice that the directory-name argument did not begin with `/`. UNIX assumes that a path specifier that does not begin with `/` is relative to your current directory. Now when you list the contents of your home directory, you will see that a directory called `subdir` has been created.

```
$ ls -l
total 50
-rw-------   1 dave     group      959 Jun  9 11:31 command2
-rw-------   1 dave     group      959 Jun  9 11:31 command3
-rw-------   1 dave     group      973 Jun  9 11:44 commands
-rw-------   1 dave     group     4630 May 27 20:55 customers.z
-rw-------   1 dave     group      534 May 27 19:26 letter
-rw-------   1 dave     group      263 Jun 11 09:28 inventory
-rw-------   1 dave     group     9365 May 27 20:56 mailing
-rw-------   1 dave     group      391 May 27 11:24 mbox
-rw-------   1 dave     group     1873 May 27 20:53 payroll
drwx------   2 dave     group        0 Jun  9 11:21 subdir
$
```

Notice that UNIX displays the name of the new directory—`subdir`—in the last reported line in the listing. You have created a subdirectory in your home directory. Your home directory is still your working directory, however. The `mkdir` command does not make the newly created directory the working directory. You must use the `cd` command to make the new directory the working directory.

Keep in mind that you can also use an absolute path name for the directory-name argument. Consider this command:

```
$ mkdir /usr/dave/subdir <Return>
```

This command would have created the same directory as in the previous example.

Note that UNIX will not allow you to create a subdirectory unless you have permission to create a file in that directory. As you know, UNIX provides for controlled access for files and directories. Other users, such as `/usr/terrie`, or system logins such as root, may not grant you permission to write to their directories. If you can't write to a directory, you can't create a subdirectory or a file in that directory, either.

If you try to create a directory in the directory /usr or /root, for example, you will receive an error message. This means that no one else can create a subdirectory in your directory unless you give them permission to do so. You can imagine how cluttered with extraneous files your (and the system's) directories could become if anyone could put files and directories there. Chapter 9 presents a more detailed discussion on file and directory permissions.

Here is what happens when you try to create a subdirectory named subdir2 in the system subdirectory /usr:

```
$ pwd <Return>
/usr/dave
$ cd /usr <Return>
$ pwd <Return>
/usr
$ mkdir subdir2 <Return>
unable to create subdir2; insufficient permission
$
```

Notice that UNIX displays an error message indicating that it is unable to create subdir2. Or, the error may look something like this:

```
mkdir: "subdir2": Permission denied
```

The usr directory, or your equivalent user directory, is owned by root or some other system owner. Your system administrator can enable users to add directories to /usr by changing the access modes for the directory. (Again, see Chapter 9 for more information on access modes and file permissions.)

Now change back to your home directory, this time using the name of your home directory. Then create another directory as follows:

```
$ cd /usr/dave <Return>
$ mkdir subdir2 <Return>
$
```

The new subdirectory, subdir2, is another child directory of /usr/dave. The mkdir command created subdir2 relative to the working directory, /usr/dave, because the directory-name argument did not begin with the / character. Although creating new directories relative to your home directory is simple, you can always specify the new directory by giving an absolute path name as the directory-name argument.

Moving Files between Directories with mv

In Chapter 6, you learned how to copy files. When you copy a file, the result is another file—additional to the original. Sometimes, however, you want to move a file to another directory or to a new name within a directory. The mv command enables you to move and rename files without creating another copy of the file. Now that you are learning about directory management, you can benefit from using mv in your directory-level work.

A good way to organize your files is to group them—by category, context, or application—into subdirectories. In Chapter 6, you learned how to use the wild-card character, the asterisk (*), with the ls command. You can always move files one at a time, but you can also move them using wild cards if their names are similar.

Before you use a wild-card argument with mv, however, it is a good idea to issue the ls command to review the names of the files that the wild-card argument will match. In the following example, the files that contain the leading characters comma will match files in the directory /usr/dave:

```
$ ls -l comma* <Return>
total 50
-rw-------     1 dave     group     959 Jun  9 11:31 command2
-rw-------     1 dave     group     959 Jun  9 11:31 command3
-rw-------     1 dave     group     973 Jun  9 11:44 commands
$
```

The listing of the matches to the comma* argument shows three files. When you verify that the three files are the correct ones to match with another command, you are ready to move the files. You move files to a subdirectory with the mv command. You can use wild cards with the mv command much as you do with the ls command.

To move the three files containing the pattern comma* to the directory subdir1, you type the following:

```
$ mv comma* subdir1 <Return>
$
```

Before you give wild-card arguments with a command that copies, moves, deletes, or otherwise changes matching files, first use the ls command with the wild-card argument. In this way, you can confirm that the wild-card argument matches only the intended file names. If files are matched that you did not intend, the ls command will show them. You can then change the formation of the wild-card argument to exclude the "extra" files. When the file-name argument is correct, use it with the copy, move, delete, or any other file-changing command.

If you list the files in your home directory, you will see that the files you moved are no longer listed in the directory:

```
$ ls <Return>
customers.z
letter
mailing
mbox
payroll
subdir1
$
```

Listing the files in the subdirectory shows that the files have indeed been moved to that directory:

```
$ ls subdir1 <Return>
command2
command3
commands
$
```

You can also search through all your subdirectories and display their contents using a process called *recursion*. You specify recursion by using the -R flag with the ls command. The recursion option tells UNIX to list the contents of any subdirectories found no matter how many levels of directories are in your directory structure.

Although the term "recursion" seems fairly technical, you can think of a recursive directory listing as the process of listing all of the branches of the directory tree, beginning from your current position. In addition to listing directory names, the ls -R command lists each directory's files.

You can move your files around as often as you want. After you move them, however, you may forget where the moved files are located. If you can't remember where they are, use the ls -R command to get a full listing of the file names in your directories. Later, you will see how to use the find command to locate a file in case you forget where you left it.

Renaming Files with mv

Even though the command name does not imply it, you can use the mv command to rename existing files. The process of renaming a file is actually the process of moving a new name into the file's directory entry. The general form of the mv command when renaming a file is as follows:

```
mv oldname newname
```

The argument represented by *oldname* is the file's name in the directory before you issue the command. The second argument, represented by *newname*, is the name the file will have after the command is executed.

Using mv to give a file a new name is very useful for preserving the contents of a file that otherwise would be overwritten by an application that uses the old file name. For example, the SCO Office Portfolio program writes a file named .applist when you select the applications that your version of Office Portfolio will display. Before you start Office Portfolio to configure a different list of applications, you can rename the .applist file to another name so that the new .applist does not overwrite the old configuration information. The renaming command looks like this:

$ **mv .applist .applist.old** <Return>

After the renaming, you can create a new .applist, but you will still have the original values and configurations in the descriptive file name .applist.old in case you need to reference them at a later time.

If you have many such versions, you may want to use an even more descriptive file-name extension, such as one that specifies the month during which you renamed the most current .applist file, such as .applist.jan..

Linking Several Names to One File with ln

To save disk space, you can maintain only one copy of a file and still have several directory entries for it. You use the ln command to *link* additional directory entries to an existing file or a directory entry.

To understand the concept of links, remember that UNIX tracks a file's identity by using the file's i-number in the i-node table. The file's name and i-number are both stored in a directory entry. The directory's i-number entry, in effect, points UNIX to the i-node that holds a file's storage information. When you give a file-name argument, UNIX looks at the names in the directory and finds the named entry. UNIX then uses the associated i-number to access the contents of the file. It is therefore possible (and often beneficial) for two or more directory entries to "point" to the same i-number (same file) even when the names used for the file are different.

Although the technical details concerning links are interesting, most users need a more fundamental explanation. You can think of a link as a nickname for a file. For example, a person may be known by his co-workers at a fast-food restaurant as "William." William's classmates at school may know him as "Bill." To his family, perhaps he is known as "Willie." He may even be known by his track teammates as "Flash." Even though these names are different, they all "point" to the same person.

An individual file can have nicknames or *aliases* through linking. In one directory, for example, a file can be named contacts. In the directory that holds greeting-card names, the same file can be called card_people. Although there are two directory entries consisting of two distinct names, the directory entries are both linked to the same file.

Linking a file enables you to access the file from more than one directory without using the full path name for the file. In many cases, linking by using a shorter alias to a file with a long, hard-to-remember name enables you to simplify your command lines.

To create a link in the subdirectory `subdir1` for the file `commands`, which is located in the `/usr/dave` directory, you enter the following:

```
$ cd subdir1 <Return>
$ ln /usr/dave/commands commands <Return>
$ ls <Return>
commands
$ cd /usr/dave <Return>
$
```

In this example, the file link `/usr/dave/subdir1/commands` was created as a link to `/usr/dave/commands`. When you change to `/usr/dave/subdir1`, you can refer to `commands` and access the same file as you would from the home directory.

If the file you are linking to (the first file) does not exist, you will get the following error message:

```
$ ln filename subdir1/filename <Return>
ln: cannot access filename
$
```

As you gain understanding of file and directory management, you may find occasion to create links to your files. Linking files across directories is more conservative in terms of disk usage than copying files in order to have them available in more than one directory.

TIP Linking files ensures that any changes you make to a file when you have accessed it by using one name will also appear as changes when you access the file by using another name. Although the file may be known by two or more names, using any of the names changes only the single file.

Deleting Files with `rm`

Disk space can fill up quickly, so it is often necessary to clean up your directories by erasing files you no longer need. Even if your system has plenty of disk space, you need to perform a good "housecleaning" on the contents of your directories from time to time. To erase files you no longer need, use the `rm` command. As the command's name suggests, `rm` *removes* files.

Because it is easy to erase files, it is also easy to mistakenly erase important files that you may need later. Once you erase a file, it is gone. In most cases, it is extremely difficult and sometimes impossible to retrieve an erased file. Always make sure that your system administrator frequently makes a backup copy of files.

Be careful when you specify which files you want to remove with the `rm` command. If you delete a file you don't want removed, you must have a backup of the file in order to restore it. Otherwise the file is lost.

Table 7.1 lists the options most commonly used with the `rm` command.

Table 7.1
Commonly Used Options for the `rm` Command

Option	Action
`-r`	Causes `rm` to *recursively* delete the entire contents of the directories and the directories themselves.
`-i`	Causes `rm` to ask *interactively* whether to erase each file, and if used with the `-r` option, whether to ask about each directory.

The `rm` command, like the `ls` command, has a recursion option. Be extremely careful, however, when using the `-r` option with the `rm` command. It is good practice to always use the interactive flag `-i` whenever you use the `-r` flag. The interactive flag `-i` causes `rm` to ask you whether to delete each file. As you are learning to delete files, you may want to use the `-i` option with every `rm` command as a "safety net."

Before you issue the `rm` command with the `-r` option, think about the branch of the file system that the command would delete. It's easy to forget your place in the directory system. If your home directory is your working directory, the following command will remove all files and directories from your home directory!

```
$ rm -r .  <Return>
$
```

In most cases, you will be removing files from your current directory. For example, to remove the file named `payroll`, you issue the following command:

```
$ rm payroll <Return>
$
```

You can use wild cards with the `rm` command to remove a group of files. Be especially careful, however, when using wild cards, or you may erase files you need. As mentioned previously, it is good practice to use the interactive option `-i` when using the `rm` command.

The `-i` option causes UNIX to ask you to verify whether or not you want to remove each file. In this example, the `-i` is used with `rm` on a list of files produced by the wild-card designation `command?`:

```
$  rm command? -i  . <Return>
$  command2 ? n <Return>
$  command3 ? n <Return>
$  commands ? n <Return>
$
```

In the example, UNIX asks you before it attempts to delete each file.

Copying Directories and Subdirectories

During your UNIX file-management and processing work, you will use commands that alter file and directory contents. If you are planning to alter several files in a directory, you can add a margin of safety to your command work by creating a copy of the files before you alter them. The copy command enables you to specify a source directory that contains original files and a destination directory where you want to place the copies of the source files. If, in the process of working with the original files, you make a mistake, or change your mind about an action you took, you can always copy the files back to your working directory from the directory where you copied them.

 Some implementations offer the copy command as a means of copying one directory's contents to another directory. The copy command as discussed in this section follows the convention of SCO UNIX System V/386. In some implementations of UNIX, copy works identically to cp. Check your system documentation to determine the presence and actions of copy on your system.

If you have some doubt that the contents of two directories are alike, you can confirm your suspicions using the dircmp command. dircmp is especially useful when you need to compare your working directory to the directory where you copied files with copy. Using dircmp, you can see whether you need to copy additional files which have been added to your working directory since the original copy. Both copy and dircmp are discussed in the following sections.

Copying Directories and Subdirectories with copy

At times, you want to save some files and make copies of them so that you can modify the copies or the originals. You use the copy command to copy the entire contents of a directory to a directory that you specify.

To copy the entire contents of a directory to another directory, specify the *from* (source) and the *to* (destination) directories as arguments with the copy command as follows:

```
copy sourcedir destinationdir
```

In this general form of the command, copy copies the contents of the source direct- ory (specified by *sourcedir*) to the destination directory (*destinationdir*).

Issuing options with copy (see table 7.2) can make the command more versatile.

Table 7.2
Commonly Used Options for the copy Command

Option	Action
-a	Causes copy to ask you before copying.
-r	Causes copy to copy all files in each subdirectory of the directory you are copying.
-m	Sets the modification and access times for the file to that of the source file. If not specified, copy uses the time of the copy.
-n	Copies only files that do not already exist in the destination directory.

The -a flag causes the copy command to ask you whether or not you want to copy each file. This technique is especially useful when you want to copy several different files but not all of them. Consider the following example:

```
$ copy -a subdir2 subdir3 <Return>
copy file subdir2/command2? y
copy file subdir2/command3? y
copy file subdir2/commands? n
$ ls subdir3 <Return>
command2
command3
$ copy subdir2 subdir3
$
```

Notice in the second listing that the -a flag is not issued with copy. In this listing, the command will not prompt you before the copy. Note also that if the file exists, copy will overwrite the existing file without informing you. You can confirm that the files were copied by using ls, as in the following sequence:

```
$ ls subdir3 <Return>
command2
command3
commands
$
```

Use the -n flag to specify that the file you are copying to must be a new file:

```
$ copy -n subdir2 subdir3 <Return>
copy:   cannot overwrite subdir3/command2
copy:   cannot overwrite subdir3/command3
copy:   cannot overwrite subdir3/commands
$
```

Comparing copy with cp

In Chapter 6, you learned how to copy files with the cp command. The copy command differs from the cp command on most UNIX systems. On the AIX system, cp acts the same as copy. Other implementations are different. You must specify a full path name with the cp command. Also, if a subdirectory does not exist, copy will create it. This is not true with the cp command.

For example, suppose that subdir4 does not exist. If you use the cp command to copy the contents of subdir2 to subdir4, you will receive an error message similar to the following:

```
$ cp subdir2/* subdir4 <Return>
cp subdir4 not found
$
```

By using the copy command, subdir4 is created, and the contents of the directory are copied as follows:

```
$ copy subdir2 subdir4 <Return>
$ ls subdir4 <Return>
command2
command3
commands
$
```

There are no flags available with the cp command. The copy command, however, offers options for recursion, prompting, and setting the modification and access times for the files. See table 7.2 for an explanation of these commonly used options.

Being Careful with Wild Cards and Recursion . . .

When you use wild-card and recursion features with any UNIX commands, always be aware of the potential dangers involved. As with the rm command, you need to be careful with the copy command. Using recursion with the copy command can be dangerous. Consider the following example:

```
$ copy -r * * <Return>
$
```

This command will copy all directories into themselves and fill your file system and disk space in an endless loop! If you do issue a command like this, press the interrupt key (either <Del> or <^C>, depending on your system) to stop the command from running further. Then contact your system administrator for help in restoring your files to their original state.

Comparing Files and Directories with `dircmp`

UNIX provides you with ways to compare your files and directories. This feature can be useful to determine whether you are missing a file from an application or whether you have updated certain files.

To compare the contents of two directories, you use the `dircmp` (for *compare directory*) command as follows:

```
$ dircmp subdir subdir3 <Return>
(screen "blips" twice)
$
```

If you try this command on your system, your screen will flash at you quickly. This is because `dircmp` creates several pages of output. You can pipe the output of `dircmp` into the `more` command like this:

```
$ dircmp subdir subdir3 | more <Return>
```

Or you can redirect the output to a file and then either view or print the file, as in the following example:

```
$ dircmp subdir subdir3 > cmpfil <Return>
$ more cmpfil <Return>
$
```

Now you can manipulate the file named `cmpfil` so that you can check any information you need.

You can use the dot character `.` with `dircmp` to specify the current working directory. To see a full `dircmp` report, compare two very different directories. Comparing directories with great differences isn't useful in your work, but it does show you how the output is formatted without your having to copy a directory.

```
$ dircmp . subdir > cmpfil2 <Return>
$ more cmpfil2 <Return>
Jun  09 11:27 1990  . only and subdir only Page 1
./.exrc
./.profile
./cmfil2
./cmpfil
./customers.z
./inventory
./letter
./mailing
./mbox
./mkdroot
./payroll
./session
./subdir
```

```
./subdir2
./subdir2/command2
./subdir2/command3
./subdir2/commands
./subdir3
./subdir3/command2
./subdir3/command3
./subdir3/commands
./subdir4
./subdir4/command2
./subdir4/command3
./subdir4/commands
./temp1
./temp2
Jun  09 11:27 1990  Comparison of . subdir Page 1
directory             .
$
```

The contents of `subdir2` and `subdir` are identical. This is how identical directories would compare:

```
$ copy subdir2 subdir > cmpfil3 <Return>
$ more cmpfil3 <Return>
Jun  09 11:30 1990  Comparison of subdir subdir2 Page 1
directory             .
same                  ./command2
same                  ./command3
same                  ./commands
$
```

When you issue `dircmp` on two files whose contents are different, each of which is located in a different directory, you receive information about the difference in file content. To illustrate, the following sequence appends an extra line of text to the end of the `commands` file in the `/usr/dave` directory.

```
$ pwd <Return>
$ /usr/dave <Return>
$ cat >> commands <Return>
extra command <Return>              (typed by user)
<^D>                                (terminates keyboard input)
$
```

The `cat` command issued with no source-file argument gets its input from the keyboard. In effect, `cat` copies your keystrokes until you press <^D>. <^D> is the UNIX end-of-file indicator. In this case, the "file" is comprised of your keystrokes. Your keystrokes are appended to the existing contents of `commands` because the `cat` command's output is redirected to `commands` through the >> symbol. The net effect of this sequence is that the file named `commands` in `/usr/dave/subdir` contains one fewer line than the file it was originally copied from.

Now, if you issue a `dircmp` command, the difference will be indicated, along with the other comparison output as follows:

```
$ dircmp . subdir > cmpfil5 <Return>
$ more cmpfil5 <Return>
Jun  09 11:44 1990  . only and subdir only Page 1
./.exrc
./.profile
./cmfil2
./cmpfil
./cmpfil3
./cmpfil4
./cmpfil5
./customers.z
./inventory
./letter
./mailing
./mbox
./mkdroot
./payroll
./session
./subdir
./subdir/command2
./subdir/command3
./subdir/commands
./subdir2
./subdir2/command2
./subdir2/command3
./subdir2/commands
./subdir3
./subdir3/command2
./subdir3/command3
./subdir3/commands
./subdir4
./subdir4/command2
./subdir4/command3
./subdir4/commands
./temp1
./temp2

Jun  09 11:44 1990  Comparison of . subdir Page 1

directory          .
same               ./command2
same               ./command3
different          ./commands
$
```

Note that the last line in the file tells you that the file named `commands` in the home directory is different from the file named `commands` in the subdirectories.

Specifying the −d flag with the `dircmp` command causes `dircmp` to list the specific differences in the files:

```
$ dircmp -d . subdir <Return>
Jun  09 11:47 1990  . only and subdir only Page 1
./.exrc
./.profile
./customers.z
./inventory
./letter
./mailing
./mbox
./payroll
./session
./subdir
./subdir/command2
./subdir/command3
./subdir/commands
./subdir2
./subdir2/command2
./subdir2/command3
./subdir2/commands
./subdir3
./subdir3/command2

./subdir3/command3
./subdir3/commands
./subdir4
./subdir4/command2
./subdir4/command3
./subdir4/commands
Jun  09 11:47 1990  Comparison of . subdir Page 1

directory        .
same             ./command2
same             ./command3
different        ./commands
Jun  09 11:47 1990  diff of ./commands in . and subdir Page 1

183d182
> extra command
$
```

The differences are listed in the same format as the `diff` command. For more information about the `diff` command, see Chapter 10.

Finding a File with `find`

When you work with many files, it can sometimes be difficult to remember where you placed a file. The `find` command enables you to locate a file. With the `find` command, you specify a path name and an expression in the following form:

```
find pathname expression
```

For example, to locate the file named `commands`, use the following sequence:

```
$ find . -name commands -print <Return>
./subdir3/commands
./subdir4/commands
./subdir/commands
./subdir2/commands
./commands
$
```

You must specify the `-name` flag with the `find` command in order for `find` to print to standard output the full path name(s) of where it located the file. The `find` command generally returns a true or false value. This is especially useful in writing UNIX programs called "shell programs." (Refer to Chapters 14 and 15 for more information on shell programming and returning values from UNIX commands.)

If you want to search more than one user's directory, you can specify a list of path names with the `find` command. `find` automatically searches through the entire directory structure specified by the path names.

Table 7.3 lists the commonly used expressions for the `find` command. These items are called *expressions*, because they return a true or false value when they are evaluated.

Table 7.3
Commonly Used Expressions for the `find` Command

Option	*Action*
`-name file`	Finds files matching the given name specified by `file`
`-user uname`	Finds files matching the given user name specified by `uname`
`-group gname`	Finds files matching the given group name specified by `gname`
`-print`	Causes `find` to print the full path names of the files which match the `find` expression

The `user` expression for the `find` command enables you to match files for a particular user. To find all the files for the user named `mary` for example, use the following command:

$ **find /usr —user mary —print** <Return>

The path name `/usr` tells the `find` command to search all files in all user directories which are owned by user `mary`.

Similarly, you can match files for a group of users. To find all the files for the group `depta`, for example, you enter the following:

$ **find /usr —group depta —print** <Return>

Other options are available with the `find` command for a number of different criteria. Refer to the Command Reference for a complete list of expressions and options for the `find` command.

Summary

You have seen ways to further manage your files and to manage your directories. You can check to see which directory in which you are working. You can create, move, copy, and delete files and directories. You can link several names to one copy of a file. You can also locate a file. With these skills you can keep your files organized so you can use them more easily.

This chapter covered the following key points:

❏ You can display the current directory by using the `pwd` command.

❏ Use the `cd` command to change from the current directory to another directory.

❏ Display other directories in the system by using the `ls` command.

❏ You create new directories with the `mkdir` command.

❏ Use the `mv` command to move directories and to rename existing files.

❏ You can compare files and directories by using the `dircmp` command.

❏ You use the `ln` command to *link* additional directory entries to an existing file or a directory entry.

❏ To erase files you no longer need, use the `rm` command.

❏ You use the `copy` command to copy the entire contents of a directory to a directory that you specify.

❏ If you forget where you placed a file, you can use the `find` command to locate it.

In Chapter 8, you will see commands that work with devices. These commands inform you about your terminal-to-UNIX communications link and disk-storage resource.

Managing Devices

You learned about devices and device drivers in Chapter 3. In Chapter 4, you got a glimpse of how the system administrator works with the many UNIX system devices. As an ordinary user, you do not have to contend with the details of most system devices. As a result, you won't have to learn many commands that manage or report the status of devices.

There are, however, certain device-related commands that you may have occasion to use during your UNIX system-level work. In this chapter, you learn about five serial-port and terminal-related commands, as well as two disk-related commands. In addition, you'll learn more terminal and disk-related concepts that will round out your understanding of devices.

Key Terms Used in This Chapter

TTY	The system's name for the terminal and its associated communications line.
`/etc/termcap`	The file containing codes for special terminal capabilities.
High function terminal (*HFT*)	A terminal, usually the built-in system console, that incorporates special features based on the display hardware.
Pixel	The smallest distinct point of illumination on a terminal display. Characters and images are composed of pixels.
Screen attributes	A program-controlled characteristic of characters on a video display. Attributes include reverse video, blinking, graphics, normal text, and others.

Tab	An ASCII character interpreted by capable terminals as an indicator to skip to the next tab stop position of a line.
Logical block	The allocation and buffering size in bytes of disk storage. A logical block is some multiple of 512 bytes and most often is 1024 bytes. Block sizes may vary from implementation to implementation of UNIX.
Fragmented file	A file with non-adjacent physical disk storage blocks. A fragmented file requires more disk-head movement to retrieve the file than an unfragmented file.

Using the Device-Related Terminal Commands

UNIX can assert some control over how your terminal appears to function. UNIX doesn't really control your terminal itself, but rather controls the way that the device driver—and programs and data files that use the device driver—deal with your terminal. This section introduces the commands that UNIX provides for ordinary users so that they can handle some of the controllable features of terminal communication.

Determining Your Terminal's Identity with `tty`

In the "olden days" of computing, terminals were actually teletype machines. Early computer terminology shortened the teletype reference to TTY. Today, *TTY* is a general term used to describe a terminal and its associated communications electronics. UNIX systems use the term TTY to denote terminals, and sometimes printers and other serial communication-based hardware. For the purpose of this discussion, you can take the meaning of TTY to represent one of the system's terminals connected through a system communications line.

Viewing the TTY Device Names

For each communications line capable of supporting a terminal, a UNIX system has a corresponding special device file in the /dev directory. The UNIX screen messages reference terminals by using the special device file name. Recall that device files are not ordinary data or program files, but rather device entries in the file system. Device files enable commands to use devices as easily as they use ordinary files as arguments or as redirection sources and destinations.

The first three characters of the TTY device file names in the /dev directory are tty. Other characters or numbers can follow tty in the file names; these characters or numbers serve to differentiate among the devices.

You can easily see the TTY devices—numbered from 1 to 99—included in your system by issuing the following command:

$ **ls -C /dev/tty[0-9][0-9]** <Return>

This command uses the wild-card bracket characters [] to provide two 0-9 ranges for the last two characters of the file-name argument. The ranges list all file names in the /dev directory that begin with tty, followed by the numbers 0 through 99. The -C option for ls produces a columnar output. The command's output looks like this:

```
/dev/tty01  /dev/tty03  /dev/tty05  /dev/tty07  /dev/tty09  /dev/tty11
/dev/tty02  /dev/tty04  /dev/tty06  /dev/tty08  /dev/tty10  /dev/tty12
$
```

You can see that there are many ttys listed. The files reported on your particular system may vary from this listing.

To see other tty devices, try the same command using /dev/tty* as the file specification. To see pseudo-TTY devices, use /dev/*tty* as the file specification for the ls command. The wild-card "front end" and "back end" to tty specifies any file containing tty in its name.

Issuing the tty Command

In order to specify your logged terminal in a command (by its tty name or full device path name) you must know which of the many TTYs you are using. UNIX provides the tty command specifically so that you can make this determination. Issuing the command is simple. At the prompt, enter the following:

$ **tty** <Return>

The system responds with your terminal's tty name, as in the following listing:

/dev/tty01

You can use this reported name to refer to your terminal.

Remember that your terminal is the standard input and standard output "file" for commands and programs. If a command reports an error, your terminal is the standard error-message file as well.

To see how UNIX automatically assigns standard input and output, look at the following example of the cat command. For the example, consider that a text file named words is in the working directory. Then enter the following command:

$ **cat words** <Return>

The text of the file `words` appears on-screen. In this example, the text appears as follows:

```
Devices and ordinary files are interchangeable
in UNIX command lines. This interchangeability
is called device and file independence.
$
```

There is nothing novel here. The `cat` command works as you expect it to. Now, to see how UNIX handles standard output automatically, try the same command, but this time redirect its output to your terminal as follows:

$ **cat words >/dev/tty01** <Return>

Now look at the output. It's the same as the first `cat` command. All you did with the second `cat` command was to direct the command's output to the same device that UNIX automatically directs output to—your terminal. The exercise illustrates that UNIX is busy directing inputs and outputs behind the scenes. Although you can't directly see it, UNIX provides the standard input and output arguments to your commands for you.

If you find that you are using your TTY name frequently during a session, you might benefit from assigning the name to a variable. You can make the assignment of an unknown terminal name with a single command by using a technique called *command expansion*.

Recall from Chapter 5 that if you enclose a command in a pair of backquotes (also called accent grave characters `), the shell executes the command and then substitutes the enclosed command's output as an argument. The following variable assignment illustrates this principle:

$ **me=`tty`** <Return>

The variable named `me` is created and assigned the output of the `tty` command. Note that the literal `tty` is not assigned. You can confirm the value of `me` using `set`, or by echoing the value as in the following:

$ **echo $me** <Return>
/dev/tty01
$

With the assignment made, you can take advantage of the shell's interpretation of metastrings. As you recall, the shell treats in a special way any items that begin with the $ in commands. The shell recognizes the argument prefixed by the $ as a variable name and substitutes the variable's value as the actual argument. With the value of /dev/tty01 in the variable `me`, you can use the argument $me anywhere you would enter /dev/tty01.

Clearing Your Screen Display with `clear`

When you are working at the UNIX command prompt, your screen often becomes cluttered with your commands and the outputs of your commands. Sometimes, users prefer to issue a command on a clean screen. Most UNIX implementations provide the `clear` command for you to use to erase the screen. If you are using a hard-copy (printing) terminal, `clear` advances the paper to the top of the next page.

Most terminals include many built-in features, such as hardware-settable tab stops, automatic carriage return after a line feed, and screen erasing. The `clear` command takes advantage of the terminal's screen-clearing function if the feature is available. If the terminal has no screen-clearing function, `clear` outputs enough newline characters to scroll any existing text off the screen. The new screen is clear just by eliminating previous lines.

The only argument that you might use with `clear` is the name of your terminal, as listed in the `/etc/termcap` terminal capability file. The `clear` command consults `/etc/termcap` to establish the character or character sequence that invokes the terminal's screen-clearing function. Because `clear` arranges the clearing sequence automatically, you don't have to worry about specifying the character sequence. If you don't know the type of terminal you are using (as listed in the `/etc/termcap` file), ask your system administrator.

Viewing `termcap` Terminal Names

To see some of the terminal-name listings in `/etc/termcap`, you can selectively view lines from the file that contain the names. Terminal names in `/etc/termcap` are separated by the | character. The | character is ideal as a search criterion for the `grep` command, which is intended to show lines with terminal names in them.

Of course, the | command is interpreted by the shell as signifying a piping operation. You can, however, take away the special piping interpretation of | by preceding it with a \ character, as you learned in chapter 5. An example `grep` search of `/etc/termcap` looks like the following:

```
$ grep \| /etc/termcap | head -20 <Return>
sa|arpanet|network:co#80:os:am:
se|ethernet|network:co#80:os:am:
su|dumb|un|unknown:co#80:os:am:
sd|du|dialup:co#80:os:am:
li|ansi|ansi80x25|Ansi standard crt:\
ln|ansi-nam|ansinam|Ansi standard crt without automargin:\
bt|b26:li#29:tc=ansi:
da|dosansi|ANSI.SYS standard crt:\
ip|ipc|intelpc|Intel IPC:\
f1|free100|liberty freedom 100:\
```

```
f2|free110|Freedom 110:\
t9|ti931|Texas Instruments 931 VDT:\
t1|ti924|Texas Instruments 924 VDT 7 bit:\
t2|ti924-8|Texas Instruments 924 VDT 8 bit :\
t6|ti926|Texas Instruments 926 VDT:\
S0|sk8620|Seiko 8620:\
Al|lisa|apple lisa xenix console display (white on black):\
e10|esp925|esprit925|esprit tvi925 emulation:if=/usr/lib/tabset/stdcrt:\
e9|espHAZ|esprit|esprit 6310 in hazeltine emulation mode:\
mt|macterm|macintosh MacTerm in vt-100 mode:\
$
```

In this example, note that the output of grep was piped to the head command.
The head command—with the argument -20—held the output to the first 20 lines
that grep found. The field listed before the first | in each line is the manu-
facturer's code for the terminal entry. The second field is the terminal name used
by the system. Fields separated by additional | characters are synonymous terminal
names and descriptions of the terminal's entry in the file. (A synonymous name for
a terminal is an alternative spelling for the terminal-capability file entry for that
terminal.)

Most users don't have to include the terminal-type argument to use clear. If you
do not include a terminal type as an argument for clear, the system consults the
terminal-type variable, named TERM (if it is assigned). Many users assign their
terminal type to TERM automatically by including the assignment in their
.profile or .login file. You can determine whether your terminal type is
defined in your .profile file by issuing the following command:

> $ **grep TERM .profile** <Return>

Note that if you are using the C shell, your .profile file is called the .login
file. You can substitute that file name in these examples. See Chapter 5 for
more information.

The grep command reports the assignment line from the file if the line exists.
If no assignment exists, grep will not issue a report. An example of a reported
assignment looks like the following:

> TERM=vt100

Some systems prompt you for your terminal type when you log on to the system.
The prompt is generated by a command in the .profile file and looks like the
following:

> TERM = (unknown)

You respond to the prompt with your terminal's name; the prompt line looks
similar to the following:

> TERM = (unknown) **vt100**<Return>
> Terminal type is vt100

If your TERM variable is not automatically assigned, you can easily assign it at the command prompt. Bourne-shell users enter the following:

$ **TERM=*terminal type*** <Return>

terminal type is the name of the terminal as given in /etc/termcap. To make the TERM variable available to subshells, you export the variable with the following command:

$ **export TERM** <Return>

You can remind yourself of your TERM variable's contents by issuing the following command:

echo $TERM <Return>

If your terminal is a DEC VT-100, you will see the following:

```
vt100
$
```

You can test for the presence of the terminal type name that you assign to TERM by following a command sequence as shown in the following:

```
$ TERM=vt100;export TERM <Return>
$ grep $TERM\| /etc/termcap <Return>
d1|vt100|vt-100|pt100|pt-100|dec vt100:\
s4|svt100|1220/PC, Sperry in VT100 mode:\
```

If the name you assigned exists in /etc/termcap, the lines which contain the name you specified are output on-screen. If you don't see any output lines, check the spelling of your terminal type. You may have made a spelling error that makes the value in TERM incorrect. Commands that consult TERM for terminal names assume that the terminal has no special capabilities if the name is not listed in /etc/termcap.

It is a good idea to assign your terminal type to the TERM variable when you start a session. Many UNIX commands and applications such as the screen editor vi, can take advantage of your terminal's capabilities when TERM is assigned a correct value.

Issuing the clear Command

The syntax for clear is simple:

```
clear term
```

term is the optional name of the terminal you are using. Again note that in order to use the terminal's special clearing capabilities, *term* must represent a terminal name which is listed in the /etc/termcap file. Otherwise, clear feeds enough blank lines to clear your screen as though you had a "dumb" or undefined terminal. If your TERM variable is defined, simply enter the following:

$ **clear** <Return>

By combining clear and echo in a command sequence, you can leave a short message on your screen. Consider the following command:

$ **clear;echo '\n\n\n\n   Be back in 5 minutes'** <Return>

This command produces the output shown in figure 8.1.

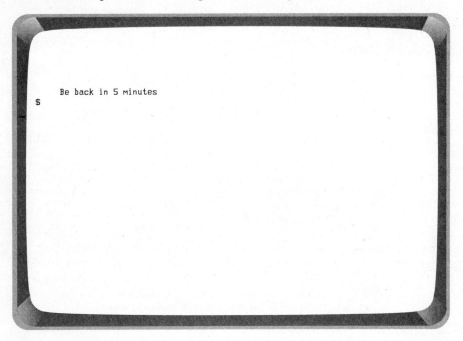

Fig. 8.1. *Screen output of a combined* clear *and* echo *command line.*

Notice that the command line you typed is not displayed on-screen. Figure 8.1 shows only the message echoed by the *second* command in the sequence. The first command in the sequence, clear, cleared the screen containing the command line. The next command, echo, printed the text of the message. Notice that the message text is not at the top of the cleared screen. The \n entries are included in the message given in the command to cause newlines to be output, thus moving the active line down the screen for each \n. From an outsider's point of view, you are using your screen as a message screen.

WARNING

Notice that the message in the preceding example—`Be back in 5 minutes`—is potentially dangerous. Never leave your terminal logged on in an untrusted working environment when you are not working with the terminal. Someone who knows you are away from the terminal could use your account to gain access to the system.

Setting and Seeing TTY Options with `stty`

To the UNIX system, your terminal is your human-to-machine interface—your gateway to UNIX computing. Although other hardware items have advanced significantly in the past few years, most UNIX terminals have remained largely unchanged. The `stty` or *set TTY* command enables the UNIX user to set and view many operational parameters of a terminal communications line.

Traditionally, terminals have been connected to UNIX systems through serial interfaces. Serial interfaces enable greater distances between the terminal and the computer than other communications methods, such as parallel connections. Serial interfaces have other advantages as well.

For example, serial communications connections require fewer physical wires for a minimal connection than other methods do. Serial connections can be made with three wires; parallel connections require at least eight. Because of these advantages, serial communications will remain the predominant communications method for multiterminal UNIX systems.

Not surprisingly, UNIX offers the `stty` command to enable control by the user of certain communications parameters. The `stty` command's control isn't limited to communications parameters, however. Over the years, `stty` has been upgraded by UNIX system contributors to include a number of input/output related capabilities. Today, `stty` is useful for setting and viewing non-serial communication parameters, too.

About High Function Terminals . . .

Many smaller UNIX systems, such as workstations or personal-computer based systems, take advantage of the built-in screen and keyboard. These built-in devices are treated by UNIX as terminals. Nearly always, the device drivers associated with these built-in "terminals" take advantage of the special functionality of the hardware of the devices. One term for these built-in terminals is *High Function Terminal* or HFT. The VGA screen on the IBM PS/2 AIX system, for instance, is an HFT capable of displaying color, bit-mapped graphics, and extended ASCII characters. The direct hardware connection of the PS/2's HFT screen enables AIX to communicate with the screen at very high rates that are many times faster than the serial-communication rates of standard terminals.

About High Function Terminals . . .(continued)

The display of some Sun Microsystems workstations, such as the 4/110, incorporate three separate screen-driver cables, which conduct red, green, and blue signals to the display. The display's viewing surface is divided into hundreds of thousands of points called *pixels*. The electron beam in the picture tube of the display scans across each pixel, and the electron energy excites the special phosphorus on the viewing surface, which in turn causes the surface to glow. A white glow results from the electron beam's scanning of pixels, with the red, green, and blue signals present in equal proportion. A red glow comes from the enabling of the red signal only. Purple results from a mix of red and blue signals. In fact, an entire rainbow of colors is possible, based on the correct combinations of reds, blues, and greens.

The same basic principle is at work with all color displays. The number of colors that a display can render in a pixel is directly related to the number of combinations of red, green, and blue that the screen's driving electronics can differentiate.

Even though HFTs are not serial-communications devices, the `stty` command includes options to set some operations of HFTs. Although `stty` reports about serial parameters such as baud rate and parity, HFTs do not use the serial-communications settings of `stty`.

The capabilities of `stty` are divided into related categories or *modes*. Modes are groups of options to the `stty` command. You don't present a mode to `stty`. You give `stty` options which belong to a mode category. Looking at the mode categories of `stty` options can help you understand the many options of `stty`. Table 8.1 shows the various modes of `stty` as well as a description of the area of each mode's control.

Table 8.1
Modes for the `stty` Command

Mode	Description
Control	Manages serial-communication parameters for the terminal line
Input	Controls the interpretation of data coming from the terminal to the UNIX system
Output	Controls those aspects of data sent by the UNIX system to the terminal
Local	Controls the interpretation of special characters and case conversion
Assignment	Establishes characters that the system will use for back spacing, end-of-file, kill, and other actions
Combination	Provides options that combine two or more functions based on other `stty` options

As an ordinary user, you will most likely never use all of the options offered with the stty command. Note that some implementations of UNIX offer an expanded number of stty options. In this chapter, you'll read about and see examples of the most commonly used options. The stty examples here are compliant with the SVID variants of UNIX. The BSD stty options are slightly different in some cases.

Understanding the Syntax of stty

You'll learn about stty by reading about each mode's options. This approach will enable you to better understand the scope of stty. The various modes' options serve as arguments in stty syntax. The general syntax of the stty command is as follows:

```
stty [-a] [-g] [argument1 argument2 . . .]
```

When you issue the stty command with no arguments, stty reports the current settings but does not change any setting. The -a option instructs stty to display all settings.

The -g option instructs stty to output the settings in a form that can be used for an abbreviated, redirected input to another stty command. The -g option is useful for storing the settings of stty in a file or variable for subsequent resetting to the previous value.

argument1 and argument2 are also optional. They instruct stty to make a setting corresponding to the given key words. If one or more key words are given as arguments to stty, no report of settings is returned to the screen. You can give one or more setting key words in any order as arguments to stty.

Reporting Current TTY Settings

You use stty most often when you want a report of the current settings of the TTY (terminal) communications link to the system. The command reports the I/O parameters of the standard input device on the standard output device. In other words, you see information about your terminal on your screen. To use stty in its simplest reporting form, enter the command at the prompt as follows:

```
$ stty <Return>
speed 9600 baud;    ispeed 9600 baud;    ospeed 9600 baud;
-parity hupcl clocal
swtch = ^@; susp = ^@;
brkint -inpck -istrip icrnl onlcr
echo echoe echok
```

What you see in the command's report are the most common of the current TTY settings. A setting beginning with a minus sign (–) indicates that the action of the option is not in place.

NOTE Don't confuse the association of the minus character in an `stty` setting with the minus character that denotes an option in a command line. When reading `stty` settings, you can substitute the word "not" for the minus sign. Each item in the report corresponds to one parameter that `stty` can control.

Although you can refer to table 8.2 for any of the common settings associated with your terminal-to-UNIX link, the most common settings you may reference are `speed` and `parity`. You recall that the system's speed and parity settings must match those established on your terminal.

Table 8.2
Common STTY Settings and Descriptions

Option	Description
Control Mode	
`speed 9600 baud`	The combined input-and-output baud rate of the serial-communications port.
`ispeed 9600 baud`	The input baud rate of the port.
`ospeed 9600 baud`	The output baud rate of the port.
`-parity`	Parity is not included.
`hupcl`	The line is hung up (modem disconnected) after the last clear.
`clocal`	The communications line is directly connected to the system (local) rather than through a modem.
Assignment Mode	
`swtch = ^@`	The < ^@ > character is assigned to the switch function.
`susp = ^@;`	The < ^@ > character is assigned to the suspend function.
Input Mode	
`brkint`	Signals an interupt when a break is detected.
`-inpck`	Input parity error-checking is not enabled.
`-istrip`	Input characters are not stripped to 7 bits.
`icrnl`	Changes a carriage-return character to a newline character.
Output Mode	
`onlcr`	Sends both a carriage return and newline to the terminal instead of just a newline.
Local Mode	
`echo`	Echoes every character typed.
`echoe`	Blanks an erased character.
`echok`	Outputs a newline character after a kill character.

You do not have to establish any input-output parameters in order to use your terminal. All TTY parameters are initialized for you when you log on to the system. In fact, even if you change one or more parameters, the default settings will be initialized again when you (or someone else) log on the same terminal the next time.

The simple (no options) form of the `stty` command shows you the most common settings to the TTY, but it does not show you all of them. To see all of the settings, you use the `-a` (*all*) option. Try the command in the following form:

```
$ stty -a <Return>
```

This time, the system responds with a more complete listing. This listing reports all TTY settings for the terminal you are using. The report looks like the following:

```
speed 9600 baud;   ispeed 9600 baud;   ospeed 9600 baud;
line = 0; intr = DEL; quit = ^\; erase = ^H; kill = ^U; eof = ^D;
eol = ^@; swtch = ^@;susp = ^@;
-parenb -parodd cs8 -cstopb hupcl cread clocal -loblk - ctsflow -rtsflow
-ignbrk brkint ignpar -parmrk -inpck -istrip -inlcr -igncr icrnl -iuclc
ixon ixany -ixoff
isig icanon -xcase echo echoe echok -echonl -noflsh -iexten -tostop
opost -olcuc onlcr -ocrnl -onocr -onlret -ofill -ofdel
```

You see all of the settings you saw as output of the simple `stty` command as well as many more. Table 8.3 lists the options of the `stty` command when issued with the `-a` option.

Table 8.3 mentions certain special characters, such as the interrupt, kill, quit, and erase characters.

A control character is assigned to the erase, kill, interrupt, quit, EOF, EOL, switch, or special-function characters. The control character is preceded by a caret (^) character in the assignment. For example, the end-of-file character is <^D>.

For more information on the meanings and format of these special characters, see Chapter 5 and Appendix D.

The `stty` command offers the `-g` option to produce the report output in an abbreviated form. The report form gives the hexadecimal values of the settings. To see the hexadecimal values, enter the following command:

```
$ $ stty -g <Return>
```

You see the reported settings as follows:

```
d06:5:cbd:3b:7f:1c:8:15:4:0:0:0:0
```

To you, this report may seem even more cryptic than the standard report. Actually, the intention of the `-g` option is not to produce an output for you to read, but rather, to produce an output suitable for redirection as input to another `stty` command.

Table 8.3
Options of stty -a

Option	Description
Control Mode	
parenb (-parenb)	Enables (disables) parity generation and detection.
parodd (-parodd)	Selects odd (even) parity.
0	Hangs up the phone line (the modem) immediately.
50 75 110 134 150 200 300 600 1200 1800 2400 4800 9600 19200	Sets the baud rate of the terminal to one of these rates, if possible.
ispeed 50 75 110 134 150 1200 1800 3400 4800 9600 19200	Sets line-input baud rate separately to one of these rates.
ospeed 50 75 110 134 150 1200 1800 3400 4800 9600 19200	Sets line-output baud rate separately to one of these baud rates.
hupcl (-hupcl)	Hangs up (does not hang up) the modem connection on the last close.
hup (-hup)	The same as hupcl (-hupcl).
cstopb (-cstopb)	Uses two (one) stop bits per character.
cread (-cread)	Enables (disables) the receiver.
clocal (-clocal)	Assumes a line without (with) modem control.
ctsflow (-ctsflow)	Enables CTS (*clear to send*) protocol for a modem or non-modem communication line.
rtsflow (-rtsflow)	Enables RTS (*request to send*) signaling for a modem or non-modem line.
Input Modes	
ignbrk (-ignbrk)	Ignores (does not ignore) break on input.
brkint (-brkint)	Signals (does not signal) an interrupt on a break.
ignpar (-ignpar)	Ignores (does not ignore) parity errors.

Table 8.3—continued

Option	Description
parmrk (-parmrk)	Marks (does not mark) parity errors.
inpck (-inpck)	Enables (disables) input parity checking.
istrip (-istrip)	Strips (does not strip) input characters to 7 bits.
inlcr (-inlcr)	Maps (does not map) newline to a carriage return on input from the terminal.
igncr (-igncr)	Ignores (does not ignore) a carriage return on input from the terminal.
icrnl (-icrnl)	Maps (does not map) a carriage return to a newline character on input from the terminal.
iuclc (-iuclc)	Maps (does not map) uppercase letters to lowercase on input.
ixon (-ixon)	Enables (disables) start/stop output control. Output is stopped by sending an ASCII DC3 (XOFF) and started by sending an ASCII DC1 (XON). On the keyboard, XOFF is < ^ S>, and XON is < ^ Q>.
ixany (-ixany)	Allows any character (only < ^ Q>) to restart output to the terminal.
ixoff (-ixoff)	Requests that the system send (not send) start/stop characters to the terminal when the system's input queue is nearly empty or full.

Output Modes

Option	Description
opost (-opost)	Post-processes output (does not post-process output; ignores all other output modes).
olcuc (-olcuc)	Maps (does not map) lowercase alphabetic characters to uppercase on output to the terminal.
onlcr (-onlcr)	Maps (does not map) a newline to a carriage-return/line-feed on output to the terminal.
ocrnl (-ocrnl)	Maps (does not map) a carriage return to a newline on output from the terminal.
onocr (-onocr)	Does not (does) output carriage returns at column zero (the first-line position) of the terminal. *Note:* This option's format is the reverse of the others; the default is to *not* output the result.
onlret (-onlret)	On the terminal, the newline performs (does not perform) the CR function in addition to the line-feed function.

Table 8.3—continued

Option	Description
Local Modes	
isig (-isig)	Enables (disables) the checking of characters against the special interrupt and quit characters.
icanon (-icanon)	Enables (disables) canonical (unprocessed) input (erase and kill processing).
xcase (-xcase)	Canonical (unprocessed) upper/lowercase presentation.
echo (-echo)	Echoes back (does not echo) every character typed at the keyboard.
echoe (-echoe)	Echoes (does not echo) an erase character as a space.
echok (-echok)	Echoes (does not echo) a newline after a kill character.
noflsh (-noflsh)	Disables (enables) a buffer flush after an interrupt or quit.
Combination Modes	
evenp or parity	Enables even parity and a character size of 7 bits.
oddp	Enables odd parity and a character size of 7 bits.
-parity -evenp -oddp	Disables parity and sets character size of 8 bits.
raw (-raw or cooked)	Enables (disables) raw input and output (no erase, kill, interrupt, quit, EOT, or output post-processing).
nl (-nl)	Unsets (sets) icrnl, onlcr. -nl unsets inlcr, igncr, ocrnl, and onlret.
lcase (-lcase)	Sets (unsets) xcase, iuclc, and olcuc.
LCASE (-LCASE)	Produces the same results as lcase or -lcase).
sane	Resets all options needed to reasonable values.

Note: This option is useful when a terminal's current stty settings are totally improper (insane). |

For example, you may want to change some of the TTY settings for a temporary purpose. Before you make the changes, you can "save" the current settings in a file or a variable. While working with changes that you intend to use during a single session, save the old settings in a variable. If you are using the Bourne shell, enter the following command:

```
$ OLDTTY=`stty -g` <Return>
```

As you know from Chapter 5, the variable OLDTTY is created and assigned the output of the stty -g command. The accent grave (backquote ") characters that enclose the command tell the shell to substitute the output of the command in the assignment. As a result of this assignment command, OLDTTY contains the hexadecimal version of the TTY settings.

After saving the current settings, you can modify settings with stty. The TTY uses the new settings. When you are finished with the new settings and want to return to the original settings, you can issue a stty command using the variable OLDTTY as an argument as in the following:

> $ **stty $OLDTTY** <Return>

The shell extracts the hexadecimal setting list from the OLDTTY variable and substitutes the list as an argument list for the stty command. As a result, the TTY assignments revert to the original settings. This variable method of setting the TTY saves many keystrokes and ensures that you don't mistakenly omit the previous value of a changed item.

If you commonly use two or more TTY option combinations, you can redirect the output of stty -g to a file for subsequent use in reverting to previous settings. The advantage of redirecting the output to a file instead of a variable is that the file is more permanent. When you log off, the OLDTTY variable is lost. To use the variable in your next session, you have to reassign it. The file named oldtty, however, will be there in your next session. To direct the output of stty to a file, enter the following:

> $ **stty -g > oldtty** <Return>

To reestablish the old TTY values, enter the following command:

> $ **stty < oldtty** <Return>

The stty command will accept arguments from the file as though you had typed them from your keyboard.

Controlling the SCO Console with `setcolor`

The setcolor command is available for SCO UNIX and XENIX users. The European version of setcolor is setcolour. Both commands are identical. The setcolor command controls screen color and other screen attributes of the console terminal on an SCO system.

 If you do not use an SCO system, you may want to skim this section for general information on screen control. Your system may have a command equivalent to SCO's setcolor. For example, the AIX PS/2 system includes the display command that serves the same purpose. Check with your system administrator about commands that control the colors on your terminal.

The `setcolor` command controls screen colors by adjusting the attributes of the characters presented on the screen. Table 8.4 lists the attributes used by `setcolor` to determine when to impose an assigned color.

Table 8.4
Character Attributes Used by the `setcolor` Command

Attribute	Description
Normal foreground	The color of text corresponding to the characters printed on a cleared screen.
Normal Background	The color corresponding to a clear screen.
Reverse	The colors corresponding to the foreground and background of reverse-video output. (If normal video is white on black, reverse video is black on white.)
Graphics	The colors corresponding to the foreground and background colors of graphics characters (extended line and box-drawing characters).

Understanding Video Attributes

To understand how to use `setcolor` with screen attributes, you must first understand the attributes associated with characters presented on-screen. Normal foreground text is ordinary text with no distinction. You see normal foreground text when you issue UNIX commands. Normal background is the color (or lack of color) that you see directly behind each character of normal text.

Reverse text or video is an attribute that programs control. Programs often utilize reverse video for the purpose of emphasizing the text. By default, reverse text consists of black characters on a white background. Most UNIX commands do not utilize the reverse-video attribute, but many applications programs do.

A capable terminal goes into reverse-video mode after receiving a special character sequence called an *escape* sequence. In fact, most terminals' special attributes, such as underlining, color, character width, and graphics modes, are initialized by escape sequences. The graphics attribute is the attribute associated with line-drawing characters. You connect line-drawing characters to make boxes, block borders, screen dividers, and other non-alphabetical geometric shapes. Some terminals are capable of producing line-graphic characters, but not all terminals are.

The `setcolor` command's control works with only an SCO-type display, which is based on a PC-type display adapter. Terminals complying with the SCO version of the `ansi` termcap entry also correctly respond to escape sequences initiated by the `setcolor` command. The terminal emulator program, TERM, from Century Software, for example, incorporates an `scoansi` emulation that enables correct color control of the emulation by `setcolor`.

The `setcolor` command is an SCO enhancement to UNIX and is available on SCO systems only. `setcolor` may not work properly on terminals other than the built-in system console display. Depending on your SCO system hardware, some `setcolor` features may be unavailable to you.

Understanding the Syntax of `setcolor`

The syntax for the `setcolor` command is as follows:

```
setcolor [-nbrgopc] [argument1] [argument2. . .]
```

When issued with no options, the `setcolor` command displays a color grid of available colors and a listing of options. Figure 8.2 is the display you see when you issue `setcolor` with no options or arguments.

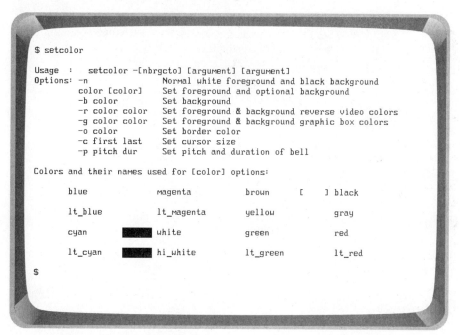

```
$ setcolor

Usage  :   setcolor -[nbrgcto] [argument] [argument]
Options: -n              Normal white foreground and black background
         color [color]   Set foreground and optional background
         -b color        Set background
         -r color color  Set foreground & background reverse video colors
         -g color color  Set foreground & background graphic box colors
         -o color        Set border color
         -c first last    Set cursor size
         -p pitch dur    Set pitch and duration of bell

Colors and their names used for [color] options:

    blue            magenta         brown      [    ] black

    lt_blue         lt_magenta      yellow          gray

    cyan         ████  white        green           red

    lt_cyan      ████  hi_white      lt_green        lt_red

$
```

Fig. 8.2. *The* `setcolor` *Palette screen.*

Note that in this book, figure 8.2 is a black-and-white rendition of the color screen. On your color display, however, you'll see a colored rectangle beside each of the color names.

You can issue `setcolor` alone to remind yourself of its syntax or the color choices. You issue `setcolor` or `setcolour` (the European version) with options to control the colors of the screen. You can specify one or more options. Table 8.5 lists the options available with `setcolor`.

Table 8.5
Commonly Used Options for the `setcolor` Command

Option	Action
-n	Sets the screen to normal (white characters on black).
-b *color*	Sets the background to the specified *color*.
-r *color1 color2*	Sets the foreground color of the reverse-video characters to *color1*, and the background color of the reverse-video characters to *color2*.
-g *color1 color2*	Sets the foreground color of the graphics characters to *color1*, and the background color of the graphics characters to *color2*.
-o *color*	Sets the color of the screen's overscan area (the border of some displays) to *color*.
-p *pitch duration*	Sets the pitch of the console's bell signal to the number of microseconds specified by *pitch*. Sets the duration of one bell signal to the number of 1/5 seconds specified by *duration*.
-c *first last*	Sets the scan lines of the cursor to *first* and *last* to control the size and position of the cursor.

The color arguments available for use with `setcolor` are the following:

```
blue        magenta      brown      black
lt_blue     lt_magenta   yellow     gray
cyan        white        green      red
lt_cyan     hi_white     lt_green   lt_red
```

To control the color of normal text, use the `setcolor` command with one color argument as in the following:

```
setcolor color
```

This command sets the foreground of normal text to the specified *color*, but does not affect other screen colors.

To include two color arguments with `setcolor`, use the following syntax:

```
setcolor color1 color2
```

This command sets both the foreground and also the background colors of normal text, but does not affect other screen colors.

Using `setcolor` To Change Colors and Backgrounds

If you have a color terminal that responds to `setcolor`, you can vary your normal text color for UNIX and other work. You can, for example, view white letters on a blue background by issuing the following command:

    $ **setcolor white blue** <Return>

This command uses a form of `setcolor` syntax in which you use no options, but give the color arguments for the default normal text. If you now run an application that uses reverse-video text, such as SCO's Office Portfolio, you can change the reverse video from the default black letters on white to blue letters on white by using the following command:

    $ **setcolor -r blue white** <Return>

Applications such as Office Portfolio use line-graphics characters. To establish white lines against a blue background, use the following command:

    $ **setcolor -g white blue** <Return>

If you pick a screen-color scheme that you don't like, you can revert to the default screen attributes by using the following command:

    $ **setcolor -n** <Return>

The −n (*normal*) option resets the screen to normal values. The −n screen attributes are the same as when the system was turned on.

You can clear your screen with `clear` after setting a background color. That way, you can see what the background color looks like immediately and change it if you want to.

Two good examples of how `setcolor` affects the look of an applications program can be seen in figures 8.3 and 8.4. The screens show the opening menu of the SCO Office Portfolio application. Office Portfolio contains normal, reversed, and line-graphics screen elements.

In figure 8.3, you see white letters on a black background. The white boxes are white-line graphics characters on a black background. The white areas containing black text, such as the word `Application`, or the number `13` date on the calendar, are reverse-video attribute areas.

Although figure 8.4 shows the same menu as figure 8.3, the `setcolor` command has reversed the screen's look. Normal foreground was set to black; normal background was set to white. Graphics lines were set to black on a white background; reverse video was set to white on a black background. Again, remember that the screen figures in this book are rendered in black and white, but you can experiment with combinations in any available color.

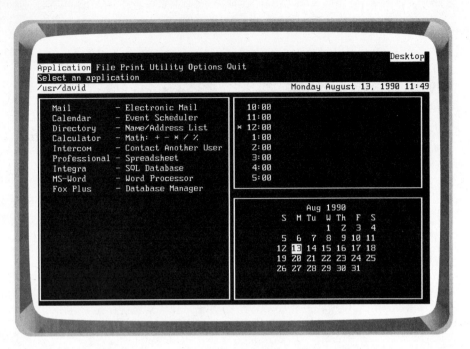

Fig. 8.3. *The Office Portfolio screen with normal attributes set.*

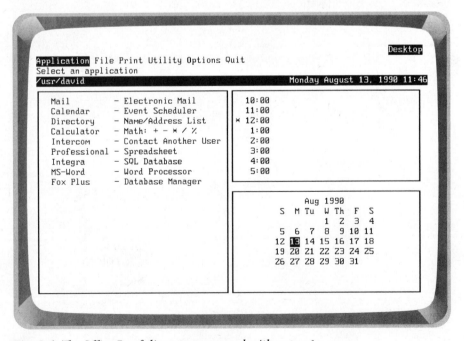

Fig. 8.4. *The Office Portfolio screen reversed with* `setcolor`.

Controlling the AIX PS/2 Display with `display`

The AIX `display` command is similar to the SCO `setcolor` command. `display` is an enhanced command that is not part of the normal UNIX command set. The `display` command controls the built-in system-console display of the computer. `display` controls the background and foreground colors of normal text.

The colors available with `display` come from the active palette. By default, the active palette contains 8 possible background colors and 16 possible foreground colors. The `display` command also controls the selection of the active palette and the current display font. This presentation will not discuss the palette and font-selection capabilities of `display`. You can assume that the default active palette and font are suitable for normal use. AIX enables virtual terminal operation for the system console. You can activate several virtual terminals at one time. Each virtual terminal may have its own `display` colors set.

 The `display` command for setting screen colors is available to AIX users. Other implementations of UNIX may use the `display` command for other **NOTE** purposes. Therefore, you should try the commands in this section only if you are an AIX primary console user.

Issuing the `display` Command

The general form of the `display` command is as follows:

> `display [-b colornum]` or `display [-f colornum]`

The `-b` option is the *background* option. The `-f` option is the *foreground* option. You cannot issue both a `-b` and a `-f` in the same `display` command. Issuing the `display` command with no color-number arguments for the included option produces a color grid (palette) and enables the arrow keys. You can then use the arrow keys to select the desired color.

The `-b` option with no color argument lists the active palette of 8 background colors and prompts you to select a number corresponding to the color you want as the new background color.

The `-b` option with a number argument (from 1 to 8) sets the background color to the color that corresponds to the selected number. The numbers for colors are based on the active palette.

The `-f` option with no color argument lists the active palette of 16 foreground colors and prompts you to select a number corresponding to the color you want as the new foreground color.

The `-f` option with a number argument (from 1 to 16) sets the foreground color to the color that corresponds with the selected number.

The colors available for foreground selection are shown in table 8.6.

Table 8.6
Foreground Colors for the `display` Command

Color	Number	Color	Number
Black	1	Gray	9
Red	2	Bright red	10
Green	3	Bright green	11
Yellow	4	Brown	12
Blue	5	Bright blue	13
Magenta	6	Bright magenta	14
Cyan	7	Bright cyan	15
White	8	Bright white	16

When you include a color argument with the `display` command, you use the number that corresponds to the color you want. All 16 colors are available for foreground colors. For background color, you can use color numbers 1 through 8. If you use a number that is not in the proper range for either foreground or background, you see an `illegal argument` error message, and the current colors remain unchanged.

Using `display` To Change Screen Colors and Backgrounds

When most AIX PS/2 systems boot, the main console display shows green characters on a black background. The display looks very similar to a green phosphor monochrome terminal display. To change the green foreground color by selecting from a displayed palette, issue the following command:

```
$ display -f <Return>
```

This command produces a color-selection screen that shows the current foreground colors as well as background colors of the default palette. At the top of the screen, in the center, you see a sample window containing the current color of text against the current background color. The color palette is arranged horizontally. The text FOREGROUND COLORS is highlighted. If you press the down-arrow key, the highlight moves below the palette to the BACKGROUND text. The up-arrow key returns the highlight to the FOREGROUND COLORS highlight. By highlighting either item of text, you elect to select the color for that item.

With FOREGROUND COLORS selected, press the right-arrow key. You'll notice that one of the numbers above the colors in the palette is highlighted. The text in the sample window changes to match the selected color. As you press the right-arrow key again, the next number to the right is highlighted, and the sample text changes color. The left-arrow key moves the highlight to the next number on the left. By using the right- and left-arrow keys, you can position the highlight to the number of the color you want for the foreground. If you select BACKGROUND COLORS, you can use the same exercise to select the desired background color.

When you have selected the colors you want, press <S> (or <s>) for *save*. The display command terminates. The UNIX prompt is back with the new colors. You can terminate the display command without saving changes by pressing <Q> (or <q>) for *quit*.

You don't have to use the display selection screen to change screen colors. You can set either the foreground or the background color by issuing the display command with the appropriate option and the number of the desired color as an argument. To set the foreground to bright white, issue the following command:

$ **display -f 16** <Return>

To set the background color to blue, issue the following command:

$ **display -b 5** <Return>

Changing the foreground and background colors of your screen from time to time helps prolong the life of the CRT.

Setting Tabs on Your Terminal with tabs

A *tab* is an ASCII character that instructs a terminal, printer, or other printing device to skip from the current printing position to the next established tab stop. The number of character positions skipped is determined by the relative position of the next tab-stop setting. A terminal must incorporate tab capability to enable tab-character action. A terminal must have hardware-settable tab stops in order to be set by the tabs command.

By default, UNIX's "standard" tab stops are 8 characters apart. You can alter your terminal's tab stops by using the tabs command. Altering your tab stops (or simply tabs) gives you more control over the appearance of text on your display or printer.

If you are preparing an outline, you may want to indent each level of the outline by 3 characters in addition to the preceding level. Screenplay writers, for example, follow a strict format for indentation based on action, dialog, and screen direction. Not all levels of indentation in a screenplay are based on repetitive tabs. Some tab stops are arbitrary. One tab stop may be 5 character positions in from the left margin while the next tab may be set 20 characters further. tabs gives you control over repetitive and arbitrary tab-stop settings.

Understanding the Tab Character

Many people confuse a series of space characters with a tab character when they view both on-screen. If a terminal has a tab stop at the 8th character position on a line, pressing the <Tab> key will cause the cursor to skip the first seven character positions and stop on the 8th. You can position the cursor in the 8th character position by pressing the space bar seven times.

 This discussion of tabs and character position assumes that you do not count the character positions taken up during command-line input by the UNIX command prompt.

When you view two indented lines that result from tabbing and spacing an equal distance, you can't tell which line is indented by a tab and which line is indented by spaces. The difference involves the terminal's interpretation of the tab character.

To more clearly see the difference, think of a stream of characters coming from the keyboard and going to a file. If you press the <Tab> key, a tab character goes into the file. If you press the <space bar> seven times, seven space characters go into the file.

You can actually create this character stream using the cat command. cat gets its input from the standard input, which is your keyboard. You can direct the output of cat to a file. cat is useful for creating short text files. Here's an example that involves a tab character. Enter the following command:

    $ **cat > tabfile** <Return>

The cursor drops to the next line and awaits your keystrokes as the standard input. The first key that you press is <Tab>; the cursor skips 7 character positions and stops on position 8 on the line. Position 8 is UNIX's default first tab stop. With the default tab stops set to 8, your screen looks like the following:

                <—this is a tab stop. <Return> (*This line started with a tab*)
                <—this is 7 spaces. <Return>
    < ^D><Return>
    $

The <^D> character in the last input line is UNIX's end-of-file (EOF) character. The EOF character signals cat that you are finished entering characters from the keyboard. You always end a text file you create using cat with a < ^D>. When you press the final <Return>, cat writes the characters to the file.

Now look at the tabfile contents by issuing the following command:

    $ **cat tabfile** <Return>

The command sends the contents of tabfile to the screen, and you see the following:

                <—this is a tab stop.
                <—this is 7 spaces.

Notice that the two lines of text start at the same column position on their respective lines. From this view, the contents of the first seven characters of each line appear to be spaces. Actually, the first line contains a tab character as the first character. The first line's second character is the < character, which begins the readable text message. By changing the terminal's tab stops from the default of 8, the difference in the lines' beginning positions becomes more apparent.

To set tab stops an equal distance from the last tab (called a *repetitive-tab specification*), issue the `tabs` command with the tab stop as an option. To set tabs at every two positions, issue the following command:

```
$ tabs -2 <Return>
```

Some terminals may show the cursor rapidly scanning the screen as the terminal establishes new tab settings. Other terminals won't respond to the `tabs` command with any action other than to establish the new settings.

The preceding command sets a repetitive tab stop every two positions. To see the effect of the new tab settings on the contents of `tabfile`, issue the `cat` command again and look at the line positioning, as in the following sequence:

```
$ cat tabfile <Return>
 <—this is a tab stop.
     <—this is 7 spaces.
$
```

You can easily see that the terminal treated the tab character in the first line as a special character and tabbed to the first stop at column two. The terminal treated the tab character in a special way when the default tab stops of 8 were in effect as well. You couldn't discern the treatment just by viewing the first `cat` example of the contents of `tabfile`.

You can set non-default tab stops for some specific purpose and then reestablish the default settings when the special purpose is finished. You can set the default tabs to 8 by issuing the `tabs` command with no options as in the following:

```
$ tabs <Return>
```

Remember that you will see a corresponding number of spaces displayed between a tab character and the next printable character when you alter tabs, but only the tab character is sent (and stored) when you press a tab key.

Understanding the Syntax of `tabs`

The general form of the `tabs` command is as follows:

```
tabs [tabspec] [-Tterminal] [+mnum]
```

When you issue `tabs` with no options, the command sets the terminal's tabs to the default of 8.

The `tabspec` is an optional entry from one of the following three categories:

1. A repetitive specification given as a single number such as `-2`.

   This is the tab-specification category used in the `tabfile` examples in the previous section.

2. An arbitrary format given as an ascending series of numbers separated by commas.

   Up to 40 numbers can be given in `tabspec`. An example series can be `1,12,20,32,40`. Numbers in the series can be expressed as an additive of the preceding number, as in `1,+11,+8,+12,+8`. These two example tab specification series result in identical tab stops.

   A `--file` specification is given when the first line of `file` contains the desired tab specification. Note that one `-` character delimits the option and another `-` is part of the file specification. If you assign a file name, such as `$HOME\tbspec`, to a variable such as `TABS1`, be sure that the assignment looks like the following:

   `$` **`TABS1=-$HOME\tbspec`** <Return>

   You then issue the command as follows:

   `$` **`tabs -$TABS1`** <Return>

   If you name the file on the command line, just remember to use two minus-sign characters in front of the literal file name.

3. A "canned" tab specification represented by a code.

   Canned specifications establish tabs based on the requirements of language-compiler programs. Ordinary users seldom use one of the canned specifications. Consult the Command Reference for descriptions of the canned tab specification options.

The `-Tterminal` option represents the type of terminal being set according to `/etc/termcap`. `terminal` is either the `termcap` name of your terminal or the variable metastring `$TERM`. If your `$TERM` variable is already assigned and exported, you can omit the `-T` option because `tabs` will already have the terminal type.

The `-mnum` option enables a left-margin setting on capable terminals. You provide a number value for `num` that moves all given tab stops over by that number. Be aware that only certain terminals are capable of setting hardware margins.

Determining Tab Problems

Some terminals and built-in consoles do not respond to the `tabs` command. If you don't see the correct tab stops when viewing output after setting tabs with `tabs`, you can use another command to establish a correctly formatted output. The `newform` command issued with the `-itabspec` option replaces tab characters in the output with spaces that correspond to `tabspec`.

To view a text file containing tabs on the standard output, and to establish tabs at every 5th position, use the following syntax:

```
newform -i-5textfile <Return>
```

You provide the name of the text file you want to see in place of `textfile`. (The file name you use with the `newform` command should be a text file—not a binary file.)

You can vary the tab stops using this syntax by varying the tab specification that follows the `-i` option. Although `newform` has other formatting purposes, you are most likely to use it to establish tabbed output on your terminal. The other uses for `newform` are not presented in this book. If you want more information on the `newform` command, consult your User's Manual.

If you use an arbitrary tab specification with `tabs`, and you mistakenly get one of the tab stops out of ascending sequence, you will see an error message like the following:

```
illegal tabs
```

When you see this message, check your tab specification and reissue the `tabs` command with your corrections.

When you attempt to set two different tab stops to the same number value, `tabs` displays the following message:

```
illegal increment
```

This type of error occurs most often when a + increment is given for one stop, while another stop is an absolute number value. For example, the tab specification `2,+2,4` results in the second and third stops equaling 4. This tab specification will result in the `illegal increment` error.

If you enter a canned tab specification code erroneously by making a typographical error, you will see the following error message:

```
unknown tab code
```

To correct this situation, reissue the `tabs` command with a legal canned code.

The `tabs` command clears up to 20 tabs before setting new tabs. It is possible for terminals with hardware-settable tabs to have over 20 tab stops set. If you press over 20 tab keys, you may find that the remaining tab stops have not been cleared. Using over 20 tabs on a single line is unlikely, so you will probably never encounter this situation. Just be aware that you may encounter unexpected tab stops beyond the 20th tab stop.

Using the Disk Device-Related Commands

So far in this chapter, you've seen commands that deal with terminal devices. UNIX provides many commands that deal with disk drives as devices. This section covers two commands—df and du—that deal with disk devices. Other disk-related UNIX commands deal with the file systems that are stored on disk drives. Although the system administrator handles most of the administration of disk devices, this section gives you the opportunity to see which disk commands you can work with as a user. In the process, you'll get a bit more understanding of how UNIX organizes and maintains its file system.

Determining Available Disk Space with df

The df command reports the available space and available i-nodes of the file system. Recall that your files are saved and stored on the system's disk drive(s). Your ability to save the files you create depends on the availability of sufficient free disk space. If your system has a separate mounted user file system, your files are stored on the portion of the system disk that is allocated to the user file system. Because you are a cooperative "citizen" in a multiuser UNIX setting, you should be aware of the resources available to you and your fellow UNIX users.

The df command enables you to determine the file-storage resource. Before you read about the command, you should understand more about disk storage under the UNIX operating system. The next section will help you understand. Don't worry about memorizing the principles presented. You need only gain a fundamental understanding of disk-storage techniques to see more clearly how df does its job and what its report means.

Understanding Blocks

For storage and tracking efficiency, files are stored on a disk in some multiple of 512-byte sectors. This multiple is called a *logical block*, or simply a *block*. Most often, UNIX systems use two 512-byte sectors to form a 1024 byte (or 1K) logical block. A logical block's size is the primary multiplier of the size of disk buffers. In other words, the disk-buffer space in memory will hold a number of logical blocks with no excess buffer space wasted.

When you create, copy, or modify a file, UNIX handles the chore of saving the contents of the file. The UNIX file-storage mechanism reserves space for a file. UNIX reserves enough blocks on the disk to hold the file. With a minimum space allocation block of 1024 bytes, even a 5-byte file will reduce available disk space by 1024 bytes. A 1025-byte file will not fit in a 1024-byte block, so an additional block is allocated to the file to store the additional byte. The 1025-byte file reduces the disk's available space by 2048 bytes.

Although it may seem that wasting space at the end of some blocks is the result of poor design, there is a good reason to allocate disk space in blocks. Remember that

UNIX must translate the file name into the physical location of the data on the disk. The physical locations of the disk are based on the block numbers of the file system(s) on the disk. As users delete files, the block space made available by the deletions is again available for the next new file or the expansion of an existing file. Deleting small files leaves blocks isolated within areas of allocated blocks. When a large file is saved, some of the blocks used to save the file are the isolated small blocks. The result is that the large file's blocks are spread across the disk as block-sized pieces of the file. In their physical relationship, these blocks are noncontiguous. This type of file is called a *fragmented* file.

To access all of the blocks of a fragmented file, the disk drive's head(s) must move to different disk cylinders, thus slowing a file's access. You can imagine the number of disk-head movements necessary to collect all parts of a fragmented 10K file if the block size is 1 byte. With a 1024-byte block, the file could be gathered in from the disk using 10 head movements at the most. The simple rule is that the larger the block size, the less the problem with fragmentation.

If most of the files on the system are large (for example, over 10K), the sum of the "wasted" space in the files' final blocks is only a small percentage of the total disk space. If most of the files are small (for example, under 100 bytes), a significant percentage of the disk's potential storage capacity is lost due to the unused portions of the files' blocks. In actual practice, the file sizes of UNIX systems vary greatly. The block size is selected by system designers to offer the best space utilization versus block access.

Understanding I-Nodes

When a file system is created, the person creating the file system (usually the system administrator) establishes the number of i-nodes in the file system's i-table. You recall that i-nodes are used by UNIX as the absolute identifiers of files, and therefore, their disk locations. The entry of a file's name in a directory is linked to the i-table by the i-node number or simply *i-number*.

The number of files that a file system (or subsequently a disk) can store is not only limited by the number of storage blocks, but also by the number of available i-nodes. For example, a file system consisting of 1000 blocks and 500 i-nodes will be unable to store a new file when it is storing 500 1K or smaller-sized files. The available space in this condition is still 500 blocks. No new files can be stored in those 500 blocks because no i-nodes in the i-table are available to link a new file's name. Although the available blocks and i-nodes in this example are purposefully small, the example serves to illustrate how the number of i-nodes must be balanced against the average file size in order to get the most from the disk's storage capabilities.

To take advantage of memory's speed, the i-table is read into memory from the disk when the system boots. The UNIX filing mechanism consults the memory based i-table to do file work. On the disk, the i-table is stored in a special block called the *superblock*. Every few seconds, the system updates the disk-based superblock to ensure that the superblock reflects the status of the memory-based i-table. If the system were to lose power, the superblock would contain information about the file system that would be, at the most, a few seconds out of date. Repairing the differences between the superblock and the entries in the directories would not be an overwhelming job.

Before shutting the system down, the system administrator uses the shutdown command. The shutdown command carries out the proper sequence of events for gracefully stopping the computer, including updating the superblock. After a successful shutdown, the superblock contains information about i-nodes that agrees with the entries in the directories.

Issuing the df Command

You issue the df command to see a report about the available disk space and available i-nodes. You normally issue the command if you save a large number of files (use many i-nodes) or if you save very large files (use many disk blocks). If your system is well maintained by your system administrator, you will not have to worry about running out of disk resources without warning. The system administrator will take preventative measures to keep the file-system resources available. If you don't have a full-time administrator, or you run your own stand-alone system, you should use df as your own preventative measure.

The form of df that you will use contains no options or arguments. The df command's options vary from implementation to implementation, as does the form of the command's output report. The df command, issued with no options, produces a default report that includes the information useful to you. Issue the command as follows:

```
$ df <Return>
```

The df command will consult an appropriate file for your system that lists the mounted file systems. The consulted file varies from system to system. On the SCO UNIX system, the file is called /etc/mnttab. On AIX, the file is called /etc/filesystems. Normally, df consults the values in the superblock for the file systems.

The SCO df response looks like this:

```
/          (/dev/root      ):    16238 blocks     9516 i-nodes
```

The first column, the /, represents the file system being reported. In this case, the file system is the root file system. The second column, containing the text in parentheses, is the device name of the file system. The third column reports the number of available disk blocks, and the last column reports the available i-nodes.

Because the superblock is updated "after the fact," the df report may be slightly off. Only under exceptional circumstances, such as power outage, will differences between the superblock and the file system be significant.

The report returned by df varies from implementation to implementation. As another example, here is an AIX report:

Device	Mounted on	Total	free	%used	ifree	%iused
/dev/hd33	/u	9228	9224	0%	971	1%
/dev/hd34	/que1	7268	3920	46%	506	34%
/dev/hd35	/	37040	3424	91%	1865	52%
/dev/hd38	/que1/tmp	5428	5376	1%	560	3%

The column heading Device indicates the system's device name for the file system, which IBM refers to as a *minidisk*. Users are most interested in the row beginning with /dev/hd33, which is the user file system. The AIX report shows the total number of kilobytes allocated to the file system under the heading Total. This total can be directly translated into blocks because each block is 1K. The column titled free shows the number of blocks available for allocation. The first %used heading gives the approximate percentage of the blocks of the file system allocation that is currently occupied. The iused heading gives the number of i-nodes used in the file system's i-table, and the percentage used is shown in the next column under the second %used heading. The Mounted on shows the point in the hierarchical file structure where each file-system storage begins.

The /u file system is normally one of the largest file systems on an AIX installation. You would expect a large user file system because /u is where the bulk of user file activity takes place. If the user file system row shows that the percentage of i-nodes or blocks used exceeds around 95%, you may want to point out this condition to the system administrator.

WARNING

You should be cautious about trying shell procedures (see Chapters 14 and 15) that create or copy files in a looping program flow. If the loop fails to terminate, or if the file arguments used as input are too general, such as when they include directory wild cards, you can easily exhaust the remaining disk space or i-nodes.

Another common problem that results in the exhaustion of available blocks is extensive file concatenation. Recall that the cat command can *concatenate* or join input files as an output file. If you concatenate using directory wild cards in the input specification, the resulting output file can be huge and take all available blocks. When a file system fills, you will see a message such as the following:

```
No room on slice:0
```

The designated slice refers to the file system which has filled. If you see a similar message or one that indicates that the supply of disk blocks or i-nodes is exhausted, the file you were saving has not been committed to the disk. Trying to save the file again will do no good. Other users trying to save files, either through applications or UNIX commands, will also see the message on their terminals.

If the file-system resource is exhausted, you should leave your terminal as it is and get help from the system administrator or a support person. Don't log off or clear your screen. The information on your screen and others users' screens, may help the system administrator determine whose work has not been properly saved. As a short-term recovery method, the system administrator may delete some unused user files, thus freeing enough space or i-nodes for pending work to be saved. As a longer-term measure, additional disk hardware may be installed, or the resources of existing hardware reallocated. By using df to keep an eye on available disk resources, you may be able to avoid the loss of your own work and inform the system administrator so that he can avoid the loss of other users' work.

Seeing Your Block Usage with du

The df command is useful for monitoring the overall availability of resource on the disk, but is not useful for determining the amount of disk resource used by individual files or directories of files. The du command is useful for determining the number of blocks occupied by files.

You use du to see the size of your files. Knowing a file's size gives you a quick way of determining whether a file is getting larger or smaller. You can see when an appended file, such as a log file, has become sufficiently large that you want to truncate it to free up storage space. You also can use du simply because you want to compare your file-storage usage with another user.

Understanding the Syntax of du

In its default format, you can issue the du command without options. For an ordinary user, the du command has two useful options. The general syntax of du is as follows:

```
du [-sa] [names]
```

Issued without arguments, du will report the block count total for all of the files in readable directories in the file system.

The -s option gives the grand total for the reported files.

The -a option causes an output line to be generated for each file.

The optional names argument names the files or directories that du is to access for the report. You supply a file specification or directory specification in place of names.

Issuing the du Command

Because you will most likely use du to determine the size of your own files or their grand-total block count, you will use two basic forms of du. The first form reports the total block count of your home directory's files and its child branches' files. du works through directories recursively, so when you specify your home directory as the names argument, you will get a count of all of your files in your home directory and subsequent subdirectories of your home directory.

The du examples use the $HOME metastring for substitution of your home directory's name. Be sure that HOME is assigned, or use the name of your home directory in place of $HOME.

Issue the following command:

$ **du −a $HOME** <Return>

du recursively processes your home directory and reports as follows:

```
    2          /usr/david/.profile
    1          /usr/david/clipdir
    1          /usr/david/wastebasket
    4          /usr/david/mbox
    0          /usr/david/mailfolders/.receipts
    0          /usr/david/mailfolders/mbox
    1          /usr/david/mailfolders
    2          /usr/david/.appllist
    1          /usr/david/mw.ini
    1          /usr/david/mytext/notes1
    1          /usr/david/mytext/notes2
    1          /usr/david/mytext/notes3
    4          /usr/david/mytext
    1          /usr/david/bin/colors1
    2          /usr/david/bin
    1          /usr/david/fox
    5          /usr/david/syntax.dcx
    1          /usr/david/words
    1          /usr/david/tabfile
   27          /usr/david
```

Notice that the first column shows the number of blocks occupied by the file or directory. Files with 0 blocks are empty files. Empty files occupy no disk space, even though they have directory entries. Any files in a subdirectory of the directory specified as the argument are reported before the directory itself. The block size reported for a directory does not include the files in the directory. If you add all of the block numbers in this report, you will get the total reported by the report's last line.

If you simply want a grand total of blocks for your home directory and its subdirectories, use the −s option as in the following command:

```
$ du −s $HOME  <Return>
27         /usr/david
$
```

Notice that the command reports the total line as the same total displayed in the previous du command. Use this form of du if you have dozens of files in your home directory. If you need to investigate a large grand total, you can then issue du with the −a option to see which (if any) files are taking the most space.

If you want to see directory-block totals, but don't want to see the sizes of individual files, you can issue du with no options, but with your home directory as an argument. Issue the following command:

```
$ du $HOME <Return>
```

The command outputs a report similar to the following:

```
1          /usr/david/clipdir
1          /usr/david/wastebasket
1          /usr/david/mailfolders
4          /usr/david/mytext
2          /usr/david/bin
1          /usr/david/fox
27         /usr/david
$
```

Issued with no options, du reports each subdirectory of /usr/david on its own line, but does not report individual files.

Summary

In this chapter, you learned about some user-oriented, device-related commands. You also learned a bit more about disk drives, the file system, and your terminal. The key points covered in this chapter include the following:

❏ You can determine your terminal's device name with tty.

❏ The purpose of the TERM variable is to store your terminal's termcap name for subsequent use by many UNIX commands.

❏ You can erase your screen with clear.

❏ You use stty to set and display your TTY option settings.

❏ SCO-console users control display colors with setcolor.

❏ AIX-console users control display colors with display.

❏ The tabs command sets hardware-settable tabs in your terminal.

❏ The df command reports available disk space and i-nodes for all mounted file systems.

❏ The du command reports the block usage of files and directories.

In the next chapter, you'll learn about a group of commands that directly relate to your participation in the UNIX multiuser, multitasking environment.

9

Participating in a Multiuser Environment

As you learned in Chapter 5, UNIX is a multiuser operating system that includes multitasking capabilities. Unlike an operating system such as MS-DOS, which supports only one user, the UNIX operating system can support many users on one system. This support capability defines the term *multiuser*.

UNIX also can work on several tasks concurrently—a capability known as *multitasking*. Because a computer's operation is very fast, each user gets the feeling that he or she is the only user on the system. UNIX gives the user this impression by "time-sharing" the processing power and storage capabilities of one computer among more than one user.

UNIX monitors a list—also known as a *queue*—of tasks that are waiting to be done. These tasks can include user jobs, operating-system tasks, mail, and background jobs. UNIX schedules "slices" of system time for each task. In "human time," each time slice is extremely short—a fraction of a second. In computer time, a time slice is a time period adequate for a program to progress through hundreds or thousands of instructions. The length of the time slice for each task may depend on the relative priority each task is assigned by the system administrator. UNIX works on one task from the queue for awhile, and then puts the task aside to begin work on another task, and so on. It then returns to the first task and works on it again. UNIX continues these cycles until it finishes a task and takes the task out of the queue. This process is all "invisible" to you, the user.

One advantage of this time-sharing feature is that you can run a specified program *in the background*. While the program is running in the background, you can continue entering commands and working with other material. UNIX employs the time-sharing method to balance your immediate commands and the ones running in the background.

The notion of background processing isn't as foreign as you might think. If you are given the tasks of filling a bucket from a slow faucet and retrieving a sponge from

241

the garage, you can do the two tasks in sequence or simultaneously. Chances are, you'll put the bucket under the faucet and begin filling it. You don't have to stand there and watch. The bucket fills on its own. You can proceed with your work by retrieving the sponge from the garage while the bucket is filling in the background. You don't worry about the filling bucket until that task is complete.

UNIX schedules many tasks in the background. You can execute many commands and programs in the background. In fact, if you have a long-running program that you can only "sit there and watch," you may as well run it in the background and move on to another task.

For the most part, UNIX handles all of this time-sharing and tasking. UNIX does, however, need to know what tasks you want to accomplish. This chapter defines the commands you will find useful for handling the multiprocessing capabilities of UNIX.

Key Terms Used in This Chapter

Queue	A list of tasks to be performed.
Process	A series of instructions, more commonly known as a *running program*—a program in the act of executing.
Background processing	A process placed in a process queue and removed from terminal control.
Password	A unique word, intended to be known only by the user. The password is used by the operating system to verify the user's identity.
Superuser	A UNIX login that allows access to the root directory, and is not restricted by file permissions. This login is generally confined to those persons responsible for administering the system. The superuser's login name is `root`.
File permission	A means to control the modes of access different users have to a UNIX file. Each file has read, write, and execute permissions.
Print spooler	The UNIX system program that is responsible for queuing and controlling the printing of files.

Exploring the Multiuser Environment

Because you are seldom alone while working with UNIX, you often need to find out what is going on in your UNIX environment. Your executing programs—also called *processes*—share computer resources with the processes of other users. UNIX even initiates its own processes.

At certain times, you may realize that a process you began needs to be terminated because you used incorrect data, or because the process is "hung" and can't successfully be completed. At other times, your system password may need to be changed to ensure security for the system. Perhaps you have been assigned multiple logins. While working on a task, you may forget what login name you used to initiate the task (see Chapter 5 for a detailed description of how UNIX uses logins). At other times, you may want to write to another user on the system and have a need to know who is on the system.

UNIX provides commands that enable you to operate in this kind of multitasking/multiuser computing environment. Some commands, such as chmod, give you control over other users' access to your files. Commands like lp are your gateways to the shared resources of the system's printers. The ps and kill commands help you track and control your processes. In this chapter, you'll learn about these and the many other commands that reveal the multiuser/multitasking flavor of UNIX.

Changing Your Password with `passwd`

The passwd command gives you the flexibility to interactively create or change your password. In most situations, your system administrator assigns a password to your account when the account is set up (see Chapter 5 for information on login and password procedures). You may, however, want to change that "generic" password and replace it with one that you are more likely to remember. Or, if your account contains no password, you may want to create one to prevent others from using your account.

As you learned in Chapter 5, not all UNIX systems require you to enter a password to log on to the system. Some UNIX systems have more relaxed security provisions than others. If the system administrator chooses, some terminals are automatically logged on when the system is up.

In the following example, the passwd command is used to change the password for the user named Amanda:

```
$ passwd <Return>
Changing password for amanda
Old password: <password> <Return>
New password: <new password> <Return>
Retype new password: <new password> <Return>
$
```

In this example, after Amanda types **passwd** and presses <Return>, UNIX presents the message Changing password for amanda. The next message prompts Amanda to enter her old password. After she presses <Return>, UNIX prompts for the new password. After she presses <Return> again, UNIX prompts her to verify the new password by retyping it. Notice that for security purposes, UNIX does not display any of the typed-in passwords.

NOTE Each password is stored in an encrypted form. If you forget your password, there is no way you can recover it, so you will need to ask your system administrator to give you a new password. Although each user can change his or her individual password, only the system administrator can issue a new password on an existing account without knowing the old password. This function is reserved for the system administrator to maintain system security.

When you use `passwd` to change your password, type your entries carefully. The `passwd` command checks to ensure that you do not make typing mistakes when entering a new password. In the following screen dialogue, the user named David attempts to change his password. Notice that David makes several mistakes, which the `passwd` command detects and reports.

```
$ passwd <Return>
Old password: (user enters password)
Last successful password change for david: Tue Mar 27 09:06:45 1990
Last unsuccessful password change for david: NEVER

        Choose password

You can choose whether you pick your own password,
or have the system create one for you.
    1. Pick your own password
    2. Pronounceable password will be generated for you
```

In this specific implementation of UNIX, the `passwd` command supplies a report to the user about the status of his old password. David is prompted to select from two methods of acquiring a new password. On this system, the `passwd` command can select a password for users if they want. David elects to select his own password by entering **1**:

```
Enter choice (default is 1): 1 <Return>
New password: (user enters david)
You may not re-use the same password.
passwd: illegal password; try again
```

The `passwd` command detects that the user has entered his login name as his password. The system refuses to allow a user's password to be the same as his login name:

```
New password: (user enters Rambo)
Re-enter new password: (user enters rambo)
passwd: They don't match; try again
```

The user enters `Rambo` as his password choice, but mistakenly types a lowercase `r` when re-entering the password. Because UNIX is case-sensitive, the password attempt is rejected again. David is prompted to try again:

```
New password: (user enters Rambo)
Re-enter new password: (user enters Ranbo)
passwd: They don't match; too many tries; try again later
Password request denied.
Reason: cannot get new password.
$
```

This time, David made a minor typing mistake when re-entering the new password. The `passwd` command detects the problem. Because the user has made three failed attempts to change his password, the `passwd` command issues a termination message and exits back to the UNIX prompt. David will have to try again.

Remember that the exact operation of `passwd` varies from system to system. The variation is due to the command itself, as well as security provisions in specific implementations of UNIX. Some systems cause passwords to expire every few weeks. When a password expires, the user is prompted during the login process to change his password. If you have difficulty changing your password, consult your system administrator.

Finding Out Who Is Using the System

The `who` command and its related commands—`whodo` and `whoami`—enable you to find out who is logged in on the system.

`who` lists the login names, terminal lines, and login times of users who are currently logged in. Other options available with `who` display other information.

The `whoami` variation of the `who` command identifies the invoking user. The `am i` or `amI` parts of this command are actually options to the `who` command. Because the output of `whoami` differs from the output of `who`, it is convenient to think of `whoami` as a separate command, even though it really isn't separate from `who`.

The `whodo` command lists the user, the terminal line, and the processes currently being used. `whodo` is a kind of hybrid between `who` and the `ps` (*process status*) command. Unlike `whoami`, `whodo` is an independent command.

Identifying the User with `who am i`

The UNIX environment allows more than one person to share the same terminal. Most users can access several terminals. As a result, many users have more than one login to accommodate group affiliations or access to applications programs. As soon as one user logs out of a session on a terminal, another user can log in on the same terminal.

Because of this capability to access several terminals, you may not remember either your terminal number or which login you used. In most situations, the screen displays the system prompt with no information as to who is logged on to the system. The who am i form of the who command identifies the user who is logged on to the terminal, as well as the terminal's TTY number. The command displays the user's login name, as in the following example:

```
$ who am i <Return>
rick tty04 June 9 15:15
$
```

In response to the who am i command, the system responds with the identity of the logged-in user—rick—as well as the terminal rick is logged into and the time he logged in.

Determining Who is Doing What with whodo

When you start programs, each program is given a process ID number that uniquely identifies the process. The kernel keeps track of the user ID that initiated each process as well. The output of whodo reports both user identification and process information for a user's processes.

The whodo command lists the user, the terminal line, and the processes currently being run. If the response time of the system seems to be slow, for example, you can issue whodo to check which processes are running and who is responsible for running them.

Consider this example:

```
$ whodo <Return>
Tue Sep  4 15:46:18 1990
andiron

tty2a     root       15:40
    ?      1288          0:03 sh
    ?      1288          0:00 whodo
$
```

In this output, you see that the superuser (root) is logged in at the terminal tty2a of the system named andiron. The superuser has been logged in for just over 15 minutes. The second line shows the process information for root. Notice that the whodo command "captured" itself in this report as one of the running processes.

Finding Out Who is On the System with who

The purpose of the who command is to find out who is logged in on the system. who lists the login names, terminal lines, and login times of users who are currently logged in.

who is useful in many situations. For example, you may want to communicate with someone on the computer using the `write` command. To find out if that person is on the system, use the `who` command. Or, you may want to see when certain users are logged in to the computer to keep track of their time spent on the computer.

Several options are available with the `who` command and its variations. Table 9.1 lists the options available with `who` and its output variations.

Table 9.1
Commonly Used Options for the who Command

Option	Action
-u	Lists only *users* who are currently logged in.
-T	Adds a field, commonly known as the "state" field, which indicates whether others can write to the *terminal*. A plus (+) state means that the terminal can be written to; a minus (–) state means that the terminal cannot be written to; and a question-mark (?) state means that the terminal line is bad.
-l	Lists only those terminal *lines* available for login. The -l option causes the word LOGIN to be displayed in the NAME field. The "state" field is not displayed.
-a	Turns on *all* options except -q and -s.
-r	Displays the *run* level of the init program.
-t	Lists the last change to the system *time* clock.
-H	Displays *headers* above each column. (This option is available only with more recent implementations of UNIX.)
-q	Also called the *quick* who. The -q option displays only the names and the number of users, ignoring all other options. (This option is available only with more recent implementations of UNIX.)
-p	Lists currently active *processes* started by the system init program.
-d	Lists all processes that have *died* (terminated for any reason) and have not yet been respawned.
-s	Lists the name, line, and time fields. This is the default display for the who command.

The options listed in table 9.1 will display the following fields if they are defined:

```
NAME   LINE   TIME   ACTIVITY   PID   COMMENT
```

These fields will be displayed unless directed otherwise by a selected option. The default behavior of the `who` command is the same as that when issued with the -s option. The other options used with the command will display the LINE, TIME, ACTIVITY, and PID fields unless otherwise stated, and the COMMENT field if stated.

The output format of the who command can include the display of up to eight fields at one time. Table 9.2 describes the fields displayed in the output format, depending on the option used. The actual field-name heading text appears if the −H option is included.

Table 9.2
Output Format for the who Command

Field	Description
NAME	Lists the user's login name.
+ − ?	This "state" field lists whether other users can write to the terminal. + in this column means that other users can write to the terminal; − means that other users cannot write to the terminal; ? means that the terminal line is bad.
LINE	Lists the line or terminal being used.
TIME	Lists the time the user logged in.
ACTIVITY	Lists the hours and minutes since the last activity on that line. A period character (.) is displayed if activity occurred within the last minute of system time. If more than 24 hours elapsed since the line s was used, or if it has not been used since the system boot, the word old is displayed.
PID	Lists the process ID number of the user's login shell.
COMMENT	Lists the contents of the comment field if comments have been included.
EXIT	When present, the EXIT field contains the termination and exit values of dead processes.

To display who is on the system, use the following form:

```
$ who <Return>
root      console       June  9 07:48
vince     tty02         June  9 13:45
cheryl    tty03         June  9 09:24
rick      tty04         June  9 15:15
$
```

In this example, the system responds to the who command by displaying a list of who is logged in on the system, the terminal lines they are using, and what time they logged in. The first line, for example, indicates that root has been logged in at the console since 07:48.

To get a quick list of who is on the system, use the who command with the −q option, as follows:

```
$ who -q <Return>
cheryl amanda rick
# users=3
$
```

This command shows that three users are currently logged on the system: cheryl, amanda, and rick.

To get more extensive information, use the who command with the -H, u, and T options, as follows:

```
$ who -HuT <Return>
NAME      LINE      TIME            IDLE    PID     COMMENTS
root      -console  Jun  10 06:48   .       10
amanda    +tty03    Jun  10 09:53   0:20    37
cheryl    +tty02    Jun  10 13:44   .       36      Admin
$
```

The -H option causes the who command to display headings above the columns. The -u option causes who to display only those users who are currently logged in—in this case, root, amanda, and cheryl. Because the -T option was used, the command also displays the "state" field before the line to indicate whether someone else can write to that terminal. In this case, the console cannot be written to because it contains a minus sign (-) in front of it. Amanda and Cheryl's terminal lines have a + in front of them, indicating that their terminals can be written to.

Changing the Group Ownership of Files with chgrp

A company is often organized into groups, such as payroll, accounting, sales, vendors, services, and so on. In the UNIX world, users are also divided administratively into groups. Each group is identified by a specific group number and a group name. A record of these items is stored in the etc/group file. The etc/group file contains a listing of the group number and the group members for each group.

A user may be a member of many groups. The system administrator sets up the default group for the user—that is, the group the user is listed in every time he or she logs in. The user can switch to any group of which he is a member to access the files in that particular group. (A later section details the process of switching groups.) For example, a user in the service group may need access to sales organization files to see whether a service contract was sold to the customer.

A file is "owned" by the user who created it. Other than the superuser, a file's owner is the only user who has absolute control over the access permissions for the file. When a file is created, it is assigned your user ID number and your current group ID number. If you allow it, all the members of your group will be able to access this file. You use the chmod command (covered in a later section) to change access modes for the file so that it can be accessed by your group and other users. By setting the group access mode for a file to r (for *read* access), anyone in your group can read the file. At times, however, you may want a different group to be able to access your files. You can use the chgrp command to change the group ownership of a file and enable the members of a different group to access your file.

 Before you use chgrp, you need some information about group membership, file ownership, and so on. You can use the ls -l command to obtain this information. The ls -l command displays a long listing of the files, including the information you need to use chgrp. (See Chapter 6 for more information on the ls command.)

In some situations, you may be listed in several groups in the etc/group file. If you have distinct department affiliations, for instance, you may have distinct group affiliations that match. See the section on the newgrp command to find out how to switch your current group ID to one of the other IDs.

In the next example, the chgrp command grants a specified group—group number 130—the permission to access the sales file:

```
$ chgrp 130 sales <Return>
$
```

The sales file now has group ownership of group 130.

The group argument can be either the group ID number or the group name. In the following example, the user named David belongs to two groups: ateam and other. David created a directory named ateam.work for use while he was logged in as a member of the ateam group. While working with his ateam group affiliation, David created a report named initial.rep, which he intends members of the other group to be able to access. Now, David must use chgrp to change the file's group ownership to other:

```
$ ls -ld ateam.work <Return>
drwxrwx---  2 david    ateam    48 Jun  5 11:45 ateam.work
$
```

The ls -ld command issued from David's directory lists information about the ateam.work directory itself (-d)—not its contents. You can see that the group ownership of this directory is the ateam group:

```
$ cd ateam.work <Return>
$ ls -l initial.rep <Return>
-rw-rw----  1 david    ateam    412 Aug  4 18:47 initial.rep
$
```

The group ownership of initial.rep is ateam; members of the other group cannot access the file:

```
$ chgrp other initial.rep <Return>
```

The chgrp command changes the file's group ownership to other so that members of the other group can read and write the file as indicated by the -rw-rw- - - - field in the following ls command:

```
$ ls -l initial.rep <Return>
-rw-rw- - - -  1 david   other    412 Aug  4 18:47 initial.rep
$
```

Now you see that the group has been changed from ateam to other. You'll learn more about group and public access modes in an upcoming section on the chmod command.

Switching Groups with newgrp

As a user, you may sometimes be listed in more than one group. The /etc/passwd file lists the groups you are assigned to by the system administrator at the time of login. At times, however, you need to access files and programs in a group other than your current group.

Whereas chgrp changes the group affiliations of files, newgrp changes the group affiliation of a single user. The new group affiliation lasts throughout the user's session, or until the user uses newgrp again.

For example, if you belong to the budget group and are assigned the task of totaling expense accounts for the marketing group, you may need access to the marketing files that contain expense reports. Because you are member of the group that owns the expense reports file, you can use the newgrp command to switch to this group.

If you need to access files and programs in another group, you can use the newgrp command to switch to that group, provided that you are listed as a member of the group in the etc/group file.

 You can use the desired group name as an argument to the newgrp command to gain access to a particular group. Or, you can use newgrp without an argument; you will then be assigned to the group given in the /etc/passwd file, which is your default login group.

The only option available with the newgrp command is the minus (–) option, which logs you into your default login group ID. You will be logged in again to your default group, so your current login shell (along with its environment) is terminated, and a new login shell is started.

The following sequence shows you how to change from your login group to another group:

```
$ id <Return>
uid=174(amanda) gid=27(budget)
$ newgrp records <Return>
$ id <Return>
uid=174(amanda) gid=29(expenses)
$
```

In this example, the id command lists the user, amanda, and her current group ID, 27 (the budget group). In the next line, the newgrp command changes amanda's group affiliation to 29 (the expenses group). The system responds by listing the same user ID for amanda along with the new group name and ID.

The id command lists the user and group IDs. Changing to a new group does not affect the user ID. User and group IDs are the numbers associated with the user login name and group affiliation name. The system uses ID numbers to track users and groups.

The next example shows how you can use newgrp with the – option to change back to your default login group and automatically log back in. Note that your default login group is the first group listed in your /etc/passwd file entry:

```
$ newgrp – <Return>
uid=174(amanda) gid=27(budget)
$
```

In this example, Amanda's group is changed back to her default group—the budget group. The – option causes the environmental variables to be re-established to their original login values. If you want to change to your default group and retain the same login name, issue the newgrp command without arguments.

Setting File and Directory Permissions with chmod

UNIX users can read and write files. In addition, users can execute files such as shell procedures and binary programs. If you look at the process of accessing files based on the mode of access, these modes are called *read*, *write*, and *execute*. This ability to read, write, or execute a file is called a permission.

Read (r) permission allows a file to be read and copied. If you use read permission with a directory, you can list the contents of the directory.

Write (w) permission allows a file to be altered. This includes editing it and appending to it. If you use write permission with a directory, you can add or delete files in that designated directory.

Execute (x) permission allows you to run the file as a program by typing the file's name. When you are granted execute permission for use with a directory, you have search permission for the directory; you also have the power to make that directory your current directory.

UNIX divides the read, write, and execute modes of its users into three categories. The three categories are independent and pertain only to the users who fit into each category. The categories are as follows:

- Owner—the user ID who created the file or directory
- Group—the group ID affiliated with the file
- Others—public access to a file by all other users beyond the file's owner and the file's group-affiliated users

You can arrange the three access categories in a row and list the possible modes of access below each category:

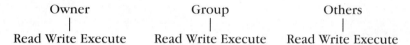

Owner | Group | Others

Read Write Execute   Read Write Execute   Read Write Execute

Each file has a set of access-mode attributes associated with its i-node entry. These attributes contain read, write, and execute access attributes for each of the categories: Owner, Group, and Others. You can see these attributes in the output of the `ls -l` command. The first field of this command displays a series of `rwx` and `-` characters:

```
$ ls -ld ateam.work <Return>
drwxrwx---  2 david  ateam   48 Sep  4 18:45 ateam.work
$ ls -l initial.rep <Return>
-rw-rw----  1 david  ateam  412 Sep  4 18:47 initial.rep
$
```

The first field in each of these directory entries shows the access modes of each file. The first file is a directory. As you recall, the first column of the attributes field of a directory shows a `d`. The first column of an ordinary file, like the file listed second, shows a `-`.

The second through fourth columns describe the owner's access permissions. An `r` in the second column indicates read permission for the owner. A `w` in the third column indicates write permission for the owner. An `x` in the fourth column indicates execute permission for the owner. Execute permission on a directory is the capability to list the directory. Execute permission for other files is the capability to run the files' program contents. When a `-` appears in place of an `r`, `w`, or `x` character, the corresponding permission is *not* granted.

The permissions for members of the same group as the file's group affiliation are listed in the next three columns. Again, the permissions for the group are listed as `r`, `w`, and `x`. Members of the file's affiliated group can access the file in any mode for which access permission is granted.

The final three columns in the attribute field of the `ls -l` listing are for Others. Others are users who are neither the file's owner, nor members of the group affiliated with the file. These users are sometimes referred to as "the public" since they have no ownership or affiliation to the file. Again, the three Others fields represent read, write, and execute permissions, or the lack of permission as a −.

At the time of login, a file-creation mask is initialized to a default value and used to set permissions for the files you create. Normally, only user read, write, and execute privileges are granted by default for your files by the file-creation mask mechanism. Only you or the superuser can alter the permission settings of your files.

You can alter file- and directory-permission modes by using the chmod command. The read, write, and execute permissions are defined in this mode. Through chmod, you indicate the permissions you grant to the file owner (yourself), to members of your group, and to others. In other words, the owner selectively grants some combination of read, write, and execute permissions to himself and the members of other categories.

Only the owner of a file and superuser can change the permissions.

Common uses of the chmod command include the following:

- Removing owner write permissions from a file to protect it from accidentally being erased
- Making a file private by removing read permission for other users while keeping the file readable by yourself and other group members
- Removing group and others permissions so that only you will have access to the file

If you have an important speech finished in a text file, for example, and don't want to accidentally erase the speech, you can remove your write permission from the owner's access mode. If you write a handy shell procedure that other users want to copy, you can grant read permission to others.

Or, suppose that you are a member of the ateam group mentioned in a previous example. You want other members of the ateam group to be able to read and edit the file initial.rep, so you need to assign read and write permissions to the group by using the chmod command.

With some more recent implementations or versions of UNIX, you can "lock" a file so that it can be accessed by only one user or program at a time. Locking a file ensures that only one copy of the file can be changed at any point in time. Otherwise, two users could use a line editor like ed to edit the file at the same time, and the last user to write his edited version back to disk would overwrite the other user's version of the file.

With three categories of users (user, group, and others) and three access permissions (read, write, and execute) for each category, arguments to the chmod command can become complicated. If you need to change many permissions, the chmod command accepts an absolute form of permission arguments (sometimes called the *numeric* method) that indicates the exact settings for all permissions. For changing one or two permissions, a symbolic form of permission arguments (the *symbolic* method) indicates particular permissions to be set. Each form is discussed in its own section.

Using the Absolute Mode with chmod

A four-digit octal number (numbers 0-7) describes the file permissions to chmod in the absolute method. Each digit is the encoded permissions for the digit's corresponding user category. This number is a result of combining any of the basic modes and adding their numeric values together.

The values for any one digit are derived from adding the value of the permissions from the following list:

No permission................ add 0

Execute permission........ add 1

Read permission............ add 2

Write permission........... add 4

Notice that if you add all of the values from the list, the result is 7. The number 7 represents read, write, and execute permission values. For read and write permissions, the value is 2 + 4, or 6. Read-only permission is 2. Write-only permission is 4. Read and execute permission is 2 + 1, or 3. No permission (you cannot read, write, or execute the file) is 0.

Remember that adding the permission values produces one digit. You will want to set permissions on three categories: yourself, your group, and everyone else. In the absolute method, each of these categories has its own digit, and the value of each digit is calculated using the values shown in the value list. In the four-digit octal chmod argument, the first (leftmost) digit has a special significance and will be discussed later. The second digit represents owner permissions. The third digit represents group permissions, and the fourth digit represents all others' permissions.

For example, consider the following specifications:

0400 (basic mode) owner read

0200 (basic mode) owner write

0100 (basic mode) owner execute

0040 (basic mode) group read

The sum of these basic mode values results in a four-digit octal number of 0740, representing the absolute mode value.

Table 9.3 includes the definitions and numeric value of the basic modes.

Table 9.3
Basic Modes Table

Mode	Definition
4000	Sets user ID on execution
2000	Prior to Release 3, sets group ID on execution
1000	Reserved
0400	Sets read permissions for the owner
0200	Sets write permissions for the owner
0100	Sets execute (search) permissions for the owner
0040	Sets read permissions for the group
0020	Sets write permissions for the group
0010	Sets execute (search) permissions for the group
0004	Sets read permissions for others
0002	Sets write permissions for others
0001	Sets execute (search) permissions for others

The absolute mode is better suited for setting all modes at once because it results in a shorter command which is less prone to typographical errors and omissions.

The symbolic mode is most useful when you want to alter specific modes. By using the symbolic mode, you can add or take away a permission without having to consider the current state of other permissions. In plain English, a symbolic chmod argument would sound like this: "Add read permission to whatever the others' permission is now." The symbolic mode is discussed in the next section.

Using the Symbolic Mode with chmod

Use of the symbolic form of chmod is suggested for altering specific modes. The symbolic mode consists of three parts:

- The "who string," which indicates which user is affected
- The operator (the operation indicator), which lists the action taken
- The "permission string," which lists the affected permissions

On the command line, these parts take the following form:

```
chmod who + or – or = permissions files
```

Now take a closer look at each of these parts.

A combination of the following letters can be used with the "who string."

Letter	Meaning
u	The user
g	The group
o	Others

The following are the three possible operators:

Operator	Action
+	Adds the desired permissions
–	Removes the listed permissions
=	Assigns absolutely the indicated permissions

 When using the + and – operators, only the stated permissions are affected. Use of the = option affects all permissions; those not mentioned are turned off.

Use of the following letters forms the "permission string":

Letter	Permission
r	Read permission
w	Write permission
x	Execute permission
s	Set user ID (with o), or set group ID (with g)
–l	New with Release 3, this option produces mandatory file-locking during access

An example of a symbolic mode would be as follows:

> $ **chmod g+r inventory** <Return>

This statement grants read permission (r) to group members (g) for the file named inventory.

Another example, using more than one operator-permission sequence, would be as follows:

> $ **g+r-w inventory** <Return>

This statement grants read permission (r) and removes write permission (–w) for group members (g) for the file named inventory.

TIP

If you are using more than one symbolic mode, separate the modes with a comma. Consider the following sequence:

```
$ chmod go-r, u-w, inventory <Return>
```

This statement removes read permission (-r) for group and others (go), and adds user write permission (u+w) for the file named inventory.

Using chmod

If you don't want other users listing the files in one of your directories, or being able to change to your directory using cd, you can change the execute mode to – for the categories you want to keep out. In effect, you're hiding the directory from other user's commands. To conceal a directory, use the following command:

```
$ chmod go -rx status <Return>
$
```

This command removes both execute and read permission (-rx). Members of group and others (go) are no longer allowed to use cd to change to the directory, nor are they able to list the directory contents.

To make a file read-only using the absolute-mode method, form the argument for the chmod command as in:

```
$ chmod 0444 inventory <Return>
$
```

This command grants everyone read-only access to the file named inventory. As you recall, a number 4 in a mode category means "read permission granted." By assigning user, group, and others a 4, everyone that logs into the system can read the file.

The following command uses the symbolic method:

```
$ chmod ugo=r status <Return>
$
```

This command grants everyone (ugo) read permission (r) for the file named inventory.

A shell script (procedure) is a text file containing commands. When you assign execute permission(s) to a script file, you can type the file's name, and the shell will execute the files commands. To make a shell script executable, use the following command:

```
$ chmod u+x listfile <Return>
$
```

This command makes the file called listfile executable (+x) to the user only (u); the user types the file name to execute the file. You'll learn more about shell procedures in Chapters 14 and 15.

Controlling File Permissions with umask

The umask command controls the establishment of permissions with newly created files. You use the command to set the creation mask to the value of your choice. The umask value is set by default in your .profile file. In most cases, the default permissions are set to read, write, and execute for the owner, and no permissions for the group and others.

In computer terminology, a *mask* is a value that is used to cover (like a mask) some other value. The final value depends on the value that the mask does not cover. If you apply masking tape to a part of a surface, for example, and then spray paint on the surface, the paint will only "come through" in the areas not masked.

The value of the umask is actually the value that is taken away from the 777 value for a file. 7 in the umask value will mask the 7 in a file mode because 7−7=0. A 7 in the umask, therefore, results in no permissions for the user(s) in that category. A 3 in the umask value means that the file has a read permission set for the corresponding category. Again, starting with 7 and masking with (subtracting) 3 gives 4, and 4 in octal mode is the read permission. UNIX starts with 7's in the user, group, and others categories, and then subtracts the corresponding number in the umask value. The permissions for the created file are the results of the subtraction.

 If you don't feel comfortable using umask, you can ask the system administrator for assistance. In most cases, the appropriate umask value is established for you by default.

To see your present umask settings, simply type **umask** with no argument and press <Return>:

```
$ umask <Return>
022
$
```

In this example, the current value of the creation mask is set to give the user all permissions. Group members and others are limited; the command prevents them from having write permission.

You specify the mask by using a three-digit octal number. The first digit denotes the owner permissions. The second digit controls group permissions, and the third digit controls permissions for others. This three-digit number may be preceded by a zero (refer to table 9.3 for the code for these digits). Remember that the umask values will be subtracted from 777 to obtain the file-creation permissions when a file is created.

When you alter the creation mask, keep in mind that the changes only apply to files being created. You cannot change the creation mask on files that already exist.

Changing File Ownership with chown

As discussed in a previous section, when you create a file, UNIX gives you the ownership of that file. The chown command enables you to change the ownership of the file. This command is used most often by the system administrator. If, however, you need to grant another user ownership of a file, thus giving up your owner permissions, you can use the chown command.

Perhaps you maintain a file containing scheduling information for work load. When you are promoted, someone else takes your old position and your old job-related files. You can give the ownership of the files, like the scheduling file, to the new user. The new user then has control of the file and doesn't have to bother you to change the file's access modes.

To give another user ownership of your file, use the following command:

```
$ chown cheryl inventory <Return>
$
```

This makes the user named cheryl the true owner of the file named inventory. Now, only cheryl (and the superuser) has absolute control of the file.

Switching between Accounts with su

There may be times when you need to change your user ID, but you do not want to log out of the system. For instance, if you are a system administrator working under an ordinary login, not root, you can use su to become the root user. In fact, the command name su is derived from its common use of switching to the *super user*.

You can use the su command to switch between accounts (if you have multiple accounts on the system) or to use someone else's account. If you do not provide a *username* argument, it is assumed that you want root privileges. If this is not the case and you want to log in to someone else's account, you need to provide the password for whichever account you want to use. The only way you can get the password is to get it directly from the owner of the account.

To change your user ID, use the following command:

```
$ su amanda <Return>
passwd:
$
```

Remember when using `su` that you must type the password for the account just as if you were logging in. To return to your login account, simply enter `<^D>`.

Displaying the Name of the Current System with `uname`

The `uname` command displays the *name* of the current system. This command is especially useful if you are working on a multisystem network. You can use this command to find out information about the system you are using.

This information is most useful when you are attempting to obtain information by logging into a remote system to access files. You may also want to know the version of the operating system on another system to check for compatibility.

The `uname` command has six options, which are listed in table 9.4.

Table 9.4
Commonly Used Options for the `uname` Command

Option	Action
-s	Shows the *system* name known to the local installation.
-n	Shows the *node* name. The node name is the name by which the system is known to a communications network.
-r	Shows the operating system *release* number.
-v	Shows the operating system *version*.
-m	Shows the name of the *machine* hardware.
-a	Shows *all* of the above.

To find out the name of your system, use the following command:

```
$ uname <Return>
andiron
$
```

This command generates a response with the system name, in this case, `andiron`.

To find out the current system version, use the following command:

```
$ uname -v <Return>
2
$
```

This command generates a response with the system version, in this case 2. As you know, options, arguments, and even commands can depend on the version of UNIX you are using. If you are having trouble getting a command or shell script to execute, you may want to check the version of the operating system. The version might not accept your command line without modification of some option, argument, or even the command.

Reporting on the Multiprocessing Environment

Previous sections discussed UNIX as a multiuser, multitasking operating system. UNIX uses a "time-share" method to make it possible for UNIX to attend to several tasks concurrently. UNIX provides several commands to help you keep track of what is going on.

Most of the time, you are unaware of how UNIX schedules and executes users' commands. Your programs, commands, subshells, background processes, and system programs which were initiated on your behalf are all tracked by UNIX. You can see into the "invisible" world of process status by using certain UNIX commands.

Users need to access shared services such as disk drives and printers in a timely fashion. A user can't afford to wait for someone else's report to finish printing to get the command prompt back after issuing his own print request. To provide speedier access to shared services, UNIX employs queues of pending jobs. A user sends a report to a printer, and UNIX intercepts the report and keeps it in a spooler file until the printer can get to it. Once the print file is spooled, the user continues working while the printer service manages the file's printing. Again, the queued services offered by UNIX are somewhat "invisible" to the user. However, UNIX offers commands that enable users to view printer status and control the printer queue.

Reporting on the Status of Processes with ps

A program and its associated data in the act of executing is called an "active process." The chown command, for example, is just a command until it begins to execute in computer memory. Then it is considered a process running under the supervision of the kernel.

Because UNIX is a time-sharing system, it needs to keep track of the information it acquires when switching back and forth between tasks. To accomplish this, UNIX assigns a process identification number (PID) to each process. The process ID is the number printed on the screen when you place the ampersand character (&) after a command to run the command in the background. All processes are assigned numbers. Normally, however, you don't see the numbers.

You use the ps (*process status*) command to report the status of the processes on the current terminal. Suppose that you want to ensure speedy processing of a command, so you start the command on the system early—before too many users log in and load up the system. You want to be able to check the amount of computer time the command had been using, obtain the process ID number to terminate the command, or verify which commands are running. All of this information can be obtained with the ps command.

Another common use of the ps command is to see background jobs and to see what is happening on the system. Because background processes don't communicate with your screen and keyboard in most cases, you need the ps command to track their progress.

In its listing, the ps command displays the following default headings as indicators of the information presented in the fields below each heading:

    PID TTY TIME COMMAND

Each of these headings is explained as follows:

Field	Explanation
PID	The process identification number
TTY	The terminal where the process originated
TIME	The cumulative execution time for the process in minutes and seconds
COMMAND	The name of the command being executed

There may be times, however, when you need to know more than what the default listing provides. To generate a display of this additional information, you can invoke some of the options listed in table 9.5.

Table 9.5
Commonly Used Options for the ps Command

Option	Action
-e	Shows information about all processes, not just the ones used with your terminal
-d	Shows information about all processes except process group leaders
-a	Displays a "full" listing
-l	Displays a "long" listing
-t *tlist*	Restricts the listing to data about the processes associated with the terminals specified in *tlist*

The ps command gives only an approximate picture of process status because things can and do change while the command is running. Your ps command is a snapshot of the process status at the instant that the ps command executed. The snapshot includes the ps command itself.

In the following example, three commands are shown. The first command is the shell. The second command is the `sort` command (used to sort the file named `inventory`), and the third command is the `ps` command you are presently running.

To find out what processes you currently have running, use the following command:

```
$ ps <Return>
PID     TTY     TIME    COMMAND
65      01      0:07    -sh
71      01      0:14    sort inventory
231     03      0:09    ps
$
```

To obtain a full listing, use the following command:

```
$ ps -f <Return>
UID        PID     PPID    C     STIME       TTY    TIME    COMMAND
amanda     65      1       0     11:40:11    01     0:06    -sh
amanda     71      65      61    11:42:01    01     0:14    sort
inventory
amanda     231     65      80    14:26:02    03     0:10    ps -f
$
```

To list processes for two terminals, use the following command:

```
$ ps -t "01 02" <Return>
PID     TTY     TIME    COMMAND
 32     01      0:05    sh
 36     02      0:09    sh
235     02      0:16    vi calendar
$
```

In this example, the `-t` option is used to restrict the listing to the processes associated with terminals 1 and 2. Terminal 1 is running the shell command (`PID32`) and using `vi` to edit the calendar (`PID235`). The cumulative time for each process is also listed.

Stopping Background Commands with `kill`

Normally, when you are running a command that is not in the background, you can stop it by pressing an interrupt key, such as <Del>, <Break>, or <^C>. However, when you put a command in the background, pressing an interrupt key will not stop the command. Because a background process is not under terminal control, keyboard input of any of the interrupt key sequences is ignored. The only way you can stop background commands is to use the `kill` command.

You may need to stop a job you are running in the background for several reasons. For example, if a process is waiting for input that it cannot get, it may go into an infinite loop. Or, perhaps you made a mistake and used the wrong file for input. You may have made a typing error in the command or issued a command that will never stop on its own. You can use the kill command to get out of these situations. The kill command sends signals to a program to demand a termination.

The format for using the kill command is as follows:

```
$ kill pid_number <Return>
$
```

This command terminates (kills) the command specified by the *pid_number*.

You can also log in on another terminal and give the kill instructions from there. In order to issue the kill command, however, you need the PID number of the process. To find the PID number associated with each process, refer to the ps command described in the preceding section.

If your login has permission, you can use the command ps -e to see all the processes running on the system. If you don't have permission, you will just see your own processes.

A process containing a PID value of 0 has a special meaning. Using the 0 PID value with the kill command signals all processes in the process group and sends a terminate signal to your login shell and to all the processes it has started up. This does not include the shell. The shell is not affected by the terminate signal, but all other processes are, so this command kills all normal background jobs. Remember that only superusers can send signals for processes other than their own.

Under certain circumstances, the kill command will not terminate a background process. Sometimes, as a result of certain programming techniques, a background process may be immune to the kill command. After issuing the kill command, use the ps command to verify that the process has been terminated. If the process is still listed, you may need to use the kill -9 variation of the kill command. The disadvantage to using this version of the command is that you could lose the contents of the file.

Unfortunately, the kill -9 command does not allow a command to finish and clean up what it is doing before it terminates. If, for example, you are using this version of the command to terminate a process that is currently updating a file, the command would terminate the process in the middle of the present activity, and you could lose your new data.

In most cases, you do not need the -9 option; the kill command issued without arguments will stop most processes.

To kill all background jobs, use the following command:

```
$ kill 0 <Return>
terminated
$
```

Sometimes commands that run in the background initiate more than one process, and tracking down all the PID numbers can be tedious. Because the kill 0 command terminates *all* processes started by the login shell, it provides a faster and less tedious means of terminating processes.

To kill a background process using the PID number, first use the ps command to obtain the number, and then use the following command:

```
$ kill 3712 <Return>
vi: 3712 terminated
$
```

In this example, the vi process, PID 3712 was terminated.

Printing Your Work

Now that you have become familiar with some of the multitasking commands, you should learn how to print your data to one of the printers on your system. This section discusses the lp, lpstat, and cancel commands, which enable you to print a short, unformatted file, check when it will be printed, and stop it from printing.

Sending a File to a Print Spooler with lp

As part of the UNIX multiuser system, more than one user may send a file to the printer at the same time. To handle this situation, UNIX uses a *print spooler*. A print spooler is responsible for queuing and controlling the printing of files. The spooler assigns an identification number to each print job and places it in a queue in the same order as it was received. The files are then printed one after another in the order in which they are queued.

The lp (*line print*) command sends a file to the print spooler where it stays in the queue and waits for its turn to be printed.

 The lp command is used for UNIX System V. The same command for versions of UNIX other than System V is the lpr command. Check your User Reference Manual to find out more about this version of the UNIX print command.

The format for using the lp command to send a file to the printer is as follows:

```
$ lp janstatus <Return>
request-id is pr1-37 (1 file)
$
```

In this example, the `lp` command takes as its argument the file name `janstatus`. The system responds with a `request-id`. This contains the printer identification number (`pr1`) and a second number that identifies only this particular print job (`-37`). If you need information on where this file is in the print queue or if you want to terminate the process, you need this number.

The `lp` command adds a "banner" page to your file. This page was designed for a multiuser system, in which more than one person uses the printer at a time. The banner page makes it easier to separate printed files because it contains the user's login name, the `request-id` of the file, and the date and time the file was printed. Once the banner is printed, the file itself is printed with no break at the bottom of pages and no margins.

Because your UNIX system may have more than one printer connected to it, the `lp` command takes this possibility into consideration. The `-d` option enables you to specify the printer of your choice. The format for using `lp` with the `-d` option is as follows:

```
$ lp -d pr2 inventory <Return>
$
```

This example specifies the printer identified as `pr2` to print the file named `inventory`.

If you do not use the `-d` option, the default printer will be used. The default printer is the main printer configured for your system.

You may also need to print multiple files. To print multiple files, make sure that the file names are separated by a space. The format for this option is as follows:

```
$ lp inventory shipments purchases <Return>
$
```

When you issue a command to print multiple files, one banner is printed, and the files are considered as one print-file request.

If you need to print more than one copy of the file, use the following format:

```
$ lp -n10 inventory <Return>
$
```

This command prints ten copies of the same file, `inventory`.

Checking the Print Status of a File with `lpstat`

The `lpstat` (*line printer status*) command enables you to find out where your file is located in the print queue. It will also show you the status of all the files you have sent to the printer. The `lpstat` command tells you how many requests are in front of you, which printers are installed, and which printers are available.

You can use options with `lpstat` to obtain additional information. Table 9.6 lists the options available with the `lpstat` command.

Table 9.6
Commonly Used Options for the `lpstat` Command

Option	Action
-a	Shows whether the listed devices are *accepting* printing requests
-c	Shows the name of each printer *class* and lists the printers in each class
-d	Shows the system *default* printer name
-o	Shows the status of *output* requests
-p	Shows the status of *printers*
-r	Shows the `lp` *request* scheduler status
-s	Shows a *status* summary containing the information provided by the options -c, -d, -r, and -v
-t	Shows all (*total*) status information
-u	Shows output requests status from *users*
-v	Shows the name of each printer and the path name of the associated *device*

To find out which printer is the system default printer, use the following command:

```
$ lpstat -d <Return>
system default destination: printer2
$
```

In this case, the `lpstat` command defines the default printer as `printer 2`.

To find the status of your printing request, use the following command:

```
$ lpstat <Return>
printer 2-27    cheryl    789    June 13  17:08    on printer2
$
```

This example shows that the user named Cheryl, who used a request ID of 27, submitted a 789-character file, on June 13 at 17:08, to printer2. The job is now printing on printer 2.

When more than one printer is connected to a system, you will need a way to identify the printer known to the system as printer 1, 2, 3, and so on, so that you can determine which printer is best suited to your needs. This information is contained in a special device file corresponding to each printer. To find out which devices correspond to which printers, use the following form:

```
$ lpstat -v <Return>
device for printer1:   /dev/lp
device for printer2:   /dev/hplp
$
```

In this example, the printer known to the system as `printer1` is a line printer (`/dev/lp`). The printer known to the system as `printer2` is a laser printer (`/hplp`).

Canceling a Print Request with `cancel`

Sometimes you need to cancel a print request you made with the `lp` command. Suppose that you accidentally specified the wrong file to print or selected the wrong printer. Maybe you just changed your mind and want to cancel the print request. You can cancel a print job using the `cancel` command.

To use `cancel`, you need the request ID (the ID is displayed by the `lp` command) or the name of the printer. Using the request ID halts the printing job whether it is waiting to be printed or in the process of being printed. Using the printer name halts just a request that is in the act of being printed.

To halt a printing job by using the request ID, use the following form:

```
$ lp filename
request id is printer2 -241 (1 file)
$ cancel printer2-241
```

To halt a job that is currently on the printer, use the following form:

```
$ cancel printer2
```

If you issue a `cancel` command and the system returns a `nonexistent` in the `comment` field, it simply means that the print job was completed.

```
$ cancel printer2-241 <Return>
cancel: request "pr2-241 nonexistent
$
```

Formatting and Printing Files with `pr`

As you learned in a previous section, the `lp` command sends data to the printer. This data is unformatted, with no page breaks, no headers, and no page sizes. To print files in a formatted state, use the `pr` command. `pr` sends the contents of named files to the standard output. The default standard output is the screen; to send the output to some place other than the default, use the | (pipe) command, which is discussed in Chapter 5.

The pr command, issued without options, begins each page with a five-line header, and ends the page with a five-line trailer, or footer. The trailer contains blank lines. The header contains two blank lines, a line, the page number, the date and time, and the file name, followed by two more blank lines. Once a file is formatted with the pr command, you can use the lp command to send the file to the printer.

The pr command has many options. Table 9.7 defines the most common of these options.

Table 9.7
Commonly Used Options for the pr Command

Option	Action
-a	Puts the first input line to the first column, the second input line to the second column, and so on, providing multicolumn output.
-m	Uses one column per file to *merge* and display all input files simultaneously.
-d	*Double*-spaces the output.
-h*header*	Replaces the default header with the string specified by *header*.
-p	*Pauses* before beginning each page when the output is directed to a terminal. A bell sounds; the system waits for you to press <Return> before continuing.
-f	Creates a new page using a *form-feed* character.
-t	Suppresses the five-line header and *trailer* normally supplied with each page.

To format and display a file on-screen, use the following form:

```
$ pr inventory <Return>
June  3  13:04  1990  inventory  Page 1

Washington,  650   125   100
Florida,     900   325   130
New York,    1150  325   130
$
```

In this example, the screen displays the header and page 1 of the formatted file, inventory.

At times, you store information in separate files so that you can keep your file size smaller. Smaller-sized files are easier to work with. On occasion, however, you may need to view information from all the files in a certain category in a side-by-side view so that you can compare the data or combine the data into a report. To merge files side by side, use the following form:

```
$ pr -m inventory    shipments    backlog <Return>
June 3 13:04 1990 inventory Page 1
Washington,      650              125            100
Florida,         900              259            175
New York,       1150              325            130
```

Using the Scheduling Commands

The UNIX environment provides many ways to handle command execution. UNIX enables the user to create lists of commands and specify when they are to be run. The `at` command, for example, takes a list of commands typed at the keyboard and runs them at the time specified in the command. The `batch` command is similar to the `at` command, but `batch` runs commands when the system finds time for them, rather than allowing the user to specify a particular time. The `cron` command allows for commands to be run periodically. The next sections discuss these scheduling commands.

Running Commands at Specified Times with `at`

The `at` command is used to run a series of commands at a time specified by the user. The `at` command takes two arguments—the time you want the command executed and the command line to be executed. The format for specifying the time is `hour:minute`. The `hour` must be a two-digit string entered in military time. The command line can contain any command that would normally be entered on a shell command line.

The `at` command always runs in the background, thus freeing up the resources but still accomplishing the job.

Like other UNIX task-scheduling commands, you can use `at` to schedule lengthy jobs to be run a time when the computer is less busy. You can also use the command to send reminders via `mail` at later dates and to run database queries late at night.

The `at` command has two options:

Option	Action
-l	*Lists* the job numbers for tasks scheduled by `at`.
-r	*Removes* the specified job number from the queue of jobs scheduled by `at` to cancel that particular job.

Consider this example:

```
$ at 15:00 mail inventory < cheryl <Return>
$
```

In this example, the file named `inventory` will be mailed to `cheryl` at 3:00 p.m.

Running Long Tasks with `batch`

UNIX offers you the flexibility of taking a list of commands and running them while you continue to work at something else. The `batch` command enables you to run long tasks that don't need your immediate attention. In fact, you don't even need to be logged in to the system when the command list runs.

You use the `batch` command to optimize your time at the computer. Perhaps you have a list of commands that do not require any keyboard input. The `batch` command enables you to run your list of commands and continue working on another project at the computer.

The `batch` command also enables you to schedule large jobs at times when the jobs will not interfere with your system's performance. For example, you may have a batch job that takes a considerable amount of time, such as three hours, that you would like to run through the night to be ready for the next day's meeting.

The format for issuing the `batch` commands is to enter the list of commands on the line that follows the command; then terminate the commands by entering a `<^D>`. You can also use a file of commands by using input redirection (see Chapter 5).

To run a command from a file, use the following form;

```
$ batch < inventory <Return>
$
```

To run a command when the system finds the time, use the following form:

```
$ batch <Return>
spell inventory > errors
$
```

The `batch` command is similar to the `at` command. However, with `batch`, you do not specify the time when the commands should be run. Using `batch` is similar to running a job in the background. With `batch`, however, you can log out and still have the job processed. `batch` also differs from the `cron` command. `cron` runs jobs from time to time instead of just once.

Scheduling Commands with `cron`

The `cron` command is used to run—on a regular basis—certain commands that are listed in a `crontab` file. Users do not directly execute the `cron` command. Rather, the system administrator activates the `cron` command during system startup. Because most users do not have root privileges, most users do not have access to the `cron` command.

The `cron` command, however, uses the information in the `crontab` file, which is available to users. You use the `crontab` command to create files that `cron` reads.

Setting Up a Schedule of Commands with `crontab`

The `crontab` command is a way to create a list of commands that will be executed on a regular schedule. The commands are scheduled to run at a specified time, such as once a month, once an hour, once a day, and so on. The list of commands must be included in the `crontab` file, which is created with the `crontab` command. Once you create the `crontab` file, `cron` will read and execute the listed commands at the specified times. The `crontab` command also enables you to view the list of commands you included in the file and cancel the list if you want.

Each user has only one `crontab` file that is created when the `crontab` command is issued. This file is placed in a directory that is read by the `cron` command. Each line in the `crontab` file contains a time pattern and a command. The command is executed according to a specified time pattern. Table 9.8 lists the time field options available with `crontab`.

Table 9.8
Time-Field Options for the `crontab` Command

Field	Range
Minute	0-59
Hour	0-23 (midnight is 0)
Day of month	1-31
Month of year	1-12
Day of week	0-6 (Sunday is 0)

Each call to the `crontab` file overwrites the previous `crontab` file.

The format of the `crontab` file must include six fields in each line, separated by spaces or tabs. The time is specified in the first five fields, and the command to be run is contained in the sixth field. The output of commands run by `crontab` is mailed to you unless you use redirection.

For example, you might include the following list in your `crontab` file in order to run the `mail` command:

```
0 1 1 * * mail
```

In this example, the `mail` command would be run on the first of every month at 1:00 a.m. The asterisk (*) is used to indicate all legal values.

The `crontab` command has two options. The `-r` option *removes* the current `crontab` file from the `crontab` directory. The `-l` option *lists* the contents of the current `crontab` file.

Suppose that your company has a yearly deadline of April 5th for managers to submit their quarterly reports by 11 a.m. `crontab` enables you to schedule in this event by entering it into the `crontab` file. Each year, you will be mailed a message to remind you of this event:

```
0 1 05 04 * echo quarterly reports due today at 11 a.m.
```

This example would mail a message to you once a year reminding you that quarterly reports are due April 5th at 11:00 a.m.

Scheduling the Priority of Commands with `nice`

The `nice` command is used to run a command at a specific scheduling priority. The priority level is determined by the number argument (higher numbers mean lower priorities). The default is set to 10. The priority is incremented, if the number argument is present, by that amount up to a limit of 20.

The format of the `nice` command is as follows:

```
nice [ - increment] command [argument...]
```

The superuser can make the priority of commands higher than normal by using a negative priority specification, such as `--10`.

Checking Current Events with `news`

The `news` command provides a form-system bulletin board where items of interest to people on the network can be posted. A company-sponsored ski trip, an item for sale, or even a birth announcement are possibilities for a news file. Items of importance, such as a visit by a foreign dignitary, would also be directed to users on the network.

A news directory on the system contains all of the "news" files. Issuing the `news` command with no arguments checks to see which files are current (added since the last time you accessed news) and displays the file along with a header listing the newest file first.

The `news` command includes three options, which are listed in table 9.9.

Table 9.9
Commonly Used Options for the `news` Command

Option	Action
-a	Lists *all* news files, whether or not they are current
-n	Lists the *names* of the current news items without listing their contents
-s	Lists the number of current news items

Once a news item is displayed, if you do not want to continue viewing it, you can use an interrupt key, such as <Del> or <^C>, to stop the display and continue to the next item. If you do not want to remain in `news`, simply enter two interrupts within one second to terminate the `news` command.

To list current news items, use the following format:

```
$ news -n <Return>
wellness seminar  (root)  Fri  Jul  13  14:32:19  1990
stress seminar    (root)  Fri  Jul  13  12:06:51  1990
$
```

In this example, using the `news` command with the -n option produces the list of current news topics, in this case the wellness seminar and the stress seminar, without listing any of the contents.

To check a particular news file, use the following form:

```
$ news wellness seminar <Return>
wellness seminar   (root)  Fri  Jul  13  03:24:27   1990
There will be a wellness seminar tomorrow in the
Conference Center. All are invited to attend.
$
```

In this example, `news` is used with the argument `wellness seminar` to call up that particular topic from the list of news items. Along with the listing, the entire contents of this news item is displayed on-screen.

To check the latest news, use the following form:

```
$ news <Return>
aerobics classes        (root)  Sat  Jul 14  15:10:03  1990
The aerobics classes are scheduled to begin next week. They
will consist of four sessions—one per week. For more
details, contact Amanda at extension 555.
$
```

Summary

This chapter presented the commands you need to function effectively in a multiuser environment. The chapter covered the following key points:

❏ You can change your password with the passwd command.

❏ You can find out who is using the system with the who command and its variations, whodo and who am i.

❏ The newgrp command enables you to switch between groups.

❏ You can change the group ownership of files by using chgrp.

❏ Set file and directory permissions with the chmod command.

❏ Use umask to control your file permissions.

❏ You can hand over file ownership by using the chown command.

❏ To switch between accounts, use the su command.

❏ Display the name of your system by issuing the uname command.

❏ Obtain a listing of the active processes with ps.

❏ Stop background commands with the kill command.

❏ Use the lp command to direct output to the line printer; cancel a request by using the cancel command.

❏ Format a file with pr before sending it to the line printer.

❏ Schedule tasks by using the at, batch, and crontab commands.

❏ You can schedule the priority of commands by using the nice command.

❏ Get an update on the current news items listed on the system with the news command.

Being able to use these commands puts you in control of task management. In the next chapter, you learn about the important file-processing commands.

10

Processing Files

UNIX provides several commands that you can use with text files to perform some useful tasks at the operating-system prompt. These tasks include sorting the contents of your files into alphabetical or numeric order, comparing the contents of your files and listing the differences between them, chopping up a file into pieces—either horizontally or vertically—putting those pieces of files together, and adding line numbers to files.

You also can perform comparisons on other types of files; UNIX enables you to determine what type of file you are working with before you attempt to perform any of these tasks.

In this chapter, you see how to accomplish these tasks using the powerful commands provided by the UNIX system.

Key Terms Used in This Chapter

ASCII code	A 7-bit number representing a character or other key on the keyboard.
Text file	A file containing characters or ASCII code. Text files contrast with binary files, which contain bytes of data. Text files are more meaningful to humans. Binary files are more meaningful to machines.
Field	A fixed or variable-length number of characters, which taken together, form a piece of data such as a date or name.
Record	A collection of fields which form a set of information about an item. Several records are used to form a file.
Sort	To place in order, usually in alphabetical and/or numeric sequence.

277

Sort key   Within a record, the field that determines the correct order for a sort.

Delimiter   A character that indicates the end of a field and the start of another, such as the blank character that separates parts of a UNIX command, or the comma or blank space that separates parts of a data record.

End-of-line   A special character at the end of a line to denote where the end is located, sometimes referred to as <CR> or <Return>.

Performing Basic File Operations

So far, you've learned commands that help you manage your UNIX computing environment. You know how to copy, delete, rename and remove files. You also know how to create, move, copy, and remove subdirectories. In this chapter, you learn the commands that process files. Processing files, like managing them, is a part of basic file operations. When you manage files, you deal with each file as an entity. When you process files, you manipulate the contents of the files to produce a resulting output that is useful to you.

UNIX provides many commands that enable you to process files. Most files that you will manipulate will be ASCII text files containing information written in plain English. ASCII characters are encoded bytes that software and hardware interpret as characters and symbols. You've learned about ASCII characters that have control functions, such as Tab <^I> and EOF <^D>. Although these control characters are not exactly "plain English," they do have assigned meanings in a character-device context.

Binary files, in contrast, consist of bytes of data or instructions whose interpretation is determined by the programs that use the data. To an ordinary user, binary data appears to have no rhyme or reason. To the program that created it, however, the data in a binary file makes perfect sense. When you view the output of a binary file on your terminal screen, the output looks like nonsense. Your terminal beeps, flashes, displays strings of meaningless characters, and may even hang. Your screen device is doing the job of interpreting bytes as ASCII characters and is misinterpreting the binary data.

Although applications and certain commands work well with binary data, people don't. A computer's internal vocabulary consists of sequences of ones and zeros; a user's vocabulary consists of words and number representations. The basic file operations you learn in this chapter will enable you to do practical, everyday work with the contents of text files. You will be directing the computing power of UNIX to do work that is of value to you.

Determining a File's Type with `file`

Before you attempt to perform the various types of processing on a text file, it is useful to determine whether or not a file is in fact a text file. Suppose that you want to sort a file. Because sorts are performed in ASCII-character order, it doesn't make sense to sort types of files other than text files. If a file doesn't contain ASCII characters, the sort will not work properly.

You've heard the expression, "You can't judge a book by its cover." Neither can you judge a file by its name. In the first case, you have to read the book to make an accurate judgment. In UNIX, however, provides you with the `file` command so that you can make an "educated guess" about a file's contents.

The `file` command is programmed to perform a series of tests on a file's contents. The command first consults the `/etc/magic` file for additional information to aid the command's determination. `file` classifies a file based on the results of the tests. Because `file` must attempt to classify a file's type based on a limited examination, it occasionally makes errors. `file` is generally correct when it classifies a file as an ASCII file, however. For your file-processing work, you will find `file` to be a useful command.

Some of the types of files you will encounter using `file` include the following:

File Type	Meaning
ASCII-text files	Files readable by humans
Packed data files	Compressed text or binary files
Directory files	The directories you use
Pure executable files	Programs you execute
C-program text files	Source code for programs
Object files	Compiled source code
Archive files	Files held in archive format

Different implementations of `file` recognize other types of files than those just listed, but all implementations recognize ASCII text files. This chapter focuses on your work with ASCII text files. You don't have to worry about the other file types. An ordinary user doesn't have to manipulate nontext files.

To determine a file's type, you type **file**, then the name of the file you want to test, and press <Return>, as follows:

```
$ file payroll <Return>
payroll:      ascii text
$
```

file is a nondestructive command, so feel free to experiment with it. Try the command with several different types of files. You will get responses similar to the following:

```
$ file subdir <Return>
subdir:         directory
$
```

In this example, file reports that subdir is a directory. Using file to test for a directory is easier than using ls -l and looking at the file-type attribute.

Consider the next example:

```
$ file customers.z <Return>
customers.z:    packed data
$
```

file reports that customer.z is a packed file. file can recognize packed data even if you rename the file so that the .z extension (which indicates that the file has been packed) has been removed.

Like the other file-accessing commands, file issues an error diagnostic message when you give a file name as an argument and the file does not exist:

```
$ file comma <Return>
comma:          cannot open, No such file or directory
$
```

If you get this message, you may have entered a typographical error, or the file may not be in your working directory. Check the spelling of the name and use the file's full or relative path name if necessary.

As with other commands that accept file-name arguments, you can use wild cards in the file name. If you use a wild-card pattern that reports more files than will fit on-screen, you can pipe the output to more or pg to break the output into screen-sized chunks. The following command is an example of a file command that includes wild cards and is piped to more:

```
$ file * | more <Return>
```

This full wild-card version of file is especially useful for "scouting out" a new directory.

Two primary options are available with the file command (see table 10.1). The -f flag, for example, enables you to use a list of file names as input to the file command. You also can use the -m option with the SCO UNIX version of file to change the access time for the file to the current time. Without the -m option, file does not modify a file's access time. (See Chapter 6 for more information on access times.)

Table 10.1
Commonly Used Options for the `file` Command

Option	Action
-f *namesfile*	Uses the list of file names in the file *namesfile*
-m	Causes the `file` command to set the access time for the file (SCO UNIX)

The `-f` option is particularly useful when you want to determine the file types for several files rather than just one. You can redirect the output of the `find` or `ls` command to a file. You can then edit the file using `ed` or `vi` to "fine tune" the included file names. Later, you use the edited file of file names as input to `file`. Consider the following command:

```
$ ls -C > tempfile <Return>
$ file -f tempfile <Return>
      <file type listing>
$ rm tempfile <Return>
```

In this example, the `ls` command along with the `-C` (*column* format) option sends the working directory's file names to the file `tempfile`. The `ls -C` command produces output in columns so that the included file names can be used as redirected-input arguments for another command. The `file -f` command includes the `-f` option's argument, `tempfile`. `file` reports the file types of the files included in `tempfile`. The `rm` command removes `tempfile` because its contents are no longer needed.

Splitting a File with `split`

Now that you have a means of determining which files are ASCII text files, you can turn your attention to the first file-processing command you will learn in this chapter. Suppose that you have an especially large file that you want to process in smaller chunks or batches. You may, for example, want to make a phone call to every customer on your customer list. If you want to call 10 customers a day, you can split your customer file into pieces of 10 records each.

The `split` command enables you to split the file into whatever size pieces you want.

Consider the file called `payroll`, which contains the following records:

```
   Name                Number    Address
  Adams, John G.      345678901 3 Oak Lane          Richmond   VA  23280
  Bowers, Frances P.  123456789 87 Sunshine Circle  Orlando    FL  30335
  Cooper, Howard L.   289306315 237 Springside Way  Oakland    CA  90034
  Davis, Willie F.    584830585 590 English Avenue  Boston     MA  00222
```

```
Edwards, Michael J.  872211509 4322 Central Drive     Spokane     WA  11789
Fisher, Richard A.    437901885 491 Ivy Trail         Greenville  SC  29605
Gardner, Sandra M.    456123098 135 Peachtree Street  Atlanta     GA  30399
Hall, Lisa L.         602349571 3348 Pacific Blvd      San Diego   CA  90002
Ingram, Martha W.     424941654 280 Northern Place    Chicago     IL  53411
Jackson, Steven E.    710084236 6 Ranchers Court      Houston     TX  47528
King, Sarah V.        098765432 46 Fox Street         Gary        IN  87765
Lender, David H.      914702355 1024 Coconut Walk     Key West    FL  33333
Martin, Roxanne C.    845761029 598 Technology Park   Newark      NJ  84905
Navarro, Patrick S.   633890071 2349 Meadow Glen      Green Bay   WI  55456
Osborne, Greg J.      270326794 112 Lakewood Village  Raleigh     NC  33419
Paris, Robert G.      110874459 17 Lucky Street       Denver      CO  63673
Quinn, Betty S.       345678901 90834 Cactus Run      Phoenix     AZ  55588
Rogers, Kevin A.      777889999 35 Mountain Climb     Martinsburg WV  10117
Shoemaker, Pete F.    459124755 671 Sandy Plains      Tulsa       OK  41225
Taylor, Nancy M.      333003333 18 Church Street      Scranton    PA  71778
Underwood, Helen B.   654098327 2479 Spinning Hill    Reno        NV  02788
Vaughn, Alice K.      901327450 56 Silver Creek Road  St. Louis   MO  89055
Wilson, Larry D.      265432891 10565 179th Street    New York    NY  10013
Xu, Ming H.           957098459 Postal Route 12906    Anchorage   AK  58640
Young, Sonja P.       028665121 345 Parish Place      Metarie     LA  23789
Zane, Daniel J.       934567870 5565 Key Drive        Washington  DC  56789
```

The payroll file was created with the vi editor. The first line is a heading containing field descriptions. Note the blank space in the first character position before the field heading Name. Because the space character is lower in the ASCII order of the alphabet, the heading line will sort to the beginning of this particular file.

With the split command, you can divide a file into pieces. The default setting for the split command is to split the file into 1,000-line pieces. Because there are nowhere near 1,000 lines in the file, the default split command would not serve any purpose. You can, however, specify the number of lines that split uses to split the file. The split command produces one or more files and gives them the default name x, with aa appended for the first file, ab for the second, and so on for however many files are needed. The original file remains untouched.

Consider the following example:

```
$ split payroll <Return>
$
```

The default split command, issued for the payroll file, generates a file named xaa, which contains 27 lines—the 26 individual listings and the one header listing. Because the payroll file is well under 1,000 lines, the default split criteria split the source file into a single resulting file. To make split useful for small text files, you need to give a smaller number of lines as the split criteria.

To tell `split` how many lines to put into each chunk of the file, you specify the number as an option, as in the following example. Include a file-name prefix, such as `pay`, to specify a name for the files other than the default `x`.

```
$ split -10 payroll pay <Return>
$
```

This example generates three files containing 10, 10, and 6 lines. The files are named `payaa`, `payab`, and `payac`, respectively.

Use the `cat` command to display the contents of the files as follows:

```
$ cat payaa <Return>
    Name             Number    Address
Adams, John G.      345678901 3 Oak Lane            Richmond    VA  23280
Bowers, Frances P. 123456789 87 Sunshine Circle     Orlando     FL  30335
Cooper, Howard L.   289306315 237 Springside Way     Oakland     CA  90034
Davis, Willie F.    584830585 590 English Avenue     Boston      MA  00222
Edwards, Michael J.872211509 4322 Central Drive      Spokane     WA  11789
Fisher, Richard A.  437901885 491 Ivy Trail          Greenville  SC  29605
Gardner, Sandra M. 456123098 135 Peachtree Street   Atlanta     GA  30399
Hall, Lisa L.       602349571 3348 Pacific Blvd      San Diego   CA  90002
Ingram, Martha W.  424941654 280 Northern Place     Chicago     IL  53411
$
```

```
$ cat payab <Return>
Jackson, Steven E. 710084236 6 Ranchers Court       Houston     TX  47528
King, Sarah V.      098765432 46 Fox Street          Gary        IN  87765
Lender, David H.    914702355 1024 Coconut Walk      Key West    FL  33333
Martin, Roxanne C. 845761029 598 Technology Park    Newark      NJ  84905
Navarro, Patrick S.633890071 2349 Meadow Glen        Green Bay   WI  55456
Osborne, Greg J.    270326794 112 Lakewood Village  Raleigh     NC  33419
Paris, Robert G.    110874459 17 Lucky Street        Denver      CO  63673
Quinn, Betty S.     345678901 90834 Cactus Run       Phoenix     AZ  55588
Rogers, Kevin A.    777889999 35 Mountain Climb      Martinsburg WV  10117
Shoemaker, Pete F. 459124755 671 Sandy Plains       Tulsa       OK  41225
$
```

```
$ cat payac <Return>
Taylor, Nancy M.    333003333 18 Church Street       Scranton    PA  71778
Underwood, Helen B.654098327 2479 Spinning Hill      Reno        NV  02788
Vaughn, Alice K.    901327450 56 Silver Creek Road  St.  Louis   MO  89055
Wilson, Larry D.    265432891 10565 179th Street     New York    NY  10013
Xu, Ming H.         957098459 Postal Route 12906     Anchorage   AK  58640
Young, Sonja P.     028665121 345 Parish Place       Metarie     LA  23789
Zane, Daniel J.     934567870 5565 Key Drive         Washington  DC  56789
$
```

The following `split` command generates 14 files, 13 containing 2 lines and one file containing the final line:

```
$ split -2 payroll pay <Return>
$
```

You can try using the `split` command on your large files. When you split large files, you may want to organize the files into a separate directory, especially if you expect to have a large number of pieces to work with.

Sorting Files with `sort`

Notice that the `payroll` file discussed in the preceding section was sorted alphabetically by the first few characters of each line or record in the file. This grouping of characters is called a *field*, and is comprised of the employee's last name in each line.

There is only one sort order—the ASCII character order. You may, however, want your data ordered in a manner other than the way you originally entered the information into the file. UNIX provides the `sort` command to change the ordering of records in your files.

The simple form of the `sort` command sorts records in ASCII-character order, using the first field in the file as the sort key. The capability to sort a file means that you can create a file like `payroll`, in which the records are out of alphabetical order, but sort the file into alphabetical order. Sorting records is common to database-management applications programs, but not common for operating systems.

The following command sorts the `payroll` file:

```
$ sort payroll <Return>
  Name                 Number      Address
Adams, John G.       345678901 3 Oak Lane           Richmond    VA  23280
Bowers, Frances P.   123456789 87 Sunshine Circle   Orlando     FL  30335
Cooper, Howard L.    289306315 237 Springside Way   Oakland     CA  90034
Davis, Willie F.     584830585 590 English Avenue   Boston      MA  00222
Edwards, Michael J.  872211509 4322 Central Drive   Spokane     WA  11789
Fisher, Richard A.   437901885 491 Ivy Trail        Greenville  SC  29605
Gardner, Sandra M.   456123098 135 Peachtree Street Atlanta     GA  30399
Hall, Lisa L.        602349571 3348 Pacific Blvd    San Diego   CA  90002
Ingram, Martha W.    424941654 280 Northern Place   Chicago     IL  53411
Jackson, Steven E.   710084236 6 Ranchers Court     Houston     TX  47528
King, Sarah V.       098765432 46 Fox Street        Gary        IN  87765
Lender, David H.     914702355 1024 Coconut Walk    Key West    FL  33333
Martin, Roxanne C.   845761029 598 Technology Park  Newark      NJ  84905
Navarro, Patrick S.  633890071 2349 Meadow Glen     Green Bay   WI  55456
Osborne, Greg J.     270326794 112 Lakewood Village Raleigh     NC  33419
```

```
Paris, Robert G.        110874459 17 Lucky Street        Denver        CO  63673
Quinn, Betty S.         345678901 90834 Cactus Run       Phoenix       AZ  55588
Rogers, Kevin A.        777889999 35 Mountain Climb       Martinsburg  WV  10117
Shoemaker, Pete F.      459124755 671 Sandy Plains        Tulsa         OK  41225
Taylor, Nancy M.        333003333 18 Church Street        Scranton      PA  71778
Underwood, Helen B.     654098327 2479 Spinning Hill      Reno          NV  02788
Vaughn, Alice K.        901327450 56 Silver Creek Road St. Louis       MO  89055
Wilson, Larry D.        265432891 10565 179th Street      New York      NY  10013
Xu, Ming H.             957098459 Postal Route 12906      Anchorage     AK  58640
Young, Sonja P.         028665121 345 Parish Place        Metarie       LA  23789
Zane, Daniel J.         934567870 5565 Key Drive          Washington    DC  56789
$
```

The `sort` command also contains several options. Table 10.2 lists the options most commonly used with the `sort` command.

Table 10.2
Commonly Used Options for the `sort` Command

Option	Action
`-c`	Verifies that the file is already sorted. If the file is already sorted, there is no output.
`-o`*outfile*	Causes `sort` to place the sorted output in a file—whose name is represented by *outfile*—rather than standard output.

You may find it more useful to write the output of `sort` to a file than to the screen. Use the `-o` flag to write the sorted file to a new file:

```
$ sort -o pays payroll <Return>
$
```

The `payroll` file is already ordered in the default order. To sort the file by a different field, you specify the fields to use as the *sort key*. The `sort` command sorts the file based on the contents of the key field when you give the numbered position of the field as an argument.

For example, to sort the file using the Social Security number, you specify position 3 as the sort key. The `sort` command starts counting fields at 0 and uses the first occurrence of a space or tab character as the default field delimiter. The resulting fields break so that the Social Security number is the third field.

In order for `sort` to determine where the fields start and stop, you must specify a field *delimiter*. The payroll file uses a blank space as the field delimiter. There also can be any number of blank spaces following the middle initial in the employee's name. The `sort` command provides the `-b` flag to ignore any leading blanks in the field on which you are sorting. By using delimiters and the available options, you sort the `payroll` file by Social Security number as follows:

```
$ sort -o payss -b +3 -4 payroll <Return>
$ cat payss <Return>
Young, Sonja P.       028665121 345 Parish Place      Metarie     LA  23789
King, Sarah V.        098765432 46 Fox Street         Gary        IN  87765
Paris, Robert G.      110874459 17 Lucky Street       Denver      CO  63673
Bowers, Frances P.    123456789 87 Sunshine Circle    Orlando     FL  30335
Wilson, Larry D.      265432891 10565 179th Street    New York    NY  10013
Osborne, Greg J.      270326794 112 Lakewood Village  Raleigh     NC  33419
Cooper, Howard L.     289306315 237 Springside Way    Oakland     CA  90034
Taylor, Nancy M.      333003333 18 Church Street       Scranton    PA  71778
Adams, John G.        345678901 3 Oak Lane            Richmond    VA  23280
Quinn, Betty S.       345678901 90834 Cactus Run      Phoenix     AZ  55588
Ingram, Martha W.     424941654 280 Northern Place    Chicago     IL  53411
Fisher, Richard A.    437901885 491 Ivy Trail         Greenville  SC  29605
Gardner, Sandra M.    456123098 135 Peachtree Street  Atlanta     GA  30399
Shoemaker, Pete F.    459124755 671 Sandy Plains      Tulsa       OK  41225
Davis, Willie F.      584830585 590 English Avenue    Boston      MA  00222
Hall, Lisa L.         602349571 3348 Pacific Blvd     San Diego   CA  90002
Navarro, Patrick S.   633890071 2349 Meadow Glen      Green Bay   WI  55456
Underwood, Helen B.   654098327 2479 Spinning Hill    Reno        NV  02788
Jackson, Steven E.    710084236 6 Ranchers Court      Houston     TX  47528
Rogers, Kevin A.      777889999 35 Mountain Climb     Martinsburg WV  10117
Martin, Roxanne C.    845761029 598 Technology Park   Newark      NJ  84905
Edwards, Michael J.   872211509 4322 Central Drive    Spokane     WA  11789
Vaughn, Alice K.      901327450 56 Silver Creek Road  St. Louis   MO  89055
Lender, David H.      914702355 1024 Coconut Walk     Key West    FL  33333
Zane, Daniel J.       934567870 5565 Key Drive        Washington  DC  56789
Xu, Ming H.           957098459 Postal Route 12906    Anchorage   AK  58640
$
```

The -4 flag tells the sort command to use only the third field as the sort key. The default would be to use the fields from the third field to the end-of-line as the sort key(s).

The end-of-line in UNIX files is the ASCII carriage-return character— <Return>, <Enter>, or <CR>.

Another option is to sort by the employee's first name, as in the following example:

```
$ sort +1 -2 -o payfn payroll <Return>
Vaughn, Alice K.      901327450 56 Silver Creek Road St. Louis   MO  89055
Quinn, Betty S.       345678901 90834 Cactus Run     Phoenix     AZ  55588
Zane, Daniel J.       934567870 5565 Key Drive       Washington  DC  56789
Lender, David H.      914702355 1024 Coconut Walk    Key West    FL  33333
Bowers, Frances P.    123456789 87 Sunshine Circle   Orlando     FL  30335
Osborne, Greg J.      270326794 112 Lakewood Village Raleigh     NC  33419
Underwood, Helen B.   654098327 2479 Spinning Hill   Reno        NV  02788
Cooper, Howard L.     289306315 237 Springside Way   Oakland     CA  90034
```

```
Adams, John G.       345678901 3 Oak Lane           Richmond    VA  23280
Rogers, Kevin A.     777889999 35 Mountain Climb    Martinsburg WV  10117
Wilson, Larry D.     265432891 10565 179th Street   New York    NY  10013
Hall, Lisa L.        602349571 3348 Pacific Blvd    San Diego   CA  90002
Ingram, Martha W.    424941654 280 Northern Place   Chicago     IL  53411
Edwards, Michael J.  872211509 4322 Central Drive   Spokane     WA  11789
Xu, Ming H.          957098459 Postal Route 12906   Anchorage   AK  58640
Taylor, Nancy M.     333003333 18 Church Street     Scranton    PA  71778
Navarro, Patrick S.  633890071 2349 Meadow Glen     Green Bay   WI  55456
Shoemaker, Pete F.   459124755 671 Sandy Plains     Tulsa       OK  41225
Fisher, Richard A.   437901885 491 Ivy Trail        Greenville  SC  29605
Paris, Robert G.     110874459 17 Lucky Street      Denver      CO  63673
Martin, Roxanne C.   845761029 598 Technology Park  Newark      NJ  84905
Gardner, Sandra M.   456123098 135 Peachtree Street Atlanta     GA  30399
King, Sarah V.       098765432 46 Fox Street        Gary        IN  87765
Young, Sonja P.      028665121 345 Parish Place     Metarie     LA  23789
Jackson, Steven E.   710084236 6 Ranchers Court     Houston     TX  47528
Davis, Willie F.     584830585 590 English Avenue   Boston      MA  00222
$
```

You do not need the –b flag here because there is always only one blank space following the employee's last name.

Another file that shows how the sort command works is an inventory of office supplies:

```
$ cat inventory <Return>
32154 Envelopes    200   25
19856 Paper        500  100
67833 Pencils      200   20
78906 Staples       25    5
66859 Coffee        15    5
39031 Folders      100   20
29743 Pens          50   10
83459 Diskettes    100   20
90951 Stamps       250   50
56902 Cards        500  100
$
```

To sort the file in ascending numerical order (by part number), you use the default field positions, because the part number is the first field in the file. Also add the following record:

```
.part.description.#...#...
```

Be sure that the period is the first character of the record, so that it is first in a part-number sort:

```
$ sort -o sinv inventory <Return>
```

The resulting `sinv` file now contains the inventory records sorted by part number as shown by the following listing:

```
$ cat sinv <Return>
.part.description.#...#...
19856 Paper       500 100
29743 Pens          50  10
32154 Envelopes    200  25
39031 Folders      100  20
56902 Cards        500 100
66859 Coffee        15   5
67833 Pencils      200  20
78906 Staples       25   5
83459 Diskettes    100  20
90951 Stamps       250  50
$
```

Notice that the first line serves as a field heading for the remaining lines. The period character that begins the line will be sorted before the part numbers of the remaining lines.

To sort the file by the part's description, use the following command:

```
$ sort -o sninv +1 -2 inventory <Return>
56902 Cards        500 100
66859 Coffee        15   5
83459 Diskettes    100  20
32154 Envelopes    200  25
39031 Folders      100  20
19856 Paper        500 100
67833 Pencils      200  20
29743 Pens          50  10
90951 Stamps       250  50
78906 Staples       25   5
$
```

You can undoubtedly find many uses for the `sort` command. Some other uses include sorting appointments by date and time, sorting book titles by author, and sorting addresses by ZIP code for mailing.

In fact, you may want to use the `sort` command before you use some of the comparison commands presented in the next section. Try some experiments with `sort` before proceeding.

Making File Comparisons

UNIX provides several ways to compare files and show their differences. You can use these commands to determine how to merge two documents that have different modifications to the same original. For example, you may want to compare two different versions of a memo so that you can see which parts of the file are still the same and which ones are different in each file. Or, you might want to compare your current `.profile` file with an older version, held in another file name like `.profile.old`, to see the text that is different.

Displaying Common File Contents with `comm`

The `comm` command compares files and shows you differences between files by displaying data from the files in three columns. The first column consists of lines that occur only in the first file; the second column consists of lines that occur only in the second file; and the third column consists of lines that occur in both files.

The files used as input to the `comm` command must be in sorted order. With both files sorted, `comm` can compare lines using a "top-to-bottom" series of comparison tests. Recall from a previous section how to use the `sort` command to sort a file in the default order.

The files `sinv`, `sinv1`, and `sinv2` differ from one another and have been sorted. The sorted files look like this:

```
$ cat sinv <Return>
19856 Paper        500 100
29743 Pens          50  10
32154 Envelopes    200  25
39031 Folders      100  20
56902 Cards        500 100
66859 Coffee        15   5
67833 Pencils      200  20
78906 Staples       25   5
83459 Diskettes    100  20
90951 Stamps       250  50
$
$ cat sinv1 <Return>
19856 Paper        500 100
29743 Pens          50  10
32154 Envelopes    200  25
39031 Folders      100  20
56902 Cards        500 100
66859 Coffee        15   5
78906 Staples       25   5
$
$ cat sinv2 <Return>
19856 Paper        500 100
29743 Pens          50  10
32154 Envelopes    200  25
39031 Folders      100  20
```

```
66859 Coffee          15    5
78906 Staples         25    5
83459 Diskettes      100   20
90951 Stamps         250   50
$
```

You use the `comm` command on files `sinv` and `sinv1` in this manner:

$ **comm sinv sinv1** <Return>

The output of this command example produces a report with two distinct offsets as starting points for each line. The display looks like the following:

```
             19856 Paper        500 100
             29743 Pens          50  10
             32154 Envelopes    200  25
             39031 Folders      100  20
             56902 Cards        500 100
             66859 Coffee        15   5
67833 Pencils   200  20
             78906 Staples       25   5
83459 Diskettes 100  20
90951 Stamps    250  50
$
```

The offsets shown in the output align with tab settings for the terminal you are using. The following headings show the relative positions of the three columns of possible offset for a line. The two lines below the headings are from the above report and show the column alignment of the lines.

```
ONE      TWO      THREE
67833 Pencils   200  20
             78906 Staples       25   5
```

Lines contained in the first file, but not the second, are displayed beginning in the first column. Lines contained in the second file, but not the first, are displayed beginning in the second column. In this case, no line begins in the second column. Lines that are common to both files are displayed beginning in the third column. The key to which column a line belongs is the position where the line begins in the output.

Notice in the full output of the `comm` example that the records containing pencils, diskettes, and stamps are in the first column because they are in `sinv`—but not in `sinv1`. There are no records in `sinv1` that are not not in `sinv`. Therefore, there is no second column. The third column contains the records that are in both files.

Here is another example:

```
$ comm sinv1 sinv2 <Return>
                19856 Paper          500 100
                29743 Pens            50  10
                32154 Envelopes      200  25
                39031 Folders        100  20
56902 Cards         500 100
                66859 Coffee          15   5
                78906 Staples         25   5
           83459 Diskettes   100   20
           90951 Stamps          250  50
$
ONE    TWO        THREE
56902 Cards         500 100
           83459 Diskettes   100   20
                19856 Paper          500 100
```

In this example, lines begin in all three columns. Again, the heading sample shows representative lines aligning at the starting point of the columns. As you can see, by viewing a line's starting point, it's relatively easy to determine whether the line is common to both files, or contained in only one of them.

Often, you want to see the results of a file comparison based on one or two of the columns. If both files have many lines in common, for example, you may find the number of lines presented as column-3 lines to be cumbersome. You don't have to view dozens of common lines just to see a few lines of difference. The comm command enables you to specify which columns of the three-column format you do not want displayed. You tell comm which comparison-test criteria to report by specifying as an option the field number(s) you want to suppress.

To display only the common lines (that is, column 3), you use the −12 flag to suppress display of the first two columns:

```
$ comm −12 sinv1 sinv2 <Return>
19856 Paper          500 100
29743 Pens            50  10
32154 Envelopes      200  25
39031 Folders        100  20
66859 Coffee          15   5
78906 Staples         25   5
$
```

Notice that the output for the column is adjusted to the left on the display, and that the display doesn't align with the column positions used by the full comm output.

You can suppress the second and third columns and display only those lines which are unique to the first file by using the −23 flag:

```
$ comm −23 sinv1 sinv2 <Return>
56902 Cards         500 100
$
```

Likewise, you can suppress the first and third columns by using the −13 flag to show lines that are unique to the second file as in the following:

```
$ comm −13 sinv1 sinv2 <Return>
83459 Diskettes    100  20
90951 Stamps       250  50
$
```

You also can suppress all three columns with the −123 flag, but to what purpose? Nothing would ever be displayed. Nevertheless, comm will accept the −123 option and then return the command prompt.

Displaying File Differences with `diff`

The diff command is another file-comparison command with features that make it useful for reconstructing one version of a file from another version. Advanced users find diff useful for file reconstruction through the ed editor. All users can use diff to read the command's output as a "shorthand" difference report. Although the comm command works with sorted files, diff comparison files do not have to be sorted.

The general information displayed by the diff command is similar to that of the comm command. In addition to displaying the lines that are the same and the lines that are different, diff creates lines that resemble ed commands. In fact, the −e flag causes diff to create a script for use with ed so that each file can be edited to look like the other file. Refer to Chapter 12, "Using the Line Editor ed," for information on the ed text editor.

About the Advanced Uses of `diff` . . .

You can use the output of diff to reconstruct the contents of a text file. Suppose your department recently updated a large training manual from an older manual's text files. If you want to preserve the contents of the old manual, you can keep a copy of the text file under a new file name. The updated manual is also stored in a file. When the project is completed, you can either keep the files for both the old and new manuals or keep a record of the changes between them. Keeping two large files takes a great deal of disk space. In most cases, keeping a file that contains the differences between the old manual and the new manual takes much less space. With the diff command, you can create from the two files a *difference* file that can be used to reconstruct the old manual's contents from the new manual, even if the text file containing the old manual has been deleted.

---

diff takes two file arguments and compares the two files. diff then reports the actions needed to bring the first file's contents into agreement with the second file's contents. In other words, you see the differences between the files as well as the actions you need to take to make the files the same. When diff detects a difference, the command displays an action line as a "shorthand" description of the action needed to eliminate the difference in the first file compared to the second file.

The action line is one of the following forms:

- An append (add) action in the following form:
  n1 a n3,n4
- A delete action in the following form:
  n1,n2 d n3
- A change action in the following form:
  n1,n2 c n3,n4

The n1 through n4 are line numbers referring to the lines that reference the proposed change. When two or more contiguous lines are referenced, the line range is specified as the lowest line number, a delimiting comma, and the highest line number. For example, a line range of lines 5, 6, 7, and 8 is shown as 5, 8. The action line contains an action character of either a, c, or d, corresponding to a proposed action of append (add), change, or delete.

Following the action line, the output of diff also contains lines beginning with > and < characters. Next to these characters are lines of text from the files. The < and > characters indicate which of the files the adjacent line comes from. Lines from the first file are flagged by <. Lines from the second file are flagged by >. diff outputs a series of dashes to separate lines from the first file from the lines from the second file.

When you do hard copy, side-by-side comparisons, one file tends to look like another. You can miss minor differences between two versions of a speech, a procedure, or an itinerary, for example. You can use diff to spot minor differences as well as large differences.

To better understand the output of diff, look at an example comparison in which sinv1 is the first file and sinv2 is the second file. This diff command reports changes necessary in sinv1 to eliminate differences with sinv2. Additional annotation is shown at the right of each line.

```
$ diff sinv1 sinv2 <Return>
7c7,8    (an action line indicating a difference)
< 56902 Cards        500 100  (sinv1 line 7)
---      (line ownership separator)
> 83459 Diskettes    100  20  (sinv2 line 7)
> 90951 Stamps       250  50  (sinv2 line 8)
$
```

The action line, 7c7,8, is read as follows:

- Line 7 in sinv1 must be changed to lines 7 and 8 of sinv2 in order for the two files to agree in respect to this difference.
- The next line (beginning with <) is line 7 from sinv1 and represents where the difference was detected in sinv2.
- The --- dash sequence indicates that all lines from sinv1 for this difference have been reported and that the lines from sinv2 for this difference follow.
- The next two lines (each beginning with >) show the text in lines 7 and 8 of sinv2 that should replace line 7 of sinv1 if the files are to agree about this difference.

When several points of difference occur in two files, diff reports an action sequence for each difference.

As an example of using the diff command, suppose that a user compares two procedures held in text files. The user is responsible for clarifying the roles of employees in routing chapters of the company's training manual. The procedure files are named procedure.old and procedure.new. First, the user views each file on-screen by using the cat command as follows:

```
$ cat procedure.old <Return>
---Routing Procedure---
Mary sends hard copy chapters to Terrie.
Terrie copies chapter and sends copy to Steve.
Steve makes his changes on hard copy and returns copy to Terrie.
Terrie logs changes and gives package to Stacey.
Stacey sends changes back to Mary.
Mary enters changes and sends final file to Bill for printing.
If there's a problem, call Angela.
$

$ cat procedure.new <Return>
---Routing Procedure---
Writer sends file and hard copy to Mary for editing.
Mary sends hard copy chapters to Terrie.
Terrie copies chapter and sends copy to Steve.
Steve makes his changes on hard copy and returns copy to Terrie.
Terrie logs package with changes and gives package to Mary.
Mary enters changes and sends final file to Bill for printing.
$
```

As you can see, the contents of the two files look very similar, but they do contain differences. When you issue the diff command, the differences become apparent:

```
$ diff procedure.old procedure.new <Return>
1a2
> Writer sends file and hard copy to Mary for editing.
5,6c6
< Terrie logs changes and gives package to Stacey.
< Stacey sends changes back to Mary.
> Terrie logs package with changes and gives package to Mary.
> ---
8d7
< If there's a problem, call Angela.
$
```

By referencing the contents of both files, you can use this diff report to see what the user needs to communicate to the employees in order for the employees to understand the new procedure's changes.

The first difference is reported as follows:

```
1a2
> Writer sends file and hard copy to Mary for editing.
```

The user tells the employees, "We've added as the first step the writer sending his work to the editor, Mary."

The next difference is reported as follows:

```
5,6c6
< Terrie logs changes and gives package to Stacey.
< Stacey sends changes back to Mary.
> ---
> Terrie logs package with changes and gives package to Mary.
```

The user tells the employees, "We've changed the two steps where Terrie logs the changes and Stacey sends the changes back to the editor to one step where Terrie logs and sends the changes herself."

The final change to the original procedure is reported as follows:

```
8d7
< If there's a problem, call Angela.
```

The user tells the employees, "Because Angela moved to Frankfort, drop the step of reporting problems to her."

This example shows that diff gives you an interesting perspective on the differences between two files. You may find occasions to use diff in an interesting way.

Options make diff more versatile. The diff command includes several options. These options are listed in table 10.3.

Table 10.3
Commonly Used Options for the `diff` Command

Option	Action
-b	Ignores trailing *blanks* so that white space differences are ignored.
-e	Creates a script which can be used with the `ed` command to convert *file1* to *file2*.
-f	Creates a script which can be used with the `ed` command to convert *file2* to *file1*.

The -b option is useful when spotting differences in files that don't have to do with spacing or tab characters. For instance, if the second file uses 3 spaces to separate columns where the first file uses 2 spaces, `diff` with -b evaluates the white spaces as being equal.

If you are heavily involved in editing text files, you may want to investigate the use of the -e and -f options of `diff` in conjunction with `ed`.

Joining Data from Two Files with `join`

You can merge file data based on comparing files with the `join` command. `join`, like `diff` and `comm`, works with two input-file arguments. The `join` command prints a joined line for each line that has an identical *join field* in each of two files. The join field is the field `join` uses to check whether there is a corresponding record in each file.

The `join` command issued with no options compares the first field of both files. If the files are identical, the command prints the rest of the line from the first file and the rest of the line from the second file.

When you use options with `join`, you can control the makeup of the output. This control enables you to merge the information in two files into a new file consisting of data from all nonduplicated fields from the input files.

The input files to `join` must be in sorted order for the `join` command to work correctly. The sort order is based on the join field. An example of a `join` exercise begins by displaying the contents of two files sorted on the first field as a part number:

```
$ cat sinv <Return>
19856 Paper       500 100
29743 Pens         50  10
32154 Envelopes   200  25
39031 Folders     100  20
56902 Cards       500 100
66859 Coffee       15   5
```

```
67833 Pencils      200   20
78906 Staples       25    5
83459 Diskettes     100   20
90951 Stamps        250   50
$

$ cat sinv1 <Return>
19856 Paper         500  100
29743 Pens           50   10
32154 Envelopes     200   25
39031 Folders       100   20
56902 Cards         500  100
66859 Coffee         15    5
78906 Staples        25    5
$
```

Notice that the part numbers are sorted, but the two files have different numbers of records. Now issue a `join` command with no options to use the first field (the part numbers) as the default join field:

```
$ join sinv sinv1 <Return>
19856 Paper 500 100 Paper 500 100
29743 Pens 50 10 Pens 50 10
32154 Envelopes 200 25 Envelopes 200 25
39031 Folders 100 20  Folders 100 20
56902 Cards 500 100  Cards 500 100
66859 Coffee 15 5 Coffee 15 5
78906 Staples 25 5 Staples 25 5
$
```

The output of this command shows each joined line consisting of a matching line from `sinv` followed by the corresponding line from `sinv1`. Notice that the records that are in `sinv` but are not in `sinv1` are not displayed. This default output shows how joining works, but doesn't suggest any meaningful uses for the `join` command. Output from `join` becomes useful when you use options.

Several options are available with the `join` command. These options are listed in table 10.4.

Table 10.4
Commonly Used Options for the `join` Command

Option	Action
`-an`	Also creates a line for each unpairable line found in file *n* where *n* is 1 (*file1*) or 2 (*file2*).
`-es`	Replaces empty output lines with the character string *s*.
`-jn`	Specifies the *join field* as the *n*th field on the line. The default is 1.
`-tc`	Uses the character *c* as a field delimiter for both input and output.

One option available with `join` is the capability of adding—from either the first (-a1) or second (-a2) file—lines that are not "pairable." This means that there is no corresponding record in the other file. The -a option ensures that all lines from the source-comparison file will appear as output. To add lines from the first file to the standard output, use the -a flag:

```
$ join -a1 sinv sinv1 <Return>
19856 Paper 500 100 Paper 500 100
29743 Pens 50 10 Pens 50 10
32154 Envelopes 200 25 Envelopes 200 25
39031 Folders 100 20  Folders 100 20
56902 Cards 500 100  Cards 500 100
66859 Coffee 15 5 Coffee 15 5
67833 Pencils 200 20
78906 Staples 25 5 Staples 25 5
83459 Diskettes 100 20
90951 Stamps 250 50
$
```

You will notice that only the remainder (in this case, the whole line) of the line `90951 Stamps 250 50` from the first file is included because there is no corresponding line to include from the second file.

The -a flag can likewise be used for lines contained in the second file, but not the first:

```
$ join -a2 sinv sinv1 <Return>
19856 Paper 500 100 Paper 500 100
29743 Pens 50 10 Pens 50 10
32154 Envelopes 200 25 Envelopes 200 25
39031 Folders 100 20  Folders 100 20
56902 Cards 500 100  Cards 500 100
66859 Coffee 15 5 Coffee 15 5
78906 Staples 25 5 Staples 25 5
$
```

It does not matter whether or not the rest of the files are identical. The default `join` command looks only at the first field:

```
$ join sinv sinv4 <Return>
19856 Paper 500 100 Papers 500 100
29743 Pens 50 10 Pens 50 05
32154 Envelopes 200 25 Envelopes 200 25
39031 Folders 100 20  Folders 100 20
56902 Cards 500 100  Cards 500 100
66859 Coffee 15 5 Coffee 15 5
67833 Pencils 200 20 Pencils 100 20
78906 Staples 25 5 Staples 25 5
83459 Diskettes 100 20 Diskettes 100 20
90951 Stamps 250 50 Stamps 350 50
$
```

Another option available with `join`—the `-j` option—provides you with the capability to select a field to join on other than the default first field. For example, the part numbers may have changed, but the description of the part stayed the same. You can therefore use the `-j` option to join records with the same description rather than part number:

```
$ join -j 2 sinv sinv1 <Return>
Paper 19856 500 100 19856 500 100
Pens 29743 50 10 29743 50 10
Staples 78906 25 5 78906 25 5
$
```

You also can use other characters besides the blank space as a field separator, or delimiter. The `-t`c option tells `join` to consider the character given as c to be the field separator character. Some applications, for instance, produce data lists in a record format with fields separated by commas or quotes. If you use a field separator that is one of the shell's special characters, be sure to escape it with a \ character. For example, the `-t\"` option uses the quote character to determine field boundaries.

You can specify a number of filler characters for empty output fields by using the `-e` option. Instead of viewing blank fields in the output, you can specify a placeholding string for `join` to print as a substitute for blank fields. For example, you can give the option `-e '-- empty --'` to replace empty fields with the substitute text -- empty --. In this case, the single quotes that enclose the string hide the space characters from the shell's interpretation as option indicators. For information on these and other options available with `join`, see the Command Reference.

Displaying the Location of File Differences with `cmp`

UNIX provides yet another method of comparing files—a method used mainly for binary files. (You will want to use one of the other methods for comparing text files because they are easier to utilize.) The `cmp` command is useful for verifying that two versions of a binary data file, an object file, or an executable file are identical.

If you have a copy of an applications program in one of your directories and you can't seem to get it to work correctly, the program could be "corrupted." A program is said to be "corrupt" when one or more of the bytes of instruction that constitutes the file changes its binary value.

Data files can become corrupted also. Applications programs and data files can easily reach tens of thousands of bytes in length. Many data files have hundreds of thousands, even millions of bytes. When you suspect that the version of a file in your directory is corrupted, you can issue `cmp` to compare the file byte-for-byte with a supposedly identical file in another directory. Even if just one byte's value is different, cmp will report the problem.

The cmp command displays the location of differences between files as an offset number of bytes from the beginning of the file. This command is useful if you are modifying an executable program or other binary file. The cmp command is included here for illustration; you may find other uses for it.

```
$ cmp sinv sinv1 <Return>
sinv sinv1 differ: char 160, line 7
$
```

One option used with cmp is the −1 flag. The −1 flag causes cmp to print the byte number in decimal numbers, and the actual bytes that differ in octal numbers.

Consider the following command:

```
$ cmp -l sinv sinv1 <Return>
160   66   67
161   67   70
162   70   71
163   63   60
164   63   66
166  120  123
167  145  164
168  156  141
169  143  160
170  151  154
171  154  145
178   62   40
179   60   62
180   60   65
183   62   40
184   60   65
cmp: EOF on sinv1
$
```

In this listing, −1 displays the number of the byte that is different, as well as the ASCII-code numbers of the differing bytes.

Searching for Patterns in Files with grep, fgrep, and egrep

You can search a single file for a pattern with the grep, egrep, and fgrep commands. Both egrep and fgrep are variations of the grep command.

grep stands for global regular expression print. For simplicity's sake you can think of grep as get repeated characters. The egrep and fgrep commands are members of the grep family; egrep stands for extended grep; fgrep stands for fast grep.

The `grep` command searches target files for the occurrence of an expression, such as a word, that you give to `grep` as an argument. `grep` reports all occurrences of the expression along with the file name containing the match.

Suppose that you wanted to find the record for all the employees in the `payroll` file who reside in the state of Georgia. The `grep` command can do the job. You would search the file for the pattern GA and display the following line:

```
grep 'GA' payroll <Return>
Gardner, Sandra M.  456123098 135 Peachtree Street Atlanta    GA  30399
$
```

The commands `fgrep` and `egrep` work in the same general way. The `fgrep` command is a faster version of `grep`, but it is not as flexible in the pattern-matching expressions you can enter. The `fgrep` command works with fixed-string patterns only. Unless you are searching files of 10K in size or more, you won't notice the speed difference between `grep` and `fgrep`.

The `egrep` command is an extension of the `grep` command, in that you can use more complex expressions with `egrep`. You use `egrep` to search for patterns where the expression has an alternate form.

To get the records of all the employees with Florida addresses, enter the following command:

```
$ grep 'FL' payroll <Return>
Bowers, Frances P.  123456789 87 Sunshine Circle   Orlando    FL  30335
Lender, David H.    914702355 1024 Coconut Walk    Key West   FL  33333
$
```

You can use the regular expression wild-card character, the period (`.`), in an expression to match any character in a record. Using just the period within the single quotes (`' . '`) gives you every record in the file, as in the following command:

```
$ grep '.' payroll > paygrep <Return>
```

The single quotes are used to delimit the string. Quotes aren't necessary unless you want to hide spaces and special characters from the shell, but getting in the habit of enclosing the `grep` expression in quotes is a good idea.

To match any one of several characters, enclose the string in square brackets `[ ]`. For example, to match either X, Y, or Z, use `[XYZ]` as follows:

```
$ grep '[XYZ]' payroll <Return>
Jackson, Steven E.  710084236 6 Ranchers Court     Houston    TX  47528
Quinn, Betty S.     345678901 90834 Cactus Run     Phoenix    AZ  55588
Wilson, Larry D.    265432891 10565 179th Street   New York   NY  10013
Xu, Ming H.         957098459 Postal Route 12906   Anchorage  AK  58640
Young, Sonja P.     028665121 345 Parish Place      Metarie    LA  23789
Zane, Daniel J.     934567870 5565 Key Drive       Washington DC  56789
$
```

As you can see, grep matches any X, Y, or Z in a line and reports the line. When you form your search patterns, you will want to include enough characters to "weed out" unwanted matches. For example, when desired characters in the file are surrounded by spaces, a pattern of ' Z ' will prevent a match of AZ and Zane.

To combine more than one test, use the egrep command with the OR operator |. Consider the following example:

```
$ egrep '[XYZ]|GA' payroll <Return>
Gardner, Sandra M.   456123098 135 Peachtree Street  Atlanta      GA   30399
Jackson, Steven E.   710084236 6 Ranchers Court      Houston      TX   47528
Quinn, Betty S.      345678901 90834 Cactus Run       Phoenix      AZ   55588
Wilson, Larry D.     265432891 10565 179th Street     New York     NY   10013
Xu, Ming H.          957098459 Postal Route 12906     Anchorage    AK   58640
Young, Sonja P.      028665121 345 Parish Place        Metarie      LA   23789
Zane, Daniel J.      934567870 5565 Key Drive          Washington   DC   56789
$
```

In this example, you see lines resulting from the matches of X, Y, and Z that matched the [XYZ] pattern, and the first line, which matches the GA pattern. You can use the OR construction to match patterns like Jim or James or Jimmy in a single egrep command.

You may want to practice forming expressions by performing searches on your own files. Also, you may want to review the information on the ed command in Chapter 12, "Using the Line Editor ed," to review the techniques for forming string expressions.

Cutting and Pasting File Contents

You may want to create new files containing only certain columns from previous files. Or you might want to change around the order in which columns of data appear in your files. The cut and paste commands enable you to reorder columns and write them out to different files.

Extracting Columns from a File with cut

Sometimes you don't want an entire line from a file. You may be interested in a single column of characters or string of characters. The cut command enables you to specify the characters or fields you want to take from a line or lines in the file.

Table 10.5 includes the options most commonly used with the cut command.

Table 10.5
Commonly Used Options for the cut Command

Option	Action
-clist	Extracts the characters in the character positions specified in *list*. Used with a dash (−) to indicate a range of positions; used with a comma (,) to separate items in the list.
-flist	Extracts the fields in field positions specified in *list*. Used with a dash (−) to indicate a range of positions; used with a comma (,) to separate items in the list.
-dc	The character following the d is the field delimiter. −d is valid only with the −f option. cut uses the tab character for *c* if d is specified, but *c* is not.

Consider the inventory file, which contains four fields: part number, description, quantity on hand, and minimum quantity:

```
$ cat inventory <Return>
32154 Envelopes   200   25
19856 Paper       500  100
67833 Pencils     200   20
78906 Staples      25    5
66859 Coffee       15    5
39031 Folders     100   20
29743 Pens         50   10
83459 Diskettes   100   20
90951 Stamps      250   50
56902 Cards       500  100
$
```

To print only the part numbers, use the cut command as follows:

```
$ cut -c1-6 inventory <Return>
32154
19856
67833
78906
66859
39031
29743
83459
90951
56902
$
```

The −c flag specifies that the numbers following are character positions. Positions 1 through 6 in the file have been included in the output. (The sixth position is a space character in this example's output. The space character will separate the part-number field from additional fields in later examples.)

To write the output to a file, use the redirection symbol >.

```
$ cut -c1-6 > inv1 <Return>
$
```

Next cut the part descriptions and write the output to the file inv2:

```
$ cut -c7-18 inventory > inv2 <Return>
$ cat inv2 <Return>
Envelopes
Paper
Pencils
Staples
Coffee
Folders
Pens
Diskettes
Stamps
Cards
```

The file inventoryd contains the same data as the file inventory, with a comma used to delimit the fields. The −f flag enables you to use a list of field numbers, rather than character positions. The −d flag specifies the delimiter.

A blank space is assumed (as in the preceding examples) to be the default delimiter:

```
$ cut -f1,3,4 -d "," inventoryd > inv3 <Return>
$ cat inv3 <Return>
32154,200,25
19856,500,100
67833,200,20
78906,25,5
66859,15,5
39031,100,20
29743,50,10
83459,100,20
90951,250,50
56902,500,100
$
```

Putting a File Back Together with paste

You can put back together the files you operated on with cut by using the paste command. paste merges the lines of as many files as you want. For example, to merge the `inv2` and `inv1` files created with the `cut` command and to display the output, use the following command:

```
$ paste inv2 inv1 > inv4 <Return>
$ cat inv4 <Return>
Envelopes       32154
Paper           19856
Pencils         67833
Staples         78906
Coffee          66859
Folders         39031
Pens            29743
Diskettes       83459
Stamps          90951
Cards           56902
$
```

For files `inv3` and `inv2`, the output is as follows:

```
$ paste inv3 inv2 > inv5 <Return>
$ cat inv5 <Return>
32154,200,25      Envelopes
19856,500,100     Paper
67833,200,20      Pencils
78906,25,5        Staples
66859,15,5        Coffee
39031,100,20      Folders
29743,50,10       Pens
83459,100,20      Diskettes
90951,250,50      Stamps
56902,500,100     Cards
$
```

The `paste` command includes several options that specify the delimiter between the lines from each file and that enable you to merge lines from the same file onto one line. See table 10.6 for a list of these options.

Table 10.6
Commonly Used Options for the `paste` Command

Option	Action
-d*list*	Specifies the *list* of characters to use between pasted fields
-s	Merges all lines in the same file to make a single line in the output

The following section shows you how to paste line numbers onto the beginning of each line of a file.

Adding Line Numbers to a File with nl

You can add line numbers to the beginning of each line of a file by using the nl command. Numbering lines enables you to identify a line's relative position in a file. You may, for instance, number the lines of a memo so that you and another person can review the printed memo's contents by referencing line numbers.

Consider this example:

```
$ nl inventory <Return>
     1   32154 Envelopes    200   25
     2   19856 Paper        500  100
     3   67833 Pencils      200   20
     4   78906 Staples       25    5
     5   66859 Coffee        15    5
     6   39031 Folders      100   20
     7   29743 Pens          50   10
     8   83459 Diskettes    100   20
     9   90951 Stamps       250   50
    10   56902 Cards        500  100
$
```

By default, ln right-justifies the numbers, uses six positions for the line numbers, and suppresses leading zeros.

You can use several options with ln. These are listed in table 10.7.

Table 10.7
Commonly Used Options for the nl Command

Option	Action
-i*incr*	Specifies the value to use to increment for each line number. The default is 1.
-s*sep*	The character or characters to use to separate the line number from the rest of the line. The default is the tab character.
-w*width*	The width of the numbers to use for the line number. The default width is 6.
-n*format*	The specified format of the line numbers. Specify ln for left-justified with leading zeros suppressed, rn for right-justified with leading zeros suppressed, rz for right-justified with leading zeros kept. The default is rn.

To use leading zeros and right-justify the numbers, use the -nrz flag:

```
$ nl -nrz inventory <Return>
000001   32154 Envelopes    200   25
000002   19856 Paper        500  100
000003   67833 Pencils      200   20
000004   78906 Staples       25    5
000005   66859 Coffee        15    5
000006   39031 Folders      100   20
000007   29743 Pens          50   10
000008   83459 Diskettes    100   20
000009   90951 Stamps       250   50
000010   56902 Cards        500  100
$
```

You may need more room for your line numbers than the 6 places nl uses by default. Use the -w flag to change the width of the numbers. To specify a width of 20 places, for example, use the following command:

```
$ nl -nrz -w20 inventory <Return>
00000000000000000001    32154 Envelopes    200   25
00000000000000000002    19856 Paper        500  100
00000000000000000003    67833 Pencils      200   20
00000000000000000004    78906 Staples       25    5
00000000000000000005    66859 Coffee        15    5
00000000000000000006    39031 Folders      100   20
00000000000000000007    29743 Pens          50   10
00000000000000000008    83459 Diskettes    100   20
00000000000000000009    90951 Stamps       250   50
00000000000000000010    56902 Cards        500  100
$
```

Use the -s flag to specify a separator between the line number and the rest of the line. For example, use -s, to use a comma to separate the number from the rest of the line. Recall the inventoryd file containing commas for field delimiters. You can add a line-numbers field to the file and still keep commas for field delimiters. Consider this example:

```
$ nl -nrz -w4 -s, inventoryd <Return>
0001,32154,Envelopes,200,25
0002,19856,Paper,500,100
0003,67833,Pencils,200,20
0004,78906,Staples,25,5
0005,66859,Coffee,15,5
0006,39031,Folders,100,20
0007,29743,Pens,50,10
0008,83459,Diskettes,100,20
0009,90951,Stamps,250,50
0010,56902,Cards,500,100
$
```

You can specify both a starting number and an increment for the `ln` command. As you have seen, the default is to start with 1 and increment by 1. You also can use the `-nln` flag to left-justify the numbers and omit leading zeros:

```
$ nl -nln -w4 -v100 -i10 inventory <Return>
100     32154 Envelopes   200    25
110     19856 Paper       500   100
120     67833 Pencils     200    20
130     78906 Staples      25     5
140     66859 Coffee       15     5
150     39031 Folders     100    20
160     29743 Pens         50    10
170     83459 Diskettes   100    20
180     90951 Stamps      250    50
190     56902 Cards       500   100
$
```

Choosing Numbering Schemes Carefully . . .

Be careful which numbering scheme you choose with the `ln` command. If the increment is too large, as in the following example, you can end up using the same numbers over again:

```
$ nl -w4 -v1000 -i1000 inventory <Return>
1000     32154 Envelopes   200    25
2000     19856 Paper       500   100
3000     67833 Pencils     200    20
4000     78906 Staples      25     5
5000     66859 Coffee       15     5
6000     39031 Folders     100    20
7000     29743 Pens         50    10
8000     83459 Diskettes   100    20
9000     90951 Stamps      250    50
0000     56902 Cards       500   100
$
```

Removing Repeated Lines with `uniq`

In certain instances, you might have a file containing repeated lines. For example, a payroll file might gain a line each time an employee is paid. After several weeks, the file would have several lines for each employee. If you wanted to make a mailing list out of this file, you would want only one line for each employee. You can see if the employee named Lender has more than one record in the payroll file using `grep` as in the following example:

```
$ grep Lender payroll <Return>
Lender, David H.     914702355 1024 Coconut Walk     Key West   FL  33333
Lender, David H.     914702355 1024 Coconut Walk     Key West   FL  33333
Lender, David H.     914702355 1024 Coconut Walk     Key West   FL  33333
Lender, David H.     914702355 1024 Coconut Walk     Key West   FL  33333
$
```

There are 4 Lender records in the payroll file reported by grep. You need to remove the duplicates if you want to avoid mailing 3 additional mailings to Mr. Lender. To achieve this, you can use the uniq command to remove repeated lines from the file. Because the uniq command looks at adjacent lines, you first must sort the file using the sort command, and then issue the uniq -d command to view all duplicates, as in the following:

```
$ sort payroll > mailtmp <Return>
$ uniq -d mailtmp <Return>
Lender, David H.     914702355 1024 Coconut Walk     Key West   FL  33333
$
```

In this case, the Lender record is the only duplicate as reported by uniq using the -d option. Now the uniq command eliminates the duplicates leaving only the unique lines as the contents of the redirected output in mailing:

```
$ uniq mailtmp > mailing <Return>
```

The file mailing now contains one line for each group of lines in mailings that were identical. The file mailtmp can be removed.

uniq includes several options, which are listed in table 10.9.

Table 10.9
Commonly Used Options for the uniq Command

Option	Action
-u	Only lines that are *not* unique are included in the output
-d	One copy of just the repeated lines is included in the output
-c	Each line of output begins with a count of the number of times it occurred

Summary

You have seen some of the many tools provided by UNIX to perform tasks on your text files. This chapter has covered the following main points:

❏ You can identify the type of file you are working with by using the file command.

❏ Use the `sort` command to sort the contents of a text file.

❏ To split a file into more manageable-sized pieces, use `split`.

❏ Comparing the contents of two or more files is easy with the `comm` command.

❏ Use the `diff` command to see a shorthand listing of two files' differences.

❏ Use `cmp` to compare two binary files for differences.

❏ Merging the contents of two or more files is the job of the `join` command.

❏ You can find patterns in a file with `grep`.

❏ You can reorder columns in a file with `cut` and `paste`.

❏ Use `ln` to add line numbers to a file.

❏ The `uniq` command eliminates duplicate lines of a file.

In Chapter 11, you learn about the UNIX commands for automating the office environment.

Automating the Office Environment

UNIX doesn't stop at providing commands that enable you to maintain processes, files, and directories. As a member of the UNIX community, you have several advantages in conducting office business using the UNIX office-automation commands. You can use electronic communications to "talk" with other people on your system. Also, you can set up an automatic reminder service to help you keep track of your appointments, display a calendar at your terminal, and use your computer as a desktop calculator. This chapter will introduce the commands you can use to take advantage of these UNIX features.

Key Terms Used in This Chapter

Office automation   Office tasks that are run using a computerized environment.

Descriptor   Modifiers used with the date command to create a specific date and time format.

Desktop calculator   A UNIX feature that enables you to use your keyboard and terminal as a calculator.

Electronic mail   A method that enables you to send and receive messages from users on your computer system or other networked computer systems.

EOF   An abbreviation for *End of File*. An EOF signal terminates keyboard input such as input to the write command used to communicate with other users. You produce an EOF by pressing <^D>.

EOT   An abbreviation for *End of Transmission*. An EOT indicator is
                         displayed on your screen to signify the end of an interactive
                         write command session.

Understanding the Calendar-Based Commands

Several commands employ UNIX's built-in calendar capabilities to help you do
useful work. Among the features UNIX offers are the capability to display a calendar
for any year from 1 to 9999 A.D., the operation of a calendar-based reminder
service, and the capability to display and set the system date and time. These
commands are covered in the following sections.

Displaying a Calendar with `cal`

Suppose that you need to schedule a meeting, but you are not sure on what day of
the week a certain date falls. Or, perhaps you are completing a report and need to
know on what day of the week the tenth of June fell last year. Should you begin to
search for a copy of last year's calendar? No. With UNIX, the cal command does
the searching for you.

The cal command enables you to display a variety of calendar configurations.
When you type **cal** and press <Return>, UNIX displays the current month. When
issued with the *year* argument, cal displays a calendar for each month of the
indicated year. When issued with the number of the month, cal displays the
calendar for that month. The general form of the cal command is as follows:

    cal [*month*] [*year*]

The *month* argument is a number between 1 and 12 representing January through
December. The *year* argument is the *full* number of the year. For example, to
display the year of the American Bicentennial, you need to enter 1976—not 76. A
two-digit year argument is taken literally, in this case to mean the year 76 A.D.

The cal command accepts years in the range 1 through 9999, so you can
experiment with calendars from the distant past or the distant future.

To display the calendar for July, 1977, use the following command:

    $ **cal 7 1977** <Return>

This command displays the calendar for the month of July as it appeared in the year 1977:

```
        July 1977
 S  M Tu  W Th   F   S
                 1   2
 3  4  5  6  7   8   9
10 11 12 13 14  15  16
17 18 19 20 21  22  23
24 25 26 27 28  29  30
31
```

To display the calendar for the year 1960, use the following command:

$ **cal 1960** <Return>

UNIX responds as follows:

```
                                    1960
        Jan                     Feb                     Mar
 S  M Tu  W Th   F   S    S  M Tu  W Th   F   S    S  M Tu  W Th   F   S
                 1   2    1  2  3  4  5   6            1  2  3   4   5
 3  4  5  6  7   8   9    7  8  9 10 11  12  13    6  7  8  9 10  11  12
10 11 12 13 14  15  16   14 15 16 17 18  19  20   13 14 15 16 17  18  19
17 18 19 20 21  22  23   21 22 23 24 25  26  27   20 21 22 23 24  25  26
24 25 26 27 28  29  30   28 29                    27 28 29 30 31
31

        Apr                     May                     Jun
 S  M Tu  W Th   F   S    S  M Tu  W Th   F   S    S  M Tu  W Th   F   S
                 1   2    1  2  3  4  5   6   7                1  2   3   4
 3  4  5  6  7   8   9    8  9 10 11 12  13  14    5  6  7  8  9  10  11
10 11 12 13 14  15  16   15 16 17 18 19  20  21   12 13 14 15 16  17  18
17 18 19 20 21  22  23   22 23 24 25 26  27  28   19 20 21 22 23  24  25
24 25 26 27 28  29  30   29 30 31                 26 27 28 29 30

        Jul                     Aug                     Sep
 S  M Tu  W Th   F   S    S  M Tu  W Th   F   S    S  M Tu  W Th   F   S
                 1   2    1  2  3  4  5   6                    1  2   3
 3  4  5  6  7   8   9    7  8  9 10 11  12  13    4  5  6  7  8   9  10
10 11 12 13 14  15  16   14 15 16 17 18  19  20   11 12 13 14 15  16  17
17 18 19 20 21  22  23   21 22 23 24 25  26  27   18 19 20 21 22  23  24
24 25 26 27 28  29  30   28 29 30 31              25 26 27 28 29  30
31

        Oct                     Nov                     Dec
 S  M Tu  W Th   F   S    S  M Tu  W Th   F   S    S  M Tu  W Th   F   S
                     1       1  2  3  4   5                    1  2   3
 2  3  4  5  6   7   8    6  7  8  9 10  11  12    4  5  6  7  8   9  10
 9 10 11 12 13  14  15   13 14 15 16 17  18  19   11 12 13 14 15  16  17
16 17 18 19 20  21  22   20 21 22 23 24  25  26   18 19 20 21 22  23  24
23 24 25 26 27  28  29   27 28 29 30              25 26 27 28 29  30  31
30 31
```

Displaying the calendar for an entire year may produce too much data for a screen to hold. In this case, it's best to pipe the output of `cal` to `pg` or `more`, so that you can display the calendar one screen at a time:

```
$ cal 1960 | more <Return>
```

About the Julian-to-Gregorian Calendar Switch . . .

The documentation for most UNIX systems invites you to try the calendar for September, 1752, because something interesting happened that month. That month, England switched from the Julian calendar system, the calendar which had been in effect since the days of Julius Caesar, to the Gregorian calendar system.

The Julian system, which had been devised by Caesar's chief astronomer, was not precise, and yearly astronomical occurrences began to creep forward a few days each hundred years. For example, the Julian calendar might determine that the moon was to be in a certain position on one day. In reality, the moon wouldn't be in that position until several days later.

In 1582, Pope Gregory XIII developed a calendar that adjusted this imprecision, but the British did not accept these corrections until 1752—170 years after the Gregorian calendar was first implemented in much of Europe.

Although the Gregorian calendar system corrects the Julian calendar's imprecision, to adjust the date to the astronomical occurrences, the British had to "drop" 11 days in the month of September, 1752. The following listing shows what happened:

```
$ cal sep 1752 <Return>
      September 1752
   S  M Tu  W Th  F  S
            1  2 14 15 16
   17 18 19 20 21 22 23
   24 25 26 27 28 29 30
```

Be assured that `cal`'s version of the calendar that month is *correct*.

Accessing a Reminder System with `calendar`

The `cal` command makes it possible for you to view the calendar for a specific month and year. The `calendar` command, on the other hand, takes date-based information a step further. Contrary to what its name might imply, `calendar` does *not* create calendar displays. The `calendar` command is the main component of a date-triggered reminder service for individual users.

To use this reminder service, you first create a file called `calendar` in your home directory. This file should contain a line describing each scheduled event (for example, a meeting, a conference, or other appointment) along with corresponding date and time. The date and time can appear anywhere in the line.

You can enter the date and time in several formats. `calendar` recognizes entries which are given in the following month-day formats:

```
December 25
dec.25
12/25
```

Note that the `calendar` command does not recognize the European day-month order, such as `25 December`.

A sample `calendar` file could be structured as follows:

```
7/10 Quarterly reports due
july 11 9 a.m. Staff meeting
12/3 Regional director's meeting 8 a.m.
4/12 Has the quarterly report been published?
```

The `calendar` file can be created with any UNIX editor, such as `ed` or `vi`. A screen editor such as `vi` displays the selected file on-screen and enables the user to move freely through it, inserting text and making other changes.

Once you have decided that you want to use the `calendar` reminder service, it is best to include the `calendar` command in your `.profile` file (see Chapter 5). Then, you will have a list showing the things you need to do for that day and the following day mailed to you automatically when you log in. (If it's Friday, the following day extends to Monday, including the weekend.) If you decide you want to manually access the command, simply type **calendar** at the system prompt and press <Return>.

The `calendar` command is of no use unless the `calendar` file exists. This file must reside in your home directory. When you invoke `calendar`, UNIX looks for the file `calendar` *only* in the current directory, so you should be in your home directory when you execute `calendar`. You can, however, link a file named `calendar` in each of your common directories to the `calendar` file in your home directory. See Chapter 10 and the Command Reference for more information on linking files.

As another example, assume that the date is July 10. Use `calendar` to remind yourself of what has to be done (the reminders are taken from the example `calendar` file created in the previous paragraphs). After logging in to the system, use the following command:

```
$ calendar <Return>
7/10 Quarterly reports due
july 11 7 p.m. Staff meeting
$
```

The `calendar` command will display reminders for the day you invoke the command as well as the following day. Note that several different date formats are used in this example.

Displaying the Date and Time with `date`

The `date` command displays the current date and time. You can use the command to provide date information for `.login` files or simply to check the time. The `date` command also provides special formatting options that you can use to change the appearance of the displayed date and time.

NOTE

The `date` command is capable of setting the time of the system's internal clock. The command uses this internal clock as its source of time. Even though any user can use `date` to see a display of the time and date, only the superuser can use the `date` command to set the system clock. If you notice that the time or date are incorrect, tell your system administrator immediately.

If you do not specify a format with `date`, the date and time are displayed as in the following example:

```
$ date <Return>
Thur Apr 12  14:02:12 EDT 1990
$
```

In this default format, the date and time output of `date` displays an abbreviation for the day of the week and the month. The time is displayed in hours, minutes, and seconds. The command also displays the abbreviation for the system's time zone, followed by the full year number. The clock time is presented in 24-hour (military) format. The system tracks time in GMT and converts the time to the time zone you are in for reporting date and time.

You can optionally use text strings and *descriptors* to change the format of this display. A descriptor is a modifier used with the `date` command to create a specified date and time format. A percent character (`%`) precedes each descriptor. The `%` character indicates to `date` that a special format follows. In the displayed output, the `date` command substitutes formatted letters or numbers in place of the designated descriptor. By selecting an appropriate group of descriptors, you can create almost any date and time format you want. Descriptors that can be used to change the format are listed in table 11.1.

Table 11.1
Descriptors for the date Command

Descriptor	Action
%n	Inserts a newline character
%t	Inserts a tab character
%m	Represents the month number (1-12)
%d	Represents the day number (1-31)
%y	Represents the two digits of the year (00-99)
%D	Uses the format mm/dd/yy to display the date
%H	Represents the hour (00-23)
%M	Represents the minute (00-59)
%S	Represents the second (00-59)
%T	Uses the format HH:MM:SS to display the time
%j	Represents the day of the year (001-366)
%w	Represents the day of the week (0-6; Sunday is 0)
%a	Represents the day's name (Sunday-Saturday)
%h	Represents the month's name (January-December)
%r	Represents the time in AM/PM notation
%%	Prints a single % symbol

To display the time in a format you establish, use the plus-sign (+) option indicator followed by a format specification. If the format contains spaces or special characters, enclose the entire format within single or double quotation marks. Descriptors are case-sensitive, so be sure to use the correct upper- or lowercase letter. An example format option is shown in the following command:

```
$ date   '+Today's date is %d/%m/%y' <Return>
Today's date is 17/6/90
$
```

In this example, the text string '+Today's date is %d/%m/%y' is enclosed within single quotes. The single quotes make the string a single argument. The descriptors used in this argument display the date in just the day, month, year format. All text within the quotes is displayed exactly as you entered it. Here's how the date example format is interpreted:

Command Element	Result
Today's date is	This is text that is displayed literally as Today's date is.
%d	In place of this descriptor, date displays the day of the month as a number. In this, case, the number 17 is displayed.
/	Because the / date separator is not output as part of this command's descriptors, you must enter the / character between the %d and the %m descriptors if you want a standard date presentation.
%m	In place of this month descriptor, date outputs the month of the year as a number. In this case the number 6 is displayed.
/	Again, you supply the literal / character to separate the month from the year in the output.
%y	In place of this year descriptor, date outputs the last two numbers of the year. In this case the number is 90.

As you can see, using text strings and descriptors in a date format enables you to control the look of the displayed output. You can create more elaborate formats by combining text and descriptors. To save yourself the effort of typing an elaborate format several times during a session, you can assign the format to an environment variable. Here's an example you can try:

```
$ FULL='%nThe Date today is %a %h %d, 19%n\ <Return>
> The Time is exactly %r%nHave a nice day!%n' <Return>
$ export FULL <Return>
```

The first step in this example assigns the format string to the variable FULL and then exports the variable. The FULL variable is now available to your current shell and subsequent subshells.

The formatted text is enclosed within single quotes to hide spaces and other special characters from the shell during command-line scanning.

Notice the use of %n descriptors in the assignment. The %n descriptors output newline characters. In this format, %n descriptors place a blank line before the readable text, separate the output to two lines, and finally, leave a blank line between the viewable text and the shell prompt.

To use the format, enter the date command as follows:

```
$ date +$FULL <Return>
The Date today is Fri Aug 31, 1990
The Time is exactly 11:29:06 AM
Have a nice day!
$
```

If you don't understand how the descriptors and text result in this output, refer to table 11.1 for an the explanation of the descriptors used, and compare the explanation with the displayed output. Before long, you'll be creating interesting `date`-command formats for your own use.

Understanding the Communications Commands

You've learned about the UNIX text-file commands, device commands, and filing system. These system facilities constitute the core of a written message-communications system. It seems only natural that UNIX provides commands that build on this core to provide you with an electronic means to communicate with other users on the system. Many UNIX systems incorporate networking hardware and software that enables users to communicate with other UNIX systems and their users.

In a UNIX-automated office, you eliminate most paper-message notes, memos, and other forms of paper correspondence. In their place, you use your terminal to enter messages that the system "delivers" to other users. In this section, you will learn about the UNIX communications features.

Many of the remote features of the mail system depend on the installation on your system of the UUCP utilities. See Chapter 4 for a description of UUCP.

The communications facilities of UNIX offer several levels of communications—including file transfers, remote login capabilities, and extensive message systems that can link hundreds of UNIX systems. These facilities are discussed in the following sections.

Sending and Receiving Mail

Two UNIX commands—`mail` and `write`—enable you to to send and receive messages from other users on the UNIX system. The features of the existing mail utility depend on the release number of the UNIX operating system. This chapter's discussion of the `mail` command concentrates on the options associated with System V, Release 3. The basic concepts, however, are the same in all releases. If you are presently using a release other than Release 3, refer to your User's Manual for particulars.

On some systems, the command to access mail facilities is `mailx`. If your system uses the `mailx` command, you will substitute `mailx` where you see `mail`.

UNIX `mail` is a terminal-based, electronic-message system. Within your system, a mailing address is a user's login name. A user can send and retrieve his or her mail from any terminal on the system. The mailing system doesn't just provide for routing and delivering the messages you send and receive. It also provides capabilities to manage the mail that you receive.

Several sets of options are available with the `mail` command. Tables 11.2 and 11.3 outline the options available for use in sending mail and dealing with mail sent to you.

Table 11.2
Options for Sending Mail

Option	Action
-o	Suppresses the address optimization facility. *Address optimization* is the process of selecting the best routing for hold-and-forward network mail addresses.
-s	Suppresses the addition of a new line at the top of the message being sent.
-w	Sends a message to a remote user without waiting for the remote-transfer program to be completed.
-t	Causes a destination line to be added to the message. This line takes the following form: To: *list of intended receivers* **Note:** Not all implementations of `mail` accept options for sending mail.

Table 11.3
Options for Retrieving Mail

Option	Action
-e	Tells you whether mail is available without displaying the list of mail items. This option displays 0 for mail and 1 for no mail.
-h	Lists numbered messages containing each item of mail, with a header indicating the sender, date, and message size. Displays a ? prompt following the list.
-p	Eliminates the prompt asking for an individual response while displaying all mail messages.
-q	An interrupt signal used to cause mail to quit. Usually terminates the printing of a message.
-r	Displays messages in the order in which they were sent.
-f*file*	Reads the mail from the specified *file* instead of from the default file.
-F*person*	Causes all incoming mail to be forwarded to specified *person* (s) by modifying an empty mail file.

Sending Mail to Other Users

You can send a message to someone by addressing the message to the intended party and then typing the contents of that message. You can also send a file to someone by including that file in the mail message. This method is discussed in the next section.

To use the first method, type **mail**, followed by the login name of the person you want to send the mail to. Press <Return>. Then enter the message and terminate the transaction as follows:

```
$ mail amanda <Return>
Good morning!  This is going to be a hectic day. Please
remember our scheduled meeting at noon. <Return>
<^D>
$
```

In this example, the command line, which includes the address argument amanda, tells mail where to send the message. The mail command then drops the cursor to the next line and awaits your input. Your input is the message to be sent. You enter text until you are finished with the message. When you are finished, press <Return> to begin a blank line, and then press <^D> as the EOF indicator. The <^D> indicates the end of the message. When mail detects the EOF character, the message is sent, and the command prompt returns.

This example points out the simplicity of sending a short mail message using mail. You can experiment by sending yourself mail. Just use your login name as an argument with mail.

You can end your mail message by entering the <^D> at the end of a line. Or, you can simply type a period (.) as the first character on a new line, and then press <Return>. The period is taken to mean "this is the end of the message." The period is not sent with the message.

Sending a mail message that you compose within mail is the most common method for communicating with other users on the network. You can also send a file to someone by using redirection (see the next section, "Sending a File").

You can make corrections in the message only on the line you are currently typing. You cannot correct any errors once they are entered. If you have many errors in your message and you want to abandon the mail operation without sending the message, press the interrupt key two times. (The interrupt key is <^C>, <Del>, or <Break>, depending on your system.)

When you type mail messages, mail breaks the line at the right margin and wraps the last partial word to the next line. Often, the result of this wraparound is split words in the right margin. You can, however, avoid this problem. Press <Return> at the end of lines—before they wrap—instead of relying on the wraparound method to determine when to go to the next line.

Sending a File with `mail`

In addition to sending simple messages with the `mail` command, you can also send information that is stored in ASCII text files. Rather than typing the contents of a message from within `mail`, you can use redirection with the `mail` command to indicate the source of the message (in other words, the file name being sent). You can redirect memos, lists, ASCII data files, and other text files through `mail`.

Be sure that the permission mode for `others` for the redirected file is r. The file's `other` access mode must be r also. (See Chapter 9 for an explanation of the `chmod` command.

Consider this example, in which a text file containing inventory information is redirected to `mail`:

```
$ mail cheryl < inventory <Return>
$
```

When you issue this command, the file named `inventory` is sent to the user named `cheryl`. The redirection symbol < performs the redirection.

About "Dead Letters" . . .

In some cases, the mail you send cannot be delivered. Your mail may not be delivered to your intended party, for example, if you have entered an incorrect login name, or the login name you specified no longer exists or has been changed. In such a situation, you are informed by a message on your screen, and a copy of the undelivered mail is mailed back to you.

If you cancel the message you are composing within `mail` by pressing an interrupt key—such as <^C>, <Break>, or <Del>—twice during input, on some systems, the `mail` command copies the message to a file in your current directory named `dead.letter`. You can also create a `dead.letter` file by mailing a message to a directory instead of a user.

Don't worry about being unaware that you've created a dead letter. The system informs you. You can edit the `dead.letter` message if you want, and then mail it at a later time. The `dead.letter` file is overwritten with each new piece of dead mail so that the last piece of dead mail received is actually the current contents of the `dead.letter` file.

Mailing to a User on a Remote System

Recall from Chapter 4 that many UNIX systems are connected by a point-to-point network through the facilities of the UUCP command suite. A system of remote communications through `mail` is available to many users, so you may be able to use remote mail on your system. Ask your system administrator for details about your remote-mailing capabilities.

To communicate with someone on a remote system linked to yours, you need to use a modified form of the address argument. Each system has a machine name or site name that identifies the computer. You include the site name of the remote system as a component of the target user's mail address.

Be aware that the process of connecting, routing, and delivering remote mail is not instantaneous. Depending on the routing and delivery schedule, delivery can take place within a few minutes, or it can take as long as several hours. Your system administrator can advise you about the typical time it takes to deliver mail to different sites.

To form a UUCP-style remote-address argument, enter the the name of the remote system, followed by an exclamation mark (!), and then include the login name of the person you are sending the message to, as in the following example:

```
$ mail ricksvax!amanda <Return>
Please bring enough copies of the product spec to
the 3 p.m. meeting.
<^D>
$
```

In this example, a mail message is being sent to amanda on the remote system. The remote system's site name is ricksvax. The communications facilities of UUCP (or other networking software) arrange the details of connecting the local system with ricksvax. You don't need to deal with the communications details to use remote mail. Once the message is received by ricksvax, the mail facilities on that computer use the address text that follows the first exclamation mark to deliver the mail to amanda.

Some systems support the alias command, which enables you to assign a long address to a shorter string. You can use this "aliased" string as an address; mail will substitute the full address. Here is an example:

```
$ alias davesol queps2!andiron!david <Return>
$ mail davesol <Return>
```

Receiving Mail

To receive mail, type **mail** at the system prompt and press <Return>. The last message received is displayed, followed by a ? prompt. Table 11.4 lists the variety of responses that can be used as subcommands at the mail command's ? prompt.

Table 11.4
Subcommands for the `mail` Command

Subcommand	Result
<Return>	Proceeds to the next message.
+	Proceeds to the next message.
−	Returns to the preceding message.
d or dp	Proceeds to the next message after deleting the message just displayed.
dn	Deletes the message number specified by n and does not go to the next message.
dq	Quits mail after deleting the current message.
h	Lists a window of headers (description of numbered messages), including the current message.
hn	Displays the header for the message specified by n.
ha	Displays all message headers.
hd	Lists headers for messages that are marked for deletion.
n	Proceeds to the next message.
p	Redisplays the message.
q	Quits and puts undeleted mail back into the `mail` file.
s*file*	Deletes the message from the system `mail` file and saves it in the designated *file*. If you do not define the file, it saves the message in the `mbox` file in your home directory.
<^D>	Works the same as q.
x	Exits `mail` with all messages unchanged as though you hadn't used the `mail` command.
y	Same as s.
?	Displays `mail` commands.

To check your mail, use the following command:

```
$ mail <Return>
>from vincent  Mon  Jun 18 09:28:14 1990
Luncheon meeting
?
```

This command enables you to read the mail message. You can then decide what you want to do with the message and respond at the ? prompt with the appropriate subcommand (see table 11.4).

You can get some idea of a typical `mail` session by viewing the screen dialog of a user named David as he accesses his mail. The session appears in the following example.

In the first two lines, David confirms his working directory:

```
$ pwd <Return>
/usr/david
```

David then uses the `file` command to determine whether his `mbox` message-saving file has any messages stored in it:

```
$ file mbox <Return>
mbox:           empty
```

The `file` command reports a file type of `empty` when no information exists in a file. The `empty` type means that the file has 0 bytes in it.

Next, David issues the `mail` command to review new mail:

```
$ mail <Return>
SCO System V Mail (version 3.2)  Type ? for help.
"/usr/spool/mail/david": 2 messages 2 new
N  2 terrie@andiron.UUCP Sat Sep  1 21:56    14/451   Reports Due Tuesday
N  1 root@andiron.UUCP   Sat Sep  1 21:51    18/596   File Clean-up
?
```

`mail` displays its version number on the first line and then reports that two messages are in David's system-mail file, `/usr/spool/mail/david`. The next two lines are message headers that identify the new mail messages.

Notice that the message headers begin with `SN` followed by a number. The number is the `mail` command-prompt identifier for the message. At the `?` prompt (seen later in the sequence) you can identify the message you want to work with using this number. To the right of the message ID number is the name and machine name of the sender. At the right of each line, you see the subject of each message.

To view his messages, starting with message 1, David presses <Return>:

```
? <Return>
Message  1:
From root Sat Sep  1 21:51:53 1990
From: root@andiron.UUCP (Superuser)
X-Mailer: SCO System V Mail (version 3.2)
To: david
Subject: File Clean-up
Date: Sat, 1 Sep 90 16:51:49 EST
Message-ID:  <9009012151.aa00238@andiron.UUCP>
Status: R

On September 10th, the systems group is going to optimize the hard disk.
Please delete any unused or duplicate files from your directories.
```

```
If you have seldom used files that show more than 10,000 bytes in an
ls-1 listing, use pack to compress the files. You can unpack them
with unpack when you need to use the files.

Your cooperation is appreciated.
        John Aberle
?
```

The lines in front of the message body are status and identification lines. The appearance of these lines varies from system to system. When David reads the body of his message, he elects to save the message to his mbox file. He can enter a **s** command at the ? prompt, but he also can press <Return> both to mark this message for saving to mbox and also to display the next message.

```
? <Return>
Message  2:
From terrie Sat Sep  1 21:56:01 1990
From: terrie@andiron.UUCP (Terrie Lynn)
X-Mailer: SCO System V Mail (version 3.2)
To: david
Subject: Reports Due Tuesday
Date: Sat, 1 Sep 90 16:55:59 EST
Message-ID:  <9009012156.aa00255@andiron.UUCP>
Status: R

Just a friendly reminder that your sales analysis report is due
Tuesday by 4:00 PM. You can mail the report to me at my login if
you do it in vi. Otherwise, I'll look for it in the departmental
mail box.

TL
?
```

David reads this message too, but he answers a phone call before he can respond to the ? prompt. When the call is completed, he turns to his terminal and instinctively presses a <Return> at the ? prompt:

```
? <Return>
Can't go beyond last message.
?
```

David forgot that there were only two new messages in his mail. His pressing <Return> to bring up the next message was greeted by an error message from mail. David decides to exit his mail session with the new messages left in the same state they were before he began the session. He presses the **x** (exit) command and returns to the UNIX $ prompt:

```
?x <Return>
$
```

Later, when activities are not as hectic, David reviews his mail again. You can follow the sequence:

```
$ mail <Return>
SCO System V Mail (version 3.2)  Type ? for help.
"/usr/spool/mail/david": 2 messages 2 new
N  2 terrie@andiron.UUCP Sat Sep  1 21:56   14/451    Reports Due Tuesday
N  1 root@andiron.UUCP   Sat Sep  1 21:51   18/596    File Clean-up
?
```

The same two new messages are pending. David hasn't received additional mail since he reviewed and exited in the previous session. David is a little worried about the report that is the subject of message 2, so he enters **2** at the ? prompt to bring that message up for display first:

```
?2 <Return>
Message  2:
From terrie Sat Sep  1 21:56:01 1990
From: terrie@andiron.UUCP (Terrie Lynn)
X-Mailer: SCO System V Mail (version 3.2)
To: david
Subject: Reports Due Tuesday
Date: Sat, 1 Sep 90 16:55:59 EST
Message-ID:  <9009012156.aa00255@andiron.UUCP>
Status: R

Just a friendly reminder that your sales analysis report is due
Tuesday by 4:00 PM. You can mail the report to me at my login if
you do it in vi. Otherwise, I'll look for it in the departmental
mail box.

TLS
?
```

David makes himself a note to do the report and decides that the message doesn't have to be saved to mbox for subsequent review. To delete the message completely, he enters **d** at the ? prompt:

```
?d <Return>
?
```

Now he looks at message 1 by entering **1** at the prompt.

```
?1 <Return>
Message  1:
From root Sat Sep  1 21:51:53 1990
From: root@andiron.UUCP (Superuser)
X-Mailer: SCO System V Mail (version 3.2)
To: david
Subject: File Clean-up
Date: Sat, 1 Sep 90 16:51:49 EST
```

```
Message-ID: <9009012151.aa00238@andiron.UUCP>
Status: R

On September 10th, the systems group is going to optimize the hard disk.
Please delete any unused or duplicate files from your directories.

If you have seldom used files that show more than 10,000 bytes in a
ls-l listing, use pack to compress the files. You can unpack them
with unpack when you need to use the files.

Your cooperation is appreciated.

        John Aberle
?
```

David elects to save in `mbox` the message from the system administrator. Because there are no more new messages, David can save this message and quit the mail session by entering **q** at the prompt.

```
?q
Saved 1 message in /usr/david/mbox
Held 0 messages in /usr/spool/mail/david.
$
```

As a final message, `mail` reports its disposition of the messages acted on during the session and returns to the UNIX prompt.

As a useful habit, David occasionally looks at the size of his `mbox` file to ensure that it doesn't grow too large. Too many messages can become unwieldy. He does this by issuing the `ls -l` command as follows:

```
$ ls -l mbox <Return>
-rw--------   1 david     group      617 Sep  1 17:04 mbox
$
```

As you can see, `mbox` contains only 617 bytes. When the file gets to be 10K bytes, David can truncate (empty) the file but retain its directory entry by using the following command:

```
$ cat < /dev/null > mbox <Return>
```

The device `/dev/null` isn't a physical device, but a software simulation of a "do-nothing" device. When you copy to `/dev/null`, the output "disappears." When you copy from `/dev/null`, the device immediately outputs an EOF signal so that nothing is copied, and the output file contains nothing. In other words, the file is truncated to a length of 0, but isn't actually removed.

Sending Messages without Mail

The `write` command enables you to have direct interactive communication with other logged-in users. Once the connection is established, you can exchange comments just as if you were meeting face-to-face. You can use the `write` command in conjunction with the `mesg` and `wall` commands.

Communicating with Other Users with `write`

To use the `write` command, type **write** followed by the `login` name of the person you want to communicate with. Then press <Return>. This step establishes the connection. Once the connection is made, two bell signals are sent to your terminal. You can proceed typing; each line will be transmitted to the other terminal after you press <Return>.

To terminate the `write` command, include at the beginning of the line an EOF (End-of-File) signal—either a <^D> or an interrupt signal such as <Break>, <^C>, or <Del>. This step causes `EOT` (End of transmission) to by displayed on the other terminal, thus signifying the end of the transmission.

In the event a user is logged in to more than one terminal, you can use a terminal argument to designate which terminal you want to use, as in the following example:

```
$ write rick tty12 <Return>
$
```

In this example, the user named `rick` is logged into more than one terminal, but is physically at terminal 12 (`tty12`). To direct correspondence to terminal 12, you include `tty12` in the terminal argument.

If you are using the `write` command and want to use a different command, you can use the exclamation-point character (`!`) at the beginning of a line to temporarily suspend the `write` command. The write mode resumes when the command completes.

Keep in mind when using the `write` command that the person you want to communicate with must be logged into the system; the `mail` command, on the other hand, works whether or not the person is logged in. The `write` command also provides messages that can be saved.

The following screen sequence shows the `write` message facility in action. Two users, David and Terrie, are working in offices at opposite ends of the building during the weekend. Terrie wants to see whether any other users are working today, so she issues the `who` command as follows:

```
$ who <Return>
david        tty01        Sep   2  10:05
terrie       tty2a        Sep   2  12:18
$
```

Terrie sees that she and David are the only users logged in. Terrie decides to send David a message, but because he is known as Dave, she sends the message to `dave`, not `david`:

```
$ write dave <Return>
dave is not logged on.
$
```

The `write` command issues an error message that tells Terrie that she issued the wrong user name. She corrects the situation as follows:

```
$ write david <Return>
Permission denied.
$
```

David has disabled his messages, and Terrie's `write` command informs her that she can't write to David's terminal. (David has disabled messages with the `mesg n` command because he is working with an application that does not allow messages. The `mesg n` command is covered in a later section.) Later, when David's applications work is completed, Terrie tries again to send a message. David has used the command `mesg y`, so this `write` attempt succeeds, and Terrie types her message:

```
$ write david <Return>
It looks like we're the only two working this weekend.
$
```

David issues a `write terrie` command as a reply. David knows that the user who sent the message is `terrie` because her message header identifies her. Terrie sees David's reply as follows:

```
Message from david on andiron (tty01) [ Sun Sep  2 12:39:49 ] ...
Yes, I have not seen any others logged on all day.
```

Terrie replies as follows:

```
I'll be here till 3:30. <Return>
```

David's reply appears as follows:

```
I'm leaving at 5 to pick up the kids at my Grandmother's.
Should I lock up?
```

Terrie sends a final reply terminated with a `<^D>`.

```
Yes. I'll leave that up to you. That's all for now...OUT. <Return>
<^D>
$
```

When Terrie presses the `<^D>`, Terrie's `write` command terminates and returns to the UNIX command prompt. David's final reply appears on-screen as follows:

```
See you monday. OUT.
(end of message)
```

Because David's last message was terminated with a `<^D>` also, the `(end of message)` is displayed on Terrie's terminal. The EOM message blanks the command prompt on the current line of Terrie's screen, but Terrie presses `<Return>` to bring up another prompt.

In the next example, the user named Terrie uses the write command with redirection to send messages. Terrie's office, which is at the front of the building, overlooks the parking lot, and Terrie is informally responsible for telling other users that the snack truck has arrived. To save typing, Terrie has prepared a file containing the text of the message. To create the text file, Terrie uses the following command:

```
$ cat > break.msg <Return>
(message text lines entered)
$
```

The message is entered into the break.msg file through keyboard input. The <^D> terminates the file's keyboard input.

To view the break.msg file, she can use the cat command again as in the following:

```
$ cat break.msg <Return>
* * * * * * * * * * * * * * * * * * * * * * * * * * * * * * * * * * * * * * * *
*                                                              *
*   The Snack Truck is at the Front Door        *
*                                                              *
* * * * * * * * * * * * * * * * * * * * * * * * * * * * * * * * * * * * * * *
$
```

Terrie redirects the break.msg file to write commands to inform users that the truck has arrived:

```
$ write david < break.msg <Return>
$
```

On his terminal, David sees the following:

```
Message from terrie on andiron (tty2a) [ Tue Sep  4 9:47:28 ] ...
* * * * * * * * * * * * * * * * * * * * * * * * * * * * * * * * * * * * *
*                                                          *
*   The Snack Truck is at the Front Door      *
*                                                          *
* * * * * * * * * * * * * * * * * * * * * * * * * * * * * * * * * * * * *
(end of message)
$
```

The message from the break.msg file goes to David's terminal through write, and a <^D> output with the text file terminates Terrie's write command automatically.

You can experiment with the message capabilities of the write command by sending messages to yourself.

Controlling the Message Facility with mesg

At times, you may not want to be bothered with messages issued by the write command. As you saw in a previous section, the user named David suppressed messages to his terminal while he was working with an applications program that would be interrupted by messages. To suppress messages, you can use the mesg command with the n (no messages) argument, as follows:

```
$ mesg n <Return>
$
```

In this example, the use of the n option prevents users from sending information to your screen with write.

To restore the process of being able to receive messages, issue the following command:

```
$ mesg y <Return>
$
```

The y (yes to messages) argument enables you to receive messages.

If you prefer not to receive write messages on your screen, you can place the command mesg n in your .profile file to start each session with messages disabled. If messages disrupt your display while you are running commands or applications, you should turn messages off.

Issuing a mesg n command will not prevent you from receiving mail messages. The mesg n command only prevents messages sent with the write command from being received.

If you don't know the status of your receiving screen messages, simply type **mesg** with no arguments at the system prompt and then press <Return>. Some UNIX implementations display a 0 if messages are receivable and a 1 if they are not. Other implementations display a worded message such as messages off:.

Writing a Message to All Users with wall

The wall, or *write* to *all users* command, is usually used by the system administrator. The wall command writes a message to the terminal screens of all logged-in users. The wall command gets the message from the standard input (keyboard) or from a redirected file.

Although the command is handy for communicating with all users on the system, for the most part, wall is used to inform the users of an impending system shutdown. The wall command, when issued by the superuser, overrides a mesg n status for a user.

The `wall` command is normally located in the `/etc` directory. As you learned, `/etc` is not generally included in an ordinary user's environmental variable `PATH` list. This means that you may have to use the full path name when issuing the `wall` command.

To invoke the `wall` command, use the following form:

```
$ /etc/wall <Return>
The system will be shut down in 10 minutes
<^D>
$
```

This message is sent to all logged-in users on the system. Because the message in this example comes from the keyboard, the message is terminated with a `<^D>`.

Because the `wall` command is not found in the usual command directories, you must use the full path name with the command.

As an example of a `wall` message, Terrie issues the following command:

```
$ /etc/wall < break.msg <Return>
```

Other users see this on their screens:

```
Broadcast Message from terrie (tty2a) on andiron Fri Sep  9 9:57:38...
************************************************
*                                              *
*   The Snack Truck is at the Front Door       *
*                                              *
************************************************
$
```

Notice the word `Broadcast` in the first line of the message. Messages written by `wall` bear this `Broadcast` header. Of course, you recognize that the message is the same message Terrie sent to David in a previous example involving `write`.

Most broadcast messages are initiated by the superuser, who is logged in as `root`. You should pay close attention to these messages, because they will most likely convey system-operation information. For example, when the system is shut down, the command that stops the system progresses through several steps to ensure an orderly shutdown. One of the steps includes invoking `wall` to inform users of the impending shutdown. On the user's screen, the shutdown-message sequence looks like this:

```
Broadcast Message from root (tty01) on andiron Sun Sep  2 14:53:03...
The system will be shut down in 60 seconds.
Please log off now.
```

`wall` writes an initial message to inform users that the system is being shut down. The message indicates the length of time remaining before shutdown. When you see this message, you should wrap up your work and end your session. Shortly before the actual shutdown, users who have not yet logged off see a second message from `wall`:

```
Broadcast Message from root (tty01) on andiron Sun Sep  2 14:54:03...
THE SYSTEM IS BEING SHUT DOWN NOW ! ! !
Log off now or risk your files being damaged.
```

If you see this message, press <^D> or type **exit** (and press <Return>) until you see the login prompt. You are then logged out. Don't log back in until the system is shut down and subsequently restarted. If you are in a subshell, you may have to press <^D> or type **exit** more than once:

```
$ exit <Return>  ( exit from the subshell)
$ exit <Return>   ( exit from login shell)

andiron
Welcome to SCO System V/386
andiron!login:     (login prompt)
```

Understanding the Desktop Accessory Commands

When an office worker looks at his or her desktop, he or she sees notebooks, pencils, in-and-out mail bins, a calculator, and perhaps a sign or two made using a wide-felt tip pen from blank sheets of paper. At the corner of the desk sits the UNIX terminal. The UNIX terminal, by accessing commands, can replace many of today's desktop accessories. This section shows you how to use the `bc` command to replace a calculator. You'll also learn how to use the `banner` command to make banners, signs, and other large character-based displays.

Calculating with bc

Two UNIX programs—`bc` and `dc`—enable you to convert your computer into a desktop calculator. The `dc` command can be compared to the Hewlett-Packard calculator and many other brands of calculators in that it behaves as an interactive programmable desk calculator. It holds integers and programs using conventional stacking and has named storage locations as well. In fact, the `bc` command "calls on" the `dc` command to do many of `bc`'s operations. This section, however, is primarily about `bc`.

The `bc` command provides sophisticated mathematical capabilities to users. If you're not heavily into math, but you do occasionally use a calculator to add, subtract, multiply, and divide, the bc calculator is right for you. This section presents the bc program in its most basic form.

To use the bc desktop calculator, you start the command by typing **bc** at the system prompt and pressing <Return>. The bc command begins expecting your input. No command prompt is displayed by bc. bc simply waits for you to type in your calculations. To end the program, you enter a <^D>.

The following examples show different operations that can be performed after the bc calculator is invoked.

To add, use the following form:

5+7 <Return>
12

You see the result of an operation when you press <Return>. To multiply, use the following form:

245.45 * 3 <Return>
736.35

2 + 4 *12 <Return>
50

Don't be fooled by expecting bc to add 2+4 to get 6 and then multiply 6 times 12 to get 74. On any input line, bc performs multiplication and division operations *before* it performs addition and subtraction operations. In order to override this default *order of precedence*, so that the calculator will perform addition or subtraction before multiplication or division, you enclose the numbers to be added or subtracted in parentheses.

If you enclose in parentheses the addition operation from the previous example, the outcome of the operation is different:

(2+4)*12 <Return>
72

This time, 2 is added to 4 to make 6. Then 6 is multiplied by 12 to make 72.

bc is an integer program. Integers are whole numbers. For example, 100 divided by 3 is 33 and 1/3, or approximately 33.33333. Notice what happens when bc divides 100 by 3:

100/3 <Return>
33

The decimal portion (.33333) is truncated from the answer. You can set the number of decimal places reported to see fractional values by using the scale assignment with bc. For two decimal places, enter the following:

scale=2 <Return>

Now try a division that results in a non-integer.

```
100/3 <Return>
33.33
```

You can vary the scale as you want. The higher the scale, the greater the precision of your results. For example, a scale of 12 produces the following result:

```
scale=12 <Return>
100/3 <Return>
33.333333333333
```

Using many decimal places may improve the precision of your result, but the decimal places can clutter the screen. If you are adding and subtracting dollar values (for example, to balance your checkbook), a scale of 2 is fine. But if you are dividing dollars-and-cents amounts, you may want to increase the scale to improve accuracy.

As an example of precision-loss problems, consider a series of calculations that a user might enter. Suppose that the user must buy the boss a Christmas present on behalf of his 17 coworkers. The gift's price is $29.95. The user divides the price by the number of workers (including himself) to determine how much to collect from each worker. Using bc, the user enters the following:

```
scale=2 <Return>
29.95/18 <Return>
1.66
```

Satisfied with the answer, the user collects exactly $1.66 from his coworkers and chips in his $1.66. He takes the money to the store in an envelope and makes his $29.95 selection. When the clerk counts the money the user has collected, however, the clerk finds only $29.88. The user needs to cough up the extra 7 cents. The puzzled user returns to his terminal and enters the following sequence to bc:

```
scale=2 <Return>
1.66*18 <Return>
29.88
```

It seems that 18 times $1.66 really is only $29.88—not $29.95. The user made a judgment mistake by setting the scale to 2 for the original calculation. The small loss of precision, because of the truncation of decimal places beyond 2, was amplified 18 times. By setting the scale to 12, the results are much more precise:

```
scale=12 <Return>
29.95/18
1.663888888888
1.663888888888 * 18
29.949999999984
```

The results given with the scale set to 12 are well within the 1000th of a cent range.

You can store (save) the result of an operation by assigning the output of the operation to a memory variable. The general form of the assignment is as follows:

```
variable=expression
```

variable is a single lower-case letter within the range of a-z. The *expression* is either a literal value typed at the bc command line or the result of the calculation typed at the command line.

For example, to save the literal value 145.43 to the c memory variable, use the following command:

```
c=145.43 <Return>
```

To store the result of the expression 5*2 in memory variable t, use this command:

```
t=5*2 <Return>
```

You can temporarily store one of 26 "memories" using the letters a-z. Remember that when you exit bc, the values stored in these memories are lost.

To recall a stored value, use the following command:

```
c <Return>
145.43
```

To use a stored value in an expression, use the following command form:

```
c*2 <Return>
290.86
```

You can mix operations using memories and literal numbers in your calculations. If you try bc a few times, you'll begin to appreciate the availability of having a "calculator" right at your terminal.

Making Banners with banner

When people think of a *banner*, they often think of a long horizontal printed message like the ones that bands carry at the front of a parade. UNIX offers the banner command to produce large letters on your terminal, or, through redirection, to your printer. You will find many uses for banner.

Use the banner command to separate files from one another when printing a batch of files, to make signs, or to make titles for reports. The banner can be anything from your last name, to a short statement such as Final Progress Report. A banner can be anything meaningful to the user who created it.

To activate the `banner` command, use the following form:

$ **banner** *banner text* <Return>
$

`banner` accepts the *banner text* from the keyboard until you press <Return>.

Each word in a banner appears on a separate line. You can use double ("") or single (' ') quotation marks to combine two or more words, making them a single argument so that they appear on one line.

The following command prints banner text with one word per line, because each word is taken as a single argument.

$ **banner Register for Prize Here** <Return>

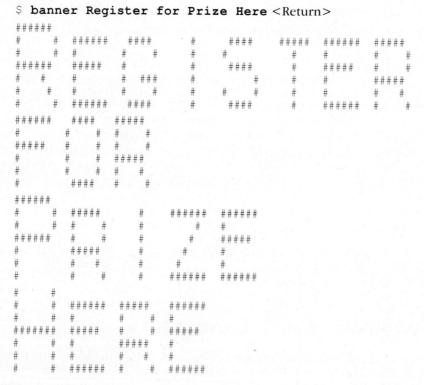

To add centering spaces to each word of a line, position each word within its own set of quotes, as in the following example:

```
$ banner ' DONATIONS' '     FOR' '     COFFEE' <Return>
```

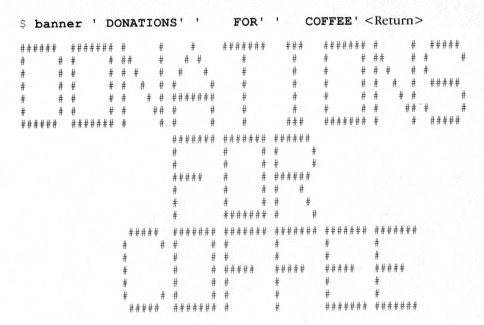

The output of `banner` can be redirected to a printer. See Chapter 5 for information on using the pipe and redirection commands with `banner`.

Summary

This chapter introduced you to the UNIX commands used to conduct office business. These include electronic communications, setting the date and time, using the on-line calculator, and reminder scheduling. You should now be able to exchange messages and files with users on your system as well as with those users on remotely connected systems. You should also be able to set up your own personal scheduling reminder system, create banners, and use the desktop-calculator capabilities of UNIX.

This chapter covered the following key points:

❏ You can display a calendar from the years 1 through 9999 A.D. with the `cal` command.

❏ The UNIX `calendar` command provides you with an on-line calendar reminder service.

❏ You can display the system date and time by using the UNIX `date` command.

❏ UNIX offers many facilities for sending and receiving mail.

❏ You can send a file to another user by using the `mail` command.

❏ You can communicate with other users on your system with the `write` and `wall` commands.

❏ You can suppress or enable the sending of messages to your terminal by using the `mesg n` or `mesg y` commands.

❏ The UNIX `bc` command provides you with an on-line, precision calculator.

❏ You can print and display large, banner-like characters and messages by using the `banner` command.

In Chapter 10, you learn about the file-processing commands.

— Part —
Three

Using Text Editors

Using ed, the UNIX Line Editor

Using vi, the UNIX Visual Editor

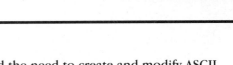

Using ed, the UNIX
Line Editor

In your work with UNIX, you will often find the need to create and modify ASCII text files. A text file can be anything from a short memo to a complete shell procedure or shell script that can automate your daily work.

As you learned in Part Two, many UNIX commands accept lists of arguments from text files. In addition, your `.profile` or `.login` file is a text file containing commands and environmental variable assignments for your login initialization. As you gain experience with UNIX, you will find many occasions to create new text files or change existing text files to suit your purposes. A text editor is your primary tool for creating and modifying text files, and the `ed` line editor is the most basic UNIX text editor.

Text editors such as `ed` enable you to enter, modify, search through, substitute, copy, and delete text. While you work with the text, it resides in a temporary file, called a *buffer*, within the system's RAM. When you finish editing the temporary file, you *save* the additions and changes by placing a permanent (but changeable) copy of the file on disk. You can then use any of UNIX's printing services to print the edited disk file, or you can use the `cat` command to display the file's contents on your terminal screen.

By today's standards, the `ed` editor is old. When `ed` was created, the hardware of the day had limited capabilities. As you learn to use `ed`, remember that it originally was designed to work with the primitive hardware that was available at the time. In the 1960's and early 1970's, users of interactive computer systems were connected to systems via slow serial lines. Many terminals were printing (hard copy) terminals, which were connected to the system either directly or through modems. Because of restrictions on data rates between the terminal and the computer, designers could use only a few characters for communication between the system and the user. As a result, system-user communication with older programs like `ed` is terse. In other words, `ed` does not present you with elaborate messages, prompts, and status indicators. In most cases, you enter single-character commands. Because of its

343

simple yet ingenious design, the editor's commands are brief, effective, and powerful.

Editors are classified according to the manner in which they interact with the user. Editors such as ed—which permit the user to work with only one line of text at a time—are called *line-oriented editors*. Line-oriented editors (sometimes called simply *line editors*) work very well in a restricted communications environment— over modem lines, for example, or on systems with slow serial-terminal interfaces.

As you learn to use ed, you also are learning the basics of another class of editor, the vi full-screen, or visual editor. The vi editor is covered in Chapter 13.

Key Terms Used in This Chapter

Line editor	A text editor that enables the user to work with only one line of text at a time
Editing buffer	A temporary file that exists within the system's RAM
Pseudo address	A symbol that represents the address of a line in the buffer
Command mode	The mode in which ed accepts instructions from the user
Text-entry mode	The mode in which ed places text into the buffer
Appending text	The process of adding text to the buffer, placing the new text after a specified line of existing text
Relative addressing	The process of addressing a line in relation to the current line or to the known address of another existing line
Absolute addressing	The process of addressing a line by assigning it an integer number (such as 1, 2, 3, and so on)
Metacharacter	A symbol that represents a class or set of characters
Marker	A hidden special character, which the user can address and ed can find

Reviewing Terminology and Conventions

Certain typographical conventions are used throughout this book to help you differentiate among the many commands, prompts, and messages used in UNIX. Most of the screen dialogue in this chapter is based on the same set of conventions outlined in the "Introduction" and used in previous chapters. Some different conventions are used in this chapter, however, to illustrate screen dialogue pertinent to ed.

One change in this chapter and the next involves the presentation of the UNIX shell prompt. Throughout the book, the $ has been used as the default presentation of the UNIX shell prompt. As you learned in previous chapters, however, you can assign the `'OMPT` variable to create a UNIX shell prompt of your own design. For example, a prompt for the user named Dennis might be as elaborate as `cMc:1:/a/usr/dennis>`.

Although the normal UNIX shell prompt is a % or a $, you can easily confuse these normal prompt characters with ed's special pseudo-address or metacharacters. To avoid confusion, in this chapter the shell prompt is shown as the > character. You'll learn about ed's special characters later in the chapter.

The only other difference in this chapter is the presentation of the terminal cursor in several of the examples of screen dialogue. The terminal cursor is presented as the underline:

—

Other than the presentation of the shell prompt and the terminal cursor, the typographical conventions for this chapter follow the format of those in the rest of this book. For more information, take time to review the section in this book's introduction called "Conventions Used in This Book."

Understanding the Editing Process

You *edit* text either by creating new text or by modifying existing text. When you create new text, you place the text in a file with an ordinary UNIX file name. When you modify existing text, you use the existing file's name to call a copy of the file into the editing session. In either case, as you edit the text, it is held in the system's memory in a storage area called a *buffer*.

As you make changes and additions to the text, these edits affect the text in the buffer—not the text stored on disk. When you are satisfied with the text in the buffer, you issue a command that writes the text from the buffer to the named file on the disk. Only when you write the text to the disk are your changes and additions made permanent.

Text editors like ed and vi are said to be *interactive* because they interact with the user during the editing session. The text editor communicates with you by displaying error messages, status messages, or sometimes nothing on-screen. A text editor such as ed also communicates with you by accepting the commands and text that you enter from the keyboard.

The UNIX text editors feature many of the same capabilities offered by full-fledged word processing programs. The primary difference between a text processor (such as ed) and a word processor is that text processors do not offer the screen and hard-copy formatting and printing functions available with word processors. In the UNIX environment, text-file formatting and printing tasks are performed by other

UNIX commands, such as lp, troff, and nroff. Your UNIX system may contain several text-editing utilities and perhaps a word processor, as well.

The ed and vi editors operate in *modes*. In *command* mode, the keystrokes you enter are accepted as command information. You use command mode to control the editing program. In *text-entry* mode, on the other hand, your keystrokes are accepted as the literal text that makes up your document. When ed is in text-entry mode, the editor acts like a typewriter. In an editing session, you can freely switch between command mode and text-entry mode as required.

You also can use an editor to modify, rearrange, delete, substitute, and search for text. You conduct these editing operations by issuing commands while the editor is in command mode. The ed editor responds to a variety of commands, but these commands have many attributes in common. Normally, a command is a single letter that corresponds to the first letter of an action's name. For example, the i command corresponds to the *i*nsert action, and the a command corresponds to the *a*ppend action.

Most commands operate on one line of text, or on a range of lines. Text lines are numbered from 1 (the top line) to the last line in the buffer (the bottom line). A line's number is the line's *address* in the text buffer. A *range* is a group of lines. An address range, therefore, is simply two addresses (separated by a comma) that identify the first and last lines of the affected range. Most ed commands accept address ranges to expand the scope of the commands' operations. Through the use of address ranges and commands, you can perform useful editing operations on your text with just a few keystrokes.

Within a line editor, one text line is considered the *current line*. The current text line is the line affected by the commands that do not specify an address. You can therefore think of the current line as an open window through which you can access a single line of text.

The term *dot* is used to describe the current line, because ed uses the period character (.) as a "shorthand" name (or *pseudo address*) for the address of the current line. You will learn more about the use of the dot character and other pseudo addresses in later sections.

Although the text buffer may contain many lines of text, remember that you can access only the current line with a command that does not specify an address or an address range. With ed, you use commands to make a line the current line. You cannot use the keyboard's cursor-control keys to move around on your screen, or to access different lines.

Understanding the Basic Operation of ed

One of the most effective ways to learn ed is to follow a sequence of operations that utilizes the editor's basic functions. This section presents examples that show you how to start ed, control the prompt, switch between command mode and text-entry mode, and control the display of help messages.

Starting ed

Starting ed is easy. ed is a command, like other UNIX commands, that you type at
the UNIX prompt. As a preliminary step, clear your terminal's screen of any
previous text. At the UNIX shell prompt (>), enter the following command:

> `> ` **`clear`** `<Return>`
> `>`

Remember that you do not enter the > shell prompt here or in future examples. If
your command prompt is customized, it may not look like the UNIX shell prompt
shown in these examples. This is all right; just remember that the > character at the
beginning of a command line represents any UNIX prompt in the following
examples. Also remember that you must press <Return> to execute the command.
As with the shell prompt, do not type the angle brackets that surround the word
Return.

Because some versions of UNIX do not include the clear command, you can
alternatively clear the screen by issuing the following command:

> `> ` **`tput clear`** `<Return>`

If your terminal does not respond to the clear command, use tput clear
when the example calls for clear.

After you issue clear or tput clear, the screen clears, leaving only the shell
prompt in the upper-left corner (home position) of the screen. Now start the ed
editor as follows:

> `> ` **`ed`** `<Return>`

This command invokes ed, and the cursor appears on-screen. Your screen should
look like this:

> `> ` **`ed`** `<Return>`
> `_` ←(*the terminal cursor*)

In this example, you start ed without naming a file to edit. When you start the
editor in this manner, ed assumes that you are creating new text and that you will
name the file later.

When you invoke ed, the program starts in command mode. This command-mode
initialization differs from most word processors, which start in text-entry mode. As
mentioned previously, ed accepts your typed commands only when it is in
command mode. Therefore, when command mode is active, you can control the
operation of ed, but you cannot enter text directly into the text buffer.

Conversely, when it is in text-entry mode, ed accepts your keystrokes only as input
for the file you are editing. You generally cannot enter commands while ed is in
text-entry mode, because ed "thinks" that you are simply entering words, not

commands. ed does, however, accept a few basic cursor-movement commands while in text-entry mode. As you will see, you can use certain commands to switch ed between text-entry mode and command mode.

To a beginner, ed's most disconcerting characteristic is the way it displays the cursor and little else. Remember, however, that you are working with a terse, line-oriented editor. ed is designed to be conservative with its dialogue. Later in this chapter, you learn a number of commands that make ed more informative.

Discovering Command Errors

Once ed is running and the cursor is on-screen, type the following ed command:

> **p** <Return>

On the next line, ed responds as follows:

?

The cursor drops to the next line. In command mode, ed displays the ? message whenever you enter an erroneous command or a command that doesn't make sense. The ? message is ed's way of saying: "You want me to do *what*?". In this case, you asked ed to display the current line by entering the p (*print*) command. (Remember that the p command tells ed to display text on-screen, *not* to print out a hard copy of the text.) But because you are editing a new (and therefore empty) file, ed cannot find a current line to print. It does not make sense to print something that does not exist, so ed questions your p command by displaying the ? message.

About the Terms Print and Display . . .

In ed, the term "printing" means the act of displaying text on-screen, rather than "printing out" a hard copy of the text file. Even though the p command is called a print command, it does not actually print anything on a hard-copy printer. Rather, p tells UNIX to display data on-screen.

In the early days of computers, most terminals were teletypes or hard-copy devices; video display monitors generally were not used. A user who wanted to view the results of an operation had to print out the data on paper. Remember that UNIX is a fairly old operating system, which came into being before video displays came into popular use. Although modern terminals and workstations nearly always use a video monitor (some even use two or more), the UNIX command terminology has not yet caught up with the times. This explains the use of the p (*print*) command to display data.

You will see the p command used throughout this chapter; remember that you use p to display text or other data on-screen, not to send the data to a printer.

Still, this does not seem like much of a response, even if you are familiar with ed's quiet nature. If you want, you can tell ed to provide more descriptive—or *verbose*—messages about erroneous commands. To invoke a verbose message about the current error involving the p command, for example, enter the following command:

> **h** <Return>

Now ed responds with the following message:

```
line out of range

_
```

The h (*help*) command gives you a brief description of the problem. When you typed **ed** and pressed <Return>, only the cursor appeared on-screen. The p (*print*) command instructed ed to print the current line in the buffer. Because no text yet existed in the buffer, ed responded with the ? message and then displayed the cursor on the next line.

Switching to Command Mode

Sometimes you may find it hard to determine which one of ed's modes is currently active. The editor's responses are so curt that you can become confused as you switch between command mode and text-input mode. If you forget that you are in the text-input mode, you might think that ed is ignoring your commands.

As a result, you may want ed to let you know when you are working in command mode. Fortunately, most versions of ed provide the option of an * (asterisk) command-mode prompt. The * prompt is displayed only when ed is in command mode. To turn on the * prompt, enter the following sequence of commands (if ed is currently active on your system, you do not have to restart ed, as shown in the first line):

> > **ed** <Return>
> **P** <Return>
> *_

As you enter commands, previous commands scroll upward on-screen. In other words, the screen's point of entry lowers. For this session of ed, the * prompt appears on every new command line; it is not displayed in text-entry mode.

Notice that the *p*rompt command, P, is an uppercase letter. Don't confuse the uppercase P command with the lowercase p command. Although the two commands are based on the same letter, they perform different operations. You can turn off the * prompt by entering another P command. Commands that alternatively turn a feature on and off are called *toggle* commands. Repeatedly entering **P** and pressing <Return> switches the ed command prompt on and off.

If you have started ed and need to quit the session, enter **q** at the * command prompt. If the buffer contains text, and if the text has not been saved to disk and given a file name, ed responds with a ? if you try to quit. If ed responds with a ?, enter **q** again and press <Return>. When you quit in this fashion, ed assumes that you want to end the session without saving the buffer's contents. You will learn how to properly quit ed later in the chapter. Use the double q command sparingly. If you make a habit of quitting ed in this "quick and dirty" manner, you eventually will lose a buffer full of data that you really wanted to keep!

Switching to Text-Entry Mode

As already mentioned, ed must be in text-entry mode to accept text into the buffer. You can add text in a number of ways. One way is to use the i (*insert*) command to switch ed into text-entry mode. As you are about to see, however, this can be a tricky process.

When you insert text, you place new text *in front* of existing text in the current line. In other words, you push existing text forward as you enter new text at the beginning of the line. Now attempt to switch from command mode to text-entry mode by using the i command, as follows:

```
*  i <Return>
?
*  _
```

Notice that ed responds to the i command with a ?. In the next line, the * command-mode prompt reappears, indicating that ed is anticipating commands rather than text. That is, ed did not accept the i command, and did switch to text-input mode. What happened?

Remember that the *i*nsert command inserts text in front of (before) the current line. Because the buffer does not yet contain any text, there is no current line. Therefore, ed doesn't know what to do and tells you so by displaying the ? error indicator. In this case, ed did not recognize the i command because it does not make sense to insert text when the buffer does not yet contain any text. Because the command was not recognized, ed stays in command mode. To you, ed's handling of the i command in this situation may seem cryptic, but remember that you are working with a terse editor.

Enabling ed's Help Facility

ed, like UNIX in general, differentiates between commands entered in upper- and lowercase letters. As you saw in a previous section, the p (*p*rint) and P (*P*rompt) commands use the same letter, but have completely different meanings to ed because of their alphabetic case. In commands such as h (*h*elp) and H (*H*elp), however, the upper- and lowercase letters simply indicate variations of the same command. This is shown in the following example.

Before learning how to enter text into an empty buffer, use the h (*help*) command to make ed more friendly. At ed's command prompt, type the following command:

```
*  h <Return>
```

As in the previous example of the the h command, ed displays a message describing the error:

```
line out of range
*
_
```

You may find it cumbersome to have to ask ed for clarification every time you make a mistake—especially if you make many command errors. Instead, you may want help messages to appear automatically when an error occurs. To enable help messages on a continual basis, enter the following command:

```
*  H <Return>
```

Again, ed responds with the following message:

```
line out of range
*
_
```

Notice that the last H command was entered in uppercase. This command prints the last error message and enters a mode that causes subsequent error messages to be displayed automatically. While you are learning to use ed, use the H command to enable automatic error messages.

Now you can enter text-entry mode and enter some text into the buffer. You can switch to text-entry mode in an empty buffer by using the append command, as shown in the following example:

```
*  a <Return>
Dear Mr. Jones: <Return>
. <Return>
```

In this example, the a (*append*) command instructs ed to append the upcoming new text to line 0 of the buffer. Zero (0) is a pseudo address that represents the beginning of the buffer. You then enter a line of text. Next, enter the dot command (a period in the very first column of a new line), to instruct ed to exit from text-entry mode and return to command mode.

To save the buffer's contents and exit from the editor, enter the following commands:

```
*  w priceletter.1ed <Return>
16
*  q <Return>
```

The w command writes the buffer to the file named `priceletter.1ed`. After the buffer is saved, the editor shows you the number of bytes saved—in this case, `16`. The q command tells `ed` to exit to UNIX.

You will learn more about these commands later in this chapter. For now, you have a basic understanding of how text is entered into the buffer and saved in a file. The following sections will help you build on this knowledge.

Running UNIX Commands from within ed

After a few minutes of dialogue with `ed`, your screen starts to become cluttered. In a previous section, you learned how to use the `clear` or `tput clear` commands to clear the screen from the shell prompt. Now, however, you are using `ed`. If you want to issue a UNIX command (such as `clear`) from within `ed`, you must precede the command with an exclamation mark (`!`), as follows:

    * **! clear** <Return>

Remember, however, that `clear` does not work on every system. If your system does not respond to the `clear` command, the following message may appear:

```
sh: clear: not found
*
```

The message informs you that UNIX did not recognize the command you just issued. The `sh` in the message means that the UNIX shell could not find the command `clear`. (For more information about the UNIX shell, see Chapter 5.)

If your system displays the preceding message (or a similar one), try entering the following:

    * **! tput clear** <Return>

The `!` (exclamation mark) is the `ed` "escape" command. If you enter the `!` command at the `ed` command-mode prompt, subsequent keystrokes are passed as commands to the UNIX shell. That is, the `!` command instructs `ed` to exit temporarily to the UNIX shell. The shell then executes the UNIX command following the `!` command. You can issue any valid UNIX command in this fashion. In most cases, after executing a UNIX command initiated from within `ed`, the shell returns to the `ed` session. This type of instruction is represented by the following generic syntax:

    * **!** *command*

This form of instruction tells UNIX to execute any UNIX command (represented in this generic syntax by *command*), and to return to `ed`. Certain UNIX commands, however, do not immediately return to `ed`. Suppose that you enter the following command:

    * **! ed** <Return>

In this case, the shell executes another copy of ed. The new copy of ed operates until you quit the session. When you finish with the second session of ed, the shell returns control to the first session of ed. When you quit the first session, ed exits to the UNIX shell. This series of steps is illustrated in the following sample dialogue:

```
*  ! ed <Return>    (Session two of ed invoked from within session one)
P <Return>          (Session two of ed begins)
*  q <Return>       (Quitting session two)
!                   (Returning to session one)
*_                  (Session one of ed resumes)
```

By using the ! command within ed to get back to UNIX, you can view file directories, copy files, and perform many other useful operations.

Creating a File in Text-Entry Mode

Now that you are familiar with the basic operation of ed's command mode, you can learn how to enter text in text-entry mode. As the following sections introduce you to ed's text-handling capabilities, you also learn more commands to expand your use of the ed command mode.

As the following examples progress, the screen dialogue shows an additive view of the screen. In most cases, current commands and messages appear at the bottom of the screen dialogue. As you type in the examples, compare your screen's appearance with the sample dialogue.

Appending Text to an Empty Buffer

You learned that ed cannot insert text when the line buffer is empty. ed provides the a (*append*) command, however, which enables you to add text to an empty buffer or to existing text.

The a command opens an *empty buffer* for text entry. If text exists, the a command opens the text buffer and adds newly input text to the file, beginning *after* the current line. ed keeps track of the lines by numbering each line. The first line of text in a file is considered line 1. Because an empty buffer contains no lines of text, however, 0 is the only valid line number in an empty buffer. To see how a line of text is entered, enter the following commands and text in the file priceletter.1ed:

```
*  a <Return>
Dear Mr. Jones: <Return>
. <Return>    (No cursor appears on this line.)
*_
```

If you make a mistake while entering text, you can press <Backspace> to move backward and erase the characters in the current line.

If, however, you press <Return> while entering text, you begin a new current line. Although the previous line is remains on-screen, you cannot simply press the up-arrow key to make it the active line again. To go back to a previous line, you must first switch back to command mode and enter a line-positioning command. For now, however, do not worry about line positioning. Instead, you should learn how to return to command mode from text-entry mode.

Exiting Text-Entry Mode and Displaying a Line

To switch from text-entry mode to command mode, use the . (dot) as an exit command. When ed encounters the . command, the editor switches from text-entry mode to command mode, and displays the * command-mode prompt. In order to act as a switch, the exit command must be placed in the first column of a blank line. When you have switched back to command mode, you can issue the p (*print*) command to display the contents of the current line as it was saved in the buffer.

The . exit command in text-entry mode is *not* the same as the . pseudo address in command mode. ed interprets the meaning of the dot or period character (.) depending on which mode ed is currently in—command mode or text-entry mode. Further, the dot is interpreted like any other text character when it appears within a line of text, so you can freely use periods to end your sentences when you are creating a text file. ed reads the dot as the exit command only when the dot appears in the first column of a blank line.

The following dialogue shows the use of the . command to change modes, and the use of the p command to review the current line from the buffer:

```
*  a <Return>
Dear Mr. Jones: <Return>
. <Return>
*  p <Return>
Dear Mr. Jones:
*  _
```

In this example, the p command displays the appended text, thereby confirming that the current line contain the text that you appended. You will learn other ways to use the p command later in the chapter.

Adding Text to an Existing File

Now that the text buffer contains some text, you can add more text to the file by using either the *a*ppend or *i*nsert commands. Remember that the i command inserts text *before* the current line (that is, the default addressed line), which in this case is line 1. The a command, on the other hand, inserts text *after* the addressed line. To insert text before the line already in the buffer, enter the following commands and text:

```
* i <Return>
Thank you for shopping at my store. <Return>
. <Return>
*
```

Note that text input is not terminated by the period at the end of the new line of text. As mentioned previously, if you want to terminate text entry and return to command mode, you must use the . (exit) command in the first column of a new line. This requirement prevents ed from interpreting an end-of-sentence period as the exit command.

Next, list both lines of the buffer to see what the new file now contains. One way to print the buffer's contents is by entering the following command:

```
* 1,3p <Return>
Dear Mr. Jones,
Thank you for shopping at my store.
*
```

In this example, you provide the p (*print*) command with a range (1, 3) of line addresses to be printed. That is, the command 1, 3p tells ed to go to line 1, display the line on-screen, then to go to line 2 and display that line on-screen, and finally to display line 3 on-screen. Like many ed commands, p accepts address ranges. Such commands operate on the first and last addresses of the specified range, and all addresses between the two. By using ranges, you can cause the commands you enter to reach beyond the current line. You will learn more about address ranges in a moment. For now, however, you should learn how to leave ed and return to the UNIX shell.

Exiting ed

At some point in your editing session, you will want to leave ed. If your text no longer needs to be modified, you should save the final edited version on disk. Fortunately, ed does not permit you to exit without first giving you the opportunity to save the file. The q (*quit*) command usually exits from ed directly. If you have not yet saved the buffer's current contents, however, ed responds to the q command by displaying the ? error indicator.

The following sample dialogue shows you what happens if you try to exit from ed without first saving the new text to disk:

```
* q <Return>
?
warning: expected 'w'
```

```
*  w priceletter.led <Return>
52
*  q <Return>
>_
```

The verbose error message (expected 'w') is displayed if the H command has been toggled on, or if you enter the h command as described previously.

To save the text to a disk file, use the w (*write*) command, and provide a file name under which the new text can be saved, as shown in the fourth line of the example. ed then writes the buffer's text to a disk file named priceletter.led. On the next line, ed reports the number of characters written to the file (the size of the file in bytes). Then use the q command to exit from ed.

 A second form of the quit command, the uppercase Q command, terminates the session, but does not provide an error message before quitting. The Q command quits without verifying whether the buffer's contents have been saved. Using the Q command can be risky because it does not prompt you to save your edited text. Use the uppercase Q command infrequently and with caution.

To make sure that the new file was indeed saved to disk, use the UNIX ls (*list files*) command at the shell prompt, as follows:

```
> ls -l priceletter.led <Return>
-rw-rw-r- 1 dennis startrek 52 May 11 16:43 priceletter.led
>
```

When issued with the -l option and a specified file name, the UNIX shell's ls command lists the saved file, if the file is stored on disk and listed in the current directory. (To interpret the information provided by the ls command, see Chapter 6.)

Reviewing the Basic Operation of ed

So far, you have been introduced to many basic ed commands and concepts. This section reviews the commands covered in the previous sections.

To start up the ed editor, enter the following command:

```
> ed <Return>
```

Remember that when you start ed, command mode is the active mode.

You can include several options with ed that give the command more capabilities. In its generic form, ed looks like the following:

```
ed [-s] [-p string] filename
```

The options are explained in table 12.1.

Table 12.1
Commonly Used Options for the ed Command

Option	Action
-s	Suppresses the display of file and buffer character counts
-p string	Displays a user-supplied prompt string, such as cMc:1:/a/usr/dennis>
filename	The name of the file to be edited or created

Several commands are useful when you are learning to use ed. Table 12.2 reviews these commands. Many commands have both a "long" form and a "shorthand" form. This table lists only the shorthand form. For information on the expanded forms of several commands, refer to Appendix E.

Table 12.2
Basic ed Commands and Messages

Command	Action
?	Not a command, but a message that indicates that you have made an error in entering a command. ? is considered ed's most basic error message.
!	When issued while ed is in command mode, the ! command acts as an escape character and tells ed that subsequent keystrokes are to be accepted as UNIX shell commands. ed then exits to the UNIX shell, where the commands are executed. Generally, control reverts to the ed editor after the command is executed.
a	Enables you to add text to the buffer *after* the current line. The a issued without parameters is a shorthand notation, and new text is appended after the current line.
h	Displays the most recent error message.
H	Redisplays the most recent error message, and turns on the automatic display of verbose error messages. H is a toggle command; repeated entry turns the display of verbose error messages on and off. When you start ed, error-message display initially is set to off.
i	Enables you to insert text before the current line in the text buffer. This is the shorthand form of the command, in which the implied address is the current line. At least one text line must be present in the buffer before ed will accept the insert command.
p	Prints (displays) the current line.

Table 12.2—(continued)

Command	Action
P	Turns on the * command-mode prompt. P is a toggle command; when used repeatedly, it turns the * prompt on and off. When you start ed, the command-mode prompt is initially set to off.
q	Quits the current editing session. If you issue the q command to exit from ed without first saving the text buffer's contents to disk, however, ed responds with the ? error indicator. If you issue a second q command, ed quits without saving the buffer's contents.
Q	Quits ed without displaying a warning prompt or verifying whether the buffer's contents have been saved.
w	Writes the text buffer's contents to the current disk file.

With the commands you have learned so far, you can create small text files quickly and efficiently. The next section shows you how to modify existing text and move around your document while editing.

Modifying Text Files

Most people make mistakes, especially when they're typing. For this reason, ed features a number of text correction and deletion commands. These commands enable you to find, replace, delete, and modify the text in the buffer. The following examples show you how to enter text and use ed's text-modification commands.

By now, you know that every command or text line must be followed by a <Return>, and that every command entry starts from the current (cursor) position. For the rest of this chapter, the <Return> will continue to appear in the text line. In most cases, the cursor will no longer appear in the sample dialogue.

Creating a New File and Appending Text

The following example should help you review and build on the concepts already discussed. Take the steps shown in the following sample dialogue:

```
> ed priceletter.2ed <Return>
? priceletter.2ed
H <Return>
cannot open input file
f <Return>
priceletter.2ed
```

In this sample dialogue, you start by instructing ed to open the file named
priceletter.2ed and read it into the text buffer. No file named
priceletter.2ed exists, however, so ed responds by displaying the ? error
message. Next, you enter the H (*Help*) command to turn on ed's verbose error
messages. The new message tells you that the specified input file cannot be opened
because it does not exist. However, ed will create a new file with the name
priceletter.2ed. When ed writes the buffer's contents to disk, the text will be
saved under this file name.

As shown in the last line of the sample dialogue, you can see the name of the
current file by issuing the f (*file name*) command. When you issue the f command
with no arguments, ed displays the current name of the file in the buffer. If you
issue the f command with a new file name as an argument, ed changes the buffer's
name to the name you specify.

Now enter text by following this example:

```
P
* H
*
Dear Mr. Jones: <Return>
<Return>
The price of fruit today is: <Return>
<Return>
Fruit<tab>Each<tab>10 Qty <Return>
<Return>
Dates<tab>0.10<tab>1.00 <Return>
Figs<tab>0.20<tab>2.00 <Return>
Kiwi<tab>0.30<tab>3.00 <Return> <^V><^G>
<Return>
The price of fruit is going up! <Return>
<Return>
Your Green Grocer, <Return>
<Return>
George <Return>
. <Return>
* w
174
* q
```

In this example, you use the P (*Prompt*) command to turn on the * prompt, and
the a (*append*) command to place ed in text-entry mode at line 1. You then enter
the letter, which includes a list of fruit and their prices.

Notice that you must press the sequence < ^V><^G> so that the computer
beeps when the list of fruit and prices is completed. When placed before a
nondisplayed character in a text file, the < ^V> character (Ctrl-V) enters the
nondisplayed character's ASCII code into the buffer. The < ^V><^G> sequence,
for example, places the ASCII code for a beep tone in the text buffer.

If a text line extends beyond the end of a terminal's defined line length, that line may or may not be wrapped and displayed on-screen. Your terminal, its setup, and your UNIX system determine line length and the way lines are wrapped on-screen. If a line does not wrap, a ! appears at the end of the line to indicate that nondisplayed text is in the buffer. Remember that the ! also is used in command mode as an escape character to the UNIX shell.

Displaying the Buffer's Contents

After you have entered the sample text shown in the preceding section, you are ready to try another variation of ed's p (*print*) command. Enter the following command at the ed command-mode prompt:

```
*  1,$p
```

The following should appear on-screen:

```
Dear Mr. Jones:
The price of fruit today is:
Fruit       Each        10 Qty
Dates       0.10        1.00
Figs        0.20        2.00
Kiwi        0.30        3.00  (bell sound)
The price of fruit is going up!
Your Green Grocer,
George
```

Remember that the p (*print*) command works with either a single line or a range of lines. When used as part of a range specification, the $ character represents the last line of the text buffer. The command 1,$p, therefore, addresses and prints every line in the buffer.

In this context, the $ acts as a *pseudo address*, representing a common address point. The $ pseudo address represents the last line in the buffer. If a buffer contains text, that buffer has a last line. The last line is a common address point; that is, every buffer that contains text has a last line. Using pseudo addresses makes specifying address ranges easier. In this case, the $ enables you to address the last line without knowing its actual line number.

The . (dot) is another pseudo-address character. The . represents the current line in the buffer; that is, the line you are currently editing. If you issue the command .,$p, for example, ed prints everything in the buffer from the current line (which is not necessarily the first line) through the final line.

ed also accepts shorthand pseudo addresses, which enable you to specify a range of lines by using only one pseudo-address character. For example, you can use the , (comma) shorthand notation rather than the 1,$ address convention shown previously. The ,p command prints the buffer's entire contents. You also can use the ; (semicolon) pseudo-address character rather than the . , $ address convention. The command ; p prints everything in the buffer, from the current line through the final line. When you want a normal view of the text, use the p (*print*) command.

Two other commands—l and n—instruct ed to display the text buffer's contents in special ways. One of these special commands is the l (*list*) command. If you want to view the entire contents of the text buffer, including tabs and special characters, enter the following command at the ed command-mode prompt:

```
*   ,l
```

Use the l command when you need to see any hidden or special characters in the text. When you use the l command to view text, <tab> characters appear as greater-than signs > on-screen, and < ^ G> (the bell sound) appears as \007. (The number 007 represents octal characters.) Long text lines are wrapped so that they appear on-screen in their entirety; a backslash (\) character shows the point at which each wrapped line is broken on-screen. If you use the l command to view the "fruit letter" example (priceletter.2ed), the file would appear on-screen as follows:

```
Dear Mr. Jones:

The price of fruit today is:

Fruit>Each>10 Qty

Dates>0.10>1.00
Figs>>0.20>2.00
Kiwi>>0.30>3.00\007 (bell sound character)

The price of fruit is going up!

Your Green Grocer,

George
```

ed also provides a display option that enables you to see the line number of each line in the text buffer. To view the buffer's contents with line numbers, enter the following command:

```
*   ,n
```

When you use the n (line number) command, ed displays each line number, followed by a tab space, and then each line of text. The rest of the text appears as it would if you had used the p command. Here is how the sample letter should look if you display it by issuing the n command:

```
1       Dear Mr. Jones:
2
3       The price of fruit today is:
4
5       Fruit       Each        10 Qty
6
7       Dates       0.10        1.00
8       Figs        0.20        2.00
```

```
9     Kiwi       0.30       3.00  (bell sound)
10
11    The price of fruit is going up!
12
13    Your Green Grocer,
14
15    George
```

You can use the l and the n commands with any address range that you might use with the p command.

Searching for Text

Now that you have some text in the buffer, you can perform a number of operations on the text. For example, you might want to search for a specific line of text and then modify or replace the line, or insert a new line adjacent to it. The following example shows you how to use ed's text-searching capabilities.

Normally, when you search for text, you want to make some modification to the line when you find it. ed enables you to just search for text, or to find text and then replace it with new text. For these tasks, ed provides a search and substitute command.

To search for text in the buffer, use the search command /text/. In the generic form of the command, text represents a character, word (partial or full), phrase, or line.

Suppose that you want to find the word price in the sample text created previously in the chapter. To have ed search for the word, enter the following command and note ed's response, as follows:

```
*  1
*  /price/ <Return>
The price of fruit today is:
```

The search command instructs ed to search *forward* through the text buffer for the first occurrence of price. When ed finds a match, the line containing the match becomes the current line, and that line is displayed.

ed's text-search capability is case-sensitive. This means that when you specify uppercase or lowercase letters in the /text/ command, ed searches for letters of the same case you specify. If the search is unsuccessful (that is, if the text buffer does *not* contain a match for the specified text), ed displays an error message.

The search pattern you specify can include alphabetical, numeric, and special characters, as well as nondisplayed characters. When you want to search for a special or nondisplayed character, however, such as < ^ G > (the bell-sound character), you must precede the character with a \ (backslash).

Unfortunately, ed's text search stops after the first occurrence of matching text is found. That is, you cannot tell ed to find *every* occurrence of a text string by using the command only once. If you want to find a second occurrence of the specified text string, you must issue the /text/ command again.

ed does, however, offer a shortcut method for finding multiple occurrences of a text string. Suppose that you want to search the sample text file priceletter.2ed for the characters 2.00. The following dialogue shows what happens when you issue the /text/ command:

```
*  /2.00/ <Return>
Figs     0.20      2.00
```

ed displays the first line in which the characters occur. You believe, however, that the characters 2.00 also appear in subsequent lines in the buffer. Rather than entering the entire command /2.00/ again for each search, you can use the shortcut form of the command, which enables you to find successive occurrences of a search string.

The shortcut search command—//—repeats the most recently completed search, as shown in the following sample dialogue:

```
*  /2.00/ <Return>
Figs     0.20      2.00
*  // <Return>
Figs     0.30      2.00
*
```

When you use the /text/ command to search for text, remember the following important rule: When a match is found, the line containing the matching text becomes the current line.

Another form of the search command, ?text?, searches *backward* rather than forward from the current line to the first line of the buffer. If the search is successful, ed stops and displays the first line that contains the specified search string. If no match is found, ed returns to the line that was current when the search began.

To repeat the most recently conducted backward search, issue the ?? command. In other words, the ?text? and ?? search commands work just like the /text/ and // commands, except that the search runs backward through the buffer rather than forward.

When you are searching for text, you need to specify only as much of the search text as is required to ensure a match. The search string or s, for example, will match for sale—but not for rent. Be sure, however, that the search string contains enough of a pattern to ensure a distinct match. A search pattern such as a will match any word in any line that contains the letter *a*.

Understanding Relative and Absolute Addressing

By default, most of ed's commands operate on the current line, so you often want to control which line is current. You already have seen how a text search redefines the current line, but you can specify a new line as the current line in other ways. By pressing <Return>, for example, you can move down one line at a time, thus displaying each line as it becomes the current line. This method only works, however, if the buffer's last line is not the current line. You can also move to a new current line by using the concept of relative and absolute addressing. The concept of addressing lines is covered in the next few sections.

Reviewing the Line Orientation of ed

To understand the concept of relative and absolute addressing, consider the "line" orientation of ed. You can think of ed's buffer as a "lined" sheet of paper. Each line on the blank, lined "paper" is numbered 1, 2, 3, and so on. If you want to write on the "paper," you need to follow some simple rules.

To write on the first line of the blank sheet of "paper," use the a (*append*) command to enter text into the buffer. The a command appends text after line 0. You can never enter text, however, on line 0. The first line of text must be placed on line number 1. You then can enter a carriage return, and ed moves down to the next line so that you can enter text on line 2. To stop entering text and return to command mode, enter a . (exit) command in the first column of a new blank line. ed does not accept the . (exit) command as text, but exits from text-entry mode and returns to command mode.

If one or more lines of text have been entered into the buffer, you can add additional text by using either the a (*append*) or i (*insert*) commands. The append command adds text *after* the addressed line. The insert command inserts text *before* the addressed line. Remember, however, that like a blank sheet of unlined paper, an empty buffer has no "lines." Therefore, you cannot use i to insert text on a blank line.

The first line on the "paper" (the buffer) is always line number 1. The last line can be any number between 1 and $, where $ represents the last line written. If only one line exists, then the first line is number 1 and the last line is also line number 1. If a page contains 5 lines of text, the first line is number 1 and the last line is number 5 (in this case, $ = 5). The intermediate lines are numbered 2, 3, and 4.

Remember that ed can edit only one line at a time; that line is called the *current line*. When you specify address ranges, you can specify the current line by using the . (dot) pseudo-address character. If you want to work with any other line, you must make that line the current line by entering the appropriate command(s).

If the buffer (sheet of paper) contains 5 lines, and the current line is line 3, then you can imagine the buffer's contents as being arranged as follows:

1 *text for line #1*   (first line)
2 *text for line #2*
3 *text for line #3*   (current line)
4 *text for line #4*
5 *text for line #5*   (last line)

You address lines of text in this buffer by *absolute* address, *pseudo* address, or *relative* address. The absolute addresses in this example are 1, 2, 3, 4, or 5 (because there are actually 5 lines of text in the buffer).

As you learned in previous sections, a line also can be addressed by its pseudo address—a symbol that represents an address. The period or dot character(.) is the pseudo address for the current line (in this case, line 3), and $ is the pseudo address for the last line in the buffer (in this case, line 5). Or, you can address two or more lines by using any valid address range. For example, 3,5 is the address range for lines 3, 4, and 5.

A pseudo address range can also be represented by a symbol. The comma (,) is the pseudo-address range for line 1 through the last line in the buffer. Entering the , is the same as specifying the address range 1,$. The semicolon (;) is the pseudo-address range for the current line through the last line in the buffer. Entering the ; is the same as specifying the address range .,$.

A line's relative address is determined according to its relationship to a specified line (whose address may or may not be known as an absolute address). For instance, the relative address $-5 addresses the last line in the buffer, minus 5 lines. The relative address .+1 specifies the line after the current line.

Using Relative and Absolute Addressing

You can make any line current by specifying its line number as an absolute address, as follows:

    [*linenumber*] or [#]

When used with a command, this option makes the specified line the current line number and executes the command on that line.

Consider the following example:

    3 <Return>

When you specify this absolute address, ed makes line 3 the current line and displays that line.

You also can move forward or backward through the text buffer by using *relative* addressing. In this case, relative addressing means deciding which line should become current, and specifying that line's position in *relation* to the current line.

Suppose that you want to move backward through the text buffer by three lines, but you are unsure of the number of the line you want to make current. You can move to the desired line by issuing the following command:

.-3 <Return>

This command addresses the current line (denoted by the dot pseudo-address character), subtracts 3 from the current line's number, and moves to the resulting address (that is, the current line's address minus 3), and displays the new current line. The new current line is relative to the old current line by a relative –3 lines.

You can also enter a number of consecutive minus signs (–) at the ed command-mode prompt; ed will move backward in the text buffer the number of lines specified by the number of minus signs entered.

If you enter three minus signs (for example ---), ed moves backward three lines from the current line, and the line whose address is .-3 becomes the current line. An easier way to accomplish this movement, however, is simply to enter a minus sign followed by the number of lines you want ed to move backward. If you enter -3, therefore, ed moves up three lines from the current line.

Similarly, you can move forward through the text buffer by using relative addressing. Suppose that you want to move forward four lines, but you are unsure of the number of the line you want to make current. You can jump to the desired line by issuing the following command:

.+4 <Return>

The command addresses the current line (.), adds 4 to the current line's number, moves to the resulting address, and displays the new current line. Again, this address is given relative to the current address.

You can use consecutive plus signs in relative addressing just as you use consecutive minus signs.

If you enter a number of consecutive plus signs (+) at the ed command-mode prompt, ed moves forward the same number of lines as there are plus signs. If you enter five plus signs (for example, +++++), ed moves forward five lines from the current line, and the line whose address is .+5 becomes the current line. An easier way to accomplish this movement, however, is simply to enter a plus sign followed by the number of lines you want ed to move forward. If you enter +5, therefore, ed moves down five lines from the current line.

These addressing techniques are illustrated by the following example text, using the file `priceletter.2ed`:

```
*  1 <Return>
Dear Mr. Jones:
*  <Return>
<Return>  (blank line)
*  <Return>
The price of fruit today is:
*
Figs ...
*  <Return>
Apples ...
*  <Return>
Oranges ...
*  <Return>
Peaches ...
```

The next sample dialogue shows an easy way to move around the buffer. Move to the last line in the buffer by entering the `$` pseudo address, and then move to the first line of the buffer by entering a 1. To move to line 2, press <Return>.

```
*  $ <Return>
George
*  1 <Return>
Dear Mr. Jones:
*  <Return>

*  <Return>
The price of fruit today is:
*  <Return>

*  <Return>
Fruit        Each        10 Qty
*  <Return>
Dates       0.10        1.00
```

This progression continues for every <Return> until the last line is displayed:

```
*  $ <Return>
George
*  <Return>
?
line out of range
*
```

A line may be addressed relative to the current line number by using the − (minus sign) or + (plus sign) relative operators, as the following example illustrates:

```
*  $ <Return>
*  -7 <Return> (Or, you can enter 7 minus signs)
Figs       0.20        2.00
*  +5 <Return> (Or, you can enter 5 plus signs)
Your Green Grocer,
```

You also can move to a line without knowing its actual line number or its relation to any other lines, by searching for a specific string of text, as shown in the following example:

```
*  $ <Return>
*  ?0.30? <Return>
Kiwi       0.30        3.00 (bell sound)
*  ?? <Return>
Kiwi       0.30        3.00 (bell sound)
*
```

As illustrated by this example, when you enter a line-number command, ed moves to the line you specify, makes that line the current line, and then displays that line. The <Return> addresses line .+1 (the next line), makes it the current line, and then displays it. In this example, the command 1 makes line number 1 the current line. If you continue to press <Return>, ed moves through the buffer line by line, displaying each line.

The command 1 is equivalent to 1p or .-#p, where # is the number. The -# (minus) and +# (plus) commands address the line -# or +# (where # is a line number) above for − and below for + the current line . (current address).

```
*  w priceletter.2ed <Return>
174
*  q <Return>
>_
```

These commands write the buffer's contents to a disk file named priceletter.2ed. ed then displays the number of bytes in the buffer. Finally, the q command ends the ed session and returns to the UNIX shell.

Loading Files and Changing File Names

Recall that the f (*filename*) command either displays or changes the current file name. If you specify a file name with the f command, ed changes the current file's name to the file name you specify. If you issue the file-name command without specifying a file name, ed displays the file name of the current file in the buffer. If the current file has no file name, however, ed displays a blank line, as shown in the following sample dialogue:

```
> ed <Return>
P <Return>
* H <Return>
* f <Return>
         (blank line)
*
```

In this example, ed is active, but the text in the buffer has no file name. You can use the e (*edit*) command to load a specific file into the text buffer. If you specify a file name (in this case, `priceletter.2ed`) with the e command, ed loads the specified file into the buffer and displays the number of lines in the file, as shown in the following dialogue:

```
* e priceletter.2ed <Return>
174
*
```

Consider another example, which uses a completely different file. Suppose that you have in the buffer a file named `inventory.jan`, which contains inventory data for the month of January. Suppose further that you are editing the contents of the file when you suddenly realize that you really needed to leave `inventory.jan` in its original state, and that you need to create a new file that is similar to `inventory.jan`, but with a few changes.

What can you do? Remember that editing takes place in the buffer, not in the saved file on disk. Because you have not yet saved the edited `inventory.jan` file to the disk, the original version of the file is still safe in permanent storage.

In such a case, ed allows you to "wipe out" the edited version of `inventory.jan`, place a fresh copy of the original `inventory.jan` file in the buffer, and use the new copy to create a separate file under a new name.

When you issue the e command without a *filename* parameter, ed deletes the contents of the buffer and re-reads the current file into the buffer. If you issue the e command with no file name, ed simply reads a fresh copy of `inventory.jan` into the buffer, overwriting the edited version of the file in the buffer. You are ready to start the editing job all over again, or you can give the file in the buffer a new file name, such as `inventory.feb`.

If you try to use the e command when the buffer does not contain a current file, ed responds with an error message, as follows:

```
* e <Return>
?
illegal or missing filename
*
```

The error occurs because the buffer does not yet have a name; ed, therefore, does not know which file to re-read into the buffer.

Now you can issue the f command with the *filename* parameter, and specify a new name for the file (for example, inventory.feb); ed changes the current file's name from inventory.jan to inventory.feb. These steps are shown in the following dialogue:

```
*  f inventory.feb <Return>
inventory.feb
*
```

Even though you have changed the file's name from inventory.jan to inventory.feb, the contents of the buffer do not change. When you save the buffer's contents to disk, the file is saved as a new file with the name inventory.feb. The contents of the original inventory.jan file are not changed.

Determining Line Numbers

At times, you want to know not only the information contained on the current line, but also the absolute address (line number) of the current line. You can get this information with the help of the = (equal) command. The following sample dialogue shows you how to use the = command:

```
*  .= <Return>
5
*
```

The address of the . pseudo address (current line) is then displayed as 5. You can find the address of other pseudo addresses in the same manner. For example, you can find the absolute address (line number) of the buffer's last line as follows:

```
*  $= <Return>
20
*
```

The last line in the buffer is line 20. You can also enter the = by itself and obtain the same result as if you entered $=.

The #= command displays the line number of the line represented by the #. The addressed line is indicated by the character in front of the =. If no line is addressed before the =, the command displays the line number of the last line. Therefore, .= displays the current line number, 3= displays 3 (not very useful), and $= or = displays the number of the last line in the buffer.

Reviewing the Process of Modifying Text

This section reviews the concepts of modifying text. The section includes tables that list the basic ed commands for modifying text, special characters used for editing, and the pseudo-address characters used with ed. For information on the complete forms of these commands, refer to Appendix E.

Table 12.3
Text-Modification Commands for ed

Command	Action
e	Re-reads the previously saved version of the current file into the buffer. If no text buffer has been saved, an error occurs.
f	Displays the current name of the text file in the buffer.
l	Displays the entire contents of the text buffer.
n	Displays a line number and a tab character before each line of text in the buffer.
/text/	Searches forward from the current line to the last line of the buffer, in order to find the specified search string (text).
?text?	Searches backward from the current line to the last line of the buffer, in order to find the specified search string (text).
//	Searches forward for the most recently defined search criteria.
??	Searches backward for the most recently defined search criteria.
#=	Displays the line number of the line specified by #

Table 12.4 lists some special characters used in the editing process.

Table 12.4
Special Characters Used with ed

Character	Action
<Tab>	You can insert tab characters into the text buffer's contents by using the keyboard's Tab key. The number of spaces moved by the Tab key depends on the configuration of the tab settings for your terminal.
<^V> [nondisplayed character]	When placed in front of a nondisplayed character in a text file, the <^V> (Ctrl-V) enters the non displayed character's ASCII code into the buffer. The <^V><^G> sequence, for example, places the ASCII code for a beep tone in the text buffer.
<Return>	In command mode, when you press <Return>, ed moves to the next line, makes that line the current line, and displays the line on-screen. If the the buffer's last line is the current line when <Return> is pressed, ed responds with an error message.
\	To strip special characters of their meaning in text searches or search-and-substitution operations, prefix special characters with a backslash (\).

Table 12.5 lists the pseudo-address characters that can be used with ed.

Table 12.5
Pseudo-Address Characters for ed

Character	Meaning
$	Represents the last line in the buffer.
,	Represents the address range 1,$ (that is, the first line through the last line of the buffer).
;	Represents the address range .,$ (that is, the current line through the last line in the buffer).
.	Represents the current line. Therefore, the command .p prints the current line's contents.
1	The number 1 makes the buffer's first line the current line and displays it. This is equivalent to the 1p command.
#	Represents any valid line number. The number 7, for example, makes the buffer's seventh line the current line and displays it. This is equivalent to the 7p command.

Performing More Advanced Editing Operations

Editing involves more, of course, than moving around in the buffer and displaying a line on-screen. When you edit, you want to enter, modify, and delete lines of text. These processes are covered in the following sections.

Understanding the Search and Substitute Process

As you edit, you occasionally may need to find and correct an error that is repeated several times throughout your text. At such times, you can use commands that search for a specified text string, and then replace it with alternative text. The ed editor provides a convenient means for fixing such errors.

To learn how to use ed's search-and-replace feature, look at the contents of the sample file named priceletter.2ed. You entered the file in a simpler format in previous sections. When this exercise is complete, the file will ultimately appear as follows:

```
Dear Mr. Jones:

The price of fruit is just going out of sight. I don't know
what it will do from day to day. I am trying my best to keep
my prices reasonable. The price of fruit in my store today
is:

Fruit        Each        10 Qty
Dates        0.10        1.00
Figs         0.20        2.00
Kiwi         0.30        3.00

Total Price              $6.00

The price of fruit may still go up!

Your Green Grocer,

George
```

To create the new copy of `priceletter.2ed`, quit the editor and enter the following commands:

```
* ed priceletter.2ed <Return>
* 1,$p <Return>
```

These commands start ed, place the file into the buffer, and display the file on your screen. In its current form, the `priceletter.2ed` file should look like this:

```
Dear Mr. Jones:

The price of fruit today is:

Fruit        Each        10 Qty
Dates        0.10        1.00
Figs         0.20        2.00
Kiwi         0.30        3.00

The price of fruit is going up!

Your Green Grocer,

George
```

As you can see, the current version of `priceletter.2ed` will need some work, if it is to look like the intended letter to Mr. Jones. You can start modifying the letter by using search-and-substitution commands, as shown in the following dialogue:

```
* s/today/in my store today/ <Return>
* p
The price of fruit in my store today is:
```

Whenever a search or search-and-substitute command is successful, the line that satisfies the search becomes the current line. If the search and substitution occur on more than one line, the last line where the substitution occurred becomes the current line. If the search fails, the line that was current when the search command was issued remains the current line.

To finish editing the existing document, enter the following commands and text:

```
*  i <Return>
The price of fruit is just going out of sight. I don't know
what it will do from day to day. I am trying my best to keep
my prices reasonable.
. <Return>
*  ,P
Dear Mr. Jones:

The price of fruit is just going out of sight. I don't know
what it will do from day to day. I am trying my best to keep
my prices reasonable. The price of fruit in my store today
is:

Fruit      Each       10 Qty
Dates      0.10       1.00
Figs       0.20       2.00
Kiwi       0.30       3.00

The price of fruit is going up!

Your Green Grocer,

George
*
```

The insert command places the inserted text just in front of the previous line—in this case, before the following line:

```
The price of fruit in my store today is:
```

The `,p` displays the entire contents of the buffer on the screen. Now, set up the following dialogue with ed:

```
*  $ <Return>
George
*  ?Kiwi? <Return>
Kiwi        0.30        3.00
*  a <Return>
<Return>
<Return> Total Price<tab><tab>$6.00 <Return>
. <Return>
*  ,p <Return>
```

In this example, the `$` pseudo address moves to the last line in the buffer and displays it. The search command `?Kiwi?` searches backward in the buffer to the line containing `Kiwi`, makes it the current line, and displays it. The append command appends text to the end of the current line (the line containing `Kiwi`). The input text is shown in the next line, and the text-entry mode is terminated by the `.` (exit) command. The final `,p` command displays the entire contents of the buffer, as shown here:

```
Dear Mr. Jones:

The price of fruit is just going out of sight. I don't know
what it will do from day to day. I am trying my best to keep
my prices reasonable. The price of fruit in my store today
is:

Fruit        Each        10 Qty
Dates        0.10        1.00
Figs         0.20        2.00
Kiwi         0.30        3.00
Total Price       $6.00

The price of fruit is going up!

Your Green Grocer,

George
```

You can use two search and substitute commands to make final changes:

```
*  1 <Return>
Dear Mr. Jones:
* s/is/may still/ <Return>
* s/going/go/ <Return>
* ,p <Return>
```

The 1 command makes line 1 the current line and displays it. The first search-and-substitute command searches for the first instance of is and replaces it with may still. The second search-and-substitute command searches for the first instance of going and replaces it with go. The ,p command displays the buffer's entire contents:

```
Dear Mr. Jones:

The price of fruit is just going out of sight. I don't know
what it will do from day to day. I am trying my best to keep
my prices reasonable. The price of fruit in my store today
is:

Fruit        Each        10 Qty
Dates        0.10        1.00
Figs         0.20        2.00
Kiwi         0.30        3.00

Total Price       $6.00

The price of fruit may still go up!

Your Green Grocer,

George
```

The letter still needs three changes. The entries in the 10 Qty column must be changed because George is having a sale this week, and Mr. Jones can buy 10 pieces of fruit for the price of 9 pieces. You can use a series of search-and-substitute commands to make the changes quickly. Before starting, remember that the current line is as follows:

```
The price of fruit may still go up!
```

You must know which line is current, so that you can tell ed to search forward or backward from that line. The following dialogue shows how the changes are made:

```
*  s?1.00?0.90? <Return>
*  s/3.00/2.70/ <Return>
*  s?2.00?1.80? <Return>
*  ,p <Return>
```

The first command searches backward from the current line to the first instance of 1.00 and replaces it with 0.90. The second command searches forward (from the new current line) to the first instance of 3.00 and replaces it with 2.70. The third command then searches backward (from the new current line) for the first instance of 2.00 and replaces it with 1.80. Remember that the variations in this file were made purposefully, so that you can learn how to change text and correct errors by using ed's search-and-substitution facility. The following example shows you how to make changes by telling ed to search for errors or original material and replace (substitute) the original text with substitute text.

The s (substitute) command is a powerful command for making changes to text lines. The command takes the following syntax:

beginning address,ending address s/rtext/stext/

In this generic form of the command, *beginning address* and *ending address* can be either line numbers or pseudo addresses. The *rtext* (or text to *replace*) option is the string that contains the error you want to replace. The *stext* option (*substitute* text) is new or correct text, which will replace the erroneous text. Notice that the two text strings are surrounded by slash (/) characters.

The address parameter for the substitute command may be zero, one, or two addresses. The address can be an implied address (.), a pseudo address ($), a global address (g), an absolute, literal address (1), or an address range (1,5).

Using Global Addressing

The process of making changes one at a time can be inconvenient and frustrating, especially if you need to make one type of change several times in a document. Several different lines of text might require the same type of correction or change. Similarly, one line of text might require several different corrections or changes. You do not always have to make changes, however, one line at a time. You can make multiple changes to a document by using a search-and-substitute command along with ed's global option.

When you use the global option g at the beginning of the substitute command, ed searches each line for the *first* occurrence of the search string. If you place the g pseudo address at the end of the substitute command, ed searches for *all* occurrences of the search string in every line. When a match occurs, ed replaces the matched text with the specified replacement text.

Assume that Mr. Jones is from Europe and is used to seeing a comma rather than a decimal point used as the delimiter in fractional numbers. For example, Mr. Jones might prefer to see $2.00 written as $2,00. You can make this change in your letter by using the following command:

```
*  g/\./s/\./\,/ <Return>
*  ,p <Return>
```

Searching for Classes and Sets of Characters

In your editing tasks, you may find it convenient to be able to search for classes or sets of characters. The ed editor makes such searches possible with the [ ] (bracket) command. You can use any group of characters with the bracket command. For example, you can use the set [0123456789] or range [0-9] to match any numeric digit in the text file. Similarly, you can specify the set [ABCDEFGHIJKLMNOPQRSTUVWXYZ] or the range [A-Z] to match any uppercase letter. The range [a-z] matches any lowercase letter, and the range [A-Za-z] matches any upper- or lowercase letter. The set [adz] matches only the lowercase letters a, d, and z.

The following dialogue illustrates the use of such character searches:

```
> ed priceletter.2ed <Return>
336
P <Return>
*  H <Return>
*  g/[01]./ <Return>
Dear Mr. Jones:

The price of fruit is just going out of sight! I don't know
what it will do from day to day. I am trying my best to keep
my prices reasonable. The price of fruit in my store today
is:

Fruit       Each        10 Qty
Dates       #.1a        1.aa
Figs        #.2a        2.aa
Kiwi        #.3@        3.@@

Total Price             $6.##
The price of fruit may still go up!
Your Green Grocer,
George
*  g/[Pp]/ <Return>
Fruit       Each        10 Qty
Dates       0.10        0.90
Figs        0.20        1.80
Kiwi        0.30        2.70

Total Price             $5.40
```

The expression g/[01]./ searches for all lines that contain a 0 or a 1. To search for all lines that contain a P or p, use g/[Pp]/. From the current position, to find the first occurrence of lines that contain these sets, omit the global pseudo address at the beginning of the command.

Deleting, Undoing, Moving, and Copying

If you do much editing of your text files, you will inevitably need to delete, move, and copy text. When you delete text, the text is removed from the buffer. When you move text, the text changes location in the buffer. When you copy text, the same text occurs elsewhere in the buffer.

In the next sections, a different example file is used to illustrate ed's deleting, moving, and copying capabilities. The file is a business letter that will set up contract details between two parties. Enter the following text, which will be named contract.miles:

```
*  ed contract.miles <Return>
?  contract.miles
P <Return>
*  H <Return>
cannot open input file
*  a <Return>
August 20, 1990 <Return>
<Return>
<Return>
Jane Miles <Return>
Vice President <Return>
World Wide Widget Corporation <Return>
1107 South State Street <Return>
Seattle, Washington  98109 <Return>
<Return>
<Return>
Dear Jane: <Return>
<Return>
This letter is to confirm our meeting at your office on
September 4, 1990. I hope that we can work out all of
the contract details in just one day. Following is a
tentative agenda for the meeting: <Return>
<Return>
<tab>1) <tab>Contract review <Return>
<tab>2) <tab>Contract changes <Return>
<tab>3) <tab>Legal review <Return>
<tab>4) <tab>Contract final draft <Return>
<tab>5) <tab>Contract signing <Return>
<Return>
```

Please let me know whether this agenda is acceptable. <Return>
<Return>
<Return>
<Return>
Sincerely yours, <Return>
<Return>
<Return>
<Return>
John Short <Return>
President <Return>
JS Distributing <Return>
<Return>
. <Return>
* **w**
contract.miles
563
*

Now, display the letter by using the , n command. This command displays line numbers along with the text; you will need to know line numbers as you work through examples later in this section. Your version of the letter should look like this:

```
*  ,n <Return>
1     August 20, 1990
2
3
4     Jane Miles
5     Vice President ·
6     World Wide Widget Corporation
7     1107 South State Street
8     Seattle, Washington  98109
9
10
11    Dear Jane:
12
13    This letter is to confirm our meeting at your office on
      September 4, 1990. I hope that we can work out all of
      the contract details in just one day. Following is a
      tentative agenda for the meeting:
14
15         1)    Contract review
16         2)    Contract changes
17         3)    Legal review
18         4)    Contract final draft
19         5)    Contract signing
20
```

```
21    Please let me know whether this agenda is acceptable.
22
23
24
25    Sincerely yours,
26
27
28
29    John Short
30    President
31    JS Distributing
32
*
```

If your letter does not look exactly like this, don't worry. You can make any changes with the techniques described in the following sections, or by using the search-and-substitute commands discussed previously.

Deleting Text

To delete the current line, use the d (*d*elete) command. If you want to delete lines 1 through 5, issue the command **1,5d**. Similarly, use the command **1,$d** or **,d** to delete everything in the buffer.

In its generic form, the delete command takes the following syntax:

```
[#,#]d
```

Practice using the delete command on the sample letter. Suppose, for example, that the agenda (lines 15 through 19) for the meeting does not seem right. You can delete lines 15 through 19 and then display the revised letter by using the following commands:

```
*  15,19d
*  ,n
```

Your letter should appear as follows:

```
1     August 20, 1990
2
3
4     Jane Miles
5     Vice President
6     World Wide Widget Corporation
7     1107 South State Street
8     Seattle, Washington  98109
9
10
```

```
11   Dear Jane:
12
13   This letter is to confirm our meeting at your office on
     September 4, 1990. I hope that we can work out all of
     the contract details in just one day. Following is a
     tentative agenda for the meeting:
14
15
16   Please let me know whether this agenda is acceptable.
17
18
19
20   Sincerely yours,
21
22
23
24   John Short
25   President
26   JS Distributing
27
*
```

Lines 15 through 19 have been deleted, and the lines below them have been renumbered.

Undoing Changes

ed is more forgiving than you might think; the editor can even help you recover if you inadvertently delete or modify a line. If you do make such a mistake, you can use the undo command to reverse the most recent change to the buffer. You can undo the actions of the most recent a, c, d, i, j, m, r, s, t, v, G, or V command.

After thinking about the agenda, you may decide that it was all right as it was originally written. How can you recover the original text? The u (*u*ndo) command provides the solution for such emergencies. You can undo the most current deletion—in this case, recover lines 15 through 19—by entering the following commands:

```
*  14 <Return>
*  u <Return>
*  ,n
```

The first command makes line 14 the current line. The u (*u*ndo) command then "undoes" the previously issued delete command, so that the deleted text is reinserted after line 14 in the buffer. The , n command displays the newly revised document, so that you can verify that the original agenda is once again in the document. The letter should once again appear as follows:

```
*  ,n <Return>
1   August 20, 1990
2
3
4   Jane Miles
5   Vice President
6   World Wide Widget Corporation
7   1107 South State Street
8   Seattle, Washington  98109
9
10
11  Dear Jane:
12
13  This letter is to confirm our meeting at your office on
    September 4, 1990. I hope that we can work out all of
    the contract details in just one day. Following is a
    tentative agenda for the meeting:
14
15       1)   Contract review
16       2)   Contract changes
17       3)   Legal review
18       4)   Contract final draft
19       5)   Contract signing
20
21  Please let me know whether this agenda is acceptable.
22
23
24
25  Sincerely yours,
26
27
28
29  John Short
30  President
31  JS Distributing
32
*
```

Moving and Copying Text

You can move text around in the buffer by using the m (*mo*ve) command. The m command has the following generic syntax:

```
[#,#]m#
```

In this generic form of the command, the options #, # represent the first and last lines of text that are to be moved. The command relocates the text after the line addressed by the # after the m. You also can use pseudo addresses in place of the #,# options.

The following example uses the `contract.miles` file. Suppose that Jane Miles has received the letter through electronic mail. She wants to reply to it but does not want to type a new letter. She can make a new letter from the existing letter, simply by moving some of the text around.

The original letter was addressed to Jane Miles and signed by John Short. This order must be reversed in the response. You can start this process by using the m (*move*) command to move lines 29 through 31 to line number 7, as follows:

    * **29,31m7** <Return>

Now, display the document as follows:

```
*  ,n <Return>
1     August 20, 1990
2
3
4     Jane Miles
5     Vice President
6     World Wide Widget Corporation
7     John Short
8     President
9     JS Distributing
10    1107 South State Street
11    Seattle, Washington  98109
12
13
14    Dear Jane:
15
16    This letter is to confirm our meeting at your office on
      September 4, 1990. I hope that we can work out all of
      the contract details in just one day. Following is a
      tentative agenda for the meeting:
17
18            1)    Contract review
19            2)    Contract changes
20            3)    Legal review
21            4)    Contract final draft
22            5)    Contract signing
23
24    Please let me know whether this agenda is acceptable.
25
26
27
28    Sincerely yours,
29
30
31
32
*
```

Next, move Jane's name, title, and company name (lines 4 through 6) to line 31 for the letter's closing, by entering the following command:

```
*  4,6m31 <Return>
```

Now take another look at the letter:

```
*  ,n <Return>
1       August 20, 1990
2
3
4       John Short
5       President
6       JS Distributing
7       1107 South State Street
8       Seattle, Washington  98109
9
10
11      Dear Jane:
12
13      This letter is to confirm our meeting at your office on
        September 4, 1990. I hope that we can work out all of
        the contract details in just one day. Following is a
        tentative agenda for the meeting:
14
15              1)      Contract review
16              2)      Contract changes
17              3)      Legal review
18              4)      Contract final draft
19              5)      Contract signing
20
21      Please let me know whether this agenda is acceptable.
22
24
25
26      Sincerely yours,
27
28
29      Jane Miles
30      Vice President
31      World Wide Widget Corporation
32
*
```

Now, suppose that the agenda needs to be broken into two identical phases; that is, suppose that Jane wants everything to be done twice. To expand the agenda, copy lines 15 through 19 to line 20.

You copy text by using the `t` (copy) command. The copy command takes the following generic syntax:

    [#,#]t#

In this generic form of the command, the options #, # represent the first and last lines of text that are to be copied. The command places a copy of the addressed lines *after* the line specified by #.

Now, copy lines 15 through 19 to line 20 by using the following command:

   * **15,19t20** \<Return\>

Display the letter once again:

```
*   ,n <Return>
1     August 20, 1990
2
3
4     John Short
5     President
6     JS Distributing
7     1107 South State Street
8     Seattle, Washington  98109
9
10
11    Dear Jane:
12
13    This letter is to confirm our meeting at your office on
      September 4, 1990. I hope that we can work out all of
      the contract details in just one day. Following is a
      tentative agenda for the meeting:
14
15          1)   Contract review
16          2)   Contract changes
17          3)   Legal review
18          4)   Contract final draft
19          5)   Contract signing
20          1)   Contract review
21          2)   Contract changes
22          3)   Legal review
23          4)   Contract final draft
24          5)   Contract signing
25
26    Please let me know whether this agenda is acceptable.
27
28
29
30    Sincerely yours,
```

```
31
32
33    Jane Miles
34    Vice President
35    World Wide Widget Corporation
36
*
```

Next, the letter's salutation should be changed from Dear Jane to Dear John. The following search-and-substitute command will handle this chore:

```
*  /Dear/s/Jane/John/  <Return>
```

You also need to substitute John's address for Jane's at the top of the letter, by using the following series of commands:

```
*  7,8d <Return>

*  i <Return>

865 North Center Street
San Jose, California   95110
.  <Return>
```

The first command deletes Jane's address from lines 7 and 8; the insert command then enters the new address into the buffer.

Now you are going to delete line number 13 and replace it with a new paragraph, by entering the following commands and text:

```
*  13d <Return>
*  a <Return>
Your letter of August 20, 1990 outlined an agenda;
however, I propose that we split the agenda into two
parts. This change is outlined as follows:
.  <Return>
```

The first command deletes line 13. You then use the append command to add a new line of text after line 13.

Finally, you should add a sentence to the letter that points out the change in agenda. Suppose that you decide simply to add a line to the agenda itself, introducing the second phase of activity. The following dialogue shows how this is done:

```
*  20i <Return>
Phase two of the contract agenda:
.  <Return>
```

The insert command inserts the text before line 20.

Now view the final revised letter:

```
*  ,n <Return>
1     August 20, 1990
2
3
4     John Short
5     President
6     JS Distributing
7     865 North Center Street
8     San Jose, California  95110
9
10
11    Dear John:
12
13    Your letter of August 20, 1990 outlined an agenda;
      however, I propose that we split the agenda into two
      parts. This change is outlined as follows:
14
15            1)    Contract review
16            2)    Contract changes
17            3)    Legal review
18            4)    Contract final draft
19            5)    Contract signing
20        Phase two of the contract agenda:
21            1)    Contract review
22            2)    Contract changes
23            3)    Legal review
24            4)    Contract final draft
25            5)    Contract signing
26
27    Please let me know whether this agenda is acceptable.
28
29
30
31    Sincerely yours,
32
33
34    Jane Miles
35    Vice President
36    World Wide Widget Corporation
37
*
```

Before going any further, save this file to disk, under the file name
contract.short.

Performing Cut and Paste Operations

As you edit text, you may want to "cut" out a portion of the buffer's contents and write that data to a disk file. You subsequently may want to "paste" the data back into the file (or into another file), by reading the disk file into the buffer.

To cut a portion of the buffer to a file on disk, you can use the following variation of ed's w (*w*rite) command:

```
[#,#]w filename
```

In this generic form of the command, #, # represents the line numbers of the first and last lines you want to cut. The write command instructs ed to write the specified lines to the disk file, represented here by `filename`.

To paste the disk file's contents into the buffer, you can use the r (*r*ead) command, as follows:

```
[#,#]r filename
```

In this generic form of the command, #, # represents the line numbers of the first and last lines that must be read from the disk file. You specify the disk file's name in place of `filename`. The read command instructs ed to read the specified lines from the disk file into the buffer; the lines are inserted into the buffer after the current line.

To practice cutting and pasting, you can make some changes to the agenda in the business letter from the preceding section. In order not to destroy the original agenda, save it out in a temporary file on disk by using the following commands:

```
* 15,25w contract.short.old <Return>
123
* q <Return>
```

The desired lines are copied to the disk file named `contract.short.old`. To verify that you really copied the lines to the new file, enter the commands shown in the following dialogue:

```
* ed <Return>
?
P
* H
cannot open file
* r contract.short.old <Return>
* ,p <Return>
```

This set of commands replaces the contents of the buffer with the contents of the temporary file `contract.short.old`, and displays the file as follows:

```
1)    Contract review
2)    Contract changes
3)    Legal review
4)    Contract final draft
5)    Contract signing
Phase two of the contract agenda:
1)    Contract review
2)    Contract changes
3)    Legal review
4)    Contract final draft
5)    Contract signing
```

ed's cut-and-paste capabilities are very powerful. With the w (*w*rite) command, you can save a single line, a range of lines, or the entire file on disk. Later, you can use the r (*r*ead) command to retrieve this file into an existing document, placing it anywhere you like within the document. Just remember that the text is placed after the current line.

Joining Lines

The j (*j*oin) command removes the <Return> characters between addressed lines, making the addressed lines one line. Consider the following sample join command:

```
[2,3]j
```

This command joins the first line addressed (line 2) through the last line addressed (that is, line 3) into a new line 2. If you do not specify a line, or if you specify only one line, the command does nothing; however, no error message is given.

Using the Change Command

ed enables you to correct mistakes in another manner, aside from using the substitution methods described in a previous section. You can use the c (*c*hange) command to eliminate unwanted text and insert replacement text. The change command takes the following generic form:

```
[#,#]c
```

In this generic form of the command, #, # represents the range of lines to be deleted from the buffer. The change command deletes the first line addressed through the last line addressed and then accepts replacement text, which you enter into the buffer.

The change command is really a combination of two commands—the delete command and the insert command. In the previous examples, when you wanted to change a line or lines of text, you first had to delete the line(s) and then perform an insert command to enter the desired text.

The change command enables you to perform the functions of both the delete and the insert commands, as shown in the following example:

```
*  3,5c <Return>
new line 3
new line 4
new line 5
.  <Return>
*
```

This set of instructions deletes lines 3 through 5 from the buffer, and replaces them with three new lines of text.

Reviewing Advanced Editing Operations

This section reviews the commands used to perform more advanced editing operations. Table 12.6 lists the shorthand form of the command. For information on the long form of the commands, see Appendix E.

Table 12.6
Advanced Editing Commands for ed

Command	Action
d	Deletes the specified range of lines from the buffer.
g	The global substitution option, which expands the scope of the search to the entire buffer or entire line. If the option precedes the command, the entire buffer is searched. If the option follows the command, the entire line is searched. The same is true for the search-and-substitute command.
m	Moves the specified range of lines to a new location in the buffer.
s	The substitute command, which searches for a specified string and replaces it with another specified string of text.
r	Reads the contents of the current file into the buffer.
t	Copies a specified range of lines to another location in the buffer.
j	The join command, which removes the carriage-return characters between addressed lines, making the addressed lines one line.
c	The change command, which eliminates unwanted text and inserts replacement text.

Introducing Markers and Metacharacters

As your skill with ed increases, you may want to take advantage of some of the more advanced capabilities of ed, including line *markers* and *metacharacters*.

Markers enable you to identify a line of text by using a character marker rather than a line number. You use the k (line mar*k*er) command to refer to each line of text symbolically. A marker command marks the addressed line with the pseudo-address character *x*, where *x* is any letter from a-z. When no address is used, the current line is marked. You can refer to this pseudo-address character by using the ` command. To go to a line marked by the letter a pseudo address, for example, you enter **`a**. This command makes the marked line current. You can use only the letters [a-z] as markers.

Metacharacters are characters whose meanings are not literal (see table 12.7). ed expands a metacharacter to a new meaning. Metacharacters should not be confused with pseudo addresses. The dot (.) metacharacter is not the same as the dot pseudo address. You can use pseudo addresses only when *addresses* are accepted; you can use metacharacters only when *characters* are accepted. When in text-entry mode, however, ed does not recognize either pseudo addresses or metacharacters.

Table 12.7
Metacharacters Used in ed

Metacharacter	Meaning
.	Represents any single character
*	Represents zero or more occurrences of the character preceding it
$	Represents the end of a line
&	A variable that takes on the value of a string in a substitution command
\	An escape character, which nullifies any special meaning that may be attached to the character that follows the backslash
^	Represents the beginning or a line in the text buffer
[]	Delineates a set of zero or more characters as a search string, where any one of the characters in the set satisfies the match criteria

This chapter does not provide a complete tutorial on the user of markers and metacharacters. For more information on the use of markers and metacharacters, see Appendix E and the Reference Manual provided with your system.

Summary

This chapter's purpose is to provide a basic introduction to the ed text editor; the chapter does not provide comprehensive descriptions of all the editor's facilities and capabilities. For more information on the many facets of ed, consult your Reference Manual.

In this chapter, you learned the following important points:

❏ ed is an interactive, but terse text editor that communicates with you as you create and modify text files.

❏ ed operates in two modes: text-entry mode and command mode. You use command mode to control the program; you use text-entry mode to enter text.

❏ ed stores the text you create in a temporary buffer; you can later make the contents of the buffer permanent by writing the contents to a disk file.

❏ The most basic ed commands enable you to append, insert, print and write text to a buffer.

❏ You can use ed to delete text and undo deletions.

❏ You can address individual lines in your file by using relative addresses, absolute addresses, and pseudo addresses.

❏ ed provides several commands that enable you to search and substitute text as well as perform cut-and-paste operations.

❏ Special characters can be used in ed to expand the editor's capabilities.

Appendix E provides a fairly complete list of ed start-up options, metacharacters, pseudo addresses, and commands. Many of the concepts discussed in this chapter appear again in the next chapter, which covers the vi editor. vi—the UNIX full-screen editing facility—uses many of the concepts and constructs of ed. You may need to refer to this chapter often as you learn about vi in Chapter 13.

Using vi, the UNIX Visual Editor

Now that you have read about the ed line editor, you're ready to learn about the UNIX full-screen editor, vi. The vi or *visual* editor is able to take advantage of today's versatile terminals. Using vi, you can move the cursor to any point on your screen to add or change text. You'll find vi useful for composing memos, modifying your .profile or .login file, creating mail messages, and working with other kinds of text files.

Before reading this chapter, thoroughly review Chapter 12 and become familiar with the ed editor. Most ed commands and other facilities are used by the vi editor. Learning vi is much easier when you have a sound understanding of ed. The time you spend learning ed will be paid back many times as you become acquainted with vi.

You'll be pleasantly suprised by vi's friendliness compared to the terse ed. If you have used word processing programs, you'll feel more at home with vi than ed. Like most word processing programs, vi is active on the complete screen—not just on a single line like ed.

vi incorporates powerful editing features such as search and replace, text-block moves, insert and append modes, extensive cursor-positioning commands, and customized terminal setup. vi has been used as the text-processing front end for hundreds of books. Scores of books have been written about vi. Learning every feature of vi requires extensive study and practice. A complete explanation of vi can easily consume two hundred pages of text.

Fortunately, you don't have to spend hours learning its operation in order to use vi to create UNIX text files. Chances are good that you will want to create and modify simple text files such as data files or shell procedures. In fact, Chapters 14 and 15 show you how to compose shell procedures to make your work with UNIX more efficient. vi is an excellent choice for creating the files you'll learn about in Chapters 14 and 15.

393

In this chapter, you'll be introduced to vi in an easy-to-learn, easy-to-use manner. The chapter does not cover the more advanced features of vi. Additional listings of commands, however, appear in Appendix F. If you want more information on advanced features and advanced text-editing operations, consult Appendix F and the Reference Manual supplied with your system.

Key Terms Used in This Chapter

Terminal configuration	The process of setting the TERM environmental variable to your terminal type. UNIX uses the TERM variable to determine your terminal's capabilities, such as underlining, reverse-video, screen-clearing method, function-key assignment, and color capability.
showmode	An option that identifies the input mode you are in.
ex	A line-oriented text processing command which forms the basis for much of vi's command functionality.
Cursor-positioning commands	Commands that you enter in the command mode to select the spot you want to be.

Getting Started with vi

Before you use vi, take some time to review Chapter 12. This chapter uses much of the same terminology defined in Chapter 12. As in Chapter 12, the typographical conventions follow those used in this book. Also as in Chapter 12, the > character is used to represent the UNIX shell prompt. Remember that your prompt may vary from the prompt shown here.

You also need to take time to check your terminal configuration. Details on that procedure are presented in the next section.

Setting Your Terminal Type

Before you execute the vi command, you must ensure that your terminal type is identified in your exportable environment. You recall from Chapter 5 that the TERM variable (if it has been defined) contains your terminal type. UNIX uses the TERM variable to determine your terminal's capabilities, such as underlining, reverse-video, screen-clearing method, function-key assignment, and color capability.

If your terminal is not properly identified by the TERM variable, "strange" characters may appear on your screen while you are using vi. Another symptom of an improper terminal setup is that blocks of characters will overwrite legible text. If you start vi and do not get the expected responses, check to see that you have set up your terminal properly. The terminal-assignment example that follows is for Bourne-shell users. If you don't know your terminal type, ask your system administrator for assistance.

To display your TERM variable setting, use the following command:

```
$ echo $TERM <Return>
      ansi
$
```

The terminal type displayed in this example is ansi. Your terminal type may be different. If your terminal type does not match the value of TERM, you will need to change it. To change your terminal type for the duration of this login session, use the following form:

```
$ set TERM=vt100 <Return>
$ export TERM <Return>
$
```

In this example, vt100 is an example of a terminal type.

Your terminal *type* is not the same as the *name* of your terminal. Your terminal type must match one of the terminal types contained in the termcap file. The termcap file is normally located in the /etc directory. If you are not familiar with the termcap file, see Chapter 8 or consult your system administrator.

Starting vi

Like ed, vi is a UNIX command. To start vi, you simply type its name at the shell prompt. If you know the name of the file that you want to create or edit, you can issue the vi command with the file name as an argument. At the shell prompt, type the following:

```
> vi <Return>
```

As with most commands, you must press <Return> at the end of a line to execute the command.

When vi becomes active, the terminal screen is cleared, and a tilde character (~) will appear on the left side of every screen line. Some versions of vi display the tilde on every other line. The ~ is the "empty-buffer" line flag. When you see a ~ character on the left, you know that that area of the buffer is empty.

Like ed, and unlike most word processing programs, vi initializes in the command-mode. Notice in the following example that the screen is blank except for the ~ blank line flags (on the left) and the cursor at the top left corner of the screen.

```
_        <— cursor
~
~
~
~
```

When you see this display, you are successfully in vi, and vi is in its command mode waiting for your first command.

Entering New Text

While in the command mode, vi interprets your keystrokes as commands. There are many vi commands. If you enter a character as a command and the character is not a command, vi sounds a beep. Don't worry if vi beeps at you during your session. The beep sound is simply an audible prompt so that you can check what you are doing and correct any errors.

Accessing the Input Mode

Before you can enter text, you must switch from the command mode to the ak form of the text-entry mode. You can enter text while in the *Append* mode or *Insert* mode. When you are beginning a new text file, as in the upcoming example, you use the append mode.

Switch vi to text-entry mode by pressing <a>. The <a> or <A> is the *a*append mode command. As you'll see, most vi commands are based on letters. Remember that you don't enter the angle brackets. They are shown here because the a is *not* echoed to your screen. You don't have to press <Return> after the <a>. As soon as you press <a>, you are in the append mode, ready to input text to the empty buffer.

Before you enter any characters, you will want to know some easy actions to correct any errors you introduce into your text. vi provides many ways to correct errors. You'll learn about several ways to position the cursor on an error (or even a non-error) in a moment. For now, you can use a few simple keys to position yourself on the error and correct it.

The most frequently used error-correction key is the <Backspace> key. Most terminals have a dedicated <Backspace> key. If yours doesn't, use the key combination <^H>. Whenever you are in the text-entry mode, use the <Backspace> (or <^H>) to delete any input errors. When you backspace over characters, vi leaves the characters on-screen, but deletes the characters from the text buffer. If your terminal offers arrow-positioning keys that vi supports, you can move the cursor to any point in your text using the appropriate arrow keys.

The following text is used to demonstrate text entry. Later, the same text is used to demonstrate the extensive cursor-positioning provisions available with vi. You will benefit from entering this "hands-on" exercise in subsequent exercises. Because you are now in the append mode, you can enter the following text:

```
If you and I should chance to meet,
I guess you wouldn't care;
I'm sure you'd pass me in the street
As if I wasn't there;
You'd never look me in the face,
My modest mug to scan,
Because I'm just a commonplace
      And Ordinary Man.

But then, it may be, you are too
A guy of every day,
Who does the job he's told to do
And takes the wife his pay;
Who makes a home and kids his care,
And works with pick or pen ...
Why, Pal, I guess we're just a pair
   Of Ordinary Men.

We plug away and make no fuss,
Our feats are never crowned;
And yet it's common coves like us
Who make the world go round.
And as we steer a steady course
By God's predestined plan,
Hats off to that almighty Force;
        THE ORDINARY MAN.
              by Robert Service
```

Completing Text Input and Saving the File

The text you have entered is a poem, but you could have entered a memo, a data list, or a shell procedure just as easily. Now that the text is entered, you save the text to a file. Before you can save the text in the buffer, you must return to the command mode by pressing <Esc> or <^C>. (Some terminals may use the <Esc> key for other purposes.)

Your "escaping" to the command mode is a fundamental vi action. Any time that you are in a text-input mode, you can press <Esc> to return to the command mode. Some vi users press <Esc> two or more times, just to ensure that they are in the command mode. Pressing <Esc> additional times isn't necessary, but it does no harm, either.

Now that you are back to command mode, your next operation is saving the file from the editing buffer to the disk. To save the file, enter the :w (both the : and the w) write command:

```
:w vi.session.1
```

This command saves the buffer to the file named vi.session.1.

vi confirms the execution of the write command by displaying the following:

```
"vi.session.1" [New file] 29 lines, 721 characters
```

 The number of lines and characters reported by vi may vary slightly depending on how faithfully you followed the example and the particular implementation of vi you use.

Quitting vi after Saving Text to a File

At this point, you have started vi, entered the text append mode, typed a file, returned to the command mode, and saved the file. The only basic vi "survival" skill you still need to know is how to quit your vi session and return to the UNIX command prompt. After you have used the :w command to save the file, you need only enter the quit command :q to quit vi.

About Backspacing in vi...

As you have seen, text is entered on the screen at the cursor. The visual capability of vi is apparent in the preceding simple demonstration. If you make a mistake while entering text, use the <Backspace> key to erase it. One major difference in operation between vi and ed is the way the <Backspace> key is used in each editor. In ed, when characters are backspaced, the characters are erased from the screen *and* the buffer. In vi, when characters are backspaced, they are not erased from the screen, but they *are* erased from the buffer.

The <Backspace> character instructs the cursor to move to the left one character position. An applications program or command can add the additional step of printing a space character in the backspaced position. The space character "blanks out" the character where the backspacing occurred. vi doesn't print the space character in the backspaced position. In the character buffer, however, the backspaced character is removed. If you type a line into vi and then backspace to the beginning of the line, the line's contents are erased, even though you see the line on your screen. If you move forward in the file so that the area containing the backspaced line is off the screen, and then move backward so that it appears again, you'll see that the backspaced line is gone.

Setting Options

vi includes several options that you may or may not choose to use. One of the most used options is the showmode option. Before you learn about the showmode option and others, start vi again, this time using the file name session.1 as an argument:

```
$ vi session.1 <Return>
```

When vi executes, you'll see the text from the first session on your screen. You may have noticed that in your first session, there was no way to determine that you were in the text-input mode while entering the exercise. You can instruct vi to inform you when you are in an input mode by using the showmode option.

Setting Showmode

Like ed, vi can cause real frustration when you don't know what mode you are in. vi includes an option called showmode that identifies the mode you are in. With showmode set to on, whenever you are in input mode, the mode type displays in the lower-left corner of the screen.

When you set the showmode option, vi displays whatever type of input mode it is in, such as regular INPUT MODE, APPEND MODE, REPLACE CHAR mode, and so on. The type of mode is displayed in the bottom left corner of the screen. To set showmode in vi, enter the following:

> `> <Esc> :set showmode`

You press <Esc> before you type the set command to ensure that vi is in the command mode.

To confirm that the mode is set, enter the following:

`:set showmode?`
`showmode` (*The showmode is displayed by* vi)

or

`:set`
`directory=/usr/tmp redraw showmatch showmode term=ibm3161`

The options displayed by set will vary depending on options set by default and your particular implementation of vi.

Issuing the set command with no arguments will show only the user-set options. You can also abbreviate the set command by using se. You can set a number of options on the same line by entering an se command such as the following:

`:se  ap eb fl magic redraw sm smd warn wm=5 ws`

Notice that the first character of input is the : (colon) character. The colon character beginning a command is special to vi. In the command mode, when you enter a :, vi turns over control or "escapes" to the ex utility. ex is a line-oriented text processing command which forms the basis for much of vi's command functionality.

The text that follows the : is passed to ex as a command string. The entered : is displayed on the last line of the screen window. The preceding se command instructs ex to set the following options:

`ap eb fl magic redraw sm smd warn wm=5 ws`

These options and their functions are explained as follows.

Option	Function
ap	The *autoprint* option prints the current line to the screen when the line is changed.
eb	The *errorbell* option causes the computer to beep when you introduce a command error.
f	The *flash* option momentarily flashes a match on the screen.
magic	The *magic* option gives metacharacters their special meaning.
redraw	The *redraw* option keeps the screen up-to-date as changes occur. If you have a slow terminal, do *not* use the redraw feature.
smd	The *show type when in input mode* option. Some implementations of vi only display INPUT MODE for all input-mode types.
warn	The *warn* option displays a warning message when an attempt is made to exit vi when the buffer is not current with the file.
wm=5	This option forces a carriage return for a whitespace character *within the margin*. The setting wm=5 instructs vi to wrap the line when a whitespace character occurs within 5 characters from the end of the line. A 0 turns wm off.
ws	The *word search* option will wrap from the <eof> (end-of-file) character to the <bof> character (beginning-of-file).

You can display all of the vi options and their present states by issuing the following command:

    :se all

If you aren't sure what options you should use with vi, don't worry. For the most part, the default options that were established for you will be sufficient for the majority of your work. Your system administrator or an advanced vi user can assist you with other options.

Understanding Cursor and Screen Positioning

When you are editing text, you need a method to position the cursor where you want to insert additional text, correct mistakes, change words, or just append text to the end of existing text. The commands that you enter in the command mode to select the spot you want are called the *cursor-positioning commands*.

A variety of cursor-positioning commands are available with vi. The exercise in this section uses the Robert Service poem you entered in a previous section. The exercise demonstrates most of the cursor-positioning commands. You can use the exercise to select some (or all) of the cursor-positioning commands to use in your vi work. For a complete list of vi commands and their functions, refer to Appendix F or the Reference Manual supplied with your system.

How To Follow the Cursor-Positioning Examples . . .

Cursor positioning moves the cursor to various areas of the screen. Because vi is a full-screen editor, illustrating vi's cursor-positioning capabilities is difficult to do in a book. To help you follow the examples, you can refer to figure 13.1. Figure 13.1 shows the complete screen. The superscript numbers above some letters indicate the sequence in which the cursor-positioning commands are entered. Each command example has a corresponding superscript number associated with it as well. While reading each command example, you can match the example's number with the corresponding position number in figure 13.1. If you made mistakes when you entered the file originally, some steps in the exercise may be slightly different on your screen.

While in the command mode, the cursor may be positioned to a number of text breaks. Text breaks are characters, words, sentences, paragraphs, screens, and sections. By using the cursor-positioning commands, you can position anywhere in the buffer the window of text that you are viewing.

For example, if you are at the end of a file, it is more efficient to move to the beginning of the file in screen-sized steps rather than in line-sized steps. If you are positioning the cursor on a particular word from a different position in the word's line, it is more efficient to move in word-sized steps rather than in character-sized steps. The following examples illustrate how efficient moves may be accomplished. Refer to figure 13.1 for orientation.

From command mode, you'll enter the <B> command to move in screen increments to the beginning of the poem. Repeatedly enter < ^ B> (or < ^ b>) until the command error beep occurs. Each entry of this command tells vi to move *backward* (toward the beginning of the file) one screen in the buffer. Repeated entry of the < ^ B> (see position 1) command will finally position vi at the first screen of the buffer. At this point, the cursor will stay on and and the terminal will beep. You've just learned your first command-mode screen-positioning command.

Now enter H (or press the <Home> key) to position (see position 2) the cursor at the first line of the screen (which is also the first line of the buffer in this screen). H is a handy command to use to orient yourself to the top of any screen.

Enter 0 to position (position 2) the cursor at the first character in the line (which is also the first character in the buffer—the word). In this example, H also positions at the cursor to the first character. The cursor should be positioned under the I of the word If in the Robert Service poem.

I[2]f you and I should chance to meet,

I[19] g[14]uess y[16]ou wouldn'[18]t care[17];[15]

I[7]'[8]m s[10]ure you'[9]d pass m[11]e in the street

As if I wasn't there;

You'd never look me in the face,

My modest mug to scan,

B[20]ecause I'm just a commonplace

       [5]A[3]nd Ordinary M[6]an.[4]

But then, it may be, you are too

A guy of every day,

Who does the job he's told to do

And takes the wife his pay;

W[21]ho makes a home and kids his care,

A[1]nd works with pick or pen ...

W[30]hy[29], P[33]a[31]l[36], I g[13]uess we're just [37]a[35] p[34]a[32]ir

       [23]O[22]f[24] Ordinary Men.

W[25]e pl[26]ug away and make no fuss,

Our feats are never crowned;

And y[27]et it's common coves like us

Who make the world go round.

And as we steer a steady course

By God's predestined plan,

Hats off to that almighty Force;

       THE ORDINARY MAN.

            b[12]y Robert Service

Fig. 13.1. *An illustration of the* vi *cursor-positioning commands.*

Move the cursor forward (position 3) to the words And Ordinary, by using the forward-search command:

```
/And Ordinary/
```

Notice that the forward-search command takes the same form as ed search command.

The cursor will be positioned under the A in the line. Search commands are often more efficient to use than other positioning commands because they locate matching text, even if the text is out of the window. Remember from Chapter 12 that you can search backwards using a pattern between ? characters in place of / characters.

The $ will move the cursor to the end of the line (position 4) under the . (period). The $ command is the "end of the line" positioning command.

Now move the cursor by using the circumflex character, or caret (^). This command moves you to the first non-whitespace character (position 3) of And at the beginning of the line. ^ is handy for bypassing empty beginnings of lines and getting directly to the text.

0, as you have seen, will move to the first character (position 5) of the line, which is _And. Entering 22| moves to column 22 at Man (position 6). The number 22 tells the | positioning command the number of characters the command should move. You can use numbers in most cases to further instruct positioning commands.

Move the cursor to the I in I'm (position 7) by entering 5-. This command positions the cursor back five lines from the current position at I'm.

The *word* command, w, moves the cursor forward a word, to the I'm (position 8). The command 3w[9] moves to the you'd. As you'll see, you can include a number argument with w to move a number of word positions.

Enter 0[7] to move to the first whitespace character at the beginning of the line (position 7) and enter W. The cursor should now be under the sure (position 10). The uppercase W command is very similar to the lowercase w command. The difference between w and W commands is that w recognizes punctuation, and W doesn't. In other words, W treats each element of punctuation as a separate word.

Entering 4W will move the cursor 4 words forward to me (position 11).

By now, you're getting the idea of the cursor-positioning commands. For the rest of the exercise, you'll enter commands in sequence. The command's resulting position in figure 13.1 is indicated by the superscript character. A brief explanation of the command's action accompanies each command. For a more complete explanation of these commands, see Appendix F.

Enter the following commands in sequence:

Command	Action
G-1[12]	Moves to "by Robert Service."
?guess?[13]	Searches backwards to "guess" in the second stanza.
??[14]	Searches backwards to "guess" in the first stanza.
$[15]	Moves the cursor to end of the line at the semicolon (;) character.
BBB[16]	Moves the cursor to "you."
25|[17]	Moves the cursor to column 25 "care."
^g	Displays the current location of the cursor on the last line.

Command	*Action*
3b[18]	Moves the cursor to "wouldn't," because punctuation is observed.
0[19]	Moves the cursor to the beginning of the line at "I."
7e[17]	Moves the cursor to "care;" because punctuation is observed.
7G[20]	Moves to line 7 at "Because I'm ..." in first stanza.
5+[21]	Moves to "Who ..." in second stanza.
5 <Return>[22]	Moves to "Of Ordinary ..." in second stanza.
5|[23]	Moves to column 5 or as close as it can, at "Of Ordinary..."
10|[24]	Moves to column 10 at "Of."
3_[25]	Moves down to "We ..." in third stanza.
llll or 4l[26]	Moves to "... plug ..." in third stanza.
jj or 2j[27]	Moves to "yet," two lines down.
kk or 2k[26]	Moves to "... plug ..." two lines up.
hhhh or 2h[28]	Moves to "plug ..."
kkkkk or 5k[29]	Moves to "Why makes ..." in second stanza.
16G[30]	Go to line 16 at the same column position or to "Why, Pal" in second stanza.
fa[31]	Moves forward to the first "a" from the current cursor position of "Pal."
2fa[32]	Moves forward to the 2nd "a" from the current cursor position of "pair."
^[30]	Moves to the first non-whitespace character at the beginning of the line "Why."
ta[34]	Moves forward to the character prior to "a" from the current cursor position of "Pal."
3ta[34]	Moves forward to the character prior to the 3rd "a" from the current cursor position of "pair."
Fa[35]	Moves backwards to the first "a" from the current cursor position of "a pair."
Fa[31]	Moves backwards to the "a" in "Pal."
$	Moves forward to the end of the line "pair."
3Ta[36]	Moves backwards to the character prior to the 3rd "a" at "Pal."
,[37]	Repeats the last command in the opposite direction at "a pair."
;[36]	Reverses the direction of the last command and repeats it; returns to "Pal."

In general, a vi command entered in uppercase performs the same function as the lowercase command, but in the opposite direction or sense.

For example, f moves right, F moves left, t moves right, T moves left, w moves right (respecting punctuation), W moves right (ignoring punctuation), b moves left (respecting punctuation), B moves left (respecting punctuation).

In addition to the commands described in the preceding exercise, you can move the cursor by using the arrow keys, the space bar, the <Return> key, and others. Appendix F provides a listing of these cursor-positioning commands and other vi commands.

Summary

This chapter was not meant as a complete tutorial to vi—such a tutorial would comprise an entire book! The best way to learn vi is by experimentation. Appendix F provides many types of commands that you can try with the editor.

This chapter covered the following key points:

❑ The vi editor is a combination of two types of editors: a line-oriented editor and a screen-oriented editor.

❑ Like many word processing programs, vi enables you to see a screenful of text as you work.

❑ You can use set commands and options to more fully utilize the power of vi.

❑ The cursor and screen-movement commands are the integral part of the power of vi.

In the next chapter, you learn about the basics of shell programming. You can create many of the simple shell scripts and procedures described in the next chapter by using either ed or vi.

Four

Programming the Shell

Understanding the Basics of Shell Programming

Increasing Your Productivity with Advanced Programming

Understanding the Basics of Shell Programming

As you learned in Chapter 5, the UNIX shell—the interface between the user and the operating system itself—is one of the major components of the UNIX operating system. The shell also incorporates a powerful programming language, which enables you to more easily exploit the full power of UNIX. Programmers will find many familiar concepts in shell programming, but most users can make good use of shell programming features without any knowledge of programming.

In this chapter you see how to create and execute shell programs (also known as *shell scripts* or *shell procedures*) and use some of the basic shell programming features. You also see a bit of the history and diversity of the UNIX user interface.

Most of the UNIX commands have been presented in previous chapters. In this chapter, you will look at several of these commands in a different light. Several commands will be presented in terms of their use within shells and shell scripts. Don't worry if each command's format isn't exactly like that presented in previous chapters; full explanations of any new syntax elements will be provided.

Key Terms Used in This Chapter

Shell	A program that serves as an interface between the user and the UNIX operating system. The shell accepts commands from some source (such as the keyboard or a file) and then executes those commands.
Shell procedure (or *shell program* or *shell script*)	A file containing UNIX commands that can be interpreted and executed by the shell.
C Shell	An alternative shell, so named because its built-in programming language is similar to the C programming language.

History	A mechanism in the C shell and Korn shell that keeps track of recently typed commands, allowing them to be executed without retyping.
Alias	In the C shell and Korn shell, a typing-saver that enables you to create a short name for a lengthy command.
Korn (or *K shell*)	An alternative shell created by David Korn at AT&T Bell Laboratories.
csh	The command that invokes the C shell.
ksh	The command that invokes the Korn shell.
Login shell	The shell for interpreting keyboard commands, provided by UNIX when a user logs in.
Comment	Information in a computer program intended to be useful to human readers; the comment is ignored by the computer.
Variable	An area of memory used by the shell to store various pieces of information.
Assignment	A command that places a value in a variable.
Command-line parameter	A piece of information provided as part of a command.
Environment	Information provided to a program by the operating system, including certain variable values.

Why Use Shell Programs?

Shell programs can greatly simplify day-to-day tasks in several ways. They can, for example, perform some of the following tasks:

- Save typing.

  Any time you find yourself retyping long commands or sequences of commands, a shell program can minimize typing time.

- Prevent errors.

  Because there is less to type, there is a smaller chance of typing mistakes.

- Simplify operations.

  Because complex operations can be "prepackaged" in a shell, casual users can invoke shell programs to perform tasks without needing to understand the details of how the task is accomplished.

In this chapter, you learn how to write shell programs that accomplish these tasks.

Understanding the Flavors of UNIX Shells

Before you look at shell programs, it is important to understand that different "flavors" of shell programs exist. In fact, UNIX actually contains different shells. In this section, you will get a better understanding of the definition of the "the shell" as well as its different varieties.

In UNIX, the word "shell" refers to a program, usually written in the C programming language, that serves as an intermediary between the user and the UNIX operating system. The shell's function is to accept commands, interpret them, and make them happen. When a user logs in, UNIX provides a shell to accept commands from the keyboard and execute them (that is, to do what the command specifies).

The details of how the shell accomplishes this is a matter for system programming books. What is important for you to know is that any program that accomplishes these operations—get a command, interpret it, and make it happen—may properly be termed a *shell*.

Throughout the history of UNIX, many shells have been written by ambitious programmers, and a few have attained some popularity. All shells have several things in common: they provide a way of entering commands from the keyboard and provide a programming language for writing shell programs. One shell may differ from another, however, in the specifics of how it handles these tasks.

On most machines, several shells are available. Each user can select the shell that best suits his or her needs or even switch back and forth at will. While this chapter focuses on only one of the available shells—the Bourne Shell—the chapter also introduces and discusses the other shells and their capabilities.

The Bourne Shell

The Bourne shell is the original UNIX shell, created by Steve Bourne at AT&T's Bell Laboratories. Because it is the oldest shell, it is usually considered the "standard" UNIX shell and is available on all UNIX systems. Because it is universally available, most shell programs are written using commands that the Bourne shell understands. This book focuses on the Bourne shell in most of its examples. (In fact, the shell prompt presented in most examples is usually the Bourne shell's $ prompt.) The powerful programming capabilities of the Bourne shell are the focus of this chapter and the next.

The C Shell

In the mid and late 1970's, the University of California at Berkeley (UCB) was actively committed to the development of a modified version of UNIX. The efforts of the students and faculty had far-reaching effects on the future of UNIX. Many of their enhancements have since become standard parts of UNIX (such as the vi text editor).

By the time Berkeley began working on UNIX, larger machines with greater capabilities were available, and some of the shortcomings of the Bourne shell were evident. Bill Joy at UCB set out to write a shell for UNIX that would accomplish the same task in a broad overall manner (that is, interpret commands and execute them), but whose features and capabilities were quite different from that of the Bourne shell.

The result was the *C shell*, so called because its built-in programming language, which is quite different from that of the Bourne shell, closely resembles the C programming language. This was a natural course of action for Joy to take, because most of the students and faculty involved with UNIX at Berkeley were already familiar with C. While a few of the very simplest shell programs can run using either the C shell or the Bourne shell, the vast majority cannot; they must be specifically written for one or the other. Many experienced users (especially those who are also C programmers) consider the programming language of the C shell vastly superior to that of the Bourne shell.

Spotting the C shell at a glance is easy—the C-shell prompt is a percent sign (%), rather than the dollar sign ($) used by the Bourne shell.

In addition to a different programming language, the C shell added a number of conveniences that made its day-to-day use more friendly. One in particular—the *history* feature—saves a great deal of typing. The C shell keeps track of the commands recently typed (you decide how many commands are kept; 80 is typical). At any point, you can repeat any recent command without having to retype it. Even nicer, a command can be changed and then repeated—a wonderful feature when that last long command contained a tiny typo.

Another of the C shell's powerful conveniences is the *alias*, which enables you to select a few characters to represent a lengthier command and execute the command just by typing the characters. As a simple example, suppose that you often want to list all subdirectories under the current directory (a handy thing to be able to do). The find command will do this for you, as in the following example:

```
% find . -type d -print <Return>
```

This command finds all files in the current directory (.) that are directories (-type d), and prints the names of the directories it finds (-print). Rather than type this lengthy command repeatedly, you might alias it as follows:

```
% alias sub find . -type d -print
```

Now, when you type **sub** and press <Return>, the C shell realizes that what you really want to do is `find . -type d -print`. In effect, you have created a new command that is an abbreviation for another command.

About the Versatile `find` Command . . .

The `find` command is an amazingly useful command, virtually unique among UNIX commands because of its verbose format. It enables you to search a directory and all its subdirectories for all files that meet one or more criteria, which you specify, and then to take some action on those files, such as printing them or removing them. `find` commands make wonderful examples of shell programming because they tend to be lengthy commands to type.

The `find` command has a myriad of options. Some of the more common ones are presented here.

The basic format of the find command is as follows:

```
find pathname [criteria] action
```

In this generic format, `pathname` is the directory and possible subdirectories to be searched, `criteria` (an optional argument) specifies what the files have in common, and `action` specifies what UNIX should do when files are found.

A sample `find` command is as follows:

```
$ find /usr/sue -name stuff -print <Return>
```

This command searches the directory (`/usr/sue`) and all subdirectories for files that meet the criterion (have the file name `stuff`); then, `find` takes the specified action (`-print`, that is, displays the names of all the files it finds that match the established criteria).

You can specify a wide variety of criteria. The `-name` criterion finds all files that have a particular name. To use wild cards, you surround them with quotation marks. Thus, to find all files in the current directory (`.`) and its subdirectories that have "pizza" as part of their name, you can use this command:

```
$ find . -name "*pizza*" -print <Return>
```

The `-user` criterion enables you to find files belonging to a particular user. This command finds all files in `/tmp` owned by Belinda:

```
$ find /tmp -user belinda -print <Return>
```

The `-type` criterion enables you to find certain types of files. It is followed by a d for directory or an f for regular file. Thus, the following command lists all directories under `/usr/bart`:

```
$ find /usr/bart -type d -print <Return>
```

Criteria can be combined in almost any combination. This command finds all files that are directories and that are owned by Peter:

```
$ find / -type d -user peter -print <Return>
```

About the Versatile find *Command . . . (continued)*

Note that specifying / as the directory causes find to search the entire file system. This process takes many minutes on large systems.

Many more find actions and criteria are available, along with various options. See Chapter 7 and the Command Reference for more information on the find command.

The Korn Shell

The C shell added many important capabilities not found in the Bourne shell, but many UNIX users were reluctant to use those capabilities, because the C shell differed so radically from the Bourne shell.

In the early 1980's, David Korn at Bell Labs produced what many saw as the perfect compromise: the Korn shell (or "K" shell). Unlike the C shell, the Korn shell is "backward compatible" with the Bourne shell—including its programming language. Thus, programs written for the Bourne shell can be used with the Korn shell.

In addition, the Korn shell added most of the C shell's enhancements and a few of its own. Aliases are borrowed from the C shell, along with a more powerful, yet easier-to-use history mechanism. Many UNIX users feel that the Korn shell will eventually become the standard UNIX shell, replacing the Bourne shell.

Other Shells

In addition to the most popular shells—Bourne, C, and Korn—other shells have popped up from time to time, including the following:

- DOS shells

  These shells make UNIX resemble MS-DOS. Several variants of DOS have shown up on different equipment. Although DOS shells never provide the same power and flexibility available with the more common UNIX shells, they are intended for the MS-DOS user who wants to make a painless transition to UNIX.

- Graphical User Interfaces (GUIs)

  These represent radical departures from typical UNIX shells. Rather than typing commands, users communicate with a GUI by using a mouse to "point-and-click" on desired selections and options. Many GUIs are extremely flashy, and most are easy for novices to use. GUIs typically require more expensive, powerful hardware than conventional shells. Various GUIs are available from different manufacturers; two of the up-and-coming GUIs are Open Look (AT&T), and Motif (used by Hewlett-Packard, IBM, and others).

- Various home-grown shells

  You may occasionally run across someone who has written his own shell. Just as fiction writers dream of producing the Great American Novel, so do C programmers dream of writing the next Great American Shell.

Which Shells Are Available?

By now, you are sitting at your terminal wondering, "Which shells are available to me?" The answer is that the Bourne shell is always available. Most UNIX systems available today can trace their lineage to one of two sources: AT&T, or the University of California at Berkeley. It's a safe bet that if your system harks back to Berkeley, the C shell is on your machine. If your system's ancestor came from AT&T, you may have the Korn shell.

Well, great, but what if you don't have a family tree handy?

To check for the presence of the C shell, type **csh** at the prompt and press <Return>. If you get a percent sign (%), as in the following listing, the C shell is running.

```
$ csh <Return>
% <^D>
$
```

Pressing <^D> will get you back to the Bourne shell.

On the other hand, if you receive an error message, the C shell is not available on your system:

```
$ csh <Return>
sh: csh:  not found
$
```

The same technique applies to checking for the Korn shell, except that the Korn shell's prompt is a dollar sign, just like Bourne shell's:

```
$ ksh <Return>
$
```

Understanding the Operation of Shell Programs

Throughout the discussion of UNIX in this book, you have learned to accomplish tasks by typing commands at the keyboard. Shell programs rely on the capability of the UNIX shell to accept commands not only from the keyboard, but from a file as well.

As you have seen, when you log in, UNIX starts up a shell called the *login shell*. The login shell repeatedly prompts you for commands and executes them. When you indicate to the login shell (by pressing <^D>) that no more commands are forthcoming, the shell terminates, and you are logged off.

A shell program is simply a group of standard UNIX commands—the same commands you use from the keyboard—which have been "prepackaged" into a file. They rely on the shell's ability to read commands from any source, including files. The commands contained in a shell program can be executed simply by typing the name of the file containing the commands. Doing so causes the login shell to start a new shell—a new command interpreter. The login shell waits idly while the new shell interprets and executes your shell program. When all the commands in your shell program have been completed (assuming that all goes well), the new shell terminates, and the login shell resumes.

It is important to realize that anything you can do from the keyboard can be done in a shell program, and vice versa. In both cases, the same part of UNIX—the shell—is doing the work.

Remember the following points about the login shell and shells in general:

- A login shell gets its commands from the keyboard; a shell executing a shell program gets its commands from a file.
- When a shell executing a shell program runs out of commands, it terminates, and the login shell resumes. When the login shell runs out of commands (as signified by a user pressing <^D>), the login shell terminates, and the user is logged off.

Writing Shell Programs

With a basic understanding of how the shell works, you are ready to write a simple shell program. In the next few sections, you see how to create and use shell programs to automatic repetitive tasks. A new command, echo, which is most useful in conjunction with shell programs, also is presented.

Creating a Simple Shell Program

Suppose that in your work, you often want to determine the current date and time, list the users currently logged on, and find out how much disk space is available. (This is not something a general user would typically need day-to-day, but a system administrator might want to monitor this information regularly.)

To accomplish this from the keyboard, you would use the date, who, and df commands, respectively, with the output looking something like this:

```
$ date <Return>
Sat Jun 16 14:04:10 EDT 1990
$ who <Return>
mark      ttyp1    Jun 16 14:02
pierce    ttyd0    Jun 16 13:51
andre     ttyid    Jun 16 13:05
mike      ttyj3    Jun 16 11:00
allen     ttyj4    Jun 16 13:54
elaine    ttyj5    Jun 16 13:20
$ df <Return>
/         (/dev/dsk/c1t1d0s0):   3274 blocks    2300 i-nodes
/usr      (/dev/dsk/c1t1d0s2):   8018 blocks   22678 i-nodes
/usr2     (/dev/dsk/c1t3d0s8):  74764 blocks   63380 i-nodes
/tmp      (/dev/dsk/c1t3d1s8):  19404 blocks    2429 i-nodes
$
```

Even though these commands are relatively simple to type, you might grow tired of typing them repeatedly. A shell program would simplify the task. The following example creates a shell program called status.

Shell programs are created in the same manner as any UNIX text file—usually by using a text editor, such as ed or vi. You can also use a word processor if it can create an ASCII file. (For more information on ed and vi, see Chapters 12 and 13.)

In this example, you create a file called status, which contains three lines—the same commands you would type from the keyboard:

```
date
who
df
```

You have now written a complete shell program.

Before you can use this program, you must perform a one-time operation of adding execute permission to the file, using the chmod command as follows:

$ **chmod +x status** <Return>

This command turns on execute permission for status, thus allowing the shell to identify the file as a shell program, rather than as an ordinary text file. Once this operation is performed for a shell program, it need never be done again for that shell program, even if you make changes to the shell program. (For more information on the chmod command, see Chapter 9 and the Command Reference.)

You now can execute the shell program simply by typing the name of the file as follows:

```
$ status <Return>
```

The shell recognizes this command as the name of a shell program (because a file exists by this name, and execute permission is turned on). Commands are read from the file and executed, one-by-one, just as though you had typed each command from the keyboard:

```
$ status <Return>
Sat Jun 16 14:04:10 EDT 1990
mark      ttyp1   Jun 16 14:02
pierce    ttyd0   Jun 16 13:51
andre     ttyid   Jun 16 13:05
mike      ttyj3   Jun 16 11:00
allen     ttyj4   Jun 16 13:54
elaine    ttyj5   Jun 16 13:20
/         (/dev/dsk/c1t1d0s0):    3274 blocks    2300 i-nodes
/usr      (/dev/dsk/c1t1d0s2):    8018 blocks   22678 i-nodes
/usr2     (/dev/dsk/c1t3d0s8):   74764 blocks   63380 i-nodes
/tmp      (/dev/dsk/c1t3d1s8):   19404 blocks    2429 i-nodes
$
```

All the features you have come to enjoy with other UNIX commands are available to shell programs as well. For example, you can redirect the output from a shell program to a file, just as you can with any UNIX command:

```
$ status > statusinfo <Return>
```

In effect, you have created your own "customized" UNIX command, which is built from three other standard UNIX commands.

Using Shell Programs To Automate Repetitive Tasks

Shell programs are most useful for simplifying complex, repetitive tasks. Whenever you find yourself repeatedly using the same commands that involve more than a few keystrokes, a shell program can probably simplify your work.

Consider the following example. Suppose that you often create temporary text files that contain various notes or data. You are in the habit of naming these files with the root name `temp`, as in `temp.notes` or `temp.data`, to indicate that they will not be kept for a long time. Further suppose that you often forget to remove these files when you have finished with them and, consequently, spend some amount of time hunting for these files when available disk space gets low.

Locating such files is not too difficult; the UNIX `find` command will do it for you. To display the names of all files in your home directory (and its subdirectories) with names that start with `temp`, use the following command:

```
$ find /usr/fred -name "temp*" -print <Return>
```

Now, this command admittedly does not flow easily from the fingers, and if this is a task you perform frequently, you could certainly tire quickly of trying to remember the command. This would be an excellent case for a shell program. To create the program, follow these steps:

Step 1. Using a text editor, such as `vi`, create a file with desired commands. For this example, call the file `findtemp`.

Step 2. Add execute permission, using the `chmod` command as follows:

```
$ chmod +x findtemp <Return>
```

Step 3. Execute the command by typing the name of the command and pressing <Return>:

```
$ findtemp <Return>
/usr/fred/tempstuff
/usr/fred/letters/temp.letter
/usr/fred/reports/temp.salesjunk
$
```

Once you become aware of how simple it is to collect commands into simple shell scripts, it becomes unthinkable to repeatedly type the same long commands.

An alternative method for executing shell programs is available, but the method is used less often. You can type **sh**, followed by the name of the shell program. Then press <Return>. Consider the following example:

```
$ sh findtemp <Return>
```

The advantage of this technique is that the shell program does not need execute permission. In a few rare situations in which a shell program will be used only once or twice, this alternative may involve less typing than setting execute permission with `chmod` and running the program as described in Step 2 above:

```
$ chmod +x findtemp <Return>
$ findtemp
$
```

Using the `echo` Command in Shell Programs

The `echo` command prints its arguments—everything that follows the word echo—to the terminal. Consider the following example:

```
$ echo Hello World. <Return>
Hello World.
$
```

In most cases, especially when the message is longer than one line, you surround the phrase to be printed or displayed with two sets of quotation marks, as in the following example:

```
$ echo "Hello World."
Hello World.
$
```

The quotation marks enable the shell to understand that a message is more than one line long. Once the shell spots an open quotation mark, it considers everything else part of the echo command until a closing quotation mark is found. You will see an example of a multiple-line message later in this section.

The echo command is quite useful within shell programs. For example, suppose that you have been writing the great American novel and have stored it in a file called great.am.novel. You might want to write a shell program—called check.novel—that uses the UNIX spell-checker to print a list of misspelled words. In its simplest form, the program might look like this:

```
spell great.am.novel | lp
```

The spell command produces a list of all the misspelled words in great.am.novel. The pipe symbol (|) causes the output from spell to be fed into the lp command as input. lp prints its input on the printer.

While this program will certainly get the job done, it may take several minutes. And most folks don't like a command that works for a long time without displaying a message on the screen. Consider this version of the same shell program, made slightly more user-friendly:

```
echo "Spell-checking the Great American Novel now ...
please wait."
spell great.am.novel | lp
echo "Spell-check complete."
```

Now when check.novel is invoked, it prints a friendly message about what it is doing, and the please wait serves to warn that patience is necessary. A typical execution might look like this:

```
$ check.novel <Return>
Spell-checking the Great American Novel now ... please wait.
(a slight pause)
Spell-check complete.
$
```

You can also use the echo command to provide fixed input for other commands. In this case, you include the pipe symbol (|) in the command line.

Suppose that you are a supervisor for several employees, and each Friday you need to remind them to turn in their time sheets. You might write a shell program called `ts.remind`, which contains this line:

```
echo "Please don't forget your time sheet." | mail joe fred mary
```

The `echo` command produces a one-line message, which is fed into the `mail` program as its input. The message is sent via UNIX mail to Joe, Fred, and Mary.

As mentioned previously, you can even echo multiple lines, allowing for longer messages. Just be sure to surround the message in quotation marks. Consider the following example:

```
echo "To:  Joe, Mary, and Fred
From:  Your Boss
Please don't forget that your time sheet
is due by noon today." | mail joe fred mary
```

The shell interprets the quotation marks as the beginning and ending of the message being piped to `mail`. When the shell sees the first open quotation mark, it considers everything else part of the `echo` command until the closing quotation mark is found.

Including Comments in a Shell Program

When you write shell programs, it is often helpful to include notes or explanations within the program, providing information about how the program works, what it does, or how it should be used. Such notes are of no use to the computer, but provide insight for other people who may later examine your program. They also can provide valuable reminders to you—the techniques and ideas that are fresh in your mind today may be obscure to you six months from now. Such notes, intended for use by people and not by the shell, are called *comments*.

Whenever the shell finds a line containing a pound sign (#), everything from the pound sign to the end of the line is ignored. If the line begins with a pound sign, the entire line is ignored. Here is an example:

```
# findtemp program, written 7/10/90 by
# Fred Smith. This program displays the
# current date, followed by the names of
# all files with names beginning with
# "temp" underneath my home directory.
date                           # print date and time
find /usr/fred -name "temp*" -print  # find temp files
```

The spacing of these commands is unimportant to the shell—you can arrange the comments in any way that looks pleasing to the eye. The only requirement is that a command and a comment appearing on the same line must be separated by at least one space or tab. Also notice that you can include blank lines almost anywhere within a shell program. Such lines are ignored by the shell and serve only to make the program easier for humans to read.

Using Variables in Shell Programs

As you learned in Chapter 5, a *variable* is a memory location used by the shell to store temporarily small amounts of data. Each variable is given a name (much like a file), and that name is used to access the data. The data stored in a variable is known as the variable's *value*. Variables find their greatest use in shell programs.

Unlike files, variables are retained in memory only until the shell terminates. Thus, if you set the variable from the login shell, the variable is retained until you log off. If you set the variable within a shell program, the variable is retained until the shell program terminates.

The next few sections explain how variables can be used both as typing savers and as tools to make your shell programs more powerful.

Making Variable Assignments

A variable can acquire a value in several ways; the most basic is called an *assignment*. A variable assignment has the following form:

```
variable=value
```

For example, consider the following assignment:

```
daughter=Jennifer
```

This statement creates a variable called "daughter" and places into it the value "Jennifer".

There are several important rules in variable assignments:

- There can be no space on either side of the equal sign.
- If the value contains any spaces or special characters, it must be surrounded by quotation marks. Thus, the following statement generates a cryptic error message:

```
$ daughter=Jennifer Jones <Return>
sh: Jones:  not found
```

But this statement works correctly:

```
$ daughter="Jennifer Jones" <Return>
$
```

Once a variable has a value, you can retrieve that value and use it as part of a command at any time by supplying the name of the variable, preceded by a dollar sign ($). Whenever the shell sees a dollar sign/variable-name combination, it replaces the combination with the value of the variable during the execution of the command.

For example, you could make the following variable assignment:

```
$ friends=/usr/jill/phonebook
```

Then, suppose that you issue the following command:

```
$ grep Mary $friends <Return>
```

The shell replaces $friends with the value of the variable.

The effect is the same as if you had typed the following:

```
$ grep Mary /usr/jill/phonebook <Return>
```

This command displays all the lines in /usr/jill/phonebook that contain the word "Mary."

Viewing the Value of a Variable

You can display the value of a variable by using the echo command. As with any command, when the shell sees a variable preceded by a dollar sign, the variable is removed, and its value replaces the variable. The echo command then prints the result. Consider this example:

```
$ echo $daughter <Return>
Jennifer Jones
$
```

or

```
$ echo "My daughter is $daughter." <Return>
My daughter is Jennifer Jones.
$
```

Notice in the second example that only the second daughter was replaced by the variable value, because only the second daughter was preceded by a dollar sign.

Using Variables as Typing Savers

Variables often can be used in a command simply as typing savers, to avoid repetitive typing of the same phrase.

For example, suppose that you frequently use the UNIX uucp software to transfer files from one UNIX computer to another. Files are usually copied to and from the directory /usr/spool/uucppublic. Typing the path names for this directory can quickly get tiresome. You can, however, save typing by placing this directory name in a variable, in this manner:

```
uu=/usr/spool/uucppublic
```

(Any variable name will do; **uu** is nice and short.)

Once you do this assignment, you can can reference the directory by typing **uu** in any command, as follows:

```
$ mv $uu/newfile . <Return>
```

In this example, before the shell executes the mv command it replaces the $uu with the variable's value, /usr/spool/uucppublic. The effect is just as though you had typed the following:

```
$ mv /usr/spool/uucppublic/newfile . <Return>
```

For another example, suppose that you need to send several pieces of mail to a number of users. You might save typing by setting a variable to contain the list of users:

```
users="fred mary john pete mike"
```

(Note that the quotation marks are necessary because the value contains spaces.) To send mail to these users, you can now type the following:

```
$ mail $users <Return>
```

The shell removes $users and replaces it with the variable's value, and the effect is as though you had typed the following:

```
$ mail fred mary john pete mike <Return>
```

Within shell programs, the same technique can be applied. This shell script sends a mail message to a list of users:

```
# set the list of users
users="fred mary john pete mike"
# send mail to those users
echo "To: $users
From: Mean Nasty Boss
Don't forget—your time sheets are due by
noon, or you won't get paid." | mail $users
```

Notice that $users is used twice in this script—once as part of the message in the echo command and again in the mail command. There are two advantages to using the variable this way:

• It saves typing because you only have to type the list of users once.

- Because the list of users appears in only one place, making changes to the list is easier.

As people are hired and fired, you only have to add and remove names in one place.

Placing a Value in a Variable with `read`

The `read` command provides another method, quite different from the method of variable assignment, for placing a value in a variable. This method is used almost exclusively within shell programs and, in effect, provides a way to ask questions of the user. In its simplest form, a `read` command looks like this:

```
read [variable]
```

When this command is executed, `read` waits for the user to type a line on the keyboard; whatever is typed becomes the value of the variable.

Suppose that you have created a list of all the books in your personal library, along with a shelf number where each book can be found. You have put this list and corresponding numbers in a file called `booklist`.

The following shell program, called `library`, asks you for a phrase and searches for all books within `booklist` whose title contains that phrase:

```
echo "Book name to locate? \c"
read name
grep "$name" /usr/fred/booklist
```

In the first line, the `echo` command prints the prompt—the wording of the question. Notice that the message ends with `\c`. Normally after `echo` prints its message, the cursor skips to the next line on the terminal; however, if the message ends with \c (for "continue"), the cursor remains on the same line.

The second line waits for a line to be typed and places whatever is typed in the variable name. Finally, `grep` searches for that name within the file `/usr/fred/booklist`.

A typical execution might look like this:

```
$ library <Return>
Book name to locate? Red <Return>
Hunt for Red October    Tom Clancy        Shelf 14
Red Star in Orbit       James E. Oberg    Shelf  7
Wielding a Red Sword    Piers Anthony     Shelf 22
$
```

In the next example, suppose that you often need to use the `find` command, but you also often forget the syntax of the command. This shell script, called `ffind` (for "Friendly Find") might make life simpler, because it prompts for the information it needs:

```
# A friendly find shell program, written
# 7/31/90 by James Johnson
echo "Friendly Find."
echo "What directory shall I search? \c"
read dir
echo "Filename to search for? \c"
read file
echo "Searching now ..."
find $dir -name "$file" -print
echo "Search complete."
```

Here, two questions are asked, and the values are placed in two variables. Both variables are then used in the find command. A typical use might look like this:

```
$ ffind <Return>
Friendly Find.
What directory shall I search? /etc <Return>
Filename to search for? *tab <Return>
Searching now ...
/etc/mnttab
/etc/inittab
/etc/drvtab
Search complete.
$
```

Notice that even wild cards can be used—they simply become part of the value of the variable and then are substituted into the find command. The quotation marks around $file are required to make this work; you will see why in the next section.

Combining Variables

The value for one variable can be used as part of the value of another variable. Consider the following example:

```
daughter=Mary
son=John
children="$daughter and $son"
```

A moment's thought reveals why this works. Before the shell executes that last statement, it spots the $daughter and $son, and changes the statement to the following:

```
children="Mary and John"
```

The shell then executes the statement, which assigns the value to children. (The quotation marks are necessary because the value being assigned to children contains spaces.)

The value of a variable can even be used as part of a new value for that same variable. Consider this example:

```
dogs="Fido and Spot"
dogs="$dogs and Bowser"
```

In the second statement, the shell replaces $dogs with Fido and Spot, and the statement becomes:

```
dogs="Fido and Spot and Bowser"
```

Fido and Spot and Bowser becomes the new value of dogs.

Using Command-Line Parameters for Input

Although the read command provides one method of user input, it is not the method used by most UNIX commands and programs. Most programs find the information they need on the command line. For example, if you want to count the words in a file, the wc command has to know which files you want to count. Rather than asking a question, wc inspects the command line and gets the needed file names there.

You can do the same thing in a shell program. When you type a command, the shell breaks the command into words (a word being a group of characters separated by spaces or tabs) and assigns each word to a special variable, called a *command-line parameter*. These special variables—named $1 through $9—represent the first nine words on the command line (not counting the name of the program itself). When the shell program begins, these variables already contain the proper values.

For example, suppose that you run a shell program by typing the following:

```
$ shellprog Mary had a little lamb <Return>
```

When the program begins, $1 will have the value Mary, $2 will be had, and so on through $5, which will be lamb. The remaining variables, $6 through $9, will be blank.

Consider the "friendly find" program you just saw. It asked two questions: what directory to search and what file name to search for. You can, instead, take information from the command line, as shown here:

```
# A friendly find shell program, written
# 7/31/90 by James Johnson. Version 2
echo "Friendly Find."
echo "Searching now ..."
find $1 -name "$2" -print
echo "Search complete."
```

You notice immediately that the program is much smaller than the original, because it doesn't have to ask questions. The program expects the first word on the command line to be the directory to search—its value is placed in $1—and the second word is the file name to find—placed in $2. A typical execution might look like this:

```
$ find /usr/mark core <Return>
Friendly Find.
Searching now ...
/usr/mark/checks/core
/usr/mark/genledger/core
Search complete.
$
```

This program is not very forgiving of errors. If you omit either of the required command-line parameters, the program will not work correctly. Some possible solutions to this problem are included in Chapter 15.

When you use command-line parameters, the library program becomes a one-liner:

```
grep "$1" /usr/fred/booklist
```

The program expects a single phrase on the command line and searches for book titles containing that phrase, as follows:

```
$ library Web <Return>
Charlotte's Web          E.B. White      Shelf 4
Webster's New World Dictionary           Shelf 11
$
```

Another handy variable, $*, represents all the parameters on the command line. That is, wherever $* occurs in a shell program, it is replaced by all the words on the shell program's command line. Many simple, yet helpful, shell programs can make use of $*.

Here is an example. If you use the UNIX typesetter troff, you are probably used to formatting and printing documents with a command such as this:

```
$ troff -mm chap1 chap2 | lp -dlaser <Return>
```

A nice shell script—call it format—that accomplishes the same task might look like this:

```
echo "Formatting your document ... please wait."
troff -mm $* | lp -dlaser
echo "Done."
```

You run this command by typing a line like the following:

```
$ format chap1 chap2 <Return>
Formatting your document ... please wait.
Done.
$
```

Within the `troff` command, `$*` is replaced by all the words on the command line, in this case `chap1` and `chap2`.

A Safe Remove . . .

A common error among UNIX users is removing the wrong file. Unlike some other operating systems, in UNIX, when you type **rm data** and press <Return>, the file is gone and is not recoverable by any practical means. Few mistakes will make your stomach sink as much as realizing that you have removed the wrong file.

A simple shell script can all but eliminate this danger. You can borrow the name of the MS-DOS equivalent to `rm`, and call it `del`. `del` works just like `rm`, except that instead of removing the file(s), it actually moves the file(s) to a special holding directory—call it `wastebasket`. If you delete a file and later realize that the deletion was a mistake, you can simply retrieve the file from `wastebasket`.

Create the `wastebasket` directory in the usual way:

```
$ mkdir /usr/mary/wastebasket <Return>
```

The shell script `del` looks like this:

```
mv $* /usr/mary/wastebasket
```

Henceforth, you should avoid the `rm` command when you want to get rid of files. Use the `del` shell script instead, as in this illustration:

```
$ del shopping.list recipes <Return>
```

When you type the preceding command, the shell script executes this command:

```
mv shopping.list recipes /usr/mary/wastebasket
```

Occasionally—perhaps once a week—you will want to "clean out" the contents of `wastebasket` by performing a genuine `rm` on any files therein; otherwise, old files will collect there forever. You might even set the UNIX `cron` command to do it for you automatically at regular intervals.

Using **read** versus Using Command-Line Parameters

To get information into a shell program, you can use either of the methods just described—asking questions with `read` or using command-line parameters. Which is best? It depends.

People who use a shell program only occasionally find programs that ask questions easier to use than those that expect command-line parameters. Users do not need to remember details about the program; they can execute the program simply by typing its name, confident that the program will ask for the information it needs.

Folks who use a program frequently find command-line parameters more to their liking. Such users are already familiar with the information required by the program, and they do not want to wade through lots of questions. With command-line parameters, they can simply provide the information on the command line, and away they go.

Using Special Variables

In Chapter 5, you saw a number of variables, called *special variables*, which have particular meanings and are often useful in shell programs.

The variable HOME, for example, contains the full path name of your home directory. Consider the following command:

```
$ grep "$name" /usr/mark/userlist <Return>
```

Instead of this command, you can write the following:

```
$ grep "$name" $HOME/userlist <Return>
```

There are several advantages to using a special variable in this situation:

- The command line is easier to read.
- If your home directory gets moved (as sometimes happens on large systems), you don't have to change your shell scripts.
- $HOME always represents the home directory of the person running the program. If another user wants to use your shell program, $HOME references that user's home directory, not yours.

Another variable, called LOGNAME, contains your login ID. This variable can be useful for printing greeting messages:

```
echo "Welcome, $LOGNAME!"
```

When executed, this command prints a line such as this:

```
Welcome, diedre!
```

The PATH variable contains a list of directories, separated by colons (:), which instruct the shell where to look for programs. When you type a command—and do not specify a path name as part of the command name—the shell searches the directories listed in PATH to find the requested command.

Using echo to display the value of PATH, you might see the following display:

```
$ echo $PATH <Return>
/bin:/usr/bin:.
$
```

This user's path contains three directories. When a command name is typed, the shell looks for it first in /bin, then in /usr/bin, and finally in the current directory (.). If the command is not found in any of these directories, an error message is displayed.

Suppose, for example, that you type the following command:

```
$ vi just.stuff <Return>
```

The shell first searches /bin—and does not find vi. Then the shell finds vi in /usr/bin and executes the command.

An especially handy technique to use with the PATH variable is to create a directory—typically called sh—in which you collect all your useful shell scripts. By adding this directory name to the path, you can cause the shell to search this directory when you type command names. This addition enables you to easily run your common shell scripts, regardless of the directory in which you are currently working. The following example illustrates this use of PATH:

```
$ mkdir /usr/jim/sh <Return>
$ mv ffind /usr/jim/sh <Return>
$ PATH=$PATH:/usr/jim/sh <Return>
```

These commands create a directory /usr/jim/sh into which shell programs can be placed, moves a shell program to that directory, and then adds /usr/jim/sh to the end of the PATH variable. Now the shell can find ffind regardless of your current working directory.

Among other interesting variables are the following:

The MAIL variable tells the shell where your UNIX mailbox is located. If your shell notifies you automatically when new mail arrives, it needs this information.

The PS1 variable is your shell prompt; that is, the text used by the shell to indicate that it is ready for a command. The default value is a dollar sign, but you can change your prompt by changing the value of this variable. Try this command:

```
$ PS1="Your command? " <Return>
Your command?
```

Your prompt is now Your command? instead of a dollar sign.

The TERM variable indicates the type of terminal you are using. Programs such as vi, which need to know how to manipulate your terminal, require this variable.

TZ indicates your time zone. Inside the computer, all times are kept in Greenwich Mean Time. Programs that display dates—such as the date command—examine the TZ variable and convert Greenwich Mean Time to the appropriate time. If you are in the Eastern time zone, this variable has the value EST5EDT, indicating that your time zone, referred to as "EST" (Eastern Standard Time), is five hours west of the Greenwich (or Prime) Meridian and supports Daylight Savings Time—in which case the time zone is referred to as "EDT" (Eastern Daylight Time).

You can determine the time in other time zones by changing `TZ` (in effect, fooling UNIX into thinking that you are in a different time zone) and then printing the time with the `date` command. For example, to find the time in Los Angeles (which is on Pacific Time), you can do this:

```
$ date <Return>
Sun Jun 17 16:04:53 EDT 1990
$ TZ=PST8PDT <Return>
$ date <Return>
Sun Jun 17 13:05:04 PDT 1990
$
```

`TZ` is set to `PST8PDT`, indicating Pacific Standard Time—eight hours west of Greenwich—and support of Daylight Savings Time.

More interesting yet, to display the current time in Beijing, China (after consulting a handy almanac or encyclopedia and discovering that Beijing is 8 hours east of Greenwich), change `TZ` as follows:

```
$ TZ=BST-8 <Return>
$ date <Return>
Mon Jun 18 04:07:19 BST 1990
$
```

The value `BST-8` indicates that the time zone is called "BST" (a made-up notation; there is no standard notation) and that the position is eight hours east of Greenwich (indicated by a negative eight). Since Beijing does not observe Daylight Savings Time, no notation appears after the `-8`.

For a complete discussion of these variables, see Chapter 5.

UNIX and Daylight Savings Time . . .

In 1986, Congress changed the beginning of Daylight Savings Time from the last to the first Sunday in April, thereby throwing UNIX systems everywhere into chaos. Many UNIX-based computers today still display the wrong time during most of April. System administrators get around this problem with any of several inelegant solutions. Some change the system time; some set the time zone one hour east (by altering TZ); others simply tolerate a time that is one hour off.

Newer versions of UNIX follow the new rules.

Understanding the Environment

When you run a shell program, a new shell starts up to execute the commands in the shell program. This new shell inherits a number of characteristics from your login shell. Two of these characteristics are important here:

- The new shell begins in the current working directory. Therefore, a pwd command within a shell program produces the same result as a pwd command typed from the keyboard just before the shell program began.
- The next shell receives copies of some variables. (You will shortly see which variables.)

Collectively, these and other inherited characteristics are known as the *environment*. An understanding of the environment is important for an understanding of how one shell affects another. As you will see, changes made in some places are not necessarily effective elsewhere.

Using the export Command

You have seen how to set the value of variables from the command line and within shell programs. Can variables set in one place be used in another? In some cases, yes.

Normally when new variables are created, they are accessible only within the shell in which they are created. That is, a variable set on the command line is a part of the login shell and is accessible only to the login shell; a variable set in a shell program is available only within that shell program. These limitations exist because variables are not normally placed in the environment and therefore are not inherited as new shell programs start up. They are sometimes called *local variables*.

Consider this simple shell program, called favorite, which doesn't do anything useful, but does help illustrate a point:

```
echo "My favorite color is $color."
echo "My favorite food is $food."
```

Then consider these commands:

```
$ color=blue <Return>
$ food=pizza <Return>
$ favorite <Return>
My favorite color is .
My favorite food is .
$
```

The first two commands assign the values blue and pizza to the variables color and food, respectively. The shell program favorite is then run, and—as with all shell programs—a new shell is started to execute the program. favorite displays blank values for the variables `color` and `food`, because it did not inherit the values of these variables from the user's login shell. `color` and `food` are local to the login shell, and not part of the environment.

The `export` command changes this behavior; it places one or more variables into the environment and makes them available to new shell programs:

```
$ color=blue <Return>
$ food=pizza <Return>
$ export color food <Return>
$ favorite <Return>
My favorite color is blue.
My favorite food is pizza.
$
```

Here, because food and color were exported to the environment, the shell program inherited their values and was able to print the correct values.

Using the `env` Command

The `env` command displays a list of all variables in the environment, along with their values. A typical `env` output might look like this:

```
$ env <Return>
HOME=/usr/mark
SHELL=/bin/sh
MAIL=/usr/mail/mark
LOGNAME=mark
PS1=$
TERM=vt100
RANDOM=14666
PATH=/bin:/usr/bin:/usr/mark/bin:/usr/mark/sh:.
MAILCHECK=600
TZ=EST5EDT
color=blue
food=pizza
$
```

All these variables and their values are available in the environment. They were exported either by the user (using the `export` command), or by one of the UNIX system programs when the user logged in. All are available to shell programs.

Understanding Changes to the Environment

A shell program can change its environment by changing directories or by changing the values of the variables it inherits. It is important, however, to realize that these changes are not reflected to previous shells.

Consider this simple program, called `testprog`, which illustrates this point. It prints the current working directory and then prints the value of the HOME variable. It then changes HOME, changes directory, and prints both again:

```
echo "Current working directory is \c"
pwd
echo "Variable HOME is $HOME"
HOME=/etc
cd /usr/bin
echo "New working directory is \c"
pwd
echo "Variable HOME is now $HOME"
```

When the program is run, it might produce this output:

```
$ testprog <Return>
Current working directory is /usr/fred/test
Variable HOME is /usr/fred
New working directory is /usr/bin
Variable HOME is now /etc
$
```

The program changed the directory and a variable, but if you test these values back at the command prompt, this is the result:

```
$ pwd <Return>
/usr/fred/test
$ echo $HOME <Return>
/usr/fred
$
```

As you can see, the value was changed only within the shell program—not within the login shell.

Using Special Characters in Shell Programs

Almost every piece of punctuation on the keyboard has a special meaning to the shell; Chapter 5 and this chapter described the meaning of many of these special characters. For example, Chapter 5 described the asterisk (*), used to represent a wild-card file specification; in this chapter, you saw that a dollar sign ($) is used to access the value of a variable. Even spaces and tabs have a special meaning—they're used to separate the parts of a command.

However, sometimes you will want to use these characters as part of a phrase or message; in such cases, you do not intend for them to have any special meaning. Using double quotes (" "), for example, enables you to selectively turn off the special meaning of characters.

Consider this `echo` statement, which seems to print a straightforward message:

```
echo Press <Return> to continue.
```

This command seems simple enough, but look what happens when you try it:

```
$ echo Press <Return> to continue. <Return>
sh: Return: cannot open
$
```

The shell spotted <Return> and thought you were trying to redirect input from a file called `Return`. Naturally, it couldn't find such a file, and an error message resulted. If the shell had gotten past that problem, it would further have thought you were trying to redirect output to a file because of `> to`. This is a classic case of the shell trying to attach a special meaning to two characters when none was intended.

Using quotes solves the problem:

```
$ echo "Press <Return> to continue." <Return>
Press <Return> to continue.
$
```

In this case, the quotes tell the shell to ignore the special characters, allowing `echo` to print them along with the rest of the text.

Consider another example: Suppose that you want to search a file for all lines that begin with the characters d-o-g. You may remember that the caret (^) means *beginning of line* in a search phrase (called a *regular expression*). Therefore searching for the characters ^d-o-g ought to find all lines that begin with the characters d-o-g. But look what happens:

```
$ grep ^dog mutt.papers <Return>
sh: dog: not found
Usage: grep -blcnsvi pattern file . . .
$
```

What happened? The shell spotted the caret, which—at least, on many shells—is an archaic symbol for a pipe. (The more acceptable symbol these days is the vertical bar |). The shell tried to make a pipe out of the command and failed when it couldn't find a command called `dog`. Foiled again by another misunderstood special character!

Quotes are again the solution to this problem:

```
$ grep "^dog" mutt.papers <Return>
dogs, dogs, and more dogs
dogs come in many breeds
$
```

At first glance, you may be tempted to say that the caret does have a special meaning in this command—"beginning of line." But that special meaning comes from `grep`, not from the shell! In effect, the quotes here tell the shell to keep its hands off, so that `grep` will see the caret and derive the appropriate meaning.

Quotes serve another purpose, which is really just a variation of the function discussed in the preceding example. When the shell processes a command, one of its first duties is to break the command into words by looking for spaces and tabs. Thus spaces and tabs have a special meaning to the shell: they serve as delimiters for words. When you surround a group of characters with quotes, the group becomes a single word, even though it may contain spaces.

Consider this example: You want to see if Mary Smith's name occurs in a memo. You might try to use `grep` to search for "Mary Smith" within the file named `memo` with this command:

```
$ grep Mary Smith memo <Return>
grep: can't open Smith
sales reports were given to Mary Smith, along
Please see Mary Cunningham for more information
$
```

You get an error message, however. `grep` tried to look for "Mary" in two files, `Smith` and `memo`—it considers the first word to be the search phrase and the remaining words to be file names. The use of quotes is the answer:

```
$ grep "Mary Smith" memo <Return>
sales reports were given to Mary Smith, along
$
```

The quotes identify "Mary Smith" as a single word, even though the word contains a space. The special meaning of the space is ignored; it just becomes another character in the search phrase.

A similar problem can occur—usually in shell programs—when variables are involved with programs like `grep`. Consider a shell program that uses `grep` to search for a name within a telephone listing:

```
echo "Name to locate? \c"
read name
grep $name /usr/fred/phonelist
```

If you respond to the read statement with "John," that becomes the value of the variable name, and the `grep` command that will be executed is:

```
grep John /usr/fred/phonelist
```

That command works fine. But suppose that, in response to the `read` command, you type "John Doe". Now the `grep` command becomes:

```
grep John Doe /usr/fred/phonelist
```

You have the same problem here as before: the command does not tell `grep` to search for "John Doe" in the file `/usr/fred/phonelist`. Rather, it requests a search for "John" within the files `Doe` and `/usr/fred/phonelist`. Because the file `Doe` probably doesn't exist, an error message will result. Suppose that the original `grep` statement is as follows:

```
grep "$name" /usr/fred/phonelist
```

In this situation, a value of "John Doe" for `name` results in this display:

```
grep "John Doe" /usr/fred/phonelist
```

Where quotes are necessary, two variations are available: double quotes (") and single quotes (', also called apostrophes). There is only a slight difference between them, but sometimes the difference is important.

Using Single Quotes

Single quotes, or apostrophes ('), cause the shell to ignore the special meaning of any characters found within the quotes. Consider this example:

```
echo 'You lose the bet—you owe me $5.'
```

Normally $5 would cause the shell to access the fifth command-line parameter, but because the $5 is inside single quotes, it's considered just another couple of characters.

Using Double Quotes

Like single quotes, double quotes cause the shell to ignore special characters—but not all special characters. Certain characters still retain their special meaning:

- $ indicates a shell variable.
- ` (an accent grave, or backquote) indicates command substitution (see Chapters 5 and 15 for more information).
- A set of " characters terminates the quoted text.

Thus the following command replaces the variable $name with the value of the variable name:

```
echo "My name is $name"
```

If single quotes had been used, the phrase would have been printed exactly as it appears, dollar sign and all.

Using the Backslash Character

You can use the backslash (\) to tell the shell to ignore the special meaning of one character—the character immediately following the backslash. Consider the following command:

```
$ grep "^dog" mutt.papers <Return>
```

You can write this command in the following way, with exactly the same effect:

```
$ grep \^dog mutt.papers <Return>
```

The backslash also can be used inside double quotes before a dollar sign to turn off the special meaning of that one dollar sign. Consider this example:

```
$ echo "I contributed \$25 to $charity." <Return>
```

Here, the backslash in front of the first dollar sign indicates that no special meaning should be attached to the dollar sign. It is just another character to be printed. The second dollar sign has no backslash in front of it; therefore, $charity is recognized as a variable to be replaced by a value.

Summary

In this chapter, you have seen the basic techniques of shell programming. While some shell programs are extremely complex, many helpful tasks can be accomplished with simple shell programs. These are the key points discussed:

❏ A shell is a system program that interprets commands, either from the keyboard or from a shell program. Several different shells are available on some machines, including the Bourne, C, and Korn shells.

❏ You create shell programs by placing UNIX commands—the same commands available at the keyboard—in a file and turning on execute permission for that file. You execute the program by simply typing the name of the file.

❏ Variables are temporary holding places for small amounts of information. Special variables, called command-line parameters, allow a shell program to access the information supplied on the command line when the shell program was invoked.

❏ The echo command prints its command-line arguments. It is most useful in shell programs for printing messages.

❏ The read command receives text from the keyboard and places it in a variable.

❑ The pound sign (#) enables a shell programmer to include comments—information intended for human readers and ignored by the shell.

❑ The environment contains information that is made available to shell programs. The `export` command allows information within shell variables to be placed in the environment.

❑ Quotation marks—single (') and double (")—can be used to prevent the shell from inferring meaning from special characters used within phrases and messages.

In Chapter 15, you see techniques that greatly expand the power of shell programs, including tests and loops.

15

Increasing Your Productivity with Advanced Programming

Chapter 14 provided an introduction to the power available to you with shell programs. In this chapter, you learn additional commands that are much more programming-oriented than those in Chapter 14. You expect such features as loops and decisions in a real programming language, and you will see commands that allow shells to qualify. As always, these commands are available both inside shell programs and from the keyboard.

You may want to review both Chapters 5 and 14 before working with the material in this chapter.

Key Terms Used in This Chapter

Decision	A point in a program at which one of two or more alternative courses will be taken, depending on some condition specified by the programmer.
Success	An exit status, represented numerically by zero, which indicates that a program worked correctly and produced positive results.
Failure	An exit status, represented by a number other than zero, indicating that a program did not accomplish some task. Failure can be due to an error, or it may indicate some situation—two files that are different (diff), for example, or a phrase not found (grep).
Exit status	A code indicating whether a program or command succeeded or failed and sometimes indicating why it failed.

Built-in command	Any of a handful of commands that are an integral, built-in part of the shell and do not represent programs that must be called from disk. `cd`, `if`, `for`, and `while` are examples.
Default	An action taken or an answer used if no alternative is given.
Loop	A series of program commands executed repeatedly.
Secondary prompt	The shell prompt, usually a >, by which the shell indicates that it wants you to continue with more of the preceding unfinished command.
Command	A mechanism within the shell that allows the *substitution* output from one command to be used as part of another command.
Accent grave (`` ` ``)	Also called a backquote. A pair of accent grave characters (`` `` ``) signal command substitution to the shell.
Kernel time	The amount of time the computer spends performing operating system tasks necessary to support your program. Also known as system time.
System time	Same as kernel time.
Real time	The elapsed time, as would be measured by a watch, from the moment a program starts until it ends.
User time	The amount of time the computer spends executing commands within your program (also see *kernel time* and *real time*).
Field	An individual part of data, such as a name, a phone number, or a home directory.
Delimiter	Within data, a character that separates parts of the data (called *fields*). Typically a delimiter is a punctuation symbol, such as a colon (:) or a comma (,).
Shell trace	A shell option that causes the shell to tell you what it is doing, step by step, as it executes a program.
Prototype	A first version of a program, usually written as quickly and inexpensively as possible, used to test the validity of a concept.

Making Programming Decisions

As you type commands at the keyboard, you are constantly making decisions about how to proceed. For example, after each command, you might ask yourself: "Did that work or not?" Perhaps you do one of two possible things, based on the answer.

In a shell program, which is an automated set of commands, you will sometimes want such a decision made automatically. In such a case, you typically provide two alternative sets of commands, and the shell program picks one or the other based on some criterion you specify.

The shell provides a method to make such decisions. While this method (like any shell technique) can be used at the keyboard as well as within shell programs, it is used almost exclusively in shell programs. The reason is clear: if you are typing commands from the keyboard, it is much simpler to make decisions yourself than to type the commands to have the shell make the decisions for you.

Making Decisions with `if`

The `if` command allows your program to make a decision; that is, to find out if some condition is true and alter its course of action based on the result. A *condition* is any situation you can ask about. In English, conditions often start with the word "if," as in "If John can go to the movies with me. . ." In shell programs, conditions are usually associated with an `if` as well.

The Notion of Success and Failure

In order to understand how decisions are made, it is necessary to discuss the concepts of *success* and *failure* in shell programming. Under UNIX (and most operating systems, in fact), whenever you execute a command, the operating system has a notion about whether the command succeeded or failed. Exactly what success or failure means to UNIX depends on the individual command.

If the command produces an error and then stops, it has obviously "failed." For example, sending mail to an unknown user causes the `mail` program to produce an error. That's a failure. Trying to print or list a nonexistent file produces an error and is also a failure.

For some commands, success or failure is determined by whether the command encounters some situation; success usually indicates that the command did what it set out to do. For example, the `grep` command searches for a pattern within one or more files. If it finds that pattern, `grep` has "succeeded"; otherwise, it has "failed." Likewise, `diff` checks whether two files are the same and prints any differences it finds. `diff` therefore "succeeds" if the two files are the same; it "fails" if they are different. (`diff`'s notion of success and failure may seem backward to you, but that's the way `diff`'s author decided it should be.)

For some commands, the concept of success or failure really doesn't apply. A simple `date` command, for example, really can't fail unless something is very wrong with your system. Other commands, such as `vi`, accomplish such complex tasks that to pin a single "success" or "failure" label on such a command really has no meaning.

How do you know what "success" and "failure" mean for a specific command? Usually one or the other makes some kind of sense: if the command accomplishes what it is supposed to, it succeeds; otherwise it fails.

If you can't reason it out, or if it doesn't seem to work the way you think it should, you can take two other possible approaches: the "Intellectual Approach," or the "Practical Approach."

The Intellectual Approach

The intellectual approach involves one step: Look it up. In your system documentation, usually under the heading "Diagnostics" or "Return Value" for each command, you can find what has to happen for the command to succeed or fail. The documentation will usually talk about an exit status and the various numbers that could result. For example, for `diff` the documentation might say:

"Exit status is 0 for no differences, 1 for some differences, 2 for trouble."

The actual numbers are unimportant beyond this simple rule: zero means success; anything else means failure. From this description, you can determine that `diff` succeeds if no differences are found between the two files and fails if differences or trouble are found. "Trouble" is a way of saying an error results—a file can't be found or an option is bad.

The Practical Approach

Try the practical approach. You can try a command and then ask the shell whether the command succeeded or failed by typing the following:

```
$ echo $? <Return>
```

The variable `$?` represents the exit status (success or failure) of the most recently executed command. If `echo` prints a zero, the command succeeded. Anything else indicates a failure. Here is an example in which a command searches a file called `turtles` for the word "pizza" (it being a well-known fact that all turtles love pizza):

```
$ grep pizza turtles <Return>
a well-known fact that all turtles love pizza.
$ echo $?
0
$
```

Here, `grep` finds the phrase it's looking for. That ought to count as a success, and sure enough, the `echo` command produces a zero, the number that means success. Compare that with this command, which searches the same file for the word "anchovies" (which turtles hate):

```
$ grep anchovies turtles <Return>
$ echo $?
1
$
```

Here, no phrase was found. You would expect that command to be a failure, and the `echo` command confirms this by printing a nonzero number. Here is a final example:

```
$ grep pizza turles <Return>
grep: can't open turles
$ echo $?
2
$
```

In this example, the file name was mistyped; `turles` doesn't exist, and an error results. That certainly counts as a failure, and the `echo` command prints a nonzero number.

Why do you care about the operating system's notion of success or failure? Because that's how decisions are made in a shell program. You attempt to execute a command and then ask (in "shell-ese"), "Did that succeed?" You do different things based on the answer.

The Basic Format of the `if` Command

The `if` command has a more complex format that most UNIX commands and generally occupies several lines. It has several possible formats; the simplest is as follows:

```
if
    one or more commands
then
    one or more commands
fi
```

When the shell sees this command, it executes all the commands between the `if` and the `then` (usually just a single command, but sometimes several.) The shell looks at the last of these commands, checking for success or failure. If the last command succeeded, the shell continues into the commands between the `then` and the `fi` and executes them too; otherwise, it skips these commands.

NOTE

`fi` is just "if" backwards, a logical "word" with which to end an `if` statement.

Alternatively, if only a single command follows the `if`, it can be written on the same line as the `if`.

NOTE

The `if` command is one of a handful of UNIX commands known as *built-in commands*. That is, that shell directly understands these commands and does not have to run a program to accomplish the task. Unlike most commands (such as `who` or `grep`), the `if` command is not listed under the name "if" in system directories. The most common built-in command you have seen so far is `cd`. The `for` and `while` statements, discussed later in this chapter, are also built-ins.

Consider this example. Every week your boss puts together a departmental status report in a file called `/usr/boss/status/weekly`. Every Monday you want to print a copy of the report if your boss mentions you. Otherwise, you don't particularly want to bother with it. (This may be an inexcusably self-centered attitude, but that's a topic for a different book.) Here's a shell program called `status` that will do the job:

```
if
    grep Jones /usr/boss/status/weekly >/dev/null
then
    echo "He's talking about you again."
    lp /usr/boss/status/weekly
fi
echo "Done."
```

The shell executes everything between the `if` and the `then`—in this case a single `grep` command. `grep` looks for your name (Jones) within the status report. It succeeds if it finds "Jones;" otherwise it fails. If—and only if—it succeeds, the commands between the `then` and `fi` are executed as well.

For a week in which Jones is mentioned in the boss' report, here's what the command might produce:

```
$ status <Return>
He's talking about you again.
request id is laser-3157 (1 file)
Done.
$
```

For a week in which Jones is not mentioned, the command would produce the following:

```
$ status <Return>
Done.
$
```

Notice that the output from `grep` is redirected to `/dev/null`, the UNIX "trash can;" any output sent to `/dev/null` is tossed away by UNIX. This provision is made because you only want to know if your name is found; you don't really want to see the output that `grep` produces.

The `else` Clause

The basic `if` statement enables you to say, "If this succeeds, do something." This power is greatly increased by the `else` clause, which adds a description of what to do if the `if` clause fails. The `else` clause has the following format:

```
if
    one or more commands
then
    one or more commands
else
    one or more commands
fi
```

As in the preceding example, the commands between the `if` and the `then` are always executed, with the shell watching to see whether the last command succeeds or fails.

- When the last command succeeds, the shell also executes the commands between the `then` and the `else`;
- If it fails, the shell executes the commands between the `else` and the `fi`.

One of these groups of commands is always executed, but never both.

You can use the `else` clause to make the `status` program a bit more user-friendly:

```
if grep Jones /usr/boss/status/weekly >/dev/null
then
    echo "He's talking about you again."
    lp /usr/boss/status/weekly
else
    echo "You're not discussed this week. Safe again."
fi
echo "Done."
```

The program still works the same as without the `else` clause when the `grep` statement succeeds, but if the `grep` command fails, the output looks like this:

```
$ status <Return>
You're not discussed this week. Safe again.
Done.
$
```

Here is another example. Your latest and greatest boyfriend or girlfriend works on the same computer system as you, and you like to send flirtatious one-line messages back and forth. (Maybe this is why you're concerned about whether your boss is discussing you.) Naturally, you want your messages to get to your sweetie as quickly as possible. If he or she is logged in, the `write` command is the fastest method—it blasts a message across his/her terminal; otherwise, you must resort to the `mail` command so that the message will be saved for later.

Here's a script called `flirt` that will do the job (assuming that "Mikey" is the object of your interest):

```
if echo "$*" | write mikey
then
  echo "Successfully wrote to mikey's terminal"
else
  echo "$*" | mail mikey
  echo "Sent mail to him instead."
fi
```

You can run this script by placing your message on the command line:

```
$ flirt Meet me behind the water cooler at 4 p.m. <Return>
$
```

The first `echo` statement in the script prints everything on the command line (`$*`) and sends that output to the `write` command. If `mikey` is logged in, he will see this message displayed across his terminal:

```
Message from mary (tty34) [ Fri Jun 22 15:33:26 ] ...
Meet me behind the water cooler at 4 p.m.
<EOT>
```

The `write` command thus succeeds, and the `if` command continues to execute the `echo` statement between the `then` and `else`, which causes the message `Successfully wrote to mikey's terminal` to appear on Mary's screen. The commands between the `else` and `fi` are skipped.

On the other hand, if Mikey is not logged in, the `write` command fails, producing an error message:

```
Mikey is not logged on.
```

The `if` command skips the commands between the `then` and the `else` and executes the commands between the `else` and the `fi`. This sequence sends a mail message to Mikey that looks like this:

```
From mary Fri Jun 22 15:33:26 EDT 1990
Meet me behind the water cooler at 4 p.m.
```

It also prints out a message to Mary's terminal: `Sent mail to him instead.`

Indenting Commands within an `if` Statement . . .

Shell programmers almost always indent the commands within the body of an `if` command in order to make their programs easier to read. Typically, a <Tab> stop before each statement greatly improves the readability of the program. Consider the following program:

```
if echo "$*" | write mikey
then
  echo "Successfully wrote to mikey's terminal."
else
  echo "$*" | mail mikey
  echo "Sent mail to him instead."
fi
```

Now compare it to this one:

```
if echo "$*" | write mikey
then
echo "Successfully wrote to mikey's terminal."
else
echo "$*" | mail mikey
echo "Sent mail to him instead."
fi
```

The shell doesn't care one way or the other, but the first program is easier for people to follow. Do yourself a favor, and get in the habit of indenting the commands within an `if` command.

Performing Tests with `test`

You will often find that you need to control an `if` statement in a way that cannot be expressed in the usual terms of a UNIX command's successes or failure.

For example, you might want to proceed differently based on whether or not a particular file exists. The `test` command enables you to check for conditions other than the success or failure of an operation. The command then intentionally succeeds or fails, based on whether your condition is true or false. The `test` command is almost always associated with an `if` command (or possibly with a `while` command, which is included in the discussion of loops, later in this chapter).

Using File Tests

The `test` command can determine whether a specified file meets a desired criterion. `test` has the following form:

```
test [option] filename
```

When you issue the `test` command with the `-f` option, for example, `test` checks whether the file specified by *filename* exists and is a regular file (as opposed to a directory or other special file). If *filename* is a regular file, the test succeeds. If the file either doesn't exist or is some other type of file, the test fails.

About Unix File Types . . .

`test` has many options that cause it to check a file for a particular type. What are the various types of UNIX files? There are four types, one of which comes in two varieties.

- *Regular files*—sometimes called *ordinary files*—represent any kind of file in which you store information. Text files, binary files, databases, spreadsheets, and shell programs are all examples of regular files. The overwhelming majority of UNIX files are of this type.

- *Directories*—or *directory files*—serve as tables of contents and are discussed in Chapters 5 and 7. They are the second most common type of file.

- *Device files* or *special files* represent something other than information stored on disk. Most often they represent pieces of hardware, and they are usually found in the `/dev` directory. They come in two varieties: *block devices* and *character devices*. The difference between them is totally unimportant here.

- *Pipe files*—sometimes called *FIFO files* (first-in, first-out)—are by far the rarest. Very few UNIX systems have more than a few of these. Some, in fact, may have none. FIFOs are used almost exclusively by C programmers.

How can you tell what type a particular file represents? An `ls -l` command displays the file type as the first character of each line. A dash (–) represents a regular file, a `d` represents a directory, and `c`, `b`, and `p` represent the rarer character device, block device, and pipe files, respectively.

Table 15.1 lists the most commonly used file options for the `test` command.

Table 15.1
Commonly Used Options for the `test` Command

Option	Action
`-f`	Checks whether a file exists and is a regular file
`-d`	Checks whether a file exists and is a directory
`-r`	Checks whether a file exists and is readable
`-w`	Checks whether a file exists and can be written to
`-x`	Checks whether a file exists and is executable
`-s`	Checks whether a file exists and has a size greater than zero

Suppose that you often receive mail during the day, and at the end of the day you want to print your collected mail. If your user ID is fred, and you have mail, the file /usr/mail/fred will exist. Here's a simple shell script, pmail, that prints mail if you have any waiting:

```
if test -f /usr/mail/fred
then
  echo "You have mail -- printing it now."
  lp /usr/mail/fred
else
  echo "You have no mail."
fi
```

If /usr/mail/fred exists and is a regular file, the test command succeeds and the then-else commands are executed; otherwise the else-fi group is executed.

Reversing the Meaning of Tests

Probably more common than checking to see whether a file meets a criterion is checking to see whether it doesn't. For example, at the beginning of a particular shell program, you might want to make sure that certain files and directories exist before beginning serious work. Such a test has this format:

```
test ! [option] filename
```

As you learned in Chapter 5, the exclamation mark (!) means *not* to the shell. The character tells test to check for the opposite condition.

Consider this example. Before a particular shell program can do its work, suppose that a particular directory must exist, must be available for writing to, and contains a particular file. Here's how that shell program might start:

```
if test ! -d reqd.dir
then
  echo "directory reqd.dir doesn't exist or isn't a
directory"
  exit
fi
if test ! -w reqd.dir
then
  echo "directory reqd.dir is not writable"
  exit
fi
if test ! -f reqd.dir/myfile
then
  echo "file reqd.dir/myfile doesn't exist"
  exit
fi
```

The `exit` command in the fourth line causes a shell to terminate immediately. In a shell program, the `exit` command terminates the program. If the command is typed from the keyboard, `exit` logs you off the system. In the preceding program, you want to quit if `reqd.dir` does not exist, if the file cannot be written to, or if the file doesn't exist.

Performing Variable Tests

The other—and perhaps more important—use for `test` is to check the value of a variable. This test, in turn, falls into two classes: string tests and numeric tests.

The string test has this form:

```
test value operation value
```

The values represent some piece of text or the value of a variable. The operation can be either = (see if the two values are equal) or != (see if the two values are different).

On many UNIX systems, the environment variable `LOGNAME` contains the user's ID (Chapters 5 and 14 include information on environment variables). Suppose that you have a shell program commonly used by everybody on your system. For a special occasion, you might put these lines at the beginning of that program:

```
if test "$LOGNAME" != "fran"
then
   echo "Shhhhh!  Surprise party for Fran"
   echo "at the Yellow Dog Pub after work"
   echo "Friday. Be there!"
fi
```

Now, whenever someone runs this script, the `echo` commands are executed if the `LOGNAME` variable does not contain the value `fran`, which would indicate that Fran herself is running the program.

This technique also can be used to examine a user's response to a question. For example, suppose that you use the `nroff` text-formatting package to do word processing on your system. Here's a program, called `format`, to format a document. The program asks you whether you want the document printed. If you answer no, it displays the document on-screen, using the `more` program. (You use `pg` if you have UNIX System V.)

```
echo "Do you want to print the document? \c"
read answer
if test "$answer" = "n"
   then
   nroff $* | more
else
   nroff $* | lp
fi
```

A common use for this technique is to provide default answers to questions—that is, your program will offer a suggested answer to a question, and if the user wants to accept that answer, only a <Return> need be entered.

Here is another example. You have written a shell program to produce a report and write it to a file. (Perhaps the shell uses the `awk` command, a useful UNIX tool for such tasks). The program then asks who is to receive the report. You enter a user ID, and the report is sent via mail. That much of the program might look like this:

```
awk ... awk commands >tempfile
echo "Report ready. Send it to whom?  \c"
read person
mail $person <tempfile
```

But you can do better. Suppose that in the vast majority of cases, you send these reports to your boss, Mike. Every once in a blue moon, however, you want to send it to someone else. You would like the program to suggest that Mike receive the report, and if that is acceptable, you need only press <Return>. Here's how you could do that:

```
awk ... awk commands >tempfile
echo "Report ready. Send it to whom [mike]?  \c"
read person
if test "$person" = ""
then
  person=mike
fi
mail $person <tempfile
```

When prompting for a user's ID, the `echo` statement gives a suggestion in brackets (many programs use this notation to suggest a default value). If the user presses only <Return>, `person` is set to a value of nothing, which is represented by two quotation marks with nothing between them. The `if` command tests to see whether `person` is nothing; if it is, the value `mike` is assigned to `person`.

The second class of value-testing involves testing numbers. It has the following format:

```
test value operation value
```

The values are numbers or variables that contain numbers. The operation is one of the following:

Operation	Meaning
-eq	Numbers are equal
-ne	Numbers are not equal
-lt	The first number is less than the second
-le	The number is less than or equal to the second
-gt	The first number is greater than the second
-ge	The first number is greater than or equal to the second

Suppose that your company (like many companies) does not want you to print more than a certain quantity of copies of a document. For a larger number of copies, a special department copies documents for you with high-speed copiers. Here is a quick and friendly shell program to print a file. The program asks the user which file to print and how many copies are wanted. If you request more than 10, then $copies is greater than 10, and the test command succeeds:

```
echo "File to print?  \c"
read filename
echo "How many copies?  \c"
read copies
if test "$copies" -gt "10"
then
  echo "You may only print 10 copies on this printer."
  echo "I will print one copy for you; please take it"
  echo "to the Reproduction Center in room 317 and"
  echo "ask them to make copies for you."
  copies=1
fi
lp -n$copies $filename
```

Notice that the last statement between the then and fi commands sets the number of copies to 1, so that only one copy is printed. The -n option for the lp command specifies how many copies of a document should be printed.

TIP

The test command has an alternative format that doesn't even use the word test. Rather than writing

```
test condition
```

you can instead enclose the *condition* in brackets:

```
[condition]
```

That has been done in this example:

```
if ["$answer" = "n"]
```

The word test and the brackets mean exactly the same thing.

One very helpful way of using the test statement enables you to make sure that a shell program is being used correctly. Suppose that a shell program called stuff is supposed to be run with two words on the command line. (It doesn't matter what they are or what the shell program does). The first thing the shell program would probably like to do is check that the user has, in fact, provided exactly two words on the command line.

The special shell variable $# always contains the number of words supplied on the command line. Thus, to make sure that the user provided two words, the program could start with these lines:

```
if test "$#" -ne "2"
then
   echo "This program should be run with"
   echo "two words on the command line."
   exit
fi
```

This technique is commonly used at the beginning of many shell programs.

Performing More Complex Tests

Many more complex tests are possible beyond what you have seen here. In fact, just about any combination of circumstances can be tested using the test command. A common tool for composing complex tests is the -a (and) option of test, which enables you to specify two conditions, both of which must be true in order for the test to succeed.

For example, suppose that you want to test /usr/stuff/misc to see whether it is a directory and whether you can write to it. You can perform the test in this way:

```
if test -d /usr/stuff/misc -a -w /usr/stuff/misc
then
   ... commands to be performed
fi
```

Here, you see two conditions, separated by the -a. Both must be true for the commands following then to be executed.

In fact, any number of conditions can be combined, each separated from the next by the -a option.

Many other tests and combinations of tests are possible, but these are the most common.

Using Programming Loops

One of the most important abilities of any program is performing a task repeatedly. You often write a shell program, not because a task is complex, but because it must be done many times. People get bored doing the same thing over and over. Fortunately, computers never do.

A *loop* is a generic computer term for an operation that will be performed repeatedly. In shell programs, there are two commands that enable you to repeat operations: for and while.

Performing Tasks Repeatedly with `for`

The `for` command repeatedly performs a set of commands on a list of items. The items can be anything—user names, file names, a list of veterinarians—you name it. `for` is useful any time you have a list of something and want to perform the same commands on each of those "somethings."

The `for` command has this format:

```
for variable
in list
do
   commands
done
```

Alternatively, the `for` and `in` can be written on the same line:

```
for variable in list
do
   commands
done
```

The commands between the `do` and `done` will be performed as many times as there are words in the list. The first time the commands are executed, the value of the variable will be the first item in the list; the second time, it will be the second item in the list, and so on.

Consider this simple program, `veggies`, for example:

```
for vegetable in carrots celery mushrooms broccoli
turnips
do
   echo "I like $vegetable."
done
```

The `echo` command will execute five times, because five words are listed after `in`. The first time, `$vegetable` will be `carrots`; the next time, `celery`, and so on. Running, the program looks like this:

```
$ veggies <Return>
I like carrots.
I like celery.
I like mushrooms.
I like broccoli.
I like turnips.
$
```

The relatively simple `for` statement opens up a world of time savers and typing savers. Hundreds of examples are possible. Following are several examples you may find useful.

Suppose that have eight parts of a book you want to format and print using `nroff`. Here's a shell script to do it:

```
for c in chap1 chap2 chap3 chap4 chap5 chap6 appendix1 appendix2
do
    echo "Formatting $c now."
    nroff -mm $c | lp
done
```

The commands between the `do` and `done` will execute eight times, because there are eight words in the list. The variable `c` will take successive words as its value each time through the loop. Note the `echo` statement, which simply serves to print informative messages on the screen so that the user can see what is happening.

Even better than listing the words repeatedly, you can use wild cards for the file names in the list. The preceding example could be written like this:

```
for c in chap* appendix*
do
    echo "Formatting $c now."
    nroff -mm $c | lp
done
```

You can't tell just by looking at the shell program how many times the loop will be performed—it depends on how many files in the current directory start with "chap" or "appendix."

You may recall an important point from Chapter 14: anything you can do from within a shell program can be done at the keyboard as well. If you want to use a `for` loop for a one-time task and are comfortable typing shell commands, you can type the `for` loop right at the $ prompt—there is no need to put it in a file and execute the file. Here's what you would see if you executed from the keyboard a `for` loop for the preceding example:

```
$ for c in chap* appendix* <Return>
> do <Return>
>    echo "Formatting $c now." <Return>
>    nroff -mm $c | lp <Return>
> done <Return>
Formatting chap1 now.
Formatting chap2 now.
Formatting chap3 now.
Formatting chap4 now.
Formatting chap5 now.
Formatting appendix1 now.
Formatting appendix2 now.
$
```

After you type the `for` command, the shell prompts with a > instead of the usual $. The > is known as the *secondary prompt*. The secondary prompt is used by the shell when requesting that you continue a command that was started on a previous line.

As another example, suppose that you are working in a directory that contains last year's sales reports. You are going to put together this year's sales reports by simply making changes to last year's. However, you want to keep a copy of last year's reports as well. One possible technique is to make a copy of every file in the current directory, ending the copied files' names with the suffix `.old`. For example, a file called `projected` would be copied to a file called `projected.old`.

This task cannot be done with a simple `cp` statement, but a `for` loop can do it easily:

```
for file in *
do
  cp $file $file.old
done
```

This `for` statement will execute the `cp` command for every file in the current directory, with the value of `file` set to different names each time.

Another use for the `for` loop is to send a customized piece of mail to each user in a list. Consider this shell program to send an invitation to a list of users:

```
for person in bob mary jim bettye mike linda carol
do
  echo "Dear $person,
  Don't forget Fred's 30th birthday party during lunch
  Wednesday at Billy-Bob's Bar-B-Q. Mark your calendars
  now!" | mail $person
done
```

Because seven words (users' names) appear in the list, the loop will execute seven times.

(Note that in the preceding program, the text of the mail message is not indented, even though that would have made the program look prettier. Because the text is surrounded by quotes, if it had been indented with spaces or tabs, the spaces or tabs would have become part of the mail message. That's not what you want.)

Also useful in a `for` statement is the variable $*, which represents all words on the command line. Here is a program, called `months`, that prints the calendars for selected months in 1990:

```
for month in $*
do
  echo "Printing calendar for $month/1990."
  cal $month 1990 | lp
done
```

This loop will execute as many times as there are words on the command line. A sample use might look like this:

```
$ months 3 5 9 10 <Return>
Printing calendar for 3/1990.
Printing calendar for 5/1990.
Printing calendar for 9/1990.
d
$
```

TIP

Any shell command too long to fit neatly on one line can be written on several lines if you end all lines except the last with a backslash (\). This technique is especially helpful in a `for` loop containing a long list of words:

```
for vegetable in carrots celery mushrooms \
broccoli turnips parsnips radishes \
"turnip greens" onions cabbage
do
  echo "I like $vegetable."
done
```

As the shell sees the first and second lines, the backslash tells it that the command is continued on the next line.

Normally a <Return> identifies the end of a command to the shell. The backslash takes away that special meaning, so that the <Return> is effectively ignored. Thus, the command continues (in this case over three lines) until a <Return> is found without a backslash in front of it.

Notice that even though you think of "turnip greens" as two words, because it is surrounded by quotes, the `for` loop views it as a single word.

Looping with `while`

The shell's other looping mechanism is the `while` loop. It has the following format:

```
while
  one or more commands
do
  one or more commands
done
```

You may notice a superficial resemblance between the `while` and the `if` commands. And, in fact, their workings are similar in some ways. The shell executes all the commands between the `while` and the `do`, watching to see whether the last command succeeds or fails. If the last command fails, the shell skips to the remainder of the statement and continues with the command following the `done`, if any. Otherwise, the shell executes the statements between the `do` and the `done` and then repeats the procedure, again executing the commands between `while` and `do`. This pattern continues until the last statement between `while` and `do` fails.

It is apparent that the last statement required in the `while` section is one that will succeed several times and then fail. The best candidate for this is the `read` statement.

The `read` command, you will recall from Chapter 14, waits for the user to type a line of input and places that input into a variable. `read` succeeds if the user enters a line and presses <Return>. It fails if the user signals the end of the data by pressing <^D>.

Consider this program, called `thank.you`, which prints thank-you notes to participants in a seminar:

```
echo "Enter names of participants, 1 per line."
echo "Press <^D> when done."
while
  echo "Participant:  \c"
  read name
do
  echo "Dear $name
  Thank you for attending our seminar.
  ... blah blah blah ... more text ...
  Sincerely yours," | lp
done
echo "Done."
```

This program prompts for a `participant` and waits for the user to type a name. If a line of text is typed, the thank-you note is printed and the process repeats, prompting for a new participant. When the user finally presses <^D>, the `read` command fails and the loop ends.

Note that the input for the `read` statement need not come from the keyboard. Instead, you can use a file and redirect input from the file. The syntax is rather strange here, however. The redirection appears after the `done` statement like this:

```
while
  read name
do
  echo "Dear $name
  Thank you for attending our seminar.
  ... blah blah blah ... more text ...
  Sincerely yours," | lp
done < list.of.people
echo "Done."
```

(The echo prompts have been removed because they don't really apply when data comes from a file.) As long as more lines are available from the file, the read command succeeds; when the end of file is encountered, the read command fails.

Testing with `true`

One interesting command sometimes used with a while loop is the true command. Interestingly enough, true does absolutely nothing—but it does it successfully! Its primary purpose is to serve as a command that *never* fails in a while statement.

The following is an example of a program that continuously displays the current date and time on your terminal when you're not using it:

```
while
   true
do
   clear
   date
   sleep 30
done
```

Because true never fails, the clear, date, and sleep commands between the do and done statements will be repeated forever. clear—though not a standard UNIX command—clears the screen on many UNIX computers. (On some UNIX System V computers, tput clear may do the job instead.) date prints the current date and time on the screen, and sleep 30 causes the computer to wait for 30 seconds before continuing. This display continues until the user presses <Break>.

This example shows a nice use for true. If you receive a lot of UNIX mail, you may occasionally find yourself with a mailbox full of mail you've already read. You'd like to get rid of it all, but how should you do it? Running the mail program and repeatedly pressing **d** (for delete) and <Return> seems crude. Here's a program called delete.mail that will empty your mailbox for you:

```
while
   true
do
   echo "d"
done | mail >/dev/null
```

The while loop simply prints d (for delete) continuously. That output is piped (|) to the mail program, which prints each message and then waits for input to tell it what to do with each message. The d tells it to delete the message. The redirection to /dev/null prevents you from actually seeing the messages.

There is also a command called false which (as you might suspect) also does nothing and fails at it every time! Its uses are much more obscure than those of true, and using it as part of a while statement never makes sense. In fact, false is rarely used at all.

Considering Other Useful Shell Programming Techniques

A number of additional techniques and commands are particularly useful, both from the keyboard and from within shell programs. These include command substitution, program tracing, and commands such as tee, time, and cut.

Using Command Substitution

It is not uncommon to run a command to produce some result and subsequently use that result as part of your next command. For example, suppose that you know there are files in the current directory that discuss lizards, and you want to print them on the printer. Recall that grep enables you to search for a phrase within files and that the -l option produces only the names of the files containing the phrase, not the actual lines. Thus you might type these commands:

```
$ grep -l lizards * <Return>
animals.txt
critters.nr
lizards.nr
wild.txt
$ lp animals.txt critters.nr lizards.nr wild.txt <Return>
```

The grep command produces a listing of the names of all the files in the current directory that contain the word "lizards." The lp command then prints those files to the printer.

There is a way to avoid retyping the names of the files. The technique is called *command substitution*. In the following example, a pair of accent grave marks (`` ) indicate the command substitution. The pair of `` marks (also called backquotes) enable you to use the output of one command as part of another command.

Here's how you could have solved the problem with the lizards:

```
$ lp `grep -l lizards *` <Return>
```

The shell spots the grep command inside the backquotes and executes that command first. It then takes whatever output is produced by grep and plugs that into the command line at that point. The final command becomes lp followed by the file names produced by grep.

For another simple example, suppose that you have a file which contains a list of files you want to remove. This command will delete the files:

```
$ rm `cat list` <Return>
```

`cat list` displays the contents of the file, which is then plugged into the `rm` command.

The number of interesting shell programs you can write with command substitution is far too big to list, but here are a couple of interesting suggestions.

Occasionally when UNIX software malfunctions, it leaves a file called `core` in its wake. This file is sometimes helpful for program developers, but not otherwise useful. This simple shell program, called `findcore`, searches out `core` files in your home directory and all subdirectories and removes them:

```
rm `find $HOME -name core -print`
```

The `find` command finds all files called `core` and plugs their full path name into the `rm` command, which removes them.

Another use for command substitution involves a situation in which you find yourself in a directory full of files, knowing that a particular topic is discussed in one of those files. You'd like to edit those files with the screen editor, `vi`. Here's a one-line shell program, called `viall`, which edits all files in the current directory that contain a phrase you specify on the command line:

```
vi `grep -l "$1" *`
```

To run this program, type something like this:

```
$ viall babies <Return>
```

This command runs `vi`, giving you an opportunity to edit all files containing the phrase "babies." (Note: When you edit several files within `vi`, the `:n` command takes you to the next file.)

Command substitution is also useful for assigning the output from a command to a variable. It has the following form:

```
variable=`command`
```

For example, to assign the current date and time to a variable, use the following command:

```
$ rightnow=`date` <Return>
```

Or, to assign a count of the number of lines in a file to a variable, use this command:

```
$ lines=`wc -l bigfile` <Return>
```

The next program is useful if you use a UNIX computer that can load MS-DOS files. You may often find files from MS-DOS that have the file names listed in all uppercase letters. It is annoying to have to use the Shift key to type their names. This shell program changes the characters in all the file names in the current directory to lowercase letters:

```
for file in *
do
  echo "$file - \c"
  lc=`echo $file | tr '[A-Z]' '[a-z]'`
  if [ "$file" = "$lc" ]
  then
      echo "ok."
  else
      echo "copied to $lc"
      mv $file $lc
  fi
done
```

The key to the program is in this line:

```
lc=`echo $file | tr '[A-Z]' '[a-z]'`
```

Within the backquotes (or accents graves (`)), the echo command prints the name of a file and pipes it to the tr command. The tr (for "translate") command changes characters within text; in this example, it converts uppercase to lowercase and prints the resulting name. However, instead of being printed, the new name is assigned to the variable lc.

The remainder of the shell script checks to see whether the lowercase name is different from the original name (which would mean that the original name was not in lowercase letters). If the names are different, the file is renamed with the mv command. echo statements are scattered judiciously to keep you informed of what's going on.

Finally, you can use command substitution as part of a for loop. For example, suppose that you often receive requests during the week to print certain documents, and you place the document names in a file called requests. On Friday, you format and print the documents using mmt. That shell program might look like this:

```
for doc in `cat requests`
do
  mmt $doc | lp
done
```

The cat requests command lists the contents of the file, and the contents are, in turn, plugged into the for command.

Using the `tee` Command To Divert Command Output

At times, you want to use the output from a command in two different ways. You can use the `tee` command do this. Not unlike a "T" joint in a water pipe, the `tee` program reads input, copying it both to a file and to its standard output.

For example, suppose that you are going to spell-check a document, and you want to view the misspelled words on the screen and put them into a file at the same time. Here's the command to do that job:

    $ **spell mydoc | tee bad.words** <Return>

`spell` finds the misspelled words and pipes them to `tee`. `tee` writes the words to its file `bad.words`, and also displays them on-screen.

When it occurs in the middle of a pipe, `tee` enables you to capture intermediate results. For example, suppose that you want to search a file for all the phone numbers in the 407 area code, sort them, and print them. However, you also want them saved to a file. The following command accomplishes all these tasks:

    $ **grep "(407)" phonelist | sort | tee stuff | lp** <Return>

The `grep` command finds all lines that contain `"(407)"`, and the `sort` command sorts them into numeric order. The `tee` command writes the list to the file named `stuff`, but also passes the data on to the next command in the pipe, `lp`, which prints the numbers.

Alternatively, perhaps in the preceding example you want to print the numbers to the printer and also see them on the screen. A slight change will produce that result:

    $ **grep "(407)" phonelist | sort | tee /dev/tty | lp**

`/dev/tty` is a special file that represents the terminal. `tee` thinks that it is writing to a file, but anything written to `/dev/tty` actually appears on the terminal screen.

The `tee` command has many such applications, both from the login shell and within shell programs. For more information on using `tee`, see Chapter 5.

Using the `time` Command with Shell Programs

Although never used *within* shell programs, the `time` command is sometimes used *with* shell programs. Programmers often want to get some idea of how much of the computer's time a program will require. Timing a program with your watch does not always give a good indication of how much of the computer's time is being used—because the time a program takes depends on how many other people are using the computer at that instant and what tasks or operations they are performing. The `time` command gives a much better idea.

To use the `time` command, simply place the word `time` in front of any command, whether a UNIX command, shell program, or even a program written in some other programming language. For example, to time a fairly complex shell program that requires a relatively large amount of time, use this command:

```
$ time myprog <Return>
```

`myprog` will execute as usual. Then, when the command finishes running, you may see output that looks like this:

```
real    2m1.43s
user    0m52.86s
sys     0m3.16s
$
```

Three different times are shown in this listing:

- `real` time—also called elapsed time—is the amount of time you would have measured with your watch. In this case, the program finished 2 minutes, 1.43 seconds after it started.

- `user` time is the amount of time the computer spent actually executing part of your program—in this case a bit shy of 53 seconds.

- `sys` time (system time)—also called kernel time— is the amount of time the computer spent doing things that were not actually part of your program, but had to be done because of your program. In this case it was a touch more than 3 seconds.

The distinction between user time and system time is subtle, and a true understanding requires a fairly detailed knowledge of what goes on inside UNIX—certainly more detailed than you need to get into here. The total of these two times—roughly 56 seconds in this example—is the amount of time the computer actually spent doing things on your behalf. You'll notice that 56 seconds is quite a bit short of the 2 minutes elapsed time. What was the computer doing during the rest of the time? Probably working with other people.

Using the `cut` Command To Edit Data

A number of standard UNIX commands, which are useful by themselves, turn out to be very useful in shell programs. This section discusses one of them, the `cut` command.

You learned about the `cut` command in Chapter 10. The `cut` command examines lines of data—either from a file or from a pipe—and picks out only certain columns of information that you specify, throwing the rest away. `cut` is particularly useful when a file or command produces more information than you want. The command is reminiscent of cutting columns out of a printed document.

The `cut` command has two possible forms. The first is as follows:

```
cut -clist [file]
```

list is a list of columns that interest you. The list can take several forms:

- You can specify a single column, such as `cut -c7 datafile`, for example. This command prints the seventh character from each line in `datafile` and nothing else.
- You can give a range of columns, such as `cut -c11-19 mystuff`. This command prints columns 11 through 19 from `mystuff`.
- You can specify a column, followed only by a dash (–), which tells `cut` to print from that column through the end of the line. The command `cut -c56- reclist` prints everything from column 56 through the end of each line within the file `reclist`.
- You can use any combination of the above specifications, separated by commas, with no intervening spaces. For example, the `cut` command `-c22-24,6,40- report` tells `cut` to print columns 22 through 24, followed by column 6, followed by everything from 40 to the end of line for each line in `report`.

In shell programs, you can use `cut` to thin out the information presented. For example, suppose that you want a shell program to print the names of everyone logged in and the terminal being used by each person. The `who` command presents more information than you want:

```
mark        tty24        Jun 22 23:51
fred        tty13        Jun 22 14:33
richard     tty12        Jun 22 08:27
```

By carefully counting columns, you can determine that the information you want is in columns 1 through 15. This command will give you just what you want:

```
$ who | cut -c1-15 <Return>
mark        tty24
fred        tty13
richard     tty12
$
```

`who` produces a list of users, and `cut` selects only the desired columns.

Although all versions of UNIX have a `who` command, and they all present pretty much the same information, be aware that the information is not likely to be in exactly the same column from one version to another. Though not generally noticeable, this may become important if you have a shell script that's looking at certain columns. For example, compare the first output from a `who` command—

from an AT&T 3B2/600 computer running UNIX System V—with the second output—from a Sequent computer running DYNIX Version 2.0:

```
$ who
don          xt011          Jun 25 06:50
mark         tty53          Jun 25 21:10
$ who
don        ttyp8   Jun 25 09:49
mark       ttyp1   Jun 25 21:27
```

You can see how close the outputs are, but they are not identical. The same caveat applies to most of the UNIX commands that produce columns of information, such as df and ps.

cut's second format is useful for data that is divided into fields—groups of information separated by a special character. The format is as follows:

```
cut  -ddelimiter  -flist  [file]
```

The -d option specifies the special character (called the delimiter) that separates the fields. The list has the same format as the -c option in the first format; it specifies the fields to be printed.

For example, suppose that you have a file that lists a customer's last name, first name, address, and phone number, separated by commas, similar to this:

```
Flintstone,Fred,1 Bedrock Way,555-7812
```

Each line has four fields; that is, four pieces of data, separated by commas. Suppose that you want to print just the last name and phone number. This command would do it:

```
$ cut -d, -f1,4 phonefile <Return>
Flintstone,555-7812
Rubble,555-6604
$
```

One standard UNIX file in particular contains useful information and is ready-made for processing with cut: the UNIX password file, /etc/passwd. It contains the following seven fields, each separated by colons:

1. The user's login name
2. The encrypted password (which is not of much use to shell programmers)
3. The numeric user ID
4. The numeric group ID
5. The user's full name
6. The user's home directory
7. The login shell (typically sh, csh, or ksh)

To print out a list of login names and full names, use this command:

```
$ cut -d: -f1,5 /etc/passwd <Return>
root:Root
bin:Admin
sys:Admin
adm:Admin
uucp:uucp
lp:LP Administrator
news:NetNews
belinda:Belinda Mason
douglass:Douglass Smith
scott:Scott Southland
$
```

(The first seven lines in this list are system accounts; the remaining three are real users.)

Such statements find frequent uses in shell programs. For example, here's a quick program that sends a message to all users on the computer. (This program assumes that the message itself has already been prepared in a file called msg.)

```
mail `cut -d: -f1 /etc/passwd` <msg
```

The cut command lists field 1 from each line in /etc/passwd, which is the login name. These names, in turn, are plugged into the mail command line, and mail is sent to those names from the msg file.

Tracing a Shell Program with the −x Option

As you write shell programs of ever-increasing complexity, your programs often may not work correctly the first time you try them. Sometimes, simple typing mistakes are the cause; at other times, more subtle errors will be responsible. Whatever the cause, a *shell trace* can often help you find the source of your problem. The trace causes the shell to tell you, step by step, exactly what it is doing as it executes your shell program.

Consider a simple shell program, copyold, which was presented in a previous section on the for command:

```
for file in *
do
  cp $file $file.old
done
```

To perform a shell trace, you type **sh −x** in front of the command. In this case, you type the following:

```
$ sh -x copyold <Return>
```

The command produces this output:

```
+ cp chap15 chap15.old
+ cp chap16 chap16.old
+ cp data.txt data.txt.old
+ cp letters letters.old
+ cp null null.old
+ cp s.chap15 s.chap15.old
+ cp s.chap16 s.chap16.old
```

In this case, the shell prints the actual copy commands that are executed as the `for` loop runs through its paces.

Moving Up to Advanced Commands

In addition to the commands covered in this chapter, many other commands are favored by experienced shell programmers. As your familiarity with the shell increases, you may want to experiment with some of them.

- `paste` is roughly the opposite of `cut`: it collects data from several different sources and assembles it into a single file or pipe. (See Chapter 10 for more information on `paste`.)

- `ed`, the UNIX text editor, allows data to be altered in a variety of ways. Typical uses might be converting data from uppercase to lowercase, moving columns around, changing one word to another wherever it appears, converting column-oriented data to field-oriented data, and hundreds of other tasks. (Chapter 12 covers `ed`.)

- `awk` is a programming language unto itself, especially well-suited to accepting raw data and organizing it into sophisticated reports. Producing column totals or breaking a report down by departments are trivial pursuits in `awk`. Selecting data by certain criteria—only printing data for females between the ages of 16 and 24 who drive white Mustangs and like Thousand Island salad dressing, for example—is also easy. `awk` users find they can produce impressive results in a fraction of the time it would take a conventional programmer. (See your User's Guide for more information on `awk`.)

- The `expr` command enables you to evaluate expressions within a shell program—that is, perform arithmetic. This is an important feature for truly sophisticated shell programs. (See your User's Guide for more information on `expr`.)

Comparing the Shell with Other Languages

If you are already a programmer—programming on a UNIX computer in languages such as C, COBOL, or Fortran—you may be curious how shell programs compare to programs written in other languages. No doubt, whenever a task presents itself, you ask yourself whether to write in shell or ... (fill in your favorite language).

These tips may help you decide:

- Shell programs tend to be smaller and occupy significantly less disk space than their counterparts in other languages.

- Shell programs tend to execute more slowly than their brethren in C, COBOL, and Fortran. If exceptional speed is a requirement, a shell program is probably not your first choice.

- If users can execute a shell program, they can usually look at them as well, making it difficult to keep confidential techniques secret. This drawback is not true of compiled languages, a category that includes almost all other major languages.

- Shell programs tend to be faster to develop. Programmers equally familiar with the shell and another language can usually write a shell program faster. Because people's time is the most expensive thing a company pays for, this argument perhaps carries more weight than those listed previously. In fact, the shell is often used to prototype a program, that is, to write a quick first draft of a program for testing and evaluation purposes, even though the final program will be written in another language.

Summary

In Chapters 14 and 15, you explored some of the capabilities of shell programs, but you have really only scratched the surface. Covering all the programming commands built into the shell would take much more space than is available here. However, beyond that, part of the magic of shell programming is that it uses the same UNIX commands you can use from the keyboard. As your knowledge and understanding of UNIX and UNIX commands grows, so does your ability to construct useful shell programs. It is a rare individual who can find nothing new to learn about shell programming.

This chapter covered the following main points:

- ❏ Most UNIX commands can succeed or fail, depending on whether or not they are able to perform a task.
- ❏ The special variable `$?` can be used to print the result of a command—0 for success, 1 for failure.
- ❏ The `if` command is used within a shell program to make a decision and change the course of the program based on the decision.
- ❏ The `test` command can be used in conjunction with an `if` statement to accomplish more complex decisions, including checking the condition of specific files or checking the values of variables.

❏ Loops allow commands to be executed repeatedly. Shell programs can contain two kinds of loop statements—`for` and `while`.

❏ Command substitution allows the output from one command to be used as part of another command.

❏ The `tee` command splits the output from a command, so that it can be used in two different ways, such as saving output to a file and using it in a pipe.

❏ The `time` command produces statistics about the time taken to execute a shell program or command.

❏ The `cut` command extracts desired information from a file or pipe, leaving undesired data.

❏ Shell tracing can be used to examine step-by-step what a shell program is doing.

❏ Other UNIX commands—including `awk`, `expr`, `paste`, and many others—are available to greatly increase the power of shell programs.

— Part —
Five

Command
Reference

Command
Reference

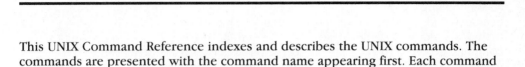

This UNIX Command Reference indexes and describes the UNIX commands. The commands are presented with the command name appearing first. Each command description begins on a new page.

A brief description of the command's purpose immediately follows the command's name. This "Purpose" section provides information on the command's action or use. Following the description of purpose is a section entitled "When To Use." This section gives you insight into when this command is most useful to you.

The next section is called "Normal Location." The section provides the name of the directory that typically contains the command as well as the names and locations of data files commonly associated with the command.

The "Common Syntax and Examples" section provides syntax information as well as examples of the command's use. When applicable, a table of options and arguments commonly used with the command follows this section. Syntax and options for this Command Reference are based on SCO UNIX System V/386 V3.2.2. Included in certain cases are notations of option variations for other implementations of UNIX.

Following this section, each command entry may optionally include a section of "Notes" and/or "Cautions." The "Notes" section, if included, indicates further information about the command, amplifying the purpose, giving insight into its efficient use, or otherwise acquainting you with the scope of the command. As appropriate, the "Cautions" section is included to make you aware of the potential ramifications of using the command.

An *Also see* notation may appear for certain commands as a reference to related or similar commands.

On some systems, the `man` (for *manual*) command is available. This command enables you to access an on-line technical reference manual which can provide you with your system's exact syntax for a command. To use the on-line manual, enter the command `man command_name`; the text for the specified `command_name` will be displayed on your screen.

Command Reference Conventions

Great effort has been taken to make the UNIX Command Reference as easy as possible to use. Yet to understand fully the syntax lines discussed, you should take time to review the conventions used in this book for presenting commands, arguments, and options. Special typeface and formatting conventions, for example, signal key properties of the terms shown in each command's syntax lines and accompanying examples. These conventions indicate what is mandatory or optional, and what components are variable. The Introduction to this book includes a section entitled "Conventions Used in This Book," which provides a complete description and explanation of these conventions. Because this Command Reference follows the same syntax conventions that apply throughout the book, refer to this section for more information.

at

Purpose

To run a single command or list of commands at a specified time. The command lines can be read from the standard input and terminated with a <^D>.

When To Use

Use at to print large reports or databases after business hours. Or, use with batch to submit jobs when the system load is lighter.

Normal Location

Two files are checked to determine whether you have permission to run the at command. If /usr/adm/cron/at.allow exists, it contains a list of users, one per line, who are allowed to use at; if your login name is missing, you cannot run at.

If at.allow is missing, UNIX looks for /usr/adm/cron/at.deny, which contains a list of all users who are *not* allowed to use at. If both files are missing, only the system administrator is allowed to run at.

Common Syntax and Examples

The syntax is as follows, shown in the three possible formats for the at command:

```
at time [date] [+increment]
at -r joblist
at -l [joblist]
```

1. The first format submits a list of one or more commands to be performed at some future time. The commands themselves are either typed at the keyboard following the command (and terminated with <^D>) or redirected from a file. You can specify the time and date to perform the commands in various ways. You can, for example, specify the time as a 1-, 2-, or 4-digit number, with the time assumed to be on a 24-hour clock. At the prompt, type the following:

   $ **at 17 < cmdlist** <Return>

   This command reads the commands in the file cmdlist and saves them for execution at 1700 (5:00 p.m.) this afternoon. If it is past 5:00 p.m., the commands are executed at 5:00 p.m. on the next day.

2. To execute commands in the file more.stuff at 10:30 am, at the prompt type the following:

   $ **at 1030 < more.stuff** <Return>

3. If you don't use a 24-hour clock, you can place am or pm after the time. At the prompt, type the following:

   $ **at 6pm < things.to.do** <Return>

4. The words noon and midnight can be used in place of a time. To execute, at midnight tonight, a list of commands located in the file late.night, at the prompt type the following:

    $ **at midnight < late.night** <Return>

5. Dates or days of the week can be added after the time. To execute the commands in the file sat.stuff on Saturday at noon, at the prompt type the following:

    $ **at noon saturday < sat.stuff** <Return>

   Three-letter abbreviations, such as sat, are allowed.

6. Some amount of time can be added to indicate a number of minutes, hours, days, weeks, months, or years from now. To execute a list of commands in the file far.things, three weeks from next Friday, at the prompt type the following:

    $ **at 6pm fri +3 weeks < far.things** <Return>

7. When commands are submitted via at, a *job-number* is displayed. The *job-number*, which is also referred to as job-id, or request-id, uniquely identifies the series of commands. If you decide not to execute the commands on schedule, at the prompt, type the following:

    $ **at -r *job-number*** <Return>.

   job-number is the number assigned to that series of commands. To see a list of all your job numbers, at the prompt type the following:

    $ **at -l** <Return>

Options

-l *job-id*	Lists the scheduled times of specified jobs. If no *job-id* is given, all currently scheduled jobs are listed.
-r *job-id*	Removes the specified job previously scheduled by the at command. The *job-id* is a job identifier returned by at.

Notes

If the file /usr/adm/cron/at.allow does exist, the superuser's login name must be included in that file.

Also see cron, batch, mail, nice, *and* ps.

banner

Purpose

To print or display large banner-like characters.

When To Use

Use any time you want to send out a large display. This command is easily attached to `mail` or any other file and is fun for sending out "Happy Birthday" messages, reminders, or similar notices through the mail. The `banner` command is also used by some UNIX system software, such as printing cover sheets for print jobs.

Normal Location

`banner` is located in the `/bin` directory.

Common Syntax and Examples

The syntax is as follows:

```
banner text
```

1. To print a banner, to the printer specified by *printername*, at the prompt type the following:

```
$ banner Happy Birthday Julie! | printername <Return>
```

2. To display a banner on-screen, at the prompt type the following:

```
$ banner Back Soon <Return>
```

3. To display two lines on-screen, at the prompt type the following:

```
$ banner "Gone for" "the Day" <Return>
```

The banner will appear in large letters as follows:

```
Gone for
the Day
```

Notes

`banner` is limited to 10 characters per line, including spaces. Use double quotation marks (" ") to place more than one word on a line.

Also see `echo`, *as well as information on redirection and piping.*

batch

Purpose

To run a command or list of commands when the system-load level permits. batch runs even if the requester has logged off the system. The output of the batch command is mailed to the requester unless some output redirection is used.

When To Use

Use batch when there is a large job to be executed and the time when it is finished is not important. Unlike at, the batch command does not designate any specific time to run.

Normal Location

Files that control queues at jobs or batch are usually located in either /user/lib/cron or /usr/lib/cron/queuedefs.

Common Syntax and Examples

The syntax is as follows:

```
batch command
```

command is any valid XENIX or UNIX command.

Notes.

The batch command is similar to the at command. However, at causes one or more commands to run at a specific time; batch causes a single command to run when nobody is using the computer or when the load on the system is light.

Also see at, cron, mail, nice, *and* ps.

bc

Purpose

The bc command provides a simple calculator and also converts from one base to another, a handy feature for programmers. For more advanced users, bc also provides a mathematical programming language, similar to the C programming language, which provides unlimited precision arithmetic.

When To Use

Use bc when you need an on-line calculator or when you need to convert from one base to another.

Normal Location

bc is located in the /usr/bin directory. To do its work, bc relies on another program, dc, which is also found in /usr/bin. A library of math scientific functions is available to bc, and these are stored in /usr/lib/lib.bc.

bc makes use of another calculator, dc, the desk calculator. dc uses a method called Reverse Polish Notation (RPN) for entering operations. If you are familiar with RPN, you may want to investigate dc, but most users find bc much easier.

Common Syntax and Examples

The syntax is as follows:

```
bc [-l]
```

Once invoked, bc waits for the user to type a mathematical operation: addition, subtraction, multiplication, or division. The operation is evaluated, and the answer is displayed. You can continue to enter operations to be evaluated until you press <^D> to exit bc.

A sample bc session looks like the following:

```
$ bc <Return>
14+7−3  <Return>
18
25.67 + 12  <Return>
37.67
<^D>
$
```

In the first equation, bc computes 14 plus 7 minus 3, and in the second, it adds two numbers.

Note that bc does not prompt in any way. After bc is invoked, you can type an equation. Also note that you can use spaces around symbols if you want (as in the 25.67 + 12 line); bc disregards these spaces.

The four arithmetic symbols are the following:

+ addition
− subtraction
⋆ multiplication
/ division

Unless you specify otherwise, bc determines how many decimal places it should display, but its guess is often different from what you want. To specify a number of decimal places, at the prompt type the following:

```
$ scale=n <Return>
```

n is the number of decimal places you want. Compare the answers given by bc before and after this command:

```
$ bc  <Return>
10/3 <Return>
3
scale=5 <Return>
10/3 <Return>
3.33333
<^D>
$
```

1. As values are computed, they are saved in any of 26 memory locations, named a through z. Use this format within bc:

   letter=equation

   For example, to add several numbers and place the result in memory location t, type the following:

   ```
   $ t = 5 + 7 + 9 + 13  <Return>
   ```

   When this line is typed, bc does not display the answer; rather it stores it in memory location t. To see the answer, type **t** and press <Return>.

2. After a value is stored in a memory location, it can be used as part of another equation. To print the value of t multiplied by 2, type the following:

   ```
   $ t * 2 <Return>
   ```

3. To compute square roots with bc, type **sqrt**, followed by a number in parentheses, as in the following example:

   ```
   $ bc <Return>
   sqrt(25) <Return>
   5
   <^D>
   $
   ```

4. The -l option to bc loads the math *library*, which makes the following complex math functions available, useful for scientists, engineers, and mathematicians:

   s sine
   c cosine
   e exponential (*e* raised to a power)

l log (natural)
a arctangent

To use these functions, supply a number in parentheses after the function you want to use. For example, to take the sine of 2, type the following:

```
$ bc -l <Return>
s(2) <Return>
.90929742682568169539
<^D>
$
```

5. bc can convert between decimal, octal, hexadecimal, or any other bases. This is a useful feature for programmers. A special memory location called an ibase contains the *input base*, the base in which numbers are keyed in. The number 8 represents octal, 10 is decimal, and 16 is hex. Similarly, obase is the base in which numbers are displayed. By setting ibase to the base you have and obase to the base you want, any type of conversion is possible.

To convert from octal to hexadecimal, type the following:

```
$ bc <Return>
obase=16 <Return>
ibase=8 <Return>
37532 <Return>
3F5A
<^D>
$
```

The number entered (**37532**) is assumed to be octal, because ibase is set to 8. The number printed is the same value in hex, because obase is set to 16.

Notes

If an equation contains several types of operations, the order of precedence rules that multiplication and division are always performed before addition and subtraction. In the equation 5 + 6 * 3, for example, the answer is 23, because 6 is first multiplied by 3 and then added to 5. You can alter this order by surrounding with parentheses the operations to be done first, as in the following example:

(5 + 6) * 3

Here the parentheses indicate that the 5 and 6 should be added first and the result multiplied by 3, for a result of 33.

Note that the trigonometric functions work with radians.

Caution

When setting both ibase and obase, set obase first.

cal

Purpose

To display on-line or to print a calendar.

When To Use

Use cal to see a particular month or year: past, present, or future. The calendar can be displayed on-screen or redirected to the printer.

Normal Location

The cal command is usually located in the /usr/bin directory.

Common Syntax and Examples

The syntax is as follows:

```
cal [month] year]
```

1. To display the month of April, 1962, on-screen, at the prompt type the following:

   ```
   $ cal 4 1962 <Return>
   ```

2. To display the entire year, at the prompt type the following:

   ```
   $ cal 1962 <Return>
   ```

Options:

month   Displays the specified month.

year   Displays the specified year.

Notes

The year must be between 1 and 9999. The month must be between 1 and 12. When no options are given, the default is the current month and year.

Cautions

Beware of supplying a 2-digit year accidentally. cal 90 does not display the calendar for 1990, but for the year 90 A.D.

The entire world has not always shared the same calendar. The cal command shows the calendar used by Great Britain and her colonies. cal also assumes that the new year always starts in January, when, in fact, this has not always been true.

calendar

Purpose

calendar is a simple reminder service that allows you to maintain a small appointment calendar on-line.

When To Use

Use calendar to maintain a list of appointments, reminders, and "to do" items.

Normal Location

The calendar command is located in /usr/bin. The program that actually does the work—which you never use directly—is /usr/lib/calprog. The appointment list that you create is called calendar in your home directory. The password file, /etc/passwd, is also required for some uses.

Common Syntax and Examples

To use calendar, you must first create a file in your home directory called calendar. The calendar file should contain a list of appointments, reminders, and things to do, one item per line. The line should begin with the date associated with the appointment or reminder. Any reasonable format can be used for the date, as long as the month comes first. A few lines from a sample calendar file look like the following:

```
Aug 17  Wash the dog
8/20  Meet with Fred McDavers of McDavers & Sons
September 19  Take dog to vet for shots
```

The syntax of calendar is as follows:

```
calendar [-]
```

When issued with no arguments, calendar simply displays the contents of the calendar file. When issued with the - option, calendar searches all users' home directories for a calendar file and sends reminders for today and tomorrow via mail. The system administrator often uses cron to have this task performed automatically each day.

Like most calendar users, you probably want to be reminded of what is on your schedule for the day when you log on. To accomplish this, place the following command in your .profile:

```
$ calendar <Return>
```

This causes calendar to look through your calendar file for all appointments and reminders for today and tomorrow, and to display any that it finds.To update your appointment/reminder list, simply edit your calendar file using any text editor, such as ed or vi.

Notes

On Friday, calendar lists reminders for Friday through Monday.

Also see cron.

cancel

Purpose

To cancel a print job used by the lp command.

When To Use

Use cancel to stop a current or queued print request. By using the job identification number, you can specify the job that you want to cancel. Specifying the name of the printer stops the current job at the printer, but does not cancel any job in the queue.

Normal Location

The cancel command is located in the /usr/bin directory. The print jobs themselves are in the /usr/spool/lp directory or one of its subdirectories.

Common Syntax and Examples

The syntax is as follows:

```
cancel [job-id/printername]
```

1. To cancel the current job on the printer named mylaser, at the prompt type the following:

   ```
   $ cancel mylaser <Return>
   ```

2. To cancel a job that is in the queue, at the prompt type the following:

   ```
   $ cancel mylaser-123 <Return>
   ```

Options

job-id   The job identification number assigned to the print job

printername   The name of the printer

Notes

The job id number for a print job is usually given when the print request is submitted with the lp command. If you forget the job id, use the lpstat command.

Unless you are the superuser (root), you can cancel only your own print jobs.

Also see lp *and* lpstat.

cat

Purpose

To concatenate (combine) two or more files into one file; to append a file onto another file; or to send a file to the screen or printer.

When To Use

Use cat to get a quick screen view of a text file or to join two text files into a combined file. By redirecting the command's output to a printer, you can get a hard copy printout of the file's contents.

Normal Location

cat is an executable file located in /bin. Normally, /bin is included in the user path, so you do not need to include the entire path name in order to use cat.

Common Syntax and Examples

The syntax is as follows:

cat [-] [-u] [-s] [-v] [-t] [-e] *filename1 filename2* . . .

Prior to Release 3, only the -s option was available.

1. To display the contents of a text file named /usr/dave/notes **on-screen**, at the prompt type the following:

   $ **cat /usr/dave/notes** <Return>

   In this example, the complete path name for notes is given. If the file you want to see is not in your working directory, you must specify a path in the *filename* argument.

2. To send the same file to a printer, at the prompt type the following:

   $ **cat notes > *printername*** <Return>

   In this example, the file notes is in your working directory. If the file is not in the working directory, you must specify a path in *filename*.

   The > symbol redirects output to the printer device.

   The *printername* is the name of the printer device that you want to print the file. Normally, the *printername* specification includes /dev as in /dev/lp0.

3. To combine two files into a third file, type the following command:

   $ **cat notes1 notes2 > notes3** <Return>

   In this example, the file-name arguments are located in the working directory.

Options

-s   Suppresses warnings about nonexistent input files.

-u   Causes output to be unbuffered.

-v   Causes most nonprinting characters to be displayed in an alternate format.

-t   Causes tab characters to be displayed as <^I>; causes form feeds (newline characters) to be displayed as <^L>. This option is not in effect unless the -v option is given.

-e   Causes a $ character to be printed at the end of each line. This option is not effect unless the -v option is given.

Notes

If you do not give a file name as an argument, or if you use cat with a single - (minus or dash) character, the keyboard will be the standard output. You can use this form of cat to create text files by redirecting output to a file and terminating keyboard input with <^D>. To start and stop screen output, use <^S> and <^Q>.

Cautions

If the output file is one of the input files, the input file's content will be lost before the copy is made. You should therefore be careful when concatenating files using wild cards in the input file names.

Consider the following command:

```
cat filename1 filename2 > filename1
```

This command will cause the original data in *filename1* to be lost. Be careful when using redirection symbols.

Also see cp, pg, *and* pr.

cd

Purpose

To change directories.

When To Use

Use cd to change from your current directory to another directory, which then becomes your current working directory. You can type simply cd at any location and be returned to your home directory. This is a quick way to get back to the top of your tree if you are buried several layers down.

Normal Location

The cd command is built into the shell; there is no associated program in any of the system directories.

Common Syntax and Examples

The syntax is as follows:

```
cd [directoryname]
```

1. To change to your home directory from any location, at the prompt type the following:

   $ **cd** <Return>

2. To move up one level from any location, at the prompt type the following:

   $ **cd** .. <Return>

3. To move down one level from any location, at the prompt type the following:

   $ **cd** *directoryname* <Return>

4. To move to a directory outside of your current path, you need to specify the full path name of where you are going. At the prompt type the following:

   $ **cd /meetings/staff/notes/july** <Return>

Notes

Before you can use cd to move to another directory, you may need to know your current location. Do this by using the pwd (*print working directory*) command.

Also see chdir, pwd, *and* sh.

chgrp

Purpose

To change the group ownership of a file or directory.

When To Use

Change the group ownership of a file or program when you need to give another group permission to use one of your files. You can specify permission for a particular group rather than making the file accessible to all others.

Normal Location

The `chgrp` command is in the `/bin` directory. A list of all valid groups and the names of all users in those groups is located in `/etc/group`.

Common Syntax and Examples

The syntax is as follows:

```
chgrp [group file(s)]
```

To change the group ownership of `filename1` to the group named "staff," at the prompt, type the following:

```
$ chgrp staff filename1 <Return>
```

You can change group ownership on either a file or a directory.

Notes

You must own the file or be the superuser to change the group id. When a file is created, it is given the creator's group id.

Cautions

On many systems, unfortunately, the system administrator is sometimes lax about making sure that the `/etc/group` file is accurate. It is possible for files to belong to groups not listed in `/etc/group` and for users to belong to groups not listed. Always take the information in `/etc/group` with a grain of salt.

Also see chmod, chown, *and* newgrp.

chmod

Purpose

To change the access permissions for a specified file or directory. chmod allows the user to control read, write, and execute access on a file or directory.

When To Use

Use chmod to protect files from being read or modified, or to allow read or modify rights to users who would not otherwise have rights.

Normal Location

The chmod command is located in the /bin directory.

Common Syntax and Examples

The syntax is as follows:

    $ chmod *access mode filename*

or

    $ chmod *action filename*

Both of these command forms accomplish the same function; the one you use is based largely on personal preference.

The first format shown is usually called the *numeric* method, because the permissions on the file are specified by a three-digit number. Each digit represents one of the three classes of users: the first digit specifies the permissions associated with the owner of the file; the second applies to users who share the owner's group, and the third digit applies to everybody else. Each digit is determined by adding up the permissions you want to apply to that class of users:

4 read permission
2 write permission
1 execute permission
0 no permission

For example, the command chmod 640 memo changes the permissions for the file memo. The first digit, 6, indicates that the owner of the file can read and write to the file (as 6 is the sum of 4 plus 2). The second digit, 4, indicates that others in the owner's group can read the file, and the last digit, 0, indicates that no one else can access the file at all.

The second form of chmod is known as the *symbolic* method, because it uses symbols (letters) in place of the numbers. Permissions are specified by listing one or more *actions*, in this format:

    [[*who*] *operation_permission*]

There must be no spaces in the action.

who is one or more of the following letters, specifying which class or classes are affected by this change:

    u   owner of the file (user)
    g   others in the owner's group
    o   everybody else (others)
    a   all three of the above classes (all users)

operation specifies whether permissions are being added, removed, or set, as in the following examples:

    +   add permissions
    −   remove permissions
    =   set permissions

permission specifies permissions that are added or removed:

    r   read
    w   write
    x   execute

1. To add write permission for the group to *filename1* and *filename2*, at the prompt type the following:

    $ **chmod g+w *filename1 filename2*** <Return>

2. To remove write permission from everybody else (others) for datafile, at the prompt type the following:

    $ **chmod o−w datafile** <Return>

3. To set the group's permission for the file named notice to read only (implied in this operation is that write and execute permissions are removed), at the prompt type the following:

    $ **chmod g=r notice** <Return>

4. To remove write and execute permissions for the file named prog1 for group and others, at the prompt type the following:

    $ **chmod go−wx prog1** <Return>

5. To add read permission for the group and take away read from others, at the prompt type the following:

    $ **chmod g+r,o−r afile** <Return>

6. To add execute permission to file abc for all users, at the prompt type the following:

    $ **chmod a+x abc** <Return>

7. If the *who* portion is omitted, chmod assumes that all users are intended. Thus to add execute permission for all users, at the prompt type the following:

    $ **chmod +x abc** <Return>

Notes

The permissions are part of a larger group of information called the *access modes*. These modes are maintained for files. chmod can manipulate all additional access modes (hence the name chmod). Manipulating these other modes are useful to advanced programmers and advanced users.

You can change the permissions on a file only if you are the owner or the superuser.

Caution

When using the symbolic method, be sure that there are no spaces anywhere in the action.

chown

Purpose

To change the ownership of one or more files.

When To Use

Use chown when you need to give a file to someone who needs full access and permission to the file. Without ownership rights, another user cannot exercise complete control over the file or change permission on the file.

Normal Location

The chown command is located in the /bin directory. A complete list of users is found in the password file, /etc/passwd.

Common Syntax and Examples

The syntax is as follows:

```
chown newowner filename(s)
```

To change the owner of *filename1* to david, at the prompt type the following:

```
$ chown david filename1 <Return>
```

Notes

You must own the file or be the superuser to change the ownership.

Caution

Once you give ownership of a file to someone else, you no longer have this ownership. To regain ownership of the file, the new owner will have to use the chown command to again make you the owner.

Also see chgrp *and* chmod.

clear

Purpose

To clear the screen or to advance one page on the printer.

When To Use

Use the clear command when you want a fresh blank screen with the prompt back at the top or when you want the printer paper to advance to the top of the next page.

Normal Location

The clear command is usually located in the /usr/bin directory, although some systems may place it in a different location.

Common Syntax and Examples

The syntax is as follows:

```
clear
```

To clear the screen, at the prompt type the following:

$ **clear** <Return>

Notes

In order for clear to work, the TERM variable must be set to the proper terminal type. If TERM is not set, or if it is incorrectly set, or if it is set to a terminal type whose screen cannot be cleared, clear does nothing.

cmp

Purpose

To compare two files and report any differences that are found.

When To Use

This command is especially suited for comparing binary files. To compare text files, use the `diff` and `diff3` commands.

Normal Location

The `cmp` command is located in the `/bin` directory.

Common Syntax and Examples

The syntax is as follows:

    cmp [-l] [-s] filename1 filename2

1. To compare *filename1* and *filename2* and display the difference, at the prompt type the following:

    $ **cmp *filename1 filename2*** <Return>

2. To compare *filename1* and *filename2* without writing any messages, at the prompt type the following:

    $ **cmp -s *filename1 filename2*** <Return>

Options

-l   Prints the byte number (in decimal) and the differing bytes (in octal) for each difference

-s   Returns an exit code only: 0 for identical files, 1 for different files, and 2 for an inaccessible or missing file

Notes

If the two files being compared are identical, no message is displayed.

Also see comm, diff, *and* diff3.

comm

Purpose

To compare two sorted files and display the differences and similarities in three columns.

When To Use

Use the comm command when you need to find not only the difference between two files but also the similarities and have them displayed for an easy comparison. The (default) three-column output includes:

First column   Displays lines that are found only in *filename1*
Second column   Displays lines that are found only in *filename2*
Third column   Displays lines that are found in both files

Normal Location

The comm command is usually located in the /usr/bin directory.

Common Syntax and Examples

The syntax is as follows:

```
comm [-123] filename1 filename2
```

1. To display the differences and similarities in a three-column output between *filename1* and *filename2*, at the prompt type the following:

    $ **comm *filename1 filename2*** <Return>

2. To display only the common lines between *filename1* and *filename2*, at the prompt type the following:

    $ **comm -12 *filename1 filename2*** <Return>

Options

-1   Suppresses printing of column one
-2   Suppresses printing of column two
-3   Suppresses printing of column three

Notes

Using all the options (-123) at once causes the command to do nothing.

Caution

Before using comm, sort the files using the sort command.

Also see cmp, diff, sort, *and* uniq.

copy

Purpose

To copy the contents of a file or directory to another location. copy leaves the source file intact as it creates a new copy.

When To Use

Use the copy command when you want to make another copy of the same file, which is good for backup purposes. You may also need to have the same file in more than one directory.

Normal Location

copy is located in the /usr/bin directory.

Common Syntax and Examples

The syntax is as follows:

```
$ copy [-alnomrv] source destination
```

The copy command copies one or more files from the source to the destination.

1. To make a copy of a single file, specify the existing name and the new name. For example, to make a copy of memo and call the copy dupmemo, at the prompt type the following:

   ```
   $ copy memo dupmemo <Return>
   ```

2. You can copy one or more files to a directory by listing all the files as the source, and listing the directory as the destination. For example, to copy the three files memo1, memo2, and memo3 to the directory /usr/fred/memodir, at the prompt type the following:

   ```
   $ copy memo1 memo2 memo3 /usr/fred/memodir <Return>
   ```

   Here all three files are copied to the directory /usr/fred/memodir, where they will retain their current names. Wild cards can also be used, as in the following example:

   ```
   $ copy memo* /usr/fred/memodir.
   ```

3. To copy all files from one directory to another, including all files in subdirectories, at the prompt type the following:

   ```
   $ copy -r /usr/mary/memos /usr/fred/memos <Return>
   ```

   This command copies all files and directories under /usr/mary/memos to /usr/fred/memos.

Options

-a   Asks the user for confirmation (a yes or no) before copying each file.

-l   Uses links instead whenever they can be used; otherwise a copy is made (links are not used for directories or special files).

-n   Requires the destination file to be a new file. If the file is not new, copy does not change the destination file.

-o   Copies the source owner and group to every file copied.

-m   Copies the modification and access times of the source file. Otherwise, the modification time is set to the time of the copy.

-r   Recursively examines each directory. Otherwise directories are ignored.

-v   Prints messages to show what the copy command is doing. The -a option overrides this option.

Notes

The owner and permission modes are not changed if the destination file already exists. If the file or directory does not exist at the destination, it is created with the same permission modes and flags as the source.

The copy command as described in this Command Reference is available only on some systems, such as XENIX. On many systems, such as UNIX System V, the cpio command provides much of the functionality of copy.

Also see cp, mv, *and* cpio.

cp

Purpose

To copy an existing file to another file or to copy a list of files into a directory.

When To Use

Use cp when you need to make a duplicate file in another location and you want to preserve the existing file. You cannot use this command to copy a file onto itself.

Normal Location

The cp command is located in the /bin directory.

Common Syntax and Examples

The syntax is as follows:

```
cp filename newfile
```

or

```
cp filename(s) directory
```

1. To copy *filename1* to *filename2*, where *filename2* does or does not already exist, at the prompt type the following:

   $ **cp filename1 filename2** <Return>

2. To copy a list of files into the directory */directory* and keep the same file names, at the prompt type the following:

   $ **cp filename1 filename2 filename3 /directory** <Return>

Caution

Be certain that the file you are copying to is not a file that you want to keep, because the file will be overwritten, and therefore lost.

Also see copy, cpio, *and* mv.

cron

Purpose

To execute commands automatically at regularly scheduled times. cron executes commands by at, batch, and crontab.

When To Use

Use cron to run commands at specified dates and times, or on any type of repeating cycle. cron is useful for sending mail out automatically as reminders or performing other such regular events as backups.

Normal Location

The actual program cron is located in the /etc directory. Users do not directly execute the cron command. Rather, cron is run automatically by the system startup program, /etc/rc. Various other files and directories are required by cron, but these vary among systems.

Common Syntax and Examples

When you start your system, the cron program starts automatically and runs continuously as long as your system is running. No syntax is given here because you never use the cron command directly.

You must supply cron with a list of commands to execute and a description of when to run the commands. On most systems, each user may have the ability to maintain a list of commands, stored in a file named by the user. Use the crontab command to submit your list of commands.

This file of commands consists of one or more lines, each line consisting of six fields, separated by spaces. The first five fields specify the times to run the command; the sixth field is the specified command:

Field 1   The number of minutes the job will run

Field 2   The number of hours the job will run

Field 3   The day of the month the job will run

Field 4   The month the job will run

Field 5   The day of the week (0=Sunday ... 6=Saturday) the job will run

Field 6   The specified command to run

Each field can be a single number, a list of numbers separated by commas, two numbers with a dash between them indicating a range, or an asterisk (*) meaning "any."

1. To send a reminder via mail every Friday at noon, include the following line in the file:

```
0 12 * * 5 echo "Stop by the store on your way home"|mail john
```

This line says "At 0 minutes after the 12th hour (noon) on any day of the month, any month of the year, 5th day of the week (Friday), execute the specified command."

2. To perform a backup every weekday, include the following line:

```
30 18 * * 1-5 find /usr/mark -print|cpio -oc >/dev/mt0
```

This line says "At 30 minutes after the 18th hour (6:30 p.m.) on any day of the month, any month of the year, 1st through 5th day of the week (Monday through Friday), execute the specified command."

3. To print your company's price list twice a day, include the following line:

```
20 9,15 * * * lp /usr/jean/price.list
```

This line says "At 20 minutes after the 9th and 15th hours (9:20 a.m. and 3:20 p.m.) on any day of the month, any month of the year, any day of the week, execute the specified command."

4. To automatically mail your employees a New Year's greeting each year, include the following line:

```
59 23 31 12 * mail barney lisa sherrie </usr/boss/new.year
```

This line says "At 59 minutes after the 23rd hour (11:59 p.m.) on the 31st day of the 12th month (December), any day of the week, execute the specified command."

Notes

On some older systems, such as UNIX System III or older versions of XENIX, there is no list of commands for each user, but a single list for the entire system, which is stored in the file `/usr/lib/crontab`. On these systems, only the superuser can modify the contents of `crontab`.

When one of your commands executed by `cron` produces output, `cron` mails the output to you.

Also see `crontab`, `at`, *and* `batch`.

crontab

Purpose

To submit a list of commands to execute on a regular schedule, to see the list you submitted, or to cancel the list.

When To Use

Use crontab any time you want to submit, modify, or cancel a list of commands that you want executed automatically on a regular cycle.

Normal Location

The crontab command is located in the /usr/bin directory. The files containing the lists of commands used by cron are kept in the /usr/lib/ cron directory. The files cron.allow and cron.deny control who is allowed to use cron and crontab. These files are usually kept in the /usr/ lib/cron directory, but this may vary on some systems.

Common Syntax and Examples

The crontab command has the following syntax:

```
crontab [-l] [-r] filename
```

crontab enables you to submit a list of commands which are located in the crontab file. The file follows the format described in the preceding entry on cron.

1. To submit a list of commands in a file called command.list, at the prompt type the following:

   $ **crontab command.list** <Return>

   If you already submitted a list, this new list replaces (overwrites) the old one.

2. To see the list of commands that cron is currently scheduling for you, at the prompt type the following:

   $ **crontab -l** <Return>

3. To cancel the list of scheduled commands, at the prompt type the following:

   $ **crontab -r** <Return>

Options

-l   Lists all crontab commands

-r   Removes all crontab commands

Notes

On some older systems, such as UNIX System III or older versions of XENIX, each user does not have a list of commands, so no `crontab` command exists. A single list of regularly scheduled commands for the entire system is stored in the file `/usr/lib/crontab`. Only the superuser can modify this file.

Also see `cron`, `at`, *and* `batch`.

csh

Purpose

The C-shell command csh is an alternative to the standard Bourne shell, sh. Both provide an interface to UNIX—a way to talk to the operating system by entering commands. csh is preferred by many users because of its timesaving features, such as command history, aliases, and many other typing-savers. It is also popular with many C programmers, because it has a built-in programming language that is quite similar to C.

When To Use

csh is not available on all systems. If it is available on your system, and you want the conveniences it offers, your system administrator can make it your standard shell.

Normal Location

The shell begins by executing commands from the .cshrc file in your home directory. The shell also executes commands from your .login file in your home directory. To log out, you type **log out** and press <Return>. This process executes commands from the .logout file, also located in your home directory. You can look at /etc/passwd for a listing of who is using what type of shell.

Common Syntax and Examples

The simple syntax for the C shell is as follows:

```
csh
```

You can use the C shell even if your system does not use the C shell automatically. First set up both a .login and .cshrc file. The C shell consults the .login file when you log in, and consults the .cshrc file upon invocation of each subshell. Your system administrator can arrange for the C shell to be your default login shell. The default prompt symbol for the C shell is the % sign, but you can configure the prompt if you want. If you are in the Bourne shell or any other common shell and you need to switch over to the C shell, at the prompt type the following:

```
$ csh <Return>
```

Options

Many flags, options, and commands can be used with the C shell. Because the C shell is an entire shell language, the following list includes only a few of the options.

-c   Reads commands from the single argument that follows.

-e   Causes the shell to exit if any command entered terminates abnormally or returns a nonzero exit status.

-f   Does not search for or execute commands from the `.cshrc` file. Causes the shell to invoke faster.

-i   Causes the shell to be interactive and prompts for its top-level input. If the input/output device is a terminal, shells are interactive without this option.

-n   Causes commands to be parsed but not executed. This option helps in syntactic checking of shell scripts.

-s   Causes commands to be taken from the standard input.

-t   Reads and executes a single line of input.

-v   Causes commands to be echoed after a history substitution, by setting the verbose variable.

-x   Echoes commands before execution.

Notes

Consult your system documentation for more information on `csh`, or refer to a book devoted exclusively to `csh`.

Also see `sh` *and* `rsh`.

cu

Purpose

To enable you to connect to another computer, usually via a modem, and to log in to that computer without logging out of your current computer. Rudimentary facilities are available for transferring data between the two computers.

When To Use

Use cu when you need to spend a short time working on another computer while remaining logged in to your current computer. To use cu, you must have a valid login ID on the other computer.

Normal Location

The cu command is usually located in the /usr/bin directory. To do its work, cu requires a rather complex database stored in several files, usually in /usr/lib/uucp. Your system administrator should have installed these required files for you.

Common Syntax and Examples

The syntax is as follows:

```
cu [-sspeed [-d] [-ldevice] [-h] [-e] [-o] telno|sysname
```

1. cu places a call to another computer and allows you to log in. If your system administrator configured your computer with information about the computer you are calling, you can simply specify the name of the computer. To call a computer known as bigben, at the prompt type the following:

   ```
   $ cu bigben <Return>
   ```

   After a brief pause, you receive a login: prompt from the computer called bigben. You can now log in and do your work. When you log off bigben, you are back on your original computer.

2. If your system administrator has not configured your computer to connect to the computer you want to call, you can still call by supplying the phone number of the other computer's modem. For example, to call the number 276-3142, at the prompt type the following:

   ```
   $ cu 2763142 <Return>
   ```

3. If your computer's modem is connected to an office PBX, so that you must dial 9 for an outside line, include 9= in front of the number. To get the outside line with the number in the previous example, at the prompt type the following:

   ```
   $ cu 9=2763142 <Return>
   ```

4. Calling by phone number can require more sophistication; you sometimes need to know the baud rate, parity, and duplex settings. This information can usually be determined with the help of the system administrator for your

system or the system you are calling. To call a system that requires 1200 baud, even parity, and half-duplex, at the prompt type the following:

```
$ cu -s1200 -e -h 9=2763142 <Return>
```

cu has many additional capabilities, accessed through what are known as *tilde commands*, because they start with a tilde (~). One in particular is crucial—the "quit" command. Normally cu exits when you log off the remote system, but if you are unable to log in for some reason, you will also be unable to log off. The "quit" command tells cu that you want to disconnect immediately. To issue a "quit," type the following:

```
<Return>
~. <Return>
```

On many systems, cu prints the name of your computer as you press the period. That's normal.

Many other tilde commands are available to make cu more useful. Consult your system documentation for more information.

Options

-s*speed*	Specifies the transmission speed. 1200 is the default value.
-d	Prints diagnostic traces.
-l*line*	Specifies the device name of the communications *line* (usually the terminal line to which the modem is connected, such as /dev/tty23). Consult your system administrator for this information.
-h	Emulates local echo.
-e	Generates even parity for data sent to the remote system.
-o	Generates odd parity for data sent to the remote system.
-n	Prompts for telephone number.
telno	Indicates the telephone number of the remote system.
sysname	Indicates the name of the computer you are calling.

Notes

You can transfer only ASCII files with the ~%take or ~%put commands. You cannot transfer binary files.

For cu to operate properly, the system administrator must correctly configure the required files in the /usr/lib/uucp directory. Further, use of cu depends on your system having the physical means of making the connection—that is, you can't place a phone call if you don't have a modem.

Cautions

cu opens devices for exclusive use. If cu terminates abnormally, the device may remain locked.

Also see cat, echo, tty, **and** stty.

cut

Purpose

To extract only selected columns or fields from data, discarding everything else.

When To Use

Use cut whenever you have data—either in a file or printed by another command—that contains columns or fields that you want to cut out.

Normal Location

The cut command is located in the /usr/bin directory.

Common Syntax and Examples

The syntax is as follows, given in cut's two distinct formats:

```
cut -c list [filenames]
cut -f list [-dchar] [-s] [filenames]
```

Either the -c or the -f option must be used, based on whether the data is arranged into columns of data (such as the output of the who command or ps command) or arranged into fields—groups of data separated by a special character called a *delimiter*. For example, in the /etc/passwd file, the data is separated into seven fields separated by colons. If you use the -f option, using the -s suppresses lines with no delimiter characters.

1. If data is organized into columns, use the -c option followed by a list of the columns to be displayed. In the following example, a data file called phonelist contains names in columns 1 through 20 of each line and phone numbers in columns 43 through 56. To display only names and phone numbers and discard all other information, at the prompt type the following:

   $ **cut -c1-20,43-56 phonebook** <Return>

   This command does not actually modify the file phonebook in any way; it affects only the information that is displayed. If you want the cut data to be stored in a file, redirect the output of the command to the desired file name.

2. If the data is organized into fields, use the -f option followed by a list of fields to be displayed. The -d option is usually required as well to specify the character that separates the fields. For example, the /etc/passwd file contains information about every user known to the system. Each line contains seven fields, separated by colons. The fifth field is the full name of the user. The seventh field from /etc/passwd contains the names of every

user known to the system. To display or print this field, at the prompt type the following:

```
$ cut -f5 -d: /etc/passwd <Return>
```

3. cut is often used as part of a pipe to extract desired information and to discard unwanted information. For example, the ps command lists four columns of data on each process: process id, terminal id, execution time, and program name. The next example displays or prints only the process id (columns two through six) and the program name (column 18 through the end of the line). At the prompt type the following:

```
$ ps | cut -c2-6,18- <Return>
```

The notation 18- means columns 18 through the end of the line.

Options

-c *list*   Specifies that information be displayed by columns (must be immediately followed by a list of columns)

-f *list*   Specifies that information will be displayed by fields (must be immediately followed by a list of fields)

-d *char*   Specifies the special character that separates fields within the data (used with the -f option)

Notes

Do not leave spaces in the lists of fields or columns. If the character specified in the -d option has a special meaning to the shell (such as a pipe symbol |), the symbol should be surrounded by single quotes, as in -d'|'.

Also see paste.

cpio

Purpose

To create or restore backup tapes and disks or to copy a directory tree (a directory and all its subdirectories) to another directory.

When To Use

Use cpio to create backups, to restore files from a backup, or to copy a directory tree.

Normal Location

cpio is located in the /bin directory.

Common Syntax and Examples

cpio has three slightly different syntaxes, depending on which of three tasks it is performing:

```
cpio -o[dacBv]
cpio -i[BcdmrtuvfSsb6] [patterns]
cpio -p[adhlmuv] directory
```

1. Use the first syntax to create backups, giving cpio a list of files to back up and redirecting its output to the floppy or tape drive on which to save the backup. In the following example, the file named filelist contains the list of files, and the name of the disk drive is /dev/fd0. To back up these files, at the prompt type the following:

    $ **cpio -ocv < filelist > /dev/fd0** <Return>

    The c option specifies that file information be written in a way that is portable across all systems (this option is almost universally used today), and the v option tells cpio to list the files as it backs them up.

2. When creating cpio backups, you rarely have an actual list of files to back up; in almost all cases, you will use the find command to create a list of files in a set of directories. To back up Pat's home directory (and all subdirectories), at the prompt type the following:

    $ **find /usr/pat -print | cpio -ocv > /dev/fd0** <Return>

    This find command produces a list of all files in /usr/pat and its subdirectories, and this list is fed into cpio as the files to back up.

3. To restore all files from a backup, use the -i syntax, redirecting input from the backup tape or disk. At the prompt type the following:

    $ **cpio -icvd < /dev/fd0** <Return>

4. To restore only certain files from a backup, use the $-i$ syntax and specify the file(s) you want restored. Type the following:

   $ **cpio -icvd /usr/pat/stuff /usr/pat/junk < /dev/fd0** <Return>

5. You can use wild cards, but they must be surrounded by double quotes (" "). To restore all files in /usr/pat that start with the letter p, type the following:

   $ **cpio -icvd "/usr/pat/p*" < /dev/fd0** <Return>

6. A slightly different variation produces a listing of all files on the tape or disk, without restoring them. At the prompt type the following:

   $ **cpio -icvt < /dev/fd0** <Return>

7. Use the third syntax for cpio for copying a directory tree to another directory. As with the $-o$ syntax, find expects to receive a list of files to copy. The find command is almost always used to generate this list.

   To copy a directory tree, change to the directory representing the top of the tree to be copied. To copy everything in that directory and all subdirectories to the directory /usr/mark/stuff, type the following:

   $ **find . -print | cpio -pvd /usr/mark/stuff** <Return>

Options

-a   When copying files with $-p$ or $-o$, gives the copied file the same access time as the original file.

-b   Reverses the order of bytes contained in each word.

-B   Uses I/O blocks of 5120 bytes (improves performance with tape drives).

-c   Writes indexing information in text form (always use this option with the $-i$ and $-o$ options).

-d   Creates directories as needed (usually desirable with the $-i$ and $-p$ forms).

-f   Copies all files *except* those that match the pattern (use with $-i$ option).

-l   Uses links whenever possible to save disk space.

-m   Retains correct file-modification time (usually desirable when restoring backups with $-i$).

-r   Interactively renames files when restoring with $-i$.

-t   Lists a table of contents instead of restoring files (use with $-i$).

-u   Copies files unconditionally (without this option, cpio does not allow an older file to replace a younger file).

-v   Enables the verbose mode, which lists the file being processed on-screen.

-6   Processes backups that were written under Version 6 UNIX (rarely needed now).

Notes

Other options may be available on some systems. Consult your system documentation for more information.

`cpio` usually fits more data on disks or tapes than does `tar`, the other popular UNIX backup program.

Cautions

Be careful to type the redirection symbols in the correct direction.

`cpio` backups are not compatible with `cr` or `tar` backups.

date

Purpose

To display or set the system date and time.

When To Use

Use the `date` command to display the system date and time. The superuser can use `date` to set the system date and time.

Normal Location

The `date` command is located in the `/bin` directory.

Common Syntax and Examples

The `date` command has two possible syntaxes:

```
date [+format]
date [mmddhhmm[yy]]
```

With the first syntax, you can display the current date and time. When you issue `date` with no options, the date and time are displayed in a standard format, as follows:

```
$ date <Return>
Sun Aug 19 17:06:17 EDT 1990
$
```

By using an option, you can specify exactly how to display the date and/or time. This format is usually used in shell programs rather than executed from the keyboard. The option always begins with a plus sign (+) and consists of some combination of characters and special character pairs. Special character pairs, the first of which is always a percent sign (%), indicate which parts of the time and date are to be printed and how.

1. To display the current month, day of the month, and day of the week, at the prompt type the following:

```
$ date +"%a, %h %d" <Return>
Sun, Aug 19
$
```

From the table of options, note that `%a` represents the day of the week, `%h` is the name of the month, and `%d` is the day of the month. The spaces and the comma are printed literally as they appear in the command line. The double quotes are necessary if there are spaces in the format.

2. To print the current time in a.m./p.m. notation, at the prompt type the following:

```
$ date +%r
05:25:05 PM
$
```

3. The second syntax can be used only by the system administrator to set the system date and time. *mm* is the month, *dd* is the year, *hh* is the hour (on a 24-hour clock), *mm* is the minute, and *yy* is the year. If *yy* is omitted, the year is unchanged. To set the date to noon on September 27, at the prompt type the following:

   $ **date 09271200** <Return>

Options

%m	Displays the month as a two-digit number, 01 through 12
%d	Displays the day of the month as a two-digit number, 01 through 31
%y	Displays the last two digits of the year, 00 through 99
%D	Displays the date in *mm/dd/yy* format
%H	Displays the hour as a two-digit number, 00 through 23
%M	Displays the minute as a two-digit number, 00 through 59
%S	Displays the second as a two-digit number, 00 through 59
%T	Displays the time in *HH:MM:SS* format, 24-hour clock
%j	Displays the day of the year as a three-digit number, 001 through 366
%w	Displays the day of the week as a one-digit number, 0 through 7 for Sunday through Saturday
%a	Displays an abbreviated weekday, Sun through Sat
%h	Displays an abbreviated month name, Jan through Dec
%r	Displays the time in a.m./p.m. notation, HH:MM:SS XM

Cautions

It is not a good practice to change the date while more than one person is using the system. File-access and modification dates and times depend on the system time as established by date. Certain commands that are executed chronologically by crontab may execute prematurely if a date is mistakenly entered as a future date.

dc

Purpose

To use an on-line arbitrary precision calculator.

When To Use

Use dc to do precision arithmetic. dc is a stacking, Reverse Polish calculator. dc takes its input from standard input, the screen, or a file. dc operates on decimal integers, but you can specify a base and fractional digits.

Normal Location

dc is an executable file located in the /usr/bin directory.

Common Syntax and Examples

The syntax is as follows:

    dc

or

    dc program file

1. To invoke the dc calculator, at the prompt type the following:

    $ **dc** <Return>

2. To run a dc program file called file1, at the prompt type the following:

    $ **dc file1** <Return>

Options

With dc, many constructions are available. Only a few of these constructions are listed here.

number	Pushes the value of the specified number on the stack.
+-/*%^	The top two values on the stack are added, subtracted, multiplied, divided, remaindered, or exponentiated. The two entries are popped off the stack, and the result is pushed on the stack in their place.
c	Pops all values on the stack, or the stack is cleared.
d	Duplicates the top value on the stack.
i	Pops or removes the top value on the stack.
p	Prints the top value on the stack.
f	Prints all values on the stack.
q	Exits the program.

Notes

bc is a preprocessor for dc. bc provides infix notation and syntax similar to the C language. For interactive use, bc is preferred to dc.

Also see bc.

df

Purpose

To report the amount of free disk space.

When To Use

Use df to check on the load of a specific file system or all mounted file systems. df tells you how many blocks are left available for use. This information helps you to monitor system space and usage.

Normal Location

The df command is located in the /bin directory. Information on the various file systems is kept in the mount table, /etc/mnttab. Other associated files are located in the /dev directory.

Common Syntax and Examples

The syntax is as follows:

```
df [-tfv] [filesystems]
```

1. To list information about all mounted file systems, at the prompt type the following:

    $ **df** <Return>

2. To list information about a file system that is on a floppy disk, at the prompt type the following:

    $ **df /dev/fd0** <Return>

Options

-i   Lists the number of free and used i-nodes (the default).

-t   Lists the number of allocated blocks along with the number of free blocks available.

-f   Causes df to count the actual number of free disk blocks, rather than to accept the information stored in the mount table (useful when you suspect that the disk or memory is corrupted).

-v   Lists the number and percentage of used blocks (not available on many systems).

Notes

The device names for floppy disks vary among implementations of UNIX. You should verify the device names of the drive containing the floppy disk that you are using.

diff

Purpose

To compare the contents of two files and show the differences.

When To Use

Use `diff` when you want to know what differences, if any, exist between two files.

Normal Location

The `diff` command is located in the `/bin` directory. If the `-h` option is used, another program, `/usr/lib/diffh`, does some of the work.

Common Syntax and Examples

The syntax is as follows:

```
diff [-efbh] filename1 filename2
```

`diff` compares the two files. If they are identical, no output is produced. If they differ, `diff` shows the differences between the two files. Because the second file is usually a version of the first file that has been changed, `diff` explains the differences in a way that indicates which changes were probably made to the second file.

To compare two memos called `memo.1989` and `memo.1990`, at the prompt type the following:

```
$ diff memo.1989 memo.1990 <Return>
```

In this example, `diff` produces output because the two files are not identical. Lines preceded by < appear only in `memo.1989`; lines preceded by > appear only in `memo.1990`. `diff` finds three sets of differences, illustrating the three possible types of differences: additions, changes, and deletions.

```
22a23,27
> At this year's sales meeting we will
> be discussing the progress of our
> new overseas division.  Jack Smith,
> Vice President, of international sales,
> will speak.
42,43c47,48
< and the 14 markets averaged sales
< of $1.2 million last year.
> and the 16 markets averaged sales
> of $1.4 million last year.
57,58d61
< Special tax laws considerations
< helped this year's profits.
$
```

The first set of differences starts with 22a23,27, indicating that lines were *added* to the second file that are not in the first—in this case lines 23 through 27. diff then shows the lines themselves, preceded by the > to indicate that they occur in the second file. The 22 tells you that if these five lines occurred in the first file, they would be found after line 22.

The next set of differences is marked with 42,43c47,48, indicating that lines were *changed*. Two lines in the first file, lines 42 and 43, were changed in the second file. However, because of the lines added earlier in the file, the changed lines are at lines 47 and 48 in the second file. diff then shows the two lines from both files.

The last set of differences is marked with 57,58d61, indicating that lines 57 and 58 in the first file were *deleted* from the second file. If they occurred in the second file, they would appear after line 61. diff displays the two lines from the first file.

Options

-e   Displays a script that the ed editor command can use to transform the first file into the second. This format is more difficult to read, but can be useful in shell programs that use the ed editor.

-f   Similar to -e, but produces commands to transform the second file into the first (not used often).

-b   Causes diff to ignore differences in blanks (spaces and tabs). If, for example, the only difference between corresponding lines in the two files is that one contains extra blanks, diff considers them the same.

-h   Causes diff to do a quicker job—a "half-hearted" process—in that diff works correctly only if the differences are small.

Notes

On some systems, diff can also determine the differences between two directories.

Also see dircmp.

diff3

Purpose

To compare three files.

When To Use

Use diff3 to compare three versions of a file at the same time.

Normal Location

diff3 is a shell program located in the /usr/bin directory. Another program, /usr/lib/diff3prog, is never called directly by the user, but actually does the work.

Common Syntax and Examples

The syntax is as follows:

        diff3 [-ex3] *filename1 filename2 filename3*

To compare three files, *filename1*, *filename2*, and *filename3*, at the prompt type the following:

        $ **diff3 *filename1 filename2 filename3*** <Return>

Options

   -e   Creates a script for the ed editor that places into *filename1* all changes between *filename2* and *filename3*

   -x   Creates a script to incorporate changes from all files

   -3   Creates a script to incorporate changes in *filename3*

Caution

On most systems, diff3 does not work on files larger than 64K characters.

Also see comm, cmp, **and** diff.

dircmp

Purpose

To compare directories and list information on the files that are unique to each directory. dircmp also indicates whether two files of the same name are unique.

When To Use

Use dircmp to compare all the files within two directories. This command is useful for deleting duplicate files or for backing up to another directory.

Normal Location

dircmp is an executable file that is located in /bin.

Common Syntax and Examples

The syntax is as follows:

```
$ dircmp [-ds] filename1 filename2
```

To compare the two directories, Memos and Meetings, at the prompt type the following:

```
$ dircmp Memos Meetings <Return>
```

Options

-d   Compares two files of the same name in both directories

-s   Suppresses all messages

-wn Changes the width of the output to *n* number of characters

Also see cmp *and* diff.

`diskcp, diskcmp`

Purpose

To copy or compare floppy diskettes.

When To Use

Use `diskcp` to make an exact copy of one floppy onto another. Use `diskcmp` to compare the contents of one floppy disk with the contents of another.

Normal Location

The `diskcp` and `diskcmp` files are both located in `/usr/bin`.

Common Syntax and Examples

The syntax is as follows, shown for both commands:

```
diskcp [-fds] [format]
diskcmp [-fs] [format]
```

format is the target format of the floppy, such as one of the following:
`-48ds9`, `-96ds9`, `-96ds15`, `-135ds9`, or `-135ds18`.

1. To make a copy of one diskette to another high-density blank diskette that needs to be formatted at the same time, at the prompt type the following:

   $ **diskcp −f −096ds15** <Return>

2. To make a copy as above and to display the checksum value, at the prompt type the following:

   $ **diskcp −f −s −096ds15** <Return>

Options

`-f` Formats the floppy before copying

`-d` For dual-floppy drives, copies directly onto the source diskette

`-s` Compares the contents of the source and target diskettes

Notes

Most errors occur with `diskcp` when a copy is attempted onto an unformatted target floppy. `diskcp` formats the target and attempts to copy again if it encounters a write error the first time.

`diskcp` and `diskcmp` are extensions provided by the Santa Cruz Operation.

Caution

These commands are not found on all systems.

Also see `cp` *and* `cpio`.

du

Purpose

To summarize and display disk usage.

When To Use

Use du to list the number of blocks (512-byte blocks) in files or directories.

Normal Location

du is an executable file located in /bin.

Common Syntax and Examples

The syntax is as follows:

```
du [-ars] filename
```

filename is any file or directory.

1. To list the total disk usage for the /usr file system, at the prompt type the following:

    $ **du -s /usr** <Return>

2. To list the total disk usage of a directory tree and all its subdirectories, at the prompt type the following:

    $ **du /usr/tanya** <Return>

Options

-a Displays the disk usage for each file listed.

-r Displays messages on files or directories that du could not access, read, or open (these files are normally not included in the estimated disk usage, nor are they mentioned).

-s Displays only the grand total figure for each file or directory given.

Notes

If no file name is given, the current directory is assumed.

echo

Purpose

To display messages to the standard output or to display the value of a shell variable or parameter.

When To Use

Use echo to display the value of a shell variable, or to print messages within shell programs. echo can also be used in a pipe to send information to another command's standard input.

Normal Location

Because the echo command is used so frequently in shell programs, on most systems it is built into the shell, and its use does not actually cause a program to be executed. For special programming situations in which an actual program is required, a program echo exists in the /bin directory, which duplicates the functionality of the built-in command.

Common Syntax and Examples

The syntax is as follows:

```
echo arguments
```

The echo command prints its arguments, usually text or variables, to the standard output. The arguments are usually surrounded by double quotes (" ").

1. Within a shell program, use echo to print a greeting, such as the following:

```
$ echo "Welcome to my shell program." <Return>
```

2. To print the value of a shell environment variable, such as TERM, at the prompt type the following:

```
$ echo "Your terminal is a $TERM." <Return>
```

In this example, the echo command prints the text as shown, except that $TERM is replaced by the value of the TERM variable. The resulting display to the terminal looks like the following:

```
Your terminal is a vt100.
```

3. You can include special characters in the text, as in the following example:

```
$ echo "Mary had\nA little lamb." <Return>
```

The \n is a special character representing a new line. When it appears in the text, a skip to the next line occurs at that point. The result of the preceding command shows the newline skip:

```
Mary had
A little lamb.
```

4. The echo command is often used in conjunction with pipes, especially in shell programs. Following is an example of an automatic-backup program that sends mail to Pete, letting him know that the backup is complete:

```
echo "Backup complete." | mail pete
```

Here the output of the echo command, rather than being displayed on the terminal, is fed into the mail command as its input, and becomes the message that is sent to Pete.

Options

\b   Displays the backspace character.

\c   Prevents a skip to the next line. Normally, echo automatically skips to the next line after printing the text. When this special character appears at the end of the text, echo continues on the same line.

\f   Displays the form-feed character.

\n   Displays the newline character.

\r   Displays a carriage return.

\t   Displays a tab.

\\   Displays a backslash character.

\num   Displays the character whose octal ASCII value is the number specified by num. \033, for example, displays an <Esc> character, because the ASCII value of <Esc> is octal 33.

Cautions

Because the echo command is built into the shell, it can behave differently or have different options, depending on the shell you are using. In particular, be careful when using echo within the C shell (csh).

Also see sh *and* csh.

ed, red

Purpose

To edit (make changes to) a file, especially when using systems or terminals that do not support more powerful editors such as vi. The restricted editor, red, is useful in conjunction with the restricted shell, rsh. When properly set up by the system administrator, it restricts the files that can be edited.

When To Use

Use ed or red to edit files when more powerful editors, such as vi, are not available. While less powerful than other text editors, ed is useful because it is available on all UNIX machines and works on all terminals.

ed works in a fashion similar to the full-screen editor, vi, in that ed reads into its buffer the file that you want to work on, thus making all changes to what is only a copy of your file. You must, in fact, write out a new copy of the file to save your changes. red is the restricted version of ed; red allows editing of files only in the current directory. red also prohibits the execution of commands via the ! (known as the bang escape) command.

Normal Location

The temporary file is located in /tmp/epid, where pid is the process ID number. In case of a terminal lock-up, all work on your ed file is saved in the file ed.hup. The command ed itself is an executable program that is located in /bin.

Common Syntax and Examples

The syntax is as follows:

```
ed [-] [-p text] [filename]
```

1. To invoke ed and read filename into the buffer for editing, at the prompt type the following:

    $ **ed filename** <Return>

2. To save your changes to a file named filename, in command mode, at the prompt type the following:

    $ **w filename** <Return>

3. To exit ed, in command mode, at the prompt type the following:

    $ **q** <Return>

4. To enter into command mode, at the prompt type the following:

    $ **.** <Return>

5. To enter into input mode, at the prompt type the following:

    $ **a** <Return>

ed is used in two modes: text-input and command. You cannot do text typing on the file when ed is in command mode. Command-mode editing is done with commands that specify the line or series of lines that are to be edited.

Options

ed is an entire line-editing language, with many commands and arguments available. See Chapter 12 and Appendix E for more information on ed.

–   Suppresses the messages that follow the e, r, and q commands. Also suppresses the diagnostics from the e, q, and ! commands.

-p *text*   Allows a prompt string.

Notes

The – option is available only in UNIX versions later than Version 3. The red command prohibits execution of sh (C) commands via the ! command. red simply displays an error message when attempting to go beyond the restrictions.

Also see vi *and* grep.

env

Purpose

To report your current environment or to modify it with an argument.

When To Use

Use the `env` command with a given argument to change your environment setup and then execute the command under the new environment.

Normal Location

`env` is an executable file that is located in `/bin`.

Common Syntax and Examples

        env [-] [*name=value*] [*command arguments*]

1. To display your current environment, at the prompt type the following:

    $ **env** <Return>

2. To change your environment temporarily and add a shell variable, at the prompt type the following:

    $ **env TZ=MST7MDT date** <Return>

   This command temporarily displays the date and time in Mountain Standard time. When the `date` command is finished, the previous value of the `TZ` variable takes effect again.

Options

–   Ignores the inherited environment. The given command is then executed with the environment specified.

name=value   Adds changes in this form to the current environment before the given command is run.

Notes

If you do not specify a command, your current environment is displayed with one *name=value* pair per line. In System V, `env` replaces the older `printenv` command. The current `printenv` is simply a link to the `env` command.

Also see `sh`.

file

Purpose

To determine the type of one or more files.

When To Use

Use file to determine what kind of information a file contains. file looks at the beginning of the file for a *magic number*—a special code number used by UNIX to identify certain types of files. For text files, which have no magic numbers, file examines the first 512 characters for hints about what kind of data is in the file.

Normal Location

The file command is located in the /bin directory. The list of magic numbers is in /etc/magic.

Common Syntax and Examples

The syntax is as follows:

```
file [-c] [-ffilename] [-mfilename]
```

1. To display file information on the file status, at the prompt type the following:

   $ **file status** <Return>

   This command displays information about the type of file, such as directory, data, ASCII text, C-program source, or archive.

2. To display the file types of all the files in the current directory, you can use a wild-card argument; at the prompt, type the following:

   $ **file *** <Return>

Options

-c	Checks the /etc/magic file for format errors.
-f*filename*	Checks the files listed in *filename*.
-m *filename*	Does one of two things, depending on the UNIX version:
	IBM AIX and System V: Uses *filename* as the magic file instead of the default /etc/magic.
	SCO UNIX: -m sets the access time for the examined file to the current time. Otherwise, the access time remains unchanged.

Notes

This command, originally developed for Berkeley UNIX, cannot be implemented in all versions of UNIX.

Also see find.

find

Purpose

To search through specified directories, including all subdirectories, for files that match the given criteria.

When To Use

Use find to locate all files that have certain characteristics. You might, for example, want to find all files owned by jim, or all files with a name beginning with memo, or all files modified in the last seven days. find can print the names of the files that meet these criteria or execute any UNIX command on the files, such as printing them with lp or removing them with rm.

Normal Location

The find command is located in the /bin directory.

Common Syntax and Examples

The syntax is as follows:

```
find pathlist criteria action
```

pathlist is a list of one or more directories to be searched. Implied is that all subdirectories will be searched as well.

criteria is a list of one or more options that specify the characteristics of the files for which you are looking.

action is what you want find to do when it finds a file that meets the specified criteria.

1. To find all files in Tanya's directories whose name starts with letter, at the prompt type the following:

```
$ find /usr/tanya -name "letter*" -print <Return>
```

Here the path list—the directory to be searched—is /usr/tanya; the search criterion is that the file's name must begin with letter; the action upon finding such a file is to print its name. The double quotes are necessary when wild cards are used.

2. To remove all files named core, at the prompt type the following:

```
$ find / -name core -exec rm {} \; <Return>
```

The path list is the root directory, so the entire file system is searched. The criterion is that the file's name must be core. When found, the command following the -exec is executed. The braces ({}) indicate where the file name should appear in the rm command. The backslash-semicolon (\;) is required by find to terminate the -exec action.

3. To print the names of all files that have been modified in the last seven days and back them up to nine-track tape (via the `cpio` command), at the prompt type the following:

   $ **find /usr/mark —mtime —7 —print | cpio —ocv > /dev/mt0** <Return>

   The criterion —mtime —7 specifies files that were modified in seven days or less. The list of files meeting this criterion is piped into `cpio`, which backs up the specified files.

4. To list the names of all files that were not modified in the past year, at the prompt type the following:

   $ **find /usr/mark —mtime +365 —print** <Return>

   The criterion —mtime +365 specifies files that were not modified in 365 days or more.

Options

—name *filename*	Specifies files whose names match *filename*. Wild cards can be used if they are surrounded by double quotes (" ").
—type *x*	Specifies files of type *x*, where *x* is d for directory, f for regular file, c for character device, b for block device, or p for named pipe.
—perm	Specifies files with a designated permission, expressed numerically as the octal mode. For example, —perm 777 finds files with read, write, and execute permissions set for the user, group, and others. A minus in front of the permissions specifies that *at least* the permissions indicated must be turned on.
—links *n*	Specifies files that have *n* number of links.
—user *name*	Specifies files owned by the user specified by *name*.
—group *name*	Specifies files belonging to the group specified in *name*.
—size *n*	Specifies files *n* blocks in size (a block is 512 bytes). Use +*n* for files larger than *n* blocks and —*n* for files smaller than *n* blocks.
—atime *days*	Specifies files that were last accessed *days* days ago. Use —*days* for files accessed less than *days* days ago and +*days* for files that were last accessed more than *days* days ago.
—mtime *days*	Specifies files that were last modified *days* days ago. Use —*days* for files modified less than *days* days ago and +*days* for files that were last modified more than *days* days ago.

-newer *filename*   Specifies files that were modified more recently than the file *filename*.

-inum *n*   Specifies a file whose i-number is *n*. This is useful to the system administrator, because UNIX sometimes reports files not by name, but by i-number.

Several criteria can be specified in a single command; find will find files which meet *all* the specified criteria. For example, to find all files which are larger than 10 blocks in size and are owned by the user named Leslie, at the prompt type the following:

     $ **find / -size +10 -user leslie -print** <Return>

The recognized actions are as follows:

-print   Prints the names of the files found.

-exec *cmd* \;   Executes the specified command every time a file is found. If { } appears in the command, it is replaced by the name of the file.

-ok *cmd* \;   Works similarly to -exec, except that every time a file is found, find prints the resulting command with a question mark and asks whether you want to perform the command. Press **y** to execute the command; press any other key to skip it.

Other options are as follows:

-o   Signifies *or*. Place this between two criteria to specify that you are looking for files meeting either of the criteria. Criteria must be surrounded by \ (and \ ). For example, to find all files owned by Jack or Jill, at the prompt type the following:

     $ **find / \(-user jack -o -user jill \) -print** <Return>

!   Signifies *not*. Place this before a criterion to specify that you are looking for files which do not meet the criterion. For example, to find files in Monica's directories that she doesn't own, at the prompt type the following:

     $ **find /usr/monica ! -user monica -print** <Return>

Notes

find is unusual among the UNIX commands in that its options are words, not letters.

Also see cpio.

finger

Purpose

To display information about users on the system.

When To Use

Use finger to list information about the users on the system. By default, finger lists the login name, the user's full name, the terminal name, how long the terminal has been idle, login time, office location, and phone number (if this is public information).

Normal Location

finger is an executable file that resides in /bin. To include information for the plan section of the displayed finger information, you need to place the file .plan or .project in your home directory, and you can reference the files as $HOME/.plan or $HOME/.project.

Common Syntax and Examples

The syntax is as follows:

```
finger [-bfilpqsw] [user1 user2 ...]
```

1. To display information in long format about jeffj, at the prompt type the following:

    $ **finger jeffj** <Return>

2. To display all users with idle time at the prompt type the following:

    $ **finger -i** <Return>

Options

-b   Provides a briefer long output of users
-f   Suppresses header line
-i   Displays a quick list of users with idle time
-l   Displays a long format
-p   Suppresses printing of the .plan files
-q   Displays a quick list of users
-s   Displays a short format
-w   Displays a narrow format of specified users

Notes

finger is a Berkeley UNIX command, not available on all systems. The comments displayed by the finger command correspond to what is contained in the /etc/passwd file. Idle time is computed as the elapsed time since any activity has occurred on the given terminal. The corresponding device file is /dev/tty??.

Also see who.

grep, egrep, fgrep

Purpose

To search files for lines containing a specified phrase or pattern.

When To Use

Use one of these commands when you need to find all lines in a file or files that contain a phrase or pattern, or when you want to determine which files contain a phrase or pattern. fgrep (for *fast grep*) is the fastest of the three commands, but can search only for fixed phrases. grep, though slightly slower, is more powerful because it can search not only for phrases, but for patterns as well, which are technically known as *regular expressions*. egrep (*extended grep*) is slightly slower still, but is the most powerful of the three: it can search for combinations of regular expressions.

Normal Location

On most systems grep is located in the /bin directory. fgrep and egrep may be located in /bin or /usr/bin.

Common Syntax and Examples

The three commands have slightly different options available, and in fact the options vary depending on the system. Common syntaxes are as follows:

```
fgrep [-vxcilnbf] [nde] phrase [files]
grep [-vcilnbsf] pattern [files]
egrep [-vcilnbf] [-e] pattern [files]
```

1. To display all lines in a file named Memo that contain the word computer, at the prompt type the following:

   $ **fgrep computer Memo** <Return>

   Any of the three commands can accomplish this task, but fgrep is the fastest.

2. To display all lines that contain a number in any file in the current directory, at the prompt type the following:

   $ **grep "[0-9]" *** <Return>

   The pattern [0-9] is a regular expression indicating a digit. Whenever the phrase or pattern contains any special characters (the brackets, in this case) or a space, the phrase should be enclosed within double quotes. In this case, only grep or egrep can do this job, with grep being the faster of the two. fgrep cannot find regular expressions.

3. To display all lines that contain either the words Jack or Jill in the file named people, at the prompt type the following:

   $ **egrep "Jack|Jill" people** <Return>

Options

-v	Displays all lines in which the phrase or pattern is not found.
-c	Displays only a count of the number of lines containing the phrase or pattern.
-i	Ignores upper- or lowercase differences.
-x	Performs an exact comparison (fgrep only). Finds lines that precisely match the phrase, with no additional characters.
-l	Lists only the names of the files in which the phrase or pattern is found, rather than the lines themselves.
-n	Displays the line number before each matching line.
-b	Displays the disk-block number before each matching line.
-s	Provides a silent search (grep only). Suppresses messages about files that can't be found (useful in shell programs).
-e*expr*	Designates an expression (fgrep and egrep only). The phrase or pattern to find immediately follows the -e. This option is useful when the phrase begins with a minus (-). Without -e, the minus would be mistaken for an option.
-f*filename*	Indicates the file containing a list of phrases or patterns to search for. For example, in fgrep -flist letter*, the file containing a list of phrases is list. fgrep prints all lines in all files beginning with letter that contain one of the phrases found in list. (This option works with fgrep and egrep only.)

Notes

In a perfect world, only one command would perform searching, rather than three. The authors of UNIX wanted to perform simple searches very quickly, without having to invoke more complex commands. The resulting compromise was a choice of three programs—fgrep, grep, and egrep—ranging from the fast and simple to the slower but more powerful.

grep gets its name from an ed command which has the format g/*RE*/p. This command *globally* searches for a *regular expression* and *prints* the lines it finds, which fairly well summarizes what grep does.

Also see ed.

head

Purpose

To display the first few lines of a file.

When To Use

Use head to display the first few lines (10 lines by default) of a file to standard output. This command is useful when you want to check the contents of a file without viewing the entire file. You often use head because you have forgotten what kind of things were listed in a specified file and want to get an idea of what is in the file.

head is similar to its counterpart, tail, which displays the final lines of a file.

Normal Location

head is an executable file that is located in /bin.

Common Syntax and Examples

The syntax is as follows:

```
head [-count] [file ...]
```

count is the number of lines to be displayed.

-count specifies a number of lines other than the default of 10. -1, for example, lists only the first line of the specified file.

To display the first 20 lines of the file alist, at the prompt type the following:

```
$ head -20 alist <Return>
```

Notes

head is a Berkeley UNIX command, not found on all systems. On other systems, a utility called sed can be used to accomplish the same thing with a little more typing, as in the following command:

```
$ sed -n 1,10p filename <Return>
```

Here, you change the 10 to alter the number of lines printed.

Also see tail.

join

Purpose

To join lines from two separate files that have the same join field.

When To Use

Use `join` when combining database types of files or files that contain lists of information. To join files, the files must have a common field.

Normal Location

`join` is an executable file located in `/bin`.

Common Syntax and Examples

The syntax is as follows:

```
join [-options] filename1 filename2
```

1. To join the files `Houses` and `Apartments`, using a comma as the field separator, at the prompt type the following:

   $ **join -t, Houses Apartments** <Return>

2. To display unmatched lines from the files `Houses` and `Apartments`, at the prompt type the following:

   $ **join -a2 Houses Apartments** <Return>

3. To join two files by using a field other than the first field, you must sort the other field first and then pipe the sorted output to the `join` command. To join the files `Houses` and `Apartments` by their fourth field, at the prompt type the following:

   $ **sort +2 -4 Houses ; join -jl 4 - Apartments** <Return>

   This command joins `Houses` by the fourth field. The minus sign (−) causes the `join` command to use this output as the first field. Using the `-j` option uses the fourth field of the first file as the join field.

Options

-a *n*	Displays each unpairable line, where *n* is either *filename1* or *filename2*.
-e *string*	Replaces empty output fields with *string*.
-j *n m*	Joins the *m*th field of file *n*. If *n* is omitted, the *m*th field of each file is used.

-o *list*   Displays all output with the fields specified in *list*. In this list, each element will have the form n.m, where *n* is the file number and *m* is the field number.

-t *char*   Specifies *char* as the field separator in the input and the output. Blanks are the default separator.

Notes

To use a tab character as a field separator (the -t option), you must enclose it in single quotation marks (' '). Each file will be sorted by its join field, which by default is the first field.

Also see comm *and* sort.

kill

Purpose

To terminate a running process or a group of processes.

When To Use

Use the kill command to stop one or more processes from running. This action may be necessary if you have started a background process and then decide to stop it for some reason, or if a program malfunctions and causes a terminal to lock up.

Normal Location

The kill command is located in the /bin directory.

Common Syntax and Examples

The syntax is as follows:

```
kill [-signal] process-ids
```

Every program running on a UNIX computer is assigned a unique number, called a *process ID*, or *PID*. To stop a process with kill, you must specify this process ID. The process ID of a background process is displayed by the shell when you start the process. If you forget, the ps command will list your processes and their associated PID numbers.

The kill command sends a message—called a *signal*—to a process, asking it to stop. There are at least 15 different signals that can be sent (more on most UNIX systems), but only two of them are of interest to most users. If you're interested in the entire repertoire of signals, many systems have the file /usr/include/sys/signal.h which lists all the signals for your system.

1. To stop a process, you should first try a "plain vanilla" kill. Suppose that you determined using ps that the process you want to kill has a process ID number of 2034. At the prompt you would type the following:

   $ **kill 2034** <Return>

   This sends a signal called a *software-termination signal*, which requests the specified process to stop. Sending a software-termination signal is like politely asking a process to stop; a well-behaved program will obey, but a malfunctioning program may ignore the request. Some programs, for various reasons, are intentionally written to ignore this signal.

2. If a simple kill fails, use the -9 option, by typing the following:

   $ **kill -9 2034** <Return>

   This causes kill to send a different message, known as a "sure kill." A process cannot ignore or refuse this signal; it has to stop.

At least 13 more signals can be sent to a process beyond the two discussed here, but most of them are of interest only to advanced programmers.

Options

-9   Provides a sure kill; when used, the process cannot refuse to stop.

-15 Functions as a software-termination signal, rather than an option you specify. This is the default signal sent by the kill command when no options are specified.

Notes

You must be the superuser in order to kill any processes other than your own.

When attempting to stop a process, you should always try a plain vanilla kill first, and then use the ps command to see whether the process stopped. This sequence requests the process to stop, but gives it a chance to tidy up first. The sure kill (-9) stops a process dead in its tracks, with no chance to clean up, removing temporary files it created, for example.

Cautions

Do not kill a series of processes without rechecking the process ID number each time; this number may change after your most recent execution of kill.

Do *not* kill the following processes:

Process	Meaning
swapper	The first process on the system
init	The parent process of the first shell for every user
logger	The location of the system error messages
update	Flushes the buffer
cron	The process scheduler
lpsched	Leave running, unless it itself seems to be locked up

Also see ps.

line

Purpose

To read one line at a time from standard input.

When To Use

Use `line` in shell scripts to read the user-input line from standard input and then write it to standard output.

Normal Location

`line` is an executable file located in `/bin`.

Common Syntax and Examples

The syntax is as follows:

```
line
```

To read from standard input and append a line entered onto the file `staff1`, at the prompt type the following:

```
$ echo  'Enter the input line here' <Return>
$ line >> staff1 <Return>
```

Also see `echo`.

ln

Purpose

To create another link to a file; that is, to add a new name to an existing file.

When To Use

Use ln to add another name to an existing file. Unlike cp, the ln command does not copy data or create a new file; it simply gives another name to the file. The file can now be accessed either by its original name or by the link.

Normal Location

The ln command is located in the /bin directory.

Common Syntax and Examples

The syntaxes of the ln command are as follows:

```
ln [-f] filename1 filename2
```

or

```
ln [-f] filenames directory
```

1. Use the first syntax to create a new name for an existing file. Suppose that you have a file named very.long.name, and you are tired of typing its name repeatedly. You can give it a shorter alternate name, such as v, by typing the following:

   $ **ln very.long.name v** <Return>

   Now, very.long.name and v are both names for the same file and can be used interchangeably. In a directory listing, both names will appear.

2. A file can have links in other directories. Suppose that Jim has a file in his directory called chart, and that you need to examine this file often while preparing a memo. To save yourself the trouble of repeatedly typing a full path name, you can use the following command as you begin work:

   $ **ln /usr/jim/data/chart jims.chart** <Return>

   This command creates the new name jims.chart in the current directory. Now when you access jims.chart in the current directory, you are accessing the same file as /usr/jim/data/chart.

3. Any number of files can be linked to another directory, using the second syntax form. If you have three files called table1, table2, and table3 in your home directory, /usr/barbara, you can create links to them all. At the prompt type the following:

   $ **ln /usr/barbara/table*** . <Return>

   In this syntax, you specify a directory at the end of the command (in this case ., the current directory). This example creates links in the current directory to all files in /usr/barbara that begin with table.

Options

The `ln` command has one option: `-f`. This option creates a link without prompting you with further questions. Normally, if you try to create a link to a file for which you do not have write permission, `ln` displays the current permissions and asks whether you want to link to the file anyway. Responding with a **y** causes the link to be made. If the `-f` option is used, no questions are asked; `ln` makes the link if at all possible.

Notes

Any file may have any number of links. Each represents a name by which the file is known, and all names may be used interchangeably.

The `ls -l` command tells you how many links a file has—that is, by how many names it is known. However, it is not always easy to tell what a file's other names actually are. A few hints follow:

- The `ls -i` command lists file names along with each file's i-number, which is the internal identification for a file within UNIX. If two or more of the names listed by an `ls -i` have the same i-number, they represent the same file.

- The `find` command with the `-inum` option can be used to find all names for a particular file.

You can remove links by using the `rm` command. If a file has two or more names and `rm` is performed on one of the names, the file itself is not removed, only the name. The data itself is deleted when the last name is removed. Note that there is nothing wrong with removing the original name and leaving only links. UNIX disregards which name is the original and which are the links; the file is preserved as long as there is a name by which it can be accessed.

Each directory has at least two names, because there are at least two ways to access it. In its parent directory, the directory is known by the name you specify with the `mkdir` command. Within itself, each directory is known as
. (current directory). Therefore, the `ls -l` command always shows at least two links for all directories. Most have more.

Also see `cm, mv, and` `rm`.

lp

Purpose

To send a request to the line printer.

When To Use

Use to create a hard-copy printout of a file by sending the file to the printer. If no files are specified, the standard input (usually the keyboard) is used to send text to the printer.

Normal Location

The `lp` command is located in the `/usr/bin` directory.

Common Syntax and Examples

The syntax is as follows:

```
lp [-cdmnostw] [filename]
```

The `lp` command invokes the UNIX print spooler. Your prompt will return immediately, even before the printer has begun printing your file. This feature has two important ramifications. First, your terminal is not tied up while your file is being printed so that you can continue working on other things. Second, if several people try to print at the same time, the spooler ensures that the first user's printing is completed before the other user's file begins printing. Files are printed on a first-come first-served basis.

1. To print a copy of the file named `memo` to the printer, at the prompt type the following:

   ```
   $ lp memo <Return>
   ```

   This command causes the file to go to the default printer.

2. To print the file `workout.sched` on the printer `laser1`, and to create a copy so that changes made after the file is sent to the print spooler do not affect the current printout, at the prompt type the following:

   ```
   $ lp -c -dlaser1 workout.sched <Return>
   ```

2. To print the file `workout.sched` on the printer called `laser1`, and to be notified by mail when printing is complete, at the prompt type the following:

   ```
   $ lp -m nddlaser1 workout.sched <Return>
   ```

Options

-c	Causes the lp command to make its own copy of the file so that changes made to the original file do not affect current printing.
-d *dest*	Specifies the name of the printer on which the file is to be printed (you can obtain a complete list of available printers with the lpstat command).
-m	Notifies the user by mail when printing is complete.
-n*num*	Specifies the number of copies to be printed.
-o*option*	Specifies an *option* specific to the printer.
-s	Suppresses messages, including the request-id.
-t*title*	Prints the *title* on the banner sheet.
-w	Notifies the user by terminal message when the request is complete (if you are not logged in, notification is sent by mail).

Notes

The lpr command was used in earlier versions of UNIX. The lp command was developed for the multiprinter environments.

By default, *dest* in -d *dest* is taken from your environment-variable setup LPDEST. If you are using the same printer for most of your work, it may be convenient to set up your LPDEST with the printer name.

If you have a variety of printers to choose from, use the lpstat -a option to determine which printers are accepting requests.

Also see lpstat.

lpstat

Purpose

To print the current status of the lp print spooler.

When To Use

Use this command to determine the location of your print request in the queue. Use also to display information about the printers available on your system.

Normal Location

The lpstat command is located in the /usr/bin directory. Files associated with lpstat are located in the /usr/spool/lp directory and its subdirectories.

Common Syntax and Examples

The syntax is as follows:

```
lpstat [-acdfoprsStuv]
```

1. To get information about the status of the print queue for the printer laser1, at the prompt type the following:

    $ **lpstat -dlaser1** <Return>

    The information given will be the print-job ID name and number, the command (such as lp) used to issue the print job, the size of the file, the date and time the request was sent, and to which printer the request was sent.

2. To display all printing requests made by the users Chelsea and Fletch, at the prompt type the following:

    $ **lpstat -uchelsea,fletch** <Return>

Options

-a*list*	Displays the status of the devices specified in *list*.
-c*list*	Displays the name of each class and the printers belonging to each class specified in *list*.
-d	Displays the system default printer.
-o*list*	Displays the status of output requests specified in *list*.
-p*list* D 1	Displays the status of the printers listed in *list*. If the -D option is used, a brief description of each printer in the list is given. If the -1 option is used, a full description is given.

-r   Displays the status of the lp request scheduler.

-s   Displays a status summary. This includes information obtained
                with the -c, d, r, and v options.

-t   Displays all status information.

-u*list*   Displays the status of the output requests from the users given
                in the *list*.

-v*list*   Displays the names of printers and the path names of the
                devices associated with them.

Also see cancel *and* lp.

ls

Purpose

To list the contents of directories.

When To Use

Use to display the contents of a specified directory along with any other information you request by using options. The current directory is used as the default unless you specify otherwise. Directory contents are listed in alphabetical order.

Normal Location

The `ls` command is located in the `/bin` directory. `ls` uses the `/etc/passwd` file to determine the names of users, and it uses `/etc/group` to determine the names of groups.

Common Syntax and Examples

The syntax is as follows:

```
$ ls [-ACFRabcdfgilmnopqrstux] [filename]
```

1. To display all files, including any hidden files in the current directory, at the prompt type the following:

```
$ ls -a <Return>
```

2. To display detailed information, including file permissions, at the prompt type the following:

```
$ ls -l <Return>
```

You can specify just one or two files with these options if you do not want to list the entire directory.

Options

Many options are available with the `ls` command. Only the most common are listed in the table that follows.

-a   Lists all entries, including . (dot) files.

-C   Lists output in multicolumns, sorted downward.

-F   Places a slash (/) after each file name if the file is a directory and places an asterisk (*) after each executable file.

-l   Lists in long format the display mode, number of links, owner, group, file size (in bytes), and the time of last modification for each file.

-n   Functions the same as the -l option, except that the owner and group ID numbers are printed instead of names.

-q   Replaces nonprinting characters in file names with the question-mark character (?).

-R   Lists recursively the subdirectories encountered.

-s   Lists the file size in blocks.

-t   Sorts by time modified (latest first).

-u   Sorts by last time accessed.

-x   Lists output in multicolumns, sorted across.

Notes

The newline and tab characters are considered printing characters in file names.

Also see ln.

mail

Purpose

To read and send electronic mail.

When To Use

You can use mail to communicate with other people connected on your system. mail is a convenient tool that can be used within departments or entire companies that are spread over many cities, or, internationally, with people who are properly set up to receive and send mail.

Normal Location

The mail program is usually located in the /bin directory. The files associated with this command are the following:

$HOME/.mailrc is your personal start-up file. This file stores your incoming mail.

$HOME/mbox is a secondary storage file. After you read a piece of mail, if you do not specify a specific place to store the mail, it is placed in the mbox file.

/usr/spool/mail functions as the "post-office" directory.

/usr/lib/mail/mail.help lists all help message files.

/usr/lib/mail/mailrc is the system (optional) start-up file.

/tmp/R[emqsx] holds temporary files.

Common Syntax and Examples

The syntax is as follows:

```
$ mail [-efFhHubBrsuU] [username]
```

1. To read mail that has been sent to you, at the prompt type the following:

```
$ mail <Return>
```

2. To send mail, type **mail** followed by one or more user names, as in the following:

```
$ mail fred barney <Return>
```

On many systems, you will be prompted for a subject; if so, enter a brief one-line description of the subject of your message and press <Return> (older systems do not ask for a subject). Next, enter the text of your message. You can type as long a message as you want. When your message is complete, press <^D>.

3. When sending any message longer than a few lines, it is usually convenient to prepare your message in a text editor. Use vi or ed to create a file of any length containing your message. If you name the file msg, you can send the message by typing:

```
$ mail fred barney < msg <Return>
```

4. If your system is properly configured, you can send mail to users on other systems. For example, to send mail to Joe who works on a computer named andiron:

> $ **mail andiron!joe** <Return>

Options

Sending and receiving mail is such an important activity that many people and companies have sought to write better and more powerful mail programs. Consequently, a number of mail programs (called *mailers*) exist on various systems, and many can accept additional options. Only the more common options are shown here; your system may have others.

-e	Tests for the presence of mail.
-f *filename*	Reads messages from the specified *filename* instead of from the mailbox; if no file name is given, mail is read from mbox.
-F	Tells mail that all your mail should be forwarded to another user. This is useful if you have two login ID's, one of which you do not use often. It can also be useful if you are on vacation and want someone else to check your mail.
-h *number*	Displays the *number* of network "hops" made so far (useful for network software to avoid infinite delivery loops).
-H	Displays header summary only.
-i	Ignores interrupts.
-n	Does not initialize from the system default mailrc file.
-N	Does not display the initial header summary (opposite of the -H option).
-r *address*	Passes the address to the network-delivery software.
-s *subject*	Sets the subject header field to *subject*.
-u *user*	Reads the specified user's mailbox.
-V	Converts uucp-style addresses to internet standards.

Notes

Many remote features of mail work only if UUCP is installed on your system. As UNIX has become more popular, many additional mailers have become popular. Thus, your system may have another program in addition to mail that is easier to use and more powerful. mailx and elm are two of these. Many manufacturers and software suppliers also provide their own mailers as add-on options.

Also see write.

mesg

Purpose

To set permission to either accept or deny messages sent to your terminal or workstation.

When To Use

Use to deny permission by turning mesg off if you do not want your screen interrupted with messages from other users.

Normal Location

mesg is an executable file that is located in /bin. The mesg command affects terminals listed in /dev/tty??.

Common Syntax and Examples

The syntax is as follows:

```
$ mesg [n] [y]
```

1. To prevent your screen from being interrupted with messages sent by other users, at the prompt type the following:

   ```
   $ mesg n <Return>
   ```

2. To turn the capability back on so that you can now receive messages, at the prompt type the following:

   ```
   $ mesg y <Return>
   ```

Notes

The superuser is always allowed message-write privileges, regardless of permission settings by the receiving end. Message permission has no effect on mail.

This command works the same as using the chmod command and removing the write permission on your terminal, as in the following command line:

```
$ chmod go-w /dev/tty?? <Return>
```

Also see chmod *and* write.

mkdir

Purpose

To create a directory.

When To Use

Use mkdir to create a new directory.

Normal Location

The mkdir command is located in the /bin directory.

Common Syntax and Examples

The syntax is as follows:

mkdir *directoryname*

To create a subdirectory called memos in the current directory, at the prompt type the following:

$ **mkdir memos** <Return>

Options

The basic mkdir command has no options. On many systems, however, more powerful versions of mkdir are available which accept some options.

-h   Creates hidden directories instead of ordinary directories

-m *mode*   Sets the mode of the directory (mode here is in octal format; see chmod)

-p   Creates the subdirectories listed if they do not already exist

Also see rmdir.

more

Purpose

To view a file one screen at a time.

When To Use

Use the more command to display the file one full screen at a time. This is especially helpful when viewing a large file. By pressing <Return>, you can advance one line at a time. Using the <space bar> advances you to the next screen (usually set around 22 or 24 lines).

Normal Location

The more command is usually located in the /usr/bin directory. more looks in the /etc/termcap file to determine the terminal characteristics and the window size. more also looks into your environment to check if you have the MORE variable set to any options. The help file is located in /usr/lib/more.help.

Common Syntax and Examples

The syntax is as follows:

```
$ more [-cdfnsuvw] [+linenumber] [+/pattern] [filename]
```

Options

-c	Avoids screen scrolling by drawing each page at the top of the screen and erasing each line just before it draws over it (works only if the terminal is capable of clearing to the end of a line)
-d	Writes the message Hit space to continue, Rubout to abort at the end of each screen
-f	Counts logical lines instead of screen lines; long lines that wrap are not counted
-n	Sizes the window desired by n number of lines
-s	Condenses multiple blank lines into one blank line (especially useful with nroff files)
-u	Suppresses the underlining capability of more
-v	Displays control characters that are not normally interpreted
-w	Waits for you to press a key before exiting more when the end of the file is reached

+linenumber   Indicates which line to begin with in the file

+/pattern   Searches for the specified pattern (usually just a phrase) and begins displaying the file at that point

Notes

At the bottom of the screen, more displays the percentage of the file already viewed. This percentage is given by characters, not by lines. This display is seen only if more is reading from a file, as this does not happen through the use of a pipe.

This utility was developed at the University of California at Berkeley and is usually available only on systems that are derived from Berkeley UNIX. If more is not available on your system, pg, a similar program, probably is.

Also see env.

mv

Purpose

To move or rename files or directories.

When To Use

Use mv to move a file to another location.

Normal Location

The mv command is located in the /bin directory.

Common Syntax and Examples

The syntax is as follows:

```
$ mv [-f] filename1 filename2
```

filename1 is the name of the file being moved, and filename2 is the new name of the file. filename2 can also be a directory. filename1 does not necessarily have to change names.

To move a file in your current directory called /taxreprt/june/chelsea to /taxreprt/july/chelsea, at the prompt type the following:

```
$ mv chelsea ../july/chelsea <Return>
```

This moves the file chelsea up one and then down into the july directory, where it retains the original file name chelsea.

Options

One option—-f—available with mv overwrites any existing files, regardless of permission settings. Use this option carefully.

Notes

A file that does not have write permissions first prompts you by displaying the permission mode. If you respond with a **y** for yes, the file is overwritten.

mv will not move a file onto itself.

mv can only rename directories; it cannot physically move them.

If filename1 and filename2 reside in two different file sytems, mv copies the file and deletes the original. The owner name becomes that of the copying process; any linking relationship with other files is lost.

Caution

You can easily write over a file that allows write privileges.

Also see cp *and* copy.

newgrp

Purpose

To change the group affiliation of a single user.

When To Use

Use the newgrp command to switch to another group. You must be a member of the group you want to change to. You may want to change groups, for example, if another department or group owns a set of programs that you need to use.

Normal Location

newgrp is an executable file that is located in /bin. The /etc/group file lists all groups and ID numbers and may list the members of the particular groups. /etc/passwd is the password file, which contains your user ID number and your primary group ID.

Common Syntax and Examples

The syntax is as follows:

        newgrp [-] [group]

1. To change into the group called engineer for your current session, at the prompt type the following:

        $ **newgrp engineer** <Return>

2. To change back from the engineer group to your default group (which is found in /etc/passwd), at the prompt type the following:

        $ **newgrp** <Return>

Options

The minus sign (−) option available with newgrp logs you into your default login group ID.

Notes

The newgrp command terminates your current shell and then executes the shell associated with your new group.

Also see chgrp.

news

Purpose

To see current system news and review news articles.

When To Use

Use news to read articles that have been posted by the system administrator or other users. The UNIX news command is a convenient way of allowing users to post messages covering a variety of subjects of general interest to users on the system.

Normal Location

The news command is located in the /usr/bin directory. Each news article is a file that is located in the /usr/news directory. Each user has a file named .news_time in his or her home directory that tracks when the last news article was read; this identifies which news articles have been posted since a particular user last looked at the news.

Common Syntax and Examples

The syntax is as follows:

```
news [-ans] [item]
```

1. To display all new news items, at the prompt type the following:

    $ **news** <Return>

2. To display a specific news article called bonus, at the prompt type the following:

    $ **news bonus** <Return>

3. To display the number of new items that you have not read, at the prompt type the following:

    $ **news -s** <Return>

Options

-a   Displays all news items regardless of the time set in the .news_time file.

-n   Displays the names of all current items without listing their contents and without changing the file-modification time.

-s   Displays how many current news items you have without displaying their names or contents and without changing the modification time.

Notes

You may have news invoked automatically for you when logging in by including news -n in your .profile file or in the system's /etc/profile file.

You must have read/write permissions on the directory /usr/news in order to create a news file.

Also see ps.

nice

Purpose

To run a command at a higher or lower priority than usual.

When To Use

Use nice to indicate to UNIX that a command can be executed at a more leisurely pace than usual. UNIX usually takes great pains to ensure that all users on the system are given equal access to the computer's resources. nice tells UNIX that you are willing to be treated at a disadvantage; in effect, you are saying that your program is less important and that you are willing to give other users better performance at the cost of slower speed to your program. You will use nice typically on programs you start before lunch or at the end of the day, when you don't expect results for some hours anyway.

Normal Location

The nice command is located in the /bin directory.

Common Syntax and Examples

The syntax is as follows:

```
nice [-increment] command [argument ...]
```

The -increment tells UNIX how much to lower the priority. -1 indicates a very minor lowering; the maximum, -19, indicates that your command should always be attended to last. The command is any UNIX command, almost always a background command ending with an ampersand (&). argument is any other argument or command to run in conjunction with the given command.

1. To run a spell-check program in the background at a lower priority, at the prompt type the following:

   ```
   $ nice spell my.memo > bad.words & <Return>
   ```

   nice informs UNIX that the spell command should be executed at a lower priority, giving other users access to the computer's memory and disk before you. The program will take noticeably longer to execute.

2. To lower the priority on a sort to its minimum possible value, at the prompt type the following:

   ```
   $ nice -19 sort old.list -o new.list & <Return>
   ```

   Note that in this case the computer will look for almost anything else to do before giving attention to your program.

3. To increase priority on a program, use two minus signs (--). At the prompt type the following:

   ```
   $ nice --10 shutdown <Return>
   ```

This command, which can only be used by the superuser, increases the priority of the `shutdown` command, causing it to run faster than usual. Other users will notice that their programs will slow down, because your program is "hogging" the computer.

Options

    -increment   Decreases the priority by the amount specified in *increment*

    --increment Increases the priority by the amount specified in *increment*

Notes

You normally need superuser authority to raise the priority level of a command.

The `nice` priority range varies on UNIX systems. Most range from 0-39 with the default being 20 for commands. Others may have a range from 1-19 with the default being at level 10.

This description of `nice` applies to that of the Bourne Shell. The C-Shell has its own `nice` commands.

Cautions

Increasing the priority can dramatically slow down the system for other users. Use the `nice` command only in emergencies.

nl

Purpose

To display a file with line numbers indicated.

When To Use

Use nl to add line numbers in a variety of fashions to a file. For programs or documents that will be passed around, the line numbers are useful reference points.

Normal Location

nl is an executable file that is located in /bin.

Common Syntax and Examples

The syntax is as follows:

```
nl [-bfhiInpsvw]
```

1. To number all lines in the file budget and to separate the line number and text with periods (. . . .), at the prompt type the following:

   $ **nl -ba -s**.... **budget** <Return>

2. The following example begins numbering a file with the number 100, with line number increments of 10 and an allowance of 5 characters for the number, including any leading zeros in the number. At the prompt type the following:

   $ **nl -v100 -i10 -w5 -nrz** <Return>

Options

-b *type*	Specifies which page *body* lines are to be numbered; options for *type* are the following:

a:	numbers *all* lines
t:	numbers printable *text* only
n:	gives *no* line numbering
p *pattern*	numbers only those lines that contain the specified *pattern*.

-f *type*	Specifies which page *footers* should be numbered; options for *type* are the same as in -b *type*.
-h *type*	Specifies which page *headers* to number; options for *type* are the same as in -b *type*.
-i *num*	*Increments* page numbers by *num*; the default is 1.
-I *num*	Specifies the number of adjacent blank lines to be counted and numbered as a group; the default varies from 1 or 2 on UNIX systems.

-n *format*		Specifies the line *numbering* format to be used; formats are the following:

        ln: left justified, leading zeros suppressed

        rn: right justified, leading zeros suppressed

        rz: right justified, leading zeros kept

-p   Prevents new numbering at each *page*

-s *sep*   *Separates* the text from the line number by the character specified by *sep* (Tab is the default *sep* character); if no *sep* is given with the -s, no separation occurs between the line number and text.

-v *startnum* Specifies number from which to begin numbering; the default number is 1.

-w *width*   Specifies the number of characters in the line number; the default width is 6 characters.

Notes

nl views the text as logical pages, with each page consisting of a header, a body, and a footer section. Logical pages are signaled by the following set of characters:

    Start of header   \:\:\:

    Start of body   \:\:

    Start of footer   \:

You can name only one file at a time on the command line.

Also see pr.

nroff, troff

Purpose

To provide text formatting programs.

When To Use

nroff is designed for use with character-type printers, such as the daisy-wheel and most dot-matrix printers. troff is designed for use with phototypesetters and laser printers that have much more sophisticated typesetting capabilities.

Normal Location

If you have the text processing package installed, you will find several files useful:

/usr/lib/suftab contains the suffix hyphenation tables.

/usr/lib/tmac/tmac* contains standard macro files.

/usr/lib/macros/* also contains standard macro files.

/usr/lib/font/* contains the width tables for troff.

/usr/lib/term/* contains the workstation driving tables for nroff.

Common Syntax and Examples

The syntax is as follows:

nroff [*options*] *filename*

or

troff [*options*] *filename*

Options

The text processing languages for UNIX are powerful and complex. Entire books are devoted to these text processors, which fully detail the operation and commands available. This section describes only a few of the available options.

-a	Displays an ASCII approximation of the output (troff only).
-b	Reports only the status of the typesetter (troff only).
-e	Outputs text in equally spaced words in adjusted lines, using full resolution of the device (nroff only).
-f	Does not feed paper on output or stop the typesetter at the end (troff only).
-h	Uses horizontal tabs in the output; tabs are every 8 characters (nroff only).
-i	Reads from the input file after the input files are all read (nroff and troff).

-m name	Prepends the ASCII text macro file /usr/lib/tmac/tmac.name to the input files (nroff and troff).
-n *num*	Numbers the first printed page with *num*; do not use this with -o (nroff and troff).
-o *list*	Prints only the pages listed in *list*, in which the page numbers are separated by commas (nroff and troff).
-p *num*	Prints all characters in the point size specified by *num* (troff only).
-q	Invokes the simultaneous input/output mode of the .rd request; nroff echoes the .rd prompt but does not echo the input. To end this, type in two consecutive newline characters (nroff and troff).
-r aN	Sets register a to N. This is useful for automatic numbering of sections, paragraphs, lines, and so on (nroff and troff).
-s *num*	Stops after every *num* pages; resumes when a newline character is entered. Default *num* is 1 (nroff and troff).
-u *n*	Overstrikes the character for bolding effects *n* times; the default is 0 (nroff only).
-z	Prints only the messages produced by .tm requests (nroff and troff).

Also see lp.

pack, pcat

Purpose

To compress files.

When To Use

Use `pack` to compress a file, encoding its contents so as to reduce the size of the file by as much as 40%. If displayed, packed files appear to contain garbage characters. The `unpack` command can reverse the process, expanding and decoding the file back to its original condition. `pack` is useful for files that you do not access often, but want to keep; by packing the files, they occupy significantly less disk space. `pack` is also useful when files are transferred over phone lines from one computer to another. Because of their smaller size, packed files can be transmitted quickly and cheaply and then unpacked at their destination.

`pcat` enables you to examine a packed file without unpacking it.

Normal Location

`pack` and `pcat` are executable files located in `/usr/bin`.

Common Syntax and Examples

The syntax is as follows:

```
pack [-] filename
```
or
```
pcat filename
```

1. To pack the files `accounts` and `bigfile`, at the prompt type the following:

    `$ `**`pack accounts bigfile`**` <Return>`

    As `pack` compresses the files, it renames them, appending the suffix `.z` to each name. Thus, `accounts` becomes `accounts.z`, and `bigfile` becomes `bigfile.z`.

2. To display information about the compressed files `accounts` and `bigfile`, at the prompt type the following:

    `$ `**`pack - accounts bigfile`**` <Return>`

3. To view the packed file `bigfile`, at the prompt type the following:

    `$ `**`pcat bigfile`**` <Return>`

    The system automatically attaches the suffix `.z` to the end of `bigfile`.

Options

The `-` (minus sign) option is available with `pack`. When issued with the `-`, `pack` provides statistical information on the input file.

Notes

pack can fail for a number of reasons. Packing will not occur if any of the following conditions are present:

- The file is already packed.
- The file is a directory.
- The file has links.
- The file cannot be opened.
- A file called *name*.z already exists.
- No disk space will be saved by the pack.
- The .z file cannot be created.
- An I/O error occurs during the process.
- The file name contains more than 12 characters.

pcat will fail if the following conditions are present:

- The file cannot be opened.
- The file is not an output of pack.
- The file name contains more than 12 characters (not including the .z extension).

Also see unpack.

passwd

Purpose

To change your login password.

When To Use

Use the `passwd` command to change your login password whenever you believe it is necessary, or when system security requires a change. Your system may be set up with a default password aging system that can force you to change your password at various intervals for security purposes.

Normal Location

The `/etc/passwd` file contains user ID numbers and also contains an encrypted version of user passwords. The `/etc/d_passwd` file contains a list of dialup passwords, stored in encrypted form. The `/etc/opasswd` file is the previous version of the password file. The configurable settings for `passwd` are located in `/etc/default/passwd`. The default restrictions are located in `/etc/auth/system/default`. You will find the following executable files in `/bin`: `passwd`, `passwd.orig`, `pwadmin`, `pwadmin.orig`, and `pwcheck`. You may not find all files on all systems.

Common Syntax and Examples

The syntax is as follows:

```
passwd
```

To change your password, you must first be logged in. At the prompt type the following:

```
$ passwd <Return>
```

The system responds, asking you to enter your old password. Once this entry passes, the system asks you to type in your new password, which does not appear on the screen to safeguard security. The system will ask you for your new password twice: This precaution ensures that you did not mistype or make another error. When you enter your new password again, you are returned to the prompt, and your password is changed.

Options

The system administrator may place on passwords a series of options and restrictions. These options and checks, however, require you to be the superuser. For more information on checks, such as minimum/maximum length, obviousness check, authentication checks, and password-aging options, refer to a system administrator's guide on password controls.

Notes

To change a password, you must know the old password.

Only the superuser can create a null password by removing a user's password in the `/etc/passwd` file. Password restrictions vary from system to system, depending on how strictly the system administrator sets the requirements.

Cautions

Do not forget your password. If you do, a system administrator or someone with superuser authority must remove your password from the `/etc/passwd` file and have you choose a new one. Absolutely no file exists that lists user passwords in a humanly readable format. No one but you will, or should, know your password.

Also see `login`.

paste

Purpose

To merge files or lines of files together.

When To Use

Use `paste` when combining columns of text from two or more files and sending the output to another file or standard output. Or, you can use this command to join all lines in the same file to form one long line.

Normal Location

`paste` is an executable file that is located in `/usr/bin`.

Common Syntax and Examples

The syntax is as follows:

    paste [-sd] *filename*

1. To paste the files `boys` and `girls` together and place the combined output in the file `all`, with each input line column separated by a tab (the default), at the prompt type the following:

    $ **paste boys girls > all** <Return>

2. The following example pastes the files `boys` and `girls` together and places the output in the file `all`. + and = are used as the column separators (+ for the first separator and = for the second). At the prompt type the following:

    $ **paste -d"+=" boys girls > all** <Return>

Options

With the `-d` *list* option, the character specified in *list* is used as the column separator (the tab is default). The *list* can include as many characters as columns to be joined. (Special characters must be enclosed in quotes.) You can use the following notations with `-d`:

`\n`   The newline character

`\t`   A tab

`\\`   A backslash

`\0`   An empty string, not a null character

`c`   An extended character.

`-s`   Joins files serially instead of in parallel. Each file is processed separately and then all lines in the file are merged onto one line. Then the next file is processed.

Notes

Output lines are restricted to 511 characters. You cannot use more than 12 input files at once unless you use the `-s` option.

Also see `cut`, `grep`, *and* `join`.

pg

Purpose

To view files one full screen at a time.

When To Use

pg is similar to the cat and more commands, except that with pg you can back up and view previously passed information. When printing with pg, headers are included on the page. Several commands are associated with the pg command that make it more versatile and powerful than some other paginators.

Normal Location

pg is an executable file that is located in /bin. The /etc/termcap file is examined to determine terminal type. The /tmp/pg* file is a temporary file that is used when input is from a pipe command.

Common Syntax and Examples

The syntax is as follows:

    pg [-cefpns +linenum -num +/pattern/] filename

To use pg when reading a file such as the system news file, at the prompt type the following:

    $ **news | pg** <Return>

Options

The list that follows includes only the options available with the pg command. Several subcommands are also available for pg, but these are beyond the scope of this Command Reference.

-c   Clears the screen and moves the cursor to the home position (if clear_screen is not defined in terminfo, this does not work).

-e   Eliminates the pause at the end of each file.

-f   Does not split lines; otherwise, pg splits lines longer than one screen width.

-n   Specifies a letter that will end the session; usually commands end with the newline character.

-p *string*   Specifies *string* as the prompt.

-s   Highlights all displayed messages and prompts, usually in inverse video.

-num	Specifies the number of lines per window; default is 23 for a typical 24-line screen.
+linenum	Begins at *linenum* in the file.
+/pattern/	Begins at the first line that contains the *pattern* specified.

Notes

To determine terminal attributes, pg examines the terminfo file for the terminal specified by the environment variable TERM. Several subcommands can be issued with the pg command after it issues its prompt. A few that may be of interest are q or Q for QUIT pg, and h for help.

Also see cat, grep, *and* more.

pr

Purpose

To format and write files to standard output.

When To Use

Use pr to format files to output on the screen or printer. Numbering and placing files into columns is common practice with pr. By default, the header on each page includes the page number, date, time, and name of the file.

Normal Location

pr is an executable file that is located in /bin.

Common Syntax and Examples

The syntax is as follows:

    pr [-adefhilmnoprstw +-num] [filename]

1. To print the files Men and Boys as a double-spaced, three-column listing with the header "Males," at the prompt type the following:

       $ pr -3dh "Males" Men Boys <Return>

2. To print the files Women and Girls side-by-side on the paper with the header "Females," at the prompt type the following:

       $ pr -m -h "Females" Women Girls | print <Return>

3. To print the file Men onto the file Boys and expand the columns to 10, 19, 28, 37, ..., at the prompt type the following:

       $ pr -e9 -t Men Boys | print <Return>

Options

-a	Prints multicolumn output across the page.
-d	Double-spaces the output.
-e *charnum*	Expands tabs to positions *num*+1, 2*num*+1, 3*num*+1, and so on. The *num* default is 8. Specify *char* as any character (no digits) to become the input tab character.
-f	Uses a form-feed character to advance to a new page. Usually, linefeeds are printed to advance to the next page.
-h *string*	Displays *string* as the page header instead of the file name.
-i *charnum*	Replaces white spaces in the output wherever possible by inserting tabs to character positions *num*+1, 2*num*+1, 3*num*+1, and so on. The *num* default is 8. Specify *char* as any character (no digits) to become the output tab character.
-l *num*	Sets page length to *num* lines. The default is 66 lines.

-m	Merges and outputs all input files simultaneously, one file per column. This overrides the *-num* and -k options.
-n *charnum*	Numbers the output lines by *num* width. The default is 5. *char* specifies the character used to separate the number from the text. (Specifying *char* is optional here.) If this is used in conjunction with the -m option, the entire output line will receive one number.
-o *num*	Offsets each line from the left margin by *num* characters. The default is 0.
-p	Causes pr to pause before each page. The terminal bell sounds and waits for you to press <Return>.
-r	Suppresses error messages when pr cannot open a file.
-s *char*	Separates columns by the single *char*. Tab is the default.
-t	Suppresses the header and footer banners. Stops after the last line of each file without spacing to the end of the page.
-w *num*	Sets the page width to *num* characters for multicolumn output. The default is 72.
+ *num*	Starts printing with *num* page. The default is 1.
- *num*	Produces *num* column output. The default is 1.

Also see cat *and* pg.

ps

Purpose

To report the status of processes currently running on the system.

When To Use

Use ps when you need to look up statistics about processes that are running on the system. If you need to kill a process, issue the ps command to determine its process ID number.

Normal Location

ps is an executable file that is located in /bin.

Common Syntax and Examples

The syntax is as follows:

```
ps [-adefglnpstu]
```

1. To display as much information as possible about all processes running on the system, at the prompt type the following:

   $ **ps -aelf** <Return>

2. To display the processes that are running from your terminal, at the prompt type the following:

   $ **ps** <Return>

3. To display the processes that the user named Tanya has running, at the prompt type the following:

   $ **ps -f -utanya** <Return>

Options

-a	Displays all process information regarding the current terminal, but not including group leaders.
-d	Displays all process information, not including group leaders.
-e	Displays all process information.
-f	Produces a full listing of processes on the current terminal only.
-g *list*	Lists process information only on the process groups specified in *list*. This is a list of group leaders' processes, indicating their PID numbers.
-l	Produces a long listing of the processes. This includes complete information on each process.

-n *namelist* Uses *namelist* as the system name file. Every executable program has a file name that gives information about variables used in the program. The default name is /unix.

-p *list* Lists only process information on process ID numbers given in *list*.

-s *swapdev* Uses the specified *swapdev* as an alternative swap device. The default is /dev/swap. This option is helpful for examining core files.

-t *list* Lists process information only about terminals given in *list*. (This can be a list of terminal ID's separated by commas or by spaces and enclosed in double quotation marks.)

-u *list* Lists process information only on the user ID's or login names specified in *list*. Login names are displayed with the -f option; otherwise, only the user ID numbers are given.

Notes

Only those options associated with the ps command are listed under Options. To determine the precise meaning of the columns in a ps listing, refer to a system administration guide.

Cautions

Be sure to use the ps command immediately before issuing a command that relies on the correct ID number, such as the kill command.

Process ID numbers do change frequently and need to be checked.

The ps command can give you only a close approximation of the current status.

Also see kill *and* nice.

pwd

Purpose

To print the working directory.

When To Use

Use pwd to determine where you are in your hierarchical directory tree. pwd displays your current location.

Normal Location

pwd is an executable file that is located in /bin.

Common Syntax and Examples

The syntax is as follows:

```
pwd
```

To display your current location in the system, at the prompt type the following:

```
$ pwd <Return>
```

Notes

All directories listed are separated by the slash (/). The last directory given is where you are.

If the messages "Cannot Open ..." and "Read error in ..." are displayed, this indicates possible file-system trouble. Refer to a system administration guide for further information.

Also see cd.

rm

Purpose

To remove files or to remove file links.

When To Use

Use rm to remove one or more files from a directory.

Normal Location

rm is located in the /bin directory.

Common Syntax and Examples

The syntax is as follows:

```
rm [-fri] filenames
```

1. To remove a file called junk, at the prompt type the following:

   $ **rm junk** <Return>

2. To remove all files with names beginning with memo, at the prompt type the following:

   $ **rm memo*** <Return>

3. To remove the old directory and everything in it including subdirectories, at the prompt type the following:

   $ **rm -r old** <Return>

4. To have the system list each file one at a time in the current directory, asking you interactively if you want to remove it, at the prompt type the following:

   $ **rm -i *** <Return>

Options

-f   Removes files without first asking for confirmation (normally, rm asks for confirmation if you attempt to remove a file for which you do not have write permission).

-i   Asks interactively for each file if the file should be removed. If you respond with **y**, the file is removed; no other response, including pressing <Return>, deletes the file.

-r   Recursively removes the contents of directories if any of the names to be removed are directories. This option can be dangerous, because a simple command can remove an unexpectedly large number of files.

Notes

To delete a file, you must have write permission on the directory in which the file resides. Write permission on the file itself is not necessary.

If a file has multiple links, `rm` only removes a link; no data is lost. Only when the last link to a file is removed, is the data itself removed.

Cautions

Beware of the `-r` option. Avoid its use if possible.

Also see `rmdir` *and* `ln`.

rmdir

Purpose

To remove directories.

When To Use

Use rmdir to remove directories from your tree.

Normal Location

rmdir is an executable file that is located in /bin.

Common Syntax and Examples

The syntax is as follows:

        rmdir [-ps] *dirname*

To remove the empty directory Accounts, at the prompt type the following:

        $ **rmdir Accounts** <Return>

If Accounts contains any files, rmdir will refuse to remove the directory.

Options

The following options are not available on some systems.

-p   Removes the named directory and any parent directories that become
      empty as a result. A message may be displayed as to whether the entire
      path or part of the path was removed with the named directories.

-s   Suppresses any message generated from the -p option.

Notes

rmdir does not remove the root directory of a mounted file system. A
directory is considered empty when it contains only the entries dot (.)
and dot dot (..).

You must have write permission in the parent directory in order to remove a
directory.

Also see rm.

rsh

Purpose

To invoke a restricted shell. This is a tighter, more restrictive, version of the standard Bourne-shell interpreter.

When To Use

rsh is a highly restricted version of the standard Bourne shell, sh. Users do not normally invoke rsh themselves; rather, by making rsh the login shell for a user, the system administrator can control precisely what that user is allowed to do.

A user running under rsh will encounter these restrictions:

- User cannot change directories.
- User cannot change the value of $PATH.
- User cannot specify path or command names containing / (slash).
- User cannot redirect output—cannot use > or >>.

These restrictions are enforced once the user's .profile file is executed.

Normal Location

rsh is an executable file that is located in /bin. When you invoke rsh, the system profile in /etc/profile is executed first, and then the user's profile in $HOME/.profile is executed. Restrictions are in place after the user's .profile is read. rsh uses all the same files that sh uses.

Common Syntax and Examples

The syntax is as follows:

```
rsh [options] [arguments]
```

The options and arguments for rsh are not covered here.

Notes

When a command to be executed is a shell function, rsh simply invokes sh to execute it, allowing the user full standard shell power, while controlling the menu of commands available.

Because rsh and sh are set up and function identically, refer to the discussion on the shell, sh, in this book, or, for an in-depth discussion, refer to a book devoted to UNIX shells.

Also see csh *and* sh.

setcolor

Purpose

To set screen color.

When To Use

Use setcolor to vary the background, foreground, borders, boxes and/or the cursor size and color. The pitch and duration of the workstation bell can be adjusted as well. A range of 16 colors is available.

Normal Location

setcolor is located in /usr/bin.

Common Syntax and Examples

The syntax is as follows:

```
setcolor [-bcgnopr] argument [argument]
```

1. To list the colors available to you and the correct syntax, at the prompt type the following:

   $ **setcolor** <Return>

2. To set hi_white as the foreground color and red as the background color, at the prompt type the following:

   $ **setcolor hi_white red** <Return>

3. To set the color of the boxes, typically in pull-down type windows, at the prompt type the following:

   $ **setcolor -r yellow blue** <Return>

   This sets text in the boxes to yellow and the background color in the boxes to blue.

4. To set the pitch and duration of your workstation bell, at the prompt type the following:

   $ **setcolor -p 2500 2** <Return>

   $ **echo** <^G>

   When using the -p option, you must echo the bell sound <^G> to the screen in order to test it, as shown in the second line.

Options

-b *color*	Sets the background to the specified *color*.
-c *first last*	Sets the first and last scan lines of the cursor.
-g *color1 color2*	Sets the foreground graphic characters to color specified by *color1* and the background graphic characters to the color specified by *color2*.
-n	Sets the screen to normal: white characters on black background.
-o *color*	Sets the screen border color.
-p *pitch duration*	Sets the pitch and duration of the bell (set the pitch in a period of microseconds, and the duration in fifths of a second). You must echo a < ^ G > (bell) to the screen for this option to work.
-r *color1 color2*	Sets the foreground reverse video characters to the color specified by *color1* Sets the background reverse video characters to the color specified by *color2*.

Notes

setcolor and its European version, setcolour, are extensions of the AT&T SystemV offered by the Santa Cruz Operation. These commands may only work on SCO XENIX or SCO UNIX Operating Systems.

Your color choices depend on the type of hardware devices that you are using. The colors typically available are shown in the following list:

blue	magenta	brown	black
lt_blue	lt_magenta	yellow	gray
cyan	white	green	red
lt_cyan	hi_white	lt_green	lt_red

sh

Purpose

To invoke the UNIX system shell. The shell is a command interpreter and programming interface between the user and the operating system.

When To Use

Several shell interfaces are available on UNIX systems. sh represents the Bourne shell, which is the most commonly used shell. The shell is invoked automatically when you log in. Use sh to run a shell program or to create a subshell, a child shell process. You may have this (or any other) shell as your default shell when logging in.

Normal Location

Several files are affected by the sh command. /etc/profile is the file that the system reads and executes before executing commands found in the individual user's profile. /etc/profile is the file to use when setting up variables for all users on the system.

After the system file /etc/profile is read, the user's file $HOME/.profile is read and the commands in this file are executed. After both system and user profiles are read, the system is ready to read the commands you enter through standard input, the keyboard.

The shell normally searches for commands in several directories, specified in the variable PATH. Typically, these are system directories such as /bin and /usr/bin, which contain common UNIX commands. You can invoke commands from these directories simply by typing the name of the command. Commands located in other directories can be invoked by typing a path name to the command.

Other files that are affected by sh are /tmp/sh*, where temporary files are created when using the << (redirection symbols), and the /dev/null file, which is the source of empty files.

Common Syntax and Examples

The syntax is as follows:

```
sh [options] arguments
```

To invoke the Bourne shell from any other shell or from the Bourne shell itself, at the prompt type the following:

```
$ sh <Return>
```

Options

The Bourne shell has a set of built-in options, which are shown in the following list. Many of these options are in fact subcommands. Please refer to the section that discusses a particular command for more details and syntax instructions. Many of the commands listed have associated arguments that are optional.

:	Places comments within a shell program.
. *filename*	Executes the commands specified in *filename* and returns.
break *n*	Exits from a for-while loop and specifies *n* nested loop levels to exit.
continue *n*	Resumes the next iteration of the for-while loop and specifies *n* loop level at which to begin.
cd *dir*	Changes the current directory to *dir*.
echo	Echoes the argument to standard output.
eval *argument*	Reads *argument* to the shell and executes.
exec *argument*	Executes *argument* in place of the shell without creating a new process.
exit *n*	Exits the shell with an exit status of *n*.
export *names*	Designates *names* to be automatically exported to the environment of subsequently executed commands. If no arguments are given, all names that are exported in the shell are displayed.
getopts	Supports command syntax standards; this option parses positional parameters and checks for legal options.
hash −r *name*	Remembers the location in the search path for each *name* given. The −r causes the shell to forget all remembered locations.
newgrp *argument*	Changes the group in which you are a member.
pwd	Prints your working directory.
read *name*	Enables interactive input. One line is read from standard input and the first word is assigned to the first name, the second word to the second name and so on.
readonly *name*	Tags *names* as read only. If no names are given, a list of all read-only names is displayed.
return *n*	Causes a function value to exit with an exit value of *n*.
set *options*	Displays a list of the current shell variables, functions and their definitions if used without options.
shift *n*	Shifts the positional parameters *n* times. The default is 1. This is used for processing arguments in loops. shift 1 changes $2 to $1.

test	Evaluates conditional expressions and returns the exit value.
times	Displays the accumulated user and system times for processes run from the shell.
trap *argument n*	Reads the argument given and executes it when the shell receives the signal(s) *n*. (trap commands are executed in order of the signal number.)
type *name*	Displays the path name used if the name given was typed as a command.
ulimit *n*	Sets the limit to *n* for the number of blocks that can be used for files written by the shell. If you don't specify *n*, ulimit displays the current limit.
umask *xxx*	Sets the user-creation mask with octal permission settings of *xxx*. If you don't specify *xxx*, umask displays the current setting.
unset *name*	Removes the corresponding variable or function for each *name* given.
wait *n*	Waits for the specified process to terminate and then reports the exit status. Without *n*, waits for all current child processes.

Notes

This is only a summary of the shell commands and options available. For more information, refer to the chapters on the shell and shell programming, or to any of several books available on the shell.

Each time a shell is invoked, a new process starts up. You can use the ps command to check the processes that are running and identify the shell that started them.

Also see csh **and** rsh.

shutdown

Purpose

To properly shut down and end system operations, so that the computer can be turned off.

When To Use

Use shutdown to halt the system or to change from multiuser mode to single-user maintenance mode. shutdown notifies all users (through the wall command) that the system is being shut down and prevents any logins by additional users. If the users already logged in fail to log off within a specified period of time, shutdown forces them off.

Normal Location

shutdown is a shell program in the /etc directory.

Common Syntax and Examples

Even though most UNIX systems have a shutdown command, the syntax varies from one system to another. The usual syntax is as follows:

    shutdown

This works on most systems, although you may need to answer questions before the shutdown begins.

1. Under Unix System V, the complete syntax is as follows:

    $ **shutdown [-y] [-ggrace] [-istate]** <Return>

2. To shut the system down in 60 seconds, at the prompt type the following:

    $ **shutdown -y -g60 -i0** <Return>

Options

-y   Answers all questions "yes." This allows the shutdown to proceed without further intervention and is convenient for experienced users, who don't want to be asked repeatedly "Are you sure?"

-ggrace   Specifies the number of seconds until all users are forced off the system. For scheduled maintenance, a 10-minute grace period is common (-g600). For emergencies -g30 or even -g0 (no grace period) may be necessary.

-istate   Specifies the new state for the system. Use -i0 to shut the system down completely or -i1 to enter single-user maintenance mode.

Notes

shutdown can be executed only by the system administrator.

Cautions

The system administrator should give users on the system enough time to clean up and log off properly before the system is shut down.

You should be in the root (/) directory before executing a `shutdown`.

If you want to reboot the system, do not do so until you receive a message that the shutdown is complete. Sample messages are `System is down` (AT&T) and `Shutdown Complete` (XENIX).

Also see `wall` *and* `haltsys`.

sleep

Purpose

To suspend execution for an interval of time.

When To Use

Use `sleep` in programs and shell scripts and to display messages on-screen. After a message is echoed on-screen, the `sleep` command can be issued to allow the user enough time to read the message before other activities take over the screen.

Normal Location

`sleep` is located in `/bin`.

Common Syntax and Examples

The syntax is as follows:

```
sleep time
```

1. To echo a shutdown message on the screen and run a `shutdown` command, at the prompt type the following:

   ```
   $ echo "The system will shut down in 5 minutes" | wall <Return>
   $ echo "Please clean up and log off" | wall <Return>
   $ sleep 540; shutdown <Return>
   ```

   Note that the time must be given in seconds. You can repeat the message across the screen every minute as a reminder by issuing additional `sleep` and `echo` commands. Piping the commands through `wall` ensures that all users on the system will receive the notice.

2. The `sleep` command is often used in shell scripts and do-while routines. To echo a message across your screen every 10 minutes and issue a command such as `date`, at the prompt type the following:

   ```
   $ while true
   > do
   > echo "It's time to go home Jimmy!"
   > echo "The time now is"
   > date
   > sleep 600
   > done
   ```

Notes

Do not issue the `sleep` command over the time of 65536 seconds. If this time is exceeded, `time` sets an arbitrary value less than this period of time.

All time is specified in seconds.

sort

Purpose

To sort or merge files.

When To Use

Use sort when you want to reorder the lines in a file into some meaningful arrangement or when you want to combine two files, intermingling their lines in some order.

Normal Location

The sort command is located in the /bin directory.

Common Syntax and Examples

The syntax is as follows:

```
sort [-cmubdfinrt] [filename(s)] [-ofilename]
```

Other options may be available on some systems.

The sort command reorders the lines in a file according to a portion of each line, called the *sort key*. The sort key might be a last name if lines are to be sorted alphabetically by name, or a revenue amount if sales departments are being placed in order by gross sales. Any portion of the line can be specified as the sort key; if no sort key is specified, the entire line is used.

1. To sort a file called countries in alphabetical order and print the list to the screen, at the prompt type the following:

   $ **sort countries** <Return>

2. To sort the same file and place the sorted list in a file called sorted.list, at the prompt type the following:

   $ **sort countries -o sorted.list** <Return>

3. To sort a list of people by social security number from a file in which the social security number is the third field, and then to remove all duplicates, at the prompt type the following:

   $ **sort +2 -u people** <Return>

   The +2 option tells sort to skip the first two fields and sort using the third.

4. To merge the two files on.time and late, intermingling their lines in order, and create a file named both with both sets of lines, at the prompt type the following:

   $ **sort on.time late -o both** <Return>

Options

+*number*   Specifies that *number* fields should be skipped in looking for the sort key. For example, +5 says to skip the first five fields and use the sixth for sorting. Fields are separated by tabs, unless the −t option is used.

−b   Ignores leading blanks when determining the starting and ending positions of the sort key.

−c   Checks to see if the file is sorted. No output is produced if the file is correctly sorted.

−m   Merges only. Can be used for a faster merge if the files are already individually sorted.

−u   Keeps unique lines only; discards lines with duplicate sort keys.

−d   Follows "dictionary order." Ignores punctuation in determining order.

−f   "Folds" uppercase onto lowercase. Normally, uppercase comes before lowercase, e.g., "John" before "alan," because John begins with an uppercase letter. −f causes sort to consider both cases equivalent.

−i   Considers only standard printable ASCII characters. Control characters or nonstandard ASCII characters (such as graphics characters from the IBM extended character set) contained in the sort key are ignored.

−n   Sorts by value of total numeric expression, rather than by value of the first digit. This is required when decimal points don't line up, as in this sequence:

```
43
176
```

Here, 176 will be placed first, the 1 being less than 4, unless you use the −n option that tells sort to look at the entire number.

−r   Sorts by reverse order. Especially useful for numbers when you want larger numbers to appear before the smaller ones (as, for example, in a sort of Fortune 500 companies by revenue).

−t*char*   Separates fields by the specified character, rather than by tabs. The following example sorts a list of all the system's users, by the fifth field in the /etc/passwd file, in which fields are separated by colons:

```
$ sort −t: +4 /etc/passwd <Return>
```

Cautions

Lines longer than 1024 characters will be truncated.

spell

Purpose

To find spelling errors in files or from standard input.

When To Use

Issue the `spell` command on any file in which you wish to check the spelling. If no file name is specified, the standard input is checked. Words not occurring in or not derivable from words in a specified spelling list are printed to standard output.

Normal Location

`spell` is an executable file located in `/usr/bin`. Users can add their own words to the spelling list against which their files are checked.

Common Syntax and Examples

The syntax is as follows:

```
spell [-blivx] [+wordlist] [filenames]
```

1. To check the spelling on the file `budget` and display the list of words found incorrect to the screen (standard output), at the prompt type the following:

    $ **spell budget** <Return>

2. To check the spelling on the file `diagnosis` and additionally to check the file against the wordlist `medical`, at the prompt type the following:

    $ **spell +medical diagnosis** <Return>

Options

`-b`	Uses British spelling.
`-l`	Follows the chain of all specified files, including paths that begin with `/usr/lib`, which normally would not be included.
`-v`	Displays all words that do not literally match words in the spell list; also displays possible variations of the word.
`-x`	Displays every plausible word stem for each word checked. Displays in the form `=stem`.
`+wordlist`	Specifies an additional `wordlist`. Users can create their own word lists in addition to the system spell list.

Notes

The system spelling list used is based upon many sources. However, it does not cover extensively such specialized vocabularies as medicine, chemistry, or biology. You can add your own special words to the `spell_list` used.

`spell` ignores most `troff`, `tbl`, and `eqn` text-processing constructions.

split

Purpose

To split a large file into several smaller files.

When To Use

Use split when a single file is too large for your intended purpose. For example, most text editors cannot edit files beyond a maximum size; split may be necessary to break a large file into editable pieces. Later, cat can be used to reassemble the pieces into a single file.

Normal Location

split is located in the /usr/bin directory.

Common Syntax and Examples

The syntax is as follows:

```
split [-n] [filename]
```

split breaks the file (or the standard input, if no file is given) into 1000-line files. The first file s called xaa, the next xab, and so on, up to xzz.

1. To split the large file transactions into smaller files, at the prompt type the following:

    $ **split transactions** <Return>

2. To split the file big.file into smaller files of 25 lines each, at the prompt type the following:

    $ **split -25 big.file** <Return>

Options

The split command provides the -n option, which allows you to specify n number of lines in each file, rather than the default of 1,000 lines per file.

Also see csplit.

stty

Purpose

To set the options and attributes for a terminal. Displays the current terminal settings if no arguments are given.

When To Use

Use `stty` to change the configuration setup on your terminal. Change such items as page length, number of columns on the screen, character size, terminal mapping or how to communicate with modems. The `stty` options are the key to setting up your workstation to your taste.

Normal Location

`stty` is an executable file located in `/bin`.

Common Syntax and Examples

The syntax is as follows:

```
stty [-ag] [arguments]
```

1. To display a short listing of your terminal's current configuration, at the prompt type the following:

   $ **stty** <Return>

2. To display a long listing of your terminal's configuration, at the prompt type the following:

   $ **stty -a** <Return>

3. Occasionally, if a program crashes, it leaves your terminal in an unusual mode so that nothing seems to work right. In such a case, do the following:

   Press <^J>

   (You may get a message about something being not found. Don't worry about it.)

   Next, type very carefully:

   $ **stty sane** (but no <Return>!)

   As you are typing this, you may not see anything appear on the screen. Also, your backspace key may not work. If you make a mistake, repeat these instructions from the beginning. Do not press <Return> or <Enter>.

   Press <^J> again. When your next prompt appears, your terminal should be normal.

Options

Along with the options available with the `stty` command, many arguments are possible within the modes: control modes, input modes, output modes, local modes, control assignments, paging options, combination modes, terminal mapping, and job-control modes. To learn more about the `stty` functions with these modes, refer to a system administration guide, specifically the `termio` (M) and `vidi` (C) sections.

-a   Reports all `stty` settings.

-g   Reports all `stty` settings in a form usable by another `stty` command; that is, in a list of twelve hexadecimal numbers separated by colons. (This form is more compact than with -a).

Notes

For more information on the `stty` command, look into the topics `console`, `ioctl`, `vidi`, `tty`, `termio`, and `termios` in your Reference Manual.

Also see `tty`.

su

Purpose

To switch between user accounts.

When To Use

su enables you to switch between accounts (if you have multiple accounts on the system) or to use someone else's account. If you are the system administrator working under an ordinary login name, you can use su to become the superuser.

Normal Location

su is an executable file that is located in /bin. You can use the file /etc/default/su to control how su is used. Entries that may be placed in /etc/default/su are the following:

SULOG, which is the log file kept to record all attempts made to su to another user, or you can set it up specifically to record all attempts to become the superuser. These are kept in the /usr/adm/sulog.

PATH is the PATH environment set for non-root users.

SUPATH is the path set to /bin:/usr/bin:/etc when invoked by root.

CONSOLE logs superusers to the named device.

Other files checked are the following:

/etc/passwd is the system password file.

/etc/profile is the system profile that may be executed upon the issuance of a su command.

$HOME/.profile is a user's profile that may be executed upon the issuance of a su command.

Common Syntax and Examples

The syntax is as follows:

```
su [-] [username]
```

1. To perform one or more operations as the user named Fred, at the prompt type the following:

```
$ su fred <Return>
Password: <Enter Fred's password>
$
```

You now have all the permissions granted to Fred and can execute any number of commands. When done, press <^D> to resume your previous identity.

2. To perform one or more operations as `root`, the superuser, at the prompt type the following:

    ```
    $ su <Return>
    Password: <Enter root's password>
    $
    ```

    You now have permission to perform any command. When done, press <^D>.

Options

The – option changes not only your identity and permissions, but also sets your environment as though you actually logged in as the other user (this includes setting shell variables from the other user's profile). When you press <^D>, you restore the environment to what it was before the `su` command.

sync

Purpose

To write buffered files to the disk and update the superblock.

When To Use

Use `sync` just before a `haltsys` or `shutdown` command. `sync` flushes all buffers, writing the data to the disk, and updates the superblock from the in-memory copy. Run `sync` to ensure file-system integrity.

Normal Location

`sync` is an executable file that is located in `/bin`.

Common Syntax and Examples

The syntax is as follows:

```
sync
```

Most commonly, `sync` is used in one of the following formats:

```
sync; sync; haltsys
```

or

```
sync; sync; shutdown
```

Use of the semicolon allows multiple commands on one line. Doubling the `sync` command ensures that buffers are indeed flushed and written to the disk before the system is shut down.

tabs

Purpose

To set tab stops.

When To Use

Use the `tabs` command when you want to change the default tab settings on your terminal or workstation, if your terminal has remotely settable tabs.

Normal Location

`tabs` is an executable file located in `/bin`.

Common Syntax and Examples

The syntax is as follows:

```
tabs [tabspec] [+mn] [-Ttype]
```

tabspec is either a list of positions at which to set tabs or an option that specifies one of a set of "canned" tab stops. Most of the canned sets are especially useful for a particular programming language. If *tabspec* is omitted, tabs are set at every eighth column.

+m*n* enables you to set the left margin to *n*+1 and moves all tabs over *n* columns. If you do not indicate *n*, the default is 10.

-T*type* is the system name for the type of terminal or workstation that you are using. If you do not indicate -T, `tabs` uses the value of the environment variable TERM. (If TERM is not defined in your environment, `tabs` tries a sequence that works with most terminals.)

1. To set tab settings required by the IBM assembler, at the prompt type the following:

   $ **tabs -a** <Return>

2. To set specific tabs at 1, 10, and 20, at the prompt type the following:

   $ **tabs 1,10,20** <Return>

3. To set tabs at every five characters, at the prompt type the following:

   $ **tabs -5** <Return>

Options

The following options specify one set of canned (predetermined) tab settings.

-a   Sets tab stops at 1, 10, 16, 36, 72 (IBM S/370 assembler, first format)

-a2   Sets tab stops at 1, 10, 16, 40, 72 (IBM S/370 assembler, second format)

-c   Sets tab stops at 1, 8, 12, 16, 20, 55 (COBOL normal format)

-c2   Sets tab stops at 1, 6, 10, 14, 49 (COBOL second format)

-c3   Sets tab stops at 1, 6, 10, 14, 18, 22, 26, 30, 34, 38, 42, 46, 50, 54, 58, 62, 67 (COBOL compact format)

-f   Sets tab stops at 1, 7, 11, 15, 19, 23 (Fortran)

-p   Sets tab stops at 1, 5, 9, 13, 17, 21, 25, 29, 33, 37, 41, 45, 49, 53, 57, 61 (PL/I)

-s   Sets tab stops at 1 ,10, 55 (SNOBOL)

-u   Sets tab stops at 1, 12, 20, 44 (UNIVAC 1100 assembler)

-n   Sets repetitive tab stops at columns $1+n$, $1+2*n$, $1+3*n$, etc. (the default is -8; -0 clears all tabs)

Notes

No consistent method of clearing tabs and settings exists among the different terminals. When using the tabs command, the leftmost column is referred to as 1, even if your terminal refers to it as 0 (zero).

Cautions

Many—perhaps most—terminals today do not have settable tabs. The tabs command has no effect on these terminals.

`tail`

Purpose

To display the last part of a file.

When To Use

Use `tail` to display the last portion of a file. The default is ten lines.

Normal Location

The `tail` command is located in the `/bin` directory.

Common Syntax and Examples

The syntax is as follows:

```
tail [number [lbc] [-f] [filename]
```

1. To display the last 10 lines in the file `things.to.do`, at the prompt type the following:

   ```
   $ tail things.to.do <Return>
   ```

2. To display the last three lines in the file named `customers`, at the prompt type the following:

   ```
   $ tail -3 customers <Return>
   ```

3. To display everything—from the 100th line on—in the file named `receivables`, at the prompt type the following:

   ```
   $ tail +100 receivables <Return>
   ```

4. To display the last thousand characters in the file named `output`, at the prompt type the following:

   ```
   $ tail -1000c output <Return>
   ```

5. To display new data as it is written to the file by another program, at the prompt type the following:

   ```
   $ tail -f output <Return>
   ```

   This option is especially useful with background processes. If you start a background process that writes data to a file, you can occasionally glimpse at its progress by executing a `tail -f` command on its output file; `tail` will watch for new data to appear in the file and display it as it is written. Press `<Break>` to exit `tail`.

Options

-number	Displays the last *number* of lines in the file.
+number	Displays the remainder of the file from the line specified by *number* to the end of the file. If neither + or – precedes the *number* specification, *number* is taken to mean +*number*.
c	Indicates that a number is in characters rather than lines. For example, -500c displays the last 500 characters, not the last 500 lines.
b	Indicates that a number is in blocks of 512 bytes rather than lines. For example, -2b displays the last two blocks.
-f	Causes `tail` to continuously try to read more data from the file. -f is useful when another process is appending to the file being read by `tail`, and you want to monitor the additions as they become available.

tee

Purpose

To make two copies of the output from another program. tee copies its standard *input* to its standard *output*, but makes a copy to a file.

When To Use

Use tee when you need to both see output on-screen as well as to save that output into a file.

Normal Location

tee is an executable file located in /bin. Normally, /bin is included in the user path, so you do not need to include the entire path name to use tee.

Common Syntax and Examples

tee is almost always used in conjunction with a pipe. tee receives data from the program that precedes it in the pipe; the data continues unaltered through tee, but is also copied to a file.

The syntax is as follows:

```
tee [-a] files
```

1. To save a listing of your files into a file named list, at the prompt type the following:

   ```
   $ ls | tee list <Return>
   ```

   This not only gives you the listing of the files on-screen, but also saves the listing in a file called list.

2. To accomplish the same result as in the previous example, except to append to an existing file named lists rather than creating the file list, at the prompt type the following:

   ```
   $ ls | tee -a lists <Return>
   ```

Options

-a   Appends to a file

-i   Ignores interrupts

-u   Causes the output to be unbuffered

test

Purpose

To test a variety of conditions; in effect, to ask a true/false question.

When To Use

The `test` command is used almost exclusively within shell programs in conjunction with an `if` or `while` statement to make decisions and to take one of two alternate actions based on the result of that decision.

Normal Location

On most systems, the `test` command is built into the shell; that is, the shell directly contains this command, and does not have to find a program on disk. On systems that do not have `test` built into the shell, the command is located in the `/bin` directory.

Common Syntax and Examples

The `test` command has two syntaxes, quite different from each other, and are as follows:

```
test expr

[expr]
```

The optional `expr` represents a true/false expression—essentially a question. `test` determines whether the expression is true or false and indicates its findings to the shell via a return code. An `if` or a `while` statement can then act upon the result, causing the shell program to take one of two courses.

The second syntax, in which the brackets surround the expression, is most unusual. Even though the word `test` does not appear in the command, it is still a `test` command being executed. This syntax was added because its use causes the `if` and `while` statements in shell programs to look like similar statements from other programming languages.

`test` can be used to ask a variety of questions. For example, the following lines from a shell program determine whether the file `msg` exists, and if so it is printed to the printer:

```
if test -f msg
then lp msg
fi
```

The `-f` option causes `test` to check whether a file exists, and whether it is a regular file (one that is not a directory or device file). If true, the statement between the `then` and `fi` is executed next; otherwise it is skipped.

Options

-r *filename*	Returns true if *filename* exists and is readable.
-w *filename*	Returns true if *filename* exists and can be written to.
-x *filename*	Returns true if *filename* exists and is executable.
-f *filename*	Returns true if *filename* exists and is a regular file (a data or text file rather than a directory or device file).
-d *filename*	Returns true if *file* exists and is a directory.
-z s1	Returns true if the length of string s1 is zero (string is any text); useful in shell programs to test whether a variable contains data.
-n s1	Returns true if the length of string s1 is nonzero.
s1 = s2	Returns true if string s1 and s2 are identical.
s1 != s2	Returns true if strings s1 and s2 are not identical.
n1 -eq n2	Returns true if two numbers, n1 and n2, are equal. Related options are -ne (not equal), -lt (less than), -le (less than or equal), -gt (greater than), and -ge (greater than or equal.
!	Means "not"; if this symbol appears between the word test (or the open bracket [) and the expression, the sense of the question is reverse. For example, test -d stuff asks whether the file named stuff is a directory; test ! -d stuff asks whether it is *not* a directory.

Cautions

If the second form of the test syntax ([ ]) is used, make certain that the square brackets are delimited by blank spaces.

Also see sh.

time

Purpose

To determine how much time a program or command takes to execute.

When To Use

Use time when you want to know how long a command takes to execute or how much of the computer's time the command requires.

Normal Location

time is located in the /bin directory.

Common Syntax and Examples

The syntax is as follows:

```
time command
```

For example, to determine the time required for spell to check the file letter1 and write a list of incorrect words to the file bad.words, at the prompt type the following:

```
$ time spell letter1 > bad.words <Return>
```

The spell command is executed as usual, checking the file letter1 for misspelled words and writing a list of incorrect words to the file bad.words. When the command is finished, however, time produces output that looks like this:

```
real    1m19.68s
user    0m11.11s
sys     0m3.26s
```

Three different times are shown:

- The real time, also called *elapsed* time, indicates that 1 minute 19.68 seconds elapsed from beginning to end. This is the time you would measure with a stopwatch.

- The user time is the amount of time the computer actually spent working on your command, in this case a little more than 11 seconds.

- The sys (system) time is the amount of time the computer spent performing operating-system functions that were required by your program—3.26 seconds in this example.

The distinction between the user time and system time is subtle. The sum of the two tells you how much time the computer actually required to complete your command. The difference between this sum and the elapsed time represents time spent by the computer on other matters.

touch

Purpose

To modify the access and modification times of specified files.

When To Use

Use touch when you want to change the times of last access and modification that UNIX maintains for each file. If no time is specified, the current time is used.

Normal Location

touch is an executable file located in /bin.

Common Syntax and Examples

The syntax is as follows:

touch [-am] [*mmddhhmm[yy]*] *filenames*

1. To modify only the modification time of a file named hello to be Feb 2nd 12:43 p.m., at the prompt type the following:

   $ $ touch -m 02021243 hello <Return>

2. To modify both the access time and modification time of a file named hello to the current date and time, at the prompt type the following:

   $ touch -am hello <Return>

   or

   $ touch hello <Return>

Options

-a	Modifies the access time of the file.
-c	Does not create a new file if the file does not already exist.
-m	Modifies the modification time of the file.
mmddhhmm[yy]	The first *mm* refers to the month. *dd* refers to the day. *hh* refers to the hour. The second *mm* refers to the minutes. *yy* refers to the year (this is optional).

Notes

The -am option is also the default option.

touch is most useful in conjunction with make, a tool used extensively by programmers.

Also see date.

true, false

Purpose

The purpose of true is to serve as a command that always returns a true value in a while statement. The purpose of false is to serve as a command that always returns a non-true value in a while statement.

When To Use

true is used almost exclusively in shell programs in conjunction with the while statement. false by itself has no practical uses (see Notes).

Normal Location

true and false are located in the /bin directory, along with related programs, depending on the computer system you are using.

Common Syntax and Examples

The true and false commands have the simplest possible syntax:

```
true
false
```

Neither of these commands executes an operation, but instead, return values to the shell. true indicates to the shell that the command was performed successfully, while false indicates that the command failed. The most common (and virtually the only) use of true is in a shell program in conjunction with a while loop:

```
while
    true
do
    command
done
```

The while loop repeats *command* as long as true succeeds. Because true always succeeds, the *command* is repeated forever—or at least until the user presses <Break>.

For example, you might want to monitor the progress of some background programs by doing a ps command every 15 seconds. You can accomplish this by including the following command in your shell script:

```
while true
do
    ps
    sleep 15
done
```

On most machines, a handful of commands also exist in the /bin directory that are linked to either true or false and can be used in a shell program to determine the type of machine on which it is running. These are usually useful only in sophisticated shell programs that perform very machine-dependent functions. For example, on an AT&T 3B2 you would find these commands available:

```
pdp11
vax
u370
u3b5
u3b15
u3b2
```

These files represent (respectively) a DEC PDP-11, DEC Vax, 370 mainframe, and AT&T 3B5, 3B15, and 3B2.

On a 3B2, all these commands are linked to false, except u3b2, which is linked to true. If your shell program needs to do something special only if running on a Vax, the program might include the following:

```
if vax
then
    commands
fi
```

On a 3B2, *commands* would not be performed because vax fails. On a DEC Vax, however, *commands* would be linked to true and succeed.

Also see sh.

tty

Purpose

To find out the name of the terminal or device on which you are working.

When To Use

Use tty in a shell script to determine whether standard input is from a terminal.

Normal Location

tty is an executable file located in /bin.

Common Syntax and Examples

The syntax is as follows:

```
tty [-s]
```

To display the path name of the workstation you are on, at the prompt type the following:

```
$ tty <Return>
```

Options

-s   Suppresses output so that tty can be used in a test condition

-l   Displays the synchronous line number if the terminal or workstation is connected to one

Notes

tty -s returns an exit status of 0 if the standard input is the terminal, 2 for invalid options, and 1 if not a terminal.

Also see sh.

umask

Purpose

To set permission codes for file creation.

When To Use

Use umask in login files to set permissions automatically on newly created files. The octal digits represent the read/write/execute permissions for the owner, the group, and others. umask is a binary *masking* operation, hence the name of the command.

Normal Location

The umask command is built into the shell; that is, the shell directly understands this program. No corresponding program exists in any of the system directories. The system profile, /etc/profile, usually contains a umask command to set a default for users who do not set their own.

Common Syntax and Examples

The syntax is as follows:

    umask [000]

1. To display the current permission mask, at the prompt type the following:

    $ **umask** <Return>

2. To set permissions on your files and directories to prevent others from writing to your files, at the prompt type the following:

    $ **umask 022** <Return>

   This sets the permission code to 644 on your files and 755 on your directories.

3. To set permissions on your files and directories to prevent read, write, and execute privileges by a group or others, at the prompt type the following:

    $ **umask 077** <Return>

   This creates the permission code of 600 on your files.

Notes

Notice that umask specifies the permissions to turn *off*—it is the reverse of the chmod command.

cp and mv are not affected by umask.

Also see sh *and* chmod.

uname

Purpose

To display the name of the computer and the operating system.

When To Use

Use uname when you need to print the name of the computer or the operating system that you are using.

Normal Location

uname is located in the /bin directory.

Common Syntax and Examples

The syntax is as follows:

```
uname [-snrvma]
```

To display information about your current operating system, at the prompt type the following:

```
$ uname -a <Return>
```

The output from the uname command differs somewhat from system to system, but here are two examples:

From an AT&T 3B1:

```
crescent crescent SYSTEM5 3.51 mc68k
```

From a Sequent computer running DYNIX:

```
icicle icicle 2.0v2 DYNIX i386
```

The first two names are the name of the system and the name by which it is known through communications networks—usually the two are the same. The third and fourth items identify the version and release of the operating system, and the last item is the type of computer equipment.

Options

-a   Displays all the information otherwise supplied by the options m, n, r, s, and v

-m   Displays the hardware currently in operation

-n   Displays the *nodename* (the name that identifies the system to a network)

-r   Displays the operating-system release numbers

-s   Displays the system name

-v   Displays the operating-system version

Notes

The -s flag is the default option. Be careful not to confuse the -r, the -s, and the -v options. It is recommended that you use them together, or use the -a option to display all the system information at once. On some systems, the -S option can also be used by the system administrator to set the name of the computer.

uniq

Purpose

To display and remove repeated lines in a file.

When To Use

Use `uniq` to compare adjacent lines of a file and remove any repeated occurrences of the line and then write to a file or to standard output. (Repetitive lines must be on consecutive lines to be found.)

Suppose that your company sells auto parts and that every time a customer makes a purchase, the customer's name goes into a file. To do an advertising mailout, you want to send a piece of mail to each person only once, regardless of how many purchases that person made. If the file is sorted, `uniq` will leave only a single line for each person.

Normal Location

The `uniq` command is located in the `/usr/bin` directory.

Common Syntax and Examples

The syntax is as follows:

```
$uniq [[-udc] [+n] [-n]] [input [output]]
```

To remove any duplicate lines in the file named `firstcopy` and send the output to the file named `finalcopy`, at the prompt type the following:

```
$ uniq firstcopy finalcopy <Return>
```

Options

−u	Specifies that the output file should contain only lines that were not repeated in the input file; with this option, the output file does not contain any copy of duplicated lines.
−d	Specifies that the output file should contain a single copy of only the lines that were duplicated. Lines that occurred only once are not in the output file.
−c	Prints each line once, preceded by a number indicating how many times it appeared in the file.
n*d*n	Ignores the first n number of fields together with any blanks (a field is defined here as a string of nonspace or nontab characters delimited by blanks).
+*n*	Ignores the first n number of characters on a line (fields are skipped before characters).
input	Specifies the name of the *input* file.
output	Specifies the name of the *output* file.

Notes

If no *input* or *output* file is given, the standard input or output is used. Before you use this command, you may want to perform a sort on your file to get any repeated lines in consecutive order so that they are picked up by the uniq command.

Also see comm *and* sort.

unpack

Purpose

To reverse the file compression created by the `pack` command.

When To Use

Use `unpack` to uncompress a file. `unpack` takes the compressed file with a `.z` extension and produces an unpacked file with the `.z` extension removed.

Normal Location

`unpack` is located in the `/usr/bin` directory.

Common Syntax and Examples

The syntax is as follows:

    unpack *filename*

To unpack the packed file `huge.file.z`, at the prompt type the following:

    $ **unpack huge.file.z** <Return>

or

    $ **unpack huge.file** <Return>

Because all packed files must end in `.z`, you do not have to type that part of the file name. When the command is completed, the packed file `huge.file.z` will be gone, and the unpacked file `huge.file` will exist instead.

Notes

The `.z` extension can be removed from the input file name. `unpack` **may not** work correctly for a number of reasons:

- The file cannot be opened.
- The file was not created by `pack`.
- A file with that name without the `.z` extension already exists.
- The unpacked file could not be written to.
- The file names are too long. They cannot be longer than the maximum file name length minus two.

Also see `pack`.

vi

Purpose

vi is a full-screen, visual editor.

When To Use

You may want to use vi as a standard editor on XENIX and most UNIX systems. vi is extremely powerful and fast as a full-screen editor. Most commands are single keystrokes that perform the editing functions.

Normal Location

vi is an executable file that is located in /usr/bin.

Common Syntax and Examples

Many options, subcommands, and editing functions are associated with vi. Included in the following list are only the options used to invoke the vi editor and a few simple commands used to get into and out of the editor.

-c *command*	Allows editing to begin by executing the specified *command*; usually a search or cursor-positioning command (SCO only).
-C	Functions as an encryption option. Similar to -x, except that -x assumes that files are already encrypted (SCO only).
-l	Invokes vi with certain options that are convenient to LISP programmers.
-r *filename*	Recovers a file after a system crash.
-R	Invokes vi in read-only mode. Useful when you want to use vi to browse through a file; this option prevents you from accidentally changing the file.
-t *tag*	Causes vi to determine which file should be edited by locating a name (a *tag*) in a special table-of-contents file, called a tag file.
-w *n*	Sets the window size to *n* lines (useful on windowing terminals).

Following are some editing commands for vi:

vi *filename*	Enables vi and reads the specified *filename* into the buffer.
ZZ	Exits vi, saves, and quits.
:wq	Writes and quits out of vi.
:q	Quits the editor. Works only if no changes have been made.

:q!	Quits the editor, even if changes have been made. Changes are not saved.
h	Moves the cursor to the left.
l	Moves the cursor to the right.
j	Moves the cursor down one line.
k	Moves the cursor up one line.
o	Opens a new line below your current position.
a	Appends after your current position.
i	Enables insert mode (before your current position).
R	Enables replace or overtype mode.
r	Replaces a single character.
<Esc>	Changes from insert or append mode to command mode.

Notes

When using vi, you need to be aware of two modes: the insert mode, which enables you to type text, and the command mode, which enables you to edit your text. The <Esc> key takes you from the insert mode to the command mode, but does not return you to the insert mode.

vi is an entire language of commands that provides enormous power. vi is not as user friendly as many text editors available today, but it remains among the most powerful. The major advantage of vi is that it is available with most implementations of UNIX and smart enough to work on virtually any type of console or terminal, a capability most editors lack.

The commands available with vi are too numerous to cover here. Many new users are intimidated by the hundreds of commands, but vi can be used quite effectively with just a fraction of the available commands. The remaining commands allow you to work more efficiently with fewer keystrokes.

Refer to Chapter 13, Appendix F, and your system documentation for more information on vi.

Also see ed, vedit, *and* view.

wall

Purpose

To write a message to all the users who are currently logged on the system.

When To Use

Use this command to broadcast a message to all users who are logged on. This message usually concerns system information, such as a notification of an impending system shutdown. Your message will be preceded by the following system heading:

```
Broadcast message from root (or user) Day, Mon dd hh:mm.
```

Normal Location

`wall` is an executable file located in `/etc`. To use `wall`, you must include the entire path name.

Common Syntax and Examples

The syntax is as follows:

```
/etc/wall
```

To use `wall`, at the prompt type the following:

```
$ /etc/wall <Return>
```

Now you can type the message that you want sent to all users on the system. End the message by typing an end-of-file signal, such as < ^ D>. This sends the message, preceded by the system header, to all users on the system.

Notes

To override any protection that users have set up, you must be the superuser.

Also see `write`.

wc

Purpose

To count the number of lines, words, and characters in a file or standard input.

When To Use

Use wc any time you need to find out the number of lines, words, and/or characters in a file or in a number of different files.

Normal Location

wc is an executable file located in /bin. Normally, /bin is included in the user path, so you do not need to include the entire path name to use wc.

Common Syntax and Examples

The syntax is as follows:

wc [-l] [-w] [-c] [*filename(s)*]

1. To obtain a line count in a file named words, at the prompt type the following:

   $ **wc -l words** <Return>

2. To obtain a character count in a file named words, at the prompt type the following:

   $ **wc -c words** <Return>

3. To obtain a line, word, and character count for a file named words, at the prompt type the following:

   $ **wc -lwc words** <Return>

   or

   $ **wc words** <Return>

wc is often useful in conjunction with pipes. Counting lines is especially useful in many situations. For example, if you want to know how many files are in the current directory, at the prompt type the following:

   $ **ls | wc -l** <Return>
   27
   $

The ls command produces a list of every file in the current directory, one per line. wc -l prints the number of lines in that listing.

Options

-l   Gives a line count

-w   Gives a word count

-c   Gives a character count

Notes

The l, w, and c options can be used interchangeably. The -lwc option is the default.

who

Purpose

To obtain a list of users who are currently logged on the system.

When To Use

Use the who command when you want to find out which users are currently working on the system and at what time they logged on. You can obtain more information by using the available options.

Normal Location

who is an executable file located in /bin. The who command examines the /etc/utmp file to obtain information. If a specific file is given, that file is examined usually through the /etc/wtmp file.

Common Syntax and Examples

The syntax is as follows:

```
who [-usATHldtasqrp] [am i] [am I] [file]
```

1. To obtain a list of users who are currently on the system, at the prompt type the following:

   $ **who** <Return>

   or

   $ **who -s** <Return>

2. To obtain a more detailed listing of the users on the system, including the amount of time since the last occurrence of activity on a particular terminal line, at the prompt type the following:

   $ **who -u** <Return>

3. To find the name of the station that you are currently working on, at the prompt type the following:

   $ **who am i** <Return>

   or

   $ **who am I** <Return>

Options

am i   Lists the name of the user invoking the command, the user who is logged on, and the login time

am I   Gives the same result as the am i option

-a   Turns on all options (except -q and -s)

-b   Lists the time and date of the last reboot

-d	Lists all dead, expired processes (used to determine why a process terminated)
-H	Prints headings above the regular output
-l	Lists the lines on which the system is waiting for a login
-p	Lists all active processes spawned by the system program `init`
-q	Provides a quick `who` command, displaying only the names and the number of users
-r	Lists the current run level of the `init` process; also lists the process-termination status, process ID, and process-exit status
-s	Lists the name, line, and time fields (this is the default)
-t	Lists the last change to the system clock by `root`
-T	Adds the write-status state of the terminal
-u	Lists the users who are logged on and the last occurrence of activity on that TTY line.

Notes

The options available vary from one system to another. The `who am i` command, for example, is not available in all implementations.

Also see `date`, `mesg`, *and* `ps`.

whodo

Purpose

To find out who is on the system and what processes any users are currently running.

When To Use

Use whodo when you want a quick summary of users on the system and what processes they are invoking.

Normal Location

whodo is a Bourne-shell file located in /etc. You need to use the complete path name to run whodo.

Common Syntax and Examples

The syntax is as follows:

```
/etc/whodo
```

This command lists the users currently on the system and lists the processes that are currently running under each user. The following shows an example of the output that you might obtain from executing the command:

```
Wed May 23 21:10:03 PDT 1990
XENIX
002      jimmy      07:52
002      1656        0:58 mscreen
002      16998       0:09 mscreen
002      17000       0:09 mscreen
002      17001       0:09 mscreen
005      brian      21:01
005      17736       0:02 rn
009      shawna     20:03
009      17746       0:00 sh
009      17747       0:01 ps
```

Notes

This command is usually invoked by the system administrator. The command is not available on every system.

Also see ps *and* who.

write

Purpose

To write to another user, causing immediate display on that user's station.

When To Use

Use this command to communicate interactively with another user who is currently logged on.

Normal Location

write is an executable file located in /bin.

Common Syntax and Examples

The syntax is as follows:

```
write user [tty]
```

The *user* argument specifies the name of the user you want to write to. The *tty* option specifies the terminal to which you want to send the message.

When first invoked, this command sends the following message to the user with whom you are trying to communicate:

```
"Message from your-logname your-tty . . ."
```

This sets up communication from you to the other user. Communication is strictly one way at this point. If the other user types a similar write command, specifying you as the receiver, a two-way communication is established. Either user can terminate his or her side of the conversation by pressing < ^ D>, which causes the message <EOT> to appear on the other user's terminal.

To write to a user named Brian, at the prompt type the following:

```
$ write brian <Return>
```

If there are more than two logins for Brian, you can specify the terminal to which you want to send the message. For example, if Brian is logged onto terminal tty0001 and you want to write to Brian, at the prompt type the following:

```
$ write brian tty001 <Return>
```

Notes

To determine which terminals users are logged on, refer to the who command.

When you write to a user, it is suggested that you use a certain protocol. For example, when you initiate the write, wait for the recipient to write back. Also, at the end of each message, use (o) or -o- (for "over") to indicate that you are finished typing; it is now the other user's turn. Use (oo) or -oo- (for "over and out") to indicate that the conversation is terminated.

Also see who.

— Part —
Six

Appendixes

DOS to UNIX Command Conversions

Chart of ASCII Values

Command Finder

Special Keys and Characters

Summary of ed *Commands*

Summary of vi *Commands*

DOS-to-UNIX
Command Conversions

If you are already familiar with MS-DOS commands, you may find a command-conversion table convenient for issuing UNIX commands.

DOS Command	UNIX Command	Function
CD (CHDIR)	chdir	Change to a different working directory. DOS uses the backslash \ as a directory separator. Remember that UNIX uses the slash /.
CLS	clear	Clear the display
	tput clear	Alternative display-clearing command
COMP	diff	Compare files and report differences
COPY	copy or cp	Copy source files to destination files
	cat	Concatenate version of COPY
DATE	date	Display the current time and date
TIME		
DIR	ls -l	Display a directory listing of files
ERASE (DEL)	rm	Delete (erase) files
FC	diff	Compare files and report differences
FIND	grep	Output lines that match a given pattern
MD (MKDIR)	mkdir	Create a new directory
MODE COM*n*	stty	Manage device characteristics
MORE	more or pg	Display file contents one screen at a time

DOS Command	UNIX Command	Function
PRINT	lp	Queue files for printer service
RD (RMDIR)	rmdir	Remove (delete) an empty directory
RENAME (REN)	mv	Rename files
SORT	sort	Sort file lines alphabetically
TYPE	cat	Display a file's contents on the output
CHKDSK	fsck	Check the integrity of a file system

Chart of ASCII Values

This appendix presents the ASCII octal and decimal values for the standard 127 ASCII codes used with UNIX. The ASCII set as used by the IBM extended character devices are shown for ASCII values 128-255. Many terminals use different character images for the extended characters above 127.

In the tables, a caret character (^) represents the Control (Ctrl) key. For example, ^C represents Ctrl-C. The *Graphic Character* column displays the IBM-style graphic character. Some display hardware uses a different graphic character set.

ASCII Codes

The codes for the American Standard Code for Information Interchange (ASCII) are presented in the following table.

Decimal	Hex	Octal	Binary	Graphic Character	ASCII Meaning
0	0	0	00000000		^@ NUL (null)
1	1	1	00000001	☺	^A SOH (start-of-header)
2	2	2	00000010	●	^B STX (start-of-transmission)
3	3	3	00000011	♥	^C ETX (end-of-transmission)
4	4	4	00000100	♦	^D EOT (end-of-text)
5	5	5	00000101	♣	^E ENQ (enquiry)
6	6	6	00000110	♠	^F ACK (acknowledge)
7	7	7	00000111	·	^G BEL (bell)
8	8	10	00001000	▪	^H BS (backspace)
9	9	11	00001001	○	^I HT (horizontal tab)
10	A	12	00001010	◙	^J LF (line feed - also ^Enter)
11	B	13	00001011	♂	^K VT (vertical tab)
12	C	14	00001100	♀	^L FF (form feed)
13	D	15	00001101	♪	^M CR (carriage return)
14	E	16	00001110	♫	^N SO

Decimal	Hex	Octal	Binary	Graphic Character	ASCII Meaning
15	F	17	00001111	☼	^O SI
16	10	20	00010000	◄	^P DLE
17	11	21	00010001	►	^Q DC1
18	12	22	00010010	↕	^R DC2
19	13	23	00010011	‼	^S DC3
20	14	24	00010100	¶	^T DC4
21	15	25	00010101	§	^U NAK
22	16	26	00010110	▬	^V SYN
23	17	27	00010111	↨	^W ETB
24	18	30	00011000	↑	^X CAN (cancel)
25	19	31	00011001	↓	^Y EM
26	1A	32	00011010	→	^Z SUB (also end-of-file)
27	1B	33	00011011	←	^[ESC (Escape)
28	1C	34	00011100	∟	^\ FS (field separator)
29	1D	35	00011101	↔	^] GS
30	1E	36	00011110	▲	^^ RS (record separator)
31	1F	37	00011111	▼	^_ US
32	20	40	00100000		Space
33	21	41	00100001	!	!
34	22	42	00100010	"	"
35	23	43	00100011	#	#
36	24	44	00100100	$	$
37	25	45	00100101	%	%
38	26	46	00100110	&	&
39	27	47	00100111	'	'
40	28	50	00101000	(	(
41	29	51	00101001	)	)
42	2A	52	00101010	*	*
43	2B	53	00101011	+	+
44	2C	54	00101100	,	,
45	2D	55	00101101	-	-
46	2E	56	00101110	.	.
47	2F	57	00101111	/	/
48	30	60	00110000	0	0
49	31	61	00110001	1	1
50	32	62	00110010	2	2
51	33	63	00110011	3	3
52	34	64	00110100	4	4
53	35	65	00110101	5	5
54	36	66	00110110	6	6
55	37	67	00110111	7	7
56	38	70	00111000	8	8
57	39	71	00111001	9	9
58	3A	72	00111010	:	:
59	3B	73	00111011	;	;
60	3C	74	00111100	<	<
61	3D	75	00111101	=	=
62	3E	76	00111110	>	>
63	3F	77	00111111	?	?

Decimal	Hex	Octal	Binary	Graphic Character	ASCII Meaning
64	40	100	01000000	@	@
65	41	101	01000001	A	A
66	42	102	01000010	B	B
67	43	103	01000011	C	C
68	44	104	01000100	D	D
69	45	105	01000101	E	E
70	46	106	01000110	F	F
71	47	107	01000111	G	G
72	48	110	01001000	H	H
73	49	111	01001001	I	I
74	4A	112	01001010	J	J
75	4B	113	01001011	K	K
76	4C	114	01001100	L	L
77	4D	115	01001101	M	M
78	4E	116	01001110	N	N
79	4F	117	01001111	O	O
80	50	120	01010000	P	P
81	51	121	01010001	Q	Q
82	52	122	01010010	R	R
83	53	123	01010011	S	S
84	54	124	01010100	T	T
85	55	125	01010101	U	U
86	56	126	01010110	V	V
87	57	127	01010111	W	W
88	58	130	01011000	X	X
89	59	131	01011001	Y	Y
90	5A	132	01011010	Z	Z
91	5B	133	01011011	[	[
92	5C	134	01011100	\	\
93	5D	135	01011101	]	]
94	5E	136	01011110	^	^
95	5F	137	01011111	_	_
96	60	140	01100000	'	'
97	61	141	01100001	a	a
98	62	142	01100010	b	b
99	63	143	01100011	c	c
100	64	144	01100100	d	d
101	65	145	01100101	e	e
102	66	146	01100110	f	f
103	67	147	01100111	g	g
104	68	150	01101000	h	h
105	69	151	01101001	i	i
106	6A	152	01101010	j	j
107	6B	153	01101011	k	k
108	6C	154	01101100	l	l
109	6D	155	01101101	m	m
110	6E	156	01101110	n	n
111	6F	157	01101111	o	o
112	70	160	01110000	p	p
113	71	161	01110001	q	q

Decimal	Hex	Octal	Binary	Graphic Character	ASCII Meaning
114	72	162	01110010	r	r
115	73	163	01110011	s	s
116	74	164	01110100	t	t
117	75	165	01110101	u	u
118	76	166	01110110	v	v
119	77	167	01110111	w	w
120	78	170	01111000	x	x
121	79	171	01111001	y	y
122	7A	172	01111010	z	z
123	7B	173	01111011	{	{
124	7C	174	01111100	|	|
125	7D	175	01111101	}	}
126	7E	176	01111110	~	~
127	7F	177	01111111	Δ	Del

Extended ASCII Codes

The extended ASCII codes are presented in the following table.

Decimal	Hex	Octal	Binary	Graphic Character
128	80	200	10000000	Ç
129	81	201	10000001	ü
130	82	202	10000010	é
131	83	203	10000011	â
132	84	204	10000100	ä
133	85	205	10000101	à
134	86	206	10000110	à
135	87	207	10000111	ç
136	88	210	10001000	ê
137	89	211	10001001	ë
138	8A	212	10001010	è
139	8B	213	10001011	ï
140	8C	214	10001100	î
141	8D	215	10001101	ì
142	8E	216	10001110	Ä
143	8F	217	10001111	Å
144	90	220	10010000	É
145	91	221	10010001	æ
146	92	222	10010010	Æ
147	93	223	10010011	ô
148	94	224	10010100	ö
149	95	225	10010101	ò
150	96	226	10010110	û
151	97	227	10010111	ù
152	98	230	10011000	ÿ
153	99	231	10011001	Ö
154	9A	232	10011010	Ü
155	9B	233	10011011	¢

Decimal	Hex	Octal	Binary	Graphic Character
156	9C	234	10011100	£
157	9D	235	10011101	¥
158	9E	236	10011110	Pt
159	9F	237	10011111	ƒ
160	A0	240	10100000	á
161	A1	241	10100001	í
162	A2	242	10100010	ó
163	A3	243	10100011	ú
164	A4	244	10100100	ñ
165	A5	245	10100101	Ñ
166	A6	246	10100110	ª
167	A7	247	10100111	º
168	A8	250	10101000	¿
169	A9	251	10101001	⌐
170	AA	252	10101010	¬
171	AB	253	10101011	½
172	AC	254	10101100	¼
173	AD	255	10101101	¡
174	AE	256	10101110	«
175	AF	257	10101111	»
176	B0	260	10110000	░
177	B1	261	10110001	▒
178	B2	262	10110010	▓
179	B3	263	10110011	│
180	B4	264	10110100	┤
181	B5	265	10110101	╡
182	B6	266	10110110	╢
183	B7	267	10110111	╖
184	B8	270	10111000	╕
185	B9	271	10111001	╣
186	BA	272	10111010	║
187	BB	273	10111011	╗
188	BC	274	10111100	╝
189	BD	275	10111101	╜
190	BE	276	10111110	╛
191	BF	277	10111111	┐
192	C0	300	11000000	└
193	C1	301	11000001	┴
194	C2	302	11000010	┬
195	C3	303	11000011	├
196	C4	304	11000100	─
197	C5	305	11000101	┼
198	C6	306	11000110	╞
199	C7	307	11000111	╟
200	C8	310	11001000	╚
201	C9	311	11001001	╔
202	CA	312	11001010	╩
203	CB	313	11001011	╦
204	CC	314	11001100	╠
205	CD	315	11001101	═

Decimal	Hex	Octal	Binary	Graphic Character
206	CE	316	11001110	╬
207	CF	317	11001111	╧
208	D0	320	11010000	╨
209	D1	321	11010001	╤
210	D2	322	11010010	╥
211	D3	323	11010011	╙
212	D4	324	11010100	╘
213	D5	325	11010101	╒
214	D6	326	11010110	╓
215	D7	327	11010111	╫
216	D8	330	11011000	╪
217	D9	331	11011001	┘
218	DA	332	11011010	┌
219	DB	333	11011011	█
220	DC	334	11011100	▄
221	DD	335	11011101	▌
222	DE	336	11011110	▐
223	DF	337	11011111	▀
224	E0	340	11100000	∝
225	E1	341	11100001	β
226	E2	342	11100010	Γ
227	E3	343	11100011	π
228	E4	344	11100100	Σ
229	E5	345	11100101	σ
230	E6	346	11100110	μ
231	E7	347	11100111	τ
232	E8	350	11101000	Φ
233	E9	351	11101001	θ
234	EA	352	11101010	Ω
235	EB	353	11101011	δ
236	EC	354	11101100	∞
237	ED	355	11101101	ϕ
238	EE	356	11101110	$\in$
239	EF	357	11101111	$\cap$
240	F0	360	11110000	$\equiv$
241	F1	361	11110001	$\pm$
242	F2	362	11110010	$\geq$
243	F3	363	11110011	$\leq$
244	F4	364	11110100	$\int$
245	F5	365	11110101	$\int$
246	F6	366	11110110	$\div$
247	F7	367	11110111	$\approx$
248	F8	370	11111000	°
249	F9	371	11111001	·
250	FA	372	11111010	·
251	FB	373	11111011	√
252	FC	374	11111100	ⁿ
253	FD	375	11111101	²
254	FE	376	11111110	∎
255	FF	377	11111111	

Command Finder

This appendix categorizes the UNIX commands both alphabetically and by their function in the program.

UNIX Commands in Alphabetical Order

Command	Function
at	Execute commands at a given time
banner	Print large letters on screen or printer
batch	Execute commands when the system load allows
bc	Invoke a basic calculator utility
cal	Display calendars
calendar	Manage a calendar-based reminder service
cancel	Unschedule printer jobs
cat	Concatenate (append) files
cd	Change the directory
chgrp	Modify the group IDs of files
chmod	Modify the permissions (ownership attributes) of files
chown	Modify the owner IDs of files
clear	Erase the terminal display
cmp	Compare two files for equality
comm	Process lines common to two files
copy	Copy files and directories of files
cp	Copy files
cron	Execute scheduled commands

633

Command	Function
crypt	Encrypt the contents of a file
csh	Invoke the C shell
cu	Call another UNIX system or terminal
cut	Cut selected text from lines in a file as output
date	Display (set) the system date and time
dc	Invoke a desktop calculator utility
df	Show the amount of free disk space
diff	Display differences between two text files
dircmp	Compare directories
display	Select the display colors (AIX)
du	Show disk usage
echo	Display text on the terminal
ed	Simple line editor
egrep	Extended grep command
env	Set and report the environment variables
false	Return a nonexit value
fgrep	grep command for fixed strings
file	Display the type of files
find	Find files in the directory tree
grep	Search a file for a matching pattern
head	Display the beginning of a text file
join	Join the output of files on a relation
kill	Stop (kill) processes
line	Read one input line into a variable
ln	Make a link to a file
lp	Send output to a system printer service
lpstat	Report the status of the printer-service queue
ls	List files in directories
mail	Initiate the electronic mail system
mesg	Control message-printing on a terminal
mkdir	Create a new directory
more	Display text on screen one line at a time
mv	Move (rename) files
newgrp	Change (log) the user to a different group
news	Display text (news) items of interest to users
nice	Adjust the priority of a new process

Command	Function
nl	Provide line numbers for lines of a file
nroff	Format text for output
pack	Compress file size
passwd	Maintain user's password
paste	Merge lines of text
pcat	Display (cat) contents of packed files
pg	Display text one screen at a time
pr	Print files on the screen or redirect to a printer
ps	Display process information
pwd	Display the name of the working directory
read	Read a single argument into a variable
rm	Remove (erase) files
rmdir	Remove an empty directory
setcolor	Select the display colors (SCO)
sh	Invoke another command shell (subshell)
sleep	Suspend command execution for a specified time
sort	Collate (alphabetize) lines of a file
spell	Check the spelling of words in a file
split	Divide a file into smaller parts
stty	Make or display terminal port settings
su	Enable superuser privilege (requires root password)
sync	Flush (write) disk buffers to disk
tabs	Set the default tabs
tail	Display the ending of a text file
tee	Copy (divert) output from a pipeline to a file in a second direction
test	Test conditions
time	Report the elapsed time of a command
touch	Update the access and modification time of files
true	Return an exit value
tty	Show the device name of the current terminal
umask	Establish the file-creation mode for a user's files
uname	Print the name of the UNIX system servicing a user
uniq	Report repeated lines in a file
unpack	Expand packed files
vi	Full-screen visual editor

Command	Function
wall	Write a message to all users
wc	Count lines, words, and characters in a file
who	Display system's logged users
who am i	Report the user's login name
whodo	Determine which user is doing what process
write	Output a message on another user's terminal

UNIX Commands by Function

Function	Command
A grep command for fixed strings	fgrep
Adjust the priority of a new process	nice
An extended grep command	egrep
Call another UNIX system or terminal	cu
Change (log) user to a different group	newgrp
Change the directory	cd
Check spelling of words in a file	spell
Collate (alphabetize) lines of a file	sort
Compare directories	dircmp
Compare two files for equality	cmp
Compress file size	pack
Concatenate (append) files	cat
Control message-printing on a terminal	mesg
Copy (divert) output from a pipeline to a file	tee
Copy files and directories of files	copy
Copy files	cp
Count lines, words, and characters in a file	wc
Create a new directory	mkdir
Cut selected text from lines in a file as output	cut
Determine which user is doing what process	whodo
Display (cat) packed files' contents	pcat
Display (set) the system date and time	date
Display calendars	cal
Display differences in two text files	diff
Display process information	ps
Display the system's logged users	who

Function	Command
Display text (news) items of interest to users	news
Display text one screen at a time	more
Display text one screen at a time	pg
Display text on the terminal	echo
Display the beginning of a text file	head
Display the ending of a text file	tail
Display the name of the working directory	pwd
Display a file's type	file
Divide a file into smaller parts	split
Enable superuser privilege (requires root password)	su
Encrypt the contents of a file	crypt
Erase the terminal display	clear
Establish the file-creation mode for a user's files	umask
Execute commands at a given time	at
Execute commands when the system load allows	batch
Execute scheduled commands	cron
Expand packed files	unpack
Find files in the directory tree	find
Flush (write) disk buffers to disk	sync
Format text for ouput	nroff
Full-screen visual editor	vi
Initiate the electronic mail system	mail
Invoke a basic calculator utility	bc
Invoke a desktop calculator utility	dc
Invoke another command shell (subshell)	sh
Invoke the C shell	csh
Join the output of files on a relation	join
List files in directories	ls
Maintain a user's password	passwd
Make a link to a file	ln
Make or display terminal port settings	stty
Manage a calendar-based reminder service	calendar
Merge lines of text	paste
Modify file permissions (ownership attributes)	chmod
Modify files' group IDs	chgrp
Modify files' owner IDs	chown
Move (rename) files	mv

Function	Command
Output a message on another user's terminal	write
Print files on the screen or redirect to a printer	devicepr
Print large letters on screen or printer	banner
Print the name of the UNIX system servicing a user	uname
Process lines common to two files	comm
Provide line numbers for lines of a file	nl
Read a single argument into a variable	read
Read one input line into a variable	line
Remove (erase) files	rm
Remove an empty directory	rmdir
Report repeated lines in a file	uniq
Report the elapsed time of a command	time
Report the status of the printer service queue	lpstat
Report the user's login name	who am i
Return an exit value	true
Return a non-exit value	false
Search a file for a matching pattern	grep
Select the display colors (AIX)	display
Select the display colors (SCO)	setcolor
Send output to a system printer service	lp
Set and report the environment variables	env
Set the default tabs	tabs
Show amount of disk space still free	df
Show disk usage	du
Show the device name of the current terminal	tty
Simple line editor	ed
Stop (kill) processes	kill
Suspend execution for a specified time	sleep
Test conditions	test
Unschedule printer jobs	cancel
Update the access and modification times of files	touch
Write a message to all users	wall

Special Keys and Characters

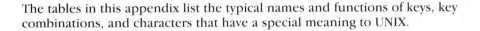

The tables in this appendix list the typical names and functions of keys, key combinations, and characters that have a special meaning to UNIX.

Special Terminal Keys and Functions

This table lists the typical names and functions of the special keys. Your keyboard may have other special keys or fewer special keys. Remember also that you do not type the angle brackets (< >) that enclose some of the key names shown here.

Key Name	Function
Esc (Escape)	Causes a return to a previous function in an applications program and some UNIX utilities.
Ctrl (Control)	Pressed simultaneously with a letter key to indicate that a terminal-control function is desired. In this book, the Ctrl key is indicated in text by the circumflex (^). For example, Ctrl-D is shown as < ^ D>. Note that the letter typed at the same time as Ctrl may be typed in either upper- or lowercase letters.
Enter	Terminates an input you are typing and sends the line to the system for processing. You must press <Enter> or <Return> before UNIX will execute your command.
Return	Return is an alternate name for <Enter>. The name Return is derived from a typewriter's carriage return (CR) action. In this book, <Enter>, <Return>, and <CR> all indicate the end of input.
Del (Delete)	Deletes the current command line or, on some systems, erases the character under the cursor.

639

Key Name	Function
Break	The Break key stops the execution of most UNIX programs and commands. During the login process, <Break> signals the system to try an alternative baud rate.
Alt (Alternate)	Pressing <Alt> simultaneously with another key gives the system an alternative value for the other key. <Alt> is often found on IBM PC-type keyboard layouts.
Backspace	Pressing <Backspace> backs the cursor one character to the left while erasing the character. On most terminals, use <Backspace> to correct mistakes.
Arrow Keys → ← ↑ ↓	Some applications programs use the arrow keys to move the cursor on-screen.
Cursor-Control Keys	Like the arrow keys, the cursor-movement keys (PgUp, PgDn, Home, and End) are used by some applications programs to move the cursor on-screen.
Function keys (F1-F12)	The function keys (F1-F12) signal the system to perform a predetermined function. The exact function assigned to each function key is determined by the application that uses function keys.

Special Command Keys and Functions

This table lists keys and key combinations that provide useful command-line control. Note that keys shown enclosed in angle brackets (< >) are nonprinting. You will not see a character on-screen when you type a nonprinting character.

Key	Meaning to UNIX
# (sharp or pound)	Erases a character to the left. The # is used on systems without active Backspace keys.
@ (at sign)	Deletes (kills) the current line. The system ignores the contents of the line.
^C (Ctrl-C)	Interrupts the current process by stopping it. <^C> is called the UNIX *interrupt* character.
Del	The Delete key. <Del> acts as the interrupt character in place of <^C> on many systems.
^D (Ctrl-D)	Stops input from the input sources of some commands, or logs you off the system. <^D> is UNIX's end-of-file (EOF) indicator.
^H (Ctrl-H)	Acts the same as the Backspace key. Use <^H> if your terminal does not have a Backspace key.
^I (Ctrl-I)	Performs a horizontal tab operation on terminals that do not have a Tab key.

Key	Meaning to UNIX
^ S (Ctrl-S)	Stops display output until < ^ Q> is pressed. In communications terminology, < ^ S> is called *XOFF*. Use < ^ S> to temporarily stop screen output from scrolling off the screen.
^ Q (Ctrl-Q)	Restarts a display that you have temporarily stopped by pressing < ^ S>. If your terminal appears to be locked, pressing < ^ Q> will sometimes restore normal operation. In communications terminology, < ^ Q> is called *XON*.

Bourne Shell Special Characters and Interpretations

Special characters enable the shell to parse a command line and to interpret the command's elements in ways that are different from the literal interpretation. This table lists the shell's special characters and the interpretation that the shell makes when those characters are used. Recall that the special interpretation occurs only when the character is encountered as part of command-line input. At other times, such as when you are running a program, these characters have no special meaning.

Character	Interpretation
$	Use the rest of the word as the contents of a previously defined variable
;	Break the command line into separate commands using the ; as the separator
\	Remove the special meaning of the character that immediately follows
"	Remove the special delimiting meaning of spaces and certain other special characters contained between a pair of double-quote (") characters
'	Remove the special meaning of any special characters contained between a pair of single-quote (') characters
`	Execute the command contained between a pair of ` characters and use the results as the argument for this position of the command line
&	Execute this command as a background process

The Expansion Characters and Their Meanings

This table lists the file-name argument expansion characters and their meanings to the shell. In a command, these characters enable the matching of file names and parts of file names based on the position of the expansion character relative to the same character position in the file names in a directory. Non-expansion characters in file-name arguments must exactly match their counterparts in the file-name pattern.

Character	Meaning to the Shell
?	Match any character in this position.
*	Match any characters.
[characters]	Match one character of the sequence of characters contained within the brackets, or one character of the range of characters contained within the brackets. If the characters are preceded by the ! character, match characters are *not* included.

Summary of ed Commands

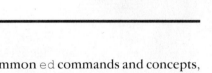

This appendix provides a summary of the more common ed commands and concepts, including start-up options, basic editing procedures, and advanced techniques. This appendix is not meant as a complete reference to ed. For more information on ed, see Chapter 12 and the Reference Manual provided with your system.

The command listings in this appendix follow two different formats. The tabular presentation of the commands lists the shorthand form of the command. Following the shorthand listings are sections that present the longer, more expanded version of the command and an accompanying explanation.

Starting ed

To start up the ed editor, enter the following command:

> **ed** <Return>

When you start ed, command mode is the active mode.

The complete syntax for ed is as follows:

    ed [-s] [-p string] [-x] [-C] [filename]

The start-up options are explained as follows:

-s	Suppresses the display of file and buffer character counts
-p string	Displays a user-supplied prompt string, such as cMc:1:/a/usr/dennis>
-x	Enables encryption and simulates an X command
-C	Enables encryption and simulates a C command
filename	The name of the file to be edited or created

643

Basic Commands and Messages

?   A message that indicates that you have made an error in entering a command. ? is considered ed's most basic error message.

!   When issued while ed is in command mode, the ! command acts as an escape character and tells ed that subsequent keystrokes are to be accepted as UNIX shell commands. ed then exits to the UNIX shell, where the commands are executed. Generally, control reverts to the ed editor after the command is executed.

a   Enables you to add text to the buffer *after* the current line. The a issued without parameters is a shorthand notation, and new text is appended after the current line.

h   Displays the most recent error message.

H   Redisplays the most recent error message, and turns on the automatic display of verbose error messages. H is a toggle command; repeated entry turns the display of verbose error messages on and off. When you start ed, error-message display initially is set to off.

i   Enables you to insert text before the current line in the text buffer. This is the shorthand form of the command, in which the implied address is the current line. At least one text line must be present in the buffer before ed will accept the insert command.

p   Prints (displays) the current line.

P   Turns on the * command-mode prompt. P is a toggle command; when used repeatedly, it turns the * prompt on and off. When you start ed, the command-mode prompt is initially set to off.

q   Quits the current editing session. If you issue the q command to exit from ed without first saving the text buffer's contents to disk, however, ed responds with the ? error indicator. If you issue a second q command, ed quits without saving the buffer's contents.

Q   Quits ed without displaying a warning prompt or verifying whether the buffer's contents have been saved.

w   Writes the text buffer's contents to the current disk file.

Several of the basic ed commands have long forms as well as shorthand forms. These commands and their complete syntax are explained in the following sections.

The Append Command

The complete syntax for the append command is as follows:

```
[#]a
text
.
```

In this generic form of the a (*a*ppend) command, the # represents any valid line number. The command 0a, for example, adds new text after line 0 or before the first line in the buffer. If the buffer is empty, the command adds the new text as the first line in the buffer. The command 3a appends new text after line 3 in the buffer. The line number, however, is optional. If you issue the append command without a line number, ed appends the new text after the current line.

The Insert Command

The complete syntax for the insert command is as follows:

```
[#]i
text
.
```

In this generic form of the i command, the # represents any valid line number. The line number is optional; if issued without a line number, i inserts text before the current line in the buffer. The command 5i, for example, opens the text buffer for insertion before line 5.

The Print (Display) Command

The complete syntax for the p (*p*rint) command is as follows:

```
[#,#]p
```

In this generic form of the p command, the #, # represents the range of lines to be printed or displayed. The command 3,7p, for example, displays lines 3, 4, 5, 6, and 7 on-screen.

The Write Command

The complete syntax for the w (*w*rite) command is as follows:

```
[#,#]w [filename]
```

In this generic form of the w command, the #, # represents the range of lines to be written to disk, in the file specified by *filename*. The command 3,7w test.doc, for example, writes lines 3, 4, 5, 6, and 7 to the disk file named test.doc. This form of the write command is useful for cut and paste operations.

If you do not specify a file name, the current file is used. If no current file exists, ed displays an error message. The w command does not change the address of dot (the current line).

If you do not specify a range of lines with the write command, ed writes the entire contents of the buffer to the named disk file.

Modifying Text

This section lists the basic ed commands for modifying text, special characters used for editing, the pseudo-address characters used with ed, and more advanced editing commands.

Text-Modification Commands

#=	Displays the line number of the line specified by #.
e	Re-reads the previously saved version of the current file into the buffer. If no text buffer has been saved, an error occurs.
f	Displays the current name of the text file in the buffer.
l	Displays the entire contents of the text buffer.
n	Displays a line number and a tab character before each line of text in the buffer.
/text/	Searches forward from the current line to the last line of the buffer, in order to find the specified search string (text).
?text?	Searches backward from the current line to the first line of the buffer, in order to find the specified search string (text).
//	Searches forward for the most recently defined search criteria.
??	Searches backward for the most recently defined search criteria.

Several of the text-modification commands have long forms as well as shorthand forms. These commands and their complete syntax are explained in the following sections.

The Equal Command

The complete syntax for the = command is as follows:

```
[#]=
```

The = command displays the specified line's number. This command enables you to determine the current line's number quickly. You also can specify a pseudo address or relative address with = in order to determine a line's number. When issued by itself, = displays the last line of the buffer.

The Edit Command

The complete syntax for the edit command is as follows:

```
e [filename]
```

When issued with no file name, the e (*edit*) command re-reads the previously saved version of the current file into the buffer. If you are editing the current file and want to start over, issue the e command without specifying a file name; ed then loads the most recently saved version of the file into the buffer, overwriting the buffer's current contents.

In this generic version of the e command, *filename* represents the name of the file you want to load into the buffer. The new file may be different from the file currently being edited. If you do not specify a file name, the current file is used.

The File Name Command

The syntax of the file name command is as follows:

```
f [filename]
```

You use the f (*file name*) command to display or change the name of the file currently in the buffer. In this form of the f command, *filename* represents the new name you want to give to the file currently in the buffer. This form of the f command changes the buffer's file name to the name you specify. If you issue the f command without specifying a file name, ed displays the name of the file currently in the buffer.

The List Command

The complete syntax for the list command is as follows:

```
[#,#]l
```

In this generic form of the l (*list*) command, the #, # options represent the range of lines to be displayed on-screen. At the completion of the list command, the current line is the last line displayed.

The Number Command

The complete syntax for the number command is as follows:

```
[#,#]n
```

In this generic form of the n (*number*) command, the #, # options represent the range of lines to be displayed on-screen. The number command is similar to the p (*print*) command, except that n displays a line number and a tab character before the line of text. At the completion of the number command, the last line printed becomes the current line.

Special Characters Used with ed

\<Tab\>	You can insert tab characters into the text buffer's contents by using the keyboard's Tab key. The number of spaces moved by the Tab key depends on the configuration of the tab settings for your terminal.
\<^V\> [*nondisplayed character*]	When placed in front of a nondisplayed character in a text file, the \<^V\> (Ctrl-V) enters the nondisplayed character's ASCII code into the buffer. The \<^V\>\<^G\> sequence, for example, places the ASCII code for a beep tone into the text buffer.
\<Return\>	In command mode, when you press \<Return\>, ed moves to the next line, makes that line the current line, and displays the line on-screen. If the buffer's last line is the current line when \<Return\> is pressed, ed responds with an error message.
\	To strip special characters of their meaning in text searches or search-and-substitution operations, prefix special characters with a backslash (\).

Pseudo-Address Characters for ed

You can address lines of text in ed by using relative, absolute, or pseudo addresses. You can use one, two, or no addresses with ed commands, depending on the command and the context in which it is used. You can use either a , (comma) or a ; (semicolon) to separate addresses. When addresses are separated by a comma, the current line does not change when the second address is calculated. When the addresses are separated by a semicolon, ed makes the first address the current line, and then calculates the second line. The semicolon is helpful for searching for the second occurrence of a search pattern.

$	Represents the last line in the buffer.
,	Represents the address range 1,$ (that is, the first line through the last line of the buffer.
;	Represents the address range .,$ (that is, the current line through the last line in the buffer).
.	Represents the current line. Therefore, the command .p prints the current line's contents.
1	The number 1 makes the buffer's first line the current line and displays it. This is equivalent to the 1p command.
#	A user-supplied value that represents any valid line number. The number 7, for example, makes the buffer's seventh line the current line and displays it. This is equivalent to the 7p command.
'*char*	Addresses the line of the buffer marked by a user-supplied character (represented here by *char*)

Advanced Editing Commands

d   The delete command, which deletes the specified range of lines from the buffer.

g   The global substitution option, which expands the scope of the search to the entire buffer or entire line. If the option precedes the command, the entire buffer is searched. If the option follows the command, the entire line is searched. The same is true for the search-and-substitute command.

m   The move command, which moves the specified range of lines to a new location in the buffer.

s   The substitute command, which searches for a specified string and replaces it with another specified string of text.

r   The read command, which reads the contents of the current file into the buffer.

t   The copy command, which copies a specified range of lines to another location in the buffer.

j   The join command, which removes the carriage-return characters between addressed lines, making the addressed lines one line.

c   The change command, which eliminates unwanted text and inserts replacement text.

Several of these advanced commands have long forms as well as shorthand forms. These commands and their complete syntax are explained in the following sections.

The Substitute Command

The s (substitute) command searches the current line for the specified search string (represented in the following generic form by *stext*). If ed finds the search string, the command replaces the string with the substitute, or replacement text (represented here by *rtext*).

```
s/stext/rtext/
[#,#]s/stext/rtext/[o]
```

In this generic form of the substitute command, the #,# options represent the line numbers at which the search operation must start and stop. If you specify the g (global) pseudo address at the beginning of the command, all lines in the buffer are searched. If a match is found on any addressed line, ed substitutes the first occurrence of *stext* with *rtext*. If no o (option) is supplied, only the first occurrence of *stext* is replaced by *rtext*. If you specify the global pseudo address as the final option, all occurrences of *stext* in the line are substituted with *rtext*. If you specify a number as the final option, only the *nth* occurrence of *stext* is replaced by *rtext*. If no match is found, ed displays an error message.

The syntax for the global substitution command is as follows:

```
g/stext1/s/stext/rtext/g
```

This command searches every line in the text buffer for *stext1* (because the global pseudo address g is given at the beginning of the command), and replaces all occurrences of *stext2* in the line (because the global pseudo address is given at the end of the command) with *rtext*.

```
[#,#]g/search text/command
[#,#]g/search/
```

The global pseudo address marks every line that matches the *search text*, and for every marked line, the command is executed. The global command moves to the first match and waits for the user to input a command and then moves to the next match and so on. All but the open text buffer and global commands are accepted.

The Copy Command

The complete syntax for the copy command is as follows:

```
[#,#]t#
```

The addressed lines of text are copied and are placed after the # address (which is specified immediately after the t command).

The Delete Command

The syntax for the delete command is as follows:

```
[#,#]d
```

This command deletes all lines, from the buffer, in the addressed range. The line remaining after the last deleted line becomes the current line.

The Move Command

The syntax for the move command is as follows:

```
[#,#]m#
```

The move command moves the set of addressed lines [#,#] after the line specified by # (which is specified immediately after the m command). To move the addressed lines to the beginning of the buffer, use m0 after the addressed range. The move command will place the text after line 0, which is the first line of the buffer.

The Read Command

The syntax of the read command is as follows:

```
[#,#]r [filename]
```

In this command, the contents of the file specified by *filename* are read from the disk and placed in the buffer after the addressed line. If no file name is given, the command reads in the contents of the current file. If there is no current file name, an error message is displayed.

The Join Command

The syntax for the join command is as follows:

```
j <Return>
```

The join command removes the <Return> characters between addressed lines, making the addressed lines one line. Consider the following sample join command:

```
[2,3]j
```

This command joins the first line addressed (line 2) through the last line addressed (that is, line 3) into a new line 2. If you do not specify a line, or if you specify only one line, the command does nothing; however, no error message is given.

The Change Command

The change command eliminates unwanted text and inserts replacement text. The syntax for the change command is as follows:

```
[#,#]c
```

In this generic form of the command, #, # represents the range of lines to be deleted from the buffer. The change command deletes the first line addressed through the last line addressed and then accepts replacement text, which you enter into the buffer.

The change command is really a combination of two commands—the delete command and the insert command. The change command enables you to perform the functions of both the delete and the insert commands, as shown in the following example:

```
*  3,5c <Return>
new line 3
new line 4
new line 5
. <Return>
*
```

This set of instructions deletes lines 3 through 5 from the buffer, and replaces them with three new lines of text.

Metacharacters Used in ed

Metacharacters are characters whose meaning is not literal. ed expands a metacharacter to a new meaning. Metacharacters should not be confused with pseudo addresses. The dot (.) metacharacter is not the same as the dot pseudo address. You can use pseudo addresses only when *addresses* are accepted; you can use metacharacters only when *characters* are accepted. When in text-entry mode, however, ed does not recognize either pseudo addresses or metacharacters.

Special note should be given to the escape (\) character, which removes special meaning from the asterisk (*) and slash (/) characters, and from any character that has a special meaning to ed.

    .   Represents any single character

    *   Represents zero or more occurrences of the character preceding it

    $ Represents the end of a line

    &   A variable that takes on the value of a string in a substitution command

    \   An escape character, which nullifies any special meaning that may be attached to the character that follows the backslash

    ^   Represents the beginning or a line in the text buffer

    []   Delineates a set of zero or more characters as a search string, where any one of the characters in the set satisfies the match criteria

The Period Metacharacter (.)

The . (period) metacharacter represents any single character. For example, to tell ed to search the buffer for the strings x+y and x-y, you specify /x.y/ as the search expression. This search expression finds all occurrences of x(*any character*)y. The period metacharacter matches any single character except the newline character.

The Asterisk Metacharacter (*)

The * (asterisk) metacharacter represents zero or more consecutive occurrences of the character preceding it. The search expression /a*/, for example, searches for zero or one or more consecutive occurrences of the letter *a*. The * metacharacter is difficult to use effectively, however, unless it is used in conjunction with other metacharacters.

The Circumflex Metacharacter (^)

The ^ metacharacter represents the beginning or a line in the text buffer. To search for an expression that appears only at the beginning of a line, use /^text/.

The Bracket Metacharacters ([ ])

The [ ] (bracket) metacharacters are used in pairs. You use these characters to delineate a set of zero or more characters as a search string. To search for all numeric characters, for example, use [01234567889]. You can abbreviate this expression as [0-9], where the - (minus sign) means that the search includes the integer numbers between 0 and 9. Thus, ed interprets the search expression /[0-9]/ to mean "search the buffer for the first occurrence of any number." You can use bracket metacharacters to search for any set of characters in the text buffer. To search for all uppercase alphabetic characters, use the search expression /[A-Z]/; to search for all lowercase alphabetic characters, use /[a-z]/. To search for all alphabetic characters, regardless of case, use [A-Za-z].

The Dollar Sign Metacharacter ($)

The $ (dollar sign) metacharacter represents the end of a line. When you specify the dollar sign metacharacter (as in the expression /text$/), ed searches for the specified search string only at the end of each line in the buffer.

The Ampersand Metacharacter (&)

The & (ampersand) metacharacter is frequently used with the substitution command. The substitution expression s/this/&isn't/ searches for the first occurrence of the word "this" on the current line, and replaces it with the words "this isn't." The & represents the characters on the left side of the substitution string. You can use the & in the substitution string as often as required.

Think of the & as a variable that takes on the value of the search string in a substitution command. From the preceding example, the & takes on the value "this" (that is, & = this).

The Backslash Metacharacter (\)

The \ (backslash) metacharacter is an escape character, which nullifies any special meaning that may be attached to the character that follows the backslash. If you want to search for a period in a sentence, for example, rather than have the period represent any single character, use the \. expression. The backslash is a very important metacharacter; it strips control characters, metacharacters, and pseudo addresses of their special characteristics, and converts them into ordinary text characters.

Markers

Markers enable you to identify a line of text by using a character marker rather than a line number. You use the k (line marker) command to refer to each line of text symbolically. A marker command marks the addressed line with the pseudo-address character *x*, where *x* is any letter from a-z. When no address is used, the current line is marked. You can refer to this pseudo-address character by using the ' command. To go to a line marked by the letter a pseudo address, for example, you enter **'a**. This command makes the marked line current. You can use only the letters [a-z] as markers.

Variations of UNIX Text Editors

UNIX includes several text editors. Some are variations of ed; others are independent programs.

ex	Provides ed functions
red	A restricted ed editor
sed	A stream ed editor
bfs **and** vedit	Read-only ed editor
vi	Screen-oriented UNIX editor

Summary of vi Commands

This appendix provides a summary of the more common vi commands in tabular format. This appendix is not meant as a complete reference to vi. For more information on vi, see Chapter 13 and the Reference Manual provided with your system.

Terminal Configuration

Before you execute the vi command, you must ensure that your terminal type is properly identified in your exportable environment. The TERM variable (if it has been defined) contains your terminal type.

The terminal-assignment example that follows is for Bourne-shell users. If you do not know your terminal type, ask your system administrator for assistance.

To display your TERM variable setting, use the following command:

```
$ echo $TERM <Return>
```

If your displayed terminal type does not match the value of TERM, you will need to change it. To change your terminal type for the duration of this login session, use the following form:

```
$ set TERM=vt100 <Return>
$ export TERM <Return>
$
```

In this example, vt100 is an example of a terminal type.

Note that your terminal *type* is not the same as the *name* of your terminal. Your terminal type must match one of the terminal types contained in the termcap file.

The termcap file is normally located in the /etc directory. If you are not familiar with the termcap file, see Chapter 8 or consult your system administrator.

Starting vi

The generic syntax for the vi command is as follows:

    vi [-t tag] [-r file] [-L] [-wn] [-R] [-x] [-C] [-c command] [filename ...]

The syntax elements are explained as follows:

-t tag	Edits the file containing the specified tag and positions the cursor in the vi editor at the tag position.
-r filename	Edits filename after an editor or system crash.
-L	Lists the name(s) of the files saved as a result of an editor or system crash.
-w#	Sets the default screen size to the size specified by #.
-R	Enters vi in the read-only mode.
-x	Encryption option.
-C	Encryption option.
-c command	Enters vi and begins by executing the editor command, command.
filename ...	filename ... specifies one or more files to be edited.

vi Modes

Command Mode

Text Input Mode

Last Line or Command Line Mode (use : / ? and !)

Numeric Arguments Used with vi Commands

You can include a numeric argument with any vi command by specifying the number of repetitions as follows:

    [#command]

The # is a positive integer between 0 and 256.

Used with the z, G, or | commands, # determines the line or column number. The default is 1 for z and |, and the end of the buffer for G.

Used with the < ^D> or < ^U> commands, # sets the scroll amount (default is 1).

Used with a, A, i, or I commands, # replicates the current input.

Used with most other commands, $ repeats the effects of the command # times. For example, 5dd deletes the current line and the following 4 lines.

Insert, Append, and Open Commands

ea*char* <Esc>	Places the character *char* at the end of the current word.
#i	Inserts the entered *text* # times before the cursor position.
#I	Inserts the entered *text* # times before the first non-whitespace character of the line.
#a	Appends the entered *text* # times after the character at the current cursor position.
#A	Appends the entered *text* # times after the last character at the end of the line.
#o	Opens the # of lines below the current line.
#O	Opens the # of lines above the current line.

Input Mode Text Editing Commands

<Backspace>	Moves the cursor one character to the left; character is deleted.
< ^W> or < ^w>	Moves the cursor to the beginning of the word to the left of the current cursor position; the word is deleted.
< ^U> or < ^u>	Deletes to the beginning of line.
<tab>	Hard tab moves one tab stop to the right.
< ^T>	Soft tab one shift width to the right.
< ^D>	Soft tab one shift width to the left.
0< ^D>	Removes soft tabs (shift widths) on the current line.
^< ^D> or ^< ^d>	Soft tab in the opposite direction.
< ^V> or < ^v> *char* or < ^Q> or < ^q> *char*	Strips *char* of its special meaning.

<@> or <^x> or <^u>	Deletes backwards to the beginning of input on the current line.
<^I> <^i>	Vertical tab.
<Return>	Performs both a line feed and a newline.
<Esc> or ^	Terminates input mode
<^G>	Sounds the computer's bell.

Cursor-Movement Commands

#h	Moves the cursor left # characters. If no # is specified, the default is 1.
#j	Moves the cursor down # lines. If no # is specified, the default is 1.
#l	Moves the cursor right # characters. The default is 1.
#k	Moves the cursor up # lines. Default is 1.
0	Moves the cursor to the beginning of the line.
^	Moves the cursor to the beginning of the line at the first non-whitespace character.
#$	Moves the cursor to the end of the line, # lines from the current location.
#w	Moves the cursor the # of words forward (considers punctuation as a separate word).
#W	Moves the cursor the # of words forward (ignores punctuation).
#b	Moves the cursor the # of words to the left (considers punctuation as a separate word).
#B	Moves the cursor the # of words to the left (ignores punctuation).
#e	Moves the cursor to the end of the # of words forward (considers punctuation as a separate word).
#E	Moves the cursor to the end of the # of words forward (ignores punctuation).
#G	Goes to line #. G moves to the end of the file.
#+	Moves the cursor to the first character # lines down from the current location.
#-	Moves the cursor to the first character # lines up from the current location.
#_	Moves the cursor to the first character #-1 lines down from the current location.
#|	Moves the cursor to column #; only valid to the end of the line.
#fchar	Moves the cursor the # of chars (a specific character) to the right.
#tchar	Moves the cursor the # of chars before (a specific character) to the right.

#F *char*	Moves the cursor the # of *char*s (a specific character) to the left.
#T *char*	Moves the cursor the # of *char*s after (a specific character) to the left.
#;	Repeats the last find command (f, t, F, T).
#,	Repeats in the opposite direction the last find command (f, t, F, T).
#H <Home>	Moves the cursor the # of lines from the top of the screen. Default is the first line (H).
#L <End>	Moves the cursor the # of lines from the bottom of the screen. Default is the first line (L).
M	Moves the cursor to the middle of the screen.
#)	Moves the cursor to the right the # of sentence(s).
#(	Moves the cursor to the left the # of sentence(s).
#}	Moves the cursor to the right the # of paragraph(s).
#{	Moves the cursor to the left the # of paragraph(s).
]]	Moves the cursor to the right (forward) a section.
[[	Moves the cursor to the left (backward) a section.
``	Moves the cursor to its prior position after a move.
''	Moves the cursor to the first character on the line where the prior cursor position was after a move.
%	Finds the matching [,], {, }, (, or) and goes to it.
< ^F> or < ^f>	Moves the cursor forward one screen.
< ^B> or < ^b>	Moves the cursor backward one screen.

Replace Commands

3cw*text* <Esc>	Replaces the next three words from the cursor with the specified *text*; <Esc> terminates input.
xp	Transposes the character under the cursor and the character to its right. This command deletes the character under the cursor, moves the cursor one character to the right, and places the character in the buffer.
#]r*char*	Replaces the # of characters with the # of single *char*s from the current cursor position.
#R*text*	Replaces the characters from the current cursor position to the right on the line with *text*; apply the change #-1 times.

`#stext`	Substitutes the # characters for `text`. Same as `#cl`.
`#Stext`	Substitutes the # of lines with one or more lines of `text`. Same as `#cc`. Text lines are blank if not filled with characters.
`#c command`	Changes the # of characters, words, lines, and so on, determined by `command`.
`#cc`	Changes the # (or more) lines; remains in input mode.
`#C`	Changes the remainder of the line, as well as #-1 of the following lines (from the current line); remains in input mode. Same as `#]c$`.

Search Commands

n or `//` or `??`	Repeats the last search command. The + or - # positions the lines specified after the match.
N	Repeats the last search command in the opposite direction.
`/text/z-`	Positions the matching line at the bottom of the screen.

Marker Commands

`mchar`	Marks the current cursor position with `char` (see colon commands). Marks are only effective for the current `vi` session.
`` `[a-z] ``	Goes to the first of the marked line.
`'[a-z]`	Goes to the marked character.
`` `[char] ``	Goes to the mark `[a-z]` and positions the cursor at the beginning of the line.
`'[char]`	Goes to the first character in the line where the mark `[a-z]` appears.

Delete and Replace Commands

`#x`	Deletes the # of `chars` under the cursor. The default x deletes the character under the cursor.
`#X`	Deletes the # of `chars` before the cursor. The default X deletes the character to the left of the cursor.
`#dl`	Deletes the # of characters.
`#dd`	Deletes the # of lines starting at the current cursor position forward in the buffer.

`#dchar`	Deletes the # of characters, words, lines, and so on, as defined by `char`.
`D`	Deletes the rest of the line from the current cursor position.
`#rchar`	Replaces the # of characters under the cursor and to the right with the character specified by `char`.
`#Rtext`	Replaces the rest of the line and appends changes # -1 times.
`#stext`	Substitutes the # of characters with `text`.
`#Stext`	Substitutes the # of lines with `text`.
`#cctext`	Changes the # of lines to `text`.
`#Ctext`	Changes the rest of the line and # -1 lines to `text`.
`~command`	Switches lower and uppercase. `command` is a user–supplied replace or change command.
`#J`	Joins # lines. The default `J` joins two lines at the current cursor location.

Undo Commands

`"#u`	Undoes the most current change, where # is the delete register number.
`U`	Undoes all changes on the current line. Once you move from the line, all changes are lost.

Move and Shift Commands

`#>`	Moves # of lines, starting at the current line, one shiftwidth (soft tab) to the right.
`#>>`	Moves the # lines from the current line, one shiftwidth (soft tab) to the right.
`#.`	Repeats the preceding command # times.
`#<char`	Determined by # `char`, shift the defined lines one shiftwidth to the left.
`#<<`	Shifts the # of lines, from the current line, one shiftwidth (soft tab) to the left.

The Write Command

`ZZ`	Writes the current file name and exits. If the current file name is up-to-date, just exits.

Shell Commands

`<^Z>`	Suspends vi and goes to the UNIX shell; return with exit.
`<kill>`	Kills the current command.
`:command`	Suspends vi and executes command in ex.
`Q or <^\> or <int><int>`	Switches from vi to ed.
`:vi`	Switches from ed to vi.
`:sh`	Switches to the UNIX shell, exits to return.
`>exit`	Switches to vi.
`#! char command`	command is executed by the shell, which uses as input the # of lines to be moved in the char (character, word, or line) command.
`#!char!args`	Uses args for the most current command and uses, as input, the # lines defined by char (character, word, or line) command.
`#!!! [args]`	Uses the most current command with args and the # of lines.

Screen-Display Commands

`<^G> or <^g>`	Displays the current file name, status, line number, and character position in vi.
`<^L> or <^l>`	Redraws the screen display.
`#<^E> or # <^e>`	Leaves the cursor in place and adds # lines to the bottom of the screen.
`# <^Y> or #<^y>`	Leaves the cursor in place and adds # lines to the top of the screen.
`#<^D> or #<^d>`	Scrolls # lines down.
`#<^U> or #<^u>`	Scrolls # lines up.
`#<^F> or #<^f> or <PgDn>`	Moves # screens forward.
`#<^B> or #<^b> or <PgUp>`	Moves # screens backward.
`#G`	Moves the cursor to line #. The default G moves to the last line in the buffer.
`#z or #zh`	Puts line # at the top of the screen. The default is the current line.
`#z+`	Puts line # at the top of the screen. The default is the first line of the next page.

`#z-` or `#zl`	Puts line `#` at the bottom of the screen. The default is the current line.
`#z^`	Puts line `#` at the bottom of the screen. The default is the last line from the previous screen.
`#z.` or `#zm`	Puts line `#` at the center of the screen. The default is the current line.

Yank and Put Commands

`"[A-Z]` or `"[a-z]` or `"[1-9]`	Selects a temporary register for yanking data from buffer into the specified register or putting data from the temporary register into the buffer.
`#"buffery`	Yanks the `#` characters forward from the cursor and places them in the named `buffer`. If `buffer` is omitted, the characters are placed in the default undo buffer.
`#"bufferyy`	Yanks (starting from the current line) `#` lines forward from the cursor and places the lines in the named `buffer`. If `buffer` is omitted, the lines are placed in the default buffer (undo buffer).
`buffer#"buffer]Y[buffer]`	Yanks (starting from the current line) `#` lines from the cursor position backward and places them in the named `buffer` (default is the undo buffer).
`buffer#"bufferybuffer`	Yanks the `#` of characters, words, lines, and so on, defined by `char` and places them in the `char`-named buffer (the default is the undo buffer).
`[#]["char]["[a-z1-9]]p`	Undoes (put the contents of the buffer from register `"[A-Za-z1-9]`) the `#` of times after the cursor.
`[#]["char]["[a-z1-9]]P`	Undoes (put the contents of the buffer from register `"[A-Za-z1-9]`) the `#` of times after the cursor.

Miscellaneous `vi` Commands

`char[a-z]`	Uses the contents of the `[a-z]` register as a `vi` command.
`comment text`	`text comments` on the screen; not stored in the file.

~	Indicates the lines that are past the end of the buffer (empty buffer lines).
<^char>	Represents the control character *char*.
<Esc>	Ends insert; also terminates an incomplete command.
<Del> or <^?>	Generates an interrupt and terminates the present mode.
<^G>	Displays the current file name.

Tags

^]	Indicates that the following word is a tag.
^V^char	Places the <Ctrl> character *char* into the buffer as though it were normal *text*.
[#]=command	Realigns lines if lisp is set.
@[a-z]	Uses the contents of the temporary register as a command.
^^	Edits the previous file.
: command	Escapes to ex.

The **ex** Utility

The syntax for ex is as follows:

```
ex [-s] [-v] [-t tag] [-r file] [-L] [-R] [-x] [-C]
   [-c command] [filename ...]
```

Options for **ex**

-s	Suppresses feedback.
-v	Evokes vi.
-t	Tags edit file with tag.
-r *filename*	Edits file after a crash.
-L	Lists files saved after a crash.
-R	Evokes ex in read-only mode.
-x	Encryption option.
-C	Encryption option.
-c *command*	Executes *command* after executing ex.
filename	Lists *filename*(s) to be edited.

Modes for **ex**

The initial state of ex is command mode, and the command-mode prompt is the colon (:). Input mode is entered by using the a, i or c command and is terminated by a . (period) in the first blank column and by a <Return>.

:ve	Prints vi version.
:q	Quits vi. Will quit only if the current buffer has been saved.
:q!	Quits vi immediately, without checking whether the current buffer has been saved.
:w	Writes the buffer to the current file name.
:w *filename*	Writes the buffer to the specified *filename*.
:w >> *filename*	Appends the buffer to the contents of named file (*filename*).
:w! *filename*	Overwrites the named file (*filename*) with the buffer contents.
if ["*char*]p [*filename*]	Puts the contents of temporary register or buffer into *filename*.
:[1$_b$, 1$_e$]w [*filename*]	Writes line group to *filename*.
:wq [*filename*]	Writes the current *filename* and quits vi.
:r [*filename*]	Reads *filename* from disk into the buffer. The contents of *filename* are placed in the buffer after the current line. The default r reads the current file name.
:r!*command*	Reads the output of *command* into a new line. The new line is entered into the buffer after the current line.
:f [*filename*] file command	Displays the current file name if *filename* is not supplied; otherwise, the current file name is changed to *filename* (supplied by the user).
:e [*filename*]	Edits *filename* without quitting vi. If no file name is supplied, the current file name is used. The buffer is cleared and *filename* is loaded. This sequence occurs only if the current buffer has been saved; otherwise, an error message is displayed.
:e! [*filename*]	Edits *filename* without saving the current buffer.
:e +[#] [*filename*]	Edits *filename*, starting at line #. When # is omitted, edit at the end of the buffer.
:e #	Edits file #.

`:x [filename]`	Writes to `filename` and exits `vi`.
`:x! [filename]`	Overwrites `filename` and exits `vi`.
`:pre`	Preserves your file. Use this command when there appears no other way to save the buffer.
`:kchar`	Marks the current line with the character `char` where the allowable characters are `[a-z]`.
`&`	Repeats the most current `ex` substitution command.
`:vi`	Returns to `vi` from `ex`.
`:sh`	Temporarily exits `vi`/`ex` to the shell. To return to `vi` from the shell, enter `exit`.
`:cd [directory]`	Changes the current directory to `directory`.
`:cd! [directory]`	Changes the current directory to previous directory.
`:rew`	Rewinds the current argument list and edits the file in the list.
`:rew!`	Rewinds the current argument list; does not save the buffer. Edits the first file in the list.
`:n`	Edits the next file in the list.
`:n[!] [filename ...]`	Edits the next file in the argument list. If ! is used, does not save the current buffer.

Colon (`ex`) Set Abbreviations and Options

`ai`	`autoindent`	Used for structured program text; supplies indent.
`ap`	`autoprint`	Prints the current line to the screen when it is changed.
`aw`	`autowrite`	Writes the buffer to the file name at any escape to the shell.
`bt`	`beautify`	Disregards nondisplayable characters on output to the screen.
`dir=text`	`directory`	Directory for `ex` temporary work files.
`eb`	`errorbells`	Beeps on a command error.
`ed`	`edcompatible`	Makes `g` and `c` compatible with `ed` editor.
`ex`	`exrc`	Use `.exrc` to set start-up options.
`fl`	`flash`	Flashing terminal screen instead of ringing bell upon error, if terminal is equipped. If not, bell still rings.

ht=*value*	hardtabs	Sets the value of hard tabs.
ic	ignore case	Ignores case in searches.
lisp	lisp	Redefines some commands for LISP program input.
list	list	Shows linefeed as a $, shows carriage return as an I, shows <tab> as ^I, and other nondisplayable characters as \xxx.
magic	magic	Special meaning is given to the metacharacters . * $ ^ [ ] << >>. See Chapter 12 and Appendix E for more information on metacharacters.
mesg	message	Turns the write privilege on in visual mode.
modeline	modelines	Checks the first and last five lines in the buffer for editing commands; if present, executes them.
nov	novice	Novice user; sets default options for a novice user.
nu	number	Places numbers at the beginning of each line on the screen.
op	optimize	Does not perform automatic carriage return; speeds up screen output for slow terminals.
open	open	Permits open and visual commands.
para=*text*	paragraph	Uses character pairs in *text* as a paragraph delimiter. These character pairs can be used by nroff.
prompt	prompt	Command mode input is prompted by a : character.
redraw	redraw	Keeps the screen up-to-date, as changes occur (takes more time).
remap	remap	Macros are repeatedly expanded.
report=#	report	Informs the user when a delete or yank affects lines greater than #. :set report? reports the effect of the last yank.
ro	readonly	The file is not to be overwritten by a write command. The w! command overrides this option.
scr=#	scroll	Determines the number of lines scrolled on end of file.

sect=*text*	sections	Defines the characters used to delimit sections. Defaults are]] and [[.
sh=*text*	shell	Sets the program to be used when a shell escape occurs (the default is /bin/sh).
sw=#	shiftwidth	Sets the shiftwidth (soft tab); the default is 8.
sm	showmatch	When brackets [ ], braces { } and parentheses ( ) are matched, vi shows the matching side of the pair (only if on the same page).
smd	showmode	Shows the type of input mode in vi.
slow	slowopen	Does not show updates during input.
tl=#	taglength	Defines the # of significant characters to be used in tags. A 0 represents all characters.
tags=*text*	tags	Defines the space-delimited list of tags for files.
term=*text*	term	Sets the terminal type to be used by vi.
terse	terse	Displays text error messages in a short or terse form.
to	timeout	Mappings for commands will be used only if they are entered before the timeout occurs.
ts=#	tabstops	Sets the value of hard tabs to #.
tty	ttytype	Displays the type of tty used by vi.
wa	writeany	Instructs vi to overwrite the current file.
warn	warn	Displays a warning message when you try to quit vi if the disk file is not current with the buffer. Displays the following error message: No write since last change.
wi=[#]	window	Sets the number of lines in the vi screen (window). Used without the #, the current number of lines is displayed.
wm=#	wrapmargin	When vi is in the append mode, forces a line feed whenever a space or hard tab is input in the wrapmargin columns.
ws	wrapscan	A search will wrap around past the end of file.

vi Map Abbreviations

`:ab`	Shows `all` macro abbreviations.
`:ab` *text param*	When in append mode, *text* is prefixed and suffixed with a break character *param*, which is interpreted and used by `vi` on the specified *text*.
`:unab`	Undo abbreviation.
`:map`	Shows `all` macro mappings.
`:map[!]` *text param*	*text* is interpreted as *param* and interpreted by the shell.
`:unmap` *text*	Strips mapping from *text*.

vi Operators

d or D	Delete
x or X	Delete character
c or C	Change
s or S	Switch
y or Y	Yank
>	Shift right
<	Shift left
J	Join
!	Shell command

Index

Computer Books From Que Mean PC Performance!

Spreadsheets

1-2-3 Database Techniques	$29.95
1-2-3 Graphics Techniques	$24.95
1-2-3 Macro Library, 3rd Edition	$39.95
1-2-3 Release 2.2 Business Applications	$39.95
1-2-3 Release 2.2 Quick Reference	$ 7.95
1-2-3 Release 2.2 QuickStart	$19.95
1-2-3 Release 2.2 Workbook and Disk	$29.95
1-2-3 Release 3 Business Applications	$39.95
1-2-3 Release 3 Quick Reference	$ 7.95
1-2-3 Release 3 QuickStart	$19.95
1-2-3 Release 3 Workbook and Disk	$29.95
1-2-3 Tips, Tricks, and Traps, 3rd Edition	$24.95
Excel Business Applications: IBM Version	$39.95
Excel Quick Reference	$ 7.95
Excel QuickStart	$19.95
Excel Tips, Tricks, and Traps	$22.95
Using 1-2-3, Special Edition	$26.95
Using 1-2-3 Release 2.2, Special Edition	$26.95
Using 1-2-3 Release 3	$27.95
Using Excel: IBM Version	$29.95
Using Lotus Spreadsheet for DeskMate	$19.95
Using Quattro Pro	$24.95
Using SuperCalc5, 2nd Edition	$29.95

Databases

dBASE III Plus Handbook, 2nd Edition	$24.95
dBASE III Plus Tips, Tricks, and Traps	$24.95
dBASE III Plus Workbook and Disk	$29.95
dBASE IV Applications Library, 2nd Edition	$39.95
dBASE IV Programming Techniques	$24.95
dBASE IV QueCards	$21.95
dBASE IV Quick Reference	$ 7.95
dBASE IV QuickStart	$19.95
dBASE IV Tips, Tricks, and Traps, 2nd Ed.	$24.95
dBASE IV Workbook and Disk	$29.95
R:BASE User's Guide, 3rd Edition	$22.95
Using Clipper	$24.95
Using DataEase	$24.95
Using dBASE IV	$27.95
Using FoxPro	$26.95
Using Paradox 3	$24.95
Using Reflex, 2nd Edition	$22.95
Using SQL	$24.95

Business Applications

Introduction to Business Software	$14.95
Introduction to Personal Computers	$19.95
Lotus Add-in Toolkit Guide	$29.95
Norton Utilities Quick Reference	$ 7.95
PC Tools Quick Reference, 2nd Edition	$ 7.95
Q&A Quick Reference	$ 7.95
Que's Computer User's Dictionary	$9.95
Que's Wizard Book	$ 9.95
Smart Tips, Tricks, and Traps	$24.95
Using Computers in Business	$22.95
Using DacEasy, 2nd Edition	$24.95
Using Dollars and Sense: IBM Version, 2nd Edition	$19.95
Using Enable/OA	$29.95
Using Harvard Project Manager	$24.95
Using Lotus Magellan	$21.95
Using Managing Your Money, 2nd Edition	$19.95
Using Microsoft Works: IBM Version	$22.95

Using Norton Utilities	$24.95
Using PC Tools Deluxe	$24.95
Using Peachtree	$22.95
Using PFS: First Choice	$22.95
Using PROCOMM PLUS	$19.95
Using Q&A, 2nd Edition	$23.95
Using Quicken	$19.95
Using Smart	$22.95
Using SmartWare II	$29.95
Using Symphony, Special Edition	$29.95

CAD

AutoCAD Advanced Techniques	$34.95
AutoCAD Quick Reference	$ 7.95
AutoCAD Sourcebook	$24.95
Using AutoCAD, 2nd Edition	$24.95
Using Generic CADD	$24.95

Word Processing

DisplayWrite QuickStart	$19.95
Microsoft Word 5 Quick Reference	$ 7.95
Microsoft Word 5 Tips, Tricks, and Traps: IBM Version	$22.95
Using DisplayWrite 4, 2nd Edition	$24.95
Using Microsoft Word 5: IBM Version	$22.95
Using MultiMate	$22.95
Using Professional Write	$22.95
Using Word for Windows	$22.95
Using WordPerfect, 3rd Edition	$21.95
Using WordPerfect 5	$24.95
Using WordPerfect 5.1, Special Edition	$24.95
Using WordStar, 2nd Edition	$21.95
WordPerfect QueCards	$21.95
WordPerfect Quick Reference	$ 7.95
WordPerfect QuickStart	$19.95
WordPerfect Tips, Tricks, and Traps, 2nd Edition	$22.95
WordPerfect 5 Workbook and Disk	$29.95
WordPerfect 5.1 Quick Reference	$ 7.95
WordPerfect 5.1 QuickStart	$19.95
WordPerfect 5.1 Tips, Tricks, and Traps	$22.95
WordPerfect 5.1 Workbook and Disk	$29.95

Hardware/Systems

DOS Power Techniques	$29.95
DOS Tips, Tricks, and Traps	$24.95
DOS Workbook and Disk, 2nd Edition	$29.95
Hard Disk Quick Reference	$ 7.95
MS-DOS Quick Reference	$ 7.95
MS-DOS QuickStart	$21.95
MS-DOS User's Guide, Special Edition	$29.95
Networking Personal Computers, 3rd Edition	$24.95
The Printer Bible	$29.95
Que's Guide to Data Recovery	$24.95
Understanding UNIX, 2nd Edition	$21.95
Upgrading and Repairing PCs	$29.95
Using DOS	$22.95
Using Microsoft Windows 3, 2nd Edition	$22.95
Using Novell NetWare	$29.95
Using OS/2	$29.95
Using PC DOS, 3rd Edition	$24.95
Using UNIX	$24.95
Using Your Hard Disk	$29.95
Windows 3 Quick Reference	$ 7.95

Desktop Publishing/Graphics

Harvard Graphics Quick Reference	$ 7.95
Using Animator	$24.95
Using Harvard Graphics	$24.95
Using Freelance Plus	$24.95
Using PageMaker: IBM Version, 2nd Edition	$24.95
Using PFS: First Publisher	$22.95
Using Ventura Publisher, 2nd Edition	$24.95
Ventura Publisher Tips, Tricks, and Traps	$24.95

Macintosh/Apple II

AppleWorks QuickStart	$19.95
The Big Mac Book	$27.95
Excel QuickStart	$19.95
Excel Tips, Tricks, and Traps	$22.95
Que's Macintosh Multimedia Handbook	$22.95
Using AppleWorks, 3rd Edition	$21.95
Using AppleWorks GS	$21.95
Using Dollars and Sense: Macintosh Version	$19.95
Using Excel: Macintosh Version	$24.95
Using FileMaker	$24.95
Using MacroMind Director	$29.95
Using MacWrite	$22.95
Using Microsoft Word 4: Macintosh Version	$24.95
Using Microsoft Works: Macintosh Version, 2nd Edition	$24.95
Using PageMaker: Macintosh Version	$24.95

Programming/Technical

Assembly Language Quick Reference	$ 7.95
C Programmer's Toolkit	$39.95
C Programming Guide, 3rd Edition	$24.95
C Quick Reference	$ 7.95
DOS and BIOS Functions Quick Reference	$ 7.95
DOS Programmer's Reference, 2nd Edition	$29.95
Oracle Programmer's Guide	$24.95
Power Graphics Programming	$24.95
QuickBASIC Advanced Techniques	$22.95
QuickBASIC Programmer's Toolkit	$39.95
QuickBASIC Quick Reference	$ 7.95
QuickPascal Programming	$22.95
SQL Programmer's Guide	$29.95
Turbo C Programming	$22.95
Turbo Pascal Advanced Techniques	$22.95
Turbo Pascal Programmer's Toolkit	$39.95
Turbo Pascal Quick Reference	$ 7.95
UNIX Programmer's Quick Reference	$ 7.95
Using Assembly Language, 2nd Edition	$29.95
Using BASIC	$19.95
Using C	$27.95
Using QuickBASIC 4	$24.95
Using Turbo Pascal	$29.95

For More Information, Call Toll Free!

1-800-428-5331

All prices and titles subject to change without notice. Non-U.S. prices may be higher. Printed in the U.S.A.